Complete

OFFICE

Handbook

Other Books by the Author

The Complete Word Book

Guide to Better Business Writing

How to Run a Meeting

Legal Secretary's Complete Handbook

The New American Dictionary of Abbreviations

The New American Handbook of Letter Writing

New Century Vest-Pocket Secretary's Handbook

The New Robert's Rules of Order

The Office Sourcebook

The Practical Writer's Guide

*The Prentice Hall Complete Book of Model Letters,
Memos, and Forms*

Prentice Hall Style Manual

Professional Secretary's Encyclopedic Dictionary

Complete
OFFICE
Handbook

MARY A. DE VRIES

PRENTICE HALL

Printed in the United States of America

Originally published as *Complete Secretary's Handbook*, 7th Edition 0-13-159674-8.

ISBN 0-13-080384-7

PRENTICE HALL
Paramus, NJ 07652

A Simon & Schuster Company

On the World Wide Web at http://www.phdirect.com

Prentice-Hall International (UK) Limited, *London*
Prentice-Hall of Australia Pty. Limited, *Sydney*
Prentice-Hall Canada Inc., *Toronto*
Prentice-Hall Hispanoamericana, S.A., *Mexico*
Prentice-Hall of India Private Limited, *New Delhi*
Prentice-Hall of Japan, Inc., *Tokyo*
Simon & Schuster Asia Pte. Ltd., *Singapore*
Editora Prentice-Hall do Brasil, Ltda., *Rio de Janeiro*

A Word About This Book

The electronic office has widened the professional horizons for secretaries and other office professionals. It has simplified many otherwise cumbersome, repetitive tasks, but it has not eliminated the need for a capable professional secretary to have a full range of office skills. The *Complete Office Handbook* reflects this philosophy.

Most office handbooks are written for a diverse audience and are used by both students and teachers and both entry- and advanced-level office professionals, as well as everyone in between. Readers are employed in organizations of all sizes, from one-room operations to large international corporations. This handbook, therefore, contains an essential blend of basic and advanced practices and procedures. Since it is a *secretarial* book intended for office personnel, it has another dual purpose—to provide discussions pertinent to an automated, electronic office environment while still describing the conventional procedures followed in offices that are not fully automated or electronically controlled.

With strong emphasis on the global economy and the technologies that link people, offices, and organizations worldwide, a substantial amount of new information has been provided in this reference. These topics are examples of some of the important new material:

Magnetic Storage Media (page 25)

Database Systems and Services (page 29)

Macros in Word Processing (page 74)

v

In addition to material on these new areas, this reference includes the latest information on new technologies while still defining the traditional practices and procedures that remain the foundation of the secretarial profession in offices of all types and sizes.

The contents of this book are organized in five parts:

I. *Techniques for General Secretarial Duties*

Part One has nine chapters that cover a broad range of practical information concerning general office practices and procedures, including various key forms of communication: records management, word processing, report writing and desktop publishing, conventional and electronic message transmission, telecommunications, meeting arrangements, travel planning, bookkeeping and accounting, and human relations.

II. *How to Write Effective Letters and Memos*

Part Two has three chapters that concentrate on the all-important area of written communication: basic letter and memo formats, important language aids, and model letters and memos.

III. *How to Write Correctly*

Part Three has four chapters that focus on language-skills guidelines for a contemporary writing style: correct word choice, spelling, word division, punctuation, and capitalization.

IV. *The Secretary's Handy Information Guide*

Part Four has one chapter that provides a variety of essential reference material for daily use: common abbreviations, weights and measures, correct forms of address, financial information, global time data, foreign currencies, and other useful facts and figures.

V. *Glossary*

Part Five has a glossary of important terms in office technology, business organization and management, accounting and bookkeeping, and business law.

The seventeen chapters and glossary in this book have been designed not only to help you perform confidently in the office today but also to prepare you for the workplace tomorrow. Hence most of the chapters deal with the major communication skills used in an office. This emphasis is based on the generally accepted view that the more effectively you can communicate—by machine, by telephone, in person, or in writing—the more successful you will be in your professional life.

Mary A. De Vries

The Secretary in a New Information Age

WORKING IN THE NEW INFORMATION AGE

This is a time of high technology in a global economy, a time when executives in their electronic offices must rely more and more on members of their support staff to manage and control the new systems. It's a time of open invitation to secretaries to abandon the familiar comforts and confinements of the past and embrace their changing role in the workplace with enthusiasm and active involvement.

The new information age has not proved to be the threat that some feared it might be. Rather, it has created an unprecedented opportunity for secretaries to enhance their job status and, ultimately, their paychecks.

The Secretary's Role in the New Information Age

CHANGES THAT HAVE OCCURRED. Most of the changes in secretarial duties that have occurred in the new information age are obvious.

- Many tasks, such as bookkeeping and word processing, are being performed with computers.

- Mail in most offices no longer means just postal messages but now includes a variety of electronic transmissions.

- Telephones are being used for countless functions from telemarketing to voice messaging.

- The horizons for research have expanded from the local library reference room to vast electronic databases nationwide.

- Checking the files in a modern office is likely to mean calling up on a computer monitor a document stored on a diskette.

These and other changes that characterize the information age are discussed in the various chapters of this book.

THE SECRETARY: YESTERDAY, TODAY, AND TOMORROW. To understand fully the impact of technological change on the secretarial profession, consider how the role of the secretary has changed in only a few decades.

1. Yesterday's secretary. As the tools for performing different tasks changed, and as new procedures were established to use these tools effectively, the role of the secretary also changed dramatically. At one time it was sufficient in many secretarial positions to perform most tasks manually or mechanically, for example:

- Handling word processing needs on a manual or electric typewriter

- Preparing letters and documents for U.S. Postal Service delivery

- Placing and receiving traditional local and long-distance telephone calls

- Sending telegrams and cables

- Organizing and filing material in conventional file folders and placing them in conventional filing cabinets

- Performing other repetitive, manual secretarial duties

Secretaries have always performed a great variety of tasks, but in the preinformation age they were frequently burdened with endlessly repetitive clerical work that had to be handled with tedious and time-consuming manual systems.

2. Today's secretary. The situation has changed for secretaries in the new information age, as they handle an extraordinary variety of tasks that now rely heavily on advanced technologies and systems, such as:

- Managing a vast array of records in a variety of mediums

- Preparing correspondence and documents for many different types of messaging systems, both paper and electronic

- Handling a variety of telecommunications functions and processing both paper and electronic forms of mail

- Making numerous contacts with clients, customers, and others not only nationwide but worldwide

- Assisting employers in implementing and operating a variety of new high-technology systems

- Supervising assistants and working cooperatively with others in the same office and in other departments and organizations

- Coordinating and managing special projects and handling special assignments

- Analyzing problems and exercising important decision-making skills

- Pursuing educational and career-development opportunities

Today's secretary does all of these things—and more.

3. *Tomorrow's secretary.* Business analysts largely agree that the secretarial role will continue to evolve in tandem with advances in technology. Many of the changes they foresee will be inevitable as the new technological systems take over many routine secretarial duties while simultaneously creating the need for much greater secretarial participation in directing and administering the use of these new systems. Secretaries of the future will be:

- Treating computers as the office standard, as typewriters once were

- Working with software systems that are more user friendly

- Relying more and more on the on-line database to locate, use, and store massive amounts of information

- Dealing with more foreign contacts but making greater use of teleconference and videoconference arrangements for meetings

- Using desktop-publishing software more often, in addition to word processing programs, for reports and other document preparation

- Using voice-mail technologies more frequently and operating workstations that integrate the various data technologies, such as facsimile and electronic mail, with the voice technologies

- Performing more management, administrative, and supervisory duties and using greater language, editing, and formatting skills but handling fewer routine tasks, such as answering the telephone

Tomorrow's secretary, therefore, will find that even more routine duties have been taken over by the new technological systems, and they will also spend even more time than today's secretary in activities concerned with controlling and managing the new technologies.

PREPARING FOR THE FUTURE

Steps You Can Take to Enhance Your Career

EDUCATION AND TRAINING. Ongoing study—both independent and formal—and retraining are essential to success in the new information age. This means that you should take advantage of every opportunity that your employer offers to learn about a new technology or system, such as attending a seminar, participating in a training program, or merely visiting someone in your firm who is an expert on the subject. College credits, business school courses, and other formal education will also widen your job opportunities, improve the opportunities for promotion and pay increases, and generally make you more competitive in the workplace.

READING. Make it a habit regularly to read books on the new technologies and trade journals that deal with topics pertinent to your employer's business or profession, as well as general office magazines such as *The Secretary*, *The Office*, and *Office Systems*. Include newsletters that keep your technical skills sharpened, such as *Word Processing: Quality Clinic*, and those that polish your general office skills, such as the *Office Skills Workshop*. Study communication books that will expand your language skills and secretarial books, such as this handbook, that report on appropriate practices and procedures for the new information-age systems.

PROFESSIONAL ASSOCIATIONS. Contact professional associations that provide information, support, and career-development opportunities. Check a directory of associations in your library for names and addresses of associations that deal with the business or profession of your employer (data processing, medical practice, education, and so on). Write to specialized secretarial associations and to the Professional Secretaries International (PSI) at 10502 N.W. Ambassador Drive, P.O. Box 20404, Kansas City, MO 64195-0404; ask for information on PSI's Certified Professional Secretaries (CPS) program. The CPS title is bestowed on those who pass a two-day, six-part examination covering a variety of topics as summarized in Chapter 17.

THE SECRETARY AS A PROFESSIONAL

Profile of a Successful Secretary

ESSENTIAL INGREDIENTS. Understanding how the new machines and systems work and what you must do to use them properly is essential to a successful career, learning more about your employer's business and your organization's position in the global economy is also a prime requisite, and continuing your education and training is a process that will pay big dividends over time. But to the total mix you need to add another critical ingredient—the personal dimension. Secretaries rarely work in isolation. They must learn how to get along with others on a daily basis and how to cope with the good and bad facets of human relations in the office.

IMPORTANT PERSONAL QUALITIES. To succeed in this evolving profession, secretaries must:

- Work effectively as team members while maintaining the ability to initiate and manage projects independently
- Be cooperative, understanding, and diplomatic in dealings with others

- Be attentive to detail and insistent on complete accuracy in their work and that of others
- Respect the need for confidentiality and the ethical requirements of their work
- Create a good personal image and a favorable company image through a businesslike appearance and a positive, cheerful attitude
- Perform their duties and deal with others honestly and in a professional manner

Without these essential personal qualities, technical skills alone will not be sufficient to carry a secretary successfully to the threshold of the twenty-first century.

THINK OF YOURSELF AS A PROFESSIONAL. It has often been said that if you think of yourself as a professional, you are more likely to function the way a professional does, and others will be more inclined to treat you like a professional. That advice, although very old, is still well suited to all secretaries in the new information age.

Contents

PART ONE

TECHNIQUES FOR GENERAL SECRETARIAL DUTIES

Chapter 1

Developing an Effective Records-Management System   3

Chapter 2

Using Productive Word Processing Techniques   59

Chapter 3

Preparing and Publishing Reports 87

Chapter 4

Handling Mail and Electronic Messages 125

Chapter 5

Using Effective Telecommunications Practices 159

Chapter 6

Making Meeting Arrangements 181

Chapter 7
_____

Making Travel Arrangements   203

Chapter 8

Keeping Company Books and Records 237

How to Keep Office and Company Records 237

Handling Petty Cash 237.   Maintaining Office Payroll Accounts 240.   Handling the Checkbook and Bank Statement 243.   Keeping Travel and Entertainment Records 248.   Handling Official Financing Statements 250.   Filing Contracts and Other Legal Documents 251.   Maintaining Securities and Property Records 252.

How to Keep Office and Company Books 256

System of Bookkeeping 256.   Basic Rules of Double-Entry Bookkeeping 258.   Journals 258.   Ledgers 261. Balance Sheet 265.   Income Statement 268. Confidentiality in Bookkeeping and Accounting 268.

How to Handle Billings and Collections 270

Calculating Charges 270.   Following Up Overdue Accounts 272.

Chapter 9

Maintaining Good Human Relations and Proper Etiquette 275

Your Professional Image 275

Etiquette in the Office 277

Daily Greetings and Use of First Names 277.   The New Employee 278.   Having Refreshments in the Office 279. Etiquette and Safety in Office Lines and Parking Lots 280.

Receiving Visitors 281

Receiving and Greeting Callers 281.   Determining the Purpose of a Call 282.   Making Callers Comfortable 283. Announcing Callers 284.   Greeting Callers Your Boss Will

---

PART TWO

HOW TO WRITE EFFECTIVE LETTERS AND MEMOS

Chapter 10

Mechanics of Business Correspondence 319

Chapter 12

Model Letters and Memos 393

PART THREE

HOW TO WRITE CORRECTLY

Chapter 13

Correct Word Usage 437

PART FOUR

THE SECRETARY'S HANDY INFORMATION GUIDE

Chapter 17

Quick-Reference Guide to Facts and Figures 579

PART FIVE

GLOSSARY OF IMPORTANT BUSINESS TERMS

Chapter 18

Glossary 661

PART ONE

TECHNIQUES FOR GENERAL SECRETARIAL DUTIES

Chapter 1

Developing an Effective Records-Management System

An effective records-management system will enable you to file and find information quickly and easily and will provide a clear guide to records-retention procedures. Your organization may have a large central file department that has a well-established filing system and well-defined rules for records retention. But you are likely to be responsible for the filing and retrieval of certain working records that are kept in your office. A well-organized records-management system is crucial to the efficient handling of paper, magnetic, microimage, and other files.

THE BASIC FILING SYSTEMS

The use of magnetic media, microimaging, and optical-disk technology has not halted the paper explosion in the business world. In most companies, 95 percent of the filing is still paper based, sometimes with duplicate files or other files maintained on other media, such as computer disks.

Regardless of the type of media used, you need to organize your material and any index to it that you use according to the rules of one of the basic filing systems. This is necessary to ensure that anyone authorized to access the files can locate material without having to decode someone's private system.

The major systems are a form of either alphabetical or numerical filing. Some offices use a combination of both forms (an alphanumeric system).

Since procedures differ from office to office, and others may have to use your system in emergencies, you may want to prepare a file manual for your office explaining the system you are using and the steps involved in (1) preparing material for filing, (2) filing it, and (3) retrieving it from the files. The files should not be open to everyone, however. Every system needs adequate controls and safeguards.

Alphabetical Filing Systems

Most filing is alphabetical, numerical, or a combination. Which system is most efficient depends on the value and complexity of the files. Each office should devise a system that is most appropriate for the type of activity involved. Experts recommend a simple system over a more complex system whenever possible.

USING NAME FILES. An easy method of filing is to classify material according to name and to file the names alphabetically.

1. *Individual files.* Open a file for each correspondent or name, if there is sufficient material. From three to ten items justify opening a separate file. In a paper file, arrange the material within the name folder by date, with the most recent date on top.

2. *Miscellaneous files.* Include a miscellaneous file for each letter of the alphabet. In a paper system, place each miscellaneous folder after the last of the name folders collected behind each individual letter of the alphabet. Arrange material in miscellaneous folders alphabetically rather than by date so that all items relating to a particular name will be together. When three to ten items accumulate for a particular name in a miscellaneous folder, set up a separate name file for those papers.

3. *Extensive correspondence with the same person.* If correspondence with the same person or firm is extensive, separate it into date periods. Folders with printed date headings are available for paper files (see Figure 1), or the dates can be typed on the folder labels. If you maintain corresponding electronic and paper files, develop an index that relates a paper file-folder label to a disk filename, if there is any difference between the two. Both may be the same, however, unless the disk filename is an abbreviated or coded version of a spelled-out paper file label.

FIGURE 1

Alphabetical Name File Arranged in Four Positions

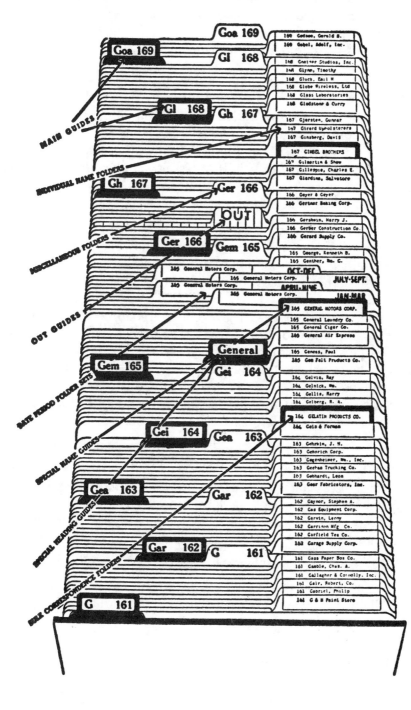

4. Correspondence with the same name. When correspondents have the same name, distinguish among them by some means, such as numbers added to the computer filenames or different-colored labels in the case of paper file folders. If you generally use blue labels and a folder for *Abernathy, Edgar, Sr.,* has a salmon label, you know immediately that there must also be a folder for *Abernathy, Edgar, Jr.,* with a blue label.

USING SUBJECT FILES. Some material is better classified by subject. But don't attempt to choose subject headings until you are thoroughly familiar with the material. Subject headings must be specific, significant, and technically correct. Select nouns whenever possible.

You can expand the subject files by adding other main subjects or by subdividing those already in use. If necessary, subheadings may be further subdivided, but for a secretary's purposes, a breakdown into main headings and subheadings is generally adequate.

1. Use of headings and subheadings in the subject files. Subject files may be arranged alphabetically or numerically; however, secretaries often prefer an alphabetical system in which main subjects are filed alphabetically, with subheadings grouped together alphabetically under each main heading.

In a *dictionary subject system,* records are stored alphabetically by specific subject, with no subheadings or subdivisions. In an *encyclopedic subject system,* main headings are organized alphabetically, and subdivisions may be established and grouped alphabetically under the appropriate main headings.

In a paper subject file that has main headings and subheadings, you will have a three-position arrangement as follows:

Alphabetical guides. These guides may be cardboard separators with the letter of the alphabet in the left position.

Main subject guides. These guides may be cardboard separators with metal or transparent plastic tabs into which the names of the main subjects can be inserted. The tabs should be in the center position. Or a "miscellaneous folder" may be used as a main subject guide.

Folders. Folders may include individual and miscellaneous:

1. *Individual folders* are folders with precut tabs in varying widths. Right-position tabs work well for the individual folders.

2. *Miscellaneous folders for each main heading* should be labeled like the guide, with a label different in color from that on the regular folders. Place the miscellaneous folder behind all other folders. The miscellaneous folder may also be used instead of the main subject guides. In that case, the folder should have a center-position tab and should be placed in front of the subhead folders.

If the subject file in your paper system has main headings, sub-headings, and further breakdowns, use guides instead of folders for the subheadings and a four-position, instead of three-position, arrangement. If you prepare an index to your corresponding computer files, follow the same breakdown of main headings and subdivisions that you have used in your paper files.

2. *Arrangement of material in paper subject file folders.* Arrange the items in a paper subject file folder by date, the same as in a name folder, with the most recent date on top. In the miscellaneous file, however, collect material alphabetically by subject rather than by date. When three to ten items on a particular subject are accumulated in the miscellaneous file, set up a separate subject folder for that topic and add it as a subheading. Place both the main heading and associated subheadings on the paper file-folder labels.

For your electronic filenames, you can develop codes such as *BDG* for Budgets or *TRV* for Travel. Whenever you maintain corresponding paper and electronic files, use the same filenames for each, or use an abbreviated or coded version of the paper filename for the computer file. Many offices require that computer filenames be established first and that the paper filename match the computer name or be a spelled-out version of it. Follow the practice of your office.

3. *Preparation of an index to the subject files.* Maintain an alphabetical index of the subjects for reference (a) to avoid filing material under a new heading when you already have a file opened for the subject and (b) to enable a substitute, an assistant, or your employer to locate material in the file. Changes are especially easy to edit into the list on a computer-prepared index, and an updated list can be printed out at any time.

Arrange the main headings and subheadings alphabetically in your index, with the main headings in full caps and the subheadings in initial caps. After each subheading, type in parentheses the main heading under which the subheading appears. *Keep the list up to date.*

Applications (Personnel)

CONTRACTS

EXPENSES AND EXPENSE ACCOUNTS

FORM LETTERS

Holidays (Personnel)
Hotels, Reservations (Travel)

INSURANCE
INVESTMENTS
Itineraries (Travel)

Leases (Contracts)

MEETINGS
Minutes (Meetings)

PERSONNEL

TRAVEL

If you use abbreviated forms of these headings for your computer filenames (or for both your computer and paper files), note both styles—a spelled-out version and an abbreviated version—on your index, for example:

Applications (Personnel): ApplPers.

Follow the rules of your software program for naming files.

USING COMBINED NAME AND SUBJECT FILES. If you have only a name file and occasionally have material that should be filed by subject, or if you have only a subject file and occasionally have material that should be filed by name, you can combine the occasional files with your main file.

In a name file, for example, you might include a file labeled "Applications" to receive the few applications that you keep in your files. In your paper files, put a cross-reference sheet under the name of the applicant in the miscellaneous folder behind the letter of the alphabet with which the applicant's last name begins. In a subject file, you might include a folder labeled with a person's name, which would be treated as another subject. Use the same cross-references on your index to the computer filenames.

USING SUBJECT-DUPLEX FILES. Some material filed by subject is further identified by numbers. This additional coding is important when the files are expanding rapidly with numerous subdivisions. Under this system, main subject headings are given a base number (such as 100), and subheadings are given auxiliary numbers or letters (such as 100.1). The file folders and index to the computer files are then positioned in numerical sequence (100, 100.1, 100.2, and so on). As in the case of a straight numerical system, described in the next section, the subject-duplex system necessitates maintaining an alphabetical index to the numbers.

USING GEOGRAPHIC FILES. The geographic system is a less common adaptation of an alphabetical system.

1. *Setting up a geographic system.* Under this system, sometimes used in sales departments, material may be classified first according to the name of the state, then according to the names of cities or towns, and last according to the names of companies and correspondents in each city or town. The breakdown may also include counties or regions. This type of file also requires an alphabetical cross-index to the names of customers.

2. *Use of the system.* A geographic system is often used by organizations in which a review of the sales or other activity in any given territory is of more importance than the name of a company or individual. The system would also be useful in activities such as market research, direct-mail advertising, and weather forecasting.

Numerical Filing Systems

A numerical filing system uses numbers that are arranged sequentially. It also may be combined with a name or subject. This is an indirect method of filing since it must be used in connection with an alphabetical cross-index that shows what the number stands for.

TYPES OF NUMERIC SYSTEMS. The following are a few of the many possible types of numeric systems.

1. In a *consecutive-number file system*, material is filed in ascending order (1, 2, 3, and so on). Although this is a simple system and the

easiest to learn, in a paper file all of the added file folders pile up at the end.

2. In a *terminal-digit file system,* numbers are divided into units, for example, 45-67-89. The digits on the right (89) may refer to a file drawer, those in the center (67) may refer to a file folder number, and those on the left (45) may refer to the order of papers in the folder (45-67-89, 46-67-89, 47-67-89, and so on).

3. In a *coded-number file system,* the numbers and letters identify a specific person or product, for example, license plate numbers or social security numbers.

4. In a *chronological file,* material is arranged in chronological order, with the most recent document on top. This file is used in addition to, not instead of, other filing systems. It is helpful when one is trying to locate material the content of which has been forgotten while the time period is remembered. It is also a logical arrangement for follow-up files, which are concerned with the date an action was taken.

5. In a *decimal filing system,* based on the Dewey decimal system, records are classified under ten or fewer principal headings, 000 to 900. Each heading is divided into ten or fewer subheadings, numbered from 10 to 90, preceded by the applicable hundreds digit. Each subheading may be subdivided into ten or fewer headings, which are numbered from 1 to 9, preceded by the appropriate hundreds and tens digits. If necessary, these headings may be further subdivided and numbered from .1 to .10, and so on, under the appropriate full number.

ADVANTAGES AND DISADVANTAGES OF NUMERICAL FILING. The advantages of a numerical system are rapidity of refiling, the opportunity for indefinite expansion, and the ability of data-processing systems to work more effectively with numbers. Among the disadvantages are the need to maintain an auxiliary alphabetical index to the numbers and the potential for misfiles from an error in a digit or from misreading large numbers.

The numerical system is well suited, however, to files in which each of the jobs, clients, or subjects has a number that acts as an identification mark (such as insurance policies, medical records, requisitions, orders, bills, and statements), for the filing of confidential records, for handling a rapidly growing file, and in files in which extensive permanent cross-reference is necessary.

INDEXING AND ALPHABETIZING GUIDELINES

Basic Indexing Rules

Indexing, as applied to filing, is the arrangement of names for filing purposes. You must know how names are indexed before you can alphabetize them. Although a computer filename may be an abbreviated version of a full name, an alphabetical index to your computer files should follow the same alphabetizing rules as those used for file-folder labels in a paper system.

INDIVIDUAL NAMES. Individual names are indexed by the last name, followed by the first name or initial, and concluding with any additional names or initials.

Name	Index as
L. Vosburgh Lyons	Lyons, L. Vosburgh
James G. Mellon	Mellon, James G.
R. S. Andrews	Andrews, R. S.

BUSINESS CONCERNS, ORGANIZATIONS, AND INSTITUTIONS. When organization names are composed of names of individuals, follow the order that applies to individual names; otherwise, each word in the name is considered in the order in which it appears.

Name	Index as
James G. Mellon & Son	Mellon, James G. & Son
J. P. Goode, Inc.	Goode, J. P., Inc.
Myron, Bache & Adams Co.	Myron, Bache & Adams Co.
National City Bank	National City Bank
National Development Co.	National Development Co.

When an institutional name contains the name of the type of institution, such as "Bank of America" or "University of Illinois," the distinctive word is used first for filing purposes.

Name	*Index as*
Bank of America	America, Bank (of)
University of Illinois	Illinois, University (of)

Basic Alphabetizing Rules

BASIC RULES. Although authorities differ in certain instances, the following rules for alphabetizing are widely accepted in the business world. Alphabetize by words, according to the first word in the name *as indexed*. When the first word of two or more names is the same, alphabetize according to the second word, then according to the third, and so on.

Index and File as
Brown, Albert A.
Brown, George
Brownell, Edward

NAMES OF UNEQUAL LENGTH. The basic rule of alphabetizing by words results in the following simple rules: When two or more names are of unequal length but contain the same word or words and are spelled the same up to and including the last word of the shorter name, index and file the shorter name first.

Order
Brown, G.
Brown, George
Brown, George A.
State Bank
State Bank and Trust Company

PRECEDENCE OF LETTERS. Follow these rules in indexing and alphabetizing letters.

1. Letters used as words. One or more single letters used as words are treated as words. The group beginning with letter names is arranged alphabetically and precedes word names.

Order

A A Club

A C E Letter Co.

AWVS

Abbey Coat Co.

Admiration Cigar Co.

2. Ampersand symbol. The ampersand symbol (&) is not considered a letter and is disregarded in determining alphabetical sequence.

Index and File as

A & B Co.

Abernathy Stores, Inc.

Adams Hardware, Inc.

Adams & Rawlins, Inc.

HYPHENATED NAMES. Treat names composed of letters, words, or syllables joined by one or more hyphens as one word. When the hyphen is used instead of a comma in a firm name, the individual parts of the name are treated as separate words. You know that the hyphen replaces the comma when the names of two individuals make up the firm name.

Index and File as

Evers-Harper & Co.
  (*hyphen used instead of comma*)

Evers, Warren D.

Ever-Sharp Products Corp.

Up-Stairs Dress Co.

Upton-Smith, Edward L.

ABBREVIATIONS. Abbreviations, such as *Chas., Co., Geo., Jas., St.,* and *Wm.,* are alphabetized in the same sequence as if spelled in full. Some secretaries spell them out on paper file labels for ease in filing.

Names	*Index and File as*
St. John's Church	Saint John's Church
Jas. Sanders	Sanders, James
Jane Sanders	Sanders, Jane
Wm. Smith	Smith, William
Willis Smith	Smith, Willis

Sometimes an abbreviated name is the actual legal name of the person or company. In this case, use the abbreviated spelling in filing.

COMPOUND FIRM NAMES. When a firm name consists of a compound word that is sometimes spelled as one word, sometimes as two or more words, index as written but treat it as one word in alphabetizing. *Exception:* Compound *geographic* names, such as a city or region, are often treated as two words.

Index and File as

Lockport Engine Co.

Lock Port Fisheries

Lockport Mansions, Inc.

New Amsterdam Bakery, Inc.

New York City Bank

Newark Rubber Co.

North, R. S.

North East Commodities, Inc.

Northeastern Burlap Co.

Opinions differ about whether compound names, such as *Lock Port*, should be treated as one or two words in alphabetizing. Adopt a rule and follow it uniformly.

SR., JR., II, III. You may retain designations that follow names, such as *Jr.* or *III* (Third), in indexing and filing and alphabetize according to the designation. The order is as follows: II (Second), III (Third), Jr., Sr. But some organizations ignore seniority terms and arrange identical names by address instead.

Index and File as
White, John, II
White, John, III
White, John, Jr.
White, John, Sr.

LAST NAMES WITH PREFIXES. When an individual last name is compounded with a prefix, such as *D', De, Del, De la, Di, Fitz, L', La, Las, lost, M', Mc, Mac, O', San, Santa, Ten, Van, van der, von,* and *von der,* index as written and treat the name as one word in alphabetizing, disregarding the apostrophe, the space, or the capitalization, if any.

Index and File as
Damata, J.
D'Amato, P.
D'Arcy, A. C.
De Lamara, A. D.
De La Mare, A. D.
Madison, R. L.
McIntyre, A. C.
Mean, Robert A.
Tenants' Committee, Inc.
Ten Eyck, E. M.

ARTICLES, PREPOSITIONS, AND CONJUNCTIONS. Disregard articles, prepositions, and conjunctions in determining alphabetical sequence. The words in parentheses in the following examples are disregarded.

Names	Index and File as
F. A. Madison	Madison, F. A.
The Marine Bank	(The) Marine Bank
Geo. Mathews	Mathews, Geo.
Society of Arts and Sciences	Society (of) Arts (and) Sciences
Society for the Prevention of Cruelty to Animals	Society (for the) Prevention of Cruelty to Animals

ARTICLES, PREPOSITIONS, AND CONJUNCTIONS IN FOREIGN LANGUAGES. Consider an article in a name in a foreign language as part of the word that immediately follows it; treat prepositions and conjunctions as separate words in determining alphabetical sequence.

Names	Index and File as
C. H. Deramer	Deramer, C. H.
Der Amerikaner	Der Amerikaner
Société des Auteurs et Peintres	Société des Auteurs et Peintres
Société des Auteurs, Musiciens et Compositeurs	Société des Auteurs, Musiciens et Compositeurs

WORDS ENDING IN S. When a word ends in *s*, index and file it as spelled, regardless of what the *s* denotes (whether possession, with or without the apostrophe, or a singular or plural ending).

Index and File as
Girl Scout Council
Girls' Service League
Smith, John
Smith's Delicatessen
Thompson, R. S.

NAMES CONTAINING NUMBERS. When a name contains a number, alphabetize as if the number were spelled in full. If practical to do so, spelling out the names on the file labels will facilitate the filing.

Names	Index and File as
28 Sutton Place, Inc.	Twenty-eight Sutton Place, Inc.
2059 Third Ave. Corp.	Twenty Fifty-nine Third Ave. Corp.
The "21" Club	(The) "Twenty-one" Club

Exception: Numbered streets and branches of organizations numbered consecutively should be arranged in numerical sequence. Thus Branch Number 4 precedes Branch Number 5, although if the numbers were spelled out and alphabetized, Branch Number Five would precede Branch Number Four.

GOVERNMENT OFFICES. Index and file names of government offices under the names of the governing body, with the names of the departments, bureaus, or institutions as subtitles.

> *Federal*
> United States Government
>> Treasury (Dept. of)
>>> Accounts (Bur. of)
>
> *State*
> Mississippi (State of)
>> Education (Dept. of)
>>> Rural Education (Div. of)
>
> *County*
> Suffolk (County of)
>> County Clerk
>
> *City*
> Memphis, Tennessee
>> City Planning Commission

TITLES. Titles are disregarded in indexing and filing but are usually written in parentheses at the end of the name.

Exceptions: If the name of an individual contains a title and a first name, without a last name, consider the title as the first word.

Names	*Index and File as*
Dr. J. C. Adams	Adams, J. C. (Dr.)
Sister Mary Brown	Brown, Mary (Sr.)
Madame Celeste	Madame Celeste
Mrs. Helen Marsh	Marsh, Helen (Mrs.)
Count Carlos Sforza	Sforza, Carlos (Count)

If a *firm name* contains a title, consider the title as the first word.

> *Index and File as*
> King Edward Hospital
> Sir Walter Raleigh Tobacco Co.
> Uncle Sam Produce Co.

MARRIED WOMEN. Index and file the names of married women according to their married last names, followed by their first names (unless they use their maiden names or are known by other names). Show the husband's initial or name in parentheses when it is important to have this information.

Name	*Index and File as*
Mrs. Robert E. (Ada R.) Brown	Brown, Ada R. (Mrs. Robert E. Brown)
Mrs. Albert S. (Mary L.) Brown	Brown, Mary L. (Mrs. Albert S. Brown)

PRINCIPAL STORAGE MEDIA

Paper Media

Paper files are the principal storage media in most businesses, although they are frequently used in conjunction with other media. Because paper files have been in use longer than electronic, microimage, or other media, the equipment and supplies, as well as the filing procedures, are fairly standard.

EQUIPMENT AND SUPPLIES FOR PAPER FILES. Paper files are stored in containers in which folders and guides are identified by typed or printed labels. An extensive variety of containers, equipment, and supplies is available.

1. Standard office file cabinets. The traditional office file is a drawer-style cabinet. *Vertical files* are upright units of one or more drawers. *Lateral files*, often with fewer drawers, are wide versions of the drawer-style cabinet. Most standard drawer files are available in decorator colors, usually with locks; have insulated, fireproof drawers; and have a suspension system.

2. Open files. Open-shelf units are usually bookcase style, with no doors. Reference-shelf files, however, have doors that lower like a countertop. Some terminal-digit files are motorized, with a hanging (suspension) folder design. Rotary types have numerous floor-to-ceiling shelves. Since the folders are immediately visible on open shelves, color coding can be used effectively to help file clerks quickly locate material and easily spot misfiles.

3. Portable files. Some file cabinets have casters for easy movement. They may have one drawer and one shelf or two drawers. The top half may have a lid rather than a pull-out drawer.

4. Safety files. A safety file is any type of container that protects materials from theft, fire, humidity, and other damaging elements by way of locks, protective insulation, or other special features.

5. Tray files. Tray files hold cards or papers positioned in a flat, usually overlapping manner. Since the contents are thus open for immediate viewing, they are often called "visible files." Some power-driven card units have trays on shelves that can be elevated or lowered to the level of the file clerk (elevator files). Visible tray or elevator files often have cards or sheets in transparent pockets.

6. Rotary files. Large, motorized, carousel-style files (such as terminal-digit open files) will accept standard file folders and guides. Other rotary files are small, desktop units that have a rotating wheel, such as the rotary address file, in which small cards are cut or punched to fit around a circular cylinder or wheel.

7. Other cabinets and containers. A variety of boxes and other cabinets and containers are used to store supplies. Some large cabinets with doors have shelves as well as a rod for hanging clothes. Some containers are simply fiberboard or cardboard boxes with a lid and a place to affix a label. Such containers might be used to store odd-sized material or inactive file folders.

8. Specialized files. Some files have special characteristics, such as the keyboard-activated random file. Printed or typed cards have metal teeth on one edge that fit over a magnetic rod. When certain keys are depressed, one or more cards are pushed up. Other files are designed for odd-sized material, such as art and blueprint files. The style may be open shelves with vertical dividers, flat drawers, or cubes that hold rolls of paper.

9. Combination files. Any file cabinet or container that combines two or more purposes is a combination file. Some units, for example, may have a general storage compartment, shelf space, and drawer space.

10. Electronic data-processing files. Certain electronic data-processing (EDP) files are designed to hold computer printouts. Containers include shelf-style pockets for storing binders and loose sheets and cabinets with hanging binder racks or printout drawers. Some printout storage devices are on casters so that they can be wheeled in and out of a workstation.

11. Information-storage and -retrieval equipment. Large data-storage and -retrieval centers are most common in a central filing department, with special operators. A detailed index that specifies the location of each file is maintained by computer. To retrieve a folder, a special electronic device is activated by a keyboard operator to locate file containers and physically transport them to a predetermined location.

PREPARING LABELS AND GUIDES FOR PAPER FILES. Conventional paper files require file folders and guides that are labeled by designations that conform to the type of filing system being used, such as alphabetic or numeric.

1. Basic rules. Use the briefest possible designations, omitting most punctuation whenever possible. However, you may be using the same designations that are used for your corresponding computer filenames. In that case, follow the filename punctuation requirements of your software program.

Index tabs (such as *A, B, C,* and so on) need to be legible only at normal reading distance. Guide labels should be legible at 2 to 3 feet. File-drawer labels should be legible at 6 to 10 feet. (See Figure 1 for examples of labels.)

Regardless of your computer-filename capitalization style, use initial caps whenever needed on paper file-folder labels. Full caps make reading more difficult. Do not underline folder labels.

2. File-folder labels. Sometimes the only part of a file-folder label that is visible is the eighth of an inch immediately below the top. Therefore, write in the first typing space below the top, and begin in the first or second typing space from the left edge of the label, except for one- or two-character designations, which may be centered. All folder labels in the file drawer will then present an even left margin. Use initial caps and indent the second and third lines so that the first word of the first line will stand out.

For a label in a numbered subject file, leave space between the number and the first word; type the subject in block form. Avoid exceptionally long file numbers if possible. For proper arrangement of various label designations, see Figure 2. Labels may be color-coded to make it easier to identify material by subject.

3. File-guide labels. Use the largest type available. Begin the typing as high on the label as the guide tabs will permit. Center one- and two-character designations. Start all other designations in the second typing space from the left edge. Use abbreviations or short forms and omit punctuation, except for large numbers such as 10,000.

4. File-drawer labels. Use the largest type available. Center the words on the label and leave a double space above and below any detailed reference information. If you are unable to print out large-type letters with your computer, hand-letter the drawer labels. Small (pica or elite) type is not legible at a distance.

USING GUIDES IN THE PAPER FILES. Frequent guides in the paper files make filing and finding easy. Therefore, it is usually advisable to put guides between at least every six to eight folders.

Alphabetic index guides come in divisions of from 25 to 200. A 25-division index has a guide for each letter from *A* to *Z*, with *Mc* added and *XYZ* combined in the last guide. Although in alphabetizing, names beginning with *Mc* are treated in regular alphabetical sequence, *Mc* is included as a letter in a 25-division index for the convenience of those who have more than three or four names beginning with *Mc*. The *Mc* guide precedes the *M* guide. In an index with more divisions, the *Mc* guide is in its proper alphabetical position, between the *M* and the *N* guides.

To determine which division you need, count the number of drawers of filing material. The following list shows the division required for a given number of drawers.

FIGURE 2

Proper Arrangement for Label Designations

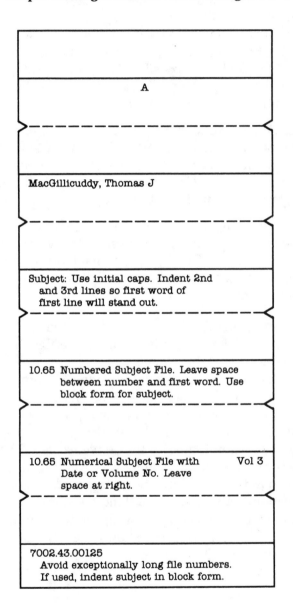

1 drawer:	25 division
2 drawers:	40 division
4 drawers:	80 division
6 drawers:	120 division
8 drawers:	160 division
12 drawers:	240 division
16 drawers:	320 division

Tabs come in different sizes and positions, for example, third cut or fifth cut. This means that they are staggered from one side of a guide or folder to the other side. You might, therefore, want to use a left-side tab for a main heading and place all others to the right for your subheadings.

USING CROSS-REFERENCES IN THE PAPER FILES. Cross-references should be used as often as necessary in all types of files—paper, electronic, or other.

1. When to use a cross-reference. Frequently, material may be filed logically under one or more names or subjects. In those cases, file a paper document under one name or subject and put a cross-reference under the other. For example, a letter from Mr. Remsen might relate to Ms. Abernathy, and the most reasonable place to file the letter might be under *Abernathy*. A cross-reference should then be made under *Remsen*. Write the cross-reference on colored cross-reference sheets, 8½ by 11 inches. They are available in most office-supply stores, or you can prepare a form on your computer similar to that illustrated in Figure 3. If Mr. Remsen has a regular folder, put the cross-reference sheet in it; if not, put it in the miscellaneous folder under the letter *R*.

2. Permanent cross-reference. A permanent cross-reference is usually maintained when a name or subject can be filed under more than one designation. For example, a permanent cross-reference should be maintained under *Simon, Franklin & Company* to *Franklin Simon & Company*. When a permanent cross-reference is desired in the paper files, make a guide to serve as a cross-reference signal and insert it in its proper alphabetical position among the regular file folders. The back of an old file folder will serve this purpose. Labels for cross-reference folders should be in a color different from the color of the labels on the regular folders. The cross-reference label should read:

FIGURE 3

Cross-Reference Sheet

CROSS-REFERENCE

Name/Subject: Remsen, S. J.   **File No:**   1102A

Re: Recommendation, George Abernathy   **Date:**   March 1, 199–

SEE

Name/Subject: Abernathy, George   **File No:**   2418C

Simon, Franklin & Co.

SEE Franklin Simon & Company

3. Storing bulky materials. If you must store odd-sized material or bulky objects (blueprints, film, and so on) in a special place, use a cross-reference sheet in the regular files.

4. When not to use cross-references. Frequent reference or the need for full information immediately may preclude the use of a standard cross-reference procedure. In such situations, use a photocopy of the document in question and place it in the regular files.

Magnetic Media

Although the use of magnetic media for information storage has outpaced the use of microimaging, the use of disks and tapes for the filing of computer-prepared documents has not surpassed paper storage, as some had predicted.

EQUIPMENT AND SUPPLIES FOR MAGNETIC MEDIA. Three common types of magnetic media are the flexible disk, hard disk, and magnetic tape.

1. Flexible disks. Flexible, or floppy, disks are small, removable disks resembling a small phonograph record, available in sizes of 3½, 5¼, and 8 inches. The amount of storage space on a flexible disk depends on the capacity provided by the manufacturer.

Individual disks may be stored in boxes, trays, or other containers designed to accommodate the different-sized disks. Covered containers keep the disks clean and protect them from physical damage. To protect your flexible disks further, do not bend the 5¼-inch floppy disk or touch the magnetic surface of any disk since dust, oil, and other residues can wipe out your data. Also, keep disks away from magnetic fields, which exist in most of your computer equipment, in telephones, and in many other places in an office, since a magnet can destroy your data. Store disks in containers, not in the drive where a power surge could wipe out or scramble the data. Locking the containers will add a measure of security, although some small containers can easily be picked up and carried away by an intruder.

Special labels are available for flexible disks, many of which have colored bars so that users can color-code the disks. A disk label is often hand-written with a felt-tipped pen that doesn't require pressure to be applied, which might damage the disk. The label designation may include information such as the software and hardware used to prepare the disk's files, the names of the files stored on the disk, and the preparation or other dates.

Individual *filenames*, which differ from the designations on the disk label, are the names, numbers, or codes of files stored on the disk. Your software will provide instructions on naming files. If, for example, you use one to eight characters plus a three-character extension, you might name the revised Henderson report HNDRSNRP.REV. The document can then be brought (called) onto the computer display screen ("loading the document") by typing its filename and striking the appropriate keys that will instruct your computer to load it.

2. Hard disks. Like a flexible disk, a permanent hard disk is a magnetic storage device. It may be built into the computer (unlike a small, removable flexible disk) or may be attached externally as an additional hard disk. Because of the vast storage capacity of a hard disk compared to that of a removable flexible disk, it can retain massive amounts of data organized in numerous files. The precise hard-disk storage procedure (i.e., the keys you must strike) depends on the hardware and software used to create your documents.

In hard-disk storage, individual files are grouped and stored in various *directories* that you can create to organize your material in main categories. Subdirectories are often developed for individual subjects or projects, which leads to a multilevel outline or index: main (or root) directory, multilevel subdirectories, and various filenames within each subdirectory. Directories, with a list of their files, can be printed out to serve as individual indexes to your hard-disk files, or they can be combined into a single detailed index to all files within all directories.

Since a hard disk is not removed and filed in a container like a flexible disk, no printed or handwritten disk labels are attached to a hard disk. However, *backup* (duplicate) copies of files on hard disks are often made on flexible disks as a precaution in case the original files on the hard disk are lost or destroyed. These backup flexible disks would be labeled as described in the preceding section.

Since hard disks are not removable for storage in a secure place, data must be protected by computer-equipment keys or passwords given only to authorized personnel, by housing the equipment in a locked room, or by some other security measure. Hard disks also must be protected against dust, excessive humidity, physical abuse, power surges, and other problems.

3. Magnetic tape. Unlike the flexible disk, a magnetic tape is a strip of magnetic material that is wound onto a reel, cartridge, or cassette. Large reels, usually associated with large mainframe computer systems, hold huge amounts of data, whereas cassettes and cartridges hold comparatively smaller amounts of information.

Since tapes are removable for storage in reel, cassette, or cartridge containers, labels can be prepared for these containers in the same way that a label would be prepared for a flexible disk. The filenames of documents stored on a tape would be comparable to the filenames devised for flexible- or hard-disk storage. Cross-references should be used freely, the same as in any other type of filing.

Cleanliness and security are also important for magnetic tape, and a suitable, safe environment must be maintained for the storage and protection of the tape containers.

Microimage Media

Although the use of computer disks for data storage has surpassed the use of microimage media, two microforms (microfilm rolls and flat forms) remain popular for long-term storage, particularly for the retention of inactive or archival material.

EQUIPMENT AND SUPPLIES FOR MICROIMAGE MEDIA. *Microfilm rolls* are available in different widths and lengths. *Microfilm flat forms* (such as microfiche, aperture cards, and micro-opaques) are filed in sheetlike forms. *Computer-output microfilm* (COM), both flat and rolled, is a computer-generated microimage media. All microimage forms are stored in containers designed for the particular size media—envelopes, trays, binders, boxes, carousels, and so on. Special equipment is needed to read the material on a display screen or to print it out in hard-copy form.

Microimage media, particularly the sheets, are filed much the same as paper media, with labels and guides, which are also prepared in a similar fashion. Container labels are used on cartridges and cassettes similar to magnetic-tape container labels. A microimage container label may specify the department and record series number, as well as any descriptive heading. Cross-references may be written directly on the container label.

Indexes to microimage records are necessary to provide a visual listing of all contents. They may be maintained with a computer in a form similar to that of disk indexes.

Security and safety measures are as important for microimage media as for other media. Although microimage media cannot be read without special equipment, which partially controls unauthorized use, other measures are nevertheless needed to secure the storage devices and to provide a clean environment, including containers that are safe for long-term film storage.

Optical-Disk Media

Optical-memory storage refers to the large-volume storage of computerized data. A relatively new technology, optical-disk applications are designed for use in handling computer-generated data as well as paper or other records that can be scanned directly into an optical-memory system.

EQUIPMENT AND SUPPLIES FOR OPTICAL-DISK STORAGE. Optical memory storage saves data in disk, tape, or card form, with optical disks being the most common.

1. CD-ROMs. The most familiar optical disk is the CD-ROM (compact disk–read-only memory), which resembles a small musical CD. This type of optical disk cannot be edited or written on. Since vast amounts of storage space are available on an optical disk, a CD-ROM can house entire encyclopedias, thousands of articles, or any other vast collection of information.

2. WORMs. The WORM optical disk is a write once–read many times metal-film disk. Once the data have been written onto it, it cannot be erased or changed but can be read over and over.

3. Erasable optical disks. Erasable optical media can be reused. The most common is the magneto-optical disk, which offers users high-speed storage and retrieval of massive amounts of data.

Optical disk systems vary but commonly consist of a computer, a scanner, and an optical-disk drive. Quality software is necessary to provide an effective system.

Documents stored in an optical-disk system can be indexed the same as those in any other disk-storage system, and optical-disk storage containers can be labeled the same as the storage containers for other media.

A clean and secure environment is also required to protect the optical-disk media. Often the same security measures devised for one type of system (such as locked premises, passwords, and other restricted access) can be applied to another system.

DATABASE STORAGE SYSTEMS AND SERVICES

Company Systems and On-Line Services

PURPOSE OF A DATABASE. A *database* is a collection of facts maintained in an organized manner. Although any conventional file of facts, such as a telephone list, could be considered a database, the term has become associated with a collection of data stored electronically. Your company may have its own computerized databases, such as a compilation of the addresses of customers and prospective customers. Or it may subscribe to an outside database service (an *on-line service*), such as a financial-reporting service (e.g., Dow Jones). Databases are an especially important application for microcomputers and are designed to store and display many types of data, including figures, text, and graphics.

HOW A DATABASE IS ORGANIZED. Special software is required to enable a computer to collect and organize data. The right database software will allow you to create a database, maintain it, and then refer to it or use it as needed. Most databases organize the particular information you provide by fields, records, and files.

A *field* refers to an individual item (such as a telephone number), a *record* is a set of fields, and a *file* is a set of records. The particular software you use will tell you how to enter the data—which keys to strike, what options you have, and so on.

HOW TO USE A COMPANY DATABASE.   If you are setting up your own database, the first step is to enter the information, just as you would have to key in the text of a document with a word processing program before you could view it or print it out. Usually, you can add, delete, or change the information you enter.

After you have entered the information, you can sort a file by fields to organize it in different ways (such as by states or by zip codes). You can then select specific records and send the information in those records to another program, such as a spreadsheet or a word processing merge file (*export it*). You can also do the reverse and bring information from an outside program into the database (*import it*). Finally, you can print out the data (*report it*).

HOW TO USE AN ON-LINE DATABASE.   An on-line service sells information electronically, just as a publisher sells information in print form. Many companies use on-line services to secure vital business information that isn't quickly or easily found elsewhere. On-line services are available nationwide, and to use them, all it takes is a computer, a modem, and a telephone. The modem connects your computer to the telephone and converts readable information into a form that will travel back and forth over the telephone lines.

On-line services exist for virtually any type of information that can be transmitted electronically, such as up-to-the-minute securities quotations, published articles in newspapers and magazines, worldwide scientific data, and different governmental information. Some large services function primarily as a centralized entry to numerous other on-line services. Check your local library for a directory of services.

Services often charge by subscription fee plus individual fees for time used. Since the cost may be high compared to another alternative, such as a visit to your local library reference room, you must evaluate your needs carefully before going on-line. If an electronic search is warranted, take steps to control your costs by controlling the time you spend on-line. Usually, you are required to type key words that identify the information you want to receive. Choose very specific key words to avoid wasting time that may produce a lot of facts and figures you don't need or want. (See Chapter 3.)

FILING AND RETRIEVAL TECHNIQUES

Preparing Material for Filing

DETERMINE IF A FILE IS REALLY NECESSARY. Files are intended to organize information so that it can be retrieved with a minimum of time and effort. Therefore, the temptation to overorganize is strong, and you need to view each new file critically.

1. Checklist for a new file. Before opening a proposed file, ask yourself these simple questions:

Will the proposed new file make it possible to locate information faster and easier than in present files?

How often will the file be used—often, occasionally, seldom?

Will the file require an increase in the number of copies of certain correspondence?

Will the file increase the number of hours devoted to filing and related duties?

Will the file affect container and other storage-space requirements?

Will the file require other new files (checkout, cross-reference, and so on) to maintain it properly?

In general, do the pros outweigh the cons?

PREPARING ELECTRONIC DATA FOR FILING. Documents and other information can be stored in the computer's memory by *saving* the information on a hard disk or flexible disk. To prepare electronic data for filing you need to do at least three things.

1. Give the document or other material you are working on a filename.
2. Determine in which directory or subdirectory you want the file to be stored, or set up a new directory if none exists for it.
3. Use the appropriate command to save the material, which will instruct your computer to store it under the filename you have given

it and in the directory or subdirectory you specify in the command. With some software, for example, to indicate that you want to save material you might type *C:\RDP\DR1.DOC*. This designation would mean that you want to store draft no. 1 (a document), which you had abbreviated as *DR1.DOC*, in a directory located on your hard disk *C* that you had called RDP (for Rural Development Project).

PREPARING PAPER DOCUMENTS FOR FILING. Filing paper documents and other material involves more steps since you have to handle the material physically and place it where you want it in the file cabinet.

1. Check to be certain the material has been released for filing. (This may be indicated by a brief notation on the document or by a rubber-stamped FILE notice.)

2. Segregate papers into the different categories: personal correspondence, business correspondence, documents, and the like. Then arrange items in each category in alphabetic order. For numeric files, code each item as described in number 6 below and arrange the items sequentially.

3. Check through all papers that are stapled to see whether they should be filed together.

4. Remove all paper clips.

5. Mend torn papers with cellophane tape.

6. If your office will permit writing or marking on file copies, use a yellow highlighting pen or erasable blue pencil to indicate on the paper where it is to be filed. (If you may not mark copies, use self-sticking, removable notes.) For a *name file*, highlight the name; for a *subject file*, write the main heading and subheading in the upper right corner. Note a guide or file number, if used, in the upper right corner. For *numerical coding*, refer to your index to the files and mark the assigned file number in the upper right corner.

7. Highlight important words to facilitate location of a particular paper when it is wanted. (But see number 6 regarding writing on file material.)

8. Make necessary cross-reference sheets as each letter or paper is handled.

Using Timesaving Equipment and Techniques

ELECTRONIC FILING TECHNIQUES. Electronic filing and finding is fast and easy. To locate a file, follow these steps:

1. Strike the appropriate keys for this purpose as described by your software. This command tells your computer that you want to "load" a document from the disk where it is stored.

2. After initiating the load command, type the name of the document you want, such as *C:\RDP\DR1.DOC,* a file described in item 3 on pages 31–32.

3. After designating which document you want to retrieve, enter the command (strike the Enter or other required key), and the material will appear on your display screen. You can now read it on the screen, edit it, or print it out as a paper copy.

PAPER FILING TECHNIQUES. Like the procedure for preparing paper items for filing, the process of *finding* material in the paper files is more involved than it is with an electronic system. You must physically locate and remove the material you want.

1. Visit showrooms and write to suppliers to request free sales literature to get ideas on new and effective filing materials and equipment, filing systems, and efficient office layouts.

2. Avoid fatigue by using filing techniques and aids such as (a) stools with rollers and (b) tables with rollers or trays that attach to file drawers. Keep heavy documents where it isn't necessary to lift or carry them far; store seldom-used materials in the higher and lower drawers or on top and bottom shelves; and always work from the side, not the front, of a file drawer.

3. File daily; large stacks of accumulated filing can complicate the task and make it tiresome.

4. Simplify the step of sorting and organizing material by using sorting trays, racks, or carts. Use rubber fingers to leaf through large stacks of correspondence. Use different-colored copy paper, according to subject, to speed the sorting process.

5. Use supplies and equipment that encourage rapid visual location, such as (a) visible files, including trays, holders, stands, looseleaf books, and desktop organizers, along with transparent guides, binder and shelf clips, and pockets; and (b) color-coded files, both file folders and storage containers. Circular, rotating files, and open-shelf filing also permit fast and easy location and retrieval, especially in combination with color coding.

6. Avoid mishaps, such as (a) toppling a file cabinet by pulling out more than one drawer at a time, (b) spilling the contents of a folder by not resting it properly after removal or by not using both hands while filing or retrieving material, or (c) ruining a folder while pulling it out by grasping only the tab.

7. Keep the size of folders manageable—open new ones if necessary. Leave several inches for such expansion in each file drawer and on each shelf.

8. Use a guide for every six to eight folders and place folders *behind* the guides. Investigate the use of file- and desk-drawer dividers to aid further in compartmentalizing and organizing contents.

9. Speed the labeling process with products such as pressure-sensitive labels, preprinted tabs, and continuous-feed labels. Some tabs are removable, and some have transparent windows for reuse.

10. Position records in their folders face up with the top toward the left; the document with the most recent date goes in front. Fold oversized papers with the data on the outside.

11. Staple an envelope on the inside of a file folder when you have small clippings or pictures that might otherwise become bent or lost.

USING COLOR CODING TO ENHANCE YOUR FILING SYSTEM. Color coding, as used on labels for paper file folders, guides, and containers, as well as on labels for other media, can be applied to any type of alphabetic or numeric filing system. It can be as simple or as intricate as you like. Quick storage and retrieval and ease in spotting misfiles are among the benefits of this technique.

Color can be applied numerically (e.g., black = 10, red = 20, green = 30, and so on) or by subject (e.g., black = Insurance; red = Real Estate; green = Investments). It can indicate action to take. Yellow, for example, might indicate action completed; red might indicate that follow-up action is needed. Some offices use color to make evaluations. Black might refer to an interested, prospective customer; red might mean a potential, but difficult, customer; green might denote an unlikely prospect.

The uses of color are almost limitless. Manufacturers of supplies and containers have complete systems already designed, and sales literature describing them is available free.

Controlling Material Taken from the Files

CONTROLLING ACCESS TO YOUR ELECTRONIC FILES. If more than one person has access to your computer, the users may be able to load your material into the computer's memory for viewing on screen or for printout on paper. In fact, if you store the material on small, removable flexible disks, someone could simply carry the disk out of your office without your knowledge. In the case of electronic mail, your messages may be sent to electronic mailboxes, or bulletin boards, where they can be read by anyone who uses the same system.

Electronic files, therefore, are subject to unauthorized use the same as paper files. But different steps must be taken to control the access to and use of electronic files.

1. Ask your employer to define clearly who should have access to your electronic files.

2. If your computer is in a location accessible to others who are not authorized to view your files or remove your flexible disks, establish appropriate security measures, such as:

   Passwords that must be given before a file can be retrieved

   Keys that lock a computer so that no one else can operate it

   Locks on storage containers and closets that house removable flexible disks

3. If certain individuals are authorized to borrow flexible disks, make a backup copy to loan out (keep the original in your office). Remember, however, that anyone who borrows a flexible disk can easily make a copy of it. Hence confidential material or very important company documents should never be removed from the office unless expressly authorized by your employer.

4. Maintain a checkout file (cards or sheets) on which you record the date of removal, disks taken, name of borrower, and date to be returned. Follow the example on page 37.

5. Place flexible disks that are released on loan in a protective jacket to protect them from the physical handling that occurs during a loan.

6. Follow your employer's policy regarding the threat of viruses (bogus programs maliciously created to disrupt or destroy disk files). A virus could infect your computer if you use disks from other offices or they use your disks in one of their infected machines. Many companies install antiviral software to detect the existence of a virus.

CONTROLLING ACCESS TO YOUR PAPER FILES. Secretaries often safeguard paper files by keeping the file cabinets locked when they are not in the office to watch them.

1. Ask your employer to define clearly who should have access to your paper files. Usually, even when others are authorized to borrow material, only the secretary is authorized to go into the files and remove the material.

2. When material is removed from the files, use *out folders* and *out guides* to occupy the position of the material that has been removed.

   Make the out folders or guides the same height as the file folders but of different-colored stock, with the word *OUT* printed in all capitals on the tab. Ruled spaces appear on the front for recording charge-out information. (See Figure 4.)

FIGURE 4

Out Card

DATE	MATERIAL	DATE REMOVED	TO BE RETURNED	CHARGE TO WHOM	REMARKS

Substitute the out folder for the regular folder that is removed. Until the regular folder is returned, file new correspondence in the out folder.

When out guides are used, accumulate new material awaiting filing elsewhere until the regular folder is returned. Out guides provide space on which to make an entry of the date, the material taken, who has it, and the date it should be returned.

Place the guide in the files where the removed material was located.

If your out guides have a pocket in which a charge-out slip (sometimes called a requisition slip) can be filed, make three copies of the slip and place one copy in the guide pocket. Clip another copy to the file material that is removed, and place a third copy in the follow-up files in case the user needs a reminder to return the material.

3. Do not, however, put an out guide in the file every time you withdraw material for your employer. Rather, use the guide only when (a) someone outside the immediate office wants the material, (b) your employer expects to take the material out of the office, or (c) you expect your employer to keep the material for a week or more.

Retrieving Lost Files

FINDING LOST ELECTRONIC FILES. Finding lost electronic files can be difficult. When the words "File Is Not Available" appear on your computer display screen, it may mean that you forgot to save the document before leaving the program or turning off your computer; if so, the material will no longer be available in the computer's memory. Usually, however, a file that appears to be lost is not really permanently lost, and you should explore possibilities such as the following:

1. If you work in a network of computers or in one of several terminals connected to a large mainframe, the document you want to find may be unavailable because it is currently being worked on by someone else who has access to it. When that person finishes, it will be available again.

2. The file you want may be stored elsewhere on a flexible disk, but you first need to rule out the possibility that it is on the hard disk. Instruct your computer to list all the files in a particular directory or on your entire hard disk. Check if the name of the file you want is listed anywhere (perhaps in the wrong directory). If it is not listed anywhere on the hard disk, look in the flexible-disk active and inactive storage containers. If you find it, bring it to your computer and either use it in one of your flexible disk drives or copy it onto your hard disk.

3. You may have typed the filename incorrectly. Perhaps you omitted the drive or used *A* when you should have used *C* for the drive designation. Or you may have typed *RPT.DOC* (Report.Document) when the extension in this case is not *DOC* but rather *FIG* (Report.Figures). You may have typed a period when a colon was required or vice versa. Or you may have typed the letter *l* whereas the filename uses the number *1*.

4. If you want a particular document but can't recall the name of it and don't recognize it on your index to filenames or in a hard-disk directory, you may be able to do a document search. Some software will search all your directories for a document that meets the criteria you specify. If the document you want appears on the list that is provided by your computer after the search, you can high-

light the name in question, or designate it however your software requires, and it will be loaded into the computer's memory and will appear on your display screen. You can then rename the document if you wish (make the same change on your index to the files) or leave it as is.

5. Read the instructions (documentation) that accompany your software for other options that may be available. If something is not clear, or if you are still having trouble retrieving the file, call the support number provided with the software vendor (usually an 800 number) and ask for help.

6. Double-check, and correct as needed, any index to the electronic files that you have been maintaining. If you use numerical file designations or codes with a combination of letters and numbers, you will have to maintain an alphabetical index to your electronic files. You may keep such an index even if your files are alphabetical so that you can print out a hard copy for ease in reference.

FINDING LOST PAPER FILES. Locating lost documents in the paper files is sometimes easier than it is with electronic files since you can physically look into the file folders and look at all the folder labels in front of you.

1. Look in the folders that precede and follow the folder where the paper should be.

2. Check under consonants that look alike, such as *N, M, W, U,* and *V.*

3. Look under vowels other than the correct one. For a name beginning with *Ca,* look under *Ce, Ci, Co,* or *Cu.*

4. Watch for abbreviations, which are easily misfiled. For example, an abbreviation of James Sanders may have been incorrectly labeled and filed under *Sanders, Jas.,* instead of *Sanders, James,* or an abbreviation of *Saint* may have been incorrectly labeled and filed under *St.* instead of *Sa.*

5. If more than one name is in the subject of the lost paper, look under each name, even though the paper should have been filed under the first name in the subject.

6. Look for a possible "charge-out" or "transferred" withdrawal that may not have been recorded.

7. Check your sorter or look behind the file cabinet or your desk or even in the wastebasket.

Streamlining the Files

HOUSECLEANING WITH ELECTRONIC FILES. One of the most overlooked tasks in electronic filing is *housecleaning,* the removal or transfer of unnecessary, old, or duplicate files from your hard disk.

1. Review your records-retention schedule to see if certain materials qualify for transfer to archives storage.

2. Print out your index to the files or a list of all directories and files on your hard disk for convenience in checking off files that are ready for transfer to flexible-disk storage.

3. Check whether a duplicate file already exists. If you have followed the recommended policy of copying (backing up) *everything* from your hard disk to a flexible disk, you will already have a duplicate copy of each hard-disk file stored on a flexible disk. However, do *not* delete any file from your hard disk until you have confirmed that a full and correct copy is available in storage on a flexible disk.

4. Review the list of files and directories on your hard disk to look for duplicate copies of files or earlier drafts that are no longer needed. Whenever you edit a document and save it, the computer retains not only the newly edited version but the previous version; the previous version has the filename extension *BAK.* Look for similar names such as *MTR22.DOC* and *MTR22.BAK.* Unless you have a reason to retain previous versions of documents, you may be able to delete the files that end with the initials *BAK.* (*Note:* A *BAK* designation refers to a copy of a document before it was changed—the previous version—but does not refer to a duplicate backup copy of the final, changed version that you make for storage on a flexible disk.)

5. Find out if your hard disk contains old versions of a software program that can be deleted (if authorized by your employer). Perhaps you recently acquired and installed on your hard disk the word processing program Microsoft Word 5.5. You may also have previous versions 4.0 and 5.0 installed on your hard disk that

could be deleted, particularly if you have retained flexible-disk copies of the older versions.

6. Look for other forms of duplication or outdated material that can either be transferred to flexible disks for permanent storage or destroyed (only if authorized by the firm's records-retention schedule and approved by your employer).

STREAMLINING YOUR PAPER FILES. It is especially important to clean out the paper files from time to time since an increasing paper volume can take up a substantial amount of office space and can become unwieldy without proper control.

1. Use hanging folders and hanging pockets. A suspension system keeps files orderly and uses file space efficiently.

Add metal frames to your cabinets. If your files did not come equipped with hanging folders and pockets, you can purchase metal frames that fit into the file drawers. Hanging folders and hanging pockets are ready to be dropped into place, and the hanging folder serves as a guide card, folder, and separator all in one.

Avoid using too many hanging folders. You will not save space if you use too many hanging folders in one drawer. A dozen of these folders would take up 3 inches of space. That would rob you of more drawer space than you would save by removing the follow block to insert a metal frame for the hanging folders.

Use hanging pockets. Pockets hold individual folders neatly in place and, unlike hanging folders, expand freely. Material is never lost by slipping under other folders onto the floor of the drawer. Folders are held firmly in place and never slip or slide under one another.

2. Use special-purpose folders. When it is necessary to transfer important material temporarily to another location, use a special-purpose folder with a clasp or tie to secure the material inside.

3. Use drawer dividing units. A portable, lightweight drawer divider is a device you can use instead of the bulky follow blocks in a file drawer. Its strong bottom stand holds folders upright and prevents loss through slipping, and it is adjustable, so that sections can be expanded or narrowed, as needed.

4. Eliminate magazines and bulky brochures. Remove old copies of magazines, brochures, and other printed material. After periodicals have been read by those who are interested, current issues should be substituted for them. If it is necessary to keep dated printed matter, however, store it in a less accessible place. Also, store material that must be kept as compactly as possible.

> Narrow pamphlets and brochures, only a fraction of the size of the folder that holds them, should be stacked in double or triple rows, lengthwise, within the folder.

> Printed matter that is clipped or bound on one edge should be equalized by alternating the papers within the folder: half of the bulky edges to the right side of the folder and half to the left.

5. Eliminate duplication. Remove duplications, which often occur in copies of memos and letters, galleys and page proofs, reprints of published letters and reports, and identical copies of published brochures.

Make only the required number of photocopies for each letter or report, and condense and centralize your files wherever possible, to avoid overlapping. If you keep a "copy file" and a "follow-up file" in addition to your employer's complete file, you may be doubling the amount of work necessary to complete your tasks.

Unless you plan to distribute additional copies of brochures or reports, do not store identical copies. Many secretaries retain three copies in the office and send the remaining copies to company storage rooms.

6. Remove thick backings of clippings and photos. Photographs and clippings that must be filed need support and protection against loss or tearing. Use light backing or celluloid envelope sheets.

7. Transfer little-used and odd-sized material. Move odd-sized, bulky material such as blueprints or tape reels out of the regular files to suitable containers and merely add a cross-reference in the regular files. Transfer correspondence, papers, and records that cannot be destroyed but are referred to only occasionally to storage to save floor space. Do not keep standard inquiries or form-letter replies. But if the inquiry represents a prospective customer or sale, add the name and address to the appropriate mailing list before destroying the inquiry.

RECORDS-RETENTION PROCEDURES

Developing a File-Retention Program

Your firm, with the advice of legal counsel concerning state and federal laws, will determine which materials must be retained and which may eventually be destroyed. Keep a current copy of your firm's records-retention policy in your office. If none is available, inquire at your local library or bookstore for current books on records retention. Also, write for a free copy of the Technical Publications Catalog, published by the Association of Records Managers and Administrators, Inc., 4200 Somerset Drive, Prairie Village, KS 66208.

GUIDELINES FOR BUSINESS MATERIAL. If your company has a firm policy concerning the retention of papers, you should be guided by this method. If no clear policy exists, ask your employer about the period of retention to be used for all types of documents and letters and for all types of media. This decision will be based on legal and company requirements as well as your employer's preferences.

Examples of records kept permanently are incorporation papers, journals and ledgers, and meeting minutes. Examples of records kept five to ten years are contracts that have expired, collection records, and evidence used in an insurance claim. Examples of records kept up to five years are meeting proxies, credit ratings of customers, and general correspondence. Examples of records kept up to one year are announcements, form letters, and duplicate copies of bank deposit slips.

GUIDELINES FOR PERSONAL MATTERS. Two factors will determine how long to keep personal papers and records: the statute of limitations and your employer's desires. Secretaries should compile for their own use a retention schedule that meets these requirements.

1. List alphabetically all types of personal papers and records in the files.

2. Make three columns to the right of the listed items.

3. In the first column, insert the statute of limitations requirements in your state or other legal requirements.

4. In the second column, state what you suggest as the period of retention. There are no established practices that can be used as guides for retention of personal papers as there are for business records.

5. Have your employer indicate in the third column his or her wish for the period of retention for each item.

6. Revise the schedule stating just one indication of years—the time approved by your employer.

PREPARING A STORAGE-CONTROL SCHEDULE. When you put files into storage, prepare a transfer sheet, or storage-control schedule, for the active files. (Standard forms are available in office-supply stores, or you can create your own.) List the following facts on your schedule:

1. File number on the storage box

2. Contents and date of contents

3. Location of storage box

4. Date to destroy contents

5. Date destroyed

6. Who authorized disposal

SAFEGUARDING YOUR FILES AND IMPORTANT DOCUMENTS. For a separate record or as part of the retention records mentioned earlier, ask your employer to indicate which business and personal material is confidential. All such items should be stored in cabinets with security locks, in bank safe deposit boxes, in a company safe, or in some other secure place approved by your employer.

Other considerations in filing and storing materials are fire, loss, humidity, and cleanliness. Each of these factors must be considered when selecting appropriate filing and storage equipment.

Transferring Files

HOW TO TRANSFER INACTIVE FILES. One of the advantages of document storage in reduced form, such as on tape or film, is that a large collection of files can be stored in a very small space. Some companies lack space for storing bulky paper files and convert them to a reduced-form media when they are ready for transfer to inactive storage. But many firms retain the paper files and transfer them to designated storage rooms. Transferring paper files requires numerous steps and good planning to accommodate large volumes of material.

1. Plan the new file well in advance of the transfer date.

2. If the entire file is to be transferred, leaving only guides in the file drawers, prepare new folders for the new file beforehand. Prepare only those folders that will be definitely needed. Use a new color for folder labels and indicate the year as well as the title.

3. If the folders and the guides are to be retained in the file, prepare a new set of inexpensive folders to hold the material in the transfer drawers. Put titles on these folders identical with those in the current file, and have them ready in advance of the transfer date.

4. If the space is available, keep the old files in the office for a few weeks until sufficient material for reference purposes accumulates in the new files.

5. Make sure that ample storage space is available for the old files and that the transfer files or boxes fit the conditions in the storage location.

6. To avoid interference with general office procedures, plan to have the transfer operation done after hours, and secure enough help to complete the entire job in one evening. Have two persons work on each drawer—one pulling out the folders and the other packing them in the transfer files. If folders and labels have not been prepared in advance, have someone do this work during the transfer operation.

7. Label all transfer files or boxes. Indicate contents of file, dates, and so on clearly on labels and affix them to the containers so that they can be easily read.

8. Pack transfer files or boxes tightly—two drawer-length transfer units will hold the contents of three filing cabinet drawers.

HOW TO ORDER AND STORE SUPPLIES

Purchasing and Distributing Supplies

Secretaries often purchase and store supplies for themselves, their employers, and other coworkers. This involves a knowledge of what is needed and when, where to go to get it, and where to store it until time for use.

REQUISITIONING SUPPLIES IN-HOUSE. A large company will have a special department that orders and stocks supplies for use in offices within the company. Usually, you will complete a company requisition form and present it at the stockroom. Supplies may not always be available, and requests should be made far enough in advance to allow for ordering if necessary. Follow the policy in your office concerning the approval of requisitions. In some offices, the secretary is responsible for authorizing the purchase of office supplies.

PURCHASING SUPPLIES FROM OUTSIDE VENDORS. In a small office, you may simply go to a local office-supply store and purchase (probably by charge account) the necessary supplies. At the time the supplies are ordered, you should keep a copy of the purchase order and check off items as they are received.

1. *Unscrupulous vendors.* Beware of deliveries from unscrupulous vendors of supplies that you did not order; such shipments should be refused at the time of delivery, if possible, or should be returned immediately after verifying that no one else ordered the material.

2. *Price comparisons.* Competition is keen in the office-products industry, and if you shop around you may realize substantial savings. Compare prices of different-sized dealers, mail-order firms, specialty dealers, telephone sales firms, warehouse stores, and cash-and-carry discount outlets.

3. *Ordering by telephone or facsimile.* If you place an order by telephone, have all the information you need written out (catalog number, quantity, and so on). Ordering by telephone or facsimile can speed delivery in many cases. Usually, you must order by credit card or have a company account with the dealer.

4. *When to order.* If you have doubts about quantities needed or how soon you will need new supplies, order far in advance, several months if necessary, and order more than you believe is needed immediately. Usually, when you order in standard packs or in quantities, the price is lower.

DISTRIBUTING SUPPLIES TO COWORKERS. When employees help themselves to supplies, the lack of control inevitably causes confusion and unexpected depletion of some items. Check the needs in your office periodically, perhaps weekly, so that you can order and distribute supplies according to a reasonable schedule. It would be inefficient to have to drop everything and rush out for supplies every time an employee ran out of paper clips or pencils.

Keep a list of what supplies you distribute and to whom you distribute them. This will tell you, after a month or two, which employees use which supplies and how soon they are likely to run out of them.

Organizing and Storing Supplies

INVENTORY-CONTROL PROCEDURES FOR OFFICE SUPPLIES. Some form of regular inventory control is needed, regardless of the size of the office, such as a list of supplies on hand and average quantity used during certain periods (e.g., monthly). Such an inventory-control sheet might have several columns, recording the quantities left on hand at certain dates (e.g., at the end of each month). When the sheet indicated that a certain supply would be exhausted in another month, it would be time to reorder. As an example, the following entry might indicate on April 30 that it is time to reorder memo pads:

		On Hand				
Item	Av. Qty. Used/Mo.	Jan. 31	Feb. 28	Mar. 31	Apr. 30	etc.
Memo Pads	12	48	36	24	12	etc.

HOW TO STORE OFFICE SUPPLIES. Lack of organization in storing supplies will complicate the task of taking inventory periodically. Store seldom-used supplies on the top and bottom shelves or toward the back in a storage closet. Group materials for ease in locating and in estimating quantities. Mark packages for quantity as they arrive—don't trust your memory to hold until the end of the month. As supplies are removed during the month, cross out that quantity and jot the new balance on the front package. At the end of the month, record the last balance on your inventory-control sheet.

HANDLING FOLLOW-UPS AND REMINDERS

A great deal of time in an office is spent following up some prior action or reminding someone to do something. A special type of system is needed to handle follow-ups and reminders, and both manual and electronic systems are widely used in offices of all sizes.

Types of Follow-up and Reminder Systems

ELECTRONIC REMINDER SYSTEMS. Many of the software programs are multifunction programs that enable you to prepare schedules, appointment calendars, address lists, and reminders.

1. *Program features.* Although programs differ in number of features offered, a typical tickler/calendar program will handle, at a minimum, appointments, deadlines, and reminders. Usually, it will set up "alarms" for any day that you designate. When you turn on your computer each morning, you will see a list of things to do that day.

2. *How to use an electronic follow-up/reminder system.* To tell your computer what things you need to be reminded about, you must identify the specific activities and enter them into the computer. Thereafter, reminders concerning these activities can be viewed on the computer display screen or printed out at any time.

Depending on your instructions to the computer, pop-up calendars, alarms, week-at-a-glance schedules, and other types of reminders will be created. You can then edit or change the information you entered as conditions change, and revised calendars, schedules, and reminders will be displayed.

Information can be organized or retrieved in various ways. For example, your employer may want to see a list of all scheduled meetings in October or a list of all important-customer birthdays or anniversaries in August.

Some programs organize projects of all sizes. You can give each task a priority, description, date, and start/finish times. The computer will then provide a to-do list each day consistent with the needs of the project and will alert you to finish things that need to be done.

PAPER REMINDER SYSTEMS. Even offices that rely heavily on electronic systems find that certain manual procedures are more convenient and practical.

1. Basic office calendars. Most secretaries need a paper desk calendar, and their employers often use both a desk calendar and, for travel and meetings, a pocket calendar. Whereas the electronic systems are useful in scheduling large projects or providing reminders of birthdays, holidays, and the like, paper calendars are more useful for jotting down on-the-spot reminders, such as a notation to call someone back tomorrow morning or a memo to meet someone for lunch in two days. Office-supply stores have a variety of calendars, and you should examine the various styles to determine which one would best meet the needs of your office.

2. How to use a paper calendar. Keep a list of events that go on the calendars year after year. Early in October, enter all recurring items, events, and engagements for the forthcoming year. If your employer makes important engagements far in advance, you may have to make up the yearly calendars even earlier.

Work from your list of events and not from the current year's calendar, since the dates change each year. The fifth of January, for example, will fall on a different day of the week each year. Also, be certain that a date for meetings or other business events does not fall on a Saturday, Sunday, or holiday. Enter notations of additional appointments or things to do as soon as you learn about them.

Keep used calendars for at least one year—longer if required by your employer. Calendars are often necessary for reference at tax-preparation time or in verifying dates such as travel periods or special engagements.

3. Checklist of recurring items. The following is a list of recurring items to enter on the appropriate calendars each year. If dates usually call for presents or cards, enter reminders about them days before the date as well as on the date.

Special family dates, such as anniversaries and birthdays

Holidays, such as Thanksgiving and Memorial Day

Meetings, such as board meetings

Payment dates, such as insurance-premium due dates

Renewal dates, such as subscriptions

Tax dates, such as quarterly tax payments

4. How to use reminder memos. Matters to come to your employer's attention in connection with any unscheduled but definite event are best handled by placing a reminder memo in an appropriately labeled folder for the event. For example, if your employer wants to be reminded to call on a certain customer the next time he or she goes to Chicago and the date of the trip has not been scheduled, make a folder marked "Chicago Trip" and insert in it the necessary reminder memo. When the date of the trip is settled, give your employer the entire folder or include the item in a schedule of matters pertaining to the trip. If the event is of such a rare occurrence that you would even need a reminder that there is such a folder, do not use a folder but make the notation on your calendar.

To remind your employer of some task, place the file on his or her desk. If your employer wants to do a certain thing in connection with the matter, attach a brief reminder to the file. For example, assume that your employer said, "I want to send a fax to Robertson on Friday if we don't hear from him." On Friday, then, you would prepare a memo stating: "You wanted to send a fax to Robertson" and would attach it to the Robertson file before placing it on your employer's desk. If possible, draft a possible message that your employer could send to Robertson and also attach it to the folder.

5. How to prepare appointment lists. If you use a computerized calendar program, you can print out an up-to-date list each morning or the

FIGURE 5

Daily Appointment Schedule

APPOINTMENTS FOR MONDAY, April 5, 19___

10:00 A.M.	Special Dictation—Speech for Ad Club
10:30	Conference—proposed personnel booklet
11:00	Mr. Simmons—new labor course
12:00	Employees' meeting—annual report on profit-sharing plan
1:00 P.M.	Luncheon at Ad Club with Y & R representatives
3:30	Mr. Dressler
4:00	Executive Committee meeting
5:00	Sales Staff meeting, through dinner

---

day before. (Be certain to add any last-minute appointments or changes that you have not yet entered in the computer.)

Each morning place on your employer's desk a combined *daily appointment list* and a list of special things to be done. You may want to prepare this list at the end of the previous day's work. Make a copy for your own reference. (See Figure 5.)

At the time of each appointment, give your employer any material he or she will need for it. For example, before the 12 noon appointment illustrated in Figure 5, hand your employer the material that has been prepared for making the report.

Some executives make a practice of calling their secretaries into their offices each morning for *daily conferences* to discuss pending matters and things to be done. Take with you a list of things to do and any material pertaining to them. Your employer will give you instructions on one matter after another.

Many executives like to see a *monthly appointment list*. Calendar-creator programs can develop calendars for any desired period, such as a month, and office-supply stores also have calendars designed for this purpose. The dates may show every Sunday in the month on the top row, every Monday on the next row, and so on, ending with every Saturday on the last row.

Figure 6 is an example of a four-week schedule, which should be updated each week. Note that it lists holidays, evening social functions, and things to be done, as well as appointments. It also indicates days the secretary plans to be out of the office. The question marks indicate uncertainty. (*WL* stands for "Weekly Letter.")

6. How to handle special reminders. An executive may find it useful to have a 3- by 5-inch or a 4- by 6-inch reminder card each evening when leaving the office. This contains not only a list of activities for the following day but also reminders of certain things that he or she should do at home. Figure 7 is an example of a reminder card for an executive who lives in the suburbs.

7. How to prepare a contact reminder file. If your employer makes numerous contacts throughout the year, it is difficult for him or her to remember every one and the circumstances of the meeting. Yet it may be necessary to be able to recall names and connections. A contact reminder file is useful for this purpose.

The data can be entered into your computer and printed out, or if your employer prefers a pocket-size file, it can be prepared in a small looseleaf notebook. Record the name of each person your employer meets, business or other affiliation, and the circumstances of the meeting. Mention any personal items that might be helpful to your employer in trying to recall the individual. Thus if the person sent flowers at Christmas or a booklet published by his or her company, or if your employer sent the individual something special, make a brief notation about it.

Follow-up Filing Techniques

MATERIAL THAT NEEDS FOLLOW-UP. The following items ordinarily call for follow-up action:

FIGURE 6

Four-Week Schedule

APPOINTMENTS

Nov. 15 Mon. –   – WL-269
              – 12:00 Noon – Preliminary Meetg. – Cleve. Engrg. Soc.
              – 3:00 P.M. – Apex Bd. Meetg.

"   16 Tues. – 1:30 P.M. – Engineering

"   17 Wed. – 5:30 P.M. – Cath. Char. – Parlor B – Cleve. Athletic Club
              – 6:00 P.M. – ? Union Club–Ohio Pub. Expenditure Coun.–WTH

"   18 Thur. – 6:30 P.M. – Foremen's Dinner – Lake Shore Ctry. Club

"   19 Fri. – 12:15 P.M. – ?Amer. Trade Assn. Executives – Public Libr.
              – 6:? P.M. – Cleve. Engrg. Soc. Panel

Nov. 22 Mon. –   – WL-270

"   23 Tues. – 1:30 P.M. – Engineering

"   24 Wed. –   – Sandusky

"   25 Thur. –   – Thanksgiving

"   26 Fri. –   – Nancy away from office all day
              – Evening   – Apex Dance – Lake Shore Ctry. Club

Nov. 29 Mon. –   – WL-271
              –   – Check to W. Shaw

"   30 Tues. – 1:30 P.M. – Engineering

Dec. 1 Wed. –   – Sandusky

"   2 Thur. –   – Talk at Cincinnati – Wm. Campbell

"   3 Fri. –   –

Dec. 6 Mon. –   – WL-272

"   7 Tues. – 1:30 P.M. – Engineering
              – 6:00 P.M. – Loyal Service Club – Carter Hotel

"   8 Wed. –   – Sandusky

"   9 Thur. –   –

"   10 Fri. – 10:00 A.M. – VCMA Meeting – Hotel Cleveland

FIGURE 7

Special Reminder Card

Reminder for WEDNESDAY, May 19 19—
Tell Mrs. Adams that her draperies will be delivered Mon.
Get exact dimensions of kitchen cabinet
  8:30—Parent-Teacher gathering at Westchester High
Pack bag for Dinner at Waldorf (White Tie)

10:30——Mr. John Brown
11:30——Portfolio Committee meeting
12:30——Luncheon for Ms. Loni Somes, Pres. Reynolds
         Inv. Assn., at Advertising Club
  2:30——Mr. Smith's office: 250 Broadway, Room 1200
       re: Texas bonds

Evening
  7:30——Reception, Grand Ballroom Waldorf-Astoria
  8:30——Dinner in honor of Dr. Thompson
       Chauffeur will return at 11:00, Park Ave. entrance

---

1. Matters that are referred to other executives or departments for information or comment

2. Correspondence or memos awaiting answer

3. Orders for future delivery, both those that you receive and those that you place

4. Items that come up for periodic consideration, such as company reports of various kinds, tax matters, and contract renewals

5. Promises to be carried out in the future

BASIC OFFICE FOLLOW-UP SYSTEM. If an incoming letter requires later action, or if an outgoing letter has not been acknowledged, a follow-up may be necessary. Secretaries often use photocopies of such correspondence placed in a special file to remind them that a matter is pending.

1. Equipment and materials needed for a follow-up system. The only equipment necessary to file photocopies of material to be followed up is a file drawer and file folders: twelve monthly folders (January–December), thirty-one daily folders (1–31), and one folder for "Future Years."

If you have a heavy volume of follow-up material, you may need two sets of folders labeled by days–one for the current month and one for the succeeding month. Tabbed guides numbered 1 through 31 and removable separators labeled by month will make it easier to locate a particular folder.

2. *Arrangement of folders by day.* Arrange the folders labeled by days in numerical order in the front of the file. Place in these folders the follow-up material for the current month. The folder labeled for the current month is at the back of the other monthly folders ready to receive any material to be followed up in the same month *next* year. Immediately following the numerical daily folders is the folder for the forthcoming month, followed by the folder for the succeeding month, and so on. Figure 8 is a diagram of the folders when April 16 is the current day.

3. *Arrangement of folders by month.* A variation of the foregoing plan is to arrange the files labeled by months in calendar sequence. Thus January is always the first month-by-month folder. Some secretaries prefer this arrangement because the folders remain in the same position. In this case, as the folder for each day is emptied, it is placed in position for the next month.

OPERATION OF A FOLLOW-UP SYSTEM. Make an extra copy of letters or memos that require a follow-up, preferably on paper of a different color. Mark on the extra copy the date on which it is to be followed up. When there is no copy of material for follow-up, write a brief memo describing what is needed and place it in the follow-up file.

Place material that is to be followed up in the current month in the proper date folders. Each day transfer the empty daily folder to the back of the folder for the forthcoming month. Thus you always have thirty-one daily folders for follow-ups, part of them for the remaining days in the current month and part of them for the first part of the forthcoming month. Place material that is to be followed up more than thirty or thirty-one days in the future in the proper month folder, regardless of the day of follow-up. See Figure 8.

On the first of each month, transfer the material from the folder for that month into the folders labeled by days. To avoid filing material for follow-up on Saturdays (if the office closes), Sundays, or holidays, reverse the folders for those days so that the blank side of the label faces the front

FIGURE 8

Diagram of Follow-up Files

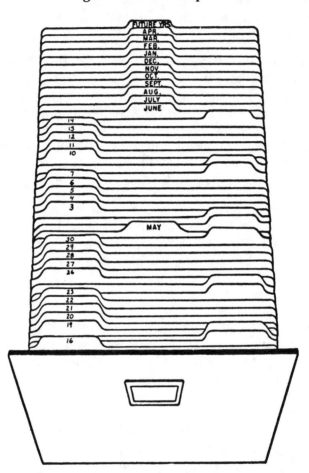

of the file. (Some secretaries tape or staple a small pocket-size calendar to the front of the file for checking weekend and holiday dates and making special notations.) The empty folder for the current month is then transferred to the rear of the other month-by-month folders—or to its proper sequence if that arrangement is used.

  1. Daily follow-up of material. If some of the matters are settled without a follow-up, destroy the copies of that correspondence or of any memos that you prepared concerning the matters. If a heavy schedule keeps you from giving attention to all the material in the daily folder, mark the less important items for follow-up on a later date. Move indefinite follow-ups forward from week to week until a definite date is established or until the matter is completed.

2. *Follow-ups on a small scale.* When you have only a small amount of correspondence or other matters to follow up, a set of follow-up file folders is not necessary. Mark the copies with the follow-up date and file them chronologically in one folder, with those marked for the earliest follow-up on top.

Chapter 2

Using Productive Word Processing Techniques

Word processing is used more than any other business software application. Every office professional needs to communicate with others, both in-house and outside the organization, and a large part of this communication is in some form of written message, regardless of how it is transmitted. Since word processing programs enable users to type, edit, and format correspondence, documents, and other material right on a personal computer, they have revolutionized the way that secretaries handle this important communications function.

The term *word processor* could mean a software program that is designed for text preparation, a machine that is devoted exclusively to handling text, or a person who enters text on a computer. But it is most often used to refer to the software application that permits text entry and manipulation.

WORD PROCESSING SYSTEMS

A *word processing system* is any machine or group of machines capable of handling text. Broadly, this includes electronic typewriters and dedicated word processors (computers designed primarily to handle text) as well as computers that run word processing applications. The two main types of word processing systems are the stand-alone system and the shared system.

The computers used in stand-alone and shared systems range in size and capability from the small personal computer to the large mainframe computer. A *personal computer* (PC), or *microcomputer*, is a small lap- or desktop computer with a central processing unit that consists of a single integrated circuit. A *small business computer*, or *minicomputer*, is an intermediate-sized computer with more power and capacity than a PC. A *large central computer*, or *mainframe computer*, is a large computer with huge capacity capable of supporting hundreds of users at a time.

Stand-Alone Computer Systems

CHARACTERISTICS OF A STAND-ALONE SYSTEM. A stand-alone system may be a computer configuration of any type or size. To be considered a stand-alone system, it must be able to operate or function by itself. Therefore, it would have to have its own keyboard, display screen, hard-disk or flexible (floppy)-disk drive mechanism, central computing logic, and printer. If it lacks one part of the configuration, such as logic or memory capacity, and has to be connected to a large mainframe computer to function, it is not a stand-alone system.

A number of stand-alone computers can be linked in some way, such as by the telephone lines or direct wiring, to communicate with one another while still maintaining their independent operating capability. In a local-area network (LAN), for example, the computers can communicate with one another through direct wiring of one terminal or machine to another.

COMPONENTS IN A STAND-ALONE SYSTEM. The main parts of a stand-alone system are the central processing unit, storage devices, display screen, keyboard, printer, and sometimes a modem.

1. Central processing unit (CPU). The CPU is the brains of a computer system. This is the control part of a system where the performance of various tasks is made possible. The CPU controls the computer by running software programs, processing the information you enter, and controlling the output of information to your display screen, printer, and modem. It performs these tasks by using two types of memory: random-access memory (RAM) and read-only memory (ROM).

Memory is measured in kilobytes (1 kilobyte = 1,024 bytes, or characters). To be certain that you can store a program that you want to run on your computer, you therefore must know how much RAM your computer has; for example, you could not run a program that requires more RAM than that which is available in your computer. (Depending on your system, you may be able to upgrade the memory, that is, add more memory, to accommodate a particular software program.)

RAM consists of electronic components called chips, which store information. This type of memory is temporary since it is in use only while the computer is operating. For instance, if you are preparing a document, it will be temporarily stored in RAM while you are working on it. Before you shut off your computer, therefore, you must save the information (transfer it to storage) on your hard disk or on a removable flexible disk.

ROM is permanent memory put into a machine during manufacture. The information in ROM cannot be changed the way a document in RAM can be edited. It can only be read by the computer system and used to tell the CPU how to interact with the other components of the system, such as the printer.

2. Storage devices. Information in a computer system is stored on permanent or removable magnetic media, such as a disk or tape.

Hard disks are permanently built into the computer or attached to it as a separate box. They can hold larger amounts of data (e.g., hundreds of megabytes, MB) than a smaller, removable flexible disk can hold. They also enable users to store, edit, and retrieve data at much faster rates of speed. Additional time is saved since a hard disk does not have to be taken in and out of the disk drive as a removable flexible disk does. Hard-disk drives convert magnetic signals from a disk into electronic signals that a computer can understand. The drives are labeled by letters, usually *C, D,* and so on.

Flexible, or *floppy, disks* (also called diskettes) are available in sizes of 5¼ inches or 3½ inches. The designation *floppy* does not accurately characterize the smaller 3½-inch disk, which is hard and rigid. Although the storage space on either size disk is much less than that on a hard disk, a high-density 5¼-inch size holds 1.2 MB of information, and a high-density 3½-inch size holds 1.44 MB of information. Floppy-disk drives are also labeled with letters, usually *A* and *B*. You may, for example, have a 5¼-inch disk drive labeled *A* and a 3½-inch disk drive labeled *B*.

Tapes are magnetic strips that are wound onto reels, cartridges, or cassettes. A *tape drive* is a device that converts the tape's magnetic signals into electronic signals for use by the computer. Although this type of storage media is less expensive than disk-storage devices, it takes longer to access data stored on tape. In general, tape storage is much less common than disk storage in business offices.

Optical disks are high-capacity storage media that resemble musical phonograph or CD records. The most common form is the CD-ROM disk, and other forms are the WORM disk and magneto disk. Because optical disks are capable of holding huge amounts of data, they are often used for database storage and multiple-application software packages. Optical disks are read by an optical-disk drive, similar to any other disk drive, or by a separate optical-disk player connected to the computer.

3. Display screen. The display screen, also called a monitor or cathode-ray tube (CRT), functions like a television screen. It is available in various sizes, the most common being 12, 13, 14, and 19 inches. The larger sizes are preferred for applications such as design, graphics, and desktop publishing. Screens may be color or monochrome. Monochrome screens may be green or amber on a black background or black on a white background.

Various devices are used to enable you to move information around on the screen. The most common devices are the keyboard and the mouse, a small handheld device that is rolled around on a hard surface to do on-screen editing. Both the keyboard and mouse are used to move a blinking dot or line called a cursor over the display screen to highlight characters, words, sentences, or larger blocks of copy that you want to edit. In the case of the keyboard, various directional keys (left, right, up, down) are pressed to propel the cursor in a certain direction.

For those who experience eyestrain from working with a display screen, *antiglare covers* can be installed over it that function much the same as sunglasses. Also, different-colored display screens (color, amber, green, and black and white) affect people in different ways, with certain colors causing more strain than others. A *privacy*, or *security*, *screen* is an attachment that makes it difficult for anyone to see what is on a display, except for the operator sitting directly in front of it.

4. Keyboard. The keyboard is the most widely used input device in a computer system. Examples of others are the mouse, a light pen, a scanner, and the human voice.

Keyboard users often develop a variety of aches and pains when using keyboards, and manufacturers of furniture and computer supplies offer various products to prevent serious problems. Computer ergonomics, in fact, is a rapidly developing field concerned with the design of adjustable chairs, wrist supports, and other products that will reduce physical discomforts and difficulties associated with workstation activity.

Although most computer keyboards resemble the QWERTY layout of a typewriter, they have additional keys such as the cursor movement keys, editing keys, function keys, and other special-purpose keys.

Cursor keys have arrows on them to designate up, down, left, and right movements of the cursor. Other movement keys are called Page Up and Page Down, which instantly move a document on the screen to the top or bottom of the page. Home and End keys rapidly move the cursor to the left or right side of the display screen.

Editing keys, such as Insert (INS) and Delete (DEL), enable you instantly to remove or insert copy that you highlight with the cursor on your display screen.

Function keys, often labeled F1, F2, and so on, are keys to which you can assign a special task and then with just one keystroke, rather than several, carry out the command.

Special keys, such as Escape (ESC), Alternate (ALT), and Control (CTRL), are used for special commands. ESC, for instance, will enable you to escape from, or leave, what is on the present screen. The ALT key, when used with another key, creates an alternate keyboard. In some programs, for example, pressing ALT and the key for the letter *U* at the same time will underline the words you type. CTRL and Page Up pressed together will move the document not to the top of the page on the screen but to the top of the first page of the document on which you are working.

5. Printer. Material prepared on a computer and viewed on its display screen can be printed out in hard-copy (paper) form. Four printers commonly used in business offices are the dot matrix, daisywheel, inkjet, and laser.

Printers vary in the size paper they will accommodate and type of paper feed used: individual sheet fed or tractor fed (connected, perforated sheets that have removable strips on each side with holes that fit over teeth used to pull the sheets through the printer). Quality, speed, and number of available fonts also vary among the printers. Some printers, for instance, can print in a fast, low-quality draft mode or a slower near-letter-quality (NLQ) mode.

Daisywheel printers, which use a flexible disk or a type wheel, usually provide excellent typewriter-quality type. They are relatively slow, however, and cannot print graphics such as a chart or graph.

Dot-matrix printers are versatile and often fast. But they are also relatively low-quality machines. The quality depends on the dots per inch that a machine will print. A NLQ printer has more pins (usually twenty-four) in its printhead than a draft-quality printer (usually nine pins). Some machines offer both draft and letter-quality modes.

Inkjet printers, which spray ink on a page to form letters, provide good-quality type and graphics and are considered superior to the NLQ dot-matrix printer. Some inkjet models are advertised as laser-quality machines.

Laser printers, the most expensive type of printer, function like a photocopier and provide very high quality text and graphics. Since they are versatile machines that can provide a variety of fonts, they are frequently used in sophisticated word processing applications and in desktop publishing.

6. Modem. A computer system must include a modem if you want to transmit or receive information with your computer over the telephone lines. A modem converts signals from electronic equipment into a form that will travel over the telephone lines to other equipment, where it is converted back into a form that the equipment can receive.

A modem transfers information at a speed measured in bauds or bits per second (bps). The modem's maximum speed is the modem's baud rate, such as a baud rate of 2,400 or 9,600. The faster the rate, the less time the transmission will take and the lower your transmission charges will be. But if you subscribe to a database service for electronic research or other purposes, ask what speed the service will accept. A 9,600 baud rate, for example, will not work with all services. Usually, a 2,400 rate is acceptable in those cases.

Shared Computer Systems

Shared systems are those that share the logic and memory of a large central computer. There are two types of shared systems: shared logic and shared resource.

SHARED-LOGIC SYSTEM. This type of system consists of "dumb" terminals (usually, only a keyboard and a display screen) connected to a large central computer. The individual workstations, therefore, share the logic and memory of the central computer.

SHARED-RESOURCE SYSTEM. This type of system also consists of individual terminals connected to a central computer. But each workstation has some memory and its own processing unit. Therefore, each terminal can function on its own when the central computer is temporarily down for repairs.

TIME SHARING. When a number of users share a computer simultaneously, it is referred to as time sharing. Often the users are in various remote locations and access the central computing source over the telephone lines. Frequently, one organization owns the central computer and sells time to outside users. Since delays are possible during times of heavy use, time sharing is less desirable for word processing than for other types of work.

Integrated Voice-Data Terminals

In the workplace of tomorrow, voice and data capabilities will be closely blended. Many firms already combine these technologies within a single terminal or workstation, and this trend is increasing:

Voice-data integration is a term applied to the concept of processing and transmitting both speech and data through the same network and of combining both speech and data in computer usage. One objective of business users is to combine voice and data communications rather than have the expense of using or maintaining separate voice networks and data networks. Rather than set up and maintain one network for text or other data preparation and transmission, such as electronic mail, and another for telephone or voice communication, such as voice mail, you would have a combined, or integrated, system capable of preparing and sending both types of messages.

Some of the use of voice-data capability today, as an integrated function, is through a device attached to the office telephone systems. In voice mail, for example, voice messages are converted into signals that are stored within a computer and later converted back to voice and played for the receiver. Research in the area of voice-data operations is concerned not only with the record-and-playback function but with the conversion of text to speech and vice versa, and the technology is steadily evolving in that direction.

Telecommunications Interfaces

USING THE TELEPHONE LINES IN COMPUTER COMMUNICATIONS. An *interface* is a link, or connection, between two systems. Computers often communicate with other computers over the telephone lines, and for this to work, the digital signals that a sending computer generates have to be converted to the analog signals that will travel over the lines. Then at the destination the signals have to be converted again from analog back to digital for the receiving computer to be able to accept the message.

Electronic Typewriters

Although computers are the clear choice for multitask operations where spreadsheets, word processing programs, database management, and other applications are carried out, many secretaries prefer electronic typewriters for preparing short letters or in-house documents. Even offices that have computers on almost every desk may still use an electronic typewriter for addressing envelopes, preparing mailing labels, and typing small or odd-sized cards and papers.

HIGH-END ELECTRONIC TYPEWRITERS. The electronic typewriter, introduced in 1978, has been evolving each year toward the personal computer. In fact, high-end electronic typewriters look more like a computer than a typewriter.

1. Personal word processors (PWPs). The larger and more sophisticated electronic typewriters are known as personal word processors and differ from the compact, portable version of the electronic typewriter in memory capacity and capabilities. The PWP, for example, has a larger display area, sometimes comparable to the display screen of a personal computer. It has a microprocessor, like a computer, and expanded memory capacity; it may have disk drives for running word processing programs. Some PWPs have a remote printer and a separate keyboard, like a stand-alone computer system.

2. Cost comparison. Although electronic typewriter sales are expected to decline and PWP sales to increase, the cost of a PWP is more akin to that of a computer system. The standard electronic typewriter, therefore, remains a relatively inexpensive alternative or supplement to the PWP or personal computer system.

LOW-END ELECTRONIC TYPEWRITERS. The standard portable electronic typewriter is widely accepted as fast and easy to use for office correspondence and preparation of short documents. Sometimes a computer system requires complex, time-consuming formatting steps to accomplish what an electronic typewriter can do with almost a single keystroke. For instance, it usually requires more steps to produce a short business letter on a computer than on an electronic typewriter. Businesses also often find that it costs less and takes less time to train employees on an electronic typewriter than on a computer.

COMPONENTS OF ELECTRONIC TYPEWRITERS. The principal components of an electronic typewriter are the memory, display, keyboard, and printer.

1. Memory. The memory of a portable electronic typewriter is substantially less than that of most computer systems. Electronic typewriters have both RAM capacity and, in high-end models, disk capacity. The disk is a 3½-inch microfloppy designed for a single disk drive. The types of memory include *document memory* (for storing a specified number of pages that can be recalled later); *phrase memory* (for storing common phrases that can be repeated later without retyping each time); *multiple-line memory* (for storing a specified number of lines that can be recalled later); and *format memory* (for storing format instructions, such as margin settings, for repeated use).

2. Display. The display may be no more than a two-line liquid crystal display (LCD) or, on high-end models, a display screen comparable to a computer monitor.

3. Keyboard. The keyboard is usually a QWERTY-style typewriter keyboard that may have additional special keys, such as cursor keys, function keys, and special keys for formatting.

4. Printer. The printer may be a separate piece of equipment in high-end models, but standard electronic typewriters double as a letter-quality daisywheel or thermal-print printer.

SPECIAL FEATURES OF ELECTRONIC TYPEWRITERS. An electronic typewriter has many features similar to those of a computer. Examples are automatic carriage return (wordwrap); text deletion, copying, and insertion; automatic centering and tabulation; dual-column formatting; text search and replace; right margin justification; automatic underlining; and address-list merge. A dictionary, thesaurus, spell checker (to locate and correct typos), and grammar checker (to locate and correct grammatical errors) can be added to the machine's memory. Since features will differ from machine to machine and from one manufacturer to another, it is helpful to request sales literature and compare the capabilities and prices of the different models.

Caring for Your Word Processing Equipment

Computer and other word processing equipment is highly sensitive, and repairs can be costly. But proper care will reduce the chances of serious, expensive problems.

1. Keep the equipment covered when not in use to eliminate dust, sprays, or other contaminants that could damage the system.

2. Avoid locations of very high or low temperatures or humidity, and keep the equipment out of direct sunlight.

3. Do not jar the equipment during moves or cleaning. Before moving the computer to another location, use the appropriate command to move the read/write heads of the hard disk to a position where they cannot destroy stored data during transit.

4. Use a surge protector to reduce the risk of power surges that might destroy data or damage the equipment. Since surge suppressors

do not fully protect equipment, however, unplug the equipment during severe storms or power fluctuations. As an ongoing safeguard, back up everything on your hard disk every day.

5. Avoid needless trading of flexible disks or use of data from another source that may be infected with a virus. Install an antiviral software program if it is necessary to share disks with others, particularly outside your office or firm.

6. Check for loose cables, inadequate electrical connections, and other external problems if your system is not functioning properly.

7. Use only properly formatted flexible disks in good condition that your system can accept.

8. Have the backup battery replaced immediately when a message on your screen alerts you that it is time.

9. Review your documentation for "troubleshooting" suggestions—tips from the manufacturer on things to check when you have a problem.

10. Don't hesitate to use the support provided by your hardware and software dealers if you cannot locate the source of a problem (use their free 800 number if they are out of town). Use the Help command if you are having difficulty running a program.

11. Provide adequate security for your files and equipment.

12. Consider purchasing a maintenance agreement for regular servicing if your equipment will receive heavy use.

NETWORKING BY COMPUTER

A *network* is a number of people working together. Computer networks, for example, provide an electronic link among people who want to share information or communicate with one another.

Information Processing on a Network

HOW A COMPUTER NETWORK WORKS. If you have been using a stand-alone computer, you probably have been preparing and printing out documents on your computer equipment and then carrying or mailing the messages to their destination. A computer network is a means to eliminate the steps of producing paper and physically transporting it elsewhere. Instead, in a computer network, you can prepare your material on the computer and, while still at your terminal, transmit it from your computer to another computer in the network.

1. Types of network connections. Networks exist in many forms, from machines wired together in a local-area network to a worldwide network that connects machines via the telephone lines or by satellite. Electronic mail is an example of communication through a network.

2. Public and private networks. Networks can be private or public. Your company, for example, may lease its own lines to provide an electronic communications link between its computers at headquarters and those in various branch offices nationally or internationally. Or your firm may subscribe to an outside communications service that provides the lines to connect your computer and those of other subscribers.

USING A NETWORK TO SAVE TIME.   An in-house or outside computer network will reduce the amount of paper processing and handling that is otherwise required. It can be a significant timesaver in organizations that are burdened with paper-based information processing and transmission.

EFFECTIVE WORD PROCESSING PROCEDURES

Understanding Your Word Processing System

The better you know your word processing system and understand what it will do, the more effectively you will be able to handle your word processing duties. Mastering word processing on a computer is dependent on giving it very clear, explicit instructions. Even electronic typewriters and dedicated word processing systems require an understanding of their functions and capabilities.

USING DIFFERENT SYSTEMS.   Just as different typewriters may have different features and capabilities, different computers and word processing software may have different capabilities. Some secretaries work in an environment where they must use different equipment. Although this may appear to double the effort and pressure to cope with different instructions and procedures, it is less likely that you will have to use different word processing programs at the same time. Rather, you will likely learn one word processing program and then use that program on the different machines. If you are familiar with the basics of a word processing system, the need to move from one machine to another will not be formidable.

LEARNING HOW TO USE YOUR WORD PROCESSING SOFTWARE. If you are using a new word processing program, take time to review key portions of the documentation (instructions). First, check the index. Most documentation has an introductory chapter on getting started that can be very useful. Start with simple tasks and use the vendor's tutorial materials. If the software is menu driven, you may be able to make your selections from the menus on the display screen without consulting the documentation. If the software is manipulated by commands, you will need to review the instructions for giving the various commands.

If you have used word processing programs before, you will already know many of the requirements of a word processing program. Although different programs, such as WordPerfect and Microsoft Word, may have different commands and use different keystrokes to carry out the commands, if you keep the vendor's keyboard template in place, it will save you a lot of time otherwise spent paging through the documentation. Don't be afraid of making mistakes. The only way to become fully at ease with a program is to start using it, use it regularly, and learn from your mistakes.

Planning and Organizing Your Word Processing Duties

Most tasks are best handled when you have everything you need at hand and you can work for long stretches without interruption. Frequent interruptions and disorganization in typewriter or computer work can lead to disastrous results such as omissions, oversights, typographical, and other errors and reduced speed and lower output. Two things in particular will help you save time in word processing: organizing your work load and planning ahead (scheduling).

ORGANIZING YOUR WORK. With both typewriter and computer preparation, know precisely what you will need before you begin. Arrange papers and other reference material that you will have to consult on your desk in the order you will need it. Place everything within reach. Once you are seated by the typewriter or computer, you shouldn't have to move away to search for a file or look up an address.

Also have all tools you might need—paper, paper clips, disks, and so on—within arm's reach. Arrange your material in the order you plan to prepare each document so that you can go from one project to another without interruption and without getting up from the keyboard between jobs.

PLANNING AHEAD. At the beginning of each day, review your calendar entries for several days ahead and schedule your work in logical categories. Except for rush work, you can segregate filing duties from word processing, research from billing, and so forth. Perhaps you have quiet periods during the day or on certain days when you could schedule word processing activities for uninterrupted periods. Or perhaps you know that a report must be completed by the end of the week.

By planning ahead, you can schedule your word processing tasks at the most advantageous times. You wouldn't, for example, want to start a large project late in the day and then have to put everything away overnight and take it all out again the next morning List your word processing projects in order of importance and handle as many priority items as you can in one sitting. Until you become expert at scheduling your own work, don't hesitate to make up long, detailed work-to-do lists and to group and regroup various tasks until everything is scheduled in the most logical, efficient order.

Preparing Documents

SELECTING EQUIPMENT. Document preparation is primarily handled by computers with word processing software and by desktop-publishing equipment. The electronic typewriter, however, is generally preferred for handling smaller projects, such as typing preprinted and multipart forms, strip labels, file-folder labels, index cards, envelopes, and some small (one- to two-page) documents.

WORD PROCESSING VERSUS DESKTOP PUBLISHING. The choice between word processing and desktop publishing for the preparation of documents depends on the complexity of the documents. An annual report or newsletter with different-sized headlines and other special features may require more variety and font choice than a word processing program can provide. A word processing program, however, which is less complex and less difficult to learn than a desktop-publishing program, is well suited to most document preparation, such as business reports, proposals, letters, memos, meeting agendas or minutes, and travel schedules. (For more about desktop publishing, see Chapter 3.)

EDITING A DOCUMENT. Editing a document on screen is much easier and takes far less time than does retyping pages on paper from scratch. Although word processing programs differ, the fundamentals of on-screen editing apply to all programs.

1. *Getting started.* When you turn on your computer to begin a word processing session, the first thing you see is a prompt, such as C>, or a menu. (The letter C refers to the disk drive that is active at that time.) The next step is to start your word processing program (follow the required keystrokes of your software). Once your word processing program appears on the display screen, you can load the document (file) you want to work on or enter a new filename for a document that you want to create. You can then begin typing the new document or edit any previous document you have called up.

2. *Entering changes.* Using either a handheld mouse or the directional keys on your keyboard, you can move the cursor around on your display screen to the word or words you want to change. By highlighting words, you can select the text that you want to delete, copy, move elsewhere, or reformat. If you make a mistake, most word processing programs have an Undo command that you can use to cancel your prior command as if you had never made it.

If your program is run by commands, you will use certain keystrokes to specify the various steps you want to take, such as change the line spacing in your document from single to double space or set new tab stops (Format command). With most programs, you can use the

Search and Replace commands to find some word, number, or symbol throughout the document and replace it with another. You might, for instance, want to find every occurrence of the word *company* and change it to *organization*. The Mail Merge command will direct your computer to merge two documents or files, such as an address list and a form letter. The documentation often lists all possible commands alphabetically for ease in finding a particular command as well as to provide an opportunity for you to view all the commands in your program at a glance.

Using special keys (see page 63) will enable you to make other changes in your document, such as switching to italic or bold type or changing a number to a superscript style (raised above the line like a footnote number). Follow the instructions of your word processing program for selecting commands, using special keys, and taking other steps to revise your document.

3. Using macros and other shortcuts. If you perform certain tasks over and over or regularly repeat several keystrokes for a certain command, you may want to create *macros*, which are a form of computer shorthand. By saving the various steps you take to accomplish something and assigning them to a function key, such as F1, you can thereafter strike just one key, F1, to accomplish what previously took several keystrokes. Your documentation will tell you how to create macros for the word processing program you are using.

Another shortcut is to type an actual abbreviation throughout your document, such as *wp* for *word processing*. Then at the end of your document you can use the Search and Replace commands to instruct your computer to find every occurrence of *wp* and change it to *word processing*.

Some secretaries save time by saving stock phrases and paragraphs in a special file called a *glossary* in certain programs. In the future, these standard blocks of copy need not be retyped in full but can be recalled from the glossary and inserted wherever you specify.

4. Formatting a document. Your word processing program will have a Format command that will let you specify how you want your document to look: margins, line spacing, indentions, justified right/left margin or centering, position of page numbers and running heads, number of columns of text, size of type, use of italics or bold type, and all the other features that together make up the layout or format of a document.

With most software, you can format characters, pages, and entire documents or portions of a document. To format a page or entire document, you would select from the options provided the measurements you want for margins, page length, columns, and the like and enter your choices (press the Enter or Return key).

To format characters, you would designate styles, such as bold, italic, or underlined, and fonts, such as 12-pitch pica. (*Note:* Even though your software may enable you to designate things such as superscript numbers or double underlining, your printed document will show these selections only if your printer is also capable of handling the various styles and fonts that you select.)

The spacing before and after punctuation marks traditionally followed in word processing applications may not be the same as that followed in desktop publishing. In desktop publishing, one space rather than two spaces may be used after a period ending a sentence, after a colon, and after a period following a figure or letter that introduces items in a list. If you are preparing a document on disk using word processing software, and the disk is to be used in your desktop-publishing department, inquire about requirements concerning spacing around punctuation.

The following list provides the standard rules for spacing in general word processing applications:

No Space
Before or after a dash, which is two hyphens
Before or after a hyphen
Between quotation marks and the matter enclosed
Between parentheses and the matter enclosed
Between any word and the punctuation following it
Between the initials that make up a single abbreviation (*C.O.D.*)
Between the initials in a traditional state abbreviation (*N.J.*)

One Space

After a comma

After a semicolon

After a period following an abbreviation

After a period in a person's name (*R. A. Jones*)

After an exclamation mark used in the body of a sentence

Before and after "×" meaning "by" (3-inch by 5-inch card)

Two Spaces

After a colon

After every sentence

After a period following a figure or letter at the beginning of a line
  in a list of items

Never separate punctuation from the word it follows. For example, do not put a dash at the beginning of a line.

If you use the same format over and over, you can save the format specifications you enter as a *stylesheet*. A stylesheet retains in computer memory the spacing, indentions, type sizes, and other aspects of your format. In future documents that need the same format, you can then simply type the document without taking time to format it. When you have finished, tell your program to "attach" the stylesheet you prepared, with the specifications already defined.

5. Using electronic spelling and grammar checkers. Your word processing software probably has a *spell checker* that will read your document, flash typos on the screen, and suggest correct spellings. Depending on the size of its directory, the *spell-check command* may catch most or all of your typographical errors. It will not, however, catch *the* when you mean *them* or *give* when you mean *gave*, since the incorrect word is spelled correctly.

A *grammar checker* works the same as a spell checker. It looks for something that doesn't conform to its set of rules. It therefore may point out something in the passive voice and suggest the active voice, or it may point out wordiness that could be deleted. As with a spell checker, you must then tell the computer either to ignore something it points out and move on to the next question or to correct it.

A *thesaurus* is a stock of words that serves as synonyms or replacements for a particular word that you highlight with your cursor on the display screen. After viewing the computer's suggested alternatives for the word in question, you can highlight the one you want to use and strike the Enter or Return key to make the substitution.

6. *Using a scanner to enter text.* A *scanner* is a device attached to a computer that converts images—text and graphics—from a previously prepared document, such as a printed book, into a form that the computer can use. By using an optical-character-recognition (OCR) conversion software program, the printed material will be transferred to and saved in your computer's memory as a word processing file ready for editing with your own word processing program. If you use WordPerfect 5.1 software, for example, and want to have a page from a book scanned into your computer, that page can then be edited with your WordPerfect program, provided the scanning software that is used will accommodate and specify WordPerfect 5.1.

Although small handheld scanners are available, full-page scanners into which the printed sheets are fed are necessary for serious business applications. Scanners vary not only in size but also in capability. Images are graded by dots per inch, with the more dots per inch, the better the resolution. Scanners are available for color work, gray-scale work (such as scanning photographs), and black-and-white work (such as scanning text or simple line drawings).

The more expensive, higher-end models provide greater accuracy in scanning, but even high-quality scanners provide only about 95 percent accuracy. Therefore, it is necessary to proofread each scanned page for errors and omissions.

7. *Using graphics in your documents.* If you prepare complex documents with different-sized headlines and other graphics, a desktop-publishing program may be more useful than a standard word processing program. However, full-feature word processing programs enable you to draw graphs and diagrams, and it is also possible to import material such as graphics files and spreadsheets from other programs directly into your word processing program's document file.

If you send documents to other people electronically or prepare documents for clients on disk, it is more convenient for the receiver to have a single document or disk that incorporates both text and graphics, rather than have one document or disk with the text on it and another with the graphics on it.

The integration of graphics and text files in a word processing program requires more skill than straight text preparation. Since you will be dealing with multiple files, it is important to have a good file-management system and to use very specific filenames. If you take those two steps and follow the instructions of your word processing software for importing files, you can prepare more complex documents without going into desktop publishing.

If you use a separate *graphics software* program to prepare the art portion of your document, you can create a variety of illustrations by selecting and manipulating shapes on the display screen. You can then enhance your basic drawing with shadings and different patterns. A quality graphics program offers more commands and tools to create drawings than does a word processing or desktop-publishing program. Also, text can be added to a graphics program, although it is difficult to edit; usually, text must be deleted and new copy typed in when a change is desired.

8. Preparing fill-in forms. Some fill-in forms are prepared and stored in the computer, whereas others are preprinted and filled in later at the typewriter or on the computer. An electronic typewriter can be used to fill in preprinted forms quickly and easily. In typing on ruled lines, you need to be certain that the typing is adjusted so that the bases of letters that extend below the line of type, such as *y*, *g*, and *p*, just touch the ruled line. This is particularly important in filling in forms and other documents that have a lot of ruled lines.

Although master forms can be created and filled in with your standard word processing program, many offices use special forms-creator and forms-finisher software to design forms especially suited to their needs and to use the computer to fill them in expertly. Since this type of software is designed exclusively for forms work, it will help you to create professional-looking forms and will help you fill them in without complex calculations and measurements.

Some forms programs provide hundreds of model forms that you can use as is or customize to your own needs. The models usually cover a variety of activities, such as general business, personnel, project planning, time management, and sales and marketing. To create additional forms with forms software, follow the instructions of the program, usually selecting options from a menu to specify what you want—how many columns, how many lines per page, and so on. You can designate the style you want for headings, such as centered heads, and then type in the names of the headings you want the computer to use.

To fill in a finished form on the computer, you may be required to use your tabulator to move from one field (location on the form) to another and fill in the appropriate data in each position. Depending on your program, you may be able to instruct the computer at a certain field to find and enter the proper information from a database. After you are finished, you can instruct the computer to store the form or print it out in hard copy, the same as you would do with any other document.

DUPLICATING DOCUMENTS

Principal Reprographic Processes

Documents are usually duplicated by making additional computer printouts or by using a photocopy machine, a mimeograph machine or spirit duplicator, or an offset press. Which equipment or method you should use depends on the quantity needed and the equipment available commercially or in your firm.

COMPUTER PRINTOUTS. Although some printers can be set to print out multiple copies of each page, this is not an efficient or economical means of duplication when large quantities are needed. The quality of a printout might be superior to photocopying or mimeographing if you use a laser or inkjet printer but might be inferior if you use a nine-pin dot-matrix printer.

PHOTOCOPIES. Making copies on a photocopy machine is by far the most common method of duplication when limited quantities are needed. Most copiers are analog, although the newer digital technology is expected to be the choice for workstations of the future in which the computer, facsimile, printer, copier, and other equipment will be integrated with voice technologies.

1. Photocopier capabilities. Your office copier may be a large-volume (up to 500,000 copies a month), high-quality, high-speed (up to 100 copies a minute) machine with special features, such as color copying, reduction and enlargement, maximum size paper of 11 by 17 inches, editing capability, automatic document feed and paper selection, and duplexing (two-sided copying). Or your machine may be a small, low-end personal copier (6–10 copies a minute; volumes of fewer than 500 copies a month) or convenience copier (10 to 45 copies a minute; volumes of up to 10,000 pages a month). Virtually all copiers use plain paper, and usually, the only additional requirement is toner.

2. Copy-usage controls. Firms frequently purchase a maintenance agreement and, when large-volume usage is common, use some type of copier-management system to manage copy costs and regulate and record (for accounting purposes) usage by various offices or for different projects. *Copier controllers* are devices that monitor and control the use of photocopiers and other equipment. They range from no more than a simple lock on the equipment to complete computerized stand-alone systems.

If your firm does not have a copier-management system, and usage is relatively light, consider designing your own *photocopy log.* To develop such a log, prepare a master form and store it in your computer for future use. Your form should have ruled columns with headings such as *Date, Number of Copies Made, By Whom,* and *Purpose* and any other information required by your firm, such as the account number to which the copy usage should be assigned for bookkeeping purposes. (In a very small office, a preruled page from an accounting columnar pad would suffice.) Keep the log next to the copy machine with a sign posted on, or next to, the copier stating that *all* users *must* make a log entry each time they make a copy.

MIMEOGRAPH AND DUPLICATOR COPIES. Although not widely used, mimeograph machines and spirit duplicators may be found in small businesses and in churches and schools where low-cost duplication is desired.

1. Mimeograph stencils. A stencil, prepared by typewriter for mimeograph machines, may produce up to 5,000 copies. An electronic stencil maker can also be used to scan documents prepared by computer and create a stencil master. Office-supply stores sell mimeograph stencils, and instructions for use and making corrections are provided with the stencils.

2. Spirit duplicator masters. A spirit master, which also is prepared by typewriter or hand drawing for a spirit duplicating machine, may produce 300 to 400 copies. Mimeograph and duplicator copies are generally confined to applications in which quality is a low priority. As with mimeograph stencils, office suppliers also sell spirit duplicator masters, and instructions on how to prepare and correct a master are provided with the package.

OFFSET PRINTING. Offset printing is a widely used method of high-quality, large-volume duplication. It is provided by most commercial print shops, and large in-house production departments may also have offset equipment.

A master, created from typed or typeset copy (e.g., prepared by word processing, desktop publishing, or other means), is placed on the press and may provide up to 50,000 copies, depending on the type of master used. Paper and plastic masters may provide up to several thousand copies, whereas aluminum masters may provide up to 50,000 copies.

BASIC OFFICE PAPERS

Principal Types of Office Paper

Secretaries use both letterhead stationery and plain cotton-content or bond-content paper in typewriter and computer document preparation. Photocopiers and other machines also use plain bond paper. Depending on the type of machine, facsimiles may use either plain paper or thermal fax paper.

RECYCLED PAPER. Many buyers insist that printing establishments and office suppliers use recycled paper. A study reported by *Paper Sales* magazine in the early 1990s indicated that more than 80 percent of the commercial printers who were polled had found that recycled paper performed as well or better than nonrecycled paper.

COTTON-CONTENT PAPERS. These papers are used primarily for the stationery of top executives and other prestige applications. If held up to the light, water-marked papers reveal a distinctive design.

1. Characteristics of content-content paper. Quality letterhead has a cotton content, usually 25, 75, or 100 percent cotton. It should be 20-pound weight or more, in a white or conservative light color.

2. Uses of cotton-content paper. Quality cotton-content paper may be used for special word processing applications as well as for stationery, where appearance is important. A high-grade sulphite bond is more suitable for nonstationery uses.

3. Cost of cotton-content paper. Cost is a determining factor in many offices, and cotton-content paper is usually more expensive than bond paper. Also, the higher the cotton content, the more expensive the paper.

SULPHITE BOND PAPERS. These papers are used for all situations in which prestige or very high quality is not a requirement.

1. Characteristics of sulphite papers. The bond paper used for most word processing projects is 20-pound weight and is graded according to brightness and opacity. A No. 1 bond is the highest quality and is often used in place of a cotton-content paper for general office stationery. It is also useful when good strength and erasability are required. A smooth paper often has the cleanest appearance with printing since toner and ink tend to look fuzzy on a rough surface. At the other end of the quality spectrum, a No. 4 bond is a lower-quality paper that may have a less attractive color cast and texture.

2. Uses of sulphite papers. A lower-quality bond (e.g., No. 4) may be used in various duplicating processes, for preparing rough drafts, and for plain-paper facsimile copies. No. 4 bond is sufficient when only adequate strength and erasing qualities are needed.

3. Cost of sulphite papers. Offices that are budget conscious should consider the lower-quality but more economical bonds for all but the important work. Some firms are also using lighter-weight (e.g., 16-pound) papers for drafts and other low-priority work to cut costs. Although heavier papers are more durable, this factor is not important in many applications as it would be in something such as forms usage, which involves considerable writing and erasing. In judging whether cost savings are warranted, it is also necessary to consider the machine being used. Computer users, for example, often find that a 20- or 24-pound paper works best in laser printers and is less likely to jam than a 16-pound stock or paper heavier than 24-pound weight.

DICTATION AND TRANSCRIPTION EQUIPMENT

Dictation Equipment and Media

Dictation can be recorded on several forms of magnetic media, such as cassettes, belts, and disks. *Discrete media* means that you can put them on and take them off the recording machine. You can also send them through the mail and erase and reuse them. *Endless-loop media* refers to continuous tape, which you don't remove; rather, the information is erased after it is transcribed so that the tape can be reused. This is a stationary system unlike the discrete equipment and media.

TYPE OF DICTATION TECHNOLOGY. Dictation technology may be either analog or digital. The digital technology, which is more recent and more expensive, is not used as widely as the analog technology.

1. *Digital technology for dictation systems.* Digital technology converts a voice into binary codes that are stored on a disk. You can therefore edit a dictation disk the same as a computer disk, inserting material on the disk anywhere without having to delete the previously stored material. You can also access documents randomly, similar to the access of computer disk files. Another similarity is that digital dictation systems may use identification codes to restrict access to authorized personnel.

Digital systems are expected to be the wave of the future as offices approach the ideal of a fully integrated workstation that combines computer, facsimile, E-mail, and other data technologies with various telecommunications voice technologies. Ultimately, voice dictation will be automatically converted to text, without transcriber intervention.

2. *Analog technology for dictation systems.* The older analog technology consists of tape-based systems, such as mini-, standard, micro-, or picocassettes. With analog systems, unlike digital systems, you cannot

insert material in the middle of a tape. Also, to locate a document you must use fast forward and move through the tape until you reach the position or document that you want rather than access the document randomly as a digital system allows.

TYPES OF DICTATION SYSTEMS. Dictation systems are available in large central systems, desktop systems for individual offices, and small pocket portables.

1. Central dictation systems. The large central systems are shared by numerous users in different offices or even in remote locations from which users access the system by touchtone telephone. In a central system, different users can be recording at the same time. When a recorder is finished, the transcriber can access the material and transcribe it. These systems can also interface with a computer to enable a firm to track and control the use and assignment of dictation and to create a voice-mail system.

2. Desktop dictation systems. The small desktop recorders are separate units for individual users, although the various independent users may share a central transcription department. With a desktop system, the person recording usually talks into a microphone. When the dictation is finished, however, the tape must be removed and delivered to the transcriber; there is no central system for the transcriber to access. Depending on the type of system used, travelers, however, can access their desk units by telephone and can dictate into a machine long distance, with the recording therefore available and waiting for the transcriber in the office.

3. Portable dictation units. The small, handheld pocket units are battery operated with built-in microphones. High-end portables have some of the same features that desktop units offer, such as voice-activated recording, variable speeds, and indexing (marking instructions or end-of-letter notations). However, all handheld pocket units are analog since digital equipment is still too large and expensive for portable use.

Travelers who use portable units can take advantage of time spent on airplanes, in cars, or in hotel rooms to complete their dictation so that it will be ready for transcription when they return to their offices (or tapes can be sent to the office by overnight express).

Preparations to Transcribe Dictation

Most secretaries want to transcribe tapes and disks as soon as possible after the recorder is finished. Being properly prepared will save the transcriber annoying interruptions while working at the typewriter or computer.

1. Become familiar with the recording and transcription units and the media used before you start. If your system is new, read the instructions thoroughly.

2. Clear your desk and organize the necessary materials for transcription—stationery, envelopes, address list, dictionary, and so on.

3. Enter your name and identification number or any other information required by your system and your office.

4. Listen to the instructions on the tapes or disks and organize the documents in order of importance, if the recorder has not already specified priority.

5. Edit and polish the first draft of the transcribed material on screen; use a spell checker and grammar checker before printout.

6. Follow your employer's preference for submitting any material to be signed, such as letters and memos.

7. Store completed tapes or disks according to office policy and filing procedure; when authorized to do so, erase nonessential data and return the tape or disk to the recorder for reuse.

Chapter 3

Preparing and Publishing Reports

HOW TO RESEARCH A REPORT

Secretaries are often asked to look up information for their employers and frequently help collect data for reports. Although you need to know where to go, you first must have at least a rough outline of the report—a logical, orderly arrangement of the topics to be discussed. During or after research, you or your employer may add, subtract, or rearrange the topics, but you always need a preliminary outline, or list, to follow in searching out information.

Using Outside Sources

PLACES TO GO. For research outside your own organization, you have several options. The most obvious place is the library, usually a public library. In a medium-sized or large city, a public library may have a good reference room. If it does not, check your telephone directory for other nearby libraries in technical-vocational schools, colleges and universities, and research and other specialized institutions. If you are looking for books, don't forget bookstores—college bookstores, general commercial establishments, and others.

Various organizations in your community and nearby communities may have the information you need. Local, state, and federal government offices; schools and institutes; local clubs and civic groups; state or national trade and professional associations; and various other business, educational, and professional groups have magazines, books, reports, and other useful material on specialized subjects. They also have knowledgeable people who can answer questions. You need not be limited to nearby facilities, however, unless you especially want to have face-to-face interviews or visit the establishment yourself. Otherwise, you can write or telephone any organization you choose anywhere you wish.

WHAT TO TAKE ALONG. Use your Yellow Pages and consult out-of-state directories for possible sources. Then make a list of names, addresses, and telephone numbers. Always explain fully what you need when contacting anyone, and try to find out the name of the most appropriate person to speak with; you may have to start by asking for a particular department or by mentioning a logical job title.

Go to interviews well prepared with a list of questions, tape recorder, camera, and anything else you need. As a matter of courtesy, however, ask your subject if he or she objects to a tape-recorded interview or to being photographed. For library work, arm yourself with a generous supply of paper and index cards. Use the cards to record each source you consult, so that later you can alphabetize the cards for ease in preparing a bibliography.

DATABASES. With a computer, a modem, and the proper software, you can access on-line databases that store vast amounts of information electronically. Numerous companies throughout the United States have developed thousands of databases that are available for public use, frequently through subscription to the service and an access charge. Different databases provide different types of information, although some of the major information-based services cover virtually every subject imaginable from newspaper articles to stock quotations to airline schedules. Some databases also provide access to numerous other databases.

Databases may be communication based rather than information based. A communication-based service, for example, might offer a subscription to an E-mail network, whereas an information-based service offers access to facts and figures similar to that found in a library reference room. Check directories and software magazines in your library for current addresses and telephone numbers of information-based on-line database services.

1. How to use a database. Usually, you can access an on-line database for research by dialing a password and your account number (provided by the vendor), placing the telephone receiver on your modem, which will enable text and graphics to move to and from your computer over the telephone lines.

Depending on the database you choose, you will likely be asked to provide key words for the topics you want to research. The database's computer will check its index after receiving your key words and select books, articles, and other material that contain information about the topics you are researching. It will then send the information it locates, frequently in the form of a list of citations or as actual abstracts of appropriate published articles, books, and other source material.

To avoid receiving huge amounts of useless information, however, be very specific in the key words you provide. For example, if you need to locate information on the ABC Company's exports to Germany, don't specify *ABC Company* alone or *Germany* alone. That will produce every imaginable fact and figure throughout the history of ABC Company or throughout the history of Germany. Rather, specifically state that you want facts on *ABC Company exports to Germany.* If you want facts pertaining to a specific year, indicate the year as well, or you will receive figures for every year the company has exported products to Germany.

2. Cost of electronic research. It is especially important to investigate the total cost of database usage. A vendor may have a connection fee, an annual or monthly subscription fee, and an access charge based on the time you are using the service. Compare costs among several major services providing the type of information you usually seek—financial data, marketing data, scientific data, educational data, and so forth.

Compare setup and service costs with the cost of finding the same information through conventional means, such as going to a library or newsstand or making a telephone call. For example, would a $10 telephone call provide the same results as a $40 connection charge to an on-line service? Would a visit to the reference room of your local library to check an encyclopedia provide the same information as a $60 access charge to a database? Or is time so short that you need an instant answer, regardless of cost? Consider these and other pertinent factors before you decide on the best research procedure for your project.

OTHER SOURCES. An *electronic clipping service* will continuously scan information being received by its database on the key words you provide and will set aside data that match your topics.

CD-ROM. The compact disk–read-only memory disk is available through magazines, catalogs, and businesses that sell computers, software, and associated products and supplies. A CD-ROM disk is an optical disk that contains vast amounts of information, such as an encyclopedia or hundreds of magazines and newspapers, with both text and graphics. A CD-ROM disk is played on a CD-ROM player (similar to a musical CD home player) or in a CD-ROM disk drive attached to a computer.

A major disadvantage of CD-ROM is that it cannot be altered. Whereas an electronic database service can provide up-to-the-minute information, a CD-ROM disk may soon become out of date. An increasingly popular use of the CD-ROM technology, however, is to package numerous software programs (word processing, accounting, and so on) on a single CD-ROM.

Using Inside Information

You may use both inside and outside sources of information. Inside material and contacts are often overlooked, although they may be the best ones and the most readily available sources.

COMPANY FILES. Your own office files—or the files in another office—have a wealth of information. If you get to know other secretaries in your organization, you will likely find them eager to help you track down some elusive fact or figure. You, in turn, should be prepared to cooperate when they are on a fact-finding mission.

INTERVIEWS. Interviews should not be restricted to outside organizations. Your company probably has numerous experts in various departments who would be happy to answer questions.

COMPANY LIBRARIES. Your own organization may have one or more libraries you could visit. Perhaps your own office has a small library. There you may find directories and other useful material.

OTHER REPORTS. Chances are that your employer is not the only one in your organization who prepares reports. Find out what reports others in the company have written. There is no need to repeat work that someone else may already have done.

REFERRALS. Don't hesitate to ask others for ideas either. People not only know about places to go, they know about other people, and such referrals can be timesavers. With a little persistence, you will soon have a long list of potential sources of information.

COMPANY DATABASES. Your firm may have computerized databases similar to public or commercial databases. It may have computer files that contain address lists, sales information, and other data frequently used by your company.

Using Your Ingenuity

Secretaries need to use ingenuity in many of their tasks. The knowledge of where to look up information is a basic requirement. If you visit an outside facility, don't be afraid that you will not know where to begin. Simply explain your problem, and you will doubtless receive all the help that you need.

Many executives want an immediate answer to a question. Use your ingenuity, then, and if it is a simple matter that would not warrant the cost of database access, think of places to telephone. (The Yellow Pages of your telephone directory will serve you well on these occasions.) Perhaps your employer wants to know the foreign-exchange rate on a particular currency. Call a commercial bank that has a foreign department. If you need to find the technical term used to describe a certain item, call the manufacturer of, or dealer in, that item if one is available in your locality.

If your fact-finding leads you to a particular reference book with a pattern of regularity, order a copy for your office or company library. If you frequently have to go to a library, become familiar with the scope of the books that are available in the reference department.

Valuable Reference Sources

Certain reference books may be useful in your fact-finding missions. Ask your local reference librarian to recommend sources for your projects.

ENCYCLOPEDIAS AND FACT BOOKS. These reference works are invaluable as sources of a wide variety of descriptive information. Become familiar with works such as the *Economic Almanac* (The Conference Board), *Encyclopaedia Britannica* (Encyclopaedia Britannica), *Facts on File* (Facts on File), *Information Please Almanac* (Houghton Mifflin), *Statistical Abstract of the United States* (U.S. Government Printing Office), *Statistical Yearbook* (United Nations), and *Van Nostrand's Scientific Encyclopedia* (Van Nostrand).

ATLASES. An atlas provides detailed maps of places and often other information such as soil and climatic conditions. Well-known atlases include the *International World Atlas* (Hammond), *Goode's World Atlas* (Rand McNally), *North American Road Atlas* (American Automobile Association), and *Rand McNally Road Atlas* (Rand McNally).

DICTIONARIES, WORD BOOKS, AND QUOTATION SOURCES. Dictionaries give spellings, pronunciations, definitions, and other information; word books show spelling, word division, and often pronunciation; and books of quotations are collections of prose, verse, and proverbs from written and spoken sources. Some of the books may be in your company's library, for example, *Bartlett's Familiar Quotations* (Little, Brown), *Black's Law Dictionary* (West), *Oxford English Dictionary* (Clarendon Press), *Roget's International Thesaurus* (Harper & Row), *Webster's New World Thesaurus* (Merriam), and *Webster's Third New International Dictionary* (Merriam).

STYLE BOOKS. Style books are intended to help you in matters such as proper capitalization, punctuation, and citation form and the treatment of written material in general. Examples are the *Prentice Hall Style Manual* (Prentice Hall), *Elements of Style* (Macmillan), *Government Printing Office Style Manual* (U.S. Government Printing Office), *Gregg Reference Manual* (McGraw-Hill), *Chicago Manual of Style* (University of Chicago Press), *Practical Writer's Guide* (New American Library), and *A Uniform System of Citation* (Harvard Law Review Association).

DIRECTORIES. This type of reference is the best source of names and addresses (and other selected facts and figures) for different professions and fields of business. Most library reference rooms have some or all of the following: *Congressional Record* (U.S. Government Printing Office), *Current Biography* (Wilson), *Directory of Corporations, Directors, and Executives* (Standard & Poor's Corp., McGraw-Hill), *Dun & Bradstreet Reference Book* (Dun & Bradstreet), *The Federal Register* (U.S. Government Printing Office), *Gale's Encyclopedia of Associations* (Gale Research), *Hotel and Motel Red Book*

(American Hotel Association Directory Corp.), *Martindale-Hubbell Law Directory* (Martindale-Hubbell), *Million Dollar Directory* (Dun & Bradstreet), *N. Y. Ayer & Son's Directory of Newspapers and Periodicals* (Ayer), *Official Airline Guide* (Official Airline Guides), *Official Congressional Directory* (U.S. Government Printing Office), *Official Guide of the Railways* (National Railway Publications Co.), *Standard & Poor's Register of Corporations, Directors, and Executives of the United States and Canada* (Standard & Poor's), and *Thomas' Register of American Manufacturers* (Thomas).

INDEXES. Indexes are guides to published material—titles, subjects, authors, dates of publication, and so on, for example, *Applied Science and Technology Index* (Wilson), *Books in Print* (Bowker), *Business Books and Serials in Print* (Bowker), *Business Periodicals Index* (Wilson), *Congressional Record Index* (U.S. Government Printing Office), *Cumulative Book Index* (Wilson), *The New York Times Index* (The New York Times), *Reader's Guide to Periodical Literature* (Wilson), *Vertical File Index* (Wilson), and *The Wall Street Journal Index* (Dow Jones Books).

BUSINESS AND FINANCIAL PUBLICATIONS. For current business and financial facts, check some of the following newspapers and periodicals: *Barron's, Business Week, The Conference Board Business Record, Current Industrial Reports, Dun & Bradstreet Reference Book, Economic Indicators, Federal Reserve Bulletin, Forbes, Fortune,* Moody's publications, Standard & Poor's publications, *Survey of Current Business, Value Line,* and *The Wall Street Journal.*

SECURITIES. Facts about investments (stocks, bonds, and so on) are available through the publications of various securities services such as Moody's manuals, Standard & Poor's publications, and the Value Line report.

DATABASES. The following are a few well-known examples of the thousands of available databases in the United States.

CompuServe Inc., Business Information Service (general service)

DIALOG Information Services, Inc.(numerous databases)

Dow Jones News/Retrieval (financial data)

New York Times Information Service (newspapers and periodicals)

LEXIS (legal data)

The Source (general service)

HOW TO ORGANIZE AND WRITE A REPORT

Many companies have adopted an in-house organization and content style for their reports, and secretaries should follow those specifications. If no particular style is mandatory, study the models in books on report writing or in style manuals such as the *Prentice Hall Style Manual*, which contains numerous model formats.

Formal and Informal Reports

FORMAL REPORTS. A formal report, usually prepared on 8½- by 11-inch paper, has all or most of the parts listed here. Reports may be single- or double-spaced, depending on the length. Very long reports are usually single-spaced.

1. Cover
2. Flyleaf (blank page between cover and title page)
3. Title page (see Figure 9)
4. Letter of transmittal (on company letterhead)
5. Table of contents (see Figure 10)
6. List of illustrations and tables
7. Abstract (summary of the report)
8. Introduction
9. Background information
10. Data analysis
11. Conclusions and recommendations
12. Appendix
13. Notes
14. Glossary
15. Bibliography
16. Index

FIGURE 9

Title Page of a Formal Report

PROPOSAL TO STANDARDIZE
COLLECTION PROCEDURES

Submitted to
Andrea T. Webster
Manager, Accounting Department
Rice Electronics
1103 Northern Boulevard
Chicago, Illinois 60607

Submitted by
Randall H. Rice, Executive Assistant
Management Consultants, Inc.
743 Third Avenue
Chicago, Illinois 60606

May 17, 1988

FIGURE 10

Table of Contents

Contents

Tables and charts are sometimes collected after the appendix or are grouped and labeled as an appendix rather than scattered throughout the report body.

INFORMAL REPORTS. Short, informal reports are often prepared on business letterhead or special memo stationery, without any of the preliminary pages, such as a title page and table of contents, that are found in a longer, semiformal or formal report. Although the informal report does not have end matter, such as an appendix and bibliography, supplementary material such as a chart or a pamphlet may be attached to the memo. The short, informal report is formatted the same as a regular correspondence memo, except that the body frequently has short topic subheads.

Parts of the Report

Your office may follow a particular pattern in both formal and informal reports. File copies can be used as guides in that case. Otherwise, observe the guidelines in the following sections:

TITLE PAGE. Usually, the title page is the front cover, but if a report is enclosed in another cover, the title page is the first page beneath the cover. The items of information on the title page are (1) the title of the report, (2) to whom submitted, (3) by whom submitted, and (4) the date submitted. See Figure 9. Keep the title short—fewer than ten words—if possible. For spacing and arrangement of items, follow the example of Figure 9.

LETTER OF TRANSMITTAL. The letter of transmittal is placed after the title page. It is usually formatted the same as any business letter and printed out on regular company letterhead. The letter should briefly, in about two paragraphs, explain the purpose and scope of the report and the sources of information used. It may acknowledge special help received and refer to special authorizations or requests. The author may also include other pertinent information or comments, such as calling attention to an important finding not included elsewhere in the report.

PREFACE. Some writers prefer to include a one-page preface instead of a transmittal letter. The preface would contain essentially the same information but would be formatted like a regular text page with the heading "Preface" instead of a chapter title.

TABLE OF CONTENTS. The table of contents consists of the numbers (if any) and titles of the chapters or topics and the number of the page on which each begins. Prepare the table of contents after the final draft of the report has been completed and the pages numbered. The sample format in Figure 10 is a double-spaced version.

LIST OF ILLUSTRATIONS. If the report has a list of illustrations and tables, prepare it in much the same style as the table of contents, with figure and table numbers, titles, and possibly leaders guiding the reader to page numbers on the right. If there are numerous exhibits, it may be preferable to have two lists, one for illustrations such as photographs and graphic matter and one for straight tabular matter such as tables and lists. The illustrations themselves may be scattered appropriately throughout the report, used as appendixes, or collected at the ends of chapters (or all of them after the last appendix). No matter where you position them, be certain that each one is mentioned in proper numerical order in the text discussion.

ABSTRACT. The report may include an abstract. This is a condensed summary of the report, briefly stating the objective and summarizing the results of the research and the author's conclusions. It may vary in length from a few paragraphs to more than a hundred pages. Many writers like to have short abstracts prepared as a list of a half dozen to a dozen numbered points.

BODY. The body of the report—the discussion and analysis of the findings—includes the introduction, the background, and each succeeding section of the data analysis—all developed logically to the final section, the conclusions and recommendations.

APPENDIX. Some reports have supplementary supporting material—tables, charts, and additional related information—that should be collected in a final chapter or section called the "Appendix(es)." Commentary in the appendix should be styled like any other text material and illustrative material like any other tables and figures in the body of the report.

NOTES. If the report does not place footnotes at the bottom of each text page, number and collect them in a special section called "Notes" at the end of the report or at the ends of chapters in the report.

GLOSSARY. If a number of technical terms are used in a report, a glossary of brief definitions may be desirable. This alphabetical list of terms is prepared either as a separate section after the notes section or as one of the appendixes before the notes section.

BIBLIOGRAPHY. A bibliography is prepared from the 3- by 5-inch cards used during research to record each source of information. It is arranged alphabetically and is placed at the end of the report just before the index.

INDEX. Many reports omit the index, but if one is used, it should be prepared as follows: Underline key words in the final draft of the report. If your computer software has indexing capability, follow the software instructions. If you prepare the index conventionally, list the underlined words or phrases on index cards, a *separate* card for each new word or phrase, with the page number(s) where the key words appear. Then group the cards by like categories before alphabetizing them. For example, assume that you have three cards, each with a word or phrase pertaining to "energy" but appearing on three different pages: (l) source of energy, page 9; (2) energy, page 17; (3) energy sources, page 19. Since you would have listed *each* page on a *separate* card, you now need to combine the data from the three cards onto one card, or index entry:

Energy 9, 17, 19

To become more familiar with the appearance of an index, examine the indexes in reports previously prepared in your office and look at the indexes in several books, including this one.

Use of Appropriate Language

WORDS. Many writers have trouble selecting clear, concrete, specific words. Thus you read about a *good* employee instead of an employee who is a *programming expert*. Or someone refers to a machine that saves *time* each day instead of a machine that saves 50 minutes each day. Or you read that a new product will be released *soon* instead of on *September 8, 19—*. Sometimes the writer simply picks the wrong word, for example, saying *infer* when *imply* is meant. Reports that are vague and imprecise are weak and uninformative. Whether you are writing the original copy or correcting someone else's work, look for myriad problems in word choice.

SENTENCES. Poor word choice can lead to weak, clumsy, or otherwise ineffective sentences. Short, simple sentences usually are stronger and clearer than long, rambling monologues. Contrary to prevalent thought in some offices, big words and long, complex sentences do *not* indicate more intelligence or better education; they merely reveal pompous, amateurish, and often tedious writing habits.

Try to use the active voice whenever you can (*I believe*) instead of the often weaker, stuffier passive voice (*It is believed that*). Then let your sentences (and paragraphs) slide one into another: "Sales have been declining; however, the sluggish economy is only partially responsible" (*not* "Sales have been declining. The sluggish economy is only partially responsible"). Use transition words such as *however, in fact,* and *therefore* to good advantage when movement from one sentence to another sounds abrupt, stiff, and awkward without them.

Avoid a lot of "there is" and "it is" beginnings. Instead of "There is a trend toward multifamily housing occurring today," try "A trend toward multifamily housing is occurring today." Making such changes may help you cut out unnecessary words too. For example, instead of "the year of 1987," simply say "1987." But don't delete words and sentences that are helpful in making the discussion flow smoothly and interestingly, even if they appear superfluous at first glance.

Generally, try to follow the requirements of the communication. A memo report, for instance, might use a more conversational style than a formal report. But all reports—as well as any other type of writing—should be written in a style and tone appropriate for the reader.

Report-Preparation Checklist: Things to Remember

The longer the report, the more things you need to check before it is released. Some secretaries make a list of everything they want to remind themselves to double-check. They go down this list one item at a time, crossing out or checking off each item when it is completed. For example:

1. Has the report been read carefully, word for word, for sense and proper language?

2. Have all typographical and other errors been corrected on the original and on all copies?

3. Are the pages numbered correctly?

4. Is the format (margins, paragraph style, and other spacing matters) attractive and consistent?

5. Has a consistent style of headings and numbering been followed throughout the report?

6. Have all statistics been checked against their sources?

7. Have all cross-references been checked?

8. Are footnotes in proper sequence with corresponding references in the text, and are the data consistent with the facts in matching bibliography entries?

9. Are mathematical tables and computations accurate?

10. Are proper names spelled correctly?

11. Are the pages arranged in proper sequence?

12. Are all pages firmly attached in the binding?

HOW TO DEVELOP A PROPER STYLE AND FORMAT

Studying the Preliminary Draft

Before preparing the final draft of a report, read over the entire handwritten or rough draft with these purposes in mind:

1. To see that each sentence makes sense and that all sentences have been arranged logically in paragraphs. If you cannot understand something in a report someone else has written, ask the meaning of the sentence or paragraph and have it clarified.

2. To correct mistakes and improve the writing style when needed.

3. To identify or supply the headings and subheadings, so that you can visualize the report in final form. Headings help to bring out the organization of the report and to disclose weaknesses in the arrangement of the material.

4. To confirm that all parts of the report are there and in the right position, including the preliminary pages, footnotes, illustrations, and end matter.

Selecting the Right Paper

Reports are usually prepared on plain white paper, 8½ by 11 inches, 20-pound substance. Use a good-quality paper for the original. Most duplicates are made by photocopier or by additional computer printouts. Numerous copies may be made by a printing or duplicating process (large quantities are usually printed). If the report is in memo form, the first page will be written on memo stationery or business letterhead.

Using a Report Binder

Staple short, informal reports in the upper left corner, or use a paper clip to secure the pages of a short memo report. Fasten formal reports along the left margin or across the top, but preferably on the side. Use brads, paper fasteners, or staples for fastening. Many formal reports, especially long ones, are presented in special holders, binders, or folders; sometimes they are laced together on the left side with a plastic comb. Check at your local office-supply store for samples.

Creating a Proper Format

DECIDING ON SINGLE OR DOUBLE SPACING. Formal reports are frequently double-spaced unless they are very long. If the report is to be duplicated or printed or if numerous copies are to be mailed, single spacing will save in printing and mailing costs. Short reports on memo stationery or business letterhead are usually single-spaced like a correspondence memo. Use a double space after subheads and between paragraphs of both single-spaced and double-spaced material. Add an additional space before the subheads.

INDENTION OF BLOCK QUOTATIONS. Indent block quotations that run eight lines or more. (Remember that every quote requires a footnote or other form of citation, and substantial quotes—such as more than 100 words from an article or more than 300 words from a book—require permission to quote from the copyright owner if the report is to be published.)

SETTING MARGINS FOR AN ATTRACTIVE APPEARANCE. Use ample and uniform margins at top, bottom, and sides of about 1¼ or 1½ inches on both sides and 1 to 1½ inches top and bottom. Never use less than a 1-inch margin, *exclusive* of the part of the page that is used for binding. Thus if ¾ of an inch is used for binding, the bound edge (left side or top) should have a margin of 1¾ inches instead of 1 inch.

The first, or opening, page of the report, of each chapter, and of each part, such as the abstract, should have a 2- to 3-inch margin at the top.

The left margin of indented material should be set even with the paragraph indentation of the main part of the report, usually ½ to 1 inch.

Numbering Pages, Titles, and Outlines

NUMBERING THE PAGES. Number the pages of the front matter starting with the table of contents and ending with the abstract—the pages that *precede* the report proper—with small roman numerals such as i, ii, iii, iv, and v. Number all pages of the report proper beginning with the Introduction and ending with the Index with arabic numerals, starting with 1. Place numbers in the upper right corner or in the center of the page, ½ inch from the bottom; place numbers of the chapter opening pages at the bottom even if other numbers appear at the top of the page. The pages of a report that is bound on the left side often use the upper right corner position for page numbers.

NUMBERING APPENDIXES. Most writers precede appendixes with a letter or number: Appendix A, Appendix B; or Appendix I, Appendix II; or Appendix 1, Appendix 2. Capital letters are often preferred when chapters have numerals. Each appendix also has a title (Appendix A: Interest Tables).

NUMBERING WITHIN THE REPORT AND PROPER INDENTATION. A report may use numbering and lettering schemes, in addition to headings, to simplify the reading. There are no fixed rules, but the following three patterns are among those commonly used. Notice that regardless of the pattern, topics of equal importance are given equal emphasis in the arrangement. Follow the style you adopt consistently throughout the report.

Pattern 1	Pattern 2	Pattern 3
I	I.	I. . . . .
1.	1.	A. . . . .
(a)	A.	1. . . . .
(b)	B.	2. . . . .
(1)	(1)	(a) . . . . .
(2)	(2)	(b) . . . . .
II	2.	B. . . . .
	II.	II. . . . .

Observe the following rules within the numbering and lettering scheme:

1. Follow roman numerals and arabic numerals with a period.

2. Do not use a period after a number or letter in parentheses.

3. Use a double space between paragraphs carrying a number or letter just as you would other paragraphs.

4. Determine how far you will indent each of the groups in your numbering and lettering scheme, indenting each successive group several spaces more than the preceding group, and maintain the same indentation plan throughout the report. Notice in the examples of three patterns how number II is aligned under number I, letter (b) under letter (a), and so on.

5. Indent the first line in a main paragraph ½ to 1 inch. Indent the first line in an indented paragraph ½ inch more than its own left margin, or use the block form.

Choosing the Right Footnote Style

Using a notes section or bottom-of-page footnotes. If there are many footnotes in a report, number them consecutively, from 1 on. In a report that is divided into chapters, begin with footnote 1 in each chapter. Place the note number (called a "superior figure" because it is set raised above the normal line of type rather than on line) at the end of the sentence in the text to which the footnote applies. Do not place numbers in the middle of sentences. In a double-spaced paragraph, it would look like this:

Only one real solution is offered:[1] To . . .

In a single-spaced paragraph it could be written on line as follows, with diagonals:

Only one real solution is offered:/2/ To . . .

If there are only a few footnotes in the report, you may use asterisks, daggers, or other similar characters instead of numbers.

If you use bottom-of-page footnotes instead of collected notes in a separate section, place the footnote at the bottom of the page on which the superior figure appears in the text. Place the footnote to a table, however, at the bottom of the table.

To separate a bottom-of-page footnote from the text, insert two lines of space below the last line of text and then add a short rule (about 2 inches); insert another line of space before beginning the footnote. Precede the footnote data with the same number or symbol used in the text. Place the number either on line or raised as a superior number. (The trend is to use numbers on line—not raised—with the actual footnote, even though the corresponding number in the text is usually a superior number in double-spaced reports.)

USING BOTH SOURCE NOTES AND FOOTNOTES. Some writers do not put footnotes at the bottoms of the text pages. They collect all of them at the end of each chapter, or after the appendixes, in a section called "Notes." Or they put only the source notes at the ends of the chapters (or end of the report) and leave expository (discussion) notes at the bottoms of the text pages as footnotes. In this case, the source notes at the end of each chapter would be numbered (starting with 1 in each chapter), and the expository notes at the bottoms of the pages might be lettered (starting with *a* in each chapter). The following list illustrates the difference between expository notes and straight source notes.

1. *Expository notes.* Follow this style for expository notes:

a. Percentages are based upon the 1980 census.

b. This system has been in operation only two years, however, as explained in D. R. Thompson, *A Comparative Study of the X-L40 and the X-L400*, Highland Digital Manufacturers Studies in Data Processing, vol. 2 (Madison, Wis., 1979), 81.

2. Source notes. Follow this style for source notes:

>   1. Melanie Clarke, *Credit and Collection Systems*, rev. ed.
> (Philadelphia: Newhouse Publications, 1981), 214–19.

>   2. Jason Stowe and Ryan McConnell, "The Credit Chase,"
> *Collection News Quarterly* 12, no. 2 (August 1982): 7–15.

MODEL FOOTNOTES. Examples of different footnotes follow. If your computer printer will not print out in italics, use underscoring:

1. Citation of a book. Follow the style in notes 1 and 2:

>   1. Robert Semenow, *Questions and Answers on Real Estate*,
> 8th ed. (Englewood Cliffs, N.J.: Prentice Hall, 1975), 111.

>   2. A. T. Watts, *The Fuel Factor*, 2 vols. (New York: Watson
> Press, 1982), 1:17.

2. Citation of an article or chapter. Follow the style in notes 3 to 6:

>   3. R. H. Lubar, "Plan for Tax Reform," *Fortune*, 19 March 1986,
> 92–96.

>   4. Morris Stevens, "Synthetics," in *The Plastic World*, ed.
> Barbara Carter and John Reubens (Baton Rouge, La.: Microplastics
> Laboratories, 1981), 91.

>   5. Daniel Westerkamp, "Seeing Is Believing," *Journal of Middle
> Managers* 40 (April 1979): 100–101.

>   6. Daniel Westerkamp, "Satellite TV Breakthrough," *Madison
> Herald*, 29 May 1989.

3. Acknowledgment or credit. Various styles are used for acknowledgments and credits. For example, the note may be an unnumbered note at the bottom of the first page of a chapter, as in the first example. Or it might be a credit line beneath an illustration, as in the second example.

>   Acknowledgment is made to Charles Berg for the data on
> housing.

>   Courtesy R. B. Majors Company.

4. Citation of unpublished material. Follow the style in notes 7 and 8:

>   7. A. T. Watts, "Indian Culture: A Lost Art" (M.A. thesis,
> University of Arizona, 1977), 401–2.

8. Marlene Lake, Foreword to "Data Processing at Benson," mimeographed (Washington, D.C.: Benson Industries, 1985), iv.

5. *Miscellaneous documents.* Follow the style of notes 9 and 10 for governmental documents and archival material.

9. U.S. Congress, Senate, Committee on Ways and Means, *Hearings on Economic Import Quotas*, 96th Cong., 2d sess., 1978. Committee Print 14.

10. Abbe Steel, proposals for Technological Park, MS. 21, M. O. Wyatt Collection, Dixon Library, Jackson, Mississippi, n.d.

6. *Short references and ibid.* Follow the style in notes 11 to 16:

11. Watts, "Indian Culture," 403.

12. Ibid., 401.

13. Lubar, "Plan for Tax Reform," 93; Watts, "Indian Culture," 400; idem, *The Fuel Factor*, 76.

14. Lubar, "Plan for Tax Reform."

15. Ibid., 92.

16. Ibid.

Choosing the Right Bibliography Style

The bibliography often contains a list of all recommended publications on the subject of the report, including all sources cited in the footnotes. If it does not include all sources cited in footnotes, it is called a "Select," or "Selected," Bibliography. (Other titles are sometimes used for this section such as "Work Cited" and "Works Consulted.")

The form in which the author's name is cited in the bibliography should be the form in which it appears on the title page of the published book being cited. Thus if the name on the title page is Robert Semenow, the form in the bibliography should be "Semenow, Robert." If, however, the name on the title page is R. Semenow, the form in the bibliography should be "Semenow, R." If an item has two or more authors, it is not necessary to reverse any names, except the one that appears first, which is reversed to aid alphabetical arrangement (*Dawes, Elaine, and Thomas Markham*).

If a bibliography contains more than one item by the same author, arrange them alphabetically according to title and use a long dash (as illustrated in the Westerkamp entry below) instead of repeating the name each time. However, *do* repeat the name if a coauthor is added.

Bibliographies may be further classified according to the types of printed material—books, book reviews, pamphlets, indexes, guides, reference works, and the like—and some reports use subheads in the bibliography and group similar references in the appropriate categories.

MODEL BIBLIOGRAPHY ENTRIES. Bibliography entries are arranged alphabetically. If your computer does not print in italic type, underscore anything that would normally be italic in printed material. If any entries are cited in the notes section(s) of the report, be certain that the data in the notes and the bibliography entries are the same, even though the arrangement of data differs.

1. Books. Follow this style for book titles:

> Semenow, Robert. *Questions and Answers on Real Estate.* Englewood Cliffs, N.J.: Prentice Hall, 1975.
>
> Watts, A. T. *The Fuel Factor.* 2 vols. New York: Watson Press, 1982.

2. Articles and chapters. Follow this style for articles and chapter titles:

> Lubar, R. H. "Plan for Tax Reform." *Fortune,* March 19, 1986, pp. 92–96.
>
> Stevens, Morris. "Synthetics." In *The Plastic World,* edited by Barbara Carter and John Reubens. Baton Rouge, La.: Microplastics Laboratories, 1981.
>
> Westerkamp, David. "Seeing Is Believing." *Journal of Middle Managers* 40 (April 1982): 100–115.
>
> _____. "Satellite TV Breakthrough." *Madison Herald,* 29 May 1979.

3. Unpublished material. Follow this style for unpublished material:

> Lake, Marlene. Foreword. "Data Processing at Benson." Mimeographed. Washington, D.C.: Benson Industries, 1978.
>
> Watts, A. T. "Indian Culture: A Lost Art." M.A. thesis, University of Arizona, 1980.

4. *Miscellaneous documents.* Follow this style for governmental documents and archival material:

> Steel, Abbe. Proposal for Technological Park. MS. 21, M. O. Wyatt Collection, Dixon Library, Jackson, Mississippi, n.d.

> U.S. Congress, Senate, Committee on Ways and Means. *Hearings on Import Quotas*. 96th Cong., 2d sess., 1978. Committee Print 14.

Choosing the Right Reference-List Style

USING A NAME-DATE REFERENCE STYLE. With this type of system, a sentence in the text might read: "This system has been in operation only two years, however (Thompson 1989: 17)." You might, then, have a section called "References" at the end of each chapter (or one large reference section after the appendixes). The alphabetical entries in the reference section will resemble the bibliography entries, except that the year will follow the name.

If an author should have two entries with the same year, you would arrange them alphabetically and label the first one 19—a and the second one 19—b.

> Thompson, D. R. 1989a. Editorial, *The New York Times*, 17 May.

> Thompson, D. R. 1989b. "Inflation," *Economic Journal*, February.

MODEL REFERENCE-LIST ENTRIES. Reference-list entries are arranged alphabetically, like the bibliography entries, and they are styled the same, except for the position of the date.

1. *Books.* Follow this style for book titles:

> Semenow, Robert. 1975. *Questions and Answers on Real Estate.* Englewood Cliffs, N.J.: Prentice Hall.

> Watts, A. T. 1982. *The Fuel Factor.* 2 vols. New York: Watson Press.

2. *Articles and chapters.* Follow this style for articles and chapter titles:

> Lubar, R. H. 1986. "Plan for Tax Reform." *Fortune*, March 19, pp. 92-96.

Stevens, Morris. 1981. "Synthetics." In *The Plastic World*, edited by Barbara Carter and John Reubens. Baton Rouge, La.: Microplastics Laboratories.

Westerkamp, David. 1982. "Seeing Is Believing." *Journal of Middle Managers* 40 (April): 100–115.

_____. 1989. "Satellite TV Breakthrough." *Madison Herald*, 29 May.

3. Unpublished material. Follow this style for unpublished material:

Lake, Marlene. 1978. Foreword. "Data Processing at Benson." Mimeographed. Washington, D.C.: Benson Industries.

Watts, A. T. 1980. "Indian Culture: A Lost Art." M.A. thesis, University of Arizona.

4. Miscellaneous documents. Follow this style for governmental documents and archival material.

Steel, Abbe. n.d. Proposal for Technological Park. MS. 21, M. O. Wyatt Collection, Dixon Library, Jackson, Mississippi.

U.S. Congress, Senate, Committee on Ways and Means. 1978. *Hearings on Import Quotas.* 96th Cong., 2d sess. Committee Print 14.

Selecting Levels of Heads and Subheads

The body of a report is usually divided into topics and subtopics with headings to identify them. Most writers already have an outline or a list of topics used in conducting research. Often these topics form the basis of the headings and subheadings in the report. In setting up the headings, keep this in mind: Topics of equal importance should be given equal emphasis.

EMPHASIS. Emphasis is shown in typed or computer-prepared material by centering and by the use of caps, spacing, underlining, or a combination of these techniques. Headings of the same relative importance should be identical in form.

PATTERNS OF HEADINGS. In preparing a long report, develop a sample of the style of headings that you intend to use throughout the report, for example:

FIRST-LEVEL SUBHEAD (centered)

Second-Level Subhead (flush left)

<u>Third-Level Subhead.</u> (underlined, indented with paragraphs, and followed by a period, with text sentence immediately following the period)

If the report requires more breakdowns, select as many of the following as you need (but keep in mind that too many levels are distracting and can make material very complicated to read), for example:

FIRST-LEVEL SUBHEAD (centered)

<u>SECOND-LEVEL SUBHEAD</u> (underlined and centered)

Third-Level Subhead (flush left)

<u>Fourth-Level Subhead</u> (underlined and flush left)

Fifth-Level Subhead. (indented, with paragraphs, and followed by a period, with text sentence immediately following the period)

<u>Sixth-Level Subhead.</u> (underlined, indented with paragraphs, and followed by a period, with text sentence immediately following the period)

Seventh-level subhead. (indented with paragraphs and followed by a period, with text sentence immediately following the period)

<u>Eighth-level subhead.</u> (underlined, indented with paragraphs, and followed by a period, with text sentence immediately following the period)

Leave two blank line spaces above a centered or flush-left heading and one line space between the heading and the text that follows. You may treat subheads that are indented with the paragraph the same as you treat paragraphs in regard to spacing above the head. Or you may leave a blank line space above any paragraph that begins with a run-in head. Heads are called *run-in heads* when a text sentence immediately follows the period after the head (some writers omit the period).

WORDING OF HEADINGS. Headings should be short, striking, and descriptive of the topic being discussed. If it is impossible for a heading to be lively and descriptive at the same time, select the descriptive heading.

Headings should be uniform in grammatical construction if possible. Thus if a subheading is introduced with a participle, other subheadings under that topic ideally would all be introduced with a participle. All important words should be capitalized in a heading that uses both uppercase and lowercase letters but not conjunctions, prepositions of fewer than five letters, and articles.

Note the effective use of short, imperative sentences in the following headings from a report outlining a plan for strengthening a company's marketing program.

> IMPROVE THE PRODUCT LINE
> Pretest New Products
> Shorten the Length of the Line
> Reduce Percentage of Low-Volume Items
> Improve Colors in Lower Price Lines
>
> STRENGTHEN FIELD SELLING EFFORTS
> Clarify Territorial Boundaries
> Relieve the Overburdened Sales Force
> Improve the Sales Compensation Plan
> Develop More Appealing Displays
> Improve Field Supervision

Setting Up the Title Page and Table of Contents

PREPARING THE TITLE PAGE. Various styles may be used for the title page of a business report. A formal report frequently has four parts: (1) the title, (2) the "submitted-to" information, (3) the "submitted-by" information, and (4) the date. When the title takes up more than one line, divide the material at a logical point. Adjectives and articles are not separated from the word they modify, a preposition is not separated from its object, and a line does not end in a conjunction. Thus the title "The Participation of the White-Collar Worker in Modern Labor Unrest" should not be divided between "Collar" and "Worker," although this division makes a more even distribution of the letters in each line. That title should be written as follows:

> THE PARTICIPATION OF THE WHITE-COLLAR WORKER
> IN MODERN LABOR UNREST

The four items on the title page are centered horizontally on the available space, exclusive of the part taken up by binding or fastening. With a left side fastening, allow ¾ inch for binding.

Leave four or more line spaces between each part on the title page, except the date, which often is positioned two blank line spaces below the "submitted-by" information (see Figure 9). You may single-space within each part on a title page, or you may double-space the title and leave a blank line space after the words "Submitted to" and "Submitted by."

SETTING UP THE TABLE OF CONTENTS. Center the table of contents horizontally and vertically on the page. Double-space a short table of contents; single-space a long one. List the chapter or topic numbers (if any) at the left, space about three times, and follow the numbers with the respective titles. List the page numbers at the right margin.

If desired, use periods as leaders to guide the reader's eye across the space between the title and the page number. Space once between each period used as a leader. Align the periods of each line with those in the line above.

Figure 10 illustrates the arrangement of chapter topics on a double-spaced table of contents.

Preparing Tables and Illustrations

SETTING UP TABLES. Although tables are more difficult to set up than most other pages, many software programs have features that simplify the procedure. The finished tables may be placed at appropriate places in the text discussion, they may be prepared on separate pages at the ends of chapters, they may be used as appendixes, or they may simply be collected in proper order after the last appendix. Follow your employer's preference or the style used in other company reports. Regardless of their position, however, be certain that each table is mentioned in the text discussion in the order numbered.

Tables may be numbered consecutively, beginning with 1, throughout the report, or they may be numbered consecutively within a chapter, often in combination with the chapter number, for example, Tables 1.1, 1.2, and 1.3; Tables 2.1 and 2.2; and Tables 3.1, 3.2, 3.3, and 3.4. (Hyphens may be used instead of periods: 2-1.)

1. How to plan the arrangement. Before setting up a table, plan the arrangement of data with these thoughts in mind:

Tables may have several parts: a number and title, column cross-headings, a stub (the list of items running down the left side), a source note, and footnotes.

Align figures at the decimal point on the right, and align words on the left (see Figure 11).

Center each word in the column headings, or align the words of each head flush left. In Figure 11 "Shares" is centered in relation to the number in the column below with the most digits, and "Held" is centered under "Shares."

2. How to determine vertical spacing. Allow one line space between the title and the subtitle (if any) or at least two line spaces between the title and the column cross-headings. Allow at least two line spaces between the column cross-headings and the items in the column. If the table is short, double-space between the items in the body to give the page a more balanced appearance. Very short tables are often prepared without any rules. A longer table may have three (or more) rules, as shown in Figure 11, before and after the cross-headings and after the last line in the table body.

3. How to prepare headings in tables. Center the title and subtitle of a table or position both lines flush left. (Remember to make an allowance if part of the left margin is to be used for binding.)

4. How to prepare captions for other illustrations. The titles of other illustrations such as photographs or charts are called "legends" or "captions." A *caption*, if used at all, is the actual title or headline, often set above the illustration. A *legend* is an explanation, often set beneath the illustration. Many authors combine the two and set both together beneath the illustration, for example:

Figure 1. Flowchart Under Reorganization. The revised chain of command can be seen in this flowchart of division chiefs and department heads.

5. Where to position footnotes to tables. Place footnotes, as illustrated in Figure 11, immediately under the body of the table. Notice that the source note precedes all other notes and a general note precedes lettered or numbered footnotes. The letters or numbers in the table body

FIGURE 11

Table Showing Proper Alignment of Words and Figures

Table I. Classification of Stockholders

December 6, 19—

	Stock-holders	Percent	Shares Held	Percent
Women	31,402	41.60	2,254,582	24.07
Men	23,285	30.84	2,161,751	23.08
Fiduciaries	14,658	19.42	1,488,444	15.89
Joint accounts	3,024	4.00	96,898	1.03
Institutions	1,164	1.54	230,773	2.46
Corporations and partnerships[a]	829	1.10	237,124	2.53
Nominees	511	0.68	2,319,731	24.77
Brokers	266	0.35	295,987	3.16
Insurance companies	233	0.31	204,729	2.19
Investment trusts	118[b]	0.16	76,459	0.82
	75,490	100.00	9,366,478	100.00

Source: Stock ledger, Philips, Henderson, and Evans.

Note: Women stockholders outnumber men by almost 11 percent.

[a] An analysis of corporations versus partnerships is shown in table II.

[b] The number of trusts declined between 1985 and 1988 but is expected to increase by early 1990.

are set as superior (raised) figures. The letters or numbers with the actual footnotes may be set raised or on line.

HANDLING OTHER ILLUSTRATIONS. Artwork and photographs should be prepared and arranged on separate sheets in the order they are mentioned in the text (be certain that mention is made of *each* piece in the text and always in the order numbered). Artwork and photographs are often called "figures" and are numbered consecutively throughout the report, beginning with the number 1 or combined with the chapter number, beginning with 1 in each chapter, for example, Figures 1.1, 1.2, and 1.3; Figures 2.1 and 2.2; and Figures 3.1, 3.2, 3.3, and 3.4.

1. Photographs. Halftones (photographs) are best submitted to a printer as black-and-white glossy prints, unless the report is to be printed in color. If desired, you can put small lines (crop marks) in the white border, using a grease pencil that will rub off, to show the portion of the photograph that you want to use.

2. Line drawings. Line drawings (charts, graphs, and so on that do not have tonal values like a halftone) may consist of pen-and-ink drawings or computer art. Follow the instructions of your software program for preparing charts, graphs, and other graphics by computer. Clear, dark lines on a clean white background are needed for sharp reproduction.

3. Marking instructions. With both line drawings and halftones, mark instructions for a printer on a tissue or acetate overlay sheet, but do *not* press down on the surface of the illustration or you will leave a crease that may show up in reproduction.

4. Working with an artist. If you retain an artist to prepare the illustrations, rather than use computer-generated graphics, explain carefully the size, quality, and general characteristics desired as well as the intended means of reproduction (for example, black-and-white offset printing). The artist must have this information to prepare the artwork in proper form for the printer to use. Any problems because of poor communication in this respect could result in costly printing charges.

Preparing and Checking the Manuscript

PREPARING THE MANUSCRIPT. The following rules should be observed in preparing manuscript copy that will be sent to an outside typesetter or draft copy that will be edited for final production using word processing software.

1. Use 8½- by ll-inch white computer or typewriter paper (e.g., bond). Make additional printouts or photocopies, but always send the original to the typesetter.

2. Use a laser or other quality printer for sharp, clean copy of any portion of the report that is to be photographed directly for reproduction (camera-ready copy).

3. Use about 6-inch lines.

4. Use double spacing.

5. Indent paragraphs at least ½ inch.

6. Prepare headings and subheadings in the position they are to occupy on the final printed page: centered, flush left, or indented with the paragraph.

7. Leave a margin of 1 to 1½ inches on all sides, and keep each page as nearly uniform in length as possible.

8. Set off eight or more lines of quoted material as a block quotation (extract) from the rest of the text by indenting all of it from the left margin or from both the left and right margins of the rest of the text.

9. Prepare footnotes double-spaced and full measure (width) on a page separate from the manuscript or in a separate notes section after the appendix (or in notes sections at the ends of the chapters). If there are very few notes, they may be placed at the bottoms of the manuscript pages. Also prepare bibliographies and reference lists on separate pages positioned at the end of the manuscript just before the index.

10. Text cross-references to material appearing in other parts of the manuscript should read "see page 000" when you submit the

manuscript to the printer. But be sure to insert the actual page numbers later when the material has been set in final page form.

11. If you need to write instructions to the printer on the manuscript, circle your comments in the margins. If you need to write instructions on a finished page that is ready to be photographed, attach a removable, self-sticking note.

12. Follow the guidelines in Chapter 17 regarding proofreading and marking copy.

CHECKING THE MANUSCRIPT. After you have prepared the manuscript, read it line for line, looking not only for obvious errors but other problems that may have escaped everyone during the writing stage.

1. Look for spelling and typographical errors, as well as missing copy. Look for errors that your computer spell checker would miss, such as the word *the* when you meant *them*.

2. Check whether punctuation, capitalization, spelling, abbreviations, and so on are consistent throughout the report.

3. Recheck the pages to be certain none is missing or out of order.

4. Check the chapter titles and subheads in the table of contents against the actual titles and heads in the body of the manuscript; the wording should be consistent.

5. For a report that is being published and distributed, double-check quoted material and illustrations to be certain that permission for their use has been obtained and that no required credit lines are missing.

6. On double-spaced manuscript to be typeset, you can make short corrections in ink by crossing out the incorrect word and writing the correct word above it. If corrections are long, make the correction by computer and print out revised pages. But you can also make long corrections by typing the revised material on a separate page and referring to it in the margin at the point of correction, for example, "Insert A from page 607 here." On the separate page with the insert, make a note such as "Insert A on page 599."

7. When you have instructions for the typesetter or printer, write them in the margin and circle them. Typesetters know they are not to set anything that is circled in the margin.

8. If you want to break up a long paragraph into two paragraphs, you may insert a paragraph sign in ink where you want a second paragraph to begin. If you want to make one paragraph out of two separate paragraphs, you may run a line in ink from the end of the first one to the first word of the second one. If you have many such corrections, print out a new page of corrected copy.

9. To separate two words accidentally typed as one, draw a vertical line in ink between them.

10. To retain material crossed out, put a row of dots in ink beneath the crossed-out words and circle the word *stet* in the margin (but re-type the crossed-out copy and print out a new page if it will not be completely legible).

11. To indicate that you want a word set in all capitals, draw three lines under it. Two lines would mean that you want *small* capital letters. One line would mean that you want the word set in italics. A wavy line would mean that you want it set in boldface type.

Using Desktop Publishing

DESKTOP-PUBLISHING SYSTEMS. A desktop-publishing (DTP) system must consist of a computer (with large storage capacity and display screen large enough to display at least one full page) and a printer (laser printers provide higher-quality type for reproduction than do dot-matrix printers) and may include other equipment such as a full-page scanner (to transfer previously typed or printed copy into the computer's memory).

Special software used in desktop publishing is available for producing complex documents such as a company magazine. For single documents such as a departmental report, a basic word processing program should be adequate. A company considering whether to add a DTP system with special software should consider how often it would be used and whether all but occasional documents could better be produced using word processing software.

Because DTP documents are extremely complex, a DTP system uses numerous files (a single document may require more than a hundred files), including document files, chapter files, and program files (the program files control the software itself).

HOW DTP WORKS. The DTP process involves taking *unformatted* text from a diskette prepared on a computer with a word processing program. This text is converted into a standard text file that can be brought into DTP for formatting. The person preparing the original text, then, does not use any tabs, extra line spaces, or other formatting devices.

HOW TO PREPARE A DISKETTE FOR DTP. Since diskettes prepared for DTP must be unformatted, everything is typed flush left, single-spaced, without any indentions or setup of lists, tables, and the like. Depending on the DTP program requirements, special elements may be "tagged," or identified, on the unformatted diskette in some way. In the following examples, the tags (descriptive words) in all capital letters are preceded by the symbol "@," which is used in one of the major software packages:

@CHAPTER TITLE = Bond Survey

@A HEAD = SURVEY PREPARATIONS

@LIST = 1. Review *The Wall Street Journal* daily.

@LIST = 2. Develop a chart to compare quotations daily and weekly.

@LETTER = Dear Jerry:
    Thanks for writing to . . .

The DTP software will then format each unformatted, tagged item. Only particular elements need to be tagged—titles, heads, examples, lists, footnotes, and so on. Normal text, such as this paragraph, would not be tagged.

If you are preparing a diskette for your firm's DTP division, ask your contact or the DTP operator for instructions on preparing the diskette, including how to tag elements and how to divide your word processing diskette into files. A long report with individual chapters, for instance, could be divided into individual files for each chapter and additional files for the front matter (such as the table of contents) and back matter (such as the index).

HOW TO MAKE PUBLISHING ARRANGEMENTS

Arranging for Design and Typemarking

If your firm uses graphics software, the illustrations for your report may be prepared on a computer, and the DTP department may provide the overall design based on the capabilities of the DTP software. Your firm may also employ professional artists or retain freelancers who design documents, prepare the artwork for them, and paste the art in spaces provided by the design. If an outside typesetter is used, someone in your firm may also mark your manuscript for specific typefaces, type sizes, column widths, spacing, and so on.

If your company does not have an art department or art and design employees, check the Yellow Pages for local art talent. Ask for cost estimates (try to get two or three), and emphasize your deadlines; once you select someone, ask to see a *layout* (a rough sketch of the proposed design).

Making Printing Arrangements

Your Yellow Pages will list local printers and where you can get your DTP-prepared document printed or where you can have your manuscript typeset and printed. Try to find two or three prospects and ask for quotes on the job. Stress your deadline to the printer, and explain precisely what you will do and what you expect the typesetter-printer to do. (If you will be doing the design and typemarking yourself, ask the printer to show you sample typefaces and also show you how to mark the manuscript properly.)

Checking Proofs

The printer or DTP department will supply one to three sets of proofs after the report has been set. Long sheets not yet divided into pages are called *galley proofs* or *galleys*. Exact pages are called *page proofs*. It may be your job to proofread the galleys or pages (or both), correct them, and return them to the printer or DTP department as soon as possible.

WHAT TO LOOK FOR. Look not only for typographical errors but for missing copy and missing or misplaced pages. Check whether all credit lines are there. Double-check the position of footnotes, figure captions and legends, titles and subheads, and so on. Facing pages (side by side) should end on the same line, without a *widow* (a very short line) falling at the top of the next page. Verify page numbers and anything else that might be missing or might contain an error. Check that no more than two successive lines on a page end with hyphens. Look for distracting white "rivers" of space (sometimes created when type is justified) running throughout pages. But try to confine your markings to problems or errors created by the typesetter. If you are using an outside typesetter, changes in copy at this stage are considered *author's alterations* and involve additional cost.

Many printers will also give you a negative proof, or press proof, of your document before it is printed. This is your last chance to look for problems. Check the proof for errors missed during earlier stages and check for proper arrangement of pages, illustrations, and copy. Keep in mind that revisions will be even more costly at this late stage of the process. Once you approve the negative, or press, proof, the document will be printed, collated, folded, and bound. The printer also may provide mailing services, or you may have an in-house mail room that handles this function.

HOW TO COPYRIGHT THE REPORT

Copyright Law

Since January 1, 1978, all published and unpublished works that are fixed in a copy or phonorecord are subject to a single system of statutory protection. Registration of a work in the Library of Congress Copyright Office, although not necessary to have a valid copyright, is necessary for bringing a court action in regard to infringement.

The maximum total term of copyright protection for works already protected by federal statute before 1978 is now seventy-five years—a first term of twenty-eight years from the date of the original copyright plus a renewal term of forty-seven years. You must apply for renewal within one year before the first twenty-eight-year term expires. Copyrights already renewed that were in their second term between December 31, 1976, and

December 31, 1977, have been automatically extended to last the full seventy-five years. (Ask the Copyright Office for Circular R15 and renewal Form RE.)

The new law sets a single copyright term with no renewal requirements. Works existing on January 1, 1978, but not copyrighted and not in the public domain are subject to automatic federal copyright protection.

The term of protection under the new law is a life-plus-50-years system (the same as most other countries have). This means that protection applies for the life of the author(s) plus 50 years after the death of the last surviving author. Protection for works made for hire and anonymous or pseudonymous works applies for 75 years from publication or 100 years from creation, whichever is shorter.

All copyright terms will run through the end (December 31) of the calendar year in which they would otherwise expire. The renewal period for works copyrighted between 1950 and 1977 will run from December 31 of the twenty-seventh year of the copyright until December 31 of the following year.

Works in the public domain are not protected under the new law, and a copyright that has been lost on a work cannot be restored, for example, if it did not meet requirements such as containing the proper copyright notice or if the terms of protection expired before renewal could be made.

Fair-Use Guidelines

The 1976 copyright law lists four criteria that are used to determine whether copying material from some source without permission or payment is fair:

1. The purpose and character of the use, including whether such use is of a commercial nature or is for nonprofit educational purposes

2. The nature of the copyrighted work

3. The amount and substantiality of the portion used in relation to the copyrighted work as a whole

4. The effect of the use upon the potential market for, or value of, the copyrighted work

Section 107 of the 1976 law states that "the fair use of a copyrighted work, including such use by reproduction in copies or phonorecords or by any other means specified by that section, for purposes such as criticism, comment, news reporting, teaching (including multiple copies for classroom use), scholarship, or research, is not an infringement of copyright." The 1976 law does not include guidelines for classroom copying, but systematic reproduction and distribution of single or multiple copies of books and periodicals by libraries (instead of their purchase) is forbidden. Spontaneous copying for classroom use must not exceed the number of students in a course, each copy must bear a copyright notice, and the amount copied must be brief.

Copyright Registration Procedure

COPYRIGHT NOTICE. For copyright to be valid, a proper notice must be published in a printed work. This notice must include (1) the letter *c* in a circle (and may also include the word *copyright* or the abbreviation *copr.*), (2) the year of first publication of the work, and (3) the name of the copyright owner (*Copyright © 1988 by Prentice Hall, Inc.*). A U.S. citizen whose work includes a proper copyright notice also receives protection in all other countries that are members of the Universal Copyright Convention.

INFORMATION AND FORMS. Free registration forms are available from the Copyright Office, Library of Congress, Washington, D.C. 20559. Ask for instructions on the proper procedure for registering a work and the applicable fee to submit. Specify what kind of work—book, magazine, artwork, and so on—you want to register. If you require additional information, ask your local reference librarian for a current copyright handbook.

Chapter 4

Handling Mail and Electronic Messages

Messages are sent and received through the U.S. Postal Service and through private organizations and in-house company facilities that handle conventional mail and electronic messages. Local, national, and international transport services carry letters and packages much the same as the U.S. Postal Service. Electronic message systems—in-house, subscriber, and service bureau—use the telephone lines, satellites, or direct wiring to transmit messages electronically, with special equipment such as computers and modems, teletypewriters, and facsimiles. The secretary's duties in message transmission concern practices and procedures in handling incoming and outgoing messages.

HANDLING INCOMING MAIL

Collecting Mail and Electronic Messages

Most mail arrives by postal or private-delivery carrier or through an electronic-transmission system. One of a secretary's first duties upon arriving at the office is to access the computer's mailbox (memory) and check other equipment such as facsimiles and teletypewriters for messages that were transmitted overnight or early in the morning.

If a message has arrived through a rapid-transmission system, it may be urgent and require your employer's immediate attention. Although electronic-mail (E-mail) messages may be viewed on your computer's display screen, a common procedure is to print out a copy of all or some of such incoming messages and include the printout with the other incoming correspondence that you collect for your employer.

Conventional letters and packages that arrive by postal or private transport may be delivered to your desk by the carrier or by an employee of your mail room. Whereas postal mail arrives at a certain time of the day, electronic messages and private-delivery material may arrive at various times throughout the day.

Opening and Sorting the Mail

CATEGORIES OF MAIL. Major categories of incoming mail include correspondence (and enclosures), bills and statements (if you can distinguish them from correspondence at a glance), advertisements and circulars, and newspapers and periodicals.

PRELIMINARY SORTING. First, separate personal matters from business matters, and then separate business mail into outside and interoffice mail. Collect all priority material—that which requires immediate attention—including postal, private transport, and electronic messages. If your office has other obvious categories of incoming mail, such as purchase orders or receipts, you may want to use some of the sorting devices, such as racks or trays, available from office-supply stores.

OPENING THE MAIL. Attend to correspondence first. On incoming sealed material, use a hand or electric letter opener, taking care not to slash the contents. Immediately attach any enclosures to the letters, making certain that no enclosures are left inside the envelopes.

Open packages carefully, and place any letter that is enclosed with your other correspondence. Then place the mailing label from the box with the contents of the package. Always check packages with supplies against your purchase order, and do not accept material that you did not order or should not be receiving.

If the address of the sender is on the envelope but not on the letter, attach the envelope to the letter. Otherwise, put the opened envelopes aside until all the mail is completely processed and you know that you will not have to recheck the envelopes for overlooked contents or return addresses.

Do not destroy the envelopes when the postmark date is significant. If a letter is undated, for example, the postmark date should be recorded.

Some offices require that all mail be stamped with the date and time received.

1. Letters sent to you in error. Some mail may be sent to you in error. If you do not know the forwarding address, cross out the incorrect address, write "Not at This Address" on the envelope, and put it back in the mail. (Note that only first-class mail is forwarded without reapplying postage.) If you open a letter by mistake, write "Opened by Mistake" or "Opened in Error" on the envelope, initial it, reseal it, and put it back in the mail.

2. Letters marked "Personal" or "Confidential." Never open letters marked "Personal" or "Confidential" unless your employer has specifically asked you to do so. It is also advisable to assume that a letter written in longhand is personal, even if not marked as such, unless you know the correspondent and your employer has asked you to open the letter. If practical, hand-deliver any letter you receive that is marked "Personal" or "Confidential."

SORTING THE MAIL. Sort the correspondence (including interoffice memos) into three categories: (1) that which requires your employer's attention, (2) that which requires the attention of someone outside your office, and (3) that which requires your attention. Then segregate (4) newspapers and periodicals, (5) advertisements and circulars, (6) bills and statements, and (7) any other category of mail that your office receives.

Double-check envelopes for enclosures. If any are missing, look in the envelope that was put aside for this purpose. If the enclosure cannot be found, make a notation on the letter to that effect. When the nature of the enclosure is such that the letter cannot be answered without it, put the letter in the pile that requires your attention.

Attach large enclosures in back of a letter, small enclosures in front of it. Loose items such as cash should be put in their proper place (e.g., a cash box) and the amount and location noted on the letter, with your initials.

1. Mail requiring your employer's attention. Strive to have the incoming mail and electronic messages ready before your employer gets to the office or as quickly as possible thereafter. If the file of previous correspondence relating to a current letter will facilitate action, attach the incoming letter to the file; ask your boss if he or she wants you to type copies of incoming letters that are written in longhand.

Arrange your employer's mail in the order of importance, with the most important on top. Although express mail and electronic messages are often the most urgent, advertisers also use fast-messaging systems, so it may be necessary to segregate such material from top-priority messages for immediate attention. Ask if your employer would like you to use color-coded folders for different categories of mail.

Ask if you should annotate the mail—highlight key points in lengthy letters and perhaps jot down useful facts on them. For instance, if a letter asks your employer to speak at a luncheon, you might highlight the time, place, and so on and in the margin of the letter and point out any conflicting appointment. Depending on your copier, yellow-ink marking pens may be used to highlight words without leaving marks that will show if the letter is photocopied. Some offices, however, will not permit any writing or marking on letters. In that case, attach self-sticking, removable slips (available from office-supply stores).

2. Mail requiring attention by others. Place in separate piles the correspondence that your immediate office cannot dispose of without information or assistance from someone else in the organization as well as correspondence that should be routed to others.

Office-supply stores have standard self-sticking, removable action-requested slips that have places to check the action you want someone to take, for example:

( )   For your information

( )   For your action

( )   For your approval

( )   For your comments

( )   Please forward

( )   Please return

( )   Please review with me

( )   Please file

( )   _____

Check the action you want taken, attach the slip to the incoming correspondence, and forward it to the individual to whose attention it is directed. If necessary, also attach pertinent files or previous correspondence.

If several people should see the correspondence, use standard routing slips or devise one similar to that illustrated in Figure 12. If you use slips that already have the persons' names on them, place the numerals 1, 2, 3, and so on in front of the names on the slip in the order that each person should receive the mail. Each person will either initial the slip or cross off his or her name after seeing the material and send it on to the next person, with the routing slip still attached.

If interoffice envelopes are used, list the names on the envelope in the order you want the individuals to receive the mail. Each recipient will cross off his or her name after reviewing the material and put the envelope with material enclosed back in the interoffice mail to be delivered by a company messenger to the next person listed on the envelope.

If you attend to part of a letter before sending it to someone for further attention, mark the paragraph that has had attention. Write the date and "done" or "noted" in the margin and initial it.

3. Mail requiring your attention. Include in a separate pile the letters that you will answer for your employer's signature, as well as those that you will write over your own signature.

When you take action that your employer should be aware of, type a brief explanation of what you did, attach it to the original letter, and put it on your employer's desk for review. Most of the matters that you handle on your own will likely be routine (e.g., answering a routine inquiry or thanking someone for sending something you requested), and you need not report such items to your employer.

4. Newspapers and periodicals. Select newspapers and periodicals that your employer likes to read. Unwrap, flatten out, and put them in a folder labeled "Newspapers and Periodicals." Put the folder on his or her desk or in a briefcase if your employer prefers to take material of this kind home.

Send the other newspapers and periodicals to the persons in the organization who need them or put them on the proper shelves for reference. If your employer is paying for a periodical that he or she does not want, that is not needed by someone in the organization, or that is

FIGURE 12

Routing Slip

Date: 3/5/—		
(To be routed in the order numbered)		
2 Mrs. Edwards	*GRE*	*3/7*
1 Mr. Roberts	*LR*	*3/6*
4 Mr. Jones	*B.J.*	*3/10*
3 Ms. Nelson	*E.N.*	*3/8*
Mr. Ellis		
5 File		
Please initial, date, and forward.		

not valuable as reference material, ask if you should cancel the subscription.

   5. *Advertisements and circulars.* Do not routinely discard all so-called junk mail. The educational value of advertisements and circulars is often overlooked. They are frequently a convenient and free source of information about things such as availability and trends in new products and procedures or reminders of important meetings and other business-related events. Some of this material will doubtless interest your employer or another department in your company. An accountant, for example, might be interested in an advertisement of new accounting or tax books; also, executives are always looking for cost-cutting ideas. If an order blank is enclosed with an advertisement, clip it to the advertisement.

   Frequently, you will find solicitations for contributions in the advertisements. Put them in a separate folder and handle them in the manner described for charitable contributions in Chapter 12.

6. *Bills and statements.* Bills and statements are usually forwarded to the bookkeeper or accounts payable department. If it is the responsibility of your office to pay bills, file them until the time of the month designated for payment. If they are to be held for payment later, it is not necessary to open them until you have disposed of the other mail. In fact, if you are particularly rushed and there is a large stack of them, you might put them in a "pending" folder until you have time to attend to them.

Daily Mail Record

PURPOSE OF MAIL RECORD. Keep a simple daily record of all mail sent out of your office for action by another person. This applies to electronic messages, reports, and other material, as well as conventional letters. The purpose of the record is twofold: It serves as a check on the receipt and disposition of mail that gets misplaced and as a follow-up reminder.

HOW TO PREPARE A MAIL RECORD. For the daily mail record, you may use looseleaf sheets with vertical columns headed *Date, Description, To Whom Sent, Action to Be Taken,* and *Follow-up.* See Figure 13. If you need to distinguish among the methods of transmission for mail received, add a column labeled *Type of Transmission* in which you can specify "E-mail," "telex," and the like. You may also include this information in the *Description* column. If you keep the record with pen and ink instead of preparing it by typewriter or computer, the sheets should have lines drawn between entries. Double-space between each entry.

Under *Description*, note the date of the communication, name of sender, and the subject matter. If pertinent, and if you don't have a separate column for the type of transmission, add a note to indicate the kind of message received, such as facsimile. In the *Action to Be Taken* column, note the action that was checked on the slip that you attached to the communication before forwarding it. Write the deadline date for disposition in the follow-up column if it is necessary to follow up to see that proper action is taken. When the matter has had the necessary attention, draw a line through the entry.

In some organizations, certain department heads receive all the mail of the department so that they may assign the correspondence to the ap-

FIGURE 13

Daily Mail Record

	DAILY MAIL RECORD			
Date	Description	To Whom Sent	Action to Be Taken	Follow-up
3/5	Spellman, Preface to Corp. Sec'y, 3/3	L. Rogers	Approval	3/5
3/5	Brown of U. of Wis. request for free copy of Credits & Collections 3/3	Andrews	Reply	

propriate person for reply. In such cases, the daily mail record is particularly important.

Procedure When Your Employer Is Away

The manner in which you should handle the mail when your employer is away from the office depends on office policy and your employer's personal preference. You can adapt the procedure recommended here as needed:

1. If your employer makes a practice of telephoning the office each day, sort the correspondence according to company matters and outside matters. Also jot down the gist of each letter so that you can report readily.

2. Telephone or fax a copy of anything urgent that requires immediate personal attention if your employer does not call you.

3. Fax copies or mail photocopies of all other mail that requires your employer's personal attention.

4. Acknowledge all correspondence, whether personal or business, if your employer is to be away more than a few days.

5. Dispose of as much of the mail as possible by covering the subject of the letter in your acknowledgment or by referring letters to other people in the organization for reply.

6. Number consecutively the packets of mail that you send to your employer (e.g., 1 of 4, 2 of 4, 3 of 4, 4 of 4). In this way, he or she can tell whether or not all the mail that you sent has arrived. Numbering the packets is particularly important when your employer is traveling from place to place.

7. If your employer is on a vacation and does not want mail forwarded, hold the letters that require personal attention and indicate in your acknowledgment to the sender when he or she might expect a reply.

8. Keep the accumulated mail in folders marked "Correspondence to Be Signed," "Correspondence Requiring Your Attention," "Correspondence to Be Read" (letters that have been answered but in which your employer will probably be interested), "Reports," and "General Reading Material" (miscellaneous items of advertising and publications that your employer might want to read).

HANDLING OUTGOING MAIL

How to Prepare Messages

How you prepare a message depends in part on the method of transmission that you will use. Most messages are set up like a regular business letter or memo, although messages sent electronically are often kept short to control costs and to make it easier to read in the case of an electronic message that the recipient will view on his or her computer display screen. A letter sent by facsimile, however, which duplicates the original precisely (like a photocopy), may be prepared conventionally on regular business stationery using standard formatting procedures.

E-mail, telex messages, telegrams, and mailgrams are not transmitted on business letterhead, however, and often must be carefully edited into very brief statements. Also, instead of a traditional letter salutation and complimentary close, the memo format is more practical for E-mail and other computer or teletypewriter messages. The text itself may need to be abbreviated, too, depending on the method of transmission and the need to control costs.

Practice editing your electronic messages to reduce the word length. Notice how the following twenty-five-word message can be cut nearly in half by deleting unnecessary words and expressing the same thought clearly in only fifteen words.

> *Twenty-five words*: WE ARE IN NEED OF PRICE AND DELIVERY SCHEDULE ON YOUR AEC-1400 PROCESSOR. WE BELIEVE YOUR QUOTATION OF 14 AUGUST CONTAINS A TWO-DIGIT ERROR.

> *Fifteen words*: REQUEST NEW PRICE AND DELIVERY SCHEDULE ON AEC-1400 PROCESSOR. BELIEVE AUGUST 14 QUOTE IN ERROR.

How to Prepare Letters for Mailing

GETTING SIGNATURES ON OUTGOING MAIL. When you give your employer letters to be signed for delivery by postal mail or private transport or transmission by facsimile, separate those that were dictated from those that were composed for your employer's signature by you or someone else.

When a letter is ready for signature, some secretaries insert the flap of the envelope over the original letter and its enclosures. Many executives are interested only in the letters, however, and consider the envelopes a nuisance. Follow your employer's preference. The practice of giving your employer letters without envelopes also has this advantage: You can get the letters ready for signature more quickly, because you can wait to address the envelopes from photocopies or after the letters are returned to you. But do not file any copies until the letters have been signed and you have made any necessary late changes on the copies. Many secretaries do not make photocopies until the original is correct and has been signed; this eliminates the separate step of correcting copies in addition to the original.

ASSEMBLING THE MAIL. When the mail has been signed, bring it back to your desk and assemble it for actual mailing or electronic transmission. Check each letter for these things:

1. Has a letter being sent by conventional mail or facsimile been signed?

2. Are all enclosures included in postal or private-transport mail?

3. Are the inside address and the envelope (or mailing label) address the same on postal and private-transport mail?

4. Has your employer marked further corrections or changes that need to be added to the original or photocopies?

5. Has your employer added a postscript in ink that you should add to the final printout or to any photocopies (unless it is a personal comment, which usually should remain in ink)?

6. Does the envelope address on postal mail use the two-letter state abbreviation, and is the address surrounded by white space so that the post office's optical character reader (OCR) can sort the envelope automatically? (See Figure 14 for an example of data positioning on an OCR and barcode envelope.)

When everything is ready, organize postal and private-transport mail into like categories to prepare for folding and inserting.

FOLDING AND INSERTING LETTERS IN ENVELOPES. Since paper clips can jam postal equipment, it is preferable to staple enclosures or insert them loose in the fold of the letter. But if you must use paper clips, insert the folded letter upside down so that the paper clip is at the bottom. In all other cases, fold and insert the letter as follows:

1. Folding letters. Letters written on full-sized letterheads for insertion in long envelopes should be folded as follows: one fold from the bottom, about a third of the way up; a second fold from the bottom to within $\frac{1}{16}$ inch of the top. Insert in the envelope, top up.

Letters written on full-sized letterheads for insertion in short envelopes should be folded as follows: one fold from the bottom to within $\frac{1}{4}$ inch of the top; a second fold from right to left, about a third of the way across; a third fold from left to right within $\frac{1}{4}$ inch of the right edge. Insert with the right edge up.

FIGURE 14

OCR and Barcode Read Areas

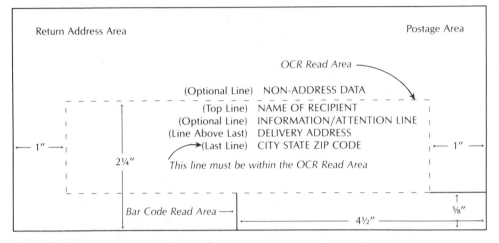

Letters written on half-sized letterheads should be folded as follows: one fold from right to left, about a third of the way across; a second fold from left to right, leaving about ¹⁄₁₆ inch between the edges at the right. Insert in a small envelope with the right edge up.

Letters should be inserted into envelopes so that when the letter is removed from the envelope and unfolded, the type side should be up.

2. Inserting enclosures. To insert like items quickly, open and flatten the flaps of several envelopes. Hold the envelopes with one hand and the enclosures with the other, sliding enclosures in, one after the other. If you have different enclosures for the envelopes, however, handle them separately to avoid slipping an enclosure into the wrong envelope.

HANDLING ENCLOSURES. Generally, follow these rules for inserting enclosures, but avoid using paper clips, as explained in the preceding section:

1. Enclosures the size of the letter. These enclosures are easily folded and inserted, with their accompanying letters, into commercial envelopes of the ordinary size. (Private-delivery companies may provide their own envelopes for your use.) If the enclosure consists of two or more sheets, staple them together but do not fasten the enclosed material to the letter. Fold the enclosure, then fold the letter, and next slip the enclosure inside the last fold of the letter. Thus when the letter is removed from the envelope, the enclosure comes out with it.

2. Enclosures larger than the letter. These enclosures include booklets, pamphlets, prospectuses, catalogs, and other printed material too large to fit into a commercial envelope of ordinary size. They are generally sent in large envelopes. Enclosures of this kind may be handled in one of the following ways:

The letter is inserted with the enclosure in the large envelope, which is sealed. In this case, for postal delivery, first-class postage is charged for both the letter and the enclosure.

A combination envelope is used. This is a large envelope with a flap that is fastened by a patent fastener of some kind but not sealed. A smaller envelope of commercial size is affixed on the front of this envelope in the process of manufacture. The letter is inserted into the small envelope, and the flap is sealed. For postal delivery, postage is affixed to the large envelope at third-class rates and to the small envelope at first-class rates.

The enclosure may be sent, unsealed, in one envelope and the letter, sealed, in another.

A letter may be enclosed with a parcel for postal delivery if postage is paid on the letter at the first-class rate.

3. Enclosures smaller than the letter. When enclosures are considerably smaller than the letter, staple them to the letter in the upper left corner, on top of the letter. If the enclosure cannot be stapled (e.g., coins), tape the objects to a card, or place them in a small, marked envelope, and then staple the card or envelope to the letter. If two or more such enclosures are sent, put the smaller one on top.

Selecting the Method of Transmission

FACTORS TO CONSIDER. When time is not critical, letters are frequently sent through the U.S. Postal Service. When time is a factor, however, or when another in-house communication vehicle is available, you need to select a method that fits your requirements in regard to time, cost of transmission, and available equipment and services.

Electronic Messages

Broadly, electronic messages include all messages transmitted through signals over the telephone lines or by satellites. Some messages are also sent by interconnected equipment, such as equipment connected through direct writing in local area networks.

Setup costs for a particular messaging system vary depending on the equipment required, whether telephone lines or satellite service must be leased, the type of subscriber service used (if any), and the subscriber service's method of charging. If your office hasn't committed to a particular type of transmission, shop around.

Check office magazines for addresses of services and suppliers, and look in your Yellow Pages under appropriate headings such as "Electronic Mail Service," "Telegraph Service," "Telephone Communications Service," "Teletypewriter Communications Systems," and "Satellite Systems." Ask for information to compare setup costs, transmission costs and speed, and other factors. If transmission charges are calculated per second or minute, for example, the longer it takes to transmit a page of material, the more expensive it will be to send each message.

SATELLITE TRANSMISSION. Some types of transmission cannot take place over the terrestrial telephone lines, and electronic systems use satellites in those cases. INTELSAT, an acronym derived from the International Telecommunications Satellite Consortium, is a communications satellite that can handle telephone, radio, and television transmission. The marine version of INTELSAT is INMARSAT. Through INMARSAT, for example, a properly equipped ship or offshore rig can contact subscribers worldwide. INMARSAT service is an automatic telecommunications service that operates similar to a telex service. Check the telephone directories for numbers and addresses.

E-MAIL. With E-mail, a computer-based form of message transmission, messages can be programmed to be sent to anyone with a receiving computer at any time (such as when telephone rates are less), and messages can be sent to more than one destination at the same time. As a high-speed form of transmission, the advantages are significant in global business, as well as in local or national communications. E-mail is frequently less expensive than a long-distance telephone call or overnight delivery and more accurate than telex.

Since computers can store data, an incoming message is said to be filed in an electronic "mailbox." A *private electronic mailbox* means that only the intended recipients can read their own mail. A *bulletin-board system* means that messages are available for all users to read. Although passwords can be used to maintain confidentiality in electronic mail, some systems have no such security measures. If your messages are private or confidential, investigate first whether the recipients use a private or bulletin-board mail system.

1. Types of E-mail systems. Large organizations often aim for greater integration of computer and word processing operations, facsimile transmission, telex, and other forms of messaging. Combining E-mail with other operations is a logical step in that direction, although the use of an E-mail system is dependent on receivers having compatible computer equipment to accept messages. Also, installation costs may be high if a firm does not already have the necessary equipment. But once the equipment is in place, there often are savings in copying, long-distance delivery, and other traditional costs.

The hardware, or equipment, used in E-mail systems is varied. Some E-mail systems are *centralized*, consisting of a number of terminals connected to a large central computer. Others rely on a *network system* with a number of independent terminals, each of which can send and receive messages on its own. A *node-to-node stand-alone electronic-mail system* is an independent computer capable of communicating with another compatible computer by using a modem and the telephone lines to send messages back and forth. (A *modem* is a computer peripheral used to effect data transmission over the telephone lines.) A *local-area network* (LAN) is a network of computers that are wired to one another locally (in the same building, for example) and communicate with one another directly, as opposed to a *wide-area network* (WAN), which uses the telephone lines or satellites to span the entire United States or most of the world. *Voice-mail systems* also send, receive, and store messages and can be accessed from almost any telephone in the world. Many business authorities believe that voice and electronic mail will eventually be integrated, with electronic mail ultimately becoming voice mail.

2. Public data networks. These services function as a clearinghouse for the electronic messages of subscribers and offer third parties access to large databases. By way of a "switching technique," subscribers to certain data networks can call the network by telephone and then reach any other computer that is part of the network. Since charges and procedures differ among available services, it is necessary to request current information including rates, types of service, and instructions on use of the service.

3. How to use E-mail. To use E-mail, you need a computer terminal or a communicating word processor. With the right equipment you can create a message of any length at any time of the day and send it to another terminal by using a modem and the telephone lines. If you use a subscriber service, follow the instructions it provides for accessing the network.

With some systems you are informed of a waiting message by a beep or other signal. You can retrieve your messages from a remote location by telephone, much the same as you can pick up messages on an answering machine from a remote location. If you are at your computer terminal, you can read your incoming messages, store them until later, print them out, or immediately create replies.

The software, or computer program, used to create E-mail messages is as varied as the hardware used in an E-mail system. Generally, when you create the messages you want to send on a computer or communicating word processor keyboard, you can edit them and print out a hard copy of your message at your own terminal. Editing with E-mail software is usually more limited than is editing with word processing software.

FACSIMILE. Facsimile, or fax, machines look like small copiers with a telephone attached. The word *facsimile* refers to both the name of a machine and the process by which exact copies of documents can be converted into signals that can be sent over the telephone lines to a receiving terminal. At the destination, a facsimile *transceiver* (a machine that can send or receive) converts the signals back into a readable form that is a precise duplicate of the original. Both text and graphics of almost any sort can be sent by facsimile.

Facsimile transmission is fast, and the machines are convenient and simple to use. Transmission of one page usually costs less than using overnight express or placing a long-distance telephone call. All that is needed to operate the machine is a telephone, if one is not built into the machine, since the facsimile itself has its own scanner and printer.

Although newer machines are generally compatible (that is, a receiving machine is likely to accept the sender's transmission without problems), facsimile paper is not so compatible, and paper manufactured to work on one machine might not work on another. Plain-paper machines, however, use ordinary paper, the same as most photocopiers, and because of the readable and easy-to-handle copies, plain-paper facsimile sales are increasing.

1. How to prepare a fax message. Facsimiles can transmit only what is already prepared, since fax machines have no keyboards. Hence they function like photocopiers, unlike the computers used in E-mail, which can compose as well as send messages. Therefore, you must compose a fax message on a typewriter or computer, add any needed graphics, print it out, and physically remove and take the finished piece to a facsimile machine for transmission.

As an alternative to the stand-alone fax machine, a fax board can be installed in personal computers, enabling PC users to create text and graphics on the computer and convert it into a fax document that can be transmitted by the computer, using a modem, to a receiving fax machine, similar to the procedure in an electronic-mail system. *PC-fax*, then, means creation of a document by computer and transmission from that computer to a *fax machine* in a different location; *E-mail* means creation of a document by computer and transmission from that computer to another *computer* in a different location.

2. How to send a fax message. To send a facsimile message from one fax machine to another, place the document in a tray or around a cylinder of the machine. The fax then scans the material, and light and dark areas are converted into signals that can travel over the telephone lines to a compatible machine at the receiving terminal. Then dial the number of the receiving terminal and push the transmit button. Include a cover sheet with your name, telephone number, and fax number (standard forms are available through office suppliers).

Facsimiles can be programmed to store data so that it can be sent automatically whenever you choose, whether or not you are there at the time. Recent machines have features such as error correction (for poor-quality telephone lines that distort a message), document reduction, programmable capability (delayed send and auto-retry), automatic feed and cut, document feeder, unattended operation, dual access (whereby a document can be scanned to memory while the fax is transmitting or receiving another document), confidential or security transmission (using a PIN code), and telephone-line or satellite-transmission capability.

3. Facsimile services. Businesses that do not own a facsimile machine can send messages through a facsimile service. Some of the international carriers provide this service, as well as numerous local businesses (check your Yellow Pages). Take your document to a nearby fax service, where the operator will put your original into the fax machine, wait for it to be transmitted or programmed for later transmission, and return the document to you. Local businesses providing fax service usually charge a fee that must be paid at the time you take the document in for transmission or that will be charged to your company account and billed later along with other charges.

TELEX. Whereas you cannot prepare a message on a facsimile machine—only send it—you can both type and send a telex message on machines commonly known as "teletypewriters." Telex is an older, slower, keyboard-to-keyboard technology. The machines have typewriterlike keyboards on which you type the message, which means that you are limited to text, whereas facsimile can send exact copies of graphics as well as text.

Since telex has been used for many years, the equipment is relatively standardized, and the cost of transmission is less than it is for some of the newer technologies and services such as electronic mail. Telex I is the original telex, and Telex II is the current name for TWX (Teletypewriter Exchange).

A *telex service* is a network of subscribers who are interconnected in the same way that E-mail subscribers are linked on an E-mail network. Your terminal may be directly connected to the service you choose, or you may have a private leased line. You can subscribe to a telex service through any major communications carrier. (Check your telephone directory.) Since the industry has been deregulated, Western Union has been able to connect you with overseas numbers, and the international carriers have been able to connect you with domestic numbers.

Telex subscribers are listed in a telex directory similar to a telephone book. This directory lists the company name, address, carrier, telex number, and telex answerback for all telex subscribers.

1. How to prepare a telex message. The quality of a conventional telex printout, which appears in all-capital letters, is inferior to other forms of transmission such as E-mail. Corrections are obvious and unattractive. Some services enable you to dial into the carrier of your choice with a computer and a modem, however, which gives you the editing capability of any computer or word processor.

After typing your message on a teletypewriter, dial the telex number at the receiving terminal and press the appropriate transmission control. The typed message is then converted to signals that travel over the telephone lines and at the destination is converted back to text and printed out on a receiving machine.

2. How to send a telex message. As a telex subscriber, you must follow the service's instructions for transmitting messages on your own communicating teletypewriter or the one supplied by the service. Usually, the system will prompt you, line by line, what to type (addressee's name, address, text of the message, and so on).

Although all telex terminals are compatible, you must follow the instructions of your service to use the equipment properly and format your message properly. When you are ready to transmit, you will probably be instructed to press a "call" button and dial the number designated by the service you are using. This will, in turn, activate your own machine's answerback mechanism. Once both parties are correctly identified, the transmission can continue. Like E-mail and fax messages, telex messages can be programmed for delivery at a later designated time (store-and-forward service).

TELETEX SERVICE. Teletex is a high-speed transmission service, much faster than telex, for high-volume users. Teletex users can also transmit messages to telex subscribers. The use of Teletex is dependent on manufacturers of the word processing equipment meeting the standards (e.g., compatibility) required by the Consultative Committee for International Telegraph and Telephone.

Teletex messages can be prepared on word processors or computers that are specially modified to send and receive such messages automatically. Therefore, unlike standard telex messages, Teletex messages look like a traditional business letter, with uppercase and lowercase letters and better print quality. Teletex has a wider range of features, too, including accents and diacritical marks. Since computers can be used, the messages also can be edited like any computer message before sending them to their destination over the telephone lines.

TELEGRAMS AND CABLES. Most communities have one or more businesses locally that will send Western Union telegrams (domestic messages) or cables (foreign messages). Since costs are calculated per word or group of words, messages should be brief.

1. How to send a telegram or cable. Most messages are sent by telephoning a Western Union office or business that provides this service (refer to your local telephone directory), where the message is sent electronically to an office near the recipient. There it is delivered to the recipient by telephone or messenger. Since charges are based on the number of words used, edit the message to eliminate all unnecessary words.

2. Using telegram forms as file copies. Even when messages are given to a Western Union office or other business providing Western Union service, the sender should keep in the office files a typed copy of the message being read over the telephone. Blank forms are available at the offices providing Western Union service. Pick up a supply for use as file copies.

MAILGRAMS. Another Western Union service, mailgram messages are also telephoned or delivered in person to a Western Union office or business that offers mailgram service. The message is transmitted electronically to a post office near the recipient, where it is printed out and delivered along with the next regular mail. Although charges are calculated by word count, like a telegram, mailgrams are less expensive than telegrams; they also take longer to reach the recipient.

INTELPOST. The U.S. Postal Service INTELPOST system enables users to send copies of documents (text and graphics) electronically to certain countries. Customers may pick up the message within an hour or a copy will be delivered in the country's regular mail.

Postal Mail

In spite of the increase in other forms of message transmission and delivery, the U.S. Postal Service remains the major national carrier of letters and documents. The following sections summarize important classes of service; for details on rates and regulations, which change frequently, contact your local post office or subscribe to the domestic and international manuals published by the U.S. Postal Service.

DOMESTIC POSTAL SERVICE. *Domestic mail* is mail sent within, among, and between the United States, its territories and possessions, the former Canal Zone, army/air force/navy post offices, and the United Nations in New York.

1. Sources of information. The *Domestic Mail Manual* covers regulations and information about rates and postage, classes of mail, special services, wrapping and mailing requirements, and collection and delivery services. The manual and looseleaf supplementary service are sold on a subscription basis. For it and other postal publications for sale, write to the Superintendent of Documents, U.S. Government Printing Office, Washington, DC 20402.

The *National Five-Digit Zip Code and Post Office Directory* lists all post offices arranged alphabetically by states. It is sold in some post offices and can be ordered from the Five-Digit Zip Code Directory Orders, National Address Information Center, 6060 Primacy Parkway, Suite 101, Memphis, TN 38188-0001.

Other booklets and brochures are available free of charge from your local post office. A newsletter, *Memo to Mailers*, is available free from the U.S. Postal Service's National Address Information Center.

2. How to send documents. It is important to select the most appropriate class of mail for the material you are sending. Many documents can be sent either through the U.S. Postal Service or by a private transport service. If time is critical, select an overnight class of delivery such as Express Mail or select first class over the slower third or fourth class.

If a regular delivery schedule is satisfactory, rather than express service or a form of high-speed electronic transmission, the following list of selected documents and other material arranged according to postal class may help you make the right choice. Notice that more than one class of mail may be used for certain material. Your choice will depend on whether you want to insure it or protect it against opening for postal inspection or aim for delivery within two or three days.

First class: invitations and announcements, bills and statements of account, nonnegotiable bonds, checks, document copies, greeting cards, letters, money orders, postcards, nonnegotiable stock certificates, photographs, tapes and cassettes, diskettes, important typewritten material or computer printouts

Registered first class: negotiable bonds, certified or endorsed-in-blank checks, currency, signed documents of value, jewelry, letters for addressee only, negotiable stock certificates

Certified first class: nonnegotiable bonds, important documents but of no significant monetary value, letters for addressee only, nonnegotiable stock certificates

Second class: newspapers, periodicals

Third class: catalogs, circulars, drawings, form letters, manuscripts, photographs, bulbs and roots, various printed matter

Fourth class: books, catalogs, manuscripts, tapes, and cassettes

3. *Minimum-size standards.* The following minimum-size standards apply to all mailable matter: All mailing pieces must be at least 0.007 inch thick, and all mailing pieces (other than keys and identification devices) that are 0.25 inch thick or less must be (1) rectangular, (2) at least 3½ inches high, and (3) at least 5 inches long. Anything less than the minimum size is prohibited from the mails.

4. *Nonstandard mail.* First-class mail weighing 1 ounce or less, single-piece rate third-class mail, and certain international mail weighing 1 ounce or less are nonstandard and subject to a surcharge in addition to the applicable postage and fees if any of the following applies: (a) length exceeds 11½ inches, (b) height exceeds 6⅛ inches, (c) thickness exceeds ¼ inch, and (d) length divided by height is less than 1.3 and more than 2.5.

CLASSES OF DOMESTIC SERVICE. The U.S. Postal Service has various classes of mail covering both single-piece and bulk-rate mailings. Since rates and regulations vary for each class and are revised from time to time, consult your local post office or a copy of the *Domestic Mail Manual* for current information.

1. Express mail. Express mail offers expedited delivery of high-priority shipments within the United States and to selected foreign countries. The five classes of domestic express service are Express Mail Next Day Service, Express Mail Second Day Service, Express Mail Custom Designed Service, Express Mail Same Day Airport Service, and Express Mail Military Service.

2. First-class mail. All mailable matter may be sent first class except for material excluded from air shipment by the Department of Transportation. Some material, in fact, *must* be sent first class, such as material sealed against postal inspection, certain handwritten or typewritten material, personal correspondence, and bills and statements of account. First-class mail, which is generally faster than second-, third-, or fourth-class mail, will be forwarded without charge for one year. For information on reduced rates through bulk mailings and application requirements, contact your local post office.

Letters, postcards, and other single pieces that weight 11 ounces or less are sent at the first-class rate. *Priority mail* is zone-rated first-class mail that weighs more than 11 ounces. *Postal cards* (U.S. Postal Service) and *postcards* (commercial), which are mailed at the first-class card rate, must be at least 3½ by 5 inches and have a rectangular shape; they may be either single or attached double cards.

Presorted first-class mail is mail presented in a manner that preserves the orientation, facing, and zip code sequence of the pieces. All pieces must be presented at one post office as part of a single mailing of not less than 500 pieces of first-class mail, each weighing 11 ounces or less. *Carrier-route first-class mail* rates apply to each piece that is part of a group of 10 or more pieces properly sorted to the same carrier route or other delivery unit.

A *ZIP + 4 presort first-class mailing* must have at least 500 pieces, each of which must contain the correct ZIP + 4 code. *ZIP + 4 barcoded mail* must have the proper ZIP + 4 barcode. (See Figure 14 for an example of barcode-read areas of an envelope.)

A *nonpresorted ZIP + 4 mailing* must contain at least 250 pieces, 85 percent of which contain the correct ZIP + 4 code. *Nonpresorted ZIP + 4 barcoded mail* must contain the correct ZIP + 4 barcode. (The U.S. Postal Service will correct and update your computer-diskette address files to add ZIP + 4 codes at no charge.)

Automation-compatible mail refers to mail that can be read and ZIP + 4 barcoded by optical character readers.

3. Second-class mail. Newspapers and periodicals may be mailed in bulk as second-class mail. All second-class publications must meet Postal Service requirements in frequency of issue, content, and printing process. They must also be authorized under one of five qualification categories: general publication, publications of institutions and societies, publications of state departments of agriculture, requested publications, and foreign publications.

4. Third-class mail. Third-class mail consists of mailable material such as circulars and printed matter that is not mailed or required to be mailed first class, is not entered as second-class mail, and weighs less than 16 ounces. Unlike first-class mail, it may not be sealed against postal inspection. Like first-class mail, it may be sent at a bulk rate if postal requirements are met.

5. Fourth-class mail. Fourth-class mail consists of mailable material that is not mailed or required to be mailed first class, is not entered as second-class mail, and weighs less than 16 ounces (except special-rate or library-rate fourth class). Any fourth-class matter may be mailed at parcel post rates based on zones. *Bound printed matter* must weigh at least 1 pound and no more than 10 pounds. Books, films, printed music, test materials, sound and video recordings, maps, and certain other material may be mailed at a *special fourth-class rate*. Colleges and certain other nonprofit organizations may mail books, recordings, and the like at a *library rate*.

SPECIAL SERVICES. *Registered mail* provides added protection to first-class mail, and insurance of up to $25,000 may be purchased on registered mail. *Certified mail* provides senders with a mailing receipt and record of delivery of first-class mail. *Insured mail* provides insurance up to $600 for third-

and fourth-class mail and third- and fourth-class mail sent at the first-class rate.

Collect on delivery (C.O.D.) mail consists of material for which the sender receives payment when collected from the receiver on delivery.

Business-reply mail (BRM) enables mailers to receive first-class mail back from customers by paying postage only on the mail that is returned by the customer. Users must apply for a permit and follow postal requirements in printing the business-reply envelopes that customers will use to respond to the sender.

Parcel airlift (PAL) service provides for air transport of parcels on a space-available basis to and from military post offices outside the forty-eight contiguous states.

Special delivery mail, available for all classes of mail except bulk third class and Express Mail, receives preferential handling and fast delivery at the destination. *Special handling* provides preferential handling, but not special delivery at the destination, when practical for third- and fourth-class mail.

INTERNATIONAL POSTAL SERVICE. Foreign or international mail is mail deposited for dispatch to points outside the United States and its territories and possessions. Foreign mail includes Postal Union mail, parcel post, Express Mail International Service, International Priority Airmail Service, and International Surface Air Lift mail.

  1. Sources of Information. International mail regulations, rates, services, wrapping and mailing requirements, and customs information are described in the *International Mail Manual*, a manual and looseleaf supplementary service sold on a subscription basis. For it and other publications for sale, write to the Superintendent of Documents, U.S. Government Printing Office, Washington, DC 20402. Contact your local post office for free booklets and brochures.

CLASSES OF INTERNATIONAL SERVICE. The U.S. Postal Service has several categories of international mail: Postal Union, parcel post, Express Mail, International Priority Airmail Service, and International Surface Air Lift (I-SAL). Since international regulations are complex, and rates vary depending on the class of service and the destination, consult your local post office.

1. Postal Union mail. Postal Union mail includes letters and cards (LC mail) and other articles (AO mail). *LC mail* consists of letters, letter packages, aerogrammes, postcards, and postal cards. *AO mail* consists of printed matter, books and sheet music, publishers' periodicals, matter for the blind, and small packets.

Letters and letter packages are personal handwritten or typewritten communications having the character of current correspondence. *Aerogrammes* are letter sheets that can be folded in the form of an envelope and sealed. *Postcards and postal cards* consist of single cards without an envelope or wrapper. *Printed matter* is paper on which letters, words, characters, figures, images, or any combination thereof, not having the character of a bill or statement or actual or personal correspondence, have been reproduced in several identical copies by any process other than handwriting or typewriting. Computer-prepared material is considered printed matter. *Matter for the blind* includes books, periodicals, and other matter in Braille or special type; embossing plates; and voice recordings and special paper for the blind. *Small packets* are small items of merchandise, commercial samples, or documents that do not have the character of current and personal correspondence.

2. Parcel Post. Parcel post may be sent to almost every country in the world, either by direct or indirect service. Merchandise is permitted but not written communication having the character of current and personal correspondence.

3. Express Mail International Service. This is a high-speed service that is exchanged with certain other countries. It includes Custom Designed and On Demand services. *Custom* mail may be picked up from any address or mailed at designated postal facilities. *On Demand* service is available at designated postal facilities for nonscheduled expedited delivery to addresses in certain countries.

4. International Priority Airmail Service. This service, which is faster than regular international airmail, is available to bulk mailers of LC and AO items sorted by the sender.

5. International Surface Air Lift. I-SAL is a bulk-mailing system that provides faster than surface delivery of publications, direct-mail pieces, and other printed materials to certain countries.

SPECIAL SERVICES. Special services are available only to certain countries (inquire at your local post office), and rates for most services vary according to the country of destination.

Special delivery offers faster delivery of postal union mail according to the regulations of the country of destination. *Special handling* entitles surface parcels, printed matter, matter for the blind, and small packets to preferential handling between the mailing point and the U.S. point of dispatch.

COD and *certified mail* are not available for international mail. *Certificates of mailing*, though, furnish evidence of mailing but no insurance against loss or damage. *Insurance* is available only for parcel post. For added security, *registered mail* is available to most countries but only for letters and letter packages, small packets, matter for the blind, and printed matter, with a small indemnity limit to most countries. A *return receipt* may be purchased at the time of mailing.

Restricted delivery limits who may receive an item. *Recall* and *change of address* services enable a sender to ask for an item to be returned or its address changed. *Reply coupons* can be purchased to prepay mail from other countries.

Private Delivery Services

AIR AND GROUND SERVICES. Private delivery services provide many of the same services that the U.S. Postal Service does. Some of these organizations transport material throughout the United States and in many foreign countries. Others serve primarily a local market. Some of them have added other message services such as facsimile and electronic mail, whereas others such as bus lines and airlines handle only letter and package delivery and consider it a sideline or secondary function. Overall, private-delivery companies handle more packages each year than the U.S. Postal Service.

A full-service organization might offer ground and air delivery, telex and facsimile, electronic mail, and messenger service and would additionally send Western Union and other messages for you. Delivery may be overnight or express service, second-day, or other schedule, depending on the carrier and the services it provides. Sometimes such organizations do not have their own delivery vehicles but act as an intermediary and simply send your material through another service. Since the services, regulations, and rates vary so widely from one service to another, you should develop a file of private services and update it periodically. Check your Yellow Pages and call the organizations operating in your area for current data.

Firms that specialize in delivery services usually offer pickup and delivery. This is not necessarily the case, however, with bus lines, airlines, and other companies. When a service has an office in your area, you may also deliver your packages to that office. Some of the private delivery services provide free mailing envelopes and cartons.

HOW TO USE PRIVATE SERVICES. Most large services will open a company account for you. Thereafter, when you have a letter or package to send, you only have to telephone the service; give your name, address, and account number; and request pickup. The organization will charge the cost to your account number and bill you later.

Caution is in order when using any delivery service. Although fast delivery services are necessary when you have an urgent shipment, such services, which are expensive, are sometimes purchased needlessly. A package that might take two to three days to arrive if it were mailed the conventional way on Friday does not need expensive overnight service if it is going to an office that won't open again until Monday.

Selecting Addressing and Mailing Equipment

The volume of work in an office changes as the organization expands its operations. One of the first places an increase becomes evident is in the level of mail activity. Whether or not the organization has a separate mailing department, it must be well equipped to handle the processing of outgoing mail properly and efficiently.

MAILING EQUIPMENT. A postage scale and a postage meter are usually the first pieces of equipment an office selects for the mail room. Scales may be purchased in an office-supply store, but a postage meter must be leased from a manufacturer that has a product approved by the U.S. Postal Service. Application to use metered stamps can be made through your local postmaster.

1. *Mail-room equipment.* The U.S. Postal Service provides a license and record book for users who lease a postage meter. After paying in

advance for the amount of postage desired, your local post office will set the machine so that you can meter mail up to the amount paid. The record book provides a place to record the amount of postage used and the current balance shown on the meter. Often it is necessary to take the meter to the post office to be reset. Some may be reset by telephoning the post office. With the computerized remote postage meter resetting (CMRS) system, users who qualify and maintain an account with the post office can reset their own meters using a one-time combination with each resetting. The design stamp you use must be approved by the post office, and metered mail must be deposited in bundles separate from mail with postage stamps.

Organizations that process a lot of outgoing mail may need automatic or semiautomatic folding and inserting machines as well as collators. An efficient mail room also has sorting trays and racks and mail-bag holders. When the volume of repeat mail—mail sent periodically to the same address—is large, some type of addressing equipment is needed. Although a small list could be maintained on multiple sheets of address labels, a longer list would require special equipment.

To help your employer select the best equipment for your needs, make a list of the factors characterizing your mail volume—how much, how often, to whom, and so on. Then write to manufacturers of addressing equipment and computer software programs for current product information. Collect sales literature on all types of addressing equipment and software.

2. Mailing lists. Most mailing lists are maintained by computer; others are processed by machines that use various types of address plates. Offices that prepare and send form letters by computer frequently use software that will merge address lists with the text of the letters. Computerized lists can be coded so that names can be recalled according to geographical location, type of business, or any other designated category.

For executives to make good judgments, they need to have all the facts pertaining to the cost of putting an address on the list, the cost of making address changes, and the cost of printing out the addresses, as well as the speed in addressing, the quality of the address after printing, and any other factors that are important in your type of work.

Very small office lists can be kept by computer and printed out on labels or envelopes. A master sheet of labels for a very small list can also be prepared by typewriter and photocopied for successive use. For medium- and small-volume mailers who want to convert to the ZIP + 4 codes or barcodes on computer or word processor lists, the Postal Service will correct diskette lists of 350 to 50,000 names at no charge.

No matter which method of list maintenance best suits your needs, set aside a time each week, or use slack moments throughout the day, to update your list so that you can use it on a moment's notice.

Efficiency in the Mail Room

THE WELL-EQUIPPED MAIL DESK. Your job of getting out the mail does not get simpler if you have a mailing department—at least not in every respect. You still have to decide the best method of sending out *your* mail. Although a knowledge of various rates and ways to use different services properly is essential, a well-equipped mail desk can prevent actual mail handling from being a wearisome task.

1. Supplies and equipment. Devices and supplies that can end some of the drudgery include electronic postage scales, postage meters, rubber stamps, colorful self-stick mailing labels, and a variety of mailing envelopes and package-sealing tapes. If you regularly send letters with special classifications, purchase a rubber stamp with the necessary information, such as "Priority Mail" or "Special Delivery."

Postage meters not only eliminate stamp licking but eliminate the need for keeping loose stamps, protect postage against loss and waste, and eliminate stamp borrowing. The equipment will also seal envelopes while applying postage. The record book or electronic record maintained with a postage meter provides an additional accounting tool and basis for cost evaluation. Some equipment will provide a record for the accounting department to use in assigning mailing costs to particular accounts.

2. Planning and record keeping. To be certain that your mail goes out when you want it to, learn the schedules for outgoing postal and private-delivery mail. If you have a company mail room, learn its schedules, capabilities, and any regulations that would affect your mailings.

If you handle your own outgoing mail, plan your work to allow time to meet any outside schedules. Facsimile and other electronically transmitted messages can be preprogrammed to go out and arrive at the time of your choice.

For purposes of control and accurate bookkeeping, keep good records of what you send, to whom, why, and the cost. If your equipment does not automatically record costs or assign costs to the appropriate accounts, have a sheet on your mail desk to record such information as soon as you prepare something for mailing—before you forget. Good records are important not only for the bookkeeper to know where to post expenses but also for purposes of reviewing how much it is costing to do certain things.

HOW TO CUT RISING MAIL COSTS. The costs of communicating increase each year, but there are ways that you can combat rising mail-room expenses:

1. Double-check to be certain that everyone on your mailing list *must* receive a copy of your communication, and regularly update your mailing list to eliminate obsolete or inaccurate addresses.

2. If you find that you often send several messages every couple of days to the same person, look into the possibility of reducing or combining several messages into one communication.

3. Try to eliminate unnecessary enclosures in postal and private-transport mail.

4. Use routing slips when practical instead of mailing numerous copies.

5. Consider microfilm if continual postal or private-transport mailings of large reports and other documents are a problem in your office.

6. Compare the costs of facsimile, E-mail, and other electronic messages instead of postal or private-transport delivery.

7. Consider bulk postal mailings, which are sent at the reduced bulk rate.

8. Note also that ZIP + 4 postal mailings can be sent at reduced cost.

9. For express mail, compare costs of electronic transmission with the costs of postal and private delivery.

10. Check at your post office whether you qualify for a carrier-route presort discount.

11. When possible, use the telephone for local contacts.

12. Use only the service you need; for example, do not pay for a more expensive fast-messaging service if regular first-class postal mail will arrive just as soon.

13. Keep your messages brief and to the point—long-windedness costs money.

14. Guard against unauthorized use of equipment and supplies.

MAIL-ROOM SECURITY. Not only must computer transmissions be protected with passwords and other security devices, but mail-room supplies and equipment must also be protected from abuse. Too often, confidential mail is not protected, postage is taken for personal use, and valuable equipment and supplies are stolen. To help organizations eliminate abuse, the Postal Service has devised a checklist of twenty-four points, as illustrated in Figure 15. A periodic check such as this can prevent potential problems from arising.

FIGURE 15

Mail-Room-Security Checklist

Checklist for better mailroom security

The Postal Inspection service offers this checklist for better mailroom security. Your suggestions of ideas and methods to make the job go safely and smoothly are welcome.—Editor

- ( ) Mailroom personnel screened.
- ( ) Location, furniture and mail flow provide maximum security.
- ( ) Access limited to authorized personnel.
- ( ) Distribution delays are eliminated.
- ( ) Postage and meter protected from theft/unauthorized use.
- ( ) High value items locked overnight.
- ( ) Accountable items verified and secured.

- ( ) Registered, Express and insured services properly used.
- ( ) Control of address labels maintained.
- ( ) Labels securely fastened to mail items.
- ( ) Postage strips overlap labels.
- ( ) Labels and cartons do not identify valuable contents.
- ( ) Return address included and duplicate address in carton.
- ( ) Presort and ZIP + 4 savings taken when applicable.
- ( ) Parcels packaged properly.
- ( ) Containers and sacks used when possible.
- ( ) Outgoing mail proper-

ly delivered to postal custody.
- ( ) Employee parking separated from dock area.
- ( ) Lost and rifled mail reported to post office.
- ( ) Supervisor can see all employees and work areas.
- ( ) Contract delivery services screened.
- ( ) Unnecessary stops by delivery vehicle are eliminated.
- ( ) Procedures established for handling unexplained packages.
- ( ) Periodic testing done for loss/quality control.

Chapter 5

Using Effective Telecommunications Practices

TELECOMMUNICATIONS IN BUSINESS

Forms of Telecommunication

Telecommunication refers to remote communication between people made possible by equipment that will transmit their messages and information over a distance, usually by way of the telephone lines. Broadly, it would include any form of information transmission, voice or data.

DATA AND VOICE COMMUNICATIONS. Telecommunication involves both data and voice. Other chapters in this book have focused on some of the major *data*-communication forms: (1) data messaging, such as facsimile, E-mail, and telex (Chapter 4); (2) data storage and access, through database networks and electronic libraries (Chapters 1 and 3); and (3) telecommuting, or working from a satellite office (Chapter 9). The other major form of telecommunication is *voice* communication, through telephone calls and the newer technologies, such as voice mail and sophisticated teleconferencing systems (Chapter 6).

THE NEED FOR GREATER EFFICIENCY IN TELEPHONE COMMUNICATION. Although trends in telephone communication point to greater productivity and efficiency through the effective use of new voice-messaging and response technologies, the frustration that accompanies traditional telephone communications has not entirely diminished. In fact, recent reports indicate that nearly three-fourths of all business calls are not completed on the first try, and more than a third of all long-distance attempts result in failure. Other trade reports suggest that an answering machine or voice-mail system would have served as well as or better than a traditional two-way telephone conversation. For example, nearly half of all telephone calls are made only to convey information, with no response required. Hence the time of two people is taken up needlessly.

Business analysts hope that in time the new voice-message technologies will make telephone usage more efficient and will eliminate the annoyances that have plagued traditional telephone-communication practices.

USING THE TELEPHONE EFFICIENTLY AND COURTEOUSLY

Your Telephone Image

In spite of the increasing use of voice-message systems, two-way telephone conversations have been and will remain a vital tool in the conduct of business. It is therefore important to consider the image you convey over the telephone by the way you speak.

THE IMPORTANCE OF VOICE AND ATTITUDE. When you greet visitors at work, they form an impression of you and your company by the way you look and act. Essentially, the same thing happens when you use the telephone to communicate, whether you do so in a two-way conversation or whether you leave a message in a voice mailbox. Callers will form an initial impression from the sound of your voice (cheerfulness, attentiveness, boredom, irritation, and so on) and your apparent willingness (or lack of it) to help them. Unfortunately, many persons cannot "hear" themselves and are unaware of problems in their telephone conversations.

Observing the Rules of Telephone Courtesy

The following simple rules constitute the basis of courteous and efficient telephone usage:

1. Answer calls promptly and return missed calls promptly.

2. When you leave your desk, arrange for someone to take your calls. Don't keep people guessing where you are and when you will return. Leave word where you can be located by telephone and the approximate time you will return. If you use an answering machine or voice mail, indicate how long you will be gone and instruct the caller on how to leave a message.

3. When making a business call, always identify yourself without waiting to be asked who is calling: "Good morning. This is Diane Schiavone, Ms. Jamison's secretary."

4. When making a number of calls on a line serving several people, try to space your calls so that others may have a chance to use their telephones.

5. Before you start a lengthy explanation or conversation with a busy person, ask if the time is convenient to talk. Then keep your telephone conversation brief but not to the point of curtness.

6. Take time to address people by their names and titles.

7. Use expressions of consideration and respect, such as "Thank you" and "I beg your pardon." A phrase such as "Yes, Mr. Adams," shows greater respect than "I see." Avoid cliches, slang, and crude expressions such as "Yeah," "Uh-huh," and "Uh-uh."

8. Don't chat with a friend who calls you during business hours; telephone abuse is a serious problem in the business world. Never chat with someone who calls your employer, except to respond politely to questions and comments.

9. In asking a caller to wait, say: "Will you please hold the line while I get the information?" Wait for the caller's reply. When you return to the telephone, thank the caller for waiting. But if it will take you some time to get the information, offer to call back. If you need to put a caller on hold for another reason, ask: "May I put you on hold?" Or "Would you like to hold?" Again, wait for a reply. Do not keep callers on hold for more than a couple minutes and check back every 30 to 40 seconds. If the delay will exceed a couple minutes, ask the caller if he or she wants to continue holding or leave a message.

10. If you have to put down the receiver for any reason, do so gently. But do not put it down with an open line since the caller might

overhear other office conversations. Your firm may have a system that plays music while the caller is on hold. (Some callers object to this, particularly if it is not adjusted properly and is too loud for comfort.)

11. Do not interrupt a caller or be impatient. Listen attentively, and do not make the other party repeat because of your inattention.

12. Do not try to talk with a cigarette, pencil, or chewing gum in your mouth.

13. Be courteous in requests and responses (stating *please, thank you,* and so on). When you have finished talking, say something such as "Thank you, Mr. Smith [using the person's name]. Good-bye." Replace the receiver gently, but let the caller hang up first.

14. If you must cut a call short, say something such as: "Excuse me, Ms. Garrison, but I have another call waiting. Could I call you back?"

How to Use the Telephone More Effectively

To become more effective in your telecommunications, make these guidelines a habit:

1. Plan your telephone conversation before placing a call. Know your facts and the points you want to cover. If necessary, have an outline of them before you while you talk. Also have all records and other material before you, especially with out-of-town calls.

2. Keep pad and pencil handy at your desk or anywhere else that you are working.

3. When you make a call, wait for six or seven rings before hanging up.

4. Speak slowly, enunciate clearly (but don't shout), and spell out words if necessary: "*Bert—B* as in boy, *e* as in Edward, *r* as in Robert, *t* as in Tom."

5. When you are making a call for your employer, be sure that he or she is ready to speak as soon as the person you are calling is on the line.

6. When you receive a call for someone who is not in the office, make a note of it and do not forget to give the person the note. (Place it on the person's desk right away if practical.)

7. Never ask a caller to wait while you get information and then stay away from the telephone so long that he or she hangs up before you return.

8. Keep short summaries of important incoming calls (Call Sheet) for your employer, especially when he or she is away from the office.

PLACING AND RECEIVING CALLS

Placing Calls

PLACING CALLS FOR YOUR EMPLOYER. Many executives prefer to place and receive calls without intervention of the secretary. In some offices, however, the secretary always places the employer's calls.

When you place a call, you may get the person called on the line before connecting your boss. Assume that you are calling Ms. Nelson for your employer Mr. Owens. When you get Ms. Nelson's secretary on the line, you might ask: "Is Ms. Nelson there for Mr. Owens of XYZ Company?" The other secretary will put Ms. Nelson on and trust to your good judgment to see that Mr. Owens comes on the line promptly. Never keep the person called (or your employer) waiting needlessly. (When a secretary calls your employer, you reciprocate the courtesy.) When Ms. Nelson comes on the line, say to her: "Here's Mr. Owens, Ms. Nelson," and establish the connection between the two at once.

If you call a close friend of your employer or a person to whom deference is due, connect your boss as soon as you talk to the secretary at the other end of the line. Tell him or her that the person called will be on the line immediately, and let your boss receive the call without further intervention from you. Some secretaries follow this procedure at all times. If you are uncertain about the best procedure, ask your boss for his or her preference and handle all calls that way thereafter.

PLACING YOUR OWN CALLS. Maintaining a pleasing tone of voice, follow these guidelines when you place calls:

1. Do not call information for a number except when you cannot find it in the telephone directory or in your custom telephone-fax book since there is usually a charge for information. Always use a person's business number unless he or she has asked you to use a home telephone number.

2. Consider the time-zone differences, illustrated in Chapter 17, so that you don't call someone during lunch time or when the person is just ready to leave the office at the end of the day.

3. Give the person you are calling ample time to answer before you hang up.

4. When someone answers your call, identify yourself immediately: "This is Kay Edwards of ABC Company." Or, when appropriate: "Good morning, Mr. Brown. This is Kay Edwards of ABC Company."

5. If the person who answers the telephone is not the one you want or does not identify himself or herself, ask pleasantly for the person you want and announce your name: "This is Kay Edwards of ABC Company. May I please speak to Mr. Brown?"

6. When you do not want any particular person, state your wishes in a nice way, preferably in the form of a request: "The rug department, please." Or: "I'd like some information about _____." Or: "Would you please take an order for _____?"

Answering Calls

ANSWERING INCOMING CALLS. When you answer your employer's telephone, convey a friendly, helpful attitude to the caller. First identify yourself.

1. *When there is no switchboard*: "ABC Company. Kay Edwards speaking."

2. *When the operator has previously answered the call*: "Advertising Department, Kay Edwards speaking." Or if several people have the same extension: "Advertising Department. This is Jody. May I help you?"

3. *Your own telephone*: "Kay Edwards." Or: "Good morning. Kay Edwards speaking."

4. *Another person's telephone*: "Mrs. Brown's office. Kay Edwards speaking."

When you answer someone else's telephone, and the person called is not available, offer to take a message. Make a record of the time of the call and the caller's name, affiliation, telephone number, and message. See that the person called gets the message immediately upon his or her return (leave it on the person's desk if practical).

When you answer your employer's telephone and a secretary tells you that "Ms. Nelson of ABC is calling Mr. Owens," ask the secretary to wait a moment and announce the call to your boss, who will then pick up the telephone and wait until Ms. Nelson is connected. Or perhaps the other secretary has learned that you are cooperative and thus puts Ms. Nelson on the line at the same time that you connect the call with your employer.

Screening Calls

Your boss may ask you to screen all incoming calls, although some executives find this practice offensive and prefer to take all calls without secretarial intervention. Follow the practice in your office. If you are expected to screen calls, and you are not familiar with the names of people who have legitimate business with your employer, it is better to err by putting through a few unnecessary calls than by delaying or rejecting important ones.

HOW TO FIND OUT WHO IS CALLING. A polite way of asking who is calling is: "May I tell Mr. Owens who's calling?" Or: "May I ask who's calling?" A legitimate caller seldom objects to giving his or her name. Almost all callers not only volunteer their names but also briefly state their business.

CALLERS WHO WILL NOT GIVE THEIR NAMES. If a caller insists on withholding his or her name, you might say: "Mr. Owens has someone with him at the moment, but if you'd like to leave your name and number, I'll ask him to call you back as soon as he's free." Then investigate the call. If your employer wants to talk to the person, call the person back in a few minutes. If you learn that the call is a nuisance call, handle it yourself.

Transferring Calls

Never transfer a call if you can take care of it yourself. But if it is necessary to transfer a call to someone else, handle it in one of the following ways.

1. State that you will refer the matter to someone else who usually handles such matters. In some cases, you will want to indicate that someone will call the person. In other cases this will not be necessary: "That's something Ms. Rogers handles. If you like, I'll tell her about it, and I'm sure she'll look into it right away." Or: "That's something Ms. Rogers handles. If you like, I'll ask her to call you back."

2. Offer to transfer the person calling to someone who can take care of the call: "That's handled by our Credit Department. If you like, I'll connect you." If the person wants to be transferred, take special care not to lose the call in the process and advise the caller what to do or which number to use in calling back if he or she is accidentally disconnected.

3. If you do not know who should handle the matter, tell the person calling that it is not handled by your department but that you will find someone who can take care of it: "That's not handled in this department. But if you like, I'll find out who handles it and ask someone to call you back." If you are making the transfer through an operator, explain the situation so that the operator will not have to ask the person calling to repeat the information: "Will you please connect Mr. Smith [or "this call"] with Ms. Rogers in the Credit Department?" Wait for the operator's reply to be sure that he or she understands correctly.

4. If you offer to transfer a caller who is annoyed because he or she has already been transferred several times, apologize, ask the caller to give you his or her name and telephone number, and state that you will get the appropriate person to return the call as soon as possible. You must then see that anything you have promised the caller receives prompt attention.

Handling Wrong Numbers

YOU GET A WRONG NUMBER. If you place a call and receive what appears to be a wrong number, immediately check the telephone number, for example: "I beg your pardon, but is this 353-2000?" If it is evident that some error was made, express regret, even if you were not responsible. If the call was placed through a long-distance operator, and it is obvious that the operator made an error in dialing, report it immediately so that you will not be charged for the call.

SOMEONE CALLS YOU BY MISTAKE. Inform the caller politely that he or she has reached a wrong number, and suggest that the caller recheck the number dialed. If your calls come through a central operator who connects a call to you through error, signal the operator and politely ask to have the call transferred to the appropriate person.

LOCAL AND LONG-DISTANCE CALLS

Local and short-distance toll calls in the United States are handled by seven regional Bell operating companies (BOCs): U.S. West, Pacific Telesis, Southwestern Bell, Bell South, Bell Atlantic, Nynex, and Ameritech. Long-distance service is provided by "other common carriers" (OCCs), sometimes called "specialized common carriers" (SCCs), such as AT&T, MCI, Sprint, and Allnet. Rates and specific services (private lines, voice-mail systems, and so on) vary, however, and it is necessary to request specific information from each company.

Station-to-Station and Person-to-Person Calls

A *station-to-station call* is made when the caller is willing to talk with any-one who answers the telephone. A *person-to-person call* is made when the caller must talk to a specific person and asks the operator to connect him or her with that particular person or extension. Rates for these calls are higher than those for station-to-station calls.

WHEN A PERSON-TO-PERSON CALL IS PREFERRED. Although a station-to-station call is less expensive, in a few cases, it is more economical to make a person-to-person call. If the person with whom you want to speak is extremely difficult to locate, use the person-to-person call, for the time spent in locating the person may run up the cost of a station-to-station call higher than the cost of a person-to-person call. (First determine if the party has a free 800 number that you could call.)

DETERMINING RATE VARIATIONS. Reduced rates apply at certain times daily and all day on Saturday and Sunday to various points. Reduced rates are also in effect at night and on Sunday on calls to many foreign countries. The rules of the long-distance carrier you use and the time at the dialing point govern the application of reduced rates. Consult the front pages of your telephone directory to find out when they are applicable, or ask the common carrier you are using for a printed rate schedule.

Out-of-Town Calls

Direct dialing of long-distance station-to-station calls is possible throughout the United States. Check your local telephone directory for a list or map of area codes. Most telephone directories have a map similar to the one in Chapter 17 and a list of area codes for selected cities in each state. Usually, it is necessary to dial "1" (or some other digit) before dialing the area code and the number.

WHEN YOU MAKE A CALLING-CARD CALL. You can request a calling card from your BOC or OCC. Through some companies, you can also use Master-Card or Visa as a calling card. After you have received your calling card and your personal security code, follow the instructions that are provided with the card.

1. *How to use the card with touchtone and rotary telephones.* Usually, from most telephones, you would dial "0," the area code, and the telephone number you want. After hearing the dial tone, you would next enter your calling-card number and security code (if any). To make additional calls, do not hang up; simply press the button for the symbol # (or other required button) and enter the next number without reentering your calling-card number. With rotary telephones, you usually dial "0," and an operator will come on the line to ask for your calling-card and security number.

2. *How to use the card with card-reader telephones.* On card-reader telephones, instead of entering the card number and security code, slide the card through the special slot and dial. (Card-reader telephones are common in airfone and railfone service.)

3. *How to use the card with person-to-person and collect calls.* To make a person-to-person call on your calling card, you usually dial "0," the area code, and the telephone number and wait for the operator. Give your calling-card number and state that you want to make a person-to-

person call. If the call is to be collect, give your own name and stay on the line until the call is completed. When a call cannot be completed at once, the operator will follow it up at your request.

WHEN YOU DO NOT KNOW THE CORRECT OUT-OF-TOWN NUMBER. When you do not know the number of the person you want to call, dial "1" (in some locations), then the area code, and next 555-1212. After an operator answers, state the city you want to call and the name and address of the person whose number you want. (There is usually a charge for information). If the person has a free 800 number, dial "1" (in some locations) and then 800 followed by 555-1212.

CHARGES ON OUT-OF-TOWN CALLS. Keep a record of all out-of-town calls you place so that you can verify the telephone bill. If your company uses an automated telephone-management system, each call may have an account number assigned to it, and with certain systems, this number will appear on your telephone bill for use by the accounting department in allocating charges to the proper customer or other expense account. If your firm does not use an automated system, you may be required to fill out certain forms for your accounting department's use. Always observe these requirements when you place a call through the company's central exchange since it may not otherwise be clear who made the call. You can also get the long-distance charge on an operator-assisted call at the time you make it if you ask the operator for it.

CHARGES FROM OUTSIDE TELEPHONES. If a call must be placed from an outside telephone, have the operator charge the call to your office telephone, use a calling card, or place the call collect. If you use a calling card, the charges will appear on a future telephone statement. With a collect call, the person receiving the call, if he or she accepts it, will then pay the charges.

TELEPHONE ABUSE. Companies are always seeking ways to reduce expenses, and cutting daily abuse is a necessary step. Your employer may require the use of access codes for long-distance calls. In other words, only authorized employees know the code that is needed to make a long-distance call on the office telephone. You can also help your employer lower expenses by using free 800 numbers when calling outside or wait for a leased line to open up. (Some secretaries become impatient and simply dial a regular long-distance call, which is more expensive.)

Other steps you can take include protecting your calling card. Do not give it to an operator in a public place where someone might overhear it. Also, consider the hours when you call for maintenance service (charges may be higher after certain hours or on weekends). These and other measures will help your employer prevent telephone abuse and cut costs.

Wide-Area Telephone Service (WATS) Calls

There are two types of WATS calls, inbound (or inward) and outbound (or outward).

INBOUND CALLS. An *inbound line* is used when a large number of calls are coming in from a wide area. Callers use your free (to them) 800 number then. If a customer calls you collect instead, you should advise the caller to hang up and call again on your firm's 800 number.

OUTBOUND CALLS. An *outbound line* is used when your firm makes a lot of calls to a particular area. If your company has a central telephone system, you will probably have to dial some code such as "7" to use the WATS line (just as you have to dial "9" with some systems to get a regular outside line).

COST OF WATS CALLS. WATS calls are billed at rates that differ from your regular telephone rates. Sometimes they are less expensive, but even if not, a firm may want a WATS line to conduct telemarketing (selling by telephone) more efficiently and to encourage customers to phone in orders.

International Calls

INTERNATIONAL DIRECT DISTANCE DIALING (IDDD). This service is available from certain cities in the United States to many countries overseas. Usually, to place a call to any of the participating countries, you dial the international access code, country code, city code, and then the local telephone number, which could be a two- to seven-digit number. Since procedures may vary among the OCCs, however, check with the carrier you use for specific information and dialing instructions.

DETERMINING THE COST OF INTERNATIONAL CALLS. Operator-assisted international calls cost more than direct-dial calls, just as they do within the

United States, and rates vary among the common carriers. Certain periods, for example, evenings and Sundays, have reduced rates. Although the time of the call is determined where the call is placed, keep in mind that there is a time differential, as illustrated by the international time chart in Chapter 17. You might call someone at 6 P.M. local time, but the caller might be awakened at 3 A.M. somewhere else.

MAKING CREDIT-CARD AND COLLECT INTERNATIONAL CALLS. Travelers often use their credit cards in the more than 100 countries that accept them. One can also place collect calls from other countries. *Teleplan* is an agreement among certain countries whereby hotels limit surcharges on international calls.

Appointment Calls

In placing a person-to-person call, you may specify a certain time that you will talk with a person. The telephone operator will try to put the call through at the exact time. The charge is the same as for a person-to-person call. The advantage of an appointment call is that it saves time. Usually, you make arrangements with the person in advance to be standing by at the selected time.

Conference Calls

BASIC CONFERENCE CALLS. Conference calls make it possible for one person to be connected simultaneously with a number of other people. No special equipment is required for a simple conference call placed through a long-distance operator. If your telephone system has a conference-call feature, however, you can place the calls without operator intervention. Suppose that your employer needs to discuss a contract provision with three or more other people (usually, any number up to ten for a basic conference call) who are in different cities. By means of a conference call your employer and the other persons can talk by long distance as though they were grouped around a conference table. In computing charges for conference calls, each party called at a different number is treated as a separate person-to-person call.

INFORMATION THE OPERATOR NEEDS. For operator assistance in arranging a conference call, dial "0" and explain that you want to make a conference call. Give full details—names, telephone numbers, time, and date—to the operator who handles the connection.

LARGE TELECONFERENCES. A basic conference call can be expanded into a large telephone or video conference arrangement. Procedures in arranging large teleconferences (audioconferences or videoconferences) are given in Chapter 6.

Mobile Calls

You can make local and long-distance radio-telephone calls to automobiles, trucks, aircraft, boats, and ships. Use the regular local or long-distance telephone lines for direct-dial calls from a mobile unit, or dial "0"; ask for the mobile, marine, or high seas operator; and give the number and name of the person you want to reach. Mobile numbers are listed in the regular telephone directory.

CELLULAR TELEPHONES. More and more executives are using cellular telephones in their cars. Whereas older mobile equipment was hampered by overloaded channels, creating long waits, new cellular technology has opened the door to more network subscribers. The wire-free cellular telephone employs radio waves to make a connection with home or office units.

Cellular technology uses small geographic cells, representing transmission centers, that can divide into even more small cells as calls increase. These cells are connected to a series of transmission towers, and switching equipment connects users to the regular local and long-distance telephone service. As a user travels in a car, a computer switches calls to the nearest cell. Through the technique of "roaming," callers can use the cellular telephone in any area into which they drive that has transmitting cells. (Check your local Yellow Pages for addresses of companies that provide cellular telephone sales, installation, and service.)

With a small radio-computer in the vehicle, callers can use a cellular telephone like any other telephone. Many cellular telephones have features that resemble those of an office telephone, such as preprogrammed numbers, voice messages, and outputs for use with a laptop computer. Some cellular telephones are integrated into the dashboard of a car for hands-free operation.

Cellular telephone calls are generally more expensive than calls made from a pay telephone. The time saved or used more effectively while in a car, however, is often considered more important than any additional cost for a cellular call.

SPECIAL BUSINESS SERVICES

BOCs, OCCs, and private commercial companies provide a variety of services, systems, and accessories for telephone communications. Whereas standardization has been largely absent in the past, the International Telegraph and Telephone Consultative Committee has prepared standards for the Integrated Services Digital Network (ISDN). With the implementation of ISDN in 1992, the industry hopes to see an improvement and standardization in a number of telecommunications areas, including the digital private branch exchange (PBX) systems. Ultimately, the ISDN will make it possible for voice, data, text, and imagery systems to converge over a global network.

Telephone Systems

Two common office telephone systems are the key, or pushbutton, system and the private branch exchange, a modern version of the old office switchboard. Although connectivity, functions, and features are becoming very similar in the two types of systems, they are still differentiated by type of connection. With the key system, telephones in different offices are interconnected and are also connected to outside lines. With an exchange, switching devices interconnect the telephones and provide access to outside lines.

The newer equipment is digital and transmits data in discrete steps based on binary digits (bits); older equipment uses a continuous analog signal. Since computers operate on a digital system, offices that want to integrate functions find that the digital telephone system is more readily linked to various computer activity.

TYPES OF EXCHANGES. Office telephone exchanges may be classified according to type (manual, computerized, and so on): The *PBX* is the basic switching facility used in business organizations. Variations are the PMBX, PABX, and CBX. The older *PMBX* is a private *manual* branch exchange operated manually. The *PABX* is a private *automatic* branch exchange in which the switching is achieved automatically by the equipment. The *CBX* is a *computerized* branch exchange whose functions are directed by a computer.

HOW AN EXCHANGE FUNCTIONS. With an exchange—unlike a key system, which consists of interconnected pushbutton telephones—the switching occurs in a central mechanism that users activate by dialing codes, such as dialing "7" or some other number to use a WATS line. An exchange is able to accommodate more telephones than a key system and is therefore more common in large organizations. An exchange operator may receive calls and make the connections with the appropriate persons, or the system may allow direct dialing without operator intervention. A variety of configurations are possible, and your particular system may differ in some respects from that in other organizations.

Special Features for Telephone Systems

Office systems often have numerous features, and new ones are evolving every day.

1. *Cost displays* provide a running total of the cost of in-progress calls.

2. *Cost reporting* tracks calls by telephone extension, department, or client account codes. Callers enter the code once the connection is made, and the charges for the call are then reported with account numbers on the telephone bill.

3. *Departmental call distribution* routes calls to salespeople equally to avoid having certain sales personnel get most of the calls.

4. *Direct inward station dialing* allows authorized people the ability to access an extension directly without going through an operator.

5. *Display messaging* provides instant information to a caller about the called person's status, for example: "Back at 2:30."

6. *Secure offhook voice announce* allows someone to interrupt a telephone conversation with an important message without the other party being able to hear it.

7. *Telecommunications devices for the deaf (TDDs)* are products available to people with hearing, speech, vision, or motion impairments.

8. *Least-cost routing (LCR)* automatically dials calls by the most economical means, such as by WATS line.

9. *Call waiting* alerts you that another call is coming in and lets you put one call on hold while you take another call.

10. *Three-way calling* is a form of conference call.

11. *Call forwarding* lets you route calls to other numbers where you are going.

12. *Memory redial* lets you redial the previously dialed number with just one or two digits rather than reentering the full number each time.

13. *Speed calling* allows you to reach up to thirty frequently called numbers by dialing just one or two digits for each number.

14. *Phone-management systems* provide a computerized accounting system to track calls, control costs, analyze data, restrict numbers, report use, prevent tampering, and generally monitor a firm's telecommunications.

15. *Music-on-hold* provides background music for callers while they are put on hold.

16. *Speakerphones* enable one to talk over the telephone hands-free while doing other tasks.

17. *Picturephones* enable callers to see each other during a telephone call.

18. *Automatic dialers* store telephone numbers so that you can dial the number thereafter by pressing just one or two buttons (see items 12 and 13).

19. *Call sequencers* indicate which incoming call is next in line. Advanced versions process unanswered calls after a specified number of rings and monitor incoming traffic.

20. *Leased lines* or *channels* are provided by OCCs to give firms a private line when they have a heavy volume of calls.

21. *Foreign-exchange (FX) lines* enable you to place or receive calls as though you were in another location. A firm thus might give the appearance of having an office in another city by using an FX line.

22. *Paging units* are limited-range pocket devices for people who are away from the office that emit a beep or other sound to indicate that the person should call the office, home, or answering service/machine.

23. *Answering services* provide trained operators to answer calls or take messages for businesses and individuals during times when the firm's or person's telephones are unattended.

24. *Automatic answering machines* record messages from callers and will play your own messages to the callers; a remote feature allows you to dial your own number from a remote location and activate the machine so that it will play back all messages to you over the telephone.

25. *Automated attendant systems* provide recordings in the form of a menu to guide a caller to automated information, for example: "To find out your account balance, press "6" [or some other number]." If none of the options provided by the automated attendant provide what a caller wants, there is usually a final option: "To speak with a representative, press "0" [or some other number]."

Voice-Processing Systems

Voice mail is a type of answering service that converts voice to data for storage and back to voice again when the message is retrieved. Broadly, voice-processing systems include any form of voice answering or response system.

' As data and voice systems become integrated, the distinction between the various types of mail (E-mail, voice mail, facsimile, and the like) will disappear. Predictions are that they will all become a form of voice mail. Currently, E-mail and voice mail, as well as fax mail and voice mail, can be used together. The data or text form is transmitted with the voice form and at the destination can be "played back" into a computer or facsimile machine for paper printout. One message system can also be used to alert the recipient about a different type of message that is also waiting. An E-mail message might alert the recipient that there is also a voice message waiting or vice versa.

SYSTEM COMPONENTS. An in-house voice-mail system requires computer-controlled hardware and software that is linked to the telephone network through an individual's telephone extension or a firm's PBX system. A touchtone, rather than rotary, telephone is needed to be able to edit a message.

Local telephone companies also provide voice-mail services, and various message services are provided by commercial establishments (refer to your local Yellow Pages). Since special features vary from one system to another, it is important to investigate state-of-the-art alternatives before deciding upon a voice-mail system.

CHARACTERISTICS OF A VOICE-MAIL SYSTEM. A voice-mail system enables you to create, store, and distribute messages that are delivered in voice form, automatically converted to data form for storage, and then automatically reconverted to voice form when retrieved. Instead of leaving a written message or PC-screen message (E-mail), voice mail leaves your spoken words to be retrieved by the recipient at his or her convenience. Since a voice-mail system can be reached from any telephone, passwords are needed to control access to it. Hence the required code must be keyed in to listen to a waiting message. A *broadcast* feature enables callers to give the same message to more than one person simultaneously. The *call, store, and foreword* function enables users to have a message stored in memory and then sent to an answering machine or voice mailbox during off-peak calling hours, when transmitting time is less expensive.

Voice mail is designed as a convenient message and response system that saves secretaries time in taking messages and in preparing and transmitting paper and electronic messages. It also can be used day or night from any location. But it does not take the place of a two-way conversational exchange provided by a traditional telephone call.

VOICE-MESSAGE ETIQUETTE. Voice-mail systems, unlike paper or electronic-text systems, have an added concern—the image that the spoken word conveys. Most of the rules of etiquette that apply to a two-way telephone conversation apply to a voice message. For example, you need to speak clearly and use a pleasant tone, projecting a professional image at all times.

TELEPHONE REFERENCE BOOKS

The Telephone Directory

Whereas the White Pages in a telephone directory provide an alphabetical listing of the business and personal telephones in your community, except unlisted numbers and newly installed telephones, the Yellow Pages consist of advertisements of products and services that you may be able to use in conducting research and shopping for items needed in your office. Most directories include other useful information, for example:

1. Information for customers with disabilities

2. Telephone service options

3. Information about custom calling (such as call waiting, call forwarding, three-way calling, and speed calling)

4. Information on placing long-distance calls

5. Information on using a calling card

6. Information on operator-assisted calls

7. A list of area codes for major cities in each state and a map of time zones and area codes

8. A list of country and city international dialing codes

9. Information on safety, emergencies, and obscene or harassing calls

10. City, county, state, and federal government numbers

11. City maps and street guides

12. A list of zip codes for important cities in the state

If you make frequent calls to cities other than those listed in your local telephone directory, you can obtain directories for those areas through your local telephone business office; inquire about the charges, which may differ from one city directory to another. Also, most libraries have copies of telephone directories for major cities nationwide.

Custom Telephone-Fax Book

You can create a custom telephone and facsimile (or other message service) book, manually or by computer, for your particular needs. Telephone- and address-book software is available to automate the development and maintenance functions.

Some computerized systems are combined packages that will help you not only develop a telephone and address book but will also enable you to print mailing labels and Rolodex files, create calendars and reminders, and provide a database of client or customer information. Some software will print out a telephone-address book in pocket size for your employer to take alone on trips, to meetings, and to other outside business activities.

BUSINESS NUMBERS FOR YOUR CUSTOM BOOK. Some telephone, facsimile, and E-mail numbers will be related to the type of work you do, the activity of your organization, and the people you and your employer call frequently at work. In addition to such numbers relating to company business, the following numbers should also be kept in your custom telephone book:

Airlines	Regional telephone company
Amtrak	Other common carriers
Car-rental agencies	Travel agencies
Express-mail offices	Equipment-repair services
Messenger services	Private-delivery services
Post office and contract stations	Building manager or superintendent
Emergency calls (fire, police, ambulance, etc.)	Residences of employees in your office
Office-supply stores	Weather
Western Union	Highway Patrol (road conditions, etc.)

PERSONAL NUMBERS FOR YOUR EMPLOYER. Also keep in your custom book the following personal numbers for your employer:

Banks	Theater ticket agencies
Brokers	Dentist
Garages	Doctors
Organizations to which he or she belongs	Family (residence and business numbers)
Restaurants	Florists
Services (dry cleaner, tailor, etc.)	Friends whom he or she calls frequently
Stores that he or she trades with	

Print out a new list when additions, deletions, and changes warrant.

Chapter 6

Making Meeting Arrangements

PREPARING FOR MEETINGS

Secretaries are often involved in meetings as a participant, an organizer, a coordinator, an assistant to someone attending or conducting the meeting, or a recorder taking minutes. Since small to large meetings occur every day in business, secretaries must be familiar with the numerous aspects of meeting arrangements.

Notifying Participants

TYPE OF NOTICE. Letting meeting participants know the details about time and place of the meeting is usually the secretary's job. How you notify people depends on the size and nature of the meeting. Notice of an informal meeting among a few persons could be handled in a variety of ways, for example, by facsimile or telephone, with follow-up letters or memos. For a very large meeting such as a convention, it is usually necessary to mail use printed forms. Numbers, then, largely determine the method of notification you use. Also, the bylaws of some organizations may specify the form that must be followed.

DETAILS IN NOTICE. Always include full details in your notice and ensure that the notices are sent far enough in advance so that recipients have time to make travel and other arrangements necessary to attend. The details should include the name of the person or organization calling the meeting and the date, time, place (not only the city and street address but the building room number), who is invited to attend, and the purpose of the

FIGURE 16

Sample Meeting Proxy

PROXY

I hereby constitute (name), (name), and (name), who are officers or directors of the Corporation, or a majority of such of them as actually are present, to act for me in my stead and as my proxy at the (meeting) of the stockholders of (company), to be held in (location), on (date), at (time), and at any adjournment or adjournments thereof, with full power and authority to act for me in my behalf, with all powers that I, the undersigned, would possess if I were personally present.

Effective Date _____

Signed (stockholder) _____

Address _____

City _____ State _____ Zip Code _____

PLEASE BE CERTAIN TO INCLUDE YOUR ADDRESS AND SIGNATURE AND THE DATE OF SIGNING. THANK YOU.

meeting. Some meetings, such as a stockholders' meeting, must follow a prescribed policy in issuing a "call," or notice. The wording of such notice, which will be given to you by the corporate secretary, must adhere to state statutes or corporate regulations, and a proxy must be enclosed (see Figure 16). Other types of meetings, too, may require proxies in order to have enough votes to constitute the quorum required to conduct business.

For a relatively small meeting, if a preliminary agenda is available, enclose a copy of it or anything else the participants should review beforehand. If the meeting location will be unfamiliar to some attendees, include directions for people arriving by car, train, or airplane. Add a statement or enclose a reply slip requesting that each person indicate *by a specific date* if he or she will attend. If a proxy form is provided, the recipient can use it to indicate whether he or she will be present or will be voting by proxy. Some notices also include a request for topics to be discussed at the meeting.

If certain individuals regularly attend the meetings, maintain their addresses by computer or in another mailing-list file. For a small group, you could print out labels by computer each time or prepare multiple sets of mailing labels to avoid frequent retyping or reprinting. No matter how you maintain the list, keep it up to date at all times.

Preparing the Agenda

The person responsible for preparing the agenda may be the corporate secretary, in the case of a corporate meeting. The conference secretary or person chairing a meeting may be responsible in other situations. For departmental meetings, the head of the department may take care of this. If you work for the person who prepares the agenda, you can be very helpful in collecting office information, organizing topics, and preparing and mailing copies to meeting participants.

HOW TO DRAFT THE AGENDA. Agenda topics, prepared on 8½- by 11-inch paper, are usually arranged in the order they will be discussed at the meeting. If the organization's bylaws do not specify a required order, the person who chairs the meeting will specify his or her preferred order. Procedures vary from office to office, but you will likely be expected to prepare at least one rough draft for the chair or corporate secretary and perhaps several if the agenda must be revised a number of times before it is complete.

ORDER OF BUSINESS. The agenda might contain some or all of the following items:

1. Call to order
2. Reading and approval of previous meeting's minutes
3. Treasurer's report
4. Other reports
5. Old business
6. New business
7. Committee appointments
8. Nominations and election of new officers
9. Announcements
10. Adjournment

For formal meetings, examine previous agendas in the files and follow the order indicated by the corporate secretary or legal counsel. A formal agenda would include more detail than the ten items just listed (see Figure 17).

FIGURE 17

Detailed Agenda for Formal Meeting

```
                     RESOURCES COUNCIL

               Agenda:  Directors' Meeting
                      August 7, 19--


               Regular Meeting, 10:00 a.m. - 12:00 noon
          Council Headquarters, 204 Lawrence Lane, Room 5,
                          Jackson, MS 39209
          Robert Saks, President, presiding (601-292-6051)


     1.   Call to order (R. Saks)                    10:00 a.m.

     2.   Roll call (voice call of directors)        10:00 a.m.

     3.   Announcements                               10:05 a.m.

          a.   Quorum (verify)

          b.   Guests (R. Saks; introduction
               and welcome)

     4.   Minutes (J. Turner; reading of             10:10 a.m.
          previous minutes; motion to approve
          as read or corrected)

     5.   Reports of officers                        10:15 a.m.

          a.   Treasurer's report (M. Quill;
               motion to approve)


          b.   Vice president (Bette Frasier;
               report on opening of overseas
               office)

     6.   Reports of committees                      10:30 a.m.

          a.   New Projects Committee (J. Heald;
               report on Department of Labor
               study)
```

FIGURE 17 (CONTINUED)

AGENDA, August 7, 19--   page 2

    b. Public Relations Committee
        (N. Slogden; report on TV
        interview)

7. Old business   10:45 a.m.

    a. Staff reorganization (R. Saks;
        review of status and present
        options)

8. New business   11:15 a.m.

    a. Governor's Task Force (R. Saks;
        discuss and recommend Council
        representation)

9. Announcements   11:45 a.m.

    a. Open House (D. Harmond; announce-
        ment of schedule for council's
        September Open House)

    b. Resources Week (R. Saks; announce-
        ment of schedule for Resources Week
        activities)

10. Adjournment (call for motion to   12:00 noon
    adjourn)

Organizing Meeting Materials

Your employer may want to take various papers and supplies to a meeting, and you can assist in organizing this material beforehand.

MEETING FOLDER. Most material, except for bulky reports and odd-sized documents, can be placed in a regular file folder or in several folders. Color-code the labels to help your employer locate papers quickly during the meeting. Collect essential correspondence and other material pertaining to the topics on the agenda as well as material pertaining to something new that your boss may want to introduce at the meeting. After the meeting, be certain to return all material to the files.

SUPPLIES. For an out-of-town meeting, extra supplies may be helpful, such as writing paper, envelopes, stamps, paper clips, cellophane tape, pencils, pen and ink, dictation belts or tapes, and computer diskettes. Some of these items may be helpful at a local meeting, too, although a well-prepared meeting room has paper and pencils at each place around the conference table.

Securing a Meeting Room

THE CONFERENCE ROOM. Some secretaries help to select and reserve the meeting room. If the meeting is to be held in a hotel or motel instead of company offices, you will need to telephone appropriate sites and request information on sizes, availability when needed, rates, and any special requirements that you have. Or your employer might ask you to reserve a conference room for an approximate number of persons at the XYZ Motel near the airport from which most participants will be arriving and leaving. You should confirm the approximate number of participants, so that the facility can reserve an appropriate-sized room.

MEALS. If morning or afternoon refreshments are desired, ask if the facility can provide them. Otherwise, inquire about delivery service from a nearby delicatessen or coffee shop. Your employer will let you know whether you should reserve a table in the dining room for lunch or whether you should ask the hotel to serve an appropriate selection from the menu to the participants in the conference room.

EQUIPMENT. Determine what special equipment must be rented—display boards, electronic bulletin boards or blackboards, projector equipment, tape recorders, computers, video equipment, microphones, and so on—

and ensure that the facility (or other suppliers) will deliver everything needed and set it all up in adequate time before the meeting. Check whether a trained operator is needed for any of the equipment.

Preparing the Meeting Room

Meetings held in your own facilities usually can be checked out and even arranged at your convenience well in advance of the meeting. In a hotel or motel conference room, you may have to wait until another meeting adjourns to check the room.

SUPPLIES. If the facility does not provide supplies, your company will have to provide pencils and pads. Put one of each at every place around the table (have extras available). Ask to have a pitcher of water and glasses delivered and located on the table. If smoking is permitted, ashtrays should be on the table too. Equipment should be set up and ready for use.

There should be a place for guests to put coats, hats, and other supplies, and enough chairs should be positioned around the table. The arrangement of tables and chairs in the room will depend on the number of participants and nature of the meeting (discussion groups, lecture presentations, equipment presentations, and so forth). Check the temperature, lighting, and ventilation. If you discover a problem, contact the hotel representative immediately. Finally, if a delicatessen or the hotel will be delivering refreshments, arrange to have a table set up at one side of the room or in an adjacent room or lobby. Participants can then interrupt the meeting whenever they please and serve themselves.

Making Accommodations for Visitors

HOTEL ROOMS. Sometimes it is necessary to make overnight hotel accommodations for out-of-town participants. The most convenient arrangement usually is to reserve a conference room and individual rooms for participants all in the same hotel or motel. A facility near the airport is a great convenience for incoming guests. Be certain to find out if spouses will accompany the participants. If numbers are indefinite or names are unknown, ask the hotel to reserve a block of rooms for an estimated number of guests.

TRAVEL. Occasionally, you may have to make partial travel arrangements as well for the participants. Usually, this is limited to car rental, taxi, or limousine service to and from the airport, Again, make reservations far enough in advance to ensure that ground transportation will be available.

WHAT TO DO AT THE MEETING

Relaying Telephone and Other Messages

TELEPHONE CALLS. Follow your employer's preference in handling calls and messages. Unless you are expected to put through important telephone calls, treat each call as if your employer were out of town. Handle what you can yourself, refer the caller to another available executive, or take messages and indicate that your boss will return the call after the meeting has adjourned.

MESSAGES. Urgent messages should be typed and quietly handed to the intended recipient. Wait to see if the person gives you a reply or asks you to handle the problem. If you are attending the meeting along with the other participants, perhaps to take the minutes, ask the secretary filling in for you to handle things the same as you would. If you are taking minutes, you cannot be interrupted or leave the meeting room.

Reading the Meeting Minutes

WHEN YOU READ THE MINUTES. If you are the recording secretary, you may be expected to read the previous meeting's minutes. Do so clearly, at a moderate pace, and in a voice loud enough for everyone to hear. There may be a tape recorder on the table recording the meeting proceedings. Be certain that you are speaking so that your voice will record properly.

WHEN SOMEONE ELSE READS THE MINUTES. Check the typed minutes carefully before you release them to anyone else. Also, check to see that all essential documents are attached—treasurer's report, budgetary information, and so on.

Following Parliamentary Procedure

RULES OF ORDER. A book on parliamentary procedure, such as *The New Robert's Rules of Order* (New American Library, New York), is a must for anyone who is frequently involved in preparing agendas and minutes and assisting with the organization and conduct of business. This book covers the rules concerning:

1. Introduction of business
2. General classification of motions
3. Motions and their order of precedence
4. Committees and informal action
5. Debate and decorum
6. Voting
7. Officers and the minutes
8. Organization and meetings
9. Officers and committees
10. Miscellaneous rules and practices

BASIC PRINCIPLES.. Business is transacted by way of motions at a meeting. *Robert's Rules of Order* lists key motions that are used today in organizations of all sizes and complexity. In formal proceedings, a motion is often referred to as a "question," and "putting a question" in parliamentary terminology means placing a motion before the meeting participants for a vote.

Motions are often classified as debatable and undebatable or as those that can be amended and those that cannot be amended. A motion "to adjourn," for example, is undebatable, whereas a motion "to postpone [something] to a certain time" is debatable. Also, a motion "to adjourn" cannot be amended, whereas a motion "to postpone to a certain time" can be amended. Motions must be handled in order of precedence, which means that a lower-rank motion cannot supersede a higher-rank motion, but a higher-rank motion can be made even though a lower-rank motion is pending. Refer to any edition of *Robert's Rules of Order* for a detailed explanation of these rules, each motion, and pertinent qualifications, such as whether a particular motion does or does not need to be seconded.

MAKING A MOTION. In formal proceedings, a person who wants some measure approved must obtain the floor by addressing the chair ("Madam Chairman" or "Mr. Chairman") and giving his or her name. After being recognized, the person makes the motion: "I move that we adopt the Newcombe proposal." Most motions require a second, so another participant must then state something such as "I second the motion" before the chair can ask for a vote.

Before asking for a vote, however, the chair will ask if there is any discussion: "The motion to adopt the Newcombe proposal has been seconded. It's now open to debate [*or* "Is there any discussion?]." After any discussion, depending on the formality of the meeting, the vote may be made by ballot, roll call, show of hands, standing, voice, or general consent.

If someone states a motion incorrectly, the chair is responsible for declaring the motion out of order. If a person behaves improperly in a meeting, the chair is also responsible for curbing such conduct: "I call the gentleman to order."

Taking the Meeting Minutes

Minutes of a formal meeting are legal records and must be accurate and complete, although not necessarily verbatim (except for resolutions, motions, and other statements). Before you start, review minutes from other meetings and notice the organization, amount of detail, phraseology, and other characteristics.

1. Quickly prepare a seating chart to help you identify speakers during the meeting.

2. Have a copy of the agenda and other documents handy in case you need to check facts and figures.

3. Summarize general discussions but record resolutions, amendments, important statements, decisions, and conclusions verbatim. Figure 18 is an example of a form you could devise to help record information at the meeting. Even though a tape recorder is often used to back up your notes, don't rely on it to supply a lot of things that you miss. It could be malfunctioning during the meeting without your knowledge.

4. Record the name of each person who makes or seconds a motion or who proposes any action or opinion.

5. Signal the chair if you miss anything or need additional information. You might arrange in advance for some sign to indicate that the chair should repeat something or to request clarification of something.

FIGURE 18

Form for Recording Motions

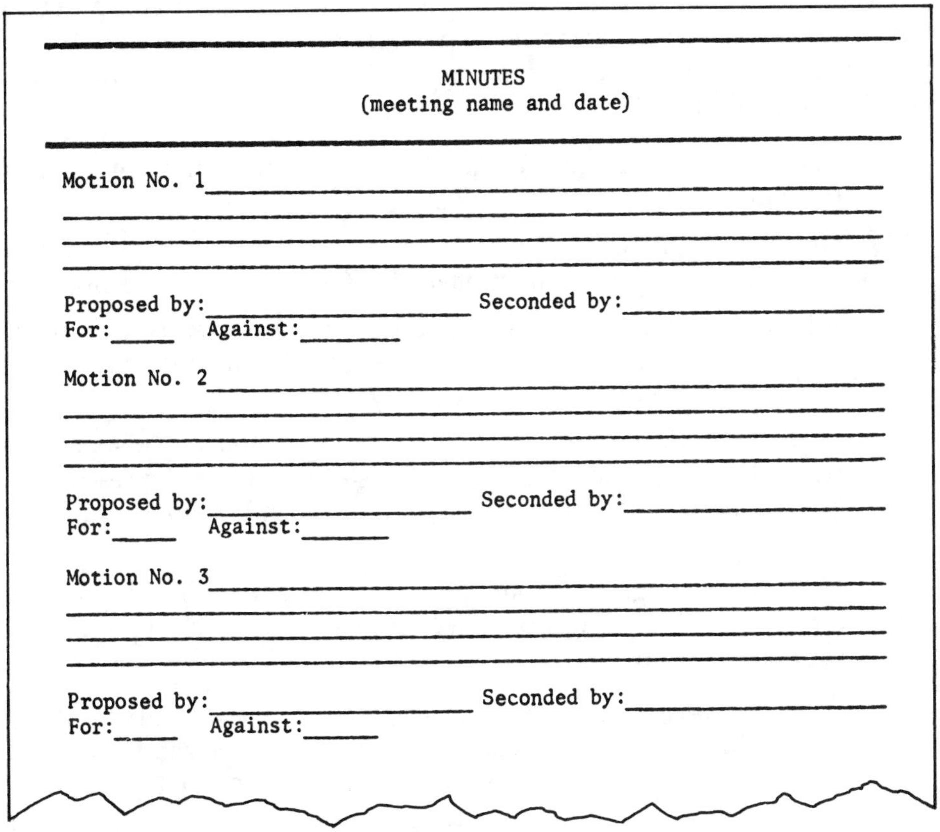

```
                              MINUTES
                      (meeting name and date)


Motion No. 1_____



Proposed by:_____  Seconded by:_____
For:_____  Against:_____

Motion No. 2_____



Proposed by:_____  Seconded by:_____
For:_____  Against:_____

Motion No. 3_____



Proposed by:_____  Seconded by:_____
For:_____  Against:_____
```

MAINTAINING THE BOOK OF MINUTES

Preparing the Meeting Minutes

ROUGH DRAFT. After the meeting, while everything is fresh in your mind, listen to the tape recording of the proceedings, correct your notes as needed, and prepare a double-spaced rough draft of the minutes. Submit this draft to your employer before preparing the final copy. After the rough draft is approved and complete, prepare the final version. If you use a computer, you need only edit in your employer's corrections rather than retype the entire document.

FINAL COPY. The final copy of the minutes should be prepared in a style consistent with previous minutes. Store the format in your computer so that you won't have to develop new specifications for the layout in future minutes. If you have no previous copy to follow, these guidelines may help (see also Figure 19):

1. Center the heading in all capitals. The heading should consist of the name of the group or company.

2. Give the day, date, hour, place, presiding officer, and type of meeting in the first paragraph. Indicate whether a quorum was present.

3. If it is a small meeting, list the names of those attending in a column or double column under the first paragraph. In the next paragraph, mention those voting by proxy.

4. Double-space the minutes if they are brief, and triple-space between headings and paragraphs. Single-space the minutes if they are long, and triple- or double-space between headings and paragraphs.

5. Use above-paragraph subheadings or margin captions. For an example of above-paragraph headings, see Figure 19. Type margin captions as follows:

   ADJOURNMENT   A motion for adjournment was made by David Michaels and seconded by Regina Novak, and the meeting was adjourned at 4:10 P.M.

6. Indent paragraphs (not essential if side captions are used) 1/2 to 1 inch and indent resolutions an additional ½ inch.

7. Indent resolutions like a blocked quotation (extract), and use all capitals for *WHEREAS* and *RESOLVED* and capitalize *That* when it follows *RESOLVED (RESOLVED That)*.

   The Board adopted the following resolution by unanimous vote:

   RESOLVED That the thanks of the Society be expressed to the Melville Chamber of Commerce for its support and assistance in the relocation of the Society's library.

FIGURE 19

Minutes for a Semiformal Directors' Meeting

ARTS AND CRAFTS SOCIETY

Board of Directors
Regular Meeting
April 14, 19--

CALL TO ORDER

A regular meeting of the Board of Directors of
the Arts and Crafts Society was called to order at
10:00 a.m., April 14, 19--, at the headquarters of
the Society, 1224 Highway 70, Suite 5, Prospect Park,
Pennsylvania 19076. The presiding officer was Abe
Jarenki, president. A quorum was present, including:

Abe Jarenki (president)
James Kirkbride (vice president)
Terry Parker (secretary)
Mary Russmore (treasurer)
Eileen Shumway (director)
Larry Stahling (director)

Voting by proxy were directors Jeffrey Shipley, Adele
Goldblum, and Harriet Conway.

MINUTES

The secretary, Terry Parker, read the minutes of
the June 5, 19--, meeting, and they were approved as
read.

FINANCES

The treasurer, Mary Russmore, presented a financial statement showing a checking account balance on
March 31, 19--, of $1,576.92 and a savings account
balance of $9,842.60 (copy attached). The treasurer's
report was approved as read.

FIGURE 19 (CONTINUED)

MINUTES, April 14, 19--   page 2

COMMITTEE REPORTS

Eileen Shumway, chair of the Special Projects Committee, reported that the next special project is the Labor Day Arts Festival, scheduled from Friday evening until noon Monday of the Labor Day weekend. A flyer with full details on the event will be mailed to all members on July 1, 19--.

NEW BUSINESS

Larry Stahling moved that the Society appoint a chair for the Christmas Arts and Crafts Fair at the next regular meeting of the directors on August 4 and that the board also adopt a theme at that meeting. The motion was seconded by James Kirkbride and passed unanimously.

ADJOURNMENT

There being no further business, the meeting was adjourned at 11:45 a.m.

_____   _____
Secretary   President

Use uppercase and lowercase letters for *Board of Directors*, *Corporation*, *Society*, and the like (for whom the minutes are being written) throughout the minutes.

8. Use uppercase and lowercase letters for round sums of money and put the amount in parentheses after it: *Four Hundred Dollars ($400.00)*. Use figures only for uneven dollars and cents: *$1,653.96*.

9. Use margins of about 1½ inches.

10. State the time of adjournment and the date for the next meeting (if not a regular meeting) in the last paragraph.

11. Add two signature lines at the bottom of the page for the secretary (on the left) and the chair (on the right).

12. Attach pertinent documents such as the treasurer's report.

Correcting the Meeting Minutes

At each meeting, the minutes of the previous meeting are read; sometimes corrections are pointed out at this time, and you will need to correct the minutes accordingly.

PROCEDURE. Follow the legal requirements of your organization in correcting the minutes. If no special requirements are indicated, follow this procedure: Draw a red or black ink line through each incorrect word, phrase, or sentence. Write the correction in ink above the line and specify in the margin at which meeting the correction was made. Include the initials of the person making the correction in the margin under the meeting date. For large corrections—too large to write above the ink line—type the new material on a separate page and note in ink in the margin of the minutes that a correction appears on a sheet at the end of the minutes. Such large corrections prepared on a separate page need to be signed by the secretary and chair the same as the actual minutes.

Indexing the Minute Book

Minutes are frequently stored in the computer, but a printout is kept chronologically in the minute book, often a three-ring binder, so that you can easily locate the minutes of a certain *date*. But what if your employer asks for the minutes that cover a specific *topic*, date unknown? An index of topics is the answer.

PREPARING AN INDEX. Although you can set up your index on 3- by 5-inch cards arranged alphabetically by topic, most secretaries maintain their index by computer, printing out a revised copy after adding the entries from each succeeding meeting. As soon as you finish preparing the minutes, list each new topic (some topics will already be in the index). Use cross-references if topics might be described in more than one way (Keynote Address: *See* Speeches). Put the topic heading flush left, and to the right list the date and where the topic is discussed in the minutes. If the same topic comes up at a future meeting, simply add the new date and location of the same key-word entry.

Zoning Proposal:	April 21, 1992, Book 12, page 5
	July 16, 1993, Book 13, page 7
	December 5, 1993, Book 13, page 31

MEETING WITH ASSISTANTS AND COWORKERS

How to Prepare and Conduct Meetings

Secretaries sometimes schedule daily or weekly conferences with assistants or trainees. Sometimes members of a secretarial staff also meet regularly or occasionally and discuss office practices or special projects.

PREPARING FOR THE MEETING. If you are attending, but not conducting, the meeting, review any preliminary information you are sent and prepare notes on the subject so that you can contribute ideas when appropriate or at least respond intelligently during the discussion. The secretary conducting the meeting may distribute pencils and paper, but to be safe, come prepared with your own supplies.

If you are in charge of the meeting, decide where to hold it—probably in your office or in the general secretarial offices. You will be expected to continue to take incoming calls and greet visitors, unless another secretary handles this for you during your meeting. Since many secretaries must maintain office activity as usual, particularly in a small office, they schedule conferences with assistants or other secretaries early in the morning, before normal business activity accelerates, or during the lunch hour. Consider the needs in your office, and select the best time for your situation.

Although secretarial meetings are often brief and informal, you should have an outline of what you want to discuss. Perhaps you want to review an assistant's problems in a particular area or perhaps you want to discuss a special project such as mailing-list conversion with other secretaries. If you want suggestions and other contributions from the others, let them know in advance what will be discussed so that they can prepare for it. You will likely set up the time and date in person if you work in the same office, so a personal reminder the day before the meeting may be adequate, rather than the written follow-up notices that are sent with certain other types of meetings. You may want to tell your coworkers to bring pencils and paper, but have extra supplies available in case they forget. You may also want to remind them to have someone take their incoming calls, if necessary, and indicate how long they should arrange to be away from their desks.

HOW TO CONDUCT THE MEETING. Although an office secretarial meeting is usually informal, you should guide the discussion. Instead of calling the meeting to order, you might simply check to see that everyone is there and say, "let's start by talking about . . ." When you ask for responses, acknowledge people one at a time and stick to your agenda or order of topics. If everyone talks at once, or if the discussion strays off course, stand up if necessary to get their attention and then remind them that time is limited, that certain things have to be discussed or decided, and that therefore it is necessary for them to speak one at a time.

Instead of formal voting, you may just "agree" on a certain division of labor or certain procedures to follow. In the case of an assistant, you may simply give daily or work assignments and suggest solutions to problems or ask if there are any problems the assistant wants to discuss. If more than one person is attending, it is not an appropriate time to criticize or reprimand anyone (in front of others). Give assistants and other participants a chance to speak and listen carefully to their comments. At the end, summarize the discussion and any decisions so that there will be no misunderstandings later.

PREPARING NOTES OR MINUTES. Everyone at an office secretarial meeting should take notes, especially if work assignments are made or decisions are reached on work procedures. Formal minutes are not needed for a routine office meeting; however, if you are conducting the meeting, take notes and keep a typed summary of each meeting in a special secretarial-meeting folder. If problems ever arise later, you may need to refer to such notes to verify that you gave someone a certain work assignment on a particular day or that you and your coworkers agreed upon a certain policy or division of labor for a special project.

ASSISTING WITH SEMINARS AND CONFERENCES

Secretaries to executives attending seminars and conferences are expected to help their employers prepare folders of meeting material to take along and to assemble supplies such as stationery and address lists (see Figure 22 in Chapter 7). Secretaries to persons arranging or conducting a meeting have additional duties. They may, for example, help in preparing a program, processing registrations, and, generally, setting up and maintaining various files pertaining to the event.

Preparing Programs and Announcements

A program committee is usually appointed for a seminar or conference to select program topics and issue invitations to prospective speakers. If you are secretary to the person responsible for preparing the program and any related announcements, you will probably have two tasks: drafting the program and coordinating the production and distribution of it, whether your manuscript copy is sent to an outside typesetter-printer or whether it is sent to your company's in-house desktop publishing division.

The size of the program and the announcements may vary. For a large conference, there may be one or more preliminary mailings followed by a package including the program and various registration forms. Some programs are large—the size of a small booklet; others are no more than a one- or two-sided 8½- by 11-inch sheet, with or without a cutoff registration form. Either way, you may have to prepare numerous drafts since program topics and speakers may change several times before a final selection is made.

INVESTIGATING PRINTING NEEDS. If your program is not printed in-house, based on the preliminary information your employer gives you, contact about three printers that are capable of preparing the materials and (if you don't have an in-house mailing department) mailing the packages. Or you may prefer to have one establishment print the programs and a different company mail them. Ask for estimates and present the written bids to your employer for approval and selection of one. Also investigate whether any airlines would be willing to print and mail the material in return for free advertising in the packages or in return for being designated official airline for the conference.

PLANNING TO MEET DEADLINES. One of the most important aspects of program and announcement preparations is the deadline. You must work out realistic dates with the printer to allow for typesetting, proofreading, corrections, printing, and mailing—all scheduled to allow participants time to decide whether to attend, to make arrangements in their own companies, to mail in advance registration fees, and so on. This entire process involves close coordination with the program committee, which may want to delay printing longer than is desirable in hopes of confirming more names of speakers or tentative topics. Keep your employer well informed of deadlines, and put all dates on your and your employer's calendar.

Handling Registration Details

Depending on the type and size of the conference, registration may be complex or simple. Some organizations devise registration cards that can be filed alphabetically (by name) like index cards. Matching lists of data are often set up by computer and coded according to program session, meals registration, and so forth. At any time, then, you can print out a list of persons registered for a particular session or planning to be present at a certain meal.

ADVANCE REGISTRATION PROCEDURES. Although the procedure for processing registration varies according to the size and nature of the meeting, advance mail registration (as opposed to on-site conference door registrations) usually involves several steps. Each incoming check must be compared to the registration form to be certain the amount is correct (bill the registrant for any balance due), and the registration must be marked or stamped paid with the amount and the date *before* the check is deposited.

Maintaining Files and Records

RECORDS FOR COMMITTEE NEEDS. Be prepared to work with the various conference committees to be certain that you are handling the registrations to meet all needs and that you have kept the records needed for you to provide any information needed by each committee. For example, the facilities committee will need to know if a particular session has so many registrations that a larger room is needed. Or perhaps the program committee will want to divide it into two groups and secure another speaker. If a session doesn't have enough registrations, they may want to cancel it. The meals committee will need to know how many luncheon, dinner, or banquet tickets have been distributed to be able to order enough meals and arrange for adequate dining- or lunch-room facilities. The budget committee will need to know how much registration money has come in and what bills have been paid or are due.

RECORDS FOR THE BOOKKEEPER. Before you start processing registration checks, discuss procedures with the bookkeeper to be certain that you are providing the information needed for him or her to record transactions and to provide satisfactory supporting documents.

CONFIRMATION PACKETS FOR REGISTRANTS. You must also send a confirmation to each person who registers in advance. This often consists of a printed packet including confirmation card, luncheon or dinner tickets, and other materials that the person must have. If time is short, you may have to hold the packet for the person to pick up at the door at the conference site. (Most on-site registration booths have a place for advance registrants to check in and another place for latecomers who have not yet registered or paid.)

DATA AND TALLY RECORDS. If you are maintaining records by computer, pertinent information must be entered (name, date and amount paid, sessions registered for, session dates and times, and so on) for each registrant. But even if you keep records by computer, maintain another file of registration cards or forms and keep up-to-the-minute tally sheets of numbers registered for each session, each meal, each tour, and any other scheduled event. Before you file a registration card or enter the data in the computer, add a tally mark to each tally sheet (one for each session, meal, and so on). Also, set up file folders for copies of each type of correspondence—speakers' correspondence, hotel or convention-site correspondence, travel correspondence, and so on. Finally, ask your employer if there are any other files or records that are needed.

PLANNING TELECONFERENCES
AND VIDEOCONFERENCES

Using the Telephone to Conduct Business

Business and professional people use the telephone lines to conduct business in both small- and large-group settings. Just as one person can use the telephone lines to talk to another person, groups of people can communicate with one another through telecommunications links. Teleconferences can be arranged for groups numbering in the thousands (some systems will accommodate up to 25,000 participants), although the complexity of the arrangements and hence the cost increases when vast numbers are involved. Although the term *teleconference* suggests a telephone-line connection, videoconferences may also use satellite transmission.

DIFFERENT KINDS OF TELECONFERENCES. A variety of teleconference arrangements are possible, some of which involve only audio communication (teleconference) and others that provide video transmission (videoconference). Not only can people communicate by voice or by a voice and visual combination, but computers and facsimiles can communicate (send and receive text and graphics) through preprogramming, without the live, on-the-spot participation of the participants.

ADVANTAGES OF TELECONFERENCING. Time and money savings are the chief benefits of audio, video, and other communication links (computers, facsimiles, electronic blackboards, and various combinations of people-machine communication). The participants avoid time-consuming and expensive long-distance travel. Since it takes far less time to set up a telephone connection among participants than it would take to make arrangements for travel and hotel facilities in a conventional meeting situation, participants can conduct their business and move on to other matters without the lengthy delays that traditional meetings involve. The savings in time and travel costs are particularly important to companies that deal with foreign clients and customers.

How to Set Up a Teleconference

Your company may already have special audio, video, and other equipment installed permanently to conduct meetings, seminars, and other small or large conferences. Sometimes this equipment will consist of strategically placed speakerphones and picturephones. In other cases, for relatively large seminars and conferences, it may consist of sophisticated cameras, monitors, computers, electronic boards, and other teleconferencing equipment. Many companies, however, would find the cost of a sophisticated conferencing setup prohibitive and instead prefer to rent the equipment necessary for occasional teleconferences or videoconferences.

The Yellow Pages of most telephone directories lists companies under "Teleconferencing Service" that will set up the type of communications link that you would like, providing any equipment that is required, such as video cameras. If your meeting will involve multiple locations, you may want to use a teleconference service.

Call at least three services and request information on the various conferencing systems they can provide, the cost of each, and what facilities, equipment, and operator knowledge will be required of your company to use the desired type of teleconference. Inquire whether a tape recording of the proceedings will be provided. Give the service (1) the date of your meeting, (2) the start-to-finish times, (3) the number of participants, and (4) their telephone numbers.

RESERVATIONS. Teleconference organizers may have different requirements for reservations. Some may need only a week's advance notice except during peak periods such as October. The sooner you make reservations, however, the sooner that notices and programs can be sent to participants.

NOTIFYING PARTICIPANTS. Ask the teleconferencing service whether it will notify participants or whether your company will be expected to do this. Participants must be given the conference date, call number, name of the moderator or chair, start-to-finish times, and any special preparation required of them. A program, an agenda, and other material must be mailed to participants in sufficient time for them to prepare for the meeting discussion. For instructions on handling other aspects of the meeting, such as the minutes, follow the guidelines given in this chapter for a conventional meeting.

Chapter 7

Making Travel Arrangements

PREPARING FOR THE BUSINESS TRIP

Business travelers rely heavily on their secretaries to help them make travel arrangements and prepare for the meetings they will attend and the contacts they will make. Although teleconferences are becoming an increasingly successful substitute for face-to-face meetings that require travel and associated arrangements, the business trip is still a major tool in conducting business both domestically and internationally. Because of the day-to-day changes in fares and services, the most important source of information is the travel agent.

Use of Travel Agents

In the complex global economy of the 1990s, a travel service is indispensable. Because of the extensive travel needs of some companies, many travel agencies offer the opportunity to open an account and be billed once a month, thus avoiding the nuisance of paying for numerous tickets throughout the month. Some firms also use company charge or travel cards, which serve essentially the same purpose. Either way, periodic billing provides a good record for your firm's accounting department.

WHAT A TRAVEL AGENT WILL DO FOR YOU. A travel agent will provide many services for business travelers. Specific services differ among the various agencies, however, and you should inquire whether a particular service you want is offered. Most agents procure tickets, plan itineraries, arrange hotel accommodations, arrange for rental cars at the destination, and perform many other services such as locating guides and translators in foreign countries.

If it is your responsibility to act as liaison between the agency and your employer, you would see to it that the desired arrangements are made without any inconvenience to your employer, and a reliable agency can be of immense help to you.

When you deal with an agency, you need make only one telephone call to find out the best schedule and best routing, even though more than one airline or other transportation may be involved. Agencies have computerized connections to airlines and other travel-related organizations to secure up-to-the-minute facts on fares and space availability as well as other information such as accommodations.

Some travel agents specialize in business clients (whose needs are different from those of vacation travelers) or at least have a division or person dealing exclusively with business travelers. Others specialize in a particular part of the world, such as the Orient.

The following services are examples of what many full-service agents will do:

1. The travel agent will provide the information you need about current and upcoming special rates on certain airlines and make arrangements for a car, limousine, or hotel courtesy vehicle to and from airports; for helicopter or other available shuttle service; and for connecting rail schedules in some cities.

2. The agent will attend to special needs of your employer, such as physical disabilities or seating preferences.

3. The agent will help travelers take advantage of money-saving foreign travel rates, such as promotional, excursion, or group rates.

4. The agent will arrange for interesting side trips to points of interest or special events in the particular area the traveler is visiting.

5. The agent will advise how and where to exchange dollars for foreign currency and will assist in getting traveler's checks or a letter of credit.

6. The agent will arrange to have a rental car waiting at the destination and will take care of personal and baggage insurance and even provide rain insurance (a sum designed to console in the event that rain mars the trip).

7. The agent will specify what documents are needed for foreign travel, such as passport, visa, and police and health certificates.

8. The agent will arrange for a foreign representative of the travel agency to meet a traveler on arrival, if desired; take care of baggage; see the traveler through customs; and assist with other problems and needs.

WHAT YOU SHOULD TELL THE TRAVEL AGENT. Get to know an agent who can work with you on a regular basis. Someone who works with you over time will more likely understand and appreciate your needs.

1. Details the agents need to know. When you ask an agent to arrange a trip for your employer, specify the number in the party, names, ages, sexes, and, if the trip includes a foreign country, citizenship. Also indicate where your party wants to go, dates of departure and return, mode and class of travel, and the approximate amount that can be spent. The travel agent will be able to tell you the classes of travel and rates that fit your budget on a particular airline or steamship, on the trains here and in foreign countries, and at hotels.

2. Special needs of your employer. Tell the agent about your employer's special needs—physical disabilities, seating preferences on airplanes, nonsmoking or dietary requirements during travel, preferences for early or late arrivals, or any other request your employer may have. Don't hesitate to ask, no matter how trivial the request may seem. It is part of an agent's job to answer questions and help to tailor a trip to the traveler's requirements.

WHEN YOUR EMPLOYER CANNOT DECIDE ON A DEFINITE ITINERARY. A traveler abroad who has all reservations made and confirmed in advance will travel with the greatest ease and comfort. But it may be impossible for your employer to know where he or she will be able to go and when. If plans are uncertain, give the travel agent the names of the places in which your employer expects to need hotel reservations, the approximate dates, and how much per day he or she (or your firm) will spend for hotel expenses. The agent will do the following things:

1. Give you the name of a desirable hotel in each place.

2. Contact each of the recommended hotels, asking them to give your requests their best attention.

3. Advise the travel agency's foreign correspondents of the approximate dates of arrival in each city.

FEES. Usually, a traveler pays no additional fee for most services of a travel agency. If plans are canceled, however, the agent may charge for the services rendered and to cover out-of-pocket expenditures such as long-distance telephone calls, facsimiles, or other communications. Some agents may add a small service charge if your employer has requested an extensive individualized itinerary that requires a lot of time for the agent to prepare. In some cases, the agent also charges for train-transportation arrangements, but not in the case of prearranged vacation package trips.

HOW TO SELECT A TRAVEL AGENT. Travel agencies are sometimes selected based on the recommendations of business associates and friends. If you or your employer has not had experience with a qualified travel agent, select one who is a member of a national organization with a grievance committee, should you ever have cause for recourse. Find out what fees and service charges may be assessed, if the agency has worldwide branches, and if someone from the agency has been to the various places your employer travels. Observe whether an agent's office displays membership in or accreditation by major carriers or has the seal of the Air Traffic Conference (ATC) or the International Transport Association (ITA).

The American Society of Travel Agents (ASTA) has members in the principal cities of the United States and Canada. The members may be recognized by the ASTA emblem, which they are permitted to display if they are in good standing. You can get the name of an ASTA member situated near your office by contacting the executive offices of the association in New York City. There are also many reliable agents that are not members of ASTA, but the code of ethics of this association is high and its members, therefore, are usually dependable and efficient.

Use of Company Travel Departments

Large firms may have their own travel offices or departments. These in-house facilities serve as a liaison between the traveling employee and the airlines, railroads, car-rental agencies, and hotels or between the employee and an outside travel agency.

OPTIONS AVAILABLE TO YOUR FIRM. Now that the personal computer has become common in organizations of all sizes, the potential has increased for many companies to access databases that provide travel information or to deal directly with airlines and other organizations. Other options are (1) to subscribe to a network service that provides travel-reservation services and miscellaneous travel information or (2) to make arrangements for a company travel department to function as a branch of an outside independent travel agency. When airline ticket printers become common in company travel departments, firms will be able to print tickets on demand and even provide seat selection.

HOW TO WORK WITH A COMPANY TRAVEL DEPARTMENT. Secretaries who work for firms that have in-house travel offices should prepare the same itinerary and other information for the in-house travel personnel that they would provide for an outside travel agent: time, date, destination, airline or other preferences, shuttle and courtesy or rental-car needs, hotel preferences, personal disabilities or special requirements, overseas guide or translator requirements, and so on. If the company travel office has several employees, try to work closely with one in particular who will become familiar with your employer's preferences and needs.

How to Get Information About Transportation

PRELIMINARY CONSIDERATIONS. Your employer will usually tell you which mode of transportation he or she intends to use. Sometimes certain information is needed to make a choice, such as:

1. What airline or railway may be used

2. Time schedules

3. Plane and train accommodations (e.g., dining and sleeping facilities)

4. Airport shuttle arrangements

5. Car-rental arrangements at destination

6. Costs

7. Baggage facilities

If your organization has a travel department, let the appropriate person know your employer's preferences and preliminary itinerary. The department will provide a schedule or several schedules, if alternatives are available. If you use an outside travel agent, provide the same information.

CHECKLIST FOR HANDLING PREPARATIONS. In arranging a business trip for your employer, here are some of the things you may be expected to do:

1. Get full transportation information from your company travel department or an outside travel agent and submit a time-and-route schedule to your employer.

2. Ask the company agent or outside travel agent to make the desired transportation and hotel reservations.

3. Confirm that tickets have been sent or will be available for pickup at the airline counter before departure.

4. Prepare the travel itinerary and appointment schedule.

5. Assemble business data and supplies to be taken on the trip.

6. Prepare baggage identification labels and furnish baggage information.

7. Make financial arrangements for the trip.

8. Give the hotel confirmations and tickets to your employer.

9. If there are to be any formal occasions, such as dinners and conventions, try to find out what type of formal attire your employer will need.

Special Secretarial Duties

When you make travel arrangements for your employer, there are many secretarial tasks relating to the necessary preparations for the trip. The following sections describe some of the essential duties in preparing for domestic and international travel.

PREPARING THE ITINERARY AND HOTEL INFORMATION. Prepare an itinerary stating points of departure and arrival, whether travel is by airline or railroad, dates and times of departure and arrival, accommodations, available car-rental facilities, and hotels. If you are working with a company travel department or an outside travel agency, the agent may prepare this itinerary. Figure 20 is an illustration of a common itinerary format.

Make three copies of the itinerary—a copy for your employer, a copy for his or her family, and a copy for the office files. Make an additional copy if anyone else in the organization needs and is entitled to it.

COMPILING AN APPOINTMENT SCHEDULE. Prepare a schedule of all appointments your employer has on the trip. Include in the schedule the following: city and state (or city and country if a foreign trip); date and time; name, firm, and address of the individual with whom your employer has an appointment; telephone number; and any remarks or special reminders about the visit. Figure 21 is an illustration of an appointment-schedule format.

If your employer has previously met any of the individuals with whom he or she is to do business, make a notation of the circumstances of the meeting. You will have this information available if you keep the contact reminder file described in Chapter 1.

ASSEMBLING DATA FOR BUSINESS APPOINTMENTS. Place together the papers relating to each matter your employer will handle on the trip, for example, letters or memos concerning the problem to be discussed and also any other pertinent information. You can use a rubber band or large paper clip to bind together the papers pertaining to each matter; label each packet clearly.

DETERMINING SUPPLIES FOR THE TRIP. Make duplicate lists of the stationery and supplies that your employer needs when going on a business trip. Use the lists as checklists when you pack the supplies so that you will not forget anything. The list in Figure 22 suggests items that might be needed.

HANDLING THE BAGGAGE. Your employer may want to know the baggage allowance that will be checked without charge on the plane ticket and the limitations on the dimensions of baggage. You can usually find this infor-

FIGURE 20

Travel Itinerary

FROM	TO	VIA	DATE & TIME	ARRIVE (EST)	ACCOMMODATION	MEAL SERVICE	CAR RENTAL	HOTEL
N.Y.	Boston	Amtrak	5/6–11:30P	5/6–5:15A	Car 106 Room A Train 467	--	Hertz--Ford	Parker House
Boston	N.Y.	Eastern	5/8–3:30P	5/8–4:45P	Flight #633	Snacks	--	Home
N.Y.	Washing.	Eastern	5/13–8:30A	5/15–9:47A	Flight #431	Breakfast	Avis--Buick	Shoreham
Washing.	Atlanta	Eastern	5/15–2:50P	5/15–7:32P	Flight #565	Dinner	--	Atlanta-Baltimore
Atlanta	Cleveland	Eastern	5/19–5:50P	5/19–10:32P	Flight #732	Dinner	--	Carter Hotel
Cleveland	Chicago	United	5/22–6:10P	5/22–7:10P CST	Flight #501	Dinner	Hertz--Chevrolet	Stevens Hotel
Chicago	New York	United	5/28–12:00N	5/28–4:00P	Flight #622	Snacks	--	Home

All Standard Time one hour earlier than Daylight Time.

Checking Out Time—3:00P.M.

FIGURE 21

Appointment Schedule

City & State	Date & Time	Appointment	Address	Phone	Remarks
Boston MA	5/7—3:30P	Williams-McGregor & Co.	125 South St.	543-3485	
	5/8—10:00A	Brown, Jones & Brown	348 South St.	211-1257	
	1:00P	Norris, at Copley Plaza, Merry-Go-Round		366-2764	Luncheon
Washington DC	5/13—11:00A	Sen. Snow	Sen. Off. Bldg.	840-4884	

Appointment Schedule May 8-28

mation in the published travel schedules from airlines or through your travel agent. People who travel a lot often increase their personal insurance coverage to compensate for damage and losses since airline and other transportation-company insurance is minimal.

1. Identification labels. Prepare identification labels for each piece of baggage, including a duplicate set that can be placed *inside* each piece. (Many persons, for security reasons, do not want their names and addresses to show on any outside labels or luggage tags.) Labels are available at ticket offices and baggage counters or can be purchased in an office-supply store. Keep a supply in the office.

2. Carry-on luggage. For short trips some executives use a carry-on combination suitcase and briefcase or an attache case with a divider that snaps down on one side. With clothes under the divider, a traveler can go from plane to appointment without having to stop at a hotel and unpack. Also, there is no time wasted for luggage pickup at the airport.

ARRANGING FOR TRAVEL FUNDS. A businessperson may use one of the following plans for keeping a supply of funds while traveling.

1. Travel advances. Some companies provide advance funds for traveling executives; others reimburse employees later. (See Figure 27 in

FIGURE 22

Checklist of Supplies for Trip

[ ] Letter and memo
stationery

[ ] Envelopes, plain

[ ] Envelopes, addressed
to company

[ ] Large mailing
envelopes

[ ] Mailing schedules

[ ] Postage stamps

[ ] Note pads

[ ] Address lists with
telephone, fax, etc.
numbers

[ ] Calendar

[ ] Global time chart

[ ] List of international
dialing codes

[ ] File folders

[ ] Business cards

[ ] Audiovisual material

[ ] Dictation equipment

[ ] Dictation belts,
tapes, disks

[ ] Computer equipment

[ ] Computer diskettes,
tapes, etc.

[ ] Mailing envelopes
for dictation and
computer media

[ ] Cash

[ ] Personal and business
checkbooks

[ ] Personal and business
credit cards

[ ] Expense form

[ ] Other forms

[ ] Pertinent files

[ ] Travel guides and
maps

[ ] Itinerary

[ ] Appointment schedule

[ ] Timetables and
schedules

[ ] Tickets

[ ] Passports, visas,
etc.

[ ] Pens and pencils

[ ] Erasers

[ ] Clips

[ ] Scissors

[ ] Rubber bands

[ ] Cellophane tape

[ ] Pins

[ ] Bottle opener

[ ] Ruler

[ ] Stamp pad and rubber
stamp

[ ] First-aid kit

Chapter 8 for an example of an expense report form.) With information supplied by your employer, you will be able to fill out the necessary company forms required for release of an advance.

2. Personal checks. A person who travels extensively usually has credit cards from the hotels where he or she stops or has a major national credit or charge card such as Visa, MasterCard, or American Express. These cards can be used as identification in cashing personal checks. Many companies open accounts at hotels at the lower corporate rate, and it is then easy for the traveler to cash checks at those hotels.

3. Traveler's checks. These checks are usually available in various denominations such as $10, $20, $50, $100, $1,000, and $5,000. Some large banks sell their own traveler's checks; others sell American Express Traveler's Checks. You can also purchase checks directly from the American Express Company. Through Cheques on Call, for example, you can telephone American Express and ask to have the checks delivered by mail anywhere in the United States.

To purchase traveler's checks for your employer at his or her or another bank, fill out the bank's application form, if required. Your employer may then have to sign the checks in the presence of the bank's representative, although some banks will allow you to mail in signature cards if your employer or the firm has an account there. If the account is particularly valuable, the bank's representative may come to your employer's office.

4. Letters of credit. A person traveling to a foreign country usually buys a letter of credit from his or her bank if funds of $1,000 or more are needed. You can fill out the application, but as in the case of traveler's checks, your employer must usually complete the transaction in the presence of the bank's representative.

A letter of credit testifies to the holder's credit standing, serves as a letter of introduction to leading banks, and can be drawn against at banks in every part of the world until the face amount of the letter of credit has been exhausted. Many travelers find it advisable to purchase both traveler's checks and a letter of credit when planning a trip to a foreign country.

BUILDING YOUR OWN TRAVEL- AND HOTEL-INFORMATION LIBRARY. Even though you may work with a company travel department or outside travel agent, keep your own office collection of road maps, timetables, and flight schedules for quick reference when you have general questions such as the usual time required for a direct flight between New York and Chicago. If your employer travels frequently, consider purchasing a hotel directory, such as *Hotel and Travel Index*, or a schedule reference, such as the *Official Airline Guide*. Visit your local library to examine copies of the various directories and travel guides to determine which might be most useful for you to have in the office. Keep in mind, however, that schedules and rates change continually, so you must still contact your company travel department or an outside travel agent, or access a travel database, for up-to-the-minute information.

Traveling with Your Employer

Some work cannot be handled by temporary office assistants in another city or foreign country. In these situations, it is more practical for the secretaries to travel with their employers.

TRAVEL ARRANGEMENTS. Your employer will specify where you are to go and when. In some cases, your transportation and hotel arrangements may be identical; in other cases, you may not visit all of the same places or stay as long in certain places.

EQUIPMENT ARRANGEMENTS. Major hotels have computer workstations and other equipment available for the use of travelers. Also, your company may have a branch office in the city you are visiting where you can make arrangements to use its equipment.

CONDUCT. A business trip involves just that—business. Although you may have free time when you can shop, sightsee, take in a play, or enjoy a meal at an interesting restaurant, it is assumed that you are there to work. Your days may be spent gathering information for your boss, checking further travel plans, taking notes at meetings, organizing your employer's travel files, preparing and processing correspondence, and so on.

When you arrive at a hotel with your employer, or drive together, he or she will take care of the tipping. Otherwise, handle this as if you were traveling alone. Keep track of, and whenever possible get receipts for, all business expenditures so that you can be reimbursed later.

Much of the time your employer may be entertaining clients or business associates. After work, you should then assume that you are on your own. But secretaries are part of the business team, representing their companies, and must dress and otherwise conduct themselves as they would at the office or at business-social events. If you are in a foreign country, respect the customs and follow proper rules of etiquette. Visit your local library or purchase guides so that you can thoroughly study the customs of a foreign country before you leave on the trip.

MAKING RESERVATIONS

Checklist of Information You Need

Today's business executive usually travels by plane, but circumstances may necessitate using an overnight sleeper. Therefore, before making reservations for the trip, you will have to know not only where your employer plans to go but also the method of transportation he or she prefers.

INFORMATION NEEDED FOR TRANSPORTATION AND HOTEL RESERVATIONS. You need the following information to make travel and hotel reservations, whether you use an outside travel agency or an in-house travel department:

1. Destination
2. Desired departure time (morning, afternoon, evening, or night)
3. Desired arrival and departure times for stopovers
4. Preferred transportation (plane, train, or automobile)
5. Travel accommodations desired (e.g., first class)
6. Whether or not a rental car is desired and vehicle preference
7. Whether or not connecting shuttle service is needed
8. Hotel preference and accommodations desired at destination
9. Special travel or destination requirements (e.g., telecommunications facilities)

How to Prepare Time and Route Data

SELECTING AN AIRLINE. Sometimes companies have a particular airline that they want employees to use (with a corporate account, it may provide discounts or other services). Otherwise, if there is more than one airline servicing the city that your employer is planning to visit, list some of the major airlines with departure and arrival times and submit the schedule so that your employer can determine which one is the most convenient.

SELECTING RAIL TRANSPORTATION. In some cases, rail transportation may be more convenient or desirable. If so, prepare a schedule showing information about departure and arrival times, railway lines to be used, and ticket information.

DESIGNATING MULTIPLE LAPS. If the contemplated trip has several laps, submit the information for each lap on a separate sheet. This information is also helpful when making reservations.

SELECTING A CAR-RENTAL AGENCY. List some of the major car-rental facilities available in each city on the itinerary, unless your company always uses a particular rental facility.

NOTING TIME CHANGES. Planes and trains are usually scheduled on standard time at the place named in the timetable—eastern standard, central standard, and so on. Call any change in time from that in your location to your employer's attention.

What to Do About Delays or Difficulty in Getting Reservations

If you cannot get space when you want it, the travel agent will find out about alternative times or will keep trying and notify you if the space later becomes available. If you request another airline and the reservation is confirmed, be certain to cancel any other reservation or request you may have made. Often, in cases of delay, travel agents can be helpful in making numerous contacts and securing space that someone else has canceled.

Securing the Tickets

COMPANY ACCOUNTS AND TRAVEL CARDS. Travel agents often make it easy to obtain and pay for tickets. Most companies whose employees travel extensively open an account with an agency (or with an airline) and with major hotels. Employees also may use a company charge or travel card. Individuals who make many trips can open similar accounts on the basis of their personal credit. Those who don't have accounts can use a consumer credit card such as Visa or MasterCard or a charge card such as American Express.

PAYMENT BY CHECK. Even if your employer does not want to use a credit or charge card or use an account with a travel agency or airline, if time is available you can telephone a travel agent, make your reservation, and pay by check. The ticket, however, is not valid until the check is received. When you make an arrangement of this kind, you must be sure that there is ample time for receipt of the check by the travel agent or airline as well as time for the ticket to be mailed or picked up.

CANCELING RESERVATIONS. Should your employer change plans, return the unused ticket and request a credit or refund. Note that even if you charge the ticket with a credit card, the unused portion must be returned before the crediting procedure can begin. Request a credit receipt to keep in your files until the credit appears on your monthly charge-card statement. If time is short, you can telephone a cancellation and fax or mail a confirming letter.

HOW TO CHECK THE TICKETS. Check tickets carefully against the information you gathered in making the reservation. With plane tickets, look for these points:

1. Are the flight numbers correct?
2. Is the departure listed at the time you requested?
3. Is the plane leaving from the airport you assumed it was leaving from?
4. Is the city of destination the city to which your employer wants to travel?
5. Is the reservation on the airline you assumed it was on?
6. Is the ticket complete?

Check train tickets carefully for information similar to that for the plane tickets: time, date, destination, train number, accommodations, and railway station. Make sure that the ticket is complete.

Making Hotel Reservations

SOURCES OF INFORMATION. Regardless of whether you are using a company travel agent or an outside travel agent, he or she will take care of hotel reservations according to your specifications or will make suggestions regarding hotel accommodations. Some firms negotiate with certain hotels for lower rates and open corporate accounts with the hotels.

1. *Maps and books.* If your employer has no hotel preference and is not familiar with the hotels in a city where he or she expects to stop, you can get detailed information in your local library by consulting the latest editions of a directory such as the *Hotel and Travel Index*, *Official Hotel and Resort Guide*, or the *Hotel/Motel Red Book*. Rand McNally and other organizations publish maps and travel books, many of which are available in libraries and bookstores. The number of rooms and the price enable you to judge the class of hotel.

2. *Other sources.* You can also call a local hotel association, write to the Chamber of Commerce in the city of destination, or access a travel-service database. For further information, write to the major hotels and request their free directories or brochures, which show distance to the airport and other key locations. Hotels can also provide details on their latest frequent-traveler discounts or discount agreements that hotels have with major airlines. Preliminary investigation of these options could mean substantial savings for your employer over time.

USING RESERVATION SERVICES. Your in-house or outside travel agent will make hotel reservations for you, or with the proper software, you can access travel services with your computer and a modem. Some credit- and charge-card organizations, certain associations, and larger hotel and motel chains provide a nationwide reservation service with free 800 numbers (consult an 800 directory or call 800-555-1212 for information.) Some airlines provide both flight and hotel reservation services. Information in the folders offered to members of the American Automobile Association guides the traveler to good hotels, inns, overnight guest houses, and motels in the United States, Canada, and Mexico.

MAKING THE RESERVATIONS. When making a hotel reservation, give your company agent or outside travel agent the name of the person for whom the reservation is to be made, the time of arrival and probable time of departure, and the type of accommodations desired. Indicate special needs such as health or exercise facilities or computer and telecommunications facilities.

1. Guaranteed reservation. State if the reservation is to be guaranteed or assured. The hotel will then hold the room until checkout time the next day. If you need to cancel, however, call before 6 P.M. (4 P.M. in resorts) to avoid being billed for the night. Request a cancellation number for your files.

2. Checkout time. Inquire about the checkout time and include this information in the memo that you give your employer before the trip. If you speak directly to someone at the hotel, get the person's name and the reservation number in case you need to make further contact concerning the reservation.

3. Room location. If your employer prefers, request a room near the elevator or midway down the hall, not at the end. Avoid a ground floor. If the hotel room has a balcony, your employer should check whether its doors lock. Patronize hotels with adequate security, such as valet parking, deadbolts, and telephone-number confidentiality.

CONFIRMING THE RESERVATION. Always get fax or other written confirmations of hotel reservations and attach them to the copy of the itinerary that your employer takes along (see Figure 20). This applies regardless of who makes the reservation.

RESERVING ROOMS FOR A LARGE MEETING. If you must reserve rooms for a large meeting, such as a conference, speak directly with the sales manager at one of the larger hotels in the city where the meeting is scheduled. Hotels provide valuable assistance in arranging for group reservations, in selecting appropriate meeting rooms and other facilities, and in handling the many other details that are involved.

USING HOUSING EXCHANGE SERVICES. Some firms participate in exchange services, whereby travelers from foreign countries are housed in employee homes and apartments while visiting the United States, and company employees are housed in homes overseas while on a foreign trip. Ask your travel agent for more details.

Making Air-Travel Arrangements

WHERE TO GET INFORMATION ABOUT FLIGHT SCHEDULES. You can get general information about air travel from travel agents, the airlines themselves, and in the *Official Airline Guides*. For up-to-the-minute schedules and rates, you must contact your company's travel department or an outside travel agent, call the airlines, or use a computerized travel service. At the same time, inquire about available shuttles, courtesy vehicles, helicopter service, or any other required ground or air service.

The best published sources of airline information are the *Official Airline Guides*. Check your local library or ask your travel agent to show you a copy. The North American edition, updated twice monthly, lists cities in the United States, Canada, and U.S. possessions alphabetically, with airline schedules for airlines servicing each city. The guide index also indicates the availability of a car-rental service and air-taxi service for each city. A world edition is updated monthly. Guides are sold by yearly subscription or single copy.

WHERE TO FIND OTHER AIR-TRAVEL INFORMATION. Your company health department or nurse can provide information on dietary hints for travelers, as well as on the use of medications while traveling. If your employer has a long domestic or international flight, check your library or bookstore or ask your travel agent about books on travel tips.

WHERE TO FIND GROUP-TRAVEL INFORMATION. If your task involves arranging air travel for a large group—perhaps for a conference—contact your company travel department or an outside travel agent. If you are seeking only preliminary information, write to several major airlines and inquire about their special services for conference travel. Some will offer a number of attractive packages, including reduced group rates and block reservations from selected cities. Some will even do a promotional mailing, free of charge, to everyone registered for the conference or to prospective attendees.

WHERE TO FIND AIRLINE-CLUB INFORMATION. Some major airlines have clubs for frequent fliers, with membership available by annual fee. Member travelers are offered special lounges and conference rooms with telephones and other amenities in airport terminals. Contact well-known national and international airlines for further information.

FINDING OUT WHAT ARRANGEMENTS YOUR EMPLOYER WANTS. Many companies require their employees to travel at the economy rate if expedient. Flights may have first class, business class, and coach, or economy, sections. Exceptions are short shuttle flights, which commonly have only one class of travel. Reservations may not be available on a shuttle flight, but the airline sometimes guarantees passage even if a second plane has to be placed in service for the scheduled flight.

1. Meal requirements. Ask your employer's preferences regarding meals and then find out whether meals or snacks will be available on a particular flight. On most flights taking place during a normal meal hour, either full meals or snacks are available. Frequently, a traveler can get a cocktail without charge at meal time in first class but must pay for it in coach service.

2. Telephone requirements. Some executives require telephone service in flight. Major airlines may offer telephone service via the airwaves (airfone service). Callers usually need to use a special credit card to insert in the telephone, and the connection is made by an operator who places the call from a telephone-company ground station.

HOW TO MAKE PLANE RESERVATIONS. Whether you deal with your company's travel department or an outside agent, be prepared with full facts before you make your contact concerning airline reservations. Get the name of the person to whom you are talking (and give that person your name), so that if you must call again to clarify any part of the itinerary, you will be able to speak with the same person.

1. Information to provide. Explain clearly what airline reservations you want. Provide the following information:

Points of departure and destination

Date and time of departure desired

Flight number (if known)

Class of accommodations desired

Any special needs (e.g., wheelchair, nonsmoking section)

2. Discount fares. An airline may offer a supersaver or an excursion rate or advertise a promotional fare, but if you are considering this, ask about any restrictions that apply.

3. Stopovers. When your employer plans to make several stopovers on the trip, or has unavoidable layovers, give your travel agent the approximate times he or she will depart from and arrive at various stops and the accommodations desired at each location. If one lap of the trip is to be by train, the agent will also make that reservation for you, as well as car-rental and shuttle needs. Remember to reconfirm any lap of the trip before departure directly with the airlines.

4. Fare reductions and refunds. If the airfare is reduced after you have purchased a ticket, ask a clerk at the ticket counter for a refund. If the reverse occurs, however, a traveler is protected against having to pay the increase.

Making Train-Travel Arrangements

WHERE TO GET INFORMATION ABOUT TRAINS. You can get information about travel by train from your company travel department and outside travel agents, directly from Amtrak, and in *The Official Railway Guide*. (Remember that rates and schedules in timetables or in a published guide will not have up-to-the-minute changes.) Check at your local library or ask your travel agent to show you a copy.

The *Official Railway Guide* is published eight times a year and contains all schedules or timetables of Amtrak and other passenger railroads in Canada and Mexico, with sample fares and a description of the accommodations on each train. It also shows connecting bus and suburban rail lines and mileage between stations and contains maps of individual roads. You can subscribe to it by the year, or single copies can be purchased.

FINDING OUT WHAT ACCOMMODATIONS YOUR EMPLOYER WANTS. Your employer might travel in the business or coach section on a plane, but he or she is not likely to travel by coach on a train unless it is a very short connection. Each timetable gives the accommodations or "equipment" offered by the scheduled trains or gives a reference to a page where that information can be obtained. You can tell from this whether the train carries a diner, club car, observation car, and the like and the type of sleeping accommodations offered.

    1. Sleeping accommodations. These accommodations may include a private bedroom or a smaller roomette intended primarily for single occupancy. Special cars are also available on some trains for handicapped persons. Tell your travel agent about any special needs of your employer.

    2. Executive sleeper service. On some routes, rail service can be as fast as plane travel. Also, some U.S. night routes offer executive sleeper service whereby the traveler can remain on the locked and unattended train until 8 A.M. the next morning.

    3. Telephone service. Railfone service is available on certain Amtrak routes. Telephone calls can be made direct to any point in the United States using a major credit card.

HOW TO MAKE THE RESERVATIONS. The procedure for making train reservations is similar to that for obtaining plane reservations. An intelligent idea of what you want before you telephone your own company travel office, a travel agent, or Amtrak will help immeasurably.

    Be sure to give complete and clear information on the point of departure and destination, time, train number or name, and the accommodations desired. For long-distance travel in the United States, trains are very limited, and you might not have a choice of time. This is also a good reason to make train reservations far in advance. When the exact reservations that you want are not available, ask the travel agent to suggest something that is available.

Making Auto-Travel Arrangements

WHERE TO GET INFORMATION ABOUT AUTOMOBILE TRAVEL. You can get information about car rentals from your company travel department or an outside travel agent and directly from the car-rental agencies. Also, the American Automobile Association and other auto clubs provide various services for their members, and airlines, railroads, hotels, and numerous other organizations provide information about and assistance in arranging car rentals.

If your employer travels by automobile a great deal, he or she may find it advantageous to be a member of the American Automobile Association, which has a travel service that can plan any trip a member wants to take by motor vehicle. Some insurance companies, such as Allstate, and gasoline companies, such as Chevron, also provide auto-club and travel services. To secure travel service, send your request to the nearest branch of the automobile association or auto club, and routings will be sent to you. Auto clubs provide a variety of services to travelers, such as:

1. Advising them how to go, where to stop, and what to see
2. Preparing special route maps
3. Providing last-minute information on weather and highway conditions
4. Assisting in selecting and securing motel and hotel accommodations in advance of the trip
5. Providing emergency road service
6. Providing bail and arrest bonds
7. Providing accident insurance
8. Offering an auto-theft reward
9. Offering discounts on car-rental and other travel services

Members of some clubs also receive road maps, travel guides, or directories covering outstanding points of interest.

FINDING OUT WHAT CAR-RENTAL ARRANGEMENTS ARE NEEDED. Your employer's preliminary itinerary and appointment schedule will suggest stopovers where a car may be needed. Ask about:

1. Specific places where a rental car or limousine is desired
2. Preferences for rental agencies
3. Preferences for make and size of car

4. Whether a cellular phone is needed

5. Method of payment to be used

6. Dates and times car is needed

7. Whether drop-off in another city is desired

Some rental agencies provide a computer printout of directions showing the easiest route to numerous local destinations. Ask your travel agent which ones provide this service in the cities your employer will visit.

How to make the reservations. On a trip involving several stops, your employer may prefer to travel from city to city by car or to have a car available for appointments within a particular city. Foreign travelers sometimes prefer a chauffeur-driven car, especially if they are on a tight schedule and are very unfamiliar with the foreign city.

Some of the major car-rental facilities at each stop should be listed on the itinerary you prepare, unless your company requires that employees use a particular agency. If you know that a car will be needed, your travel agent can telephone in advance for reservations and have a car waiting at the airport or train station. Upon arrival, your employer need only show a driver's license. Payment is usually made by company account with the rental company or with one of the major credit or charge cards. Membership in a car-rental club, offered by some of the major rental agencies, saves time at the counter since a preprinted form is readily provided and waiting each time the member rents a car.

PREPARING FOR FOREIGN TRAVEL

Many large U.S. companies maintain a foreign office or employ a representative in the country or countries in which the firm does business. Other companies rely on communications from the firm's U.S. location coupled with business trips as needed. As telecommunications are expanding abroad, along with various forms of fast messaging such as facsimile and other electronic mail, contacts in foreign countries are increasing among U.S. firms of all sizes.

Language Requirements

USE OF TRANSLATORS AND INTERPRETERS. Some of the countries of the world are multilingual, and in all cases, English is the widely accepted language of choice for business dealings. In countries where English is known only as a second or third language, if at all, translators and interpreters can be hired for service at the destination. Many businesses, however, prefer to hire their own interpreters and translators at home, as company employees or freelancers, rather than wait and use those provided by foreign customers and clients or by foreign translation services.

Whether a traveler is speaking or writing directly to a foreign contact or through an interpreter or translator, it is important to use very precise English. Translators and foreign representatives tend to interpret every word and expression literally, as explained in Chapter 11.

Etiquette Requirements

SOURCES OF INFORMATION. Libraries and bookstores have numerous books on etiquette and protocol that will help foreign travelers avoid making unintentional blunders in another country, and numerous articles have been written about the etiquette of international travel. Books, travel guides, and articles focusing on individual countries and regions are also available, and it is extremely important for a businessperson to study the customs of the countries he or she will visit—before leaving home.

RULES OF INTERNATIONAL ETIQUETTE. Rules of etiquette vary greatly from one country to another and from one region of the world to another, for example:

1. In Spain it is expected that businesspeople will get acquainted socially before conducting business.

2. It is a social gaffe in nearly all countries to use first names, except with very close friends.

3. A handshake is acceptable in Japan but a slight bow from the waist is better.

4. Touching or back slapping is taboo in the Far East and is considered bad form even in Europe.

5. It is improper to give an Italian hostess chrysanthemums since they are associated with funerals in Italy.

6. Direct eye contact is rude in the Far East but suggests sincerity in Europe.

Travel Materials Requirements

FOREIGN ITINERARY AND APPOINTMENT SCHEDULES. A detailed itinerary, which you or your travel agent may prepare, is essential on a foreign trip. Following the format of Figure 20, it should include the essentials, such as a list of meetings, dates and times, names and addresses of contacts, and special reminders (e.g., when to confirm travel arrangements or check in with the home office).

SUPPLIES AND TRAVEL INFORMATION TO TAKE ALONG. A checklist of supplies, equipment, and other material for the international traveler should include those items listed in Figure 22 to the extent practical in regard to baggage limitations or foreign customs restrictions. The foreign traveler needs a number of items that a domestic traveler can omit, such as dictionaries of the destination country's language, with English translations (or a small electronic translator); address lists and maps of hotels, rail stations, car-rental agencies, and the like; travel guides and other country-specific books; consulate numbers; exchange-rate details; and other information related to the purpose of the trip.

Foreign Currency Requirements

SOURCES OF INFORMATION. Call the international department of your firm's bank for current exchange rates just before your employer leaves. You can also check financial newspapers or access a financial database, if you have the proper software.

PURCHASING FOREIGN CURRENCY. Some businesspeople purchase small amounts of foreign currency before leaving for use with miscellaneous expenses on arrival (tips, taxis, telephone, and the like). Since banks offer better rates of exchange than hotels and other sources, remind your employer that this should be taken care of during banking hours to avoid having to go to a more expensive source after hours.

Foreign Messaging and Telecommunications Requirements

INTERNATIONAL DIALING CODES. If you don't already have a list of international direct-dialing codes, request a current list from your long-distance carrier. Since the codes may change from time to time and new country codes are added periodically, request a new list at least once a year.

INTERNATIONAL CALLING CARDS. A businessperson who travels overseas should have an international calling card (provided by long-distance carriers) that provides direct-dial service as well as operated-assisted service. A traveler can then place a direct call from any touchtone telephone by dialing an access number, authorization code, and the desired telephone number. For translation or interpreter services, ask the calling-card operator to connect you with a translator or interpreter during a call.

MAIL AND ELECTRONIC TRANSMISSIONS. Communication with your employer overseas can be accomplished by telephone, postal mail, facsimile, telex, E-mail, or any other form of message transmission or delivery available in the country your employer is visiting. To send a fax to a foreign country, you need the same information required for a telephone call: the international access code, country code, and city code.

Use of Travel Agents

SPECIAL NEEDS FOR FOREIGN TRAVEL. A company travel department or outside travel agency is essential in making foreign travel arrangements. Although you should follow the guidelines on the selection and use of a travel agent at the beginning of this chapter, in the case of foreign travel it is important to choose an agent that is experienced in making international travel arrangements and is either familiar with or specializes in the countries your firm deals with.

Securing a Passport

WHEN PASSPORTS ARE NEEDED. Passports are needed for U.S. citizens to travel to most countries with a few exceptions such as Canada, Mexico, and some Caribbean islands. Ask your travel agent or check with the embassy or consulate of the country involved for a list of admission requirements.

WHERE TO APPLY. Application for a passport, which should be made well in advance of the trip, may be executed before a clerk of a federal court, a state court authorized to naturalize aliens, an agent of the State Department, or a post office authorized to grant passports. Passport agents of the State Department are located in various U.S. cities, including New York City, San Francisco, Chicago, Los Angeles, Boston, and New Orleans. In Washington, D.C., applications are executed in the Passport Division of the Department of State. Passports currently held by a businessperson may be renewed by mail. Ask your travel agent or a nearby passport office for details.

PASSPORT INFORMATION. Write for a current copy of *Your Trip Abroad* (for sale by the Superintendent of Documents, U.S. Government Printing Office, Washington, DC 20402). This booklet discusses documents (passport, visa, and the like) that you need before you leave the United States and gives advice on dealing with problems after you arrive in the foreign country.

PROCEDURE. The following is a brief summary of the essential requirements for making application for a passport when the applicant is a native American citizen or a naturalized citizen.

1. Proof of citizenship. A native American citizen must submit a previous U.S. passport or a birth certificate with the application to prove citizenship. If this certificate is not obtainable, the applicant must submit an affidavit executed by a person who has personal knowledge of the place and date of birth. If an affidavit of a relative or attending physician cannot be obtained, an affidavit of some other reputable person, preferably a blood relation, with knowledge of the facts should be submitted. The person must have known the applicant for several years. The affidavit should state how knowledge of the place and date of birth was acquired.

2. Proof of identity. The traveler must establish his or her identification to the satisfaction of the passport agent. This may be done by presentation of one of the following documents containing the signature of the applicant and either a photograph or a physical description of the applicant:

Prior U.S. passport

Certificate of naturalization

Driver's license

Federal, state, or municipal government identity card

A naturalized citizen must present his or her naturalization papers and be identified in the same manner as a native-born citizen.

3. *Other requirements.* Two current (within six months) 2- by 2-inch black-and-white or color passport photographs must be submitted, along with the current passport fee. Check your Yellow Pages for locations where passport photographs may be obtained.

Applications of persons going abroad on business in pursuance of a contract or agreement with a federal government agency must be accompanied by a letter from the head of the firm or, in his or her absence, from the person in charge. The letter must state the position of the applicant, destination (or destinations), purpose of the trip, and approximate length of stay.

Securing a Visa

After the traveler gets a passport, the next step is to get visas for the countries that require them. You can check the Visa Fee Sheet at a local passport office for a list of countries requiring a visa and fees charged for it. Your travel agent also can tell you whether or not a visa is required.

WHERE TO GET A VISA. Visas are obtained from the embassy or consulate of the country to be visited. Generally, a passport must be presented and a visa form filled out. The various countries have a number of special requirements, such as additional photographs, police and health certificates, vaccinations, and inoculations. (Write for a copy of *Health Information for International Travel*, sold by the Superintendent of Documents, U.S. Government Printing Office, Washington, DC 20402.) Since the length of time required for processing a visa varies with the country, it is important to apply well in advance of the departure date.

Your employer may ask you to consult the *Congressional Directory* in your local library for addresses of overseas consular offices. Also, the U.S. Government Printing Office in Washington, D.C., sells a publication, *Key Officers of Foreign Service Posts*, that lists all embassies, legations, and consulates general (as well as provides other information, such as key officers).

Securing an International Driving Permit

The American Automobile Association and the American Automobile Touring Alliance have applications for an international driving permit. Two passport photos, an application fee, and a U.S. driver's license are required. Ask your travel agent for additional details.

Special Secretarial Duties

When your employer travels abroad on business, you will likely have certain duties in addition to those related to preparations for a pleasure trip, for example:

1. Ask your travel agent or the consulates for full details on the special requirements imposed on commercial travelers (as opposed to pleasure-trip visitors). This is most important.

2. Compile a list of officers and executives of each firm with which your employer does business in the foreign countries to be visited. Your employer may want this information included in a pocket-size notebook for convenience in traveling.

3. Compile pertinent data on all recent business deals completed with each firm, together with data on pending deals. You should have a separate file folder for each company or individual to be visited.

4. Write letters, for your employer's signature, requesting letters of introduction from banks, individuals, business houses, and the like to their foreign offices. Such introductions are very helpful to a commercial traveler. The following is a general example that you can adapt to your own purpose:

Mr. Alexander N. Genetes
Second Vice-President
Guaranty Trust Company
140 Broadway
New York, NY l0006

Dear Mr. Genetes:

On April 24 I am leaving for Europe on a business trip. I will call on publishers and booksellers in London, Paris, Zurich, Brussels, Amsterdam, Copenhagen, Oslo, Stockholm, and probably Barcelona. A letter from you to your correspondents in each of these cities might be helpful to me, and I would appreciate it very much if you would supply me with such a letter.

I expect to gain a good deal of firsthand information on general conditions in all of these countries, as well as more specific data on books and publishing matters. I will be happy to make available to you upon my return any information that may interest you.

Sincerely yours,

5. Write letters to the foreign firms your employer expects to visit and announce his or her travel plans, the dates of the proposed stay in the city concerned, your employer's expected local address in the foreign country, and the like. These letters are written over your employer's signature or in the name of the president of your firm. If you do not draft these letters yourself, remind your employer to dictate them well in advance of the trip.

6. Write an announcement of the planned visit to different trade or professional magazines that are published in the city or country to be visited. The announcement should give the address where your employer can be reached while there, as well as the dates of the proposed visit. If you use a skilled travel agent, he or she will prepare an itinerary of the entire trip and make extra copies for distribution.

7. Write a letter for your employer's signature six weeks or two months in advance of the trip to the following:

Travel Officer
International Trade Administration
Department of Commerce
Office of International Trade
Washington, DC 20230

This letter should state the purpose of the trip and should include the itinerary. The Department of Commerce sends airgrams, via its bulletins, to all foreign offices announcing the visit.

8. Ask your employer if you should help collect market information or locate market advisors in various countries from any of the following sources: (a) The Trade Development Group in the Department of Commerce has information on current markets and obstacles in particular countries. (b) For advance information on what to expect in a particular market and help in setting up appointments, prospective travelers can contact the respective country desk officer in the International Economic Policy Branch of the Department of Commerce. (c) Foreign commercial officers located at various U.S. embassies and consulates in other countries can advise on local business customs and help with introductions. (d) *Business America* (sold through the Superintendent of Documents, U.S. Government Printing Office, Washington, DC 20402) reports on market opportunities and lists the posts of the business liaison officers worldwide.

9. Get a letter of authority, addressed "To Whom It May Concern," from your company's president or any other person who is authorizing your employer to represent the firm. This is especially valuable in dealing with immigration or customs authorities.

10. Develop country profiles by assembling data on the trade conditions, political aspects, geography, climate, customs, and the like of each country to be visited. If your employer makes frequent trips abroad, you should also accumulate such material throughout the year from trade journals, books, governmental sources, and other organizations or publications that have appropriate information. Photocopy or mark with a yellow marking pen the items of interest. Films, videocassettes, and the like also provide useful information about these matters; ask your local reference librarian to help you compile a list of current distributors and addresses. *Background Notes* (sold by the Superintendent of Documents, U.S. Government Printing Office, Washington, DC 20402) are individual pamphlets on the countries of the world covering everything from culture to climate.

11. If your company subscribes to the Dun & Bradstreet credit service, get a card from them authorizing your employer to call on their foreign offices for credit information.

12. Establish contact with secretaries in the foreign firms your employer will visit. Offer to be of assistance to their employers when they visit the United States and ask if they will act as a contact to help your employer should the need arise while he or she is visiting their countries. Suggest forming a worldwide network not only for assistance to traveling employers but as a means of exchanging useful information throughout the year.

Travel Security

Travelers need to take special precautions against assaults, theft, and other crimes, and travel agents often recommend particular precautions in specific countries or cities. The following are general guidelines that you and your employer can observe:

1. Do not travel with more than $200 in cash. Charge or prepay travel and hotel costs as much as possible. If you use charge or credit cards, take as few as possible. Completely destroy the carbon copy used in charge forms—your card number shows on it and can easily be retrieved from a wastebasket by a thief. Check the sequence of your traveler's checks (some thieves steal only a few, hoping you won't notice).

2. Be certain that your personal insurance covers travel losses.

3. Keep your luggage with you at all times, and do not use expensive designer luggage that will readily attract a thief. Also use combination locks and luggage tags that conceal your name and address.

4. Inquire at the hotel about safe or unsafe areas to walk or park a car, and avoid dark streets, parks, and unattended parking garages.

5. Avoid using pocketbooks and similar small cases. But if you must carry a purse or small case, stay away from the curb where motorcycle thieves can snatch the object and quickly speed away. A woman can carry a shoulder bag tucked under her arm and held tightly by the strap. Men can use a money belt or, if necessary,

only a front pocket. Wrap your wallet with a heavy rubber band to prevent a pickpocket from easily sliding it out of your pocket.

6. Keep your passport with you but in a guarded or inaccessible pocket, not in an open pocket or hip pocket, and never leave it laying on a hotel or restaurant table. Photocopy the essential pages before departing on the trip, and leave one copy at the office, carry another copy in a suitcase, and place a third copy in a different location.

7. Do not wear much jewelry, especially expensive jewelry or something an inexperienced thief might assume is expensive.

8. Never enter a rental or any other car without checking the back seat to see if someone is hiding there, and park your car in a well-lit place. If you go to a garage or parking lot where you must leave it with an attendant, take the trunk key with you. Store items only in the trunk of your car and, when available, use a hotel safe for jewelry and other valuables, important computer disks, and so on.

9. Have your hotel room made up during breakfast and hang a do-not-disturb sign out the rest of the day. Turn on the television and set the volume on low.

10. Keep your room key with you even when you leave the hotel.

11. In a hotel room, use the chain lock and the deadbolt (if any). Temporary locking devices and alarms, sold commercially, can be carried by travelers to hotel rooms. Never open the door unless you know the person who is there.

12. As a precaution in case of theft, photocopy airline tickets and other important documents with numbers before departing on the trip. One copy is for the office files, and another should be kept in the traveler's suitcase; a third copy should be kept by the traveler elsewhere, apart from the original documents.

13. If you are robbed, call the police immediately, especially in a foreign country where it is difficult or impossible to file a claim after you have gone. Immediately secure a copy of the police report for use in filing an insurance claim.

14. Ask your travel agent to recommend particular carriers, hotels, and the like with a good safety record. Inquire about dates or

times to travel that are generally safer than others, and ask about special precautions that will be needed in the specific countries you or your employer will be visiting.

Customs Information

Anyone going to a foreign country should know in advance the U.S. customs laws and regulations covering purchases made in a foreign country and brought into the United States. It is also important to find out which of a traveler's personal possessions (e.g., computer equipment) must be declared before entering the destination country. A competent travel agent can provide this information or direct you to the proper source.

PRINTED INFORMATION. The government has a number of useful pamphlets on customs and other matters pertaining to international travel. Send for *Know Before You Go, Customs Hints for Returning U.S. Residents*, which furnishes travelers with the general information needed about U.S. Customs laws and regulations. Copies are available free from any local Customs office.

Chapter 8

Keeping Company Books and Records

HOW TO KEEP OFFICE AND COMPANY RECORDS

Record keeping is an ongoing task in offices of every size and occupation. In addition to handling filing and data-management activities, secretaries are often involved in various aspects of the accounting and bookkeeping functions of their companies. But whether or not you actually do the bookkeeping and preparation of financial statements in your firm, you need to be familiar with this important function since it directly or indirectly affects the way that other work is handled.

Your firm may use one or more of the many computer software programs available for maintaining the books of account, handling billings and collections, processing payroll data, and preparing financial statements. The same basic rules of accounting and bookkeeping apply whether records are prepared and maintained electronically or manually. The rules of cash and accrual accounting and the basic rules of double-entry bookkeeping, for example, apply in either case.

Handling Petty Cash

Certain small, miscellaneous expenditures cannot easily or practically be handled by check. If a package arrived with 10 cents postage due, for example, you wouldn't write a check for such a small amount. You would

237

no doubt pay it with cash from the office petty cash fund. Other examples of small expenditures usually paid from petty cash are taxi fares, occasional office supplies, delivery charges, meals, gifts, shipping costs, postage supplies, minor repairs, office refreshments, and cleaning supplies.

ESTABLISHING A PETTY CASH FUND. The person authorized to write and sign checks draws and cashes a check for a small amount, perhaps $50 or a $100—enough to last a certain period such as a month. The cash is usually placed in a locked box that is then stored in a secure place. Some secretaries keep the cash box in a locked desk drawer.

MAKING PAYMENTS FROM PETTY CASH. The secretary in charge of the petty cash fund keeps a record of every expenditure on small printed forms (available at most office supply stores) called "petty cash vouchers." The form may be as brief and simple or as detailed and complex as you like. A common form of voucher is shown in Figure 23. A standard voucher form has a place for you to initial it, to signify approval of the expenditure, and a place for the person receiving the cash to sign his or her name, to signify receipt of the specified amount. The voucher should also clearly indicate *what* the expenditure is for. Some offices want the voucher to state not only the nature of the expenditure (for example, postage) but the number of the account to which the expense will be charged later in the cash disbursements journal (for example, 201—postage).

Keep any receipts you receive whenever you make a payment from the fund. Some payment, such as carfare, will not have any proof of payment other than the voucher. But if you purchase a box of paper clips, the store will give you a cash register or written receipt. Attach any additional proof of payment, such as a receipt, to the voucher. Finally, file all vouchers (with additional receipts) numerically in a file folder. Daily—or at least frequently—verify the balance in the cash box. The total of the vouchers plus the remaining cash in the box should equal the amount of the check that was cashed and deposited in the box at the beginning of the period plus any cash that was in the box at that time.

REPLENISHING THE FUND. When the fund is getting low, or at the end of a specified period such as a month, prepare a *record of transactions* for your employer. Even if your office does not have a special computerized form for this purpose, break down the expenditures by category so that they

FIGURE 23

Petty Cash Voucher

```
┌─────────────────────────────────────────────────────┐
│                                                       │
│              PETTY CASH VOUCHER                       │
│                                                       │
├───────────────────────────────────────────────────────┤
│                                                       │
│   Date ___June 4, 1993___      No. _69_              │
│   Paid to ___John Simmons___   $14.65                │
│   For ___taxi-to sales seminar___                    │
│                                                       │
│   ─────────────────────────────────────────────────  │
│                                                       │
│   Approved by:          Payment Received by:         │
│                                                       │
│   ___E. C. K.___        ___John Simmons___           │
│                                                       │
└───────────────────────────────────────────────────────┘
```

can later be recorded in the company's cash disbursements journal. Figure 24 is an example of a simple petty cash transactions record that can be prepared by typewriter or computer.

After your employer reviews the record of transactions and replenishes the fund, place the record in the voucher file folder, in front of the group of vouchers listed on the transactions record. If only a few vouchers are involved, you may be able to staple them behind the petty cash transactions record sheet. As soon as the fund has been replenished, the entire process begins all over again.

DO'S AND DON'TS IN HANDLING PETTY CASH. Treat the record keeping for petty cash the same as you would treat any other financial record-keeping duty—with utmost accuracy and attention to detail. Never permit anyone to borrow from the fund, and if ever you doubt whether an expense is legitimate, don't hesitate to ask for approval before you process the transaction.

FIGURE 24

Petty Cash Transactions Record

PETTY CASH TRANSACTIONS RECORD
April 1 to 15, 1993

Date	Voucher	To	Receipts	Payments	Supplies	Taxi	Postage	Meals	Delivery	Misc.
4/1	—	Balance	$27.10							
4/2	30	Ronald Sayles		$4.10		$4.10				
4/7	31	Joe's Market		5.49				$5.49		
4/11	32	Postal Carrier		0.23			$0.23			
4/13	33	Markam Window Serv.		5.00						$5.00
4/13	34	Cole Manfg.		1.70						1.70
4/14	35	Office Suppliers		0.79	$0.79					
4/14	35	D. T. Uphol. Shop		7.00						7.00
4/15	—	Balance	$ 2.79							

Maintaining Office Payroll Accounts

Wherever people are employed, payroll records must be maintained. Although large organizations have special departments that handle payroll and accounting functions, in other companies, this duty is frequently assigned to a secretary or administrative assistant. Payroll records involve (1) wages and salaries paid to employees and (2) payroll and withholding taxes paid to the federal, state, and local governments. Federal requirements apply nationwide, but you should contact state and local authorities for information about records required and payments due in your state and local jurisdiction.

SETTING UP PAYROLL RECORDS. Computerized payroll programs vary greatly. Some are combined with electronic accounting and other nonaccounting functions such as the printing of mailing labels. One system, for example, will manage the payroll for up to 1,000 employees, including the recording, calculation, and preparation of wages, standard and custom deductions, W-2 forms, 1099s, and unemployment tax reports. The program includes fourteen charts of account to customize the software to a particular business. Other capabilities include check writing, billing, bank reconciliation, general ledger, accounts receivable, inventory tracking, job-cost tracking, financial report preparation, and budgeting. Transactions are recorded on paperlike records, which are then posted automatically.

Many manual time clocks have been replaced with PC-based time clocks that track employee hours and compute weekly reports. In some systems employees key in I.D. numbers rather than punch in and out on a conventional clock. The data are then processed electronically by recording and tallying hours and preparing the required payroll reports.

Computer printouts contain essentially the same data as that used on conventional printed employee compensation cards (see Figure 25). Regardless of the system used, the objective is the same: for each employee and for each pay period, you need to record the total hours worked, gross earnings, and deductions.

Payroll data for each employee are then combined and transferred to an electronic or manual payroll journal. In addition to containing the columns shown in Figure 25, a payroll journal sheet might have a column to record the check number of each employee's paycheck and columns for tax-exempt wages.

PROCESSING PAYROLL TAXES. Although state and city requirements vary, as do company insurance and retirement plans, federal law requires two principal deductions from each employee's gross earnings: Federal Insurance Contribution Act (FICA) taxes and income taxes. The FICA tax, often referred to simply as the social security tax, includes Medicare, old-age, disability, and survivor benefits. Some employers must also pay federal and state unemployment taxes. Rates as well as the bases for each tax change, often from year to year, and you should request current information from the Internal Revenue Service (IRS) each year (ask for "Circular E: The Employer's Tax Guide") and from your state taxing authority.

Income taxes must be withheld from each employee's paycheck above a certain minimum. That minimum depends on the number of withholding allowances claimed by the employee and his or her marital status. Employees file Form W-4 with their employers showing how many exemptions they claim.

Social security taxes are deducted from wages up to a certain ceiling, paid to an employee during the year. The employer then matches this amount when submitting withholdings to the federal government.

Federal unemployment taxes must be deposited by employers who paid a certain amount of wages in any calendar quarter or who at any time had one or more employees for some portion of at least one day during each of

Figure 25

Employee Compensation Record

EMPLOYEE COMPENSATION RECORD

NAME _____ SOC. SEC. NO. _____

ADDRESS _____ DATE OF BIRTH _____

PHONE _____ RATE _____ NO. OF EXEMPTIONS _____

Pay period ending	Hours worked									Earnings				Deductions						Net pay
	S	M	T	W	Th	F	S	Total regular hours	Overtime	At regular rate	At overtime rate	Total	Social security	Fed- income tax	State income tax	Group insurance	U.S. bonds	Other	

QUARTERLY TOTALS

twenty calendar weeks. However, no deduction is made from the employee's paycheck for these taxes.

PAYING PAYROLL TAXES TO THE FEDERAL GOVERNMENT. Employers must deposit payroll taxes with the federal government if their total liability—income tax withholding plus employer-employee social security tax—exceeds a specified amount per quarter. "Circular E, Employer's Tax Guide," gives current details about how much to withhold and when and where deposits must be made.

1. Special forms to use. Certain forms are used to make the required tax deposits. Form W-4, "Employer's Withholding Allowance Certificate," must be completed by each new employee and filed with the employer. Form W-2, "Wage and Tax Statement," is issued by the employer to each employee on or before January 31 of each year. Form W-3, "Transmittal of Income and Tax Statements," is sent by the employer, along with copies of W-2 forms, to the Social Security Administration on or before the last day of February. Form 940, "Employer's Annual Federal Unemployment Tax Return," is sent by the employer on or before January 31. Form 941, "Employer's Quarterly Federal Tax Return," is filed by the employer every three months. Form 8109, "Federal Tax Deposit" is sent by the employer with each deposit of income tax and deductions. Ask the IRS and your state tax department for information on other forms that your employer may be required to complete and file.

2. Maintaining confidentiality with payroll data. Since the facts and figures for these reports come from the firm's payroll records, the maintenance of thorough and accurate payroll records is essential. Furthermore, payroll information is strictly confidential, and secretaries who maintain data about employees' wages and salaries must protect and secure such records at all times.

Handling the Checkbook and Bank Statement

Except for petty cash expenditures, all major payments must be made by check. The secretary's duties vary depending on the size of the firm and the office, but professional secretaries are always prepared to assume responsibility for reconciling bank statements, organizing bills for payment, preparing supporting documents, and even filling in the check stubs and writing checks for the employer's signature.

WRITING CHECKS. When a bill arrives, it should be checked for accuracy and initialed by the person authorized to approve payment. After approval, the next step depends on whether you use an electronic check-writing program or write checks manually.

   1. Using an electronic check-writing program. With an electronic check-writing program the data for multiple checks, such as payroll checks, are calculated automatically and printed out in rapid succession. With a check-writing program for individual checks, you would key in the data (date, to whom, amount, and so on) and print out the check the same as you would prepare and print out another type of document on your computer. Some programs support numerous checking, savings, and charge accounts and will create budgets, reconcile bank statements, and provide figures for use on income tax returns.

   2. Filling out a check manually. If you do not use an electronic check-writing program for miscellaneous individual checks, it may be your job to write out a conventional check and fill in the check stub. Enter on the stub the same basic information that goes on the check: (a) date, (b) payee, (c) amount, and (d) purpose of the payment. Some offices also record the number of the account on each stub. If rent is listed in the cash disbursements journal as account number 601, for example, you would then also note "601" on the check stub when paying the rent.

   State the name of the payee accurately. Omit titles such as *Mr.* or *Dr.*, except that a check made payable to the wife of Edward Jones would require the title *Mrs.* (Mrs. Edward Jones). A check made payable to Edna Jones, however, would need no title. Capitalize principal words in the amount but write cents as a fraction, unless the entire amount is less than one dollar:

One Hundred Fifty-two and No/l00 . . . . .Dollars

Only Sixty-five Cents . . . . ~~Dollars~~

   Notice that the word *Only* precedes the amount in cases of less than one dollar and the printed word *Dollars* is crossed out. Avoid spaces where someone might alter the check. In other words, write figures close to the dollar sign ($20.00, not $ 20.00).

3. Voided checks. If you spoil a check, cross out the signature and write "Void" across the face of both the check and the stub in large letters. Then staple the voided check to the back of the stub, and when the canceled checks arrive with the next bank statement, add it to the group of canceled checks and note the voided check number on the bank statement.

4. Stop payments. Remember to add back in the amount of any check written for which you issue a stop payment. Perhaps you learn that a check is lost in the mail, and you want to be certain that it isn't cashed illegally. You should then telephone the bank immediately and ask it to stop payment on the check (usually, there is a charge for this service that will appear on your next statement as a debit). Give the bank the date, the payee's name, the amount, and the check number.

5. Electronic funds transfer. In the case of electronic funds transfer, deductions and additions occur without normal check writing or submission of deposit slips. For example, some items may not be paid by check but instead are automatically deducted from one's account (e.g., insurance premiums). Some deposits, too, may be made automatically. For funds to be transferred automatically, the holder of the bank account must sign an authorization slip with the bank so that the transfer of funds can take place on a regular basis. These items also appear on the monthly bank statement.

6. Bank reconciliation. Upon receipt of the bank statement, reconcile the balance shown by the bank with the balance shown by your checkbook as of the date of the bank statement. If your computer software does not provide automatic reconciliation, your bank statement will include a printed form that you can use for the reconciliation. To find the current bank balance using the bank's reconciliation form, you usually subtract the amount of each check you write from the previous balance and add any new deposits, the same as you would do in your personal checkbook.

After the reconciliation has been made, OK and initial it. Put the bank statement and canceled checks on your employer's desk unless previously instructed to do otherwise. (Many banks maintain checks on microfilm and then do not return the canceled checks to the customer.)

MAKING DEPOSITS. Always examine checks carefully before making deposits. Look for postdating (checks that are dated ahead), discrepancies between figures and written amounts, or problems with the signature. Then endorse each check (see Figure 26) and list it individually on the deposit slip (1) by the name of the drawer, (2) by transit number, or (3) by the place where it is payable.

The endorsement should be made across the left end on the back of each check. It should correspond *exactly* with the name of the payee. If the name of the payee is not correct, endorse the check as it is made out and then write the correct name under the endorsements. Be certain to stay within the area designated on the back of each check for the endorsement.

Endorsements may be restrictive, blank, or specific. Figure 26 illustrates each type.

1. Restrictive endorsement. A restrictive endorsement restricts or limits the endorsee's use of the funds represented by the check. When the check is endorsed to a bank for the credit of the payee, it does not require a manual endorsement. A rubber stamp or typewritten endorsement is acceptable.

The usual phrasing for a restrictive endorsement is "Pay to the Order of _____ Bank for Deposit Only. John E. Brown." If the name of the payee is incorrect, type the name as it appears on the face of the check, and then stamp or type the endorsement for deposit.

Always use a restrictive endorsement on a check that is to be deposited by mail.

2. Blank endorsement. To endorse a check in blank, the payee simply signs his or her name on the back of the check, thereby making it negotiable without further endorsement. Anyone may then cash the check. Do not endorse a check in blank on the typewriter. The endorsement should be written in ink by the payee of the check or by someone authorized to endorse checks for the payee. Never endorse a check in blank until you are ready to cash or deposit it.

3. Specific endorsement. A specific or special endorsement specifies the person to whom the check is transferred. Thus John E. Brown, the

FIGURE 26

Endorsements of Checks

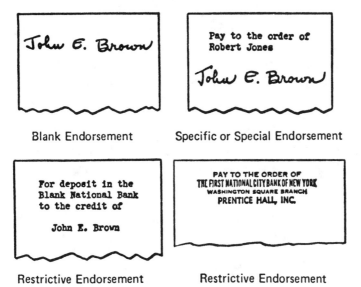

Blank Endorsement   Specific or Special Endorsement

Restrictive Endorsement   Restrictive Endorsement

payee of a check, endorses it "Pay to the Order of Robert Jones. John E. Brown." The check is then payable only to Robert Jones. A specific endorsement must be signed by the payee or someone authorized to endorse checks for the payee, but the other part of the endorsement may be written on the typewriter.

HANDLING SUPPORTING DOCUMENTS. For every check you write, a written document should be produced to "support" the check or to substantiate the amount of the check, its purpose, and so on. The most common supporting document is an invoice. When you receive a bill for something you purchased, keep a copy of the invoice. Mark the document paid and indicate the date and check number. If no supporting document is available, type a memo stating the purpose of the check and, again, mark it paid, with the date and check number. These documents should be filed in a paid bills folder or binder. Depending on the practice in your office, file the documents (1) numerically according to the paid check number you mark on each item or (2) alphabetically according to the payee's name.

Keeping Travel and Entertainment Records

Most companies require that employees document and report all travel and entertainment expenses. This step is necessary whether a traveler received travel funds in advance or whether someone is requesting reimbursement for out-of-pocket expenses. The forms used to report travel and entertainment data vary widely, although certain basic data are common to all of them. Figure 27 illustrates a simple combination travel-entertainment expense form. Office-supply stores sell other standard forms—some providing room to record much more detail—and many companies have their own forms especially designed to suit their needs. If your firm uses numerous forms, you may use a computerized forms file to record information that will be processed electronically for bookkeeping and tax-reporting purposes.

RECORDING THE DATA. The person who takes the trip or does the entertaining will likely supply rough notes (and receipts) or will be required to fill out a printed report form. If it is your job to fill in this form or enter the data into the computer, follow these basic steps:

1. Organize the receipts and notes into the categories listed on the form you will be using to record the data, for example, meals, hotels, and so on.

2. Double-check dates, names of places and persons, and all other facts and figures.

3. If any receipts or paid bills are missing for expenses such as hotels or car rental (there won't be any for miscellaneous expenses such as tips or taxi fare), let the executive know. In certain instances, you may be able to write for a copy of some missing bill.

4. After you are certain all receipts and notes pertaining to all expenditures have been properly grouped by category (for example, telephone, plane fare), list each expense in the proper column on the report form and add the amounts of the individual listings to arrive at a total for each category. Depending on your computer software, the computer may perform these calculations.

5. After you are certain that your employer has no final figures to add, print out or make as many photocopies as needed in your office.

FIGURE 27

Expense Report Form

EXPENSE REPORT

Name _____   Period Covered _____

Title _____   Department _____

Date	Transportation		Living Exp.		Enter-tainment	Phone Telegr. Postage	Misc.	Daily Total
	Auto	Plane	Train	Hotel	Meals				
Total									

Item	Current Month	Previous Month	Year to Date
Mileage Expenses Budget			

Source: Mary A. De Vries, *The Prentice-Hall Complete Secretarial Letter Book* (Englewood Cliffs, N.J.: Prentice-Hall, Inc., 1978).

FOLLOWING IRS REGULATIONS. Since federal rules and regulations may change from year to year, always keep on file the latest information. IRS publication 463, "Travel, Entertainment, and Gift Expenses," is available free from any office of the Internal Revenue Service. This publication explains what expenses you may deduct for business-related travel, entertainment, local transportation, and gifts. It discusses the reporting and record-keeping requirements for these expenses and summarizes the reimbursement and accounting rules for employees and self-employed persons.

Handling Official Financing Statements

Businesses that sell goods on credit have financing statements that debtors must sign to signify agreement to the terms of the sale. Such statements provide information about the transaction including:

1. Name and address of seller

2. Name and address of buyer

3. Good sold

4. Terms of sale (number of installments, amount of each installment payment, interest rate and other charges, period of agreement, and so on)

Often the sales agreement has numerous additional terms and conditions explaining matters such as what will happen if the buyer defaults on the payments.

A *security agreement* identifies the seller's interest in a transaction. When buyers pledge something of value (*collateral*) such as an automobile in return for a loan, they are in effect promising to give up the automobile to the seller if they fail to repay the loan. But sellers sometimes want additional protection. For example, they might want assurance that a buyer won't sell the car pledged as collateral or pledge it to another lender. To deal with such problems, a comprehensive set of laws called the Uniform Commercial Code (UCC) has been adopted by most states in whole or in part.

UNIFORM COMMERCIAL CODE. The UCC covers commercial transactions such as the sale of goods. It also covers a variety of other business matters such as investment securities, bank deposits, and secured transactions. Article 2 of the UCC covers contracts involving the sale of goods, and Article 9 covers transactions in which the seller has a security interest.

Article 9 pertains primarily to personal property and fixtures, for example, the sale of an office copier on credit. If a business sells a copier on credit, it usually retains an interest in the copier until the final payment has been made by the buyer. If the buyer fails to make the payments, the seller can repossess the copier, provided that the seller's security interest has been *perfected*. This means that a document known as a "financing statement" was filed with the appropriate governmental agency. In effect, it gives added protection to sellers who might sign an agreement with a buyer who then pledges the same collateral to someone else or who sells the pledged collateral before the contract has been paid in full.

FINANCING STATEMENTS. Check the applicable statutes in the place where the collateral is located to determine the place of filing a financing statement. Then write to the designated governmental agency and request a UCC-1 "Financing Statement" form. This form is fairly standard in the states that have adopted the UCC, but check for variations in your particular area. Other forms may also be needed such as a UCC-2 (duplicate) to file with another agency (if required) or a UCC-3 (amendment) if you want to change the original UCC-1 statement.

UCC financing statement forms are usually brief, and the secretary primarily fills in the blanks: debtor's name and address, lender's name and address, and items sold under a credit arrangement. The statement is then signed by the seller (secured party) and the buyer (debtor) before it is mailed to the designated agency for official filing. (Be sure to keep a copy for the office files.)

Filing Contracts and Other Legal Documents

A legal *contract* is an enforceable agreement between two or more parties. It must include a promise to give something, to do something, or to refrain from doing something; a *consideration* (something of value promised or given); parties who are legally capable of contracting; and a reasonable agreement among the parties as to what the contract means.

Although a contract does not have to be in writing to be valid, it usually is prepared as a computer or typewriter document that is signed by all parties. The form of a legal document will depend upon the issuer and what the instrument involves (sale of goods, labor contract, and so on). A simplified fill-in-the-blank form from your computer forms file may suffice in many cases. In others, a highly complex and detailed document prepared by an attorney may be required.

PREPARING THE DOCUMENT. Figure 28 illustrates a relatively standard form used in some law offices that can be adapted to other general needs. Prepare the document by typewriter or computer double-spaced on 8½- by 11-inch white bond paper. The specific terms of the agreement are described in the middle of the form. The exact wording should be specified by the firm's attorney or by your employer.

Print out a duplicate *original* for each signing party and make a copy for the files, as well as any additional copies requested by your employer. All parties must sign the document, and, if required, the corporate seals of the corporate parties to the agreement must be affixed and attested to by the corporate secretaries.

Some legal instruments also require an *attestation clause* to make them legal. This is a statement signed by witnesses that the parties to the agreement signed and sealed the document in their presence. An *acknowledgment* is a signed statement by the person who executes a legal instrument that the instrument is genuine. It is sworn before a notary public. The acknowledgment is prepared according to requirements in the state where it is to be recorded or used. Acknowledgments and similar legal requirements are usually prepared by an attorney.

Maintaining Securities and Property Records

To report dividend and interest income and capital gains and losses for tax purposes, federal, state, and local governments require that certain records be kept. Although state and local requirements vary from one place to another, federal regulations are the same everywhere. In the case of a corporation with large and diverse holdings, the record keeping is usually under the management of specialists in the financial area. But in many other offices the secretary may keep similar records for the company or for one or more executives in the firm. Two types of transactions in particular involve ongoing record keeping: securities transactions and real estate transactions.

FIGURE 28

Agreement between Corporations

THIS AGREEMENT, entered into on the _____ day of_____, 19—, by and between _____ CORPORATION, a corporation organized and existing under and by virtue of the laws of the State of _____, and having its office at _____, _____, hereinafter referred to as " _____," and THE _____ COMPANY, a corporation organized and existing under and by virtue of the laws of the State of _____, and having its office at_____, _____, hereinafter referred to as "_____,".

W I T N E S S E T H:

WHEREAS _____

_____; and

WHEREAS _____

_____

_____.

NOW, THEREFORE, in consideration of the premises

_____

_____.

IT IS AGREED:

1. _____

_____.

2. _____

_____.

IN WITNESS WHEREOF the parties hereto have on the day and year first above written caused these presents to be executed in their behalf and in their corporate names respectively by their proper officers hereunto duly authorized and their respective corporate seals to be hereto attached by like authority.

(Corporate Seal)   _____ CORPORATION

ATTEST: By _____
                                                President

_____
                 Secretary

(Corporate Seal)   THE _____COMPANY

ATTEST: By _____
                                            Vice President

_____
                 Secretary

(Number page in center, one-half inch from bottom.)

Source: Besse May Miller, revised by Mary A. De Vries, *Legal Secretary's Complete Handbook*, third edition (Englewood Cliffs, N.J.: Prentice-Hall, Inc. 1953, 1970, 1980).

SECURITIES RECORDS. To keep track of sales and purchases of securities, you need to record every transaction as it occurs. Often the data are keyed into the computer after a transaction has occurred, and current listings can then be printed out at any time. Investment-management software may be used to measure portfolio performance (stocks, bonds, and other securities) and develop long-range goals. The program may also prepare graphs and reports and provide figures for tax-return preparation.

If you need to keep securities records and files manually, you can use a standard form from an office-supply store or devise your own form. Individual records of transactions must be kept for each security. Figure 29 is an example of a format that could be added to your computer forms file and adapted for use in your investment record keeping.

1. Maintaining lists of investments. You may be expected to maintain a list of all investments or one list of all stocks owned, another of all bonds owned, another of mutual funds, and so on. The column headings on the form you use should include the following:

Name of stock (or bond, mutual fund, and so on)

Description

Number of shares (or face value)

Total cost (no. of shares times the cost per share)

Current market value

2. Maintaining income records. Keep a separate income (dividend or interest) record, with these column headings:

Name of stock (or bond, mutual fund, and so on)

Date of income

Amount received

Current total

REAL ESTATE RECORDS. Individuals and companies that have real estate holdings on which rental income and loss must be reported need reliable records to use in computing taxes due and in determining the profitability of the holdings. Although this type of information may be processed by a special department in a company, in some firms the secretary may be responsible for recording purchases, sales, and costs such as insurance,

FIGURE 29

Record of Securities Transactions

SECURITIES TRANSACTIONS

Name of Security _____

Exchange Where Listed _____

Broker _____ Telephone _____

Address _____

Location of Security _____

No. Shares	Certif. No.	Purchase or Sale	Date	Price/ Share	Broker's Commis.	Tax	Total Price	Net Receipt	Cap. Gain (Loss)	
									Short Term	Long Term

mortgage interest, and miscellaneous repair bills. Some real estate software will help you determine property values, income generated, amount of profit or loss, tax information, and other data.

A variation of Figure 30 can be used for this purpose to record information manually or by computer. Record all expenses such as building maintenance and real estate taxes in the "Expense" column. Depreciation and repairs such as plumbing repair are recorded in a separate column. After you adapt the form to suit your employer's needs, add the format to your computer forms file for future use.

HOW TO KEEP OFFICE AND COMPANY BOOKS

Office and company books of account may be maintained manually or with one of the numerous computer accounting programs. Electronic bookkeeping and accounting saves time primarily in the repetitive tasks and routine bookkeeping operations such as posting entries from journals to ledgers and in the calculations for and development of accounting financial statements. Accounting packages usually consist of *modules,* with each module handling a particular area of the accounting records, such as accounts receivable, payroll, or the general ledger.

Basic rules of bookkeeping and accounting apply to both manual and computer systems. For income tax purposes, for example, records must be kept on a cash or accrual basis. On a *cash basis,* cash is recorded when actually or constructively received and expenses when paid. (The IRS considers a check dated December 31 to be constructively received on December 31 even if you don't receive it until January 7 and don't deposit it until January 8.) On an *accrual basis,* income is credited to the period in which it is earned (not necessarily when received), and expenses are also assigned to the period incurred (not necessarily when paid).

System of Bookkeeping

The *system of bookkeeping* used in an office refers to the method of recording and classifying transactions. *Accounting,* on the other hand, is much broader and more complex than is bookkeeping, and it includes the analytical work such as interpreting financial data. Secretaries who work in organizations that do not have a separate accounting and bookkeeping

FIGURE 30

Real Estate Record

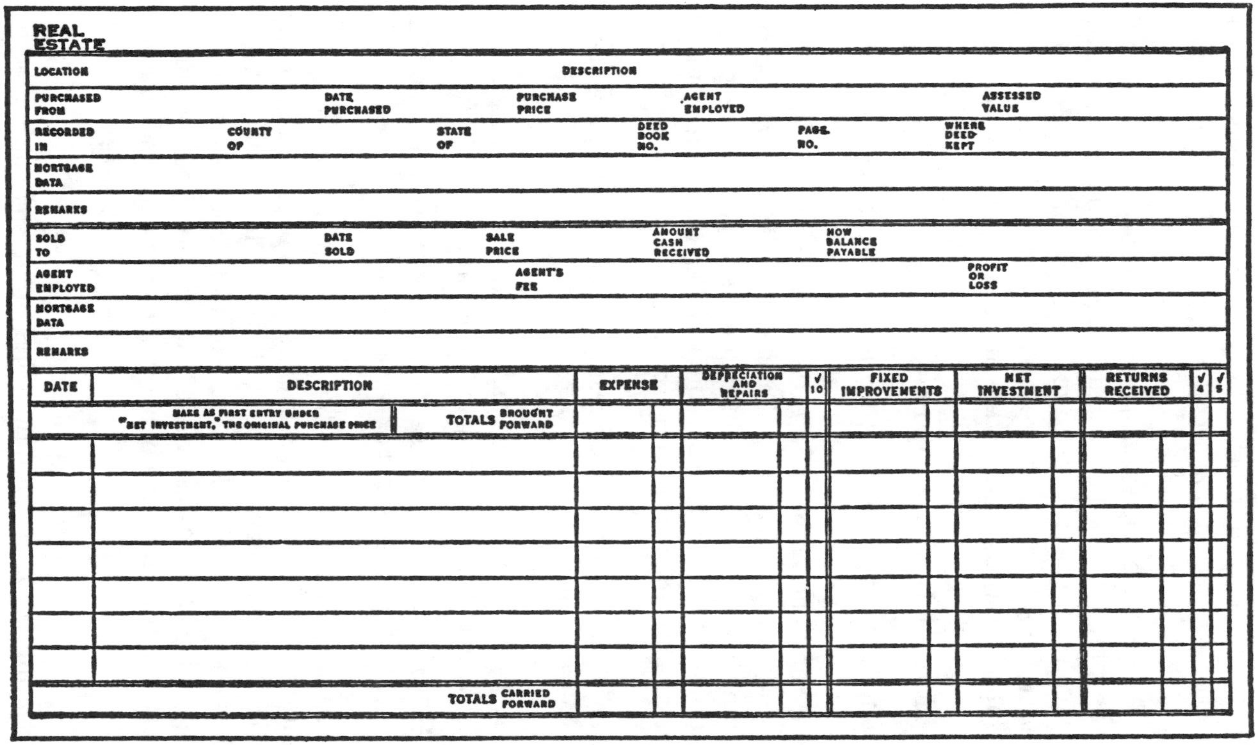
REAL ESTATE

LOCATION DESCRIPTION

PURCHASED FROM | DATE PURCHASED | PURCHASE PRICE | AGENT EMPLOYED | ASSESSED VALUE

RECORDED IN | COUNTY OF | STATE OF | DEED BOOK NO. | PAGE NO. | WHERE DEED KEPT

MORTGAGE DATA

REMARKS

SOLD TO | DATE SOLD | SALE PRICE | AMOUNT CASH RECEIVED | HOW BALANCE PAYABLE

AGENT EMPLOYED | AGENT'S FEE | PROFIT OR LOSS

MORTGAGE DATA

REMARKS

DATE	DESCRIPTION		EXPENSE	DEPRECIATION AND REPAIRS	√ 10	FIXED IMPROVEMENTS	NET INVESTMENT	RETURNS RECEIVED	√ 4	√ 5
	MAKE AS FIRST ENTRY UNDER "NET INVESTMENT," THE ORIGINAL PURCHASE PRICE	TOTALS BROUGHT FORWARD								
		TOTALS CARRIED FORWARD								

Source: Prentice-Hall Editorial Staff, revised by Mary A. De Vries, *Private Secretary's Encyclopedic Dictionary,* third edition (Englewood Cliffs, N.J.: Prentice-Hall, Inc., 1984).

staff often help with some of the mechanical aspects of bookkeeping and may even assist in certain accounting functions, such as preparing periodical financial reports.

The bookkeeping system used in most offices is called "double-entry bookkeeping." With this system, all transactions are recorded twice (in two accounts). The two basic types of books or computer files in which the transactions are recorded are called "journals" and "ledgers." The purpose of each type is explained in the following sections.

Basic Rules of Double-Entry Bookkeeping

To simplify the process of recording transactions in one of the books of account or computer files, numbers are often assigned to individual accounts, and the accounts are then arranged in numerical order in the general ledger. Each account has a debit (left) column and a credit (right) column. The principle behind double-entry bookkeeping is that each amount is entered in *both* a debit and a credit column, and the total of all debit balances must, therefore, equal the total of all credit balances.

DEBIT AND CREDIT ENTRIES. The recording of debit and credit entries is based on two basic rules:

1. *Debit entries* increase assets and expense accounts and decrease capital, income, and liability accounts.

2. *Credit entries* increase capital, income, and liability accounts and decrease assets and expense accounts.

An *asset* refers to something owned that has a money value such as furniture or cash on hand. A *liability* refers to something that is owed such as bills to be paid or taxes that will be due for payment. Assets minus liabilities equals the *capital*, that is, the difference between what a business owns and what it owes. Table 1 shows the types of entries you would make for transactions that either increase or decrease an account.

Journals

Journals are books or computer files of *original* entry—the first place you record a transaction. It doesn't matter whether you call one of these books the cash journal or cash receipts journal or the cash payments journal or

TABLE 1

Type of Entries for Each Class of Accounts

Class of Account	Type of Entry	
	When the Transaction Decreases the Account	When the Transaction Increases the Account
Asset	Credit	Debit
Liability	Debit	Credit
Capital	Debit	Credit
Income	Debit	Credit
Expense	Credit	Debit

cash disbursements journal. When cash journals are used, in addition to other special journals or a general journal, one of them—the *cash receipts journal*— is for all transactions involving the receipt of cash, and the other one—the *cash payments journal*—is used for all transactions involving the payment of cash. When such special journals are used, very few transactions remain. Those that are left are entered in a *general journal*. Finally, entries from all the journals are posted to the ledgers, which are the books or computer files of final entry.

CASH RECEIPTS JOURNAL. If you use a cash receipts journal, you will record each item of cash received during the month. Each amount must appear in two columns—a credit column and a debit column. Figure 31 illustrates how income might appear in a traditional cash receipts journal. (A check is placed in the checkmark column later when amounts are posted to the ledger.)

At the end of the month, all columns in the cash receipts journal are totaled (called "cross-footing"). The sum of debit columns must always equal the sum of the credit columns, or a mistake has been made. Column totals are then posted from the journal to the ledger.

CASH PAYMENTS JOURNAL. If you use a cash payments journal, handle the recording of cash payments the same as cash receipts. Individual entries must be recorded on a daily basis in the cash payments journal—each amount recorded in a debit column and repeated in a credit column. At

FIGURE 31

Cash Receipts Journal Entries

				Income Cr.			
				(102) Production Repairs	(103) Production Sales	Total Receipts Dr. (101)	Bank Deposits
Invoice	Date	Received From	√				
00271	Apr 5	E. Smith Co.		35.00		35.00	
00272	6	J. Morris			100.00	100.00	135.00
00273	9	W. Weiss Co.		16.00	214.00	230.00	230.00
00274	14	R. Feldman		72.00	180.00	252.00	252.00
00275	26	A. Etiozni		111.00	200.00	311.00	311.00
				234.00	694.00	928.00	928.00

CASH RECEIPTS JOURNAL April, 19XX — Page 6

the end of the month, total the columns and post each total to the appropriate ledger account. Figure 32 illustrates how cash payments might appear in a traditional cash payments journal. (Again, a check is placed in the checkmark column at the time each amount is posted to the ledger.)

GENERAL JOURNAL. If your business is small, you may use only one journal—a general journal. A general journal is also used for the transactions that do not fit logically in a cash receipts or cash payments journal (or in another special journal such as a sales journal or a purchases journal). This journal is also used to make adjusting and closing entries at the end of the accounting period. Entries from the general journal are posted to the ledger at the end of each month, just as they are posted from any of the special journals.

Figure 33 illustrates a printout of journal entries as recorded in a computer accounting system.

FIGURE 32

Cash Payments Journal Entries

| | | | | | | Office | Other, Dr. | |
| | | | | | Amount, | Exp. Dr. | | |
Ck. No.	Date	Paid to	For	√	Cr.	(204)	Item	Amount
140	Apr 1	V.C. Industries	Office Rent		1700.00		(308) Rent	1700.00
141	6	Office Supplies	Lamp		60.00	60.00		
142	11	Office Supplies	Stationary		98.00	98.00		
143	30	Postmaster	Postage		18.00		(260) Postage	18.00
					1876.00	158.00		1718.00

CASH PAYMENTS JOURNAL April, 19XX   Page 4

Ledgers

Ledgers—both subsidiary and general—are books or computer files of *final* entry (unlike the journals, which are books of original entry). The *general ledger* is the book where the miscellaneous accounts are kept.

GENERAL LEDGER. At the end of the month, columns from the journals are totaled to prepare for transfer to the general ledger. Figure 34 illustrates how the receipts would be posted in a traditional ledger, and Figure 35 illustrates how the payments would be posted in this ledger. (The notation "CR6" in the "Post Ref." column of Figure 34 refers to page 6 in the cash receipts journal. The notation "CP4" in the "Post Ref." column of Figure 35 refers to page 4 in the cash payments journal.)

The process of listing ledger accounts, showing the balance of all debits and all credits, is called "taking a trial balance." In ledgers, as in

FIGURE 33

General Journal Computer Printout

```
                        MADISON CONSULTANTS
                        GENERAL JOURNAL

                                                            PAGE 05
-------------------------------------------------------------------
TRANS DATE   ACCT. NO.   ACCT. NAME          DR.           CR.
-------------------------------------------------------------------
  41  0610   0110     STORE EQUIP          1000.00
             1200         ACCOUNTS PAYABLE                1000.00
-------------------------------------------------------------------
  42  0610   2300     SALARIES EXP         2600.00
             2410         FIT PAYABLE                      799.00
             2411         FICA PAYABLE                     115.85
             2412         INSUR. PAY                        26.00
             2413         UNION DUES PAY                    40.00
             2414         SALARIES PAY                    1619.15
-------------------------------------------------------------------
  43  0620   3460     PAYROLL TAX EXP       314.55
             2411         FICA PAYABLE                     207.75
             2415         SUTA PAYABLE                      87.20
             2416         FUTA PAYABLE                      19.60
-------------------------------------------------------------------
  44  0624   4100   . SALES RET & ALL       106.00
             2550     SALES TAX PAY           8.05
             1100         ACCOUNTS REC                     114.05
-------------------------------------------------------------------
  45  0625   1200     ACCOUNTS PAYABLE     1150.00
             4140         PURCH RET & ALL                 1150.00
-------------------------------------------------------------------
  46  0626   5160     OFFICE EQUIP          372.80
             1200         ACCOUNTS PAY                     372.80
-------------------------------------------------------------------
  47  0627   4100     SALES RET & ALL       200.00
             2550     SALES TAX PAY          12.00
             1100         ACCOUNTS REC                     212.00
-------------------------------------------------------------------
  48  0628   1360     STORE EQUIP           604.00
             1200         ACCOUNTS PAY                     604.00
-------------------------------------------------------------------
                     PAGE TOTALS           6367.40        6367.40
                                           =======        =======
```

FIGURE 34

Posting to the General Ledger from the Cash Receipts Journal

				CASH (101)				Page___1___
DATE	DEBIT	POST REF	AMOUNT	DATE	CREDIT	POST REF	AMOUNT	
19XX 4/30		CR6	928.00					

			INCOME FROM PRODUCT REPAIRS (102)				Page___2___	
DATE	DEBIT	POST REF	AMOUNT	DATE	CREDIT	POST REF	AMOUNT	
				19XX 4/30		CR6	234.00	

			INCOME FROM PRODUCT SALES (103)				Page___3___	
DATE	DEBIT	POST REF	AMOUNT	DATE	CREDIT	POST REF	AMOUNT	
				19XX 4/30		CR6	694.00	

FIGURE 35

Posting to the General Ledger from the Cash Payments Journal

			CASH (101)				Page___1___
DATE	DEBIT	POST REF	AMOUNT	DATE	CREDIT	POST REF	AMOUNT
19XX 4/30		CR6	928.00	19XX 4/30		CP4	876.00

			OFFICE EXPENSES (204)				Page___4___
DATE	DEBIT	POST REF	AMOUNT	DATE	CREDIT	POST REF	AMOUNT
19XX 4/30		CP4	158.00				

			RENT (308)				Page___5___
DATE	DEBIT	POST REF	AMOUNT	DATE	CREDIT	POST REF	AMOUNT
19XX 4/30		CP4	1700.00				

			POSTAGE (260)				Page___6___
DATE	DEBIT	POST REF	AMOUNT	DATE	CREDIT	POST REF	AMOUNT
19XX 4/30		CP4	18.00				

journals, the sum of all debits must equal the sum of all credits, and each amount must appear in both a debit and a credit column.

Figure 36 illustrates a printout of ledger entries as recorded in a computer accounting system.

Subsidiary Ledger. Your organization may use special ledgers as well as a general ledger. For example, some firms use an accounts receivable ledger and an accounts payable ledger. In the *balance form of account*, a special ledger has three columns: debit, credit, and balance. The third column—balance—would show, for example, how much a customer owes in total as of a certain date—the balance owed, in other words.

The number and types of ledgers (and journals) you use depends on the type of business your employer is engaged in and how complex your bookkeeping and accounting needs must be. The more complex the business, the more likely that operations will be computerized in a separate accounting department that handles both the record-keeping and analytical functions. Nevertheless, a secretary should be prepared to assist others who perform these functions, and a good place to start is with a general understanding of double-entry bookkeeping and a working familiarity with the principal books of original and final entry.

Balance Sheet

Two important financial statements are the balance sheet and the profit and loss, or income, statement. A *balance sheet* shows the financial status of a business on a particular date. Your employer may prepare a balance sheet at the end of each month or at the end of each quarter or only at the end of the year. The format is the same in any case, and your duties in preparing a balance sheet are also the same regardless of the time of year it is prepared.

If your computer program provides for the preparation of financial statements, you need only key in certain data or instruct the computer to locate the data already in its memory, and the computer will then perform the calculations, organize the data, and print it out in the proper format for the type of balance sheet you are preparing. Figure 37 is an example of an account form of balance sheet. Notice that the total assets equal the total liabilities and shareholders' equity.

A conventional balance sheet lists the assets of a company on the left (debit) side of a page and the liabilities and capital on the right (credit)

FIGURE 36

General Ledger Computer Printout

```
                          MADISON CONSULTANTS
                          GENERAL LEDGER
                          AS OF 06-30-XX
```

CASH				ACCOUNT NO.	800

DATE	EXPLANATION	REF	DEBIT	CREDIT	BALANCE
19XX					
0601	BEG. BAL.	---			25000.00 DR
0630	TOTAL	CR11	11200.00		36200.00 DR
0630	TOTAL	CPO3		907.23	35292.77 DR

CHANGE FUND				ACCOUNT NO.	810

DATE	EXPLANATION	REF	DEBIT	CREDIT	BALANCE
0601	BEG. BAL.	---			200.00 DR

PETTY CASH				ACCOUNT NO.	820

DATE	EXPLANATION	REF	DEBIT	CREDIT	BALANCE
0601	BEG. BAL.	---			100.00 DR

ACCOUNTS RECEIVABLE				ACCOUNT NO.	900 DR

DATE	EXPLANATION	REF	DEBIT	CREDIT	BALANCE
0601	BEG. BAL.	---			7000.00 DR
0611		J07		104.22	6895.78 DR
0618		J07		311.00	6584.78 DR
0630	TOTAL	S04	21003.00		27587.78 DR
0630	TOTAL	CR10		19102.00	8485.78 DR

FIGURE 37

Balance Sheet

```
                        THE MILL WORKS, INC.
                           Balance Sheet
                        December 31, 199-


                              ASSETS



Current assets:
  Cash and short-term investments                      $ 24,000
  Accounts receivable                                    70,000
  Inventories                                           122,000
  Prepaid expenses                                        33,000
     Total current assets                              $249,000

Fixed assets, at cost:
  Land                                    $180,000
  Buildings                                290,000
  Machinery and equipment                  175,000
                                          $645,000
  Less accumulated depreciation            160,000
     Total fixed assets                                 485,000

Other assets                                             70,000
  Total assets                                         $804,000




              LIABILITIES AND SHAREHOLDERS' EQUITY



Current liabilities:
  Accounts payable                                     $229,000
  Income taxes                                          105,000
  Other accrued liabilities                             306,000
     Total current liabilities                         $640,000

Long-term debt                                           50,000

Shareholders' equity:
  Common stock, $1 par value: 100,000 shares
    issued and outstanding                $ 50,000
  Additional paid-in capital                20,000
  Retained earnings                          44,000
     Total shareholders' equity                        $114,000
        Total liabilities and
          shareholders' equity                         $804,000
```

side. The sum of the left and right sides should be equal, or in balance. The heading of a balance sheet states the name of the business, the type of statement (balance sheet), and the date of the report.

Assets are usually given in the order of liquidity, with current assets first and fixed assets last. In other words, the current assets are more *liquid*; that is, they are more easily converted into cash. *Fixed assets* refers to permanent property used in the business. Liabilities that mature first are listed first, and those that mature last are listed last. Thus current liabilities are positioned ahead of long-term liabilities. A balance sheet is really a summary of the general ledger accounts.

Income Statement

An income statement shows the results of operating a business at the end of a specified period—whether a company made or lost money. Figures for this important financial statement are taken from the journals and ledgers. Like a balance sheet, an income statement may be generated automatically if your computer software provides for the preparation of financial statements. Before this statement (or a balance sheet) can be prepared, the journals and ledgers must be completely up to date.

A simple, short form of income statement will list what a company received, what it spent, and what it earned (assuming it received more than it spent). Management, owners, creditors, and others are very much interested in the economic picture revealed by this statement. Figure 38 illustrates an income statement covering the month of November.

Confidentiality in Bookkeeping and Accounting

Whereas accounting books, checkbooks, and other paper records can be locked in a file cabinet in a manual accounting system, information in a computerized accounting system requires extra security. Records are usually stored on diskettes, which should be protected against damage or erasure (always make backup copies) and locked in a secure location. Information retained, even temporarily, on a hard disk requires other security measures, such as the use of passwords or I.D. numbers by authorized personnel to access the information. Blank checks for a computerized check-writing system should be locked away the same as a conventional checkbook. Antiviral programs should be used or other care taken to prevent the loss of vast amounts of data through malicious destruction such

FIGURE 38

Income Statement

```
                    A. O. SCHWARZ, INC.

                    Income Statement
               Year Ended December 31, 199-


Income:
  Net sales                                    $560,000
  Dividend income                                11,900
     Total income                              $571,900


Expenses:
  Cost of goods sold             $228,500
  Selling expenses                 18,200
  Administrative expenses         102,000
  Federal income taxes             46,500
     Total expenses                             395,200
Net income:                                    $176,700
```

as a computer virus designed to destroy or disrupt payroll data and other computerized books and records. These measures are important to safe-guard material and protect the confidentiality of records pertaining to the firm, its customers, and its employees.

HOW TO HANDLE BILLINGS AND COLLECTING

Calculating Charges

Collecting money that is owed to your firm should be a preplanned function, even if your office is responsible only for occasional, miscellaneous collections. Firms that handle a huge number of transactions usually have a department especially geared to prepare invoices and process receipts electronically. In smaller firms or firms that handle a limited number of bills and receipts, the secretary may assist, manually or by computer, in calculating charges, preparing and mailing invoices, and processing incoming payments.

HOW TO DEVELOP A SYSTEM. One of the first steps is to develop a system for calculating charges if your office doesn't already have one. To do this, implement a computerized or manual system of record keeping that will account for the factors or materials that you expect someone to pay for: time, telephone calls, photocopying costs, mailing costs, supplies, merchandise, and so on. Some offices assume that some of these things are absorbed in the daily operating overhead. For instance, office stationery would not be charged to a particular customer in normal circumstances. Therefore, you need not keep track of the number of sheets of stationery used to prepare letters to a particular customer. On the other hand, perhaps your office does assign long-distance telephone charges to specific accounts. Professional persons, such as lawyers and accountants, keep track of time, telephone, photocopying, and other costs pertaining to a specific client's needs.

1. *Types of software programs.* Once you have established which costs must be borne by a customer/client, you can set up a recording procedure. Study the billing and invoice systems described in software catalogs and write to the developers for further information. (Some

firms have programs especially written to fit their own needs.) Many of these programs will track time and expenses for thousands of accounts and will generate invoices, print mailing labels, and produce reports. The invoices may be printed on blank paper or preprinted forms that you can order. With some systems you would enter the "who," "what," and "why" data and the invoice would be formatted and printed out automatically.

Different programs are designed to accommodate different-sized client or customer lists and the complexity of reporting that your firm needs. All software programs have different equipment requirements (e.g., amount of memory that your computer requires to run the program), and it is important to study the capabilities of your equipment as well as the capabilities of software programs that appeal to you.

2. Information needed for cost assignment. Some of the material listed here may be produced and recorded electronically in your office, depending on your equipment capability. Some modern equipment and systems automatically indicate charges per customer. With some telephone systems, for instance, you can precede each call with a customer code, and the telephone bill will then reflect charges per customer. Certain electronic postal equipment similarly provides a miniaccounting system. If charges are not recorded automatically, however, organize and keep receipts and other records for use in client cost assignment, for example:

Telephone message slips that identify time, date, and name of client, for verification of the telephone bill charges

A record of all time spent per employee on behalf of a client

A record of materials (e.g., photocopies) provided for work on behalf of the client

A record of postage and other mailing or fast-messaging expenses

Copies of any paid bills pertaining to other expenses incurred on behalf of a client

Many secretaries use desk calendars or devise forms to record time spent on each client. When it is time to bill the client, perhaps at the end of the month, they add up the total time spent per client. Similarly, many secretaries keep a tally sheet or log by the office photocopy machine on which they note all copies made per client. At the end of the month, or when it is time to prepare a bill, total photocopies are added together for each client. Electronic calendars can also be used on your computer to track projects, telephone calls, letters, clients, accounts, and other data for billing purposes.

Following Up Overdue Accounts

What do you do when someone doesn't pay the bill you send? Follow-ups are an everyday occurrence in the business world. Most billing and invoice software programs provide for follow-ups. They will keep a history of payments and credit balances in the computer memory so that second or third notices can be sent at the appropriate time on past-due accounts.

Sometimes routine follow-ups, such as sending second and third notices every thirty days, fail. The next step in your firm may be to write letters. Often a series of four to six letters is written, each letter worded more strongly than the previous one. Some offices also use standard collection notices available in office-supply stores (see Figure 39). Telephone calls—when the number of delinquent accounts is limited—are often effective in collection procedures too. Some firms even try calling on the customer in person. Mailgrams or some other form of fast message may be used to create a sense of urgency.

Often, when a series of collection letters is used, the final letter demanding payment by a specified date is sent by certified or registered mail. Such letters firmly insist on payment within a set period such as ten days or two weeks. The customer is told that the matter will be turned over to a lawyer or collection agency if payment is not forthcoming. Both agencies and attorneys that specialize in these matters will attempt to collect the delinquent account for a percentage of the amount that is due. As a final resort, the firm can always arrange for the attorney to sue the debtor.

STANDARD COLLECTION STATEMENTS. Letters, mailgrams, printed notices, telephone calls, and personal visits all make use of standard collection statements. How harshly or how gently each statement is worded depends on the firm's relations with the customer, the customer's attitude and intentions, the past-due amount involved, and how long overdue the account is. Each office follows a standard procedure and uses some or all of the following statements at some time:

FIGURE 39

First-Notice Collection Form

YOUR COMPANY NAME
Address/Telephone

JUST A FRIENDLY REMINDER . . . | If your check is already in the mail, please disregard this notice. If not, your prompt payment will be greatly appreciated. Thank you!

TO:

Invoice No.: _____

Date Due: _____

FIRST NOTICE

Amount Due: _____

1. You apparently forgot/overlooked your payment.

2. Please let us know if your check is in the mail.

3. May we have your check promptly?

4. Protect your credit standing by sending in your check immediately.

5. We will be happy to fill your order as soon as your past-due account is settled.

6. We value your friendship too much to resort to legal action. Won't you send us your check today?

7. Let us know if you are experiencing difficulty in making your payments. We may be able to devise a payment plan especially for you in this instance.

8. Urgent that we receive your payment by _____.

9. We must receive your check no later than _____ to avoid action by our attorney.

10. Unless we receive your full payment by _____, this matter will be turned over to the XYZ Collection Agency.

11. Payment by _____ will prevent repossession of your _____.

12. Failure to send your check has left us no choice but to instruct our attorney to proceed immediately with legal action.

PROS AND CONS OF COLLECTION EFFORTS. Although it may seem that the various collection steps involve more time and expense than an overdue account is worth, organizations nevertheless must have a system to discourage delinquency and make reasonable efforts to collect the payments that are essential for the firm to remain in business. The secretary who helps prepare the letters, printed notices, and other messages plays a vital role in maintaining the financial well-being of his or her employer.

Chapter 9

Maintaining Good Human Relations and Proper Etiquette

YOUR PROFESSIONAL IMAGE

Image—the portrait of ourselves that we present to others—is far more important than most people realize. Good skills and quality work are essential, but a poor image can cloud even the most perfect technical skills.

Your image will affect the receptiveness of coworkers to your ideas and requests—something that can be crucial when you need help or generally want to advance in your career. Clients and customers, too, will respond positively or negatively to the image you convey through dress, attitude, poise, courtesy, and ethical actions. Some of them may gain their first impression of your company through you.

In general, human relations experts recommend a helpful, cheerful, positive, and confident attitude combined with a neat, clean, conservative, and businesslike personal appearance. Specifically, they recommend that you develop as many of the following attributes as possible:

1. Develop healthful eating habits to help you look and feel better.

2. Use your dress, hair style, and so forth to convey confidence and professionalism. Experts say to dress for the job you want. To advance in many companies, this often means well-tailored businesslike apparel and an attractive and practical hair style. In other

words, dress as though you are attending a business meeting, not a rock concert or the opera.

3. Pay attention to your body language. Stand straight and walk with a confident stride. Avoid frowns and shifting, nervous glances. Look others directly in the eye when talking. Work hard to eliminate undesirable hand or other body movements and distracting habits such as chewing on a pencil.

4. Don't be tardy. Employers rank this high among their pet peeves.

5. Be courteous to *everyone* and take time to reply to any question or request, even when you're disagreeing with someone or are extremely busy and would prefer to avoid interruptions.

6. Be open to two-way communication. Always be willing to exchange ideas and learn from others.

7. Learn to accept new ideas and challenges with an air of excitement and enthusiasm rather than with debilitating fear and insecurity—it shows.

8. Learn how to work effectively under pressure. Don't interrupt your concentration with worry. Set a good pace and keep your mind on the work.

9. Have a positive attitude toward life in general and avoid negative responses that create friction at work. This includes cheerfully accepting extra work and staying late when necessary.

10. Develop a team attitude (in terms of cooperation but not at the expense of individual initiative) and be willing to accept help and delegate work to assistants.

11. Display your skills and talents—let others know what you can do. Your boss will be surprised and pleased to learn that you have untapped potential.

12. Be willing to change course or admit an error. In other words, be open to the demands of the moment. Don't avoid action or try to stay in the middle of the road simply because you are afraid you may be criticized later if you're wrong or if others disagree.

13. Never be cynical and sarcastic. It suggests an attempt to hide feelings of inferiority and insecurity.

14. Develop initiative. Become active rather than passive in offering suggestions, in asking necessary questions, and in handling tasks on your own.

15. Develop your leadership abilities. Learn how to delegate tasks, supervise assistants, and organize and manage projects on your own.

16. Read, listen, inquire—whatever is needed to become familiar with your job, your office, and your company—so that you will appear alert and knowledgeable in the presence of others.

ETIQUETTE IN THE OFFICE

Daily Greetings and Use of First Names

GREETINGS TO COWORKERS. There is no need to be unsure about whether you should greet certain people whom you do not know personally—those from another office getting on the elevator with you, a door attendant, an elevator operator, or the company president. The courtesy of saying "good morning" or "good night" to someone is universally acceptable in business. But this does *not* mean that you should try to promote a conversation with the company president.

USE OF FIRST NAMES. Most modern offices are informal, and the use of first names among fellow employees is the usual practice. But even in such offices, there are situations in which it is proper to use a title (*Mr., Ms., Mrs., Dr.*) and the person's last name. The most important rule is simple: Follow the practice that has been established in your office; ask a coworker if you are a newcomer and are uncertain. Generally, however, it is traditional to observe these common guidelines:

1. Addressing your supervisor. You should never address your boss or immediate supervisor by first name unless that person has informed you specifically that it is all right to do so. Even then, you should use a title in addressing the person in the presence of visitors. (Your boss or supervisor should extend that same courtesy to you.)

2. Addressing executives. You should never address a person of executive rank by first name, unless he or she tells you to do so. Addressing executives by title is the only practice that is accepted as conventional etiquette despite the informality that might exist in the office.

3. Addressing older men and women. It is not unusual for an older employee to prefer to be addressed by title by younger coworkers. Even if others in the office refer to an older employee by first name, it is best to wait before you take the same liberty if you are a newcomer in the office.

The New Employee

HELPING A NEW EMPLOYEE. A new employee appreciates it when coworkers provide a friendly reception and help familiarize the newcomer with the strange surroundings.

Giving a new employee a helping hand with his or her work also ensures that the employee will become productive more rapidly. It encourages the new employee to appreciate your company and to want to stay with it. But even if there were not practical reasons for making a new employee feel at home and for helping someone get started in a new job, business etiquette requires such efforts.

Many companies have an orientation program for new employees, but it does not take the place of personal friendliness and assistance from a coworker.

INTRODUCING NEWCOMERS TO COWORKERS. Make a point of seeing that new employees are properly introduced to the people with whom they will be dealing. It will help if they are also given some idea of what each person does. Names and faces are then easier to remember and newcomers get a general idea of how their jobs fit in with those of others.

INVITING NEWCOMERS TO LUNCH. Be certain to invite new employees to join you and other coworkers for lunch. This is a particularly good way to help someone new feel at home and part of the team. Take advantage of this time to find out the newcomer's interest in work-related matters and cooperative efforts such as car pools.

SCHEDULING PERIODIC CONFERENCES. For the first week or two, schedule daily 10- to 15-minute conferences to discuss both routine work and special projects and to answer any questions the newcomer has. After this initial period, you may want to schedule weekly conferences until the newcomer is thoroughly familiar with the work. Such brief meetings will help eliminate confusion and save time in the long run by increasing the newcomer's familiarity with the work and with office procedures, thereby lessening the prospects of time-consuming mistakes and later problems.

OBSERVING THE RULES WHEN YOU ARE A NEWCOMER. A newcomer should observe certain rules of etiquette. If you are the newcomer, here are a few suggestions that may help you get a practical and congenial start on a new job.

1. *Don't be a critic.* It is rude and useless to try to impress others by telling them how much better your previous employer handled matters or to point out mistakes you see them making. Once you have established a working relationship with the other workers and with your boss, your suggestions will stand a much better chance of being accepted instead of resented.

2. *Don't be too friendly too soon.* Use some restraint in your first few days on a job. Give those already on the job a chance to make the friendly advances. You not only avoid giving the impression that you are pushy and forward but also avoid forming alliances that you may later regret.

3. *Know what to do when you are invited to lunch.* On your first day, a few persons may ask you to have lunch with them. Generally, you are expected to pay for your own lunch, even if your immediate supervisor is in the group. If your immediate supervisor invites you to have lunch with him or her alone, generally the superior pays for your lunch.

Refreshments in the Office

TAKING DAILY BREAKS. Having refreshments is an established practice in American business, but a few cautions are in order:

1. Be neat. Bread or cookie crumbs, beverage stains, cluttered ashtrays, and unwashed coffee cups are unsightly.

2. Observe common table manners when eating and drinking at your desk.

3. Observe your company's policy regarding no-smoking areas.

4. Don't let your refreshments interfere with business. The excuse for a break is that it increases efficiency, but the practice of taking refreshments at work can be harmful to business if not used with discretion. If a coworker, a business caller, or an executive comes to your desk while you are taking a break, you should give your full attention to the caller, and you should never keep a visitor waiting while you finish eating or drinking.

5. Don't stretch your pause for refreshments with a second cup of coffee, an extra helping of food, or even some chewing gum.

6. Do not pause while you are taking a break to attend to personal grooming at your desk unless you are clearly alone. Application of makeup, combing of hair, filing of nails, and so on are most properly attended to in the restroom.

7. Follow the practice in your office regarding the purchase of refreshments. Often coworkers take turns in going out to get refreshments for everyone or in making coffee in the office. If there is no office coffee fund, employees should pay for their own refreshments or take turns purchasing coffee for the office coffee machine. It is perfectly proper to ask for payment from anyone who fails to pay you in advance or fails to reimburse you.

PROVIDING REFRESHMENTS FOR VISITORS. If guests arrive while you are having coffee, and your desk is near the area where they are visiting, it is usually appropriate to offer them a cup of coffee (or other beverage) also. If guests are already waiting, postpone having your refreshments until you are alone.

Each office has its own practice. In some small, professional offices, the secretary or the executive always offers the visitor a cup of coffee. In other large business reception rooms, no effort is made to offer refreshments to the numerous callers coming and going.

Etiquette and Safety in Office Lines and Parking Lots

ETIQUETTE IN OFFICE LINES. In many business situations, employees must line up and await their turns. Although no one enjoys having to wait, rules of etiquette must be followed in getting on and off elevators; lining up in the cafeteria or lunchroom; waiting for the drinking fountain; punching the time clock, morning and afternoon; and so on. Time clocks create a double problem. Latecomers may rush down the hall, without regard for their own safety or that of others, to punch the clock just before it changes from 9:00 to 9:01 A.M. In the afternoons, the rush for first place in the line to punch out is not only a breach of etiquette but is a violation of traditional company safety rules.

SAFETY IN THE PARKING LOT. Many employees tend to forget their manners, as well as their own safety and that of others, in a wild dash to get to work on time or to be the first one out of the parking lot or garage. If you calmly continue working for 5 to 10 minutes after quitting time, you will find that you can get out easily and just as soon as if you had rushed to join the traffic jam.

RECEIVING VISITORS

Receiving and Greeting Callers

METHODS OF RECEIVING CALLERS. Organizations have different methods of receiving callers. In large companies, all callers go to a reception room or desk where a trained receptionist takes care of the preliminaries and advises the secretary that a caller has arrived. (Each morning it is helpful to give the receptionist a list of callers you expect during the day.) The secretary then goes to the reception room, introduces himself or herself, and escorts the visitor to the office, if the caller has an appointment. Do not attempt to carry on a conversation at this time, but do respond cordially to any remarks or questions.

In small companies the telephone operator may double as receptionist, or a messenger or some other person who has been trained in the preliminaries may greet the visitor.

HOW TO GREET CALLERS. Formality is appropriate in greeting an office caller. Say, "How do you do?" or "Good morning," or "Good afternoon," not merely "Hello." Let the caller make the first gesture toward shaking hands. If your desk is at the entrance of the office or in a convenient or conspicuous location, you need not rise to speak to a caller unless he or she is a person of considerable importance or much older than you. After your greeting, if the caller does not volunteer any information, your next move is to ask, "May I help you?"

If a talkative caller is making small talk with you when an important businessperson enters the office to keep an appointment, but the caller does not notice the businessperson, try to draw the conversation to a pause or a close gracefully, without appearing to silence the talk. If you cut into the conversation abruptly, you will embarrass both persons.

Determining the Purpose of a Call

Depending on office policy, you may be expected to ask why a caller wants to see his or her employer, not only when the caller comes to the office unexpectedly but when telephoning for an appointment. Some employers object to this practice, believing that visitors may be offended by what they would perceive as a secretary prying into their private affairs. But certain high-level executives or those who have very hectic schedules feel compelled to maintain some control over their appointments.

If a visitor presents a business card upon arrival, you may be able to tell the reason for the visit from the card. Perhaps the caller is a sales representative. Or you may understand the purpose of the visit from previous correspondence or visits. The "voice with a smile" is never more useful than when you are trying to get information from a caller or when you must refuse to let someone see your employer. This duty requires discretion, tact, and patience. Fortunately, a visitor who makes a call in good faith rarely objects to telling the purpose of the visit.

GREETING CALLERS. You might say, "Good morning, Ms. Jones. I'm Mr. Brown's secretary. He's busy at the moment, but is there anything I can do for you?"

Or: "Good morning. I'm Mr. Brown's secretary. He's not in the office now, but is there anything I can do for you?"

Or: "Good morning, Ms. Jones. I'm Mr. Brown's secretary. What can I do for you?"

Or: "You're waiting to see Mr. Brown? I'm Sara Edwards, Mr. Brown's secretary. May I be of help?"

1. Caller states business. Assuming that the caller's business is of interest to your boss, you might say, "I'm afraid I can't arrange a definite appointment right now because I don't know what additional commitments Mr. Brown has made since I last saw him. But if you'll let me have your telephone number, I'll call you either later today or surely tomorrow morning and arrange an appointment for you. I know Mr. Brown will be glad to see you."

Or you may arrange a definite appointment on the spot; you may take the caller in to see your employer, you may arrange for the caller to see an assistant, or you may handle the matter yourself. Each situation will be different, and you should make a judgment as the occasion requires.

2. Caller refuses to state business. If office policy requires that you make every effort to find out the caller's business, you might say, "I'm afraid I'm not permitted to make appointments without letting Mr. Brown know what visitors want to discuss. Could you give me a general idea?"

Or: "Unfortunately, Mr. Brown is only able to see people by appointment. Since I make all his appointments, I'll need to know what you would like to discuss with him."

Or: "Could you let me know what you want to see Mr. Brown about? That's the first thing he always asks me to find out."

If the caller still refuses, you might say, "I'm really sorry, Ms. Jones, but I'm obligated to follow our office rules. Without some indication of the business you want to discuss, I'm not authorized to set up an appointment."

Or: "If you'd rather not say anything now, I understand. Perhaps you could write a confidential note to Mr. Brown, briefly telling him what you want to see him about and asking for an appointment. I'm sure he'll be happy to see you."

Making Callers Comfortable

Show callers where to leave their hats, coats, briefcases, and any other articles that are not needed for the appointment. Offer to hang up their coats.

When callers have to wait, ask them to have a seat. If they have to wait any length of time, provide newspapers and magazines. If callers deserve special attention, ask: "Is there anything I can do for you while you're waiting?" If they would like to look up something in the telephone directory or make a call, offer to look up a number, but do not insist. Point out a private telephone, if there is one, and be sure not to show any unnecessary interest in a private discussion.

Do not begin a conversation with waiting visitors, but if they show an inclination to talk, respond. Choose topics in which they are likely to be interested, but avoid controversial issues. Never tell your employer's friend a story you know that he or she would enjoy telling. If a visitor asks questions about the business, reply only in generalities.

Announcing Callers

When your employer is ready to receive a guest, you may do one of two things. If the caller is known to your employer and has visited the office before, you may nod and say something to the effect that "Mr. Wilson is free. Won't you go right in?" However, if it is the caller's first visit, or if the caller is an infrequent visitor, go along to the door of your employer's office, step to one side, and say, "Mr. Wilson, Mr. Smith." *Or:* "Mr. Wilson, this is Mr. Smith."

When older people or dignitaries are announced in a business office, it is usually considered proper to mention the guest's name first. The name mentioned first is the person being honored. For instance, should a church dignitary visit your employer, the polite announcement would be, "Bishop McLeish, Mr. Wilson."

CALLERS WITH AN APPOINTMENT. If you have a receptionist, give her or him a list of appointments each day. The receptionist will then be in a position to handle your callers courteously and efficiently.

When a caller with an appointment arrives, notify your employer immediately unless he or she is in a conference that cannot be interrupted. You might say something over the intercom such as, "Ms. Carter is here for her 10 o'clock appointment. May I bring her in?" If the caller is already in your office, near your desk, it is better to go into your employer's office and announce that the caller has arrived. When your employer is ready, say, "Will you come with me, Ms. Carter?" and introduce her as described earlier.

1. When a caller must wait. If your employer has to keep a caller with an appointment waiting, explain the delay, for example: "Mr.

Grant has someone with him at the moment, but he'll be free in a few minutes. Will you have a seat?" If the delay will last for any length of time, tell the caller the approximate time that it will be necessary to wait. The caller can then decide whether to wait or make a later appointment. (If you know that your employer is not going to be able to keep an appointment promptly, notify the person before he or she leaves the office.)

2. *When your employer is called away.* Say something such as, "Good morning, Mr. Hughes. Ms. Smith was called into the plant about 10 minutes ago. She should be back any minute now. Do you mind waiting?"

If an unexpected emergency will keep your employer out of the office for more than a few moments, you might explain the absence this way: "Good morning, Mr. Hughes. I'm afraid that Ms. Smith was called to the office of the chairman of the board a little while ago. I'm not sure when she'll be back. I tried to reach you, but your secretary said that you had already left. Would you like to wait, or would you prefer to come back or talk with someone else?"

CALLERS WITHOUT AN APPOINTMENT. Usually, when a person your employer will see calls at your office without an appointment, you know the person well enough to greet him or her by name: "Good morning, Ms. Douglas. It's nice to see you again." You might briefly inquire about her family or ask about her recent vacation. Then ask the nature of the unexpected visit. After you learn the purpose of the call, if you have the least doubt about whether your employer wants to see the visitor, ask.

If your employer is busy, ask the caller to wait, explaining approximately how long it will be. Unless the unexpected caller is someone your employer is always especially eager to see, the delay may make the caller realize that it is better to make an appointment. You might limit the unexpected caller's visit by saying, "Mr. Roberts has another appointment in 10 minutes, but he'll be glad to see you in the meantime."

Perhaps a crowded schedule makes it inconvenient for your employer to see the unexpected caller at that time. Explain the situation, assuring the caller that a visit at any other time would be most welcome. Offer to make a future appointment if your employer is interested.

Greeting Callers Your Boss Will See

CALLS BY FRIENDS OF YOUR EMPLOYER. Some visitors are important clients or friends whom your boss will almost always see.

1. How to announce the caller. When a friend of your employer calls, announce and escort the visitor to your employer's office.

2. What to do when your employer is away. If a visitor arrives without an appointment and your employer is out, do everything possible to make the caller comfortable (offering newspapers, for example) until your employer arrives. If your employer is not expected, express his or her regret at not seeing the caller and ask if the caller can return another time. Never ask a visitor to wait in your employer's office, unless he or she has told you to permit this. Do everything you can to make your employer's friend feel welcome, but never be overly friendly.

CALLS BY OFFICE PERSONNEL. In many business organizations today, top officials keep an open door to the office personnel. The secretary must usually make the appointments, but if the open-door policy prevails, the secretary does not inquire about the purpose of the appointment.

Always treat officers and executives of the company with respect, but it is not necessary to stand up every time an officer enters your office. You should, however, offer the caller a chair if he or she has to wait.

Occasionally, you can save time for your employer and also do a favor for a young, new employee who wants to see your employer. In an appropriate situation you might say, "What's on your mind, Joe? Anything I can do?"

If Joe hedges, you might say, "Do you want to sit down and tell me about it? Maybe I can help."

If Joe tells you about it, you might say, "I'll be glad to talk to Ms. Abbott about this, and then we'll let you know what can be done."

Or you might go to Ms. Abbott and say, "Joe Brown, a new member of the Mailing Department, has a problem he needs your advice about. If you can see him for a minute, I think you could be of help."

Or you might say to Joe, "Do you think you should discuss that with Ms. Abbott? You'll be going over the head of your immediate supervisor. Why don't you tell Mr. Jacobs [the immediate supervisor] how you feel. I have a feeling he will do anything he can to straighten things out for you."

Use your own judgment in each situation, but if a caller does not want to confide in you, do not urge the person to do so.

Handling Callers Your Boss Will Not See

When you know that your employer is not interested in the purpose of the visit or is too busy to see the caller, you might say, "I wish I could be more helpful, but Ms. Evans is concerned with some emergencies and will be involved for some time; therefore, she has to limit her appointments to matters directly connected with business activity. It will be quite a while before this situation changes, so it would probably be best for you to take up the matter with her in writing."

Or you might ask the caller if you or another person could be of help. If the caller has sales material or samples to distribute, offer to take the samples and show them to the appropriate person at an opportune time.

CALLERS SOLICITING CONTRIBUTIONS. When a caller states that his or her business is to solicit a contribution, you might say, when applicable: "Unfortunately, the demands on Mr. Lewis for donations are so numerous that he's forced to limit his contributions to those charitable causes that he's contributed to for years, and he's just not able to add to that list. I'm sure you can understand his situation." If you have any doubts about your employer's wishes, however, ask what he or she prefers in regard to new solicitations.

CALLERS YOU REFER ELSEWHERE. When you find that the purpose of a caller's visit involves a matter that should be taken up with another person in the organization, you might say, "That's something handled for Ms. Johnson by Mr. Smith. I'll be glad to make an appointment for you, or if he's not busy now, I'm sure he'll be happy to see you right away."

Or: "I wonder if you could take this up with Mr. Smith of our Sales Department. He's more familiar with the matter than Ms. Johnson and can be of more help to you."

If the caller agrees to see Mr. Smith, get Mr. Smith on the telephone and explain the situation. Then say, "Mr. Smith will be glad to see you now. Just go to the fourth floor and tell the receptionist that Mr. Smith is expecting you." Or, if necessary, tell the caller, "I'm afraid that Mr. Smith can't see you this morning, but he asked if you could come in at 11 o'clock tomorrow."

If the caller objects because he cannot see your employer personally, tell him you're sorry but the instructions are made by your employer and you have to abide by them.

PROBLEM CALLERS. Persistent and emotional callers pose a problem for both the secretary and the executive.

1. Persistent callers. Some callers simply will not accept any explanation you give for being unable to see your employer. A few may become rude or even threatening. Most problem callers are more persistent and annoying than dangerous, and with them you should be just as persistent—but polite—in making the explanations and suggestions described in the previous section. In other words, insist that you are not authorized to change procedures. But always assure the caller that he or she can write a letter to your employer and that you will be certain that your employer sees it.

2. Threatening callers. Should a caller become threatening, speak *privately* with your employer or ring for security if your company has such a system. Do not attempt to cope with someone who is abusive and potentially dangerous.

3. Emotional callers. Certain situations are emotional, although not abusive or threatening. Perhaps a man who has just lost his job is extremely upset. Female secretaries should secure male assistance—your employer or another person—in calming an emotionally troubled male caller. If the emotional caller is a woman, a female secretary may be able to calm the troubled visitor. If not, consider asking another—preferably mature—female employee to help.

4. Con artists. Businesses are sometimes troubled by unscrupulous vendors. A common tactic involves calling a secretary and stating that a previous order is almost ready to be shipped. All that is needed is some final information for the shipping order or packing slip, such as the specific delivery address and the credit-card number. To protect yourself and your employer, never divulge such information over the telephone or in person without first verifying that an order actually was placed and that it, indeed, is to be charged to a particular account or someone's credit card.

In general, be suspicious of products or services being sold (1) at an unrealistically low price, (2) by a person or organization that hasn't been in business very long, or (3) by a person or organization that has no mailing address or telephone number where you can call back later after checking the situation.

Handling Telephone Calls During a Meeting

HOW TO INTERRUPT A CONFERENCE. Try to avoid interrupting a conference, but if it is essential to enter a room where your employer is in conference, do so quietly and unobtrusively. Type on a slip of paper any message that must be delivered to someone in the conference room. If you want instructions, type the questions. Your employer can then handle the matter with a minimum of interruption. If it is essential to announce a caller to your employer while he or she is in conference, simply take in the visitor's card or type the name on a slip of paper.

When a visitor overstays an appointment, buzz your employer on the intercom to announce another appointment. In some offices, the executive has a concealed bell that can be rung unobtrusively when he or she wishes to terminate a conference. The secretary can then enter the room and remind the executive about another appointment.

HOW TO HANDLE TELEPHONE CALLS FOR A VISITOR. When there is a telephone call for a visitor, ask the person calling if it is possible for you to take a message. If so, type the message on a sheet of paper, addressing it to the visitor, and also type your name, the date, and the time at the bottom of the sheet. No visitor should be required to decipher strange handwriting.

If the person calling insists on speaking to the visitor, go into the conference room and, with a glance that takes in both your employer and the visitor, apologize for the interruption: "Excuse me, Mr. Howard [looking at the visitor], Mr. Davis is on the telephone and has asked to speak with you immediately. Do you want to take it here?" (Indicate which telephone to use.) If he says yes, put the call through. Often, however, the visitor says that he will call back, in which case you would give that message to the person calling and type out the telephone number as a reminder for the visitor.

If several people are in conference with your employer and you must deliver a message to one of them, type it and take it to that visitor, just as you would to your employer. If the visitor is wanted on the telephone, also type on the message: "Do you want to take the call in the outer office?" The visitor can then leave the conference without disturbing the others.

Seeing Callers Out

You may find it necessary to remind your employer that it is time for the next appointment—a cue to a visitor that it is time to leave. Or if your employer warns you in advance that your assistance may be needed in cutting a visit short, you might interrupt politely with a reminder that it is time for your employer to leave or to attend some other meeting. As visitors prepare to leave, help them collect their articles and show them to the door, saying "Good-bye" with a pleasant smile. If your building is large and a visitor is a stranger, point out the way or escort the person to the elevator or lobby.

MANAGING PERSONAL SKILLS AND HUMAN RELATIONS

Working for and with Others

WORKING FOR ONE PERSON.   In the modern office the employer-secretary relationship is—or should be—a matter of teamwork. Each person must respect what the other contributes to the smooth and successful functioning of the office. One of the best ways to foster such respect is to keep the channel of communication open. Talk often and try to keep your employer well informed about office activities. Similarly, try to keep informed about your employer's activities and needs. As the occasion arises, volunteer to do nonroutine tasks and openly demonstrate your willingness to participate in the successful functioning of the office.

Often it is necessary to put personal preferences and opinions aside to develop an effective working relationship. Secretaries who work for one person must recognize their responsibility in cooperating with and assisting their employers. This may mean supporting—in the office and outside—policies and practices you personally disagree with. However, it is perfectly appropriate to make recommendations and offer ideas for your employer's consideration.

Learn to accept criticism graciously and gratefully. Use it as a means to become more capable and successful. Similarly, if you see an error your employer has made, point it out tactfully. For example, if your boss makes a mathematical error in a report and if you discover the correct figure and it is minor, correct it and avoid any reference to it. If it is important, however, point out your change and ask if your boss would mind checking it. If your boss finds an error in a report prepared by an assistant working under your supervision and asks who did it, tell him or her but add that it is your responsibility. (If the error is indicative of a recurring problem, this may be an opportunity to discuss corrective steps with your assistant. If a slow assistant prevents you from completing assignments quickly, do not report this to your boss; find out why the assistant is slow and help him or her along. If that does not solve the problem, get another assistant.)

Be prepared to overlook personal traits in your employer that annoy you. If the relationship is going to work, it will take your full attention just to be supportive and cooperative and to do your part in ensuring that the relationship works for the benefit of your company at all times.

WORKING FOR MORE THAN ONE PERSON. Even when you work for two or more persons, the combination should be viewed as a team. Everyone still has the same overall objective: to contribute to the successful operations of the company.

Secretaries who work for several executives must be particularly adaptable. After all, each executive has his or her own personality and method of working. One person may be more demanding than another. One may expect you to work more independently than another. You will have to adjust your work habits to each situation.

One of the major problems concerns scheduling. If two rush jobs reach you at once, which person do you favor? Unless one executive is the superior and another the subordinate, you should avoid any appearance of favoritism. Explain any conflict that arises to *each person* and ask *all of them* for assistance in resolving the situation. It is important that each one be aware of your work load and any serious problems in scheduling. But try to avert potential problems by anticipating task and time requirements and organizing your work to accommodate each person's needs.

WORKING WITH OTHER DEPARTMENTS. In large companies, many of your contacts will be with coworkers in other departments. The training department may need to work closely with the sales staff, or the public relations office may need to work closely with the mail department. Sometimes one department is faced with a rush job and needs to call on another department for assistance and cooperation.

Be certain to contact the appropriate person in each department, and try to develop good relations with that person. When someone frequently helps you, try to reciprocate and at least make a point of expressing your appreciation at every occasion.

Avoid antagonisms that could develop when one department appears to be giving priority to someone else's request. Try to find out why. Perhaps the secretary with the priority work would be willing to let your job go first. Or perhaps there was simply a misunderstanding in handling your work. Someone may be preoccupied with a personal problem and is creating a problem for you unintentionally (always look behind the scenes before you make a hasty judgment). At any rate, aim to *discuss* problems and encourage a spirit of good human relations in your dealings with coworkers in other offices and departments.

WORKING WITH A SATELLITE OFFICE. Telecommuting is common in certain businesses and for certain positions, such as field representative. If your employer works from a location away from the company facilities, such as a home office, you will need to adjust your practices to make greater use of telephone, facsimile, and computer communication.

You may be expected to assume greater responsibility in the office if your boss is not on the premises every day. This may involve learning more about your employer's activities so that you can answer questions on your own, find documents or other material without your boss's assistance, and solve unexpected problems, such as a computer breakdown, without help or instruction from your boss. In the beginning, this may seem like a heavy burden, but in time you will become comfortable with your increased responsibility and long-distance communication.

In this type of operation it is important to clarify the limits of your authority. If you type a report, for example, to be sent to the company president, should you first fax a copy to your boss in the satellite office? Or are you authorized to proofread it and send it to the president on behalf of your boss? If your computer system fails, are you permitted to have it fixed? Or must you first telephone your boss for approval?

Make a list of situations that might arise and give the list to your boss so that he or she can indicate the preferred procedure. This will help to ensure that misunderstandings won't occur later. But if something else occurs and you are uncertain about the limits of your authority, telephone your boss and try to postpone action until you have a reply. If your boss is unavailable, ask his or her immediate supervisor or someone else designated by your boss as an emergency contact.

Initiating and Managing Projects

BECOMING AN INITIATOR. Busy executives need secretaries who can work independently. They simply don't have time to decide everything that needs to be done around the office or to help the secretary start each project. The secretary who can proceed on his or her own initiative is a great asset in any organization.

To become an initiator, you need to become a thinker and have some imagination. As you observe activity in your office, stop to think whether everything is being handled in the most efficient, logical manner. You may decide that the filing system needs streamlining or that the storeroom needs reorganizing or that better records of incoming and outgoing mail should be kept. Naturally, you're not looking for work just for the sake of looking for work. The question is whether some change or new procedure would truly improve operations. If it would and it is nothing requiring your employer's approval, start the project on your own. Think it through (pros and cons), plan the steps you must take, and then simply begin.

Your ideas may involve more than changes you can make on your own. Learn to state the needs and benefits you visualize in clear, persuasive language, so that you can present your ideas to your employer. Not all of your proposals may be accepted, but if your ideas are realistic, many of them will be. If they are accepted, again develop your own plan and simply begin. If you need the cooperation and assistance of others, find ways to motivate them as well.

COORDINATING AND MANAGING PROJECTS. Leadership qualities are important when it comes to coordinating and managing projects. Some of the most essential qualities are the ability to organize, to set priorities and standards, to delegate work, to solve problems, to motivate others, and to schedule work and meet deadlines.

1. Coordination. Coordinating a project means making everything and everyone work together effectively to achieve some ultimate common goal. If your special project is to produce a newsletter, you may need to coordinate the work of writers, artists, photographers, desktop publishing operators, and the mail room. In other words, you need to work out each aspect of production, so that everything and everyone will pull together at the right time in the right way.

2. Management. Managing a project means controlling and directing all aspects of it. To manage effectively, you need to plan the various steps, secure the assistance you need, and delegate each phase of activity to the appropriate people, setting stands and guidelines and supervising their work throughout the project. You need to schedule everything to meet your deadline and to ensure that everyone else completes his or her task as required. This means constant communication. You must decide upon and explain the standards to be followed (the scope and quality of work required—the yardstick for you and others to use in deciding whether all facets of the work are being performed satisfactorily). As problems arise, you need to deal with them, working out solutions and making decisions, often instantaneously. Generally, you need to oversee the entire project and make it work. One thing management instructors often fail to mention: you also need to have some fun.

Managing Time and Money

MANAGING YOUR OWN TIME. The way you manage your own time depends in part on the type of work you do. But, generally, experts believe that you must, first, be very critical about each thing that you do and, second, learn how to do high-priority work better. Managing your time more successfully may involve some drastic changes in your habits. Here are some steps that will get you started:

1. Set goals and write down everything you want or need to do.

2. Set priorities; that is, arrange your goals in order of importance.

3. Plan your time by scheduling each task and setting deadlines, using calendars, planners, checklists, and anything else that will help.

4. Delegate work to assistants to allow more time for important matters.

5. Learn to say no to wasteful, unnecessary intrusions.

6. Control interruptions by discouraging unnecessary visiting and by reorganizing and rescheduling your work to fit quiet and busy periods.

7. Develop better communications to avoid repeating conversations and having to redo work.

8. Avoid time-wasting, unproductive squabbles with coworkers.

9. Look for ways to improve the processing of mail, correspondence, and other recurring items.

10. Take time to do each job right the first time, since it will take much more time to do it all over later.

11. Group your activities; for example, run all errands in one trip.

12. Organize each task before you start it, so that you won't have to stop midway because of something you forgot.

13. Make use of downtime, such as when a telephone call is on hold, by planning future activities.

14. Schedule work according to your physical strength, doing the hardest jobs when you have the most energy.

15. Simplify tasks, for example, using the telephone instead of taking off time for a personal visit.

16. Avoid procrastination by starting with something you like to do.

17. Work on ways to improve your concentration and shut out nuisance distractions.

18. Make better use of available technology (machines, services, and so on) to simplify otherwise tedious, time-consuming manual tasks.

LEARNING TO BE COST CONSCIOUS. Increasing costs threaten businesses of all sizes, and wasteful habits are taboo. Since secretaries use and often purchase so many of the supplies in an office, they must be as concerned as their employers about managing money and materials. Learning to be cost conscious should be the goal of every secretary.

Here are some things that will help you eliminate waste and establish better control over office expenditures:

1. Learn to control expenditures by budgeting and anticipating your needs and expenses over selected periods such as a month or a quarter.

2. Keep accurate records to compare costs and usage from one period to another, to forecast future needs and costs, and to determine priorities.

3. Order supplies for extended periods when practical to take advantage of bulk discounts.

4. Organize your work to avoid duplication and unnecessary waste of stationery, supplies, and so on.

5. Use credit wisely to avoid unnecessary finance charges in purchasing supplies, and shop where returns are accepted and money is refunded.

6. Deal only with reliable suppliers who provide quality products and stand behind their goods.

7. Avoid unnecessary correspondence and mailings, grouping frequent communications whenever possible.

8. Eliminate unnecessary long-distance telephone calls and fast-delivery services for messages that are not urgent.

9. Read available books and articles on money management and purchasing.

10. Remember that "time is money" in business and become time-conscious as well as cost conscious.

Interviewing and Supervising Assistants

FINDING AND INTERVIEWING NEW EMPLOYEES. Many secretaries help their employers find and interview new employees.

1. Where to find prospective employees. Recruits can be obtained from many sources. Consider the ones most likely to have the type of employee you need, for example:

Employment agencies

School placement offices

Employment/unemployment bureaus

Newspaper advertisements placed by you or the applicant

References from outside sources

Contacts previously made by interested applicants

Your company's personnel department

2. How to conduct an interview. You must plan ahead for the interviews to find out what you want to know about the applicant and also to provide information to the applicant—all within the time set aside for the meeting. These are the basic steps involved:

Set a mutually convenient time.

Prepare a detailed, written description of the company and the job, listing specific tasks the applicant will have to perform.

Devise skills tests, such as a word processing test, if prepared tests are not available.

Draw up a list of specific questions you want to ask (your company may have a standard application form, but this list is necessary in addition) and take notes throughout the interview; be a good listener.

Make certain that the applicant is comfortable and at ease, and try to encourage him or her to volunteer information and indicate relative interest in skills and job duties.

If possible, review a completed application before the interview so that you can use the interview to clear up problems.

If you interview several prospective employees, follow the same procedure with each one so that your comparison will be meaningful and fair.

Summarize and type the results and present them to your employer along with any recommendations or comments that you have, after all the interviews are completed.

TRAINING AND SUPERVISING ASSISTANTS. Once the new worker is hired, the job orientation and training begin. The new employee should be made to feel at home and acquainted with not only the immediate office but general company policy and facilities as well.

Training will require (1) careful instruction and explanation of duties—presented at a pace the employee can digest—and (2) practice sessions where actual tasks are first completed under your direct supervision, often with step-by-step explanations as work proceeds. It will become evident when direct, constant supervision can be relaxed.

Once the worker is functioning alone—with the exception of occasional questions—you should still check his or her work occasionally for errors and general quality, as well as for efficiency and overall performance. (Some secretaries schedule daily, then weekly, 10- to 15-minute conferences to review work loads and answer questions.) If further guidance or discipline is required, do not hesitate to provide it. Remain alert to dissatisfaction and actively encourage open communication that will prevent such problems. Develop the same spirit of teamwork that characterizes the ideal employer-secretary relationship.

It is important throughout the worker's employment to provide motivation. An employee who has no incentive to do better probably will not. Job satisfaction is essential in any position. Compliment the new employee frequently. If criticism is necessary, offer it in a positive, constructive manner that encourages the person to work harder and gain—not lose—confidence.

Here are some of the things to cover in your training sessions:

1. Supplies—location and use

2. Forms—location and use

3. Correspondence—company practice, with samples

4. Word processing aids—how-to instructions such as the use of spell checkers and standard formats

5. Style—correspondence, reports, and so on

6. Machines—care and operation

7. Filing—procedures and location

8. Telephone—use and courtesy

9. Available facilities such as purchasing department and cafeteria

10. Company—review of product/service, personnel, and so on

11. Grammar and writing skills

12. Mail and other messaging—handling incoming and outgoing material

13. Other duties and office procedures

In spite of all efforts to find and select the right candidate and give proper training, there is always the chance that the person will not work out. The employee may be unable to adjust to the work pace or may be unable to produce work of adequate quality. If further training will not solve the problem, you will be forced to advise your employer, who may ask you to discharge the employee. It will be necessary to tell the person as gently as possible that she or he is being released. You could indicate that the employee may want to pursue further training or education or that she or he would be more suited for a different type of job or office. Be as tactful, but direct, as possible and wish the person well upon leaving.

ETHICS IN THE WORKPLACE

Written Rules

Employees are expected to observe both written and unwritten rules that pertain to ethical conduct. The written rules may specify where you may park your car, where and when you may smoke or have refreshments, the procedure to follow in reporting serious offenses, and other guidelines.

Some professions provide a written code of ethics for all employees that covers do's and don'ts when dealing with clients, how to handle confidential matters, and other ethical practices. The American Bar Association, for example, publishes a Code of Professional Ethics to which all practicing attorneys adhere. If such written rules or guidelines are available, memorize them and observe them at all time.

Unwritten Rules

In addition to following written rules or guidelines, employees are expected to observe unwritten rules that are generally based on common sense and a commonly accepted moral sense of proper behavior in the workplace. The following guidelines are examples of ethical conduct in the office.

1. Do not abuse the office telephone by using it to conduct personal business or make unnecessary personal calls to friends and relatives.

2. Do not use the office copier for your personal copying needs.

3. Do not make copies of company software or hard-copy documents for your personal use, unless you are authorized to do so.

4. Do not use the office and your time at work for personal visits with friends and relatives.

5. Do not remove (borrow or take) office supplies, files, or other items from the workplace unless you are authorized to do so.

6. Do not discuss your employer's dealings with clients or customers outside of the office.

7. Do not take part in gossip, rumors, personal attacks, or any form of covert behavior.

8. Do not force your personal (romantic) attentions on other coworkers.

9. Do not conduct unfair or unscrupulous campaigns against coworkers competing for a position or recognition.

10. Do not engage in borrowing or lending as a general rule.

11. Do not blame coworkers for your own errors and deficiencies but rather assume responsibility for your own comments and actions.

12. Do not take credit for an achievement that belongs to someone else.

Observing the Rules of Confidentiality

All organizations need to maintain a certain degree of privacy and confidentiality. The ones that deal with sensitive material or must constantly safeguard against giving an advantage to competitors have special policies and procedures in this regard. Secrecy is important even within a company office or department.

HOW TO ACT WHEN YOU ARE AWAY FROM THE OFFICE. As a rule, when you are away from the office, never discuss with others matters about your employer, the nature of your work, or matters about your company—except in generalities ("I'm a secretary; yes, I love my job"). Assume—even if you are not told—that all conversations about specific people and projects are taboo, that everything is confidential unless you have been told otherwise. In other words, it's fine to tell someone that you work for an accounting firm, but it would be a serious breach of ethics to discuss your work pertaining to one of your employer's clients. Similarly, it would be fine to tell someone that you work in the records department of a clothing manufacturer, but it would be grounds for dismissal to tell anyone what you read in one of the files.

HOW TO SAFEGUARD OFFICE MATERIAL. Employers must be able to trust the people who work for them. No business could function effectively if secretaries and others knowingly or unwittingly violated the all-important rule of confidentiality.

In addition to not discussing office matters, you should make it a practice to protect the material you work with. Keep confidential papers on your desk turned over and locked in the files the rest of the time, and keep notes and notebooks in your desk when not being used. Keep dictation and computer tapes and disks with correspondence, word processing documents, and other material locked in their file containers. Remember that messages sent to an electronic bulletin board via an electronic-mail system may be read by other people. Also, the use of electronic media by others may cause the spread of computer viruses that disable computer systems. (Antiviral software will locate and destroy many of the known computer viruses.) Keep outsiders *out* of your employer's office when he or she is away. Don't discard unused or outdated photocopies of sensitive documents without shredding them. Keep your desk, files, and other storage areas locked, with the keys well hidden from possible intruders.

Handling Human Relations Problems

WHAT TO DO ABOUT GOSSIP. A trail of office gossip passed from one employee to another by word of mouth is called a grapevine. The smart secretary regards grapevine news with caution. If you hear through this source something that seems important and that affects you and your job, directly question your employer about it. *Never* spread grapevine information. Passing on unfounded rumors can lead to unfortunate consequences and can involve you in embarrassing situations.

Remember that a rumor can have serious consequences when it gets outside the company. Even when you have no reason to doubt what you hear, strictly avoid making office matters public. Discussing the matter with a close friend in a restaurant is the same as making the news public, because you never know who may overhear you.

WHAT TO DO ABOUT PERSONAL BORROWING AND LENDING. A breakdown of scrupulous courtesy in this area can cause irreparable ill will among those who must work together. In general, it is advisable *not* to borrow if you can possibly avoid it.

If you must borrow, be sure to make it a practice to return what you have borrowed as quickly as possible. Delays lead to forgetfulness and to accidents or actual loss of things—with the inevitable disagreeable feeling on the part of the individual who was kind enough to lend you his or her belongings.

1. Borrowing money. From a practical standpoint, discretion, responsibility, and trustworthiness rank above courtesy when borrowing money—without these qualities, there is no courtesy in the transaction. Do not borrow money, even very small sums, from coworkers or people who do business with your company if you can possibly avoid it. If you must borrow lunch money, for example, be sure to return it promptly.

Borrowing a large sum of money from a coworker or someone doing business with the company is frowned upon in all business organizations. Even if a friend, out of kindness, offers you a loan, don't accept it. Banks, not friends or business associates, are appropriate sources for such purposes.

2. Lending money. If a coworker has been remiss in returning a loan, you will show more consideration by tactfully reminding him or her of the debt than by nursing a secret annoyance. Never mention the debt to others. Although a large amount of money cannot simply be forgotten, and you may have to resort to legal action to recover it, use such measures as a last alternative since they will, at the least, put a strain on your working relationship. The wisest policy is: "neither a borrower nor a lender be."

HOW TO DEAL WITH OFFICE POLITICS. *Office politics* is a general term that usually refers to games that people play to get ahead at work or perhaps to get by with something questionable.

1. Unethical practices. Competition is healthy and desirable in most circumstances, but when the motivation to gain recognition and get ahead causes irrational, unethical behavior, it is clearly unhealthy. Honest, hard work, in the spirit of teamwork and cooperation, is the only ethical way to secure a raise or promotion. This type of challenge to a coworker is natural and common. But unfair schemes and secret ploys to discredit competing coworkers are unthinkable to an honest, responsible person.

2. The unethical coworker. If you are forced to deal with a coworker who is acting questionably in efforts to gain some favor or recognition above you, do not be pushed into using similar strategy. Continue to work honestly and responsibly and be sure that your actions are fair and open for all to see. If necessary, regularly point out to your employer what you have done in your work and what you are planning to do so that any efforts by someone else to claim credit for your achievements or to sabotage them will soon be exposed. (Send your boss copies of letters and reports you write, type a summary of an idea you have—with your name on it, and so on.) You may have to be patient, but keep in mind that there is some truth to the cliche that if you give people enough rope, they will hang themselves.

3. The positive side of office politics. Although the term *office politics* often implies something shady, it also refers to legitimate maneuvers to make your worth known. Don't hesitate to use honest, ethical strategies to get a raise, get a promotion, and generally enhance your status in the company: for example, develop a reputation as a cooperative, understanding coworker by being a good listener and volunteering to help others in appropriate situations; demonstrate your worth to your employer—particularly when you are seeking a raise or promotion—by regularly making your achievements known (in writing when possible) and by periodically preparing a new, detailed job description that illustrates your merits; regularly engage in independent inquiry and study to become better informed and to polish your abilities in specific areas of work; develop your initiative to the fullest and take advantage of opportunities to handle matters on your own. Generally, work hard to enhance your competence and subtly make your employer and others aware of your expanding responsibility and capability.

HOW TO COPE WITH INJURIES AND ILLNESSES. Since office workers are vulnerable to accidents and illnesses and since these occurrences are typically unexpected, a secretary may have to make some fast decisions when something happens.

1. *What to do for an injured coworker.* Injuries and illnesses at work should be handled the same as you would handle them outside the office. The first concern must be the injured employee. Quickly give whatever first aid you can offer and then immediately summon appropriate help. With a minor illness or injury, it may be sufficient to accompany the coworker to a company nurse or doctor. With a serious accident, it will be necessary to call an ambulance instantly. If you must leave the office to accompany the injured person somewhere, ask a coworker to cover for you. Since every situation will vary, you will have to use your own judgment each time. But in each case, remember that the employee's safety and well-being come first.

2. *How to help a coworker during the recovery period.* Employees who have been ill or in an accident will need your help during their recovery. Offer to take over some of their tasks and let them know that you and others will do what you can to help handle their work loads until they are fully recovered. Your employer will no doubt divide the work among certain members of the staff or bring in temporary outside help. If you are given extra duties, it may be an inconvenience and a strain to handle the increased work load. But unless the request is unreasonable or impossible (in which case you should ask to hire temporary help), do what you can without complaining. One day the tables may be turned, and you may need the cooperation and help of your coworkers to keep your job secure while you are recovering.

HOW TO HANDLE PERSONNEL PROBLEMS. Every office, large or small, is a potential trouble spot where human relations are concerned. Even in the highly automated office where tasks involve person-machine more than person-to-person contact, there are problems that a secretary may face.

1. Serious conflicts. How do you handle a situation where you and another worker are in strong disagreement? First, you should remember that it is necessary to continue working each day with your coworkers. Arguments seldom solve anything. The sensible route is to take time to listen and try to understand the other side—before it becomes a conflict. If possible, seek a no-fault resolution. If you still disagree, do not change your opinion, but do not let it anger you that someone else has a different viewpoint. If you are in charge, you are entitled to put your decision into effect if it concerns office procedures. If it is a matter of concern to your employer, let him or her make the final decision. The important thing to remember is that patience, understanding, and a friendly attitude will go a long way in preventing disagreements from becoming battles. Although some conflict cannot be avoided, there are things you can do to minimize the probability. Stress is a cause of many forms of conflict, and you can help combat it—even encourage harmony—by staying calm and level headed when you are the one under pressure. Often it is a matter of understanding *yourself* better.

Make a list of your strengths and weaknesses and find ways to emphasize your strengths and overcome your weaknesses. Chances are that modifying your own behavior in this way will help to reduce incidences of conflict. You may be able to encourage others—subtly—to emphasize their strengths and overcome their weaknesses too; if you can't, learn to empathize with them and accept their weaknesses, but do not let them provoke you into unwanted conflict. Perhaps you simply need to work harder to win over diffident or uncooperative coworkers. If you run into disinterest or even the "cold shoulder" treatment, don't let it dissuade you.

Examine the communications function: make a list of ways to avoid misunderstandings by making your written and spoken messages clearer, by asking questions when you need more information, and by speaking only for yourself—never for others without their authorization.

2. Other people's problems. One of the most difficult situations arises when a secretary either is asked for personal help or is in a situation where it seems necessary to offer assistance. If the person in trouble is a coworker, and possibly a good friend as well, the secretary will doubtless feel compelled to offer help and comfort. There is a dangerous point that may be reached. A good rule to remember is that you never really help someone by covering for errors or problems. If someone has a drinking problem, for instance, or some emotional problem affecting his or her work, do not play doctor or psychologist and do not help the person hide it from your employer. Rather, help the person find professional guidance outside—quickly.

If the individual with a problem is your employer and you are asked to offer suggestions, do the same thing. Otherwise, if the problem is extremely serious and is clearly jeopardizing the company's welfare, you should carefully consider advising your employer's immediate superior that a threatening problem exists. (But proceed cautiously—perhaps the superior is part of the problem.) If the problem is minor, or at least not a threat to the company, what you do depends on how much it disturbs you. You can try to ignore it or ask for a transfer to another office. In any case, do *not* participate in anything illegal or immoral even if it seems the only way to save your job or help an employer in trouble. If you cannot reason with your employer, or if his or her superiors are also involved, you may *as a last resort* have to resign your position in that office or even in the entire company.

Every situation that presents itself is different in some way, and your response will have to be dictated by the seriousness of it and your own involvement. Certainly, you should not seek out individuals with problems and should not attempt to involve yourself as an amateur psychiatrist or counselor.

3. Employee grievances. Management often establishes a grievance committee or arranges for some individual to hear the grievances of employees. The theory is that employees who are given an opportunity to air their complaints and work out solutions with management will be less likely to become disgruntled or quit their jobs. You can apply this same policy to your assistants—arrange for a certain period each week for employees with grievances to talk them over with you. But if no attempt is made to solve the problems or to explain fully what can and cannot be done and why, the entire process will be a waste of everyone's time.

4. Sexual harassment. Both men and women may be subject to pressure from their superiors to grant sexual favors in return for job security, a promotion, or something else the employee deems important. This road is fraught with dangers, and no one should submit to any pressure of this sort—*ever.* In 1980 the Equal Employment Opportunity Commission declared that all forms of sexual harassment, from offensive comments to unwanted physical contact, are illegal. Victims are instructed to register complaints, and companies are required to handle such complaints.

How you handle such a situation depends on the incident, your objectives, and your sense of social justice. In serious cases, employees have brought charges against their superiors on grounds of sexual harassment.

An essential first step in cases of unwanted sexual advances is to be extraordinarily firm and clear in your *initial* response: You want the behavior to stop. Don't wait; give absolutely no hint that you are unsure or may change your mind. *Very clearly* state that under *no* circumstances could you *ever* consider an involvement *of any sort* with someone at work, that it is *completely* beyond your ability in every possible way even to imagine or discuss the possibility—*no matter what the consequences.*

If the person appears willing and perhaps eager to drop it in light of your strong position, help him or her save face by changing the subject and never mentioning it again—to anyone. But if the person continues with bribes or even threats, increase the firmness of your position. If that fails to bring it all to a halt and you are in physical danger, get out quickly and seek immediate help if necessary. In fact, serious threats and certainly physical abuse require immediate police assistance.

When you believe that sexual harassment is occurring, you have to decide what steps you want to take, legal or otherwise. Each situation will be different. It may be enough in certain cases to make clear that unless it all stops *immediately* you will have no choice but to report it; in other cases, this will be insufficient, and you will actually have to report it. If you sense that the problem will continue, keep a detailed written record of what was said or done, including the time and place and the names of any witnesses. If your request to have the unwanted behavior stop is ignored, write a letter to the offender stating your objections (keep a copy). If this also fails, follow company guidelines for reporting the harassment. If policy requires that you contact your supervisor, do so unless the threat comes from your supervisor. In that case speak to your supervisor's boss. If that also fails to produce results, file a complaint with your local office of the Equal Employment Opportunity Commission. Remember that employers are responsible for an occurrence of sexual harassment in their companies and may not legally fire or demote you for filing a complaint. Above all, remember that sexual harassment is a crime that cannot be ignored—for your own safety and well-being and for that of your coworkers.

5. Performance problems. Some problems affect or involve an employee's ability to perform. Perhaps the employee's productivity or output is low. Perhaps the quality of the employee's work is below standards. If the reasons are unknown, a performance appraisal is in order. This may involve having the employee record each step taken in performing each task—what is done and how long it takes to do it. A review of the employee's education, background, and specific job qualifications may be needed. Finally, it may be desirable to interview the employee, pointedly asking questions that will reveal the person's attitudes, understanding of work requirements, and so on.

Many things cause performance problems, and the first step is to isolate the factors that directly contribute to the problems. For instance, outmoded equipment could lead to poor performance on the job. In other cases, however, equipment and working conditions might be perfect, but the employee might be having problems at home that interfere with performance at work. These situations can be delicate, and you need to work *with* the employee, encouraging cooperation and participation, in solving the problem. Any criticism that must be given should be phrased positively and constructively (for example, "A little more practice, Joan, and I think you'll be doing letter-perfect work," *not* "You're still making mistakes, Joan").

HANDLING SOCIAL-BUSINESS RESPONSIBILITIES

Making Arrangements for Theater Tickets

The secretary's chief responsibility when an employer entertains at the theater is reserving the tickets. That is a difficult chore unless the tickets are ordered far in advance. Theaters, telephone services, and ticket agencies are listed in the telephone directory, and newspapers carry advertisements of current plays. Many hotels also have information on, and facilities for, the purchase of theater tickets, tours, and other forms of entertainment.

USING A TICKET AGENCY. On short notice, a ticket agency may be helpful. If you order tickets frequently, establish a contact at the agency and make all purchases through the same person if possible. Specify the event and the date, and the agency will deliver the tickets to you or at the theater box office. You may also specify which seats you want. An additional charge by the agency is added to the original cost of each ticket. Many agencies will allow you to charge the tickets with one of the major credit cards.

PURCHASING TICKETS AT THE BOX OFFICE. Tickets can also be purchased at the box office, but the problem of getting good seats on short notice—or getting any seats at all—remains no matter where or how you purchase the ticket. Many box offices accept credit cards.

USING A TELEPHONE SERVICE. In major cities, you can also call a telephone service such as Ticket Central for tickets and charge them with one of the major credit cards. Often you can specify the area, such as orchestra, but usually not the specific row or seat desired. Ask where you may pick up the tickets—usually at the box office. Also ask whether there is a service charge.

SENDING TICKETS THROUGH THE MAIL. Some persons prefer to have the tickets in advance rather than pick them up at the box office. If you send tickets through the mail to anyone, always include the numbers of the seats in your letter of transmittal. This information on the copy of your letter is useful if the tickets are lost.

PREPARING INFORMATION FOR YOUR EMPLOYER. When you give the theater tickets to your employer, enclose them in an envelope with the following information typed on it:

1. Day of the week and date of performance
2. Curtain time
3. Name and address of theater
4. Name of show
5. Seat numbers

Handling Presents and Holiday Cards

HELPING WITH EXTRA HOLIDAY DUTIES. Your calendar should have a notation to bring holiday lists to your employer's attention. The time depends on shopping conditions in your locality. For example, allow about six weeks before Christmas. Many private secretaries assist in the selection of cards and address and mail them. Some secretaries make suggestions for presents and help select and prepare them for mailing.

PREPARING THE HOLIDAY PRESENT LIST. Figure 40 is a suggested form to use in bringing the list of Christmas presents to your employer's attention. The form is self-explanatory. The employer makes additions or deletions, approves the presents suggested by you or decides on something else, and indicates the price range. In addition to Christmas, there are other holidays such as Hanukkah that are celebrated about the same time. It is important that you are aware of the days and knowledgeable about the various customs. To avoid duplication in your list, you should keep a similar card record for those people to whom your employer gives presents at other times of the year.

WRAPPING AND MAILING GIFTS. Appropriate holiday cards are usually sent with holiday presents. When you plan to have a store gift-wrap and mail presents, take the cards with you when you do your shopping. If a present is to be mailed, comply with the request of the Postal Service or other de-

FIGURE 40

Christmas List

CHRISTMAS LIST 19-- (Mr. Hambro)					
Name	Gift yr. before last	Gift last yr.	Amt. spent	Suggestion	Amt. to spend?
Mr. & Mrs. Nelson	cocktail glasses	gourmet cheese	$60	handcrafted vase	
Allen Pierce	humidor	manicure kit	$18	leather stationery case	

livery service and send packages early during busy holiday seasons such as Christmas. This is especially important if the packages are to be sent abroad.

HANDLING MONEY PRESENTS. All executives have a certain number of service people to whom they give presents of money each Christmas. If you help your employer handle money gifts, make a list of those to whom your employer gives money and ask him or her to indicate the amount. The list will include household employees, elevator operators, doormen and women, janitors and building superintendents (but not building managers) of apartment houses and office buildings, mail carriers, and any others who perform services throughout the year and are not tipped. The amount given household employees is usually based on salary and length of service; the amount given apartment house employees, on the rent; the amount given others, on length of service. Some executives also give presents of money to relatives and members of their families.

If the amount of money is small, $25 or less, use crisp new bills; for a larger amount, write a check. No matter what the amount or to whom given, insert it in a Christmas envelope printed for that purpose.

PREPARING CARD LISTS. Use your computer to maintain an alphabetical list of the names and addresses of people to whom your employer sends holiday cards. If your employer sends personal cards to some people and sends cards jointly with his or her spouse to others, keep separate lists. Your employer may also have a select list of cards that he or she prefers to sign. In addition, you may have to keep a separate list of customers or clients who receive company or firm cards.

When a card is received from someone who is not on the list, add the name below the regular list so that the next year, your employer can decide whether to add that person to the list. If he or she makes new contacts during the year, add them to the list, indicating where the contact was made. Your employer will cross out any names that should not be on the list.

It is important to make changes of address in your computer file. As cards are received, compare addresses shown on the envelopes with the ones on your list, and check the names on the list as you address the cards.

KEEPING RECORDS OF BIRTHDAYS. Keep a computer file or card record of those who receive presents on other occasions such as birthdays. The record should show the present given on each occasion and the approximate cost. Your employer will want to know what presents were given to a particular person on other occasions as well as on previous birthdays before making a decision about another birthday present.

SELECTING GIFTS FOR WEDDING ANNIVERSARIES. Presents on wedding anniversaries follow a tradition—each anniversary is associated with a different substance or jewel. Gift stores and jewelry stores have lists of the substance or jewel currently associated with each anniversary. Merchants' associations may revise the list from time to time, so check for recent changes before making a purchase.

Keeping Records of Donations

HOW TO HANDLE REQUESTS FOR DONATIONS. Records of donations or contributions must be kept (1) to support the income tax deduction and (2) for your employer's information. But the secretary is also concerned with record keeping for nontax purposes.

At certain times of the year, numerous organizations make drives for donations. It may be advisable to accumulate the requests in a folder and give a batch of them to your employer at an opportune time. If the request comes from a new organization, try to find something about it and present the details to your employer. Never destroy a request for a donation unless your employer has told you to do so. Some persons, particularly those in public positions, make a practice of responding, at least in a small way, to nearly every request.

HOW TO KEEP A RECORD OF DONATIONS. When your employer is considering whether to make a certain donation, he or she is interested in knowing (1) the amount donated to a specific organization the preceding year and (2) the total amount of donations for the current year. Note on each request, before giving it to your employer, the amount donated the previous year. Give the running record of donations for the current year to your employer with each request. At the end of the year, make an alphabetical list of organizations to which contributions have been made. When your employer makes a pledge payable in installments, enter the due dates on your calendar.

Sending Expressions of Sympathy

HOW TO SEND EXPRESSIONS OF SYMPATHY. Sympathy to the family of a deceased friend or acquaintance is usually expressed by (1) flowers, (2) a letter of sympathy, (3) mass cards, or (4) contributions.

1. Flowers. It is customary to send flowers to a bereaved family, except to an Orthodox Jewish family. It is appropriate to send them fruit baskets. A visiting card, with the engraved name struck out in ink and bearing a few words of sympathy, may accompany the flowers. Usually, however, the secretary orders the flowers by telephone and the florist supplies the card and writes the name of the person sending the flowers. The florist will ask you the name of the deceased, where the funeral is to be conducted, and the date and time of the service.

Flowers are appropriate at a memorial service—as for someone lost at sea—or when the deceased is to be cremated. Unarranged bouquets of cut flowers are not appropriate for a funeral service. Some kind of floral piece, a spray or a wreath, is preferable.

2. Letters of condolence. Letters of condolence are sent to a family of any faith.

3. Mass cards. Mass cards may be sent to a Roman Catholic family by a Catholic or a non-Catholic. You may obtain them from any priest. It is customary to make an offering to the church at the time of asking for the card. Although a Roman Catholic might ask a priest to say a mass for a non-Catholic, it is not in good taste to send a mass card to a non-Catholic family.

4. Contributions. Many families request that, instead of flowers, friends send contributions to charities or other organizations in which the deceased was interested. The organization sends the family a notice of the contribution. Your employer may want to write a short note to the family of a close friend or relative and tell them that he or she is sending a donation in their name even though the gift is later announced by the organization.

HOW TO ACKNOWLEDGE FLOWERS AND MASS CARDS. The secretary needs to be concerned not only with the acknowledgment itself but with the records pertaining to the replies.

1. Files to keep. In case of the death of a member of your employer's family, write descriptions of floral pieces on the back of each accompanying card. Keep separate files for fruit baskets, mass cards, and letters. Arrange all in alphabetical order. Make a separate notation of people who have sent both flowers and mass cards and of those who have written and also sent fruit baskets, flowers, or mass cards. Prepare separate lists (see Figure 41).

2. Types of acknowledgment. Authorities differ about whether good taste permits a typed acknowledgment or an engraved acknowledgment card. If there are few acknowledgments to write, undoubtedly your employer should write them in longhand. In the case of a prominent person, however, when hundreds of people send flowers, mass cards, letters, and so on, the task of acknowledging each by a handwritten letter is too formidable. Engraved acknowledgment cards may be

FIGURE 41

Lists for Acknowledgment of Cards and Flowers

```
List No. 1

                              FLOWERS

Name and Address
   (Alphabetical)          Kind of Flowers          Remarks

Brown, Mr. and Mrs. R.S.    Spray, calla lilies    See Mass list
   (Catherine and Bob)
275 E. 86th St.
New York NY 10017

Jones, Mrs. A. (Mary)       Iris, white stock      Also wire from Mr. Jones
79 W. Adams St.                                       (Tom)
Boston MA  03201
```

```
List No. 2

                              MASSES

Name and Address            Particular form of
   (Alphabetical)           card; how many masses      Remarks

Brown, Mr. and Mrs. R.S.    Society for the Propagation  See Flowers list
   (Catherine and Bob)         of the Faith

Murphy, Thomas E. (Tom)     6 masses
44 Fifth Ave.
New York NY  10017
```

used to acknowledge letters of sympathy, flowers, mass cards, or fruit baskets from persons who are unknown to the bereaved but should not be sent to close personal friends.

Also make a list of the names and addresses of those who performed outstanding services, such as doctors and nurses; priest, rabbi, or minister; editorial writers; and the like. Your employer may want to send letters of appreciation to them.

From these lists it is simple to handle the acknowledgments. The first column gives you the proper salutation (e.g., Dear Mary); from the information in the second column, you can make a special comment in your acknowledgment of the type of flowers, mass card, and so on; the column headed *Remarks* gives you other information you may need. A thank you letter should also be sent to those who gave memorial contributions to organizations. The notices from the organizations tell who made the contributions.

Your employer will select from the lists the friends to whom he or she wants to write in longhand and will dictate acknowledgments to some of the others. You can then draft and type acknowledgments to the rest of the names on the lists.

HOW TO WRITE EFFECTIVE LETTERS AND MEMOS

Chapter 10

Mechanics of Business Correspondence

HOW TO SET UP LETTERS AND MEMOS

Companies usually have preferred letter and memo formats and may require all employees to use those formats in preparing correspondence. Secretaries who prepare correspondence by computer can store the format specifications for later recall and rapid setup of future messages.

The choice of format depends on the image a company wants to portray. Some formats, such as the simplified letter, suggest a modern image, whereas others, such as the modified-block letter, suggest a conservative, traditional image. The time involved in setup may also enter into the selection of a format. For those who prepare correspondence primarily by typewriter, the number of keystrokes or operations that the layout requires may be important. A full-block or simplified format, for instance, is faster and easier to set up than are some of the other styles, such as the modified-block or official/personal format.

LETTER FORMATS

Five standard formats for letters are as follows:

1. Full block (Figure 42)
2. Block (Figure 43)
3. Modified block (Figure 44)
4. Simplified (Figure 45)
5. Official/personal (Figure 46)

FIGURE 42

Full-Block Format

[LETTERHEAD]

July 16, 19--

Ms. Sheila Jones
The Modern School for Secretaries
12 Harrington Place
Greenpoint, NJ 07201

Attention D. L. Lewis

Dear Ms. Jones:

You asked me to send you examples of letter
formats being used in offices throughout the
country. This letter is an example of the full-
block format.

This is an efficient letter form that saves time
and energy in setup. As you can see, there are no
indentions. Everything, including the date and
the complimentary close, begins at the extreme
left.

Since the dictator's name is typed in the signature, it is not necessary to include his or her
initials in the identification line.

Sincerely,

Martha Scott
Correspondence Chief

hc

FIGURE 43

Block Format

[LETTERHEAD]

                                    July 16, 19--

                                    ·Your reference 12:3:1

Mrs. Jane Carter
The Modern School for Secretaries
12 Harrington Place
Greenpoint, NJ 07201

Dear Mrs. Carter:

BLOCK LETTER FORMAT

You asked me for information about traditional
letter styles. This is an example of the block
letter, which is a compromise between the full-
block and modified-block formats.

As you can see, the inside address is placed flush
left, and the paragraph beginnings are aligned
with the left margin, as they are in the full-
block form. The dateline and reference line are
positioned slightly right of the page center, with
the dateline about two line spaces below the
letterhead and the reference line two line spaces
below the dateline. The complimentary close also
begins slightly to the right of the page center.
Both lines of the signature are aligned with the
complimentary close.

The dictator's initials are not given in the
identification line, because his or her name is
typed in the signature.

                                    Sincerely,

                                    Martha Scott
                                    Correspondence Chief

cf

Enc.

FIGURE 44

Modified-Block Format

[LETTERHEAD]

July 16, 199--

Ms. Paula Anderson
The Modern School for Secretaries
12 Harrington Place
Greenpoint, NJ 07201

Dear Ms. Anderson:

    Thank you for your letter requesting a con-
servative modified-block letter format to add to
your correspondence file.

    This format differs from the block form in
only one respect--the first line of each paragraph
is indented one-half to one inch.   The dateline is
set slightly right of the page center, two to four
line spaces below the letterhead.   The complimentary close also begins slightly to the right of
the page center.   All lines of the signature are
aligned with the complimentary close.

    Because the dictator's name is typed in the
signature line, his or her initials are not necessary in the identification line.

Sincerely,

Martha Scott
Correspondence Chief

cf

c: Michael Johnson

    P.S.   For more information about GDC filing
systems, contact our Sales Office at the letterhead address.   MS

FIGURE 45

Simplified Format

[LETTERHEAD]

July 16, 19--

Mr. William Wyatt
The Modern School for Secretaries
12 Harrington Place
Greenpoint, NJ 07201

SIMPLIFIED LETTER FORMAT

You asked for an illustration of the simplified
letter style, Mr. Wyatt. This letter is an
example of the modern, easy-to-prepare simplified
format.

Unlike the other styles, this one omits the salutation and complimentary close. But it resembles
the full-block format in that the structural parts
are all positioned flush left. The subject line
is written in all capitals, flush left, without
the word SUBJECT. The signature, too, is written
in all capitals, flush left, in one line.

Businesses that choose this style letter, Mr.
Wyatt, typically mention the recipient's name in
the opening and closing paragraphs.

MARTHA SCOTT--CORRESPONDENCE CHIEF

ml

FIGURE 46

Official/Personal Format

[LETTERHEAD]

July 16, 19--

Dear Ms. Kennedy:

Every forms file should include a sample of the official/personal letter format. It is often used with executive-size letterhead.

The structural parts of the letter differ from the modified-block arrangement only in the position of the inside address. The salutation is placed two to five line spaces below the dateline, depending on the length of the letter. The inside address is written in block form, flush with the left margin, from two to five line spaces below the final line of the signature.

The identification line, if used, should be placed two line spaces below the last line of the address and the enclosure mark two line spaces below that. Because the dictator's name is typed in the signature, it is not necessary for the letter to carry an identification line. The typist's initials may be on the file copy of the letter but should not appear on the original.

Sincerely yours,

(Mrs.) Martha Scott
Correspondence Chief

Ms. Janice Kennedy
The Modern School for Secretaries
12 Harrington Place
Greenpoint, NJ 07201

Letters prepared in these formats are reproduced on the following pages. The principal features of the various formats are described in the body of each letter.

Punctuation Style

Either mixed or open punctuation may be used in the structural parts of a letter. *Mixed punctuation* means that punctuation marks are used after the city in the inside address and after the complimentary close. *Open punctuation* means the omission of punctuation marks after these parts. Many firms with word processing equipment use open punctuation to reduce keystrokes. But whether open or mixed punctuation is used in the inside address, a colon always follows the salutation.

PRINCIPAL PARTS OF LETTERS

Dateline

The position of the dateline on the page depends on the letter format used and the length of the letter. The dateline is usually placed from two to four line spaces below the letterhead (or more if the letter is very short). It should be either flush left or slightly right of the page center, depending on the letter format.

How to write the dateline. The following suggestions should be kept in mind when preparing the dateline:

1. Date the letter the day it is dictated, not the day it is typed.
2. Write the date conventionally, all on one line (September 15, 19—). But note that the military and some other organizations place the day first and omit the comma (15 September 19—).
3. Do not use *d*, *nd*, *rd*, *st*, or *th* following the day of the month (*not* September 15th).
4. Do not abbreviate or use figures for the month (*not* Sept. 15 or 9/15).
5. Do not spell out the day of the month or the year.

Reference Line

If a file reference is given in an incoming letter, include a reference line in your reply. Place your own reference beneath the incoming reference.

HOW TO WRITE THE REFERENCE LINE. When letterheads include a printed reference notation, such as *In reply please refer to*, place your reference line after it. Otherwise, place the reference line two line spaces beneath the date.

April 20, 19—

Your File 3476
Our File 2785

Personal Notation

A letter or envelope should be marked "Personal" or "Confidential" only when no one but the addressee is supposed to see the letter but not as a device to catch the attention of a busy recipient.

HOW TO WRITE THE PERSONAL NOTATION. Type the word *Personal* or *Confidential* flush left four line spaces above the address (or two line spaces below the reference line), which is at the top of the letter. You may underline the notation to make it more noticeable.

Inside Address

WHAT THE INSIDE ADDRESS CONTAINS. The inside address includes the name and address of the addressee. In addressing an individual in a company, the inside address contains both the individual's name and that of the company and may also contain the individual's business title.

Mr. John Jones
The Mississippi Electrical Power
   and Light Company
148 West Tenth Street
Jackson, MS 39201

WHERE TO PLACE THE INSIDE ADDRESS. Begin the inside address at the left-hand margin of the letter, not less than two or more than twelve line spaces below the dateline. The exact position of the first line of the address depends on the length of the letter. The inside address should not extend beyond the middle of the page. Carry over part of an extremely long line to a second line and indent the carryover line about three character spaces.

HOW TO WRITE THE INSIDE ADDRESS. Follow these guidelines in writing the inside address:

1. The inside address should correspond exactly to the official name of the company addressed. If *Company, Co., The, Inc.*, or *&* is part of the company's official name, use the form shown by the company title. Punctuate the name according to the company's official style.

   > ABC Company Inc.
   > ABC Company, Inc.
   > ABC Co., Inc.

2. Do not precede the street number with a word or a sign or with a room number.

   > 70 Fifth Avenue (*not* No. 70 Fifth Avenue or #70 Fifth Avenue)
   > 70 Fifth Avenue, Room 305 (*not* Room 305, 70 Fifth Avenue)

   Use a *post office box number* in preference to a street address, if you know it.

3. Spell out the numerical names of streets and avenues if they are numbers of twelve or under. When figures are used, do not follow with *d, st,* or *th*. Use figures for all house numbers except *One*. Separate the house number from a numerical name of a thoroughfare with a space, a hyphen, and a space. Authorities give different rules for writing addresses, but the following are widely used forms.

   > 23 East Twelfth Street
   > 23 East 13 Street
   > One Fifth Avenue
   > 2 Fifth Avenue
   > 234 - 72 Street

4. Never abbreviate the name of a city, unless the abbreviation is standard, such as *St. Louis* and *St. Paul*. For the names of states, ter-

ritories, and U.S. possessions, use official U.S. Postal Service abbreviations.

5. Use one or two character spaces between the last letter of a state name and the first digit of the postal zip code.

6. Even if there is no street address, put the city, state, and zip code on the same line.

7. Do not abbreviate business titles or positions, such as president, secretary, and sales manager. *Mr., Ms., Mrs.,* or *Miss* precedes the individual's name even when the business title is used. (Note: *Ms.* is uncommon in other countries.) But do not use two titles referring to the same thing (*not* Dr. Morris Anderson, M.D.). If a person's business title is short, place it on the first line; if it is long, place it on the second line.

> Mr. James E. Lambert, President
> Lambert & Woolf Company
> 1005 Tower Street
> Cleveland, OH 44900
>
> Mr. George F. Moore
> Advertising Manager
> Price & Patterson
> 234 Seventh Avenue
> New York, NY 10023

The modern trend, however, is to omit the business title if it makes the address run over four lines. For example, many business writers would omit *Advertising Manager* in the preceding example.

8. In addressing an individual in a firm, corporation, or group, place the individual's name on the first line and the company's name on the second line. When addressing a letter *to the attention of* such individual, place the person's name in an attention line two lines below the address.

9. Do not hyphenate a title unless it represents a combination of two offices (*secretary-treasurer*).

10. When writing to the officer of a company who holds several offices, use only the title of the highest office, unless letters from the officer are signed differently.

11. If a letter is addressed to a particular department in a company, place the name of the company on the first line and the name of the department on the second line.

12. Type the names of two or more persons in an inside address, one above the other, with no space between them. Place the names of the person of highest rank first; if both are equal, use alphabetical order.

> Mr. Rod Boyleston
> Ms. Janice Smith
> Computer Consultants, Inc.
> 1811 First Avenue
> Milwaukee, WI 12346

Attention Line

Business letters addressed to a firm are often directed to the attention of an individual by the use of an attention line, in preference to addressing the letter to the individual. This practice ensures that the letter will be opened promptly by someone in the firm.

HOW TO WRITE THE ATTENTION LINE. Place the attention line two line spaces below the address. The word *of* is not necessary. The attention line has no punctuation and is not underscored. When a letter is addressed to a firm and includes an attention line, the salutation is general (*Ladies and Gentlemen*) because the salutation is to the firm, not the individual named in the attention line. But a letter may be addressed to a specific person and also have an attention line directing it to another person. This will ensure that the person named in the attention line will open the letter if the addressee is absent. It is permissible to direct the letter to the attention of an individual without including his or her first name or initials, if they are unknown.

> *Preferable*:   Attention Walter R. Richardson
> *Permissible*:   Attention Mr. Richardson

Salutation

WHERE TO PLACE THE SALUTATION. Place the salutation two line spaces below the inside address, flush with the left margin. If an attention line is used, place the salutation two line spaces below the attention line.

HOW TO WRITE THE SALUTATION. Capitalize the first word, the title, and the name. Do not capitalize *dear* when *my* precedes it, but do capitalize *my*, thus *My dear Mr. Jones* (formal).

Use a colon following the salutation. A comma is used only in handwritten social letters.

HOW TO SELECT THE RIGHT FORMS OF SALUTATION. An informal salutation is used in business letters whether or not the letter writer is acquainted with the addressee, thus *Dear Mr.* instead of the more formal *My dear Mr.* and the antiquated *My dear Sir.* (Formal salutations to use when addressing people in honorary or official positions are given in Chapter 17.)

1. Never use a designation of any kind after a salutation.

   Dear Mr. Roberts: (*not* Dear Mr. Roberts, C.P.A.:)

2. Never use a business title or designation of position in a salutation (except in references to high officials: *Dear Mr. President* for the president of the United States).

Right:	Dear Mr. Adams:
	Dear Mr. Secretary: (U.S. Cabinet)
Wrong:	Dear Secretary: (business firm)
	Dear Secretary Ames: (business firm)

3. If a letter addressed to a company is directed to the attention of an individual, the salutation is to the company (*Ladies and Gentlemen*), not to the individual.

4. Follow a title with the person's last name.

   Dear Professor Ames: (*not* Dear Professor:)

5. The salutation in a letter that is not addressed to any particular person or firm, such as a general letter of recommendation, is *To Whom It May Concern*. Note that each word begins with a capital letter.

6. The common salutation in a letter addressed to a group composed of men and women is *Ladies and Gentlemen*; to a married couple who both use the same last name, *Dear Mr. and Mrs. Marsh*. Several alternative salutations may be used for professionals who are hus-

band and wife and for a professional woman married to an untitled man:

> Dear *Dr.* and *Mrs.* Marsh: (She is untitled.)
> Dear *Drs.* Marsh: (Both are titled.)
> Dear *Dr.* and *Mr.* Marsh: (He is untitled.)

7. When the gender is unknown, use the person's first name or initials in the salutation.

> Dear M. L. Watson:

HOW TO ADDRESS WOMEN. Follow these rules in letters addressed to women:

1. Use *Ms.* in domestic business correspondence unless you know that the woman prefers *Mrs.* (*Ms.* is uncommon in other countries.)

> Dear Ms. Brown:

2. If the letter is addressed to a firm of women, the salutation is *Ladies* or *Mesdames.* Do not use "Dear" or "My dear" with either of these salutations.

> Ladies:
> Mesdames:

3. The usual salutation in domestic correspondence to two women with the same name is:

> Dear Mss. Smith: (married or unmarried)
> Dear Ms. Smith and Mrs. Smith: (One prefers *Mrs.*)

Subject Line

A subject line makes it unnecessary for a writer to devote the first paragraph of his or her letter to a routine explanation of the subject of the letter; it also facilitates the distribution of mail to various departments and expedites subject filing.

HOW TO WRITE THE SUBJECT LINE. Place the subject line two line spaces beneath the salutation either flush left or with a paragraph indent, depending on the letter format that is used. Only lawyers place the subject line before the salutation. In business writing it is always placed after the salutation and is considered part of the body of a letter.

The word *Subject* may be omitted from the subject line. If it is included, a colon follows it. (Lawyers use *In re* rather than *Subject*. No punctuation follows *In re*.) The important words in a subject line are always capitalized, and the line may be underscored, although the trend is to omit the underlining.

Body

HOW TO WRITE THE BODY. Follow these suggestions for preparing the body of a letter:

1. Single-space the body unless the letter contains only one or two sentences; such messages may be double-spaced if desired.

2. Double-space between paragraphs.

3. When the block or simplified format is used, begin each line flush with the left margin.

4. When an indented format (such as the modified-block or official/personal letter) is used, indent the first line of each paragraph ½ to 1 inch.

5. Always indent paragraphs when a brief letter is double-spaced.

HOW TO SET UP LISTS. These guidelines apply to itemized lists in letters or memos:

1. Indent the list ½ to 1 inch from each margin of the letter or at least from the left margin.

2. Precede each item with a number, followed by a period (or enclose the number in parentheses).

3. Begin each line of the indented material two to three character spaces to the right of the number.

4. Single-space the material within each item but double-space between items.

HOW TO WRITE DATES. Usually, in the body of a letter, the date is written as *March 5*. When the day precedes the month, write out the day: *fifth of March* (*5th of March* is permissible).

Complimentary Close

WHERE TO PLACE THE COMPLIMENTARY CLOSE. Place the complimentary close two line spaces below the last line of the letter body. Begin it slightly to the right of the page center, except in the full-block or simplified formats, where it is flush left. It should never extend beyond the right margin of the letter. In letters of more than one page, at least two lines of the body should be on the page with the close.

HOW TO WRITE THE COMPLIMENTARY CLOSE. Capitalize only the first word. Follow the complimentary close with a comma. (This is often preferred practice even when open punctuation is used in the inside address.)

HOW TO SELECT CORRECT FORMS OF COMPLIMENTARY CLOSE. As with salutations, the preferred practice today for domestic correspondence is to use an informal closing, such as *Sincerely* or *Sincerely yours*, or a warm, friendly closing, such as *Cordially*, *Cordially yours*, *Regards*, *Best regards*, or *Best wishes*. (For international correspondence, use the more reserved closing of *Sincerely* or *Sincerely yours*.) When writing to a company, *Sincerely* is preferable to *Cordially*. In strictly formal or official correspondence, use a more formal close such as *Yours very truly*, *Yours truly*, *Very truly yours*, *Very cordially yours*, *Very sincerely yours*, *Respectfully yours*, or *Respectfully*.

Signature Line

WHAT THE SIGNATURE CONTAINS. The signature to a business letter may consist of the name of the company, the handwritten signature of the writer, and the typed name of the writer and his or her business title. Some companies, such as accounting and law firms, include the firm name when the letter is contractual or gives a professional opinion. Most companies, however, omit the firm name, except in a formal document. Also, the typed name of the writer may be omitted if it appears as part of the printed letterhead.

WHERE TO PLACE THE SIGNATURE. When the firm name is included in the signature, place it two line spaces below the complimentary close, followed by the writer's name four line spaces below the firm name; the writer's position may be written either on the same line with his or her name or on the next line. When the firm name is not included, place the writer's name and position four line spaces below the complimentary close.

Align the signature with the first letter of the complimentary close. The lines of the signature should be blocked, unless an unusually long line makes it necessary to have a carryover line (which would be indented two to three character spaces). No line of the signature should extend beyond the right margin of the letter.

> David Hillsborough
> Research Coordinator and
> Activities Director

HOW TO WRITE THE SIGNATURE. Follow these rules for the correct style of the various parts of the signature:

1. Write the firm name in all capitals, exactly as it appears on the letterhead.

> Sincerely yours,
>
> ACCOUNTING SERVICE COMPANY, INC.
>
> *Keith Norwood*
>
> Keith Norwood
> Treasurer

Never use the title *Mr.* or *Ms.* in the signature line of domestic correspondence unless it is necessary to clarify that the signer is a man or woman. (In most foreign correspondence, *Ms.* should be placed in parentheses before the name since many foreign readers are unfamiliar with this title.)

> *Leslie Carter*
> (Mr.) Leslie Carter

2. Write the signature exactly as the dictator signs his or her name. (It is not necessary to type the name and title if this information is already printed at the top of the letter as part of the letterhead.)

Right:

Richard P. Miller

Richard P. Miller
President

Wrong:

Richard P. Miller

R. P. Miller
President

3. Business titles and degree letters follow the typed signature. No title precedes either the written or typed signature in domestic correspondence except *Mrs.* (unless *Mr.* or *Ms.* is necessary to clarify gender).

Bernard Frost

Bernard Frost, Ph.D.

Paula Addison

(Mrs.) Paula Addison

HOW TO WRITE SIGNATURES FOR WOMEN. These guidelines apply to the signatures of women:

1. An *unmarried woman* should not precede her typed signature with *Ms.* in parentheses in domestic correspondence unless gender would not otherwise be known (but it should be included in foreign correspondence). It is assumed that a woman wants to be addressed as *Ms.* if no title is given. *Miss* is not common in domestic business correspondence.

Nora Kingston

Nora Kingston

2. A *married woman* should omit the title *Mrs.* in domestic correspondence if she prefers to be addressed as *Ms.* Her signature line also indicates whether she prefers that you use her maiden name, mar-

ried name, or both of them combined. In strict formal usage she may, if desired, type *Mrs.* with her husband's first and last names, all in parentheses, beneath her handwritten signature.

Janet Houston

Janet Houston

Janet Farraday-Houston

Janet Farraday-Houston

Janet Houston

(Mrs.) Janet Houston

Janet Farraday — Houston

(Mrs.) Janet Farraday-Houston

Janet Houston

(Mrs. Arnold K. Houston)

Janet Farraday

Janet Farraday

3. A *widow* signs her name as she did before her husband's death (follow the forms for a married woman).

4. If a *divorcee* does not use her maiden name, she may sign her first name, with or without the initial of her maiden name, and her former husband's last name. The typed signature is the same as the written signature. A title in parentheses is omitted in domestic correspondence if she wants to be addressed as *Ms.* The typed signature also may combine her maiden name with her former husband's last name or her first name with maiden name and her former husband's last name (with no title in domestic correspondence unless she wants to be addressed as *Mrs.*). If she uses her

maiden name, she should omit the title in domestic correspondence to indicate that she prefers to be addressed as *Ms.*

Right:

Eleanor M. Davis
Eleanor M. Davis

Eleanor M. Davis
(Mrs.) Eleanor M. Davis

Eleanor M. Davis
(Mrs. Montgomery Davis)

Eleanor Montgomery Davis
Eleanor Montgomery Davis

Eleanor Montgomery Davis
(Mrs.) Eleanor Montgomery Davis

Eleanor Montgomery
Eleanor Montgomery

Wrong:

Eleanor M. Davis
(Mrs. John R. Davis)

How to Write the Secretary's Signature. When you sign your employer's name to a letter, place your initials immediately below it.

Hiram R. Jones
Hiram R. Jones
President
mg

When you sign a letter in your own name as secretary to your employer, do not include his or her initials unless another person in the organization has the same name. Always precede your employer's name by a title such as *Mr.* or *Ms.*

Right: *Elizabeth Mason*

Secretary to Mr. Nelson

Wrong: *Elizabeth Mason*

Secretary to Mr. R. S. Nelson

Identification Line

The identification line shows who dictated the letter and who typed it. The only purpose of the identification line is for reference by the business organization *writing* the letter. The dictator's name is typed in the signature unless someone other than the dictator signs it.

HOW TO WRITE THE IDENTIFICATION LINE. Unless company rules require otherwise, include nothing but your own initials in the identification line. If it is convenient, omit them on the original of the letter.

If your company requires it, place the initials of both the dictator and the transcriber flush with the left margin, two line spaces below the last line of the signature. In the official/personal style of letter (Figure 46), the identification line is usually omitted but if used is placed two line spaces below the inside address. When the person who signs the letter has not dictated it, place his or her initials first, those of the dictator next, and those of the transcriber last.

JC:MK:ul

Enclosure Notation

HOW TO WRITE THE ENCLOSURE NOTATION. When a letter contains enclosures, place the word *Enclosure* (or *Enclosures*) or the abbreviation *Enc.* (or *Encs.*) flush with the left margin two line spaces beneath the identification line. If there is more than one enclosure, indicate the number. If the enclosures are of special importance, identify them. If an enclosure is to be returned, make a notation to that effect.

RPE:es

Enclosure

RPE:es

Enc. Policy 35-4698-M (to be returned)

RPE:es

Enc. Cert. ck. $2,350 (Mtge., Nelson to Jones)

RPE:es

Enc. 2

Mailing Notation

HOW TO WRITE THE MAILING NOTATION. When a letter is sent by any method other than regular postal mail, include a notation of the exact method on the envelope and make a similar notation on the copy of the letter flush left two line spaces beneath the enclosure notation or, if none is used, two line spaces below the identification initials. To simplify preparation, some companies include the notation on the original as well as on the copies.

Copy-Distribution Notation

HOW TO WRITE COPY NOTATIONS. When a copy is to be sent to another person, place the distribution notation flush with the left margin two line spaces below all other notations.

c: Mildred Parsons
Copy to S. A. Williams
fc: Linda Caruthers

Copy, c, or *pc* is used when the copy is a photocopy or computer-printout copy; *fc,* when it is a fax copy; *rc,* when it is a reprographic copy. The abbreviation *c* and the word *Copy* are also used generally to refer to any type of copy.

HOW TO WRITE THE BLIND-COPY NOTATION. Place the blind-copy notation two line spaces below other copy notations or in the upper left portion of the letter only on the file copy and the one sent to the blind-copy recipient. A blind copy means that the addressee of the letter does not know that a copy was sent to anyone else.

bc: Samuel Felshner

Postscript

A postscript is an added thought not directly related to the body of the letter (*not* something you simply forgot to include in the body itself).

HOW TO WRITE THE POSTSCRIPT. When it is necessary to add a postscript, place it two line spaces below the identification line or the last notation on the letter. If you use a modified-block (indented) letter format (Figure 44), indent the left margin of the postscript the same as the paragraphs in the body. Place it flush left if you use a full-block (Figure 42), block (Figure 43), or simplified (Figure 45) format. You may include or omit the abbreviation *P.S.* Use *P.P.S.* with a second postscript. Place the dictator's initials immediately after the last word in the postscript.

P.S. The next committee meeting will be June 11, 19—.   FVK

Heading on Continuation Page

If the letter runs to two or more pages, use your company's continuation-page stationery or use a plain sheet for the additional page. There is no need to add the word *continued* at the bottom of the first page. The fact that no signature appears at the end of the page makes it obvious that another page follows.

HOW TO WRITE THE CONTINUATION HEADING. The heading should contain the name of the addressee (no title), the number of the page, and the date; the margins should be exactly the same as those used on the first page. Leave two or more line spaces between the continuation heading and the body of the letter.

David Jones   2   May 5, 19—

Mary Brower
September 12, 19—
page two

You should have at least two lines from the body of the letter on the continuation sheet.

MEMO FORMATS

Memo formats vary as do the sizes of memo stationery. But most styles omit the inside address, salutation, complimentary close, and signature and substitute guide words such as *To, From, Subject,* and *Date.* Figures 47 and 48 illustrate two common formats—the brief note style and the tradi-

FIGURE 47

Note Memo Format

M E M O   from

Randy Taft

```
Here's the brochure I promised
to send you, Jean.  Hope it
offers what you want.
```

<hr>

FIGURE 48

Standard Memo Format

[LETTERHEAD]

TO:	Susan Eddington	**FROM:**	Lois Stanford
SUBJECT:	Memo Format	**DATE:**	July 16, 19--

Memo styles vary from simple notes to standard
multiple-copy forms, sold in office-supply stores,
to company-designed memo letterheads. Most forms
include guide words such as To, From, and Date at
the top of the page. Some also include a subject
line at the top and a signature line at the bottom
of the page.

Paragraphs are usually positioned flush left, with
no indention. The sender's initials may be added
below the last paragraph. Other notations such as
the enclosure notation are positioned the same as
in a traditional letter.

LS

rr

Enc.

tional memo style prepared on regular business letterhead. Some organizations also purchase printed message—reply forms (speed messages) in office-supply stores. These forms are often divided into two parts, the top or left part for the sender's message and the bottom or right part for the recipient to write a reply.

The note memo is a small-sized format intended only for very brief comments to a friend or close associate. The standard memo format is an 8½- by 11-inch style used for both interoffice and certain outside correspondence such as messages to close associates in other firms, purchase orders, or other messages that need not have a formal appearance.

PRINCIPAL PARTS OF MEMOS

Guide Words

A memo heading is often printed at the top of the page just beneath the name and address. This heading consists of guide words such as *Date*, *To*, *From*, and *Subject*. Instead of typing a dateline, inside address, salutation, subject line, and so on, as you would do with a traditional letter, you simply fill in the appropriate information after each guide word (see Figure 48). Major words in the subject line are capitalized the same as they are in a letter.

Body

HOW TO WRITE THE BODY. Follow these guidelines for preparing the body of a memo:

1. The body of a memo may be single spaced or double spaced, depending on its size, the same as the body of a letter. All but very brief messages, however, are single spaced.

2. Paragraphs may be indented but are usually flush left like a block letter (see Figure 43).

3. Since a memo has no salutation, the first paragraph begins two or more line spaces after the last line of the guide words.

Signature Initials

HOW TO WRITE SIGNATURE INITIALS. Some standard printed styles of memo available in office-supply stores have a printed line at the bottom of the page for the sender to include his or her signature. But most memos omit the signature line. Some writers, however, like to have their initials typed two line spaces beneath the last line of the body, positioned slightly to the right of the page center. Others do not want their initials typed on the memo, but they include their handwritten initials in this position.

Identification Line

HOW TO WRITE THE IDENTIFICATION LINE. Place the identification line flush left two line spaces beneath the last line of the body or two line spaces below the signature initials, whichever is last. Follow the instructions for using an identification line in a letter.

Enclosure Notation

HOW TO WRITE THE ENCLOSURE NOTATION. Place the enclosure notation flush left two line spaces beneath the identification line. Follow the instructions for using an enclosure notation in a letter.

Copy-Distribution Notation

HOW TO WRITE THE COPY-DISTRIBUTION NOTATION. Place the copy-distribution notation (*c, pc, copy, rc, fc*) flush left two line spaces below all other notations. Place a blind-copy notation (*bc*) only on the file copy and the copy sent to the blind-copy recipient. Follow the instruction for using a copy-distribution notation in a letter.

Postscript

HOW TO WRITE THE POSTSCRIPT. Place a postscript—flush left or indented the same as the paragraphs in the body—two line spaces below the last notation. Follow the instructions for using a postscript in a letter.

Heading on Continuation Page

HOW TO WRITE THE CONTINUATION HEADING. Write the heading on a memo continuation page the same as you would for a letter.

ENVELOPES

OCR Addressing

HOW TO WRITE THE ADDRESS. Figures 49 and 50 show commonly used styles of address on envelopes (note the use of all capitals and omission of punctuation as preferred by the U.S. Postal Service for optical character reading).

The items in the envelope address are usually the same as those in the inside address. It is important that you use the official post office abbreviation of the state followed by the zip code. The name of a foreign country is written in capitals as the last line in an address on the envelope but usually with only initial capitals in the inside address. For a list of postal address abbreviations, consult the national zip code directory, available to the public for reference in most post offices.

Although companies have their own preferred style of address, and the envelope address should include the same data as the letter's inside address, the Postal Service recommends the following: that you write the address in block style at least 1 inch from the left edge and at least ⅝ inch from the bottom edge; that you put unit numbers such as a suite immediately after the street on the same line; that you put a box number before a station name; and that you write the address in all capitals without punctuation.

With window envelopes, the insert should show at least ¼ inch space at the left, right, and bottom edges of the window.

WHERE TO PLACE THE PERSONAL NOTATION. Place the personal notation in all capitals to the left of and two line spaces above the address block. It may be underscored. See Figure 49.

WHERE TO PLACE THE ATTENTION LINE. Place the attention line immediately beneath the company name or left of the address block on any line above the second line from the bottom of the address. See Figure 50.

FIGURE 49

Envelope with Personal Notation

[Return Address]   **[Postage]**

    PERSONAL

        MR RS JACKSON
        NORTHERN MANUFACTURING CO
        25 W 79 ST RM 600
        MILWAUKEE WI 12345

FIGURE 50

Envelope with Attention Line and Special Delivery Notation

[Return Address]   **[Postage]**

ADDRESS CORRECTION REQUESTED

                    SPECIAL DELIVERY

        FTM: 0021-1-93
        NORTHERN MANUFACTURING CO
        ATTN MR RS JACKSON
        25 W 79 ST RM 600
        MILWAUKEE WI 12345

WHERE TO PLACE THE MAIL INSTRUCTION. Place mail instructions such as *SPE-CIAL DELIVERY* in all capitals two to four line spaces below the postage area. See Figure 50.

WHERE TO PLACE ACCOUNT NUMBERS. Nonaddress data such as account numbers or dates should be placed immediately above the first line in the address block. See Figure 50.

FORMS OF ADDRESS

General Rules

Follow these guidelines in addressing men, women, and firms. (Chapter 17 provides the correct forms of address for those who hold official or honorary positions.)

TITLES. Always precede a name by a title, unless initials indicating an academic degree or *Esq.* follow the name. The use of a business title or position or of *Sr., Jr., II, III*, and the like after a name does not take the place of a title. (Some writers omit the comma before the abbreviations *Jr.* and *Sr.* in a name, but you should follow the style used by the person in question.)

> Mr. Ralph P. Edwards III, President (*not* Ralph P. Edwards III, President)

DEGREES. Initials or abbreviations indicating degrees and other honors are sometimes placed after the name of the person addressed. Use only the initials of the highest degree; more than one degree may be used, however, if the degrees are in different fields. List the degree pertaining to the person's profession first, for example, *John Jones, LL.D., Ph.D.*, if he is a practicing attorney by profession. A scholastic title is not used in combination with the abbreviation indicating that degree, but another title may be used in combination with abbreviations indicating degrees.

> Dr. Roberta E. Saunders (*preferred*) or Roberta E. Saunders, Ph.D. (*not* Roberta E. Saunders, A.B., A.M., Ph.D.)
>
> Dr. Ralph Jones (*preferred*) or Ralph Jones, M.D. (*not* Dr. Ralph Jones, M.D.)

> The Reverend Perry E. Moore, Sc.D., LL.D. (*degrees pertain to field other than title indicates*)
>
> Professor Lola Markham (*not* Professor Lola Markham, Ph.D.)

ESQUIRE. The abbreviation *Esq.* may be used in addressing prominent attorneys or other high-ranking professional men and women who do not have other titles. *Mr., Ms.,* or *Mrs.* does not precede the name when *Esq.* is used. In fact, no other title is used with *Esq.*

> Honorable Richard P. Davis (*not* Honorable Richard P. Davis, Esq.)
>
> Allison D. Wells, Esq. (*not* Ms. Allison D. Wells, Esq.)
>
> Nathan Rogers Jr., Esq. (*not* Mr. Nathan Rogers Jr., Esq.)

Note: The title *Esquire* is commonly used in England and its colonies. There it is the proper title to use in addressing the heads of business firms, banking executives, doctors, and the like (Robert E. Meadfe, Esq., M.D.; Laurence D. Goode, Esq., M.D.).

Rules for Companies

Use the single-sex designations *Messrs.* and *Mesdames* only if the companies consist solely of men or women. *Messrs.* and *Mesdames* may be used in addressing a firm—but not a company—of men and women only when the names denote *individuals*. Do not use *Messrs.* or *Mesdames* as a form of address for the corporations or other business organizations that bear impersonal names.

> American Manufacturing Company (*not* Messrs. American Manufacturing Company)
>
> Mesdames Marvin, Tobin, and Smart (*not* Mesdames Marvin, Tobin, and Smart, Inc.)
>
> James Marshall & Sons (*not* Messrs. James Marshall & Sons)

Rules for Men

TITLES. Use the title *Mr.* when a man does not have a professional or honorary title such as *Dr.,* unless initials indicating a degree or *Esq.* follow the name.

Mr. John Wyatt
Professor John Wyatt
John Wyatt, M.D.
John Wyatt, Esq.

Rules for Women

FIRM COMPOSED OF WOMEN. In addressing a firm composed of women either married or unmarried, use *Mesdames* or *Mmes.*

Mesdames Cooper and Hill

UNMARRIED WOMAN. Use *Ms.* in domestic correspondence when the woman does not have another title such as *Dr.* (*Ms.* is uncommon in other countries.)

Ms. Donna Devane

MARRIED WOMAN. Socially, a married woman is addressed by her husband's full name preceded by *Mrs.* unless she has retained her maiden name and uses it with *Ms.* In domestic business correspondence, she is addressed by her first name and her married or maiden name, as preferred, preceded by *Ms.* unless she has indicated that she prefers *Mrs.* Some women combine their maiden and married names, with or without a hyphen (Ms. [or Mrs.] Janice Evans-Sloane).

Married name:	Ms. Carol Mackenzie
	Mrs. Carol Mackenzie
	Mrs. William Mackenzie (*formal social only*)
Maiden name:	Ms. Carol Neitzer
Maiden and married names:	Ms. Carol Neitzer-Mackenzie
	Mrs. Carol Neitzer-Mackenzie

WIDOW. Follow the rules for a married woman.

DIVORCEE. If a divorcee retains her married name, use *Ms.* in domestic correspondence unless she prefers *Mrs.;* use *Ms.* if she resumes using her maiden name. Some women use combined maiden and married names preceded by *Ms.* (or *Mrs.*, if preferred). In formal social usage she may be addressed as *Ms.* with her chosen last name (maiden or married) or by her maiden name combined with her married name preceded by *Mrs.* (no first name).

Married name:	Ms. Margaret Weeks
	Mrs. Margaret Weeks
Maiden name:	Ms. Margaret Barkley
Maiden and married names:	Ms. Margaret Barkley-Weeks
	Mrs. Margaret Barkley-Weeks
	Mrs. Barkley-Weeks (*formal social only*)

WHEN A SPOUSE IS TITLED. In social usage, do not address a married woman who has no title by her husband's title. Address her as *Mrs. Robert E. Adams* or, in domestic correspondence, as *Ms. Mary Adams* or *Ms. Mary Clarke* (maiden name) if she prefers. If she is addressed jointly with her husband, the correct form is *Dr. and Mrs. Robert E. Adams* or *Dr. Robert E. Adams and Ms. Mary Adams* or *Dr. Robert E. Adams and Ms. Mary Clarke.*

If the wife is titled and the husband untitled, mention her name first: *Dr. Mary Adams and Mr. Robert E. Adams* or *Dr. Mary Clarke and Mr. Robert E. Adams.* If both are titled, use *Drs. Robert E. and Mary Adams* or *Dr. Robert E. Adams and Dr. Mary Adams* or *Dr. Robert E. Adams and Dr. Mary Clarke.*

PROFESSIONAL WOMEN. Address a woman with a professional title by her title followed by her first and last names.

> Dr. Ruth Alder
> Professor Ruth Alder
> Dean Ruth Alder
> President Ruth Alder
> Mayor Ruth Alder

UNMARRIED MAN AND WOMAN. When writing to an unmarried man and woman, address them individually, placing one name under the other, with the person of highest professional or scholastic rank listed first. If both are of equal rank, use alphabetical order.

> Mrs. Lynda Russell, Associate Director
> Mr. Adam L. Matthews, Research Assistant
> [Address]

When you do not know whether an addressee is a man or a woman, omit the title in the inside address of a letter and use the person's first name in the salutation.

M. L. Dorsey
1133 North Avenue
Prescott AZ 86301

Dear M. L. Dorsey:

Rules for Prominent Persons

PERSONS WITH NAME UNKNOWN. You should make every effort to learn the name of the person addressed, as well as his or her title. If you know the title only, address the person by the title prefaced by *The*, for example, *The Lieutenant Governor of Iowa*. The formal salutation would be *Sir* or *Madam*.

ACTING OFFICIAL. When a person is acting as an official, the word *Acting* precedes the title in the address but not in the salutation or spoken address: *Acting Mayor of Memphis, Dear Mayor Blank*.

FORMER OFFICIAL. A person who has held an official position and is entitled to be addressed as *The Honorable* is addressed as *The Honorable* after retirement. The title itself, such as *Senator* or *Governor*, is not used in the address or salutation. Even a former president is called *Mr.* An exception to this practice is the title of *Judge*. A person who has once been a judge customarily retains the title even when addressed formally. Retired officers of the armed forces retain their titles, but their retirement is indicated as, for example, *Lieutenant General John D. Blank, U.S.A., Retired*. (The military omits periods in designations such as *USA*.)

PERSONS WITH SCHOLASTIC DEGREES. In many cases, the name in the inside address is followed by the abbreviation of a scholastic degree: *Ms. Nancy Shallet, Sc.D*. (In the case of more than one degree, list the one pertaining to the person's profession first.) If you do not know whether the addressee has the degree, do not use the initials. Also, do not address a person by a scholastic title (*Dr.*) unless he or she actually possesses the degree that the title indicates (*Ph.D.*).

SPOUSES OF OFFICIALS AND DIGNITARIES. The wife of an American official does not share her husband's title. When they are addressed jointly, the address is, for example, *Ambassador and Mrs. Blank.* Nor does a husband share his wife's title. When they are addressed jointly, if he does not have a title, the contemporary forms of address are *Ambassador* Ruth Blank and *Mr.* J. W. Blank (the titled person preceding the untitled person), *Ambassador* Ruth and *Mr.* J. W. Blank, *Ambassador* and *Mr.* Blank.

WOMEN. Women in official or honorary positions are addressed just as men in similar positions, except that *Madam* replaces *Sir,* and *Ms.* or *Mrs.* replaces *Mr.*

HOW TO SELECT AND ORDER STATIONERY

Type and Size of Paper

LETTER. Traditional business letterhead is 8½ by 11 inches, and most envelopes, files, and business machines are geared to accommodate this size. It is referred to as "letterhead size," although letterheads in other sizes are used, as shown here in inches:

Baronial	5½ by 8½
Executive, or Monarch	7¼ by 10½
Official	8 by 10½
Standard	8½ by 11

MEMO. Memo sizes vary much more than letter sizes, from small note paper to the regular 8½ by 11 inches. The half-sheet, or memo size, is 5½ by 8½ inches. Standard forms of almost any size can be purchased from office suppliers. Some offices decide upon an appropriate size for their communications and have their own memo letterhead printed using the same design as found on their company letterhead stationery. In selecting a size for memo stationery to be sent outside the firm, be certain to consider the size of the envelope into which it must fit.

Letterhead Design

GENERAL CHARACTERISTICS. Businesses use letterheads to convey a desired image. The typography, logo (emblem), color, and arrangement of these items may be conservative, bold, or anything else a firm desires. The basic company stationery, used by most offices, may be white or colored stock (e.g., light beige or blue) and have black ink or color for the letterhead. The typical size is 8½ by 11 inches.

EXECUTIVE STATIONERY. Letterheads for the personal use of top executives typically possess dignity, and their chief characteristic is simplicity, attained by black or some other conservative color engraved on pure white, cream, or other pastel color paper of heavy substance and high quality. In addition to the company letterhead, the full name of the office is usually engraved at the left margin, with the title of the office the executive holds directly underneath it. The size of the sheet is sometimes smaller than standard letterhead. The two common types of paper are *laid* (with a pattern of parallel lines that give a ribbed appearance) and *wove* (with a smooth, soft finish).

An executive may use his or her business letterheads for all correspondence except answers to formal invitations, letters of condolence, or answers to letters of condolence from personal friends. For these purposes, many executives use writing paper engraved with the residence address or with both his or her name and residence address. The stationery is usually the Executive, or Monarch, size (7½ by 10½ inches).

Continuation Sheets

Continuation sheets are frequently referred to as "second sheets." Technically, the reference is inaccurate. Second sheets are papers used for making multiple copies of letters and other documents.

Continuation sheets should be of the same size and quality as the letterhead. Some firms print their name and address in small type at the top of the continuation sheet, near the left margin. Order these sheets when you order the letterhead paper. After you have placed two or three orders for stationery, you will be able to judge more accurately the proportion of continuation sheets to letterheads that you use.

Envelopes

Envelopes should be of the same quality and stock as the letterhead. The most popular sizes for business are as follows:

No. 5½ (Baronial)	4⅝ by 5¹⁵⁄₁₆
No. 6¾ (Commercial)	3⅝ by 6½
No. 7 (Executive, or Monarch)	3⅞ by 7½
No. 9 (Official)	3⅞ by 8⅞
No. 10 (Standard)	4⅛ by 9½

Nos. 6¾, 9, and 10 accommodate 8½- by 11-inch letterheads. The Executive, or Monarch, size is used with a letterhead size of 7¼ by 10½ inches. The No. 5½ Baronial is also sometimes used by business executives for personal stationery.

How to Order Stationery

JUDGING QUALITY. The quality of paper may be judged by its appearance and use characteristics.

DETERMINING WEIGHT. Paper weight (called "basis weight") is measured by the ream, which consists of 500 sheets cut to a given standard size for that grade. The weight of the ream may be 16 pounds, 20 pounds, 24 pounds, or even more (or less). Letterhead stationery is usually selected in a 20- or 24-pound weight. Lighter-weight paper may be used for foreign correspondence or other messages where cost savings through weight reduction is desired.

PLACING ORDERS. Get a written quotation that specifies the *weight* and *content* of paper and the kind of printing or engraving that will be on it. In placing your order, specify the following requirements and include sample stationery from a previous printing.

1. The quantity in sheets
2. The weight
3. The content (cotton, watermark rag, or good-grade sulphite bond)
4. The grain: parallel to writing for typewriter copies; perpendicular to writing for certain duplicating processes (discuss this with the print shop)
5. That the letterhead shall be printed on the "felt" side of the paper or the top side (all but a careless printer will do this automatically)

6. The size

7. The color

8. The previous order number if a repeat order

9. The supplier's reference number if an initial order

HOW TO ORDER SOCIAL AND BUSINESS CARDS

Social Visiting Cards

Social cards are primarily used in business for gift enclosures. They should be of medium to heavy white card stock. The approximate size of a card is 3 by 1½ or 2 inches. The printing or engraving should be in black ink. Stationery stores and printers have samples of card stocks and typefaces. When ordering for an executive, be certain to order some matching envelopes so that they may be sent with flowers or other gifts.

Initials should be avoided as much as possible, and in any case, one's given name must be written in full. It is better to write out the entire name, usually centered on the card. *Mr., Mrs., Miss,* or *Doctor* are the only titles that should be used before the name. *Doctor* is always spelled out when space permits. *Miss* may be used by single women or omitted, as desired. The card of a married or widowed woman has *Mrs.* and the husband's full name (unless she has retained her maiden name). A divorced woman uses her first name and the last name she has assumed: *Mrs.* Nancy Cantrell. If a name is very long, *Sr.* or *Jr.* may be abbreviated and capitalized, but it is preferable to write out the word in lowercase letters (*junior, senior*). An address is usually not given on a social card.

Informals

Along with the decline in the use of social cards, except as gift enclosures, has come an increase in the use of *informals,* larger cards on which one can write a short message. Although the design depends on preference, an executive's name or name and address are usually engraved (but may be printed) in black ink on white or cream-colored paper at the top of a single (rather than foldover) card. The address, if used, often appears in the upper right corner and the name is centered slightly beneath it. When the name alone is used, it is usually centered on the card. Since informals are sent in the mail, they must be 3½ by 5 inches or larger.

Business Cards

All executives who call on clients or customers or who make business calls for any reason carry business cards. You should be aware of, and able to make suggestions about, the social amenities for business calling cards: how they differ from a social card, what is the proper wording to use on them, and whether they are sent with presents from an executive to customers or clients.

STYLE FOR EXECUTIVES AND OTHER PERSONNEL. The business card is usually about 3½ by 2 inches (which may be larger than a social card). On the executive level, a business card often has the executive name in the middle of the card and his or her title and the firm name in the lower left corner, either one above the other. The address and possibly telephone and facsimile numbers are then in the lower right corner. If the business is in a large city, the street address and the city are used, but the state may be left out. If the company offices are in a small town, the name of the state is written on the same line as the town, no street address being necessary. Some very prominent executives omit their titles from the card; only the executive's name and the name of the company appear on it.

High-level executives may prefer a conservative type style engraved in black on quality parchment or white card stock. Some executives, however, prefer a more informal, modern look.

Initials and abbreviations, although not correct on social calling cards, may be used on business cards. However, the word *Company* should be written out unless the abbreviation *Co.* is part of the registered name of the firm. A title such as *Mr.* does not precede the executive's name on a business card as it does on a social card, but *M.D.* or military rank may follow the name.

On business cards of company representatives below the executive level, the firm name is usually imprinted or engraved in the center of the card and the individual's name, title, and department in the lower left corner. The address and the telephone and facsimile numbers may be in the lower right corner. Sometimes the person's name and title will be centered and the firm name will be in the left corner and the firm address in the right corner. The precise arrangement depends on personal preference.

Cards used by salespersons or other representatives to advertise a company or a product frequently carry a trademark or emblem or an eye-catching design, and the printing may be done in color. A calendar or advertising matter may appear on the back of the card. The telephone number is always on a card of this type.

Doctors and dentists frequently put their office hours on their cards. Printers and stationery stores have numerous examples of card stock, typefaces, and designs ranging from ultraconservative to ultramodern.

Cards presented to businesspeople in other countries should have the same data printed on the reverse side in the language of the other country. Use the same quality ink and design to avoid the implication that a foreign recipient is less important than a domestic recipient.

BUSINESS CARDS FOR WOMEN. The business card used by a woman is the same as that for a man, and her personal title (*Ms., Mrs.*) is included only if it would otherwise not be clear that she is female.

Women in business follow the rules for addressing women in other situations. Thus a card might read *Edna Hill, Edna Wright,* or *Edna Hill-Wright.* A woman with a professional title may use her maiden name, her married name, or a combination, with her first name and her title. For instance, when Dr. Laura Rogers marries John Edwards, she may call herself "Dr. Laura Edwards," or "Dr. Laura Rogers," or "Dr. Laura Rogers-Edwards." On her business cards she may use either "Laura Rogers, M.D.," "Laura Edwards, M.D.," or "Laura Rogers-Edwards, M.D." Military titles may also be used. Secretaries who represent their employers at meetings should have their own cards printed, following the suggestions given here.

CORRECT USE OF BUSINESS CARDS WITH GIFTS. Formerly, an executive did not enclose a business card with a gift, even though the gift was going to a client or customer, unless it accompanied a gift to a new business. Otherwise, the giving of a gift was thought to be a social gesture, requiring a social card. This rule is no longer followed strictly. Instead of using either social cards or business cards, presidents and board chairmen of large corporations sometimes have special cards printed for enclosure with holiday gifts. These special cards usually mention the company name and the name of the executive sending the gift but in no way resemble a business card. Some executives personalize their regular business cards by striking out their printed or engraved name on the front and writing a note on the front or back, signing it with their first name only. Other executives prefer to use informals or foldover note paper for short messages.

HOW AND WHEN TO REORDER CARDS. Remember to put a reorder reminder with your employer's business cards. It usually takes ten days or two weeks (perhaps longer for engraved cards). Until you have been working for your employer long enough to know his or her wishes, you should get approval before reordering. For instance, your employer may want to change the style of the card or some of the information on it.

HOW TO PREPARE INVITATIONS

Formal Invitation

A formal invitation is written in the third person and is printed or engraved, partially printed or engraved, or handwritten. Envelopes are always handwritten. With a partially printed or engraved invitation, spaces are left open to write in the guest's name, time, date, and nature of the event. Paper for a formal invitation is often heavy white or light cream stock. Printers and stationery stores have books with sample paper and sample lettering. A stiff white or ivory card may be used for partially printed or engraved invitations, and heavy white or cream writing paper may be used for handwritten invitations. The invitation should be presented in a standard format, and the letters *R.s.v.p.* in the lower left corner mean that a reply is expected. Figures 51 and 52 are examples of formal invitations showing the placement and spelling of date, hour, and address.

Formal Reply

The reply (and envelope) to a formal social invitation must be handwritten and follow the same form as the invitation. Thus you would fill out and return an R.s.v.p. card if one is enclosed with the invitation (Figure 53), or you would write a reply by hand in the third person and repeat essential data, as shown in Figure 54. For a handwritten reply, use personal writing paper and fold it in half the same as the invitation itself. A reply to a social-business function is handwritten on business letterhead.

FIGURE 51

Formal Invitation

Miss [or Ms.] Michele Green, president

The New Company

requests the pleasure of your company

at a reception

in honor of Mr. Walter Arlington

on Friday, the fourth of August

at half past six o'clock

1200 Seventh Avenue

Houston

R.s.v.p. card enclosed　　　　　　　　*Black tie*

FIGURE 52

Formal Invitation

MARCUS INDUSTRIES

[logo]

The Board of Trustees

cordially invite you to

cocktails

to celebrate Marcus Industries'

twentieth year of service

Friday, April 6th

5 to 7 p.m.

1600 Larchmont Boulevard

Cincinnati

R.s.v.p. card enclosed

FIGURE 53

Reply Card

[logo]

Mr. *Walter Steiner*

Name of Guest *Sarah Schoenfeld*

Accept ✓ Regret ____ Tele. No. *342-6107*

Cocktails, April 6th, 5–7 p.m.
1600 Larchmont Boulevard
Cincinnati

FIGURE 54

Formal Reply

Mr. and Mrs. James Forest
accept with pleasure
the kind invitation of Miss Greene
to be present at the reception
in honor of Mr. Walter Arlington
on Friday, the fourth of August
at half past six o'clock
1200 Seventh Avenue
Houston

FIGURE 55

Informal Invitation

David Cross

requests the pleasure of your company

at *Dinner*

on *Saturday, April 9, at 8 o'clock*

at *The Cross-Country Inn*

44 Lakeside Boulevard,

Burlington

R.s.v.p.
471-9033

FIGURE 56

Informal Foldover Card

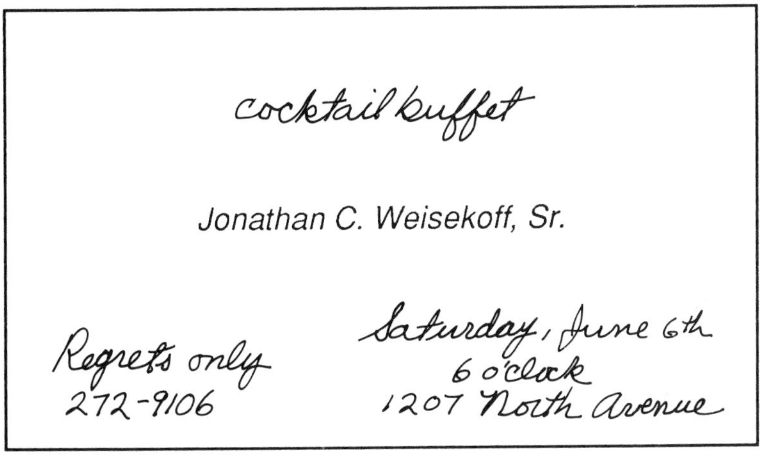

cocktail buffet

Jonathan C. Weisekoff, Sr.

Regrets only
272-9106

Saturday, June 6th
6 o'clock
1207 North Avenue

Informal Invitation

An informal invitation can be prepared by typewriter or computer on business letterhead or can be handwritten on folded note paper or calling card. Figure 55 is an example of a preprinted fill-in invitation; Figure 56 shows the front of an informal foldover card. Printers, stationery stores, and office-supply stores have examples of informal, printed invitations, partially filled in. An informal social-business invitation, such as one for a business luncheon, is commonly typed as a social-business letter on business letterhead.

Informal Reply

Your reply to an informal invitation depends on the format of the invitation itself. The R.s.v.p. notice in Figure 55 gives a telephone number, indicating that you should reply by telephone. Most of the informal business invitations that come into the office are not sent on printed cards or note paper but are prepared by typewriter or computer as a traditional letter. Replies are then sent in a letter format on business stationery.

Chapter 11

Valuable Aids for Productive Letter Writing

PLANNING A LETTER

Plan your communication as a whole before you start to write the first paragraph, following this procedure:

1. Read carefully the letter you are answering and, if office policy permits, highlight with a yellow marker the main points of the letter (if office policy does not allow marking on original letters, make a photocopy or take notes on a separate piece of paper).

2. Tell yourself the purpose of the letter.

3. Outline what your answer should contain.

4. Collect all the facts you need to reply.

5. Try to visualize your reader and adapt the letter to the recipient.

USING APPROPRIATE LANGUAGE

Stilted and Trite Expressions

A key objective in good letter writing—as in any writing—is to avoid stilted or worn-out expressions. To illustrate the improvement that results when stilted or trite phrases are eliminated, consider the following example of a business letter as originally written and then as rewritten:

STILTED AND VERBOSE LANGUAGE.   Notice the stiff, out-of-date style in this example:

> Dear Sir:
>
> Replying to your kind favor of the 15th inst. in which you inform us that the enameling sheets ordered by you have not come to hand, beg to advise we have checked up on this shipment and find same left our factory March 10 and should have reached you March 13. For your information wish to state that we are now tracing through the express company. If the shipment does not arrive by March 19, kindly wire us collect, and we will duplicate same.
>
> Regretting the inconvenience caused you, we are,
>
> Yours truly,

CLEAR AND STRAIGHTFORWARD LANGUAGE.   Here the outmoded style has been transformed into a concise, businesslike, modern style:

> Dear Mr. Bradley:
>
> The shipment of enameling sheets that you asked about left our factory on March 10. It should have been delivered to you not later than March 13, so we have asked the express company to trace the shipment immediately.
>
> If you do not receive the sheets by March 19, please call us collect, and we will start another shipment at once.
>
> We are very sorry that this delay occurred and assure you that we will do everything possible to expedite delivery.
>
> Sincerely yours,

LIST OF TRITE TERMS.   Here is a list of expressions that are stilted or trite and should be avoided.

acknowledge receipt of. Use *We received.*

advise. Used with too little discrimination and best reserved to indicate actual advice or information. Often *say* or *tell* is better—or nothing.

> *Poor*: We wish to *advise* that your order was shipped
>   April 7, 19—.
>
> *Better*: Your order was shipped April 7, 19—.

and oblige. A needless appendage.

> *Poor:* Kindly ship the enclosed order *and oblige.*
>
> *Better:* Please ship the enclosed order *immediately.*

as per; per. Correctly used with Latin words *per annum* and *per diem.* Otherwise, *a, according to,* and the like are preferred in general writing.

> *Allowable*: Five dollars *per* yard
>
> *Better:* Five dollars *a* yard
>
> *Poor:* *As per* our telephone agreement
>
> *Better:* As we agreed by telephone; or *in accordance with* our telephone agreement
>
> *Poor:* Per our contract
>
> *Better:* According to our contract

ascertain. A more pompous way of saying *find out.*

> *Poor:* Can you *ascertain* the reason for the delay?
>
> *Better:* Can you *find out* the reason for the delay?

at all times. Often used with little meaning. Better to use *always.*

> *Poor:* We are happy to hear from you *at all times.*
>
> *Better:* We are *always* happy to hear from you.

at this time. Unnecessary in most cases. Try *at present, now, currently,* or *temporarily.*

> *Poor:* We wish to advise that we are out of stock of handkerchiefs #1000 *at this time.*
>
> *Better:* Handkerchiefs #1000 are *temporarily* out of stock.

at your convenience; at an early date. Trite, vague, and unnecessary in most cases. Be specific.

> *Indefinite*: Please notify us *at an early date.*
>
> *Better:* Please let us know *within ten days.*

Vague: We would appreciate hearing from you *at your convenience.*

Better. We would appreciate hearing from you *by the tenth of May.*

beg. Do not use old-fashioned expressions such as *beg to state*, *beg to advise*, and *beg to acknowledge*.

Poor: In answer to yours of the 10th inst., *beg to state . . .*

Better. In answer (or reply) to your letter of May 10, *we are pleased . . .*

consummate. A more pretentious word for *complete*.

Poor. After we *consummate* the arrangements . . .

Better. After we *complete* the arrangements . . .

contents carefully noted. Contributes little to a business letter.

Poor. Yours of the 5th received and *contents carefully noted.*

Better. The instructions outlined in your letter of June 5 have been followed in every detail.

duly. Unnecessary.

Poor. Your request has been *duly* forwarded to our executive offices.

Better. We have sent your request to our executive offices.

enclosed please find. Needless and faulty phraseology. The word *please* has little meaning in this instance. The word *find* is used improperly.

Poor. *Enclosed please find* sample of our #1989 black film ribbon.

Better. *We are enclosing* a sample of our #1989 black film ribbon.

encounter difficulty. A more pompous and dramatic expression for *have trouble.*

> *Poor:* If you *encounter difficulty* finding volunteers . . .
>
> *Better:* If you *have trouble* finding volunteers . . .

enlighten. A pretentious way of saying *tell.*

> *Poor:* Ray will *enlighten* you about it.
>
> *Better:* Ray will *tell* you about it.

esteemed. Too flowery and effusive.

> *Poor:* We welcomed your *esteemed* favor of the 9th.
>
> *Better:* Thank you for *your letter* of April 9.

favor. Do not use the word *favor* in the sense of letter, order, or check.

> *Poor:* Thank you for your *favor* of October 5.
>
> *Better:* Thank you for your *letter* of October 5.

forward. Do not use for *send.*

> *Poor:* Please *forward* a brochure to my office.
>
> *Better:* Please *send* a brochure to my office.

have before me. A worn-out expression.

> *Poor:* I *have before me* your complaint of the 10th.
>
> *Better:* *In answer* (or *reply*) to your letter of
> November 10 . . .

hereto. Often needless.

> *Poor:* We are attaching *hereto* a copy of our contract
> covering prices on linoleum.
>
> *Better:* We are attaching a copy of our contract
> covering prices on linoleum.

herewith. Often redundant.

> *Poor.* We enclose *herewith* a copy of our booklet.
>
> *Better.* We are pleased to enclose a copy of our booklet.

in re. Avoid. Use *regarding* or *concerning*.

> *Poor.* *In re* our telephone conversation of this morning . . .
>
> *Better.* *Regarding* our telephone conversation of this morning . . .

in the event that. Use *if* or *in case*.

> *Poor.* *In the event* that you are in the city Thursday . . .
>
> *Better.* *If* you are in the city *Thursday* . . .

initiate. A pompous substitute for *start* or *begin*.

> *Poor.* She plans to *initiate* work on the project tomorrow.
>
> *Better.* She plans to *start* work on the project tomorrow.

inquire. A pompous substitute for *ask*.

> *Poor.* May I *inquire* how many attended?
>
> *Better.* May I *ask* how many attended?

it is requested that. Simply say *please*.

> *Poor.* *It is requested that* you meet us at the restaurant.
>
> *Better.* *Please* meet us at the restaurant.

line. Do not use in place of *merchandise* or *line of goods*.

> *Poor.* Our salesman Joe Whitman will gladly show you our *line*.
>
> *Better.* Our salesman Joe Whitman will gladly show you our *merchandise* (or *line of goods*).

our Ms. Becker. Use *our representative Ms. Becker* or just *Ms. Becker.*

> *Poor:* Our Ms. Becker will call on you next Tuesday, May 10.
>
> *Better:* Our representative Ms. Becker will call on you next Tuesday, May 10.

procure. Simply say *get.*

> *Poor:* Did you *procure* the supplies?
>
> *Better:* Did you *get* the supplies?

recent date. Vague and unbusinesslike. Better to give the exact date.

> *Vague:* Your letter of *recent date* . . .
>
> *Definite:* Your letter of *June 2* . . .

render. Do not use for *do* or *offer.*

> *Poor:* We would like to *render* our assistance.
>
> *Better:* We would like to *offer* our assistance.

same. A poor substitute for one of the pronouns *it, they,* or *them.*

> *Poor:* Your order of the 5th received. Will ship *same* on the 10th.
>
> *Better:* Thank you for your order of March 5. We expect to ship *it* to you by the 12th of this month.

state. Often too formal. Better to use *say* or *tell.*

> *Poor:* We wish to *state* . . .
>
> *Better:* We are pleased to *tell* you (or *let you know*) . . .

take pleasure. A trite expression. Use *are pleased, are happy,* or *are glad.*

> *Poor:* We *take pleasure* in announcing our fall line of shoes.
>
> *Better:* We *are pleased* to announce our fall line of shoes for women.

thanking you in advance. Wordy, and the tone implies that your request will be granted. A simple "thank you," however, is permissible and is used by many writers as a friendly and appreciative conclusion to a letter of request.

> *Poor:* Kindly mail me any information you may have for removing crabgrass. *Thanking you in advance* for the favor, I remain,

> *Better:* I would appreciate any information you may have for removing crabgrass. Thank you.

under separate cover. Meaningless. Better to be specific and give the method of shipping.

> *Poor:* We are sending you *under separate cover* a copy of our pamphlet "How to Grow Lawns."

> *Better:* We are pleased to send you *by third-class mail* a copy of our pamphlet "How to Grow Lawns."

valued. Too effusive. Better to omit.

> *Poor:* We appreciate your *valued* order given to our salesman Ryan McCall.

> *Better:* We appreciate the order you gave our salesman Ryan McCall.

wish to say; wish to state; would say. All are examples of needless, wordy phraseology. Simply omit.

> *Poor:* Referring to your letter of the 10th, *wish to say* that we cannot fill your order before the first of December.

> *Better:* In answer to your letter of March 10, we will be able to fill your order about December 1.

Unnecessary Words and Phrases

Many letter writers add unnecessary words to their phrases because of an erroneous idea that the padding gives emphasis or rounds out a sentence. For example, letter writers frequently speak of *"final* completion," *"month of* January," or *"close* proximity." The completion is obviously final or it is not complete. January is obviously a month. Incidents in proximity are obviously close. Here is a list of padded phrases frequently used in business letters and other writing. The italicized words are completely unnecessary and should be omitted.

It came *at a time* when we were busy.
Leather depreciates *in value* slowly.
During *the year of* 19—, prices fell.
It will cost *the sum of* one hundred dollars.
At a meeting *held* in Philadelphia, the bylaws were amended.
We will ship these shoes *at a* later *date*.
In about two weeks' *time*, the tourist season begins.
In order to reach our goal, we must work harder.
The mistake *first* began because of a misunderstanding.
A *certain* person by the name of Bill Jones is here.
The *close* proximity of these two incidents surprises me.
It happened at *the hour of* noon.
We see some good in both *of them*.
In *the city of* Columbus, residential housing is scarce.
The body is made *out* of steel.
During *the course of* the campaign, four candidates withdrew.
Perhaps it may be that you are reluctant.
Our uniform *and invariable* rule is to reward senior employees first.
Someone *or other* must be responsible.
We are now *engaged in* building a new plant.
By *means of* this device we are able to detect surface lesions.
All that is necessary *for you to do* is to use common sense.
We have discontinued *the policy of* the late renewal penalty.
Will you please *arrange to* send the booklets.

TWO WORDS WITH THE SAME MEANING. Some letter writers think that if one word does a job, two words add emphasis. Actually, the second word makes the thought less effective. Here are a few examples of "doubling."

> sincere and good wishes
> first and foremost
> appraise and determine
> experience together and contacts in
> deeds and actions
> optimism and encouragement
> refuse and decline
> unjust and unfair
> advise and inform
> at once and by return mail
> immediately and at once
> demand and insist
> right and proper
> obligation and responsibility

Favorite Words and Expressions

Avoid acquiring favorite words or expressions. They become habitual and your letters sound cut and dried. Some writers unintentionally overuse their pet expressions:

> *Poor:* *For your information,* the meeting will be Friday, August 11, 19—. A copy of the agenda is enclosed *for your information.*

> *Better:* The meeting will be Friday, August 11, 19—. A copy of the agenda is enclosed.

Short Words and Sentences

WORD LENGTH. Some people think that using a vocabulary of big words will mark them as learned, but when short, simple words will do the job as well, it merely marks them as pretentious. This does not mean that an extensive vocabulary is not an asset; the more words that writers know, the more clearly and forcibly they can express themselves. But they should never choose words of many syllables over those with few syllables unless there is an important reason for doing so. For example, in a business letter, there is seldom a justifiable reason for using *ultimate* for *final, prerogative* for *privilege, transpire* for *occur, commence* for *start, terminate* for *end,* or *converse* for *talk.*

SENTENCE LENGTH. Since the aim of a business letter is to transfer a thought to the reader in the simplest way with the greatest clarity, avoid long, complicated sentences. Break up long, stuffy sentences by making short sentences of the dependent clauses. Here is an example of a long, confusing sentence.

> Believing the physical union of the two businesses to be desirable and in the best interests of the stockholders of each corporation, the Boards of Directors have given further consideration to the matter and have agreed in principle upon a new plan that would contemplate the transfer of the business and substantially all of the assets of the A Company to B in exchange for shares of common stock of B on a basis that would permit the distribution to the A Company stockholders of one and one-half shares of B common stock for each share of A Company common stock.

Rewritten in four shorter sentences, this becomes:

> The Boards of Directors of both companies thought a merger desirable and in the best interests of the stockholders. They finally agreed on a new plan. The business and substantially all assets of the A Company will be transferred to B in exchange for B common stock. A Company stockholders will get one and one-half shares of B common stock for each share of A Company common stock.

Various Shades of Meaning

Use different words to express various shades of meaning. In this case a large vocabulary is helpful. The writer with an adequate vocabulary writes about the *aroma* of a cigar, the *fragrance* of a flower, the *scent* of perfume, and the *odor* of gas, instead of the *smell* of all these things.

Words That Antagonize

Words that carry uncomplimentary insinuations not only are tactless but often defeat the purpose of your letter. Never use a word that might humiliate or belittle the reader. Here are some expressions to avoid in letters:

claim	inferior
complaint	mistake
defective	neglect
dissatisfied	poor
error	trouble
failure	unfavorable
inability	unsatisfactory

For example, do not say "You *failed* to enclose the prospectus you mentioned." Say "The prospectus you mentioned was not enclosed."

Words That Please

Just as some words can, in certain contexts, irritate or offend a reader, other words may have the opposite impact and may tend to make a reader feel good. The following are examples of words that usually influence readers positively:

admire	please
appreciate	promise
cooperate	respect
enjoy	satisfy
genuine	success
happy	thank you
intelligent	wonderful

Action Words

In business one often wants to motivate someone to do something. Perhaps your boss wants to encourage the staff to work harder or stimulate an associate to accept a proposal. Whatever the situation, if your aim is to prompt a productive response, action words can be a useful tool. The following are examples of words that tend to motivate others to take action.

analyze	implement
benefit	launch
coordinate	monitor
create	organize
design	progress
enhance	review
generate	streamline

Nondiscriminatory Language

SEXISM. Avoid all forms of sexist language. For example, use asexual words such as *people, civilization,* or *humankind* for *mankind; salesperson* for *salesman;* and *businessperson* or *businesspeople* for *businessmen.*

> The workshop is especially useful to *businesspeople*
> (*not* businessmen).

Do not refer to personal characteristics (instead of professional capabilities) in women.

> The program is run by William Parker, manager, and
> Jeanne Troy, executive assistant (*not* William
> Parker, manager, and his lovely assistant Jeanne).

Use first and last names and personal titles of men and women in the same way.

> Mr. Rod Boylston and Ms. Amelia Steiner (*not*
> Mr. Rod Boylston and Amelia).

Refer to adults as men and women in describing a group or use neutral terms such as *staff* or *committee.*

> The men and women (*not* the men and girls) from the
> West Coast office will host this year's banquet.

Use the term *spouse* or *spouses,* not *wife* or *wives,* in general references.

> Employees and their spouses (*not* wives) are
> excluded from the contest.

Do not use *his* in general references; use *his and her* or *their.*

> Each candidate must manage *his or her* (*not* his) own
> campaign. *Or* Candidates must manage *their* own
> campaigns.

Avoid comments that refer to a person's sex.

> The speaker (*not* woman speaker) will discuss
> high-tech management.

RACIAL AND ETHNIC BIAS. Eliminate language that reveals or focuses on racial and ethnic characteristics. Delete remarks that reinforce negative attitudes and draw attention to racial and ethnic backgrounds.

> Marilee Jefferson is a chemical engineer (*not* a black
> engineer) at ABC Industries.

Delete remarks that humiliate members of a racial or an ethnic group.

> The company's English-language workshop is
> designed for Mexican and Puerto Rican employees
> (*not* "disadvantaged" minorities).

Do not divide people into general white and nonwhite groups; identify the specific heritages.

> The new training program is for Afro-American,
> Mexican-American, and Asian (*not* nonwhite)
> employees.

Do not unwittingly suggest that members of a certain heritage usually are the opposite of some admirable trait.

> Foy Chan is a capable manager (*not* an open and
> honest manager, which might imply that people of
> his heritage are often secretive and dishonest).

Delete comments that stereotype all members of various racial and ethnic groups.

> Some people are very ambitious (*not* the Japanese
> are very ambitious).

HANDICAP BIAS. Eliminate remarks that draw attention to a person's handicap or unintentionally demean the person. However, even though you should avoid comments that unnecessarily draw attention to a disability, do not foolishly pretend it does not exist when circumstances necessitate dealing with it.

> Nora, let's discuss ways to make the files more
> accessible (*not* Just ask Jane if you need
> something from the files).

Do not perpetuate negative attitudes and draw unnecessary attention to a disability; make any essential reference to a disability incidental.

> Una Macauley, who has multiple sclerosis (*not* the MS victim Una Macauley), will head the orientation seminar for handicapped employees.

Avoid comments that stereotype all people with handicaps or a certain type of handicap.

> Roy has exceptional hearing (*not* Roy has exceptional hearing since he can't see).

Do not use words and phrases that are demeaning even if common. For example, say *disabled* or *handicapped*, not *crippled*; *emotional difficulties*, not *insanity*; *seizure*, not *fit*; *slow learner*, not *retarded*; and *speech and hearing impaired*, not *deaf and dumb*.

> The cafeteria should be made more suitable for handicapped employees (*not* cripples).

Overused Intensifiers

Guard against the overuse of intensifiers—words that emphasize other words that they modify (*really* good). Usually, the following intensifiers are unnecessary:

best	really
more	somewhat
most	such
pretty	too
quite	very
rather	

Intensifiers that end with *self* are occasionally used for emphasis: The police chief *himself* broke the law. But in most cases, the following *self* intensifiers should be omitted:

herself	ourselves
himself	themselves
itself	thyself
myself	yourself
oneself	yourselves

Jargon, Buzzwords, and Gobbledygook

Jargon, buzzwords, and gobbledygook are all generally undesirable forms of slang or business shorthand. Businesspeople are often guilty of overusing words that pertain only to their own trade or profession (e.g., *interface*). Although technical or specialized language is useful and sometimes necessary, it should not be overused outside of the workplace. *Buzzwords* are words that sound important (e.g., *optimize*) but often are more vague than the specific concrete terms they replace and hence should be replaced with more appropriate terms. *Gobbledygook* is an especially vague form of jargon (e.g., *facilitize*) and should always be deleted. The following are examples of the forms of slang or business shorthand that careful writers avoid.

ballpark figure	know the ropes
bottom line	off the record
budgetwise	operative
downsize	optimize
finalize	optimum
frame of reference	parameter
gameplan	prioritize
hype	scenario
infrastructure	systematize
input	viable
interface	workup

Vague Words

Vague words lead to misunderstandings and confusion. Although general terms are useful when you don't know a specific word or don't want to restrict your comments to a specific idea, it is usually desirable to be clear and precise in your written or spoken comments.

Poor: Please *distribute* these flyers.

Better: Please *mail* these flyers.

Poor: Bring your own *tools and supplies* to the meeting.

Better: Bring your own *pens, pencils, and paper* to the meeting.

Cliches

Cliches are used so widely in business that many people do not know that the expressions they are using are trite, unimaginative, and often wordy. Readers in other countries, who translate English literally, are puzzled and confused by them. Avoid worn-out expressions such as the following:

back to square one	long shot
blessing in disguise	more or less
bury the hatchet	one fell swoop
by the grapevine	pay through the nose
come up smelling like roses	rank and file
fair shake	water under the bridge
handwriting on the wall	whole ball of wax

Misplaced Words

Sometimes when a word appears in the wrong place in a sentence it can change the meaning of the comment. Notice how the meaning changes in the following examples depending on the position of certain words:

She told her boss *only* what she had read.

She told *only* her boss what she had read.

They agreed to return the flipcharts *on Monday*.

They agreed *on Monday* to return the flipcharts.

Entering the lobby, he saw the delegates.

He saw the delegates *entering the lobby*.

A Positive Approach

Always use a positive (and tactful) approach in letters. The following examples show how much more forceful and effective a positive approach is than a negative one:

Negative: We cannot quote you a price until we have seen the specifications.

Positive: We will be glad to quote you a price as soon as we have seen the specifications.

Negative: We cannot ship these goods before August 8.

Positive: We will ship the goods on or shortly after
August 8.

FOR A BETTER LETTER BEGINNING

The opening of any letter must get the reader's attention immediately.
(See Figure 57.) The following sections describe eight concrete suggestions
that will help you develop a technique of starting a letter, even a routine
letter, in a natural and interesting manner.

Make the Opening Short

Long paragraphs are uninviting and discourage many readers; therefore,
the opening should be short. Refer to Figure 57 for examples.

Go Straight to the Point

Rambling or making long introductory comments does not capture a
reader's attention. Get right to the point of your message. This does away
with the practice of restating the contents of a letter that you are answering.

WHEN TO USE A RESTATEMENT. A brief restatement, however, sometimes
makes it easier for your correspondent to find his or her letter in the files.
Or the restatement might relieve the reader of having to refer to a copy of
the letter. In these cases, it is desirable. Ask yourself if the restatement
serves any useful purpose. Consider this example of a reply to a person
who wants to buy an oil burner:

> In reply to yours of the 15th in which you state that you
> would be interested in receiving more complete information as to
> our STEADY-HEAT Oil Burner, since you are considering
> installing a burner in your home, we are enclosing a booklet . . .

The reader knows that he is considering installing a burner and knows
that he wrote for information about the Steady-Heat burner. The date that
he wrote the letter is of no interest. Why not open the letter with the following:

FIGURE 57

Chart Showing Openings and Closings
for Various Types of Letters

	Openings	Closings
Appreciation	It was generous of you to give me so much of your time yesterday, and I appreciate your co-operation.	Thank you for your help. We're ready to serve you in every way possible.
Appreciation for messages of congratulations	I appreciated your comments about my efforts to guide the new Credit Management program.	Thanks for your thoughtful note.
Replying to requests for information booklets, and samples	The information you requested concerning the STEADY-HEAT Oil Burner is in the enclosed booklet.	When we can be of further help, please let us know.
Congratulations	I was pleased to read in this morning's paper of your appointment yesterday to the state supreme court.	You have my sincere congratulations added to all others that you must be receiving.
Complaints	Unfortunately, my last case of mayonnaise reached me in damaged condition.	I will keep the damaged case until I receive further instructions from you.
Adjustments or answering complaints	We are glad that you notified us promptly that some of your books have not yet arrived.	We very much regret the delay and hope that it will not cause you serious inconvenience.
Asking a favor	I know you must be busy with vacation time nearly here, but I have a small favor to ask of you.	I hope you'll be able to find time in your busy schedule to join us. Everyone is eager to see you again.
To Applicants	We appreciate the interest shown by your application for a position on the Prentice-Hall sales staff.	The best of luck to you, both in finding the right job and in making the most of it.

The enclosed booklet "Better Heat with Steady-Heat" will provide the information you requested about the STEADY-HEAT burner.

Avoid Stilted Openings

Participial phrases and stilted expressions bore readers and exhaust them before they reach the point of the letter.

Boring and Artificial	*Natural*
Replying to your letter of July 9 in which you request that we send you samples of our WEAREVER fabrics, we are asking . . .	Thank you, Mr. Edwards, for your request for samples of our WEAREVER fabrics.
In accordance with the authority contained in your letter of April 9th, the records of this office have been amended to show the date of your birth as January 4, 1963, instead of January 4, 1965.	In answer to your letter of April 9, we have corrected our records to show the date of your birth as January 4, 1963, instead of January 4, 1965.
It is with the deepest regret that I must decline your kind invitation to speak at the luncheon meeting of the Secretarial Association to be held on April 18.	I'm very sorry that I must decline your invitation to speak at the Secretarial Association's lunch on April 18.

Include the Reader's Name

The use of the reader's name in the opening sentence personalizes a routine letter. The use of the name in the illustrations that follow makes those opening sentences more interesting to the reader. When overdone, however, the use of the name sounds too familiar. Do not use the name more than once in a very short letter.

Refer to a Previous Contact

Take advantage in your opening of a previous contact with your reader, either by letter or in person. Reference to a mutual interest or contact requires no particular skill, but it tends to get a letter off to a good start.

> It was a pleasure to have such an interesting visit with you during my trip east last week.

> Thanks to you, Mr. Barrett, my stay in Cleveland was delightful.

Use a Pleasant Phrase

Use any appropriate statement that may trigger an agreeable attitude. Even if you are going to disagree with the reader later, don't put the bad news in the first sentence. This device is particularly helpful in adjustment letters. Here are three pleasant opening sentences:

> We appreciated your letter, Ms. Adams.

> You are very patient, Mrs. Jones.

> Your interest in better business letters, Mr. Johnson, makes writing to you a pleasure.

Use "Who," "What," "When," "Where," and "Why"

When you have good news that you know will interest an individual or group, follow newspaper style and tell your reader who, what, when, where, and why in the opening. This technique is particularly effective in sales or promotional letters. Here is an illustration:

> June [*when*] is that eagerly awaited month when motoring Americans take to the highways for their annual vacations [*why*]. Wherever [*where*] you may be planning to go this summer, our new travel information bureau [*who*] will be happy to assist [*what*] you.

Use Other Techniques of the Experts

The experts devote considerable time and effort to developing techniques that help them write attention-capturing openings. Some additional techniques they have developed are as follows:

1. Use of a question
2. Statement of an unusual or not commonly known fact
3. Telling of an interesting story
4. Use of a quotation
5. Reference to a famous name

FOR A BETTER ENDING

The closing of your letter frequently influences the reader to do what you ask—or it might have the opposite effect. The closing should add something definite to the letter or it should not be there. (See Figure 57.) The following sections describe four techniques that will help you to write closings that add to the persuasiveness of your letters.

Avoid Stilted or Formal Endings

A dull closing sentence can ruin an otherwise effective letter. For example, here is the last paragraph of a letter soliciting club memberships. The job was finished—and it was a good job—with the first paragraph. But the writer weakened the appeal of the selling paragraph because he could not resist the temptation to add this old-fashioned sentence in the closing paragraph:

> Thanking you for your kind consideration of the advantages of membership in our organization, and trusting you will see your way clear to acceptance of this invitation, we remain . . .

Suggest Only One Action

Tell the readers the *specific* action that you expect them to take. If they are given a choice of several things to do, they will probably do nothing. Concentrate on *one* action and do not mention others.

In the following closings, the alternative suggestions tend to confuse the reader; the specific suggestions are impelling and produce action.

Alternative Suggestions	*Specific Suggestions*
Write us a letter or telegram or send the enclosed card right now.	Send the enclosed card today.
If it is convenient for you to see me, please drop me a note or call me at 356-4920.	When it is convenient for you to see me, please call me at 356-4920.
Please mail this payment to arrive at our office within five days. Or if you aren't able to do that now, send us a postdated check for the same amount.	Please mail this payment to arrive at our office within five days, by Saturday, May 7, 19—.

Use Dated Action

If you expect the reader to take certain action in the future, use *dated action*. That is, tell the reader that you expect the action by a given date or within a certain number of days, not "in the near future."

The experience of an insurance company illustrates how an indefinite date can weaken a letter. The company had difficulty getting reports from examining physicians. The letters asked the doctors to return the report blanks "as soon as possible," but the company found that on an average it had to write 3.7 follow-up letters to each physician. The company then switched to dated action and called for the return of the blanks by a specific date. As a result, the average number of follow-up letters for each report was reduced to 2.1.

Here are two examples of dated-action closings:

> For us to handle this claim promptly for your patient, we will need your preliminary report by the *end of this week, July 13, 19—*.

> An *immediate reply* will enable us to complete the draft of the contract by Friday.

Use Positive Words

Negative words anywhere in a letter weaken it, because they show the writer's lack of confidence. They are doubly harmful in the closing. *Hope, may, if,* and *trust* tend to defeat the purpose of any business letter. Compare the following negative closings with the positive revisions.

Negative	*Positive*
If you will O.K. the card, we will gladly send you a copy of the bulletin. *Trusting* you will do this . . .	Your copy of this interesting bulletin is waiting for you. Just O.K. and mail the card.
Now is the time when our customers are stocking up for summer business. We *trust* you will join them by placing your requirements on the order blank enclosed.	Our customers are now stocking up for summer business. You can join them by placing your requirements on the order blank enclosed.
If you would like to have our salesperson call with samples, please so advise.	Ted Mead, someone you are going to like, will be around next Monday morning to show you samples and service your order.

INTERNATIONAL CORRESPONDENCE

Foreign letters and electronic messages are formatted the same as domestic correspondence. But other aspects of the letter-writing process differ. You need to be very literal, to *over*punctuate your messages, and to understand and respect the customs of your foreign readers.

Do's and Don'ts in Foreign Letters

THE NEED TO BE LITERAL. Many businesspeople try to make their messages sound casual and conversational by using contemporary language. Although this can be effective in domestic correspondence, it can cause problems in foreign messages. Foreign readers and translators usually don't understand American language deviants such as slang (*throw money at*), cliches (*change of heart*), and jargon (*downsize*).

Idiomatic usage is also a puzzle to foreigners. An *idiomatic expression* (*make good*) is one that is based on common usage but is not consistent with the rules of English grammar. Contractions (*it's*) are another problem to foreigners, who may have trouble finding them in their dictionaries.

To help your foreign readers and translators, (1) edit your messages to be very literal; (2) avoid slang, jargon, buzzwords, cliches, idiomatic expressions, and other language variants; and (3) avoid contractions.

THE NEED TO OVERPUNCTUATE. Although the trend in contemporary writing is to use less punctuation (fewer keystrokes for the typist and computer operator), this policy creates problems for foreign readers who need commas and other punctuation marks to avoid misreading a message. Notice how the omission of a comma in the following example could cause someone who uses English only as a second or third language to stumble over the use of the word *however*.

> *Poor:* No policy however well intentioned justifies this
> much risk.

> *Better:* No policy, however well intentioned, justifies
> this much risk.

To guide your readers through sentences that may seem simple to a domestic reader but will frustrate a foreign reader, use punctuation liberally to indicate pauses and to clarify your intended use of phrases, clauses, and other parts of the sentence.

THE NEED TO UNDERSTAND YOUR READER'S CUSTOMS. It is important to be aware of the special religious, social, and other customs of any reader, domestic or foreign. Your foreign readers may have customs that will affect the degree of formality you use (more formality is safest when you are unsure), how soon it is proper to initiate business proceedings, and what forms of address you should use (*Dr., Mr., Mrs.,* or other).

Each country has its own holidays, religious observances, business procedures, forms of address, and other customs. Purchase a book about the countries with which your firm deals, and take notes on all matters pertaining to style, tone, and other points of composition in your letters.

MODEL LETTER FILES

Using Models

Many secretaries store in their computer model letters and paragraphs that can be edited in future situations requiring almost the same letter. Often they simultaneously maintain a notebook or file folder of printouts. A large file will require an index of categories (announcements, apologies, congratulations, and so on) so that you can locate suitable models without delay. If you keep both a computer file and a binder or file folder of paper copies, be certain to use the same index for both files.

You can create your own database of models by saving samples of both outgoing and incoming letters and by composing your own examples to add to the collection. Rewrite your models from time to time to keep them current.

The secretary is concerned with two types of models: (1) those that are used mostly as a guide in composing future letters and (2) those for which all or most of the letter is repeated each time (form letters), often with the inside address and salutation merged into the basic letter of the model. Most major word processing programs have a merge feature that enables users to combine a standard text with an address list.

Using Model Letters and Paragraphs

A list of routine letters that the secretary writes and examples of them are given in Chapter 12. These letters may be used in your file of models. Copy the letters that you are likely to need, and add them to your computer and hard-copy files. Analyze your correspondence to see what other types of models you may need, and select repetitive letters and paragraphs from previous correspondence to add to your files of models.

You will find that model paragraphs can be used in many letters. For example, if you answer, instead of merely acknowledge, a letter received in your employer's absence, your opening paragraph could be the same in each letter. Add the standard paragraph to your files, but be careful not to use the same opening paragraph in frequent letters to the same person.

Using Form Letters

Situations that can be covered by form letters vary with the secretary's position. The factors that determine which messages might be sent as a form letter are (1) frequency of use, (2) purpose of the letter, and (3) the probable response of the recipient. Differences of opinion exist about the effectiveness of form letters, but if they are properly handled and personalized with your computer, there can be no logical objection to them. When the letter is purely routine or when the recipient is interested only in the information it contains, a standard letter can be used to advantage.

Chapter 12

Model Letters and Memos

CATEGORIES OF CORRESPONDENCE

Letters and Memos the Secretary Signs

Your employer's wish is the principal factor in deciding which letters you might sign. If he or she expects you to use your own judgment, the determining factor is consideration for the recipient of the letter. A writer who expects a letter to be answered by an executive might be offended if it is passed to someone else in the office. In this case, it would be poor business procedure for you to write the letter over your signature. If the recipient is interested only in the information given in answer to the letter, however, you can safely write it over your own signature. As secretaries assume more responsibility in the modern business world, letter writing becomes an increasingly important daily activity.

Examples of letters that you will often write and sign include:

1. Acknowledgments
2. Adjustments in account
3. Appointments
4. Follow-ups
5. Inquiries
6. Orders

7. Reminders

8. Requests

A pattern and models for each type of letter are illustrated in the following sections. The signature is the same in each case.

[Your handwritten signature]

Secretary to Mr. Jones

Letters and Memos Your Employer Signs

STYLE AND TONE OF LETTERS. Familiarize yourself with the tone and style of your employer's correspondence. The aim in composing a letter for someone else's signature is to write it *exactly* as that person would have dictated it. Here are three rules:

1. Follow the executive's style as closely as possible without flagrantly disregarding the rules of good letter writing. Thus if the executive has a few pet phrases, use them, but if he or she has a habit of opening letters with long participial phrases, try a natural opening, and probably your employer will approve it.

2. Adapt the tone of your letter to the tone the executive uses when dictating. Thus if the letters come quickly to the point, compose letters in that tone; if the letters are gentle and courteous, use that tone. It is particularly important to know whether the tone of the letter should convey personal friendship, a formal business relationship, or some other attitude.

3. Use the same salutation and complimentary close that your employer would use. They change with the relationship existing between the writer and the addressee. Thus if your employer uses "Dear Bob" as the salutation to Senator Robbins, you would use the same salutation in letters that you write to him for your employer's signature.

LETTERS ABOUT COMPANY BUSINESS. All the rules of good letter writing described in Chapters 10 and 11 are applicable here. One type of letter that you may send out in the company's name is the letter announcing to a firm or a customer that a donation is being given in its name to a hospital or charity in place of the usual Christmas gift.

> Dear Mr. Jones:
>
> On behalf of this company, I am happy to let you know that we are sending in your name a donation to the Children's Hospital in place of the personal gift we usually send at this season.
>
> May the coming holidays bring to you and yours good health, happiness, and a full share of those things that make this world a better place in which to live.
>
> Cordially yours,

PERSONAL BUSINESS LETTERS. Before you acquire the technical knowledge necessary to write letters about the company's business, you may be expected to handle the personal letters (e.g., congratulations, thank yous, and special greetings) that the amenities of business require.

You will write some of these letters for your employer's signature without instructions and others from a few words of instruction or from marginal notes that he or she makes on an incoming letter.

An effective personal letter must meet these requirements, in addition to those given in Chapter 11 for any letter:

1. Be sure that your letter is opportunely timed. A note of congratulations, a message of condolence, or a letter of appreciation is far more effective if it is written promptly—that is, immediately after the event.

2. Make the tone of your letter personal, so that the message is tailor-made for the *individual* reader.

3. Be cordial and friendly but not gushy.

4. Select a salutation and complimentary close that harmonize with the friendly tone of the letter. Use the reader's name in the greeting unless the letter is addressed to an organization.

5. Write with a sincerity that lends conviction to your message.

6. Have your employer sign the letter. The recipient will value the personal touch of his or her signature.

Letters and Memos Written in Your Employer's Absence

Letters that you may be expected to write over *your* signature when your employer is away include the following. Refer to the models in this chapter for examples.

1. Acknowledgments
2. Apologies
3. Appointments
4. Appreciation
5. Follow-ups
6. Goodwill
7. Inquiries
8. Orders
9. Reminders
10. Requests

MODEL BUSINESS LETTERS AND MEMOS

Acknowledgments

ACKNOWLEDGMENT WITHOUT ANSWER. The pattern for these letters is simple:

1. Respond promptly and thank the writer for any information or material you received.
2. State that your employer is out of the city or away from the office, if that is the case, and give the expected date of his or her return.
3. Assure the writer that his or her message will receive attention when your employer returns.
4. If the delay may cause inconvenience to the writer, add a note of apology.

Do not refer to an illness or other difficulties when explaining your employer's absence from the office, unless the writer knows the circumstances. Say: "Because of Mr. Peter's absence from the office, he will not be able to attend . . ."

> Dear Ms. Stevenson:
>
> Thank you for sending Mr. James the information about the Denver project. He's away on business now, but I'll bring this to his attention as soon as he returns, and I'm certain that he will contact you promptly.
>
> Please accept my apologies for this unavoidable delay.
>
> Sincerely yours,

> Dear Mr. Ames:
>
> Your letter of August 14 arrived the day after Ms. Tauber left on a two-week business trip. Since you indicated that it does not require an immediate answer, I'll hold it for prompt attention on her return.
>
> Sincerely yours,

> Dear Ms. Parker:
>
> Thank you for contacting Mr. King about the new tax forms. He is attending a convention in Philadelphia this week and will return to the office next Monday. I'll be certain to bring your letter about the new tax forms to his attention at that time.
>
> Sincerely yours,

ACKNOWLEDGMENT THAT ALSO ANSWERS. The important factor in answering, as well as acknowledging, a letter is to know the facts. Here is a suggested pattern:

1. Respond promptly and identify the incoming letter.
2. State that your employer is away if that is the case.
3. State the facts that answer the letter and express appreciation if something was received.
4. If appropriate, or desirable, state that your employer will write when he or she returns.

Dear Mr. Frederick:

Your letter reminding Mr. Stone of his promise to speak before the Managers Association at lunch on Tuesday, December 20, arrived during his absence from the office.

He will return on Monday, and I will bring your thoughtful letter to his attention then. I know that he is looking forward to speaking at the luncheon.

Sincerely yours,

Dear Mrs. Florio:

Thank you for asking to see Mr. French about office equipment.

Mr. French will be out of the office for the next month. However, Mr. Rhinesmith is responsible for all company purchases, and you may want to contact him. His office is in Room 512, and he is usually available every morning from 10 o'clock until noon. If you want to call him for an appointment, his extension is 560.

I'll see that he has this correspondence, so you may refer to it when you call.

Sincerely yours,

Dear Mr. Roberts:

Your letter asking Ms. Ainsworth to speak before the Business Club of Jackson on January 14 arrived a few days after she left town on a business trip.

However, after checking her schedule for January 14, I see that she is scheduled to make a special report to the Board of Directors on that day; apparently, it will therefore be impossible for her to address the members of your club at that time.

I know that Ms. Ainsworth will nevertheless appreciate your kind invitation and will write to you as soon as she returns to Nashville.

Sincerely yours,

Adjustments

Errors, misunderstandings, and changes in plans make it necessary for businesspeople to write letters of adjustment. Many adjustments result from the use of charge cards, credit cards, and company or individual travel accounts, and the same pattern can be applied to most of these situations.

LETTERS OF ADJUSTMENT OF BUSINESS ACCOUNTS. Companies and executives usually have accounts established for travel tickets, hotel accommodations, car rentals, office supplies, restaurant services, and other business activities. Charges are then billed to the company or the executive by itemized monthly statements. When services are involved, the statement is accompanied by a *record of charge* made at the time the service is completed. This record of charge shows the date and items of purchase, the signature of the purchaser, and the name and address of the service establishment.

Always check the items of the record of charge signed by your employer against the itemized monthly statement received. Also make certain that any cancellations of orders or reservations have been properly credited to the account. Letters that you write may include these categories: (1) when the amount of an item or the total is incorrect, (2) when a cancellation has not been credited, (3) when an item not purchased is charged to an account, and (4) when returned merchandise has not been credited.

1. *When the amount of an item is incorrect.* The same procedure would apply if the total were incorrect.

Give the person's name, the company, and the account number.

Describe the incorrect item and tell how it is incorrect.

State what the item should be, giving any documentary information that you have.

Ask for a corrected statement or enclose a check for the correct amount and ask that the error be rectified on the next statement.

Ladies and Gentlemen:

SUBJECT: Account 365-809-112, A. D. Brock, Computers, Inc.

Your statement of June 17 charges Mr. Brock's account for dining services at the Princess Hotel in Bermuda during the week of May 8 for $312.67. According to the record of charge, the total should be $302.67, or $10.00 less than the statement shows.

Enclosed is Mr. Brock's check for this month's statement, minus $10.00. Please credit Mr. Brock's account in full.

Sincerely yours,

2. When a cancellation has not been credited. Follow these steps when a bill or statement fails to credit the amount of an order that was canceled.

Give the person's name, the company, and the account number.

Give the date of the order and identify the goods or services that were requested.

Tell how and when the order was canceled.

State the amount that has been incorrectly charged.

Ask for a corrected statement or enclose a check for the correct amount and ask that the error be rectified on the next statement.

Ladies and Gentlemen:

SUBJECT: Account 711-298-067-A, Andrea R. Ace, Winston Motors

Your statement of August 15 to Ms. Ace includes a charge of $60 for 1,000 business cards. We placed this order on July 28, 199–, and were given a delivery date of August 20.

On Ms. Ace's instructions, however, I canceled this order by telephone on the morning of July 29 and also sent a letter of confirmation on that date (copy attached).

I am, therefore, enclosing Ms. Ace's check for the amount of your August 15 statement, minus the $60 charge for business cards. Please credit her account in full.

Sincerely yours,

Apologies

When there is an adequate and convincing explanation for a situation that requires an apology, a few words can be devoted to the explanation. If no justification exists, a frank admission of that fact usually has a disarming effect upon the reader. Regardless of the circumstances, any situation that requires a letter of apology requires a tone of warmth and friendliness.

LETTER OF APOLOGY. Whenever possible, follow an apology with a solution or means to rectify the situation.

Dear Ms. Morton:

I hope you will accept a sincere apology for my absence from the Credit Association meeting yesterday afternoon.

When I promised earlier in the week that I would be there, I fully intended to be present. But a meeting of our own credit department staff yesterday afternoon lasted much longer than expected, and it was impossible for me to get away.

When I see Jim Davis at lunch tomorrow, I will ask him to bring me up to date on yesterday's developments.

Sincerely yours,

EXPLANATION OF OVERSIGHT. An oversight usually deserves an explanation as well as an apology. Sending a thoughtful letter to a customer or client is a good way to improve customer relations.

Dear Mr. Clemons:

I was sorry to learn that our shipment of booklets was delivered without the free self-inking address stamp. The stamp that was promised with your order is enclosed.

Usually, the booklets are shipped from our own facility, and our packers routinely insert a stamp with each order. But because your request was a rush order, we asked the printer to ship the booklets directly to you from the print shop, bypassing our offices. Apparently, someone missed the instructions to include your stamp with the order.

Please accept our apologies for this oversight and any inconvenience it may have caused you. We appreciate your interest in our booklets and hope you will continue to find them a productive adjunct to your next mailing.

Sincerely yours,

Appointments

Here is the pattern that a letter arranging an appointment should follow:

1. Refer to the purpose of the appointment.

2. Suggest, or ask the person to whom you are writing to suggest, the time, place, and date.

3. Ask for a confirmation of the appointment.

There are three main categories of appointment letters: (1) your employer asks for an appointment, (2) you ask someone to come in to see your employer, and (3) you reply to a letter asking your employer for an appointment.

YOUR EMPLOYER ASKS FOR APPOINTMENT. Whether the letter goes out over your signature or your employer's signature, keep it brief, but be certain to provide all necessary facts.

1. You want to fix the time. Include the place, time, and date.

Dear Mr. Green:

Mr. Stone is attending a convention in Chicago next week. While he is there, he would like to discuss with you the revision of your book on tax reports.

Will it be convenient for him to call on you Tuesday afternoon, June 1, at two o'clock?

Sincerely yours,

2. You have to let the other person fix the time. If your employer is following a schedule, you might suggest a general time period such as within the next week or two; otherwise, leave it all up to the recipient.

Dear Mr. Roberts:

Ms. Gorman is returning from Washington on Friday of this week and would like to discuss with you the results of her sessions with the Labor Committee.

Will you please ask your secretary to telephone me and let me know when it will be convenient for you to see Ms. Gorman?

Sincerely yours,

YOU ASK SOMEONE TO COME IN TO SEE YOUR EMPLOYER. You may find it necessary to specify a certain time, or you may be able to let the other person choose the time.

1. You want to fix the time. Again, give the place, time, and date.

Dear Mr. Morris:

Mr. Polinski would like to know if it would be possible to see you on Monday, February 27, at 2 o'clock in his office, Room 201, to complete arrangements for the rental of your summer cottage.

Please let me know whether this time is convenient.

Sincerely yours,

2. You let the other person fix the time. You may nevertheless want to suggest a general period such as "next week."

Dear Mrs. Elwood:

The papers in connection with the trust that you are creating for your daughter are now complete, except for your signature. Mr. Watkins would like to know if you could come to his office early next week to sign them.

Please telephone me to arrange a convenient time for you.

Sincerely yours,

REPLY TO LETTER ASKING YOUR EMPLOYER FOR AN APPOINTMENT. You will either agree to the request or say no politely. If you say yes, you must again deal with the three basic facts of date, time, and place.

1. You fix a definite time. In this case, you give a specific time rather than a general period.

Dear Ms. Smith:

Mr. Brown will be glad to see you on Monday, December 27, at 2 o'clock in his office, Room 201, to discuss with you the program for the annual convention.

Sincerely yours,

2. You let the other person fix the time. Here you give the recipient a chance to suggest a time but you may want to indicate the week.

Dear Mr. Rhoades:

Mr. Ricotti will be glad to see you some time during the week of March 3 to talk over the installation of the elevator in his residence at 20 West Street.

If you will telephone me at 353-9200 we can arrange a time that will be convenient for you and Mr. Ricotti.

Sincerely yours,

3. Your employer signs the letter. The facts that are stated remain unchanged even though your employer signs the letter. However, he or she may want to add a personal closing sentence.

Dear Mr. Boyd:

I will be happy to talk with you when you are in Minneapolis next week. Would it be convenient for you to come to my office at 10 o'clock, Thursday morning, November 5? I believe this hour will give us the best opportunity to discuss your project without interruption.

It will be a pleasure to see you again.

Cordially yours,

4. You have to say no politely. The trick to writing these letters is to combine firmness with courtesy.

Dear Mr. Thomas:

Ms. Jarvis has considered very carefully all that you said in your letter of December 21. If there were any possibility that a meeting with you would be helpful, she would be glad to see you. However, she does not believe that would be the case and has asked me to let you know and to thank you for writing.

Sincerely yours,

Appreciation

A letter of appreciation is sent when someone does something helpful or commendable and is often used to promote goodwill. It should not discuss other business and should reflect genuine sincerity and honest gratitude, not merely the writer's desire to conform with the rules of etiquette. The letter should be brief, and the tone should be one of friendly informality. The factors that determine the suitable degree of informality are the following:

1. The extent to which the favor, service, or courtesy performed is personal

2. The degree of friendship existing between the writer and the recipient

3. The age and temperament of the recipient

FOR PERSONAL FAVOR OR SERVICE. In the case of an important favor such as filling in at the office during a long absence, you might offer to reciprocate or generally suggest that the recipient not hesitate to ask if ever you can be of assistance. However, appreciation for small favors and deeds also promotes good relations, and the overall tone and style of the letters are similar regardless of the magnitude of the situation.

> Dear John:
>
> Thank you so much for the ticket to the Annual Retailers' Convention and Forum. The exhibits were extremely interesting, and I particularly enjoyed the forum sessions.
>
> It was thoughtful of you to remember me. My sincere thanks for your kindness.
>
> Cordially,

FOR ASSISTANCE TO COMPANY, CLUB, OR ASSOCIATION. It is important to acknowledge all forms of special assistance with a brief letter of appreciation.

> Dear Ms. Noble:
>
> It was generous of you to spend so much time with our organization yesterday. The material you brought and the suggestions you made will be of great help in our new organization plans in the Personnel Department.
>
> We all appreciate your cooperation. My sincere thanks for your valuable help.
>
> Sincerely yours,

FOR HOSPITALITY. When the thanks involve personal attention, the letter should have an especially warm, personal tone.

Dear Ned:

I want to thank you for your hospitality during my two-week stay in Chicago. I count the evenings spent in your home as highlights of my stay in your city.

Your personal knowledge of the Merchandise Mart and the time you spent with me in the Mart greatly enhanced the pleasure and fruitfulness of my trip.

Thanks so much for your kindness.

Best regards,

FOR MESSAGE OF SYMPATHY. Keep acknowledgments pertaining to sympathy brief—usually, no more than one to three sentences.

Ladies and Gentlemen:

The members of this organization appreciate your kind expression of sympathy upon the sudden death of our treasurer, Thomas Thornhill. We feel keenly the loss of one whose ability and exceptional personal qualities have meant so much in the growth of this firm.

Please accept our sincere thanks for both your sympathetic message and your splendid tribute to Mr. Thornhill.

Sincerely,

FOR MESSAGE OF CONGRATULATIONS ABOUT A SPEECH. If the circumstances provide the opportunity, say something nice about the other person or organization in addition to expressing appreciation.

Dear Andy:

That was a fine letter you wrote to me about my talk in Milwaukee last week, and I appreciate it ever so much.

Speaking to the members of your organization was a most enjoyable experience, and I am very glad that my remarks contributed in some small way to the success of your meeting.

Cordially,

FOR FAVORABLE MENTION IN A SPEECH. You can easily adapt this letter if mention was instead made in an article or a book.

Dear Mr. Kennedy:

Thank you for the generous remarks you made in your speech before the Dry Goods Association yesterday about my part in the association's activities.

Coming from someone of your high standing among the businesspeople of this state, the compliment was especially pleasing, and I'm happy to know that you approve of my work.

Sincerely,

Collection

Large companies usually have a separate department that handles the collection of past-due accounts. In other cases, collection problems fall to each individual office or department.

When a series of follow-up letters is necessary, the tone usually progresses in each succeeding letter from a casual reminder to a firm final demand for payment before taking legal action.

1. Know the facts of each collection problem before preparing your letter.

2. Always give your client or customer a chance to pay before announcing other action.

A CASUAL REMINDER. The first letter is usually short and friendly since the payment may have been overlooked and not intentionally ignored.

Dear Mrs. Stone:

Just a friendly reminder that your payment of $82.40 for the stationery you purchased on August 12 will be very much appreciated.

If your check is already in the mail, please disregard this notice and accept our thanks. If it is not, won't you take a moment to mail it today?

Cordially yours,

A FIRM REMINDER. When it is clear that something is amiss, the tone of the letter, although not overly harsh and threatening, hints at an adverse impact on the recipient's credit standing.

Dear Mrs. Stone:

Ninety days have passed, but we have not yet received your payment of $82.40 for stationery purchased on August 12.

Since we have received no reply from you concerning this purchase, we assume the balance due is correct and that your records agree with ours. Won't you therefore send us your check immediately and protect your credit rating?

Your cooperation and prompt reply will be very much appreciated, Mrs. Stone.

Sincerely yours,

A FINAL APPEAL. This final letter before legal or other action is taken may be preceded by two other letters: (1) a discussion letter, asking the recipient to indicate, in confidence, whether he or she is having difficulties and (2) an urgent message that says the recipient must break his or her silence to avoid having serious action taken. If these efforts fail, the final appeal usually announces that a collection agency or attorney will take over shortly, and it gives the recipient one last chance to respond.

Dear Mrs. Stone:

Since you have not replied to any of my previous letters, I regret that we must take other steps to collect the past-due amount of $82.40 for stationery you purchased on August 12.

If we do not have your check within ten days, by January 1, the Morris Collection Agency will begin appropriate action in our behalf. I hope you will take this final opportunity to avoid further damage to your credit standing as well as the additional costs you may incur if legal action is required.

Send us your check by January 1, and the matter will be resolved before the Morris Collection Agency takes further action.

Sincerely,

Complaints

Anger and frustration breed many unjustified complaints. Such emotional outbursts usually involve unfair criticism and unreasonable requests for adjustments. Many complaints, however, involve actual errors and are proper and necessary.

LETTERS CALLING ATTENTION TO ERRORS IN ACCOUNT. In calling attention to an error in an account, avoid giving the impression that you are complaining. Keep the tone of your letter pleasant and remember not to use words that antagonize. The following situations often occur in business: (1) an item not purchased is charged to an account, (2) returned merchandise has not been credited to an account, and (3) the amount of an item or total is incorrect.

1. When an item not purchased is charged to the account. These letters should include the following points:

The person's name, the company name, and the number of the account

A description of the item charged in error, including the price and the date charged

Any additional pertinent information that you have

A request that the charge be investigated

A request for a corrected statement

Ladies and Gentlemen:

The June statement of Mrs. Robert Walker's account no. 14825 shows a charge of $35.85 on May 15 for three boxes of envelopes. Mrs. Walker charged three boxes for $35.85 on May 10 and three boxes for the same amount on May 20, but she did not charge anything on May 15. The six boxes that she bought were properly charged to her account.

Naturally, Mrs. Walker is concerned that someone may have used her account without her permission. Would you please investigate and let her know what happened?

Sincerely yours,

2. When returned merchandise has not been credited. Follow the same pattern as when the amount of an item is incorrect.

Ladies and Gentlemen:

On May 4 James Novak, account number 15836, returned for credit a pen and pencil set that he purchased from you on May 2. The price was $27.50, including tax.

Mr. Novak's June statement does not show this credit. A credit slip was given to him, but unfortunately, it has been misplaced. Mr. Novak would therefore appreciate it if you would verify the credit and send him a corrected statement.

In the meantime, I am enclosing Mr. Novak's check for $146.25, which is the amount of the statement less the price of the returned merchandise.

Sincerely yours,

LETTERS CRITICIZING GOODS OR SERVICES. When a product or service is unsatisfactory, the letter registering a complaint must be composed carefully. Although it is important to state the facts clearly and firmly, emotionalism should not govern the remarks or the tone of the letter. Usually, the objective is to motivate the recipient to compensate your employer for any loss suffered or to encourage the person or firm to perform better in the future. Anger, threats, insults, and the like may cause the recipient to become defensive and uncooperative. A rational and reasonable tone is generally the most effective.

Dear Mr. Schiavone:

We were disappointed to discover that your Model 290FM copier, which we leased from you on February 9, is not at all suitable for our needs. We are, therefore, asking that you replace it immediately with the larger model 291FM.

As we had emphasized to you before leasing the 290FM, our copy volume exceeds 1,000 copies a month, and we copy in quantities of 500 to 600 at a time. The 290 FM that you recommended, however, is not able to handle this volume. The lengthy cool-down period required after only twenty to thirty pages has made it impossible for us to complete our runs of 500 to 600 copies in adequate time. This delay is causing problems not only for us but for our clients.

We would like to exchange the Model 290FM for a 291FM before March 7, when our next run will occur. Please telephone me at 279-6000 on Monday, March 3, to discuss the adjustments in our lease. Thank you.

Sincerely,

Credit

Letters pertaining to credit matters involve the reputations of companies and individuals. Accuracy, honesty, and fairness are therefore essential in providing information.

PROVIDING CREDIT INFORMATION. If the person or organization asking for information provides a special blank form, fill out the required facts on that form. Otherwise, compose your own brief letter. Be accurate and honest, and show consideration for the subject's feelings and needs.

> Dear Mrs. Donnovan:
>
> Our experience with Brewster Toyland has been generally satisfactory. They have paid most of our invoices within thirty days and the rest within sixty days. Their purchases have ranged from $75 to $400 a month.
>
> Based upon our two-year relationship with Brewster Toyland, I would not hesitate to extend credit to them on purchases up to $500.
>
> If I can answer any further questions, Mrs. Donnovan, just let me know.
>
> Best regards,

REQUESTING CREDIT. When requesting certain forms of credit such as a bank credit card, one might simply ask for a credit application. In other situations, one might collect recommendations from business sources and call upon the supplier to present the backup information. Another common approach is to write a personal letter to the appropriate person in the firm from whom credit is desired.

> Dear Mr. Blakely:
>
> Along with our company's steady growth, our advertising department is facing continually increasing needs for additional printing and composition services. Since we are familiar with your reputation for quality work and prompt delivery, we would like to place some orders with you in the coming months.
>
> Our department currently purchases from $2,000 to $4,000 worth of printing and composition each month. Would you be able to extend your usual credit terms to our department for amounts within this range? I'm enclosing the name of our bank and two organizations that have provided credit to us in the past.
>
> Please let me know if you need additional information for us to establish an account with you. Thanks very much, Mr. Blakely.
>
> Sincerely,

Employee Communications

Management sends company employees a variety of letters, memos, announcements, and other forms of communication. Many of these messages are sent in memo format; others may be prepared in letter format with a salutation such as "Dear Staff Member" or "Dear Employee." Some letters are factual and straightforward such as a transmittal letter; others may be motivational, intended to encourage employees to take certain action or adopt a certain attitude. Often they are written in a warm, personal, conversational tone. One of the most common letters is the announcement (of a new employee, a promotion, a change in policy, and so on).

ANNOUNCEMENT OF STAFF APPOINTMENT. This type of appointment—introducing a new employee or a new appointment—has a friendly, upbeat tone. Although the letter should not be effusive in its praise, the staff member is usually presented in the best light, with mention of commendable background details.

TO: Members of the Training Department

FROM: Norman Stahl, Director
        Data Processing Training Department

SUBJECT: Assistant Director Appointment

I'm very happy to announce the appointment of Joanne Pressman as assistant director of our Data Processing Training Department. Joanne will assume the post vacated by Roy Carter, who recently joined our Los Angeles training staff.

Joanne comes to us from New York, where she was senior training instructor in the Data Processing Division of Standard Equipment, Inc. She taught data processing for eight years and worked closely with the data-processing training director during the past two years. As a result, she is thoroughly familiar with the scope and responsibilities of her new position and is highly qualified to handle the many challenges of the position of assistant director.

I know that Joanne will welcome your help and cooperation in becoming familiar with our department and her new duties. We all wish her much success and feel very fortunate to have her as part of our team.

LETTERS THAT SAY NO. Occasions inevitably arise when your employer has to say no to another employee. Perhaps a proposal is unacceptable, a request for a raise may be unrealistic, or it may be necessary to refuse someone's offer to help. The possibilities are endless. But all messages that say no should observe three basic rules:

1. If something is offered, thank the employee.

2. Explain—tactfully—why the offer or request is being turned down.

3. Try to encourage the employee in regard to future efforts or opportunities.

> Dear Ms. Snow:
>
> We have carefully considered your request for a salary increase of $4,000 in lieu of the $1,200 increase you were recently granted. I'm sorry to let you know, however, that our company is unable to grant an increase of that size at this time.
>
> Although your job record at Brandon Wholesalers is very satisfactory, you have only completed your first year with us. It is our current policy to offer salary increases up to $1,200 a year, but not beyond, to one-year employees in your job classification. But your next job and salary review is scheduled for June 1, and we will reevaluate your progress and the company's financial position at that time.
>
> We hope you will continue to enjoy your work at Brandon Wholesalers, Ms. Snow, and we look forward to a long and mutually rewarding association.
>
> Cordially,

TRANSMITTAL MESSAGE. People in business regularly send material back and forth. Sometimes a detailed cover letter is necessary to explain the reason for sending the material, what it is, and so on. Usually, though, material is routinely transmitted from one person to another with no detailed explanation. Brief transmittal messages are commonly typed in the memo format. Sometimes only a handwritten note is attached to the material or a routing slip. The traditional brief transmittal message should simply state what is enclosed. If it is necessary to tell the recipient why it is being sent, add a sentence or two of explanation.

TO: J. M. Aldine

FROM: A. J. Frastizi

SUBJECT: Electronic Products Survey

Here's the report you requested, Jim. Do let me know if you have any questions.

Follow-ups

If correspondence in your follow-up file (see Chapter 1) is not answered by the follow-up date, trace the letter for a reply. Your letter should cover the following points:

1. Identify the letter. Identification by date is not sufficient because your correspondent does not know what you are writing about.

2. Offer a reason for the recipient's failure to reply, without casting reflection on the recipient.

3. Enclose a copy of your original letter, unless it was very short. If so, simply repeat the contents in your follow-up letter.

COPY OF ORIGINAL LETTER NOT ENCLOSED. If you can briefly and adequately describe the unanswered correspondence, there is no need to enclose your original letter.

Ladies and Gentlemen:

On February 2 we ordered from you 200 copies of your latest bulletin, "Successful Selling Techniques," but we have not yet had an acknowledgment of the order.

Since our first order evidently went astray, please consider this a duplicate.

Sincerely yours,

COPY OF ORIGINAL LETTER ENCLOSED. Some things are too detailed to repeat in a new letter, and it is then better to enclose a copy of the original correspondence. Since the following example is a follow-up of a letter requesting a favor, it is written for your employer's signature. Notice that a reply is requested by a specific date.

Dear Ms. Roberts:

In the rush of work you probably have not had time to answer my letter of October 25 about using some of your selling ideas in our Real Estate Service, with credit to you. On the chance that this letter did not reach you, I'm enclosing a copy of it.

I would like to include your selling ideas in the next supplement of the service. This will be possible if I have your reply by December 15.

Thanks very much.

Cordially,

Goodwill

Letters of goodwill help build a favorable image of your company and develop good human relations both inside and outside the organization. Examples of such letters are letters of appreciation, offers of assistance, messages of congratulations, thank you letters, holiday and seasonal greetings, and letters of commendation.

1. Use any appropriate occasion to say something nice.

2. Write naturally and sincerely.

3. Do not use these letters for other business purposes; restrict your comments to the occasion.

Dear Ken:

Congratulations! I was really pleased—but not surprised—to learn about your promotion. I know you'll do an outstanding job, as always, and the company is truly fortunate to have you in charge of our field operations.

Best wishes, Ken, for a challenging and successful future in your new post.

Cordially,

Inquiries

Some letters simply and briefly inquire about a product or service or ask some other question. Letters that concern information received or requested include those that (1) supply information about things such as products and services, (2) acknowledge the receipt of information, and (3) answer inquiries about things such as delivery dates and prices. These letters should cover the following:

1. Identify the incoming letter and acknowledge any information received.
2. State that your employer is away if that is the case.
3. Provide the information requested, if possible.
4. Advise the writer that your employer will contact him or her upon return.

GENERAL INQUIRY. Most inquiries are brief, straightforward, and specific.

> Ladies and Gentlemen:
>
> Do you have a copier service representative in or near Jackson? If so, please send his name and telephone number.
>
> Thank you.
>
> Sincerely,

REPLY TO INQUIRIES. Be as informative and specific as possible in your first reply.

> Dear Mr. Jackson:
>
> In Ms. Cole's absence I'm replying to your inquiry about our Model ABC facsimile. This fax is in stock and available at $725. A brochure describing its many new features is enclosed.
>
> We appreciate your interest, and I hope this will be of some help to you until Ms. Cole returns next Monday, September 20. She will be happy to call you then to answer any further questions you may have.
>
> Sincerely,

Introductions

The letter of introduction may be prepared for direct mailing to the addressee or for delivery in person by the one introduced. In the latter case, the envelope should be left unsealed as a courtesy to the bearer. When there is sufficient time for the letter to reach its recipient before the arrival of the person introduced, the preferable practice is to send the note directly to the addressee.

The letter is ordinarily written in a spirit of asking a favor. It should include:

1. The name of the person being introduced
2. The purpose or reason for the introduction
3. All relevant and appropriate details, personal or business
4. A statement that any courtesy shown will be appreciated by the writer

The writer's acquaintance with the person introduced and with the recipient of the letter and also the purpose for which the letter is written determine its tone. When the writer is introducing a personal friend on both social and business bases, the tone is informal. When the writer is introducing a business associate for purely business reasons, the tone is more conservative.

A letter introducing a new sales representative is distinctly promotional. It often includes a summary of the new representative's qualifications and background for this work, as well as an assurance of the person's desire to cooperate with the reader.

INTRODUCING A PERSONAL FRIEND. Although the tone is more informal in this letter, it nevertheless includes pertinent background information about the friend.

Dear Ed:

My good friend Paul Davison plans to be in Akron next week and will present this letter to you.

Paul is very much interested in developing a house magazine for Robert Gould & Company of Cleveland, where he is in charge of the Sales Promotion Department. I have told him that you publish one of the finest house organs I have ever seen and suggested that he drop in for a chat with you.

I know that you and Paul will like each other, and I'm sure you can give him some valuable suggestions. I will certainly appreciate anything you do to assist him, and I know that Paul will be sincerely grateful for your help.

It must be about time for you to make another trip to Cleveland, and I hope you will plan to have lunch with me at the club.

Cordially,

INTRODUCING A BUSINESS OR PROFESSIONAL ASSOCIATE. The introduction written for only business reasons omits the informal comments of the preceding letter.

> Dear Ms. Bradley:
>
> I'm pleased to introduce to you a very good friend, Arthur Truesdale, chief engineer for the Acme Fisher Company.
>
> Mr. Truesdale is making a careful investigation of the heating and power plants of some of our largest industries before writing a report on the subject. He tells me that your company has one of the most modern plants in our country and that he would like very much to inspect it.
>
> Since you both might profit from knowing each other, I'm writing this letter and will greatly appreciate whatever assistance you can give Mr. Truesdale.
>
> Sincerely yours,

Orders

PLACING ORDERS. When a firm does not use a printed order form or requisition blank, orders are often written in a memo format, although the traditional letter format also may be used.

1. Indicate that your letter represents an order (or request for refund).
2. Give the name and address to which the bill should be sent.
3. List items desired, with all pertinent order data (catalog number, color, and so on).
4. State where the order should be sent and indicate if a specific delivery date is desired.

> TO: Art Supply Store
>
> FROM: J. T. Watt, Purchasing Department
>
> Please send the following item and charge it to our account number 730-01-221163.
>
> One (1) #47321 Easel, Walnut, $89.95
>
> Please deliver to our letterhead address, attention R. M. Blake. We will need this item on or before March 25.
>
> Thank you.

Ladies and Gentlemen:

On August 5 I placed an order for rental of two overhead projectors to be used at our company's September 6 seminar at the Hotel Franklin. The rental fee was paid in advance by our check no. 7808 for $47.50.

The seminar has since been postponed indefinitely, and we want to cancel our order. Please acknowledge this cancellation by mail and send us our refund of $47.50.

Thank you.

Sincerely,

Recommendations

Recommendations, or references, are commonplace in our mobile society. Not only do businesspeople recommend employees for new positions, they recommend products, services, and so on.

1. Provide as much helpful information as possible.

2. Be objective, honest, and tactful.

3. In requesting a reference from someone, be certain to show appreciation.

To Whom It May Concern:

Jennifer King was employed as our office manager from 1984 to 1987. During this time she was responsible for the management of word processing, telecommunications, filing and records management, and other office functions.

Ms. King supervised a staff of fourteen and is credited with raising employee morale and efficiency to the highest level ever experienced during my association with this company. At all times she demonstrated a thorough and expert knowledge of office skills and procedures and maintained a steady, constant flow of high-quality work.

Ms. King would be a great asset to any organization desiring smooth and efficient office functioning, and I am happy to recommend her for any position in the area of office management and administration.

Sincerely,

Reminders

Most reminders are brief, factual restatements of something someone has forgotten or may forget without the reminder. The memo format is ideal for such brief messages to coworkers and well-known business associates and customers.

1. State the facts.
2. Ask for a confirmation by letter or telephone.
3. Be tactful and do not accuse the recipient of being forgetful.

> TO: David Jocelyn
>
> FROM: Roger Misak
>
> SUBJECT: Education Committee Report
>
> Just a reminder that the Education Committee report you're preparing is due April 9. Could you drop me a note indicating the status of your project?
>
> Thanks, Dave.

Requests

Letters of request ask to have something done. Like inquiries, these letters should be specific:

1. Tell what you want, possibly why.
2. Indicate what the recipient should do.
3. Give all necessary facts.
4. Express appreciation if special effort is involved.

REQUEST FOR MISSING ENCLOSURE. If you urgently need the material, give the recipient a deadline.

> Dear Mr. Pearson:
>
> Since Mr. Symonds is out of town this week, I'm acknowledging your letter of April 12 to him. You mentioned that you were including the proposed plans for new tennis courts; however, they were not enclosed.
>
> Mr. Symonds will need the plans in order to discuss this matter with the Board of Trustees. Since they are meeting early next week, could you please send them by overnight express? Thank you very much.
>
> Sincerely,

REQUEST FOR FAVOR. All requests must be persuasive to some degree. In a request for a favor, a positive, friendly, persuasive tone is particularly important.

> Dear Nora:
>
> If you could spare a little of your time and expertise, I'd like to enlist your help for our November 7 seminar, "Computer Networking."
>
> We've decided to publish the remarks of each of the twelve scheduled speakers and mail them to the attendees shortly after the seminar. But experience tells me that most of the papers will need a close reading and some careful editing to clean up the usual typographical errors and smooth out the typically awkward language of nonwriters. Our budget, however, has no allowance for purchasing outside assistance, so we're seeking in-house talent. As editor of our company's house organ, you have precisely the expertise we urgently need. I know how busy you are, but perhaps you could oversee the editorial function and assign the actual copyediting to members of your staff.
>
> Everyone greatly respects and values your work, Nora, so I can add many voices to my own in asking this favor. I'm sure you know how important the seminar is to our company, and we truly do need your help. May we count you in?
>
> I'd appreciate a call (extension 812) from you by the end of this week. Many thanks.
>
> Best wishes,

LETTERS GRANTING REQUESTS. A friendly acknowledgment expressing pleasure in granting a request builds goodwill.

> Dear Mr. Milliken:
>
> We're glad to send you, with our compliments, the booklet "A Dozen Ways to Build Business." Your copy is being mailed today in a separate envelope.
>
> Your interest in this publication is appreciated, and we hope the booklet will prove useful to you.
>
> Cordially yours,

LETTERS EXPLAINING DELAYED ACTION. When definite action cannot be taken immediately, a note of acknowledgment is a business courtesy.

Dear Mr. Hanley:

I will be glad to send you whatever information I have on mailing-list testing that is relevant to your problem. You are right that I have been interested in this aspect of promotional work for some time, and I have accumulated a considerable amount of material.

Unfortunately, I must leave this evening on a business trip to Boston and Providence, and I will be away from the office for the next three or four days. But as soon as I return, I will check over the mailing-list material and send you anything that I think may prove helpful.

Cordially yours,

Dear Bill:

Just a short note to tell you that I have received your letter of April 24 concerning requirements for the housing project. May I have a few days to think this over?

You will hear from me further within the week, and I hope it will be possible for me to be helpful to you.

Sincerely,

Sales Promotion

In large companies, sales letters are usually prepared by specialists. In other situations, however, promotional letters may be written by your employer with your help.

1. Slant the message to arouse interest and prompt the reader to take action.

2. Describe what is being offered and tell why the customer will benefit from it.

3. Pave the way for possible further contact.

Dear Mr. Samuels:

Have we got a new copier paper for you! It's a completely new lightweight grade of paper designed and manufactured especially for your equipment.

This remarkable new lightweight substance-16 paper runs just as efficiently as the heavier sheets you've been using. Moreover, it has the same top-grade, brilliant white characteristics of the heavier paper, and it has the opacity needed for quality copying. What does all this mean? It means a big load off your budget: reduced paper costs *and* lower postage and mailing costs!

Phil Evans, our representative, will be in your city the week of July 14 and will contact you before then to arrange a convenient time to let you test samples of the new paper. In the meantime, I'm enclosing a booklet describing its many features and uses.

Best regards,

MODEL SOCIAL-BUSINESS LETTERS AND INVITATIONS

Acceptance

A personal letter accepting something should convey appreciation and enthusiasm. If certain details are not clear, the acceptance must deal specifically with these points. Otherwise, a brief note is sufficient.

ACCEPTING INVITATION TO A SPECIAL EVENT. Use an enthusiastic and appreciative tone in responding to any invitation.

Dear Mr. Nash:

I'll be delighted to be a guest of the Rand-Niles Company on the happy occasion of its fiftieth anniversary dinner.

Our association has indeed been very close, and I wouldn't miss being with you for anything in the world.

I'm looking forward to seeing you at the celebration.

Sincerely,

ACCEPTING SPEAKING INVITATION. Repeat the details conveyed in the invitation or query the writer if any essential information is not clear or was omitted.

Dear Mr. Scott:

I'm happy to accept your invitation to speak at the American Business Administrators' annual meeting on March 5 at 2 o'clock. I've always admired your organization and look forward to the opportunity to attend one of your meetings.

What do you think of the topic "The Relationship Between Business and the College of Business Administration"? This is simply a suggestion. Since you did not indicate how long you want me to speak, I will limit my address to 30 minutes unless I hear otherwise from you.

I'm eager to meet you and the other members of your society. In the meantime, if you need any information from me for your program, do let me know.

Sincerely yours,

ACCEPTING MEMBERSHIP IN PROFESSIONAL OR CIVIC ORGANIZATION. Ordinarily, association membership is handled routinely, and one does not respond personally. But occasionally a special invitation is extended personally and thus should be acknowledged personally.

Dear Ms. Foley:

Your cordial invitation for me to join the American Business Writing Association pleases me very much, and I accept with pleasure.

I realize that your membership includes many recognized authorities on the subject of business writing, both in academic ranks and in business circles. I'm highly complimented to have the opportunity to become associated with such a group.

Sincerely yours,

Birthday Greetings

Greetings on special occasions should be warm and friendly, with the degree of informality depending on the relationship of the writer and recipient. In all cases, avoid remarks about the person's age and, generally, keep the message brief.

Dear Helen:

Here's wishing you a wonderful and joyous day on December 12 and much happiness on every day that follows. A very happy birthday, Helen!

Regards,

Condolences

In any letter written to express sympathy, sincerity and tact are the most important qualities. Avoid words or sentiments that could distress the reader. Do not philosophize upon the meaning of death or quote scripture or poetry. A letter of condolence should not be long and involved. A decision about the length is based upon (1) the degree of friendship between writer and reader, (2) the situation that prompts the letter, and (3) the tastes and temperament of the reader.

Formerly, all letters of condolence were written in longhand, but today such letters to business acquaintances who are not well known to the writer may be prepared by typewriter or computer on business letterhead.

In the case of the death of an intimate friend, a handwritten letter, on personal writing paper, is correct. Some executives prefer to write letters of condolence in longhand, whether to a business or social acquaintance. In these cases, you give your employer the paper, the correct address, and perhaps a necessary fact or two.

TO A BUSINESS ASSOCIATE OF THE DECEASED. A letter pertaining to a business contact, unless a personal friend is involved, usually omits an offer of assistance during the time of bereavement.

> Dear Mr. James:
>
> It was with deep regret that I learned this morning of the sudden death of Walter Conroy. I thought of you immediately, for I realize how great the loss of your good friend and business partner of some twenty years will be to you.
>
> All of us in the furniture business will miss Walter. We admired the combination of kindness and honesty that his life represented. But since the loss to you is most direct and personal, I wanted to send you these words of sincere sympathy upon the death of a loyal friend and trusted associate.
>
> Sincerely,

TO THE WIDOW OF AN EMPLOYEE. A letter to a member of the family of the deceased may be more personal in tone, and an offer of assistance is common.

Dear Mrs. Echols:

It was with a very real sense of loss that I heard today of the death of your husband. I valued his friendship for many years. I don't believe I've ever known another man who was so loved and respected by all who knew him. It was a privilege to know Jack, whose place in our company can never be fully taken by anyone else.

My heartfelt sympathy goes out to you and your family. If there is any way in which I can be of assistance in the weeks ahead, please do not hesitate to call on me.

Sincerely,

TO SOMEONE WITH PERSONAL INJURY, ILLNESS, OR PROPERTY DAMAGE. Most unfortunate situations are potential objects of a sympathetic message. Because of the endless variety of difficulties, each letter has to be especially tailored to the individual's circumstances.

Dear Cliff:

I have been watching closely the reports in the paper each evening about your progress, and I am delighted at the news of your continued improvement. Tonight's item says that you and the doctors have won the fight, for which your many friends here are very thankful.

I hope that you will be feeling more and more like your former self from now on and that you will soon be returning home.

Sincerely,

Dear Mr. Beckman:

We were extremely sorry to learn that your warehouse was damaged by fire last night.

Perhaps there is some special service that we can perform in this emergency. If there is, please call on us.

You have been a friend and customer of Maybank Brothers for many years, and we want to be helpful in any way possible.

Sincerely yours,

Congratulations

The outstanding qualities of an expression of congratulations are (1) brevity, (2) naturalness of expression, and (3) enthusiasm. Trite, stilted phrases indicate a lack of sincerity and destroy the individuality of the letter.

Upon PROFESSIONAL OR CIVIC HONOR. All letters of congratulations should focus on the subject and never discuss other business.

> Dear Mr. Dodge:
>
> I read with mixed feelings the announcement of your election as president of Norwich University. I am delighted, of course, at this splendid tribute to your ability and achievements. But I am also keenly regretful that it will take you away from Highland. The place you hold in the life of this community will be hard to fill.
>
> The purpose of this letter, however, is to congratulate you upon the high honor that has come to you, which you so well deserve. You have my very best wishes for continued success in your new work.
>
> Sincerely yours,

Upon OUTSTANDING COMMUNITY SERVICE. Appointments outside of business present excellent opportunities to send messages that promote goodwill.

> Dear Ms. Morrison:
>
> I read with pleasure of your appointment as director of the United Cerebral Palsy Fund Drive in the community.
>
> When someone as busy as you are makes time to assist in the conduct of the affairs of the town, it's time for the rest of us to applaud the wonderful job she is doing.
>
> Please accept my sincere admiration and every good wish for your success.
>
> Sincerely,

Upon RETIREMENT. Keep the spirit of unselfish praise for the recipient, even though he or she may be completely leaving the business community.

Dear Walter:

I just learned of your forthcoming retirement from Scott Investment Company and wanted to congratulate you on your record of wise leadership that has given your company the stature it now has.

No one, upon retiring from business, has ever taken with him as high a degree of respect and good wishes from so many devoted friends and associates as you have received.

Sincerely,

UPON A BUSINESS ANNIVERSARY. Letters to customers or clients on special occasions build goodwill. One should focus on the occasion, however, and strictly avoid any sales-promotion effort.

Dear Mr. Laughlin:

We're delighted to send you our sincerest congratulations on the fortieth anniversary of The Personnel Group. All of us at Brownley Suppliers feel fortunate to have had you as a customer for many of those years.

The Personnel Group is widely known and respected for its substantial contribution to our community. You truly have something to celebrate in this anniversary year. From its inception, The Personnel Group has made steady growth and progress, gaining many new friends with every year of service.

We all look forward to your continued success and heartily salute your well-earned position in our community.

Cordially,

UPON SERVICE TO COMPANY. Employees are commonly recognized for ten, twenty, or more years with a company. A letter of recognition briefly offers congratulations and acknowledges the person's good work, devotion, special contribution, or anything else that is pertinent and appropriate. A gift may be sent if the recipient is a good friend or if the occasion is a special anniversary.

Dear Marie:

Congratulations and all good wishes to you on your twentieth anniversary at The Information Center!

Here's a little gift for you to help you celebrate this happy day. Considering your outstanding record of progress and achievement, as well as the countless friends you've made, I know this is a significant occasion for you.

Everyone shares my best wishes for continued success and satisfaction in your career. Have a very happy anniversary, Marie.

Cordially,

Declination

Letters of declination should include an expression of regret and an expression of appreciation for the invitation. An explanation of the circumstances that prevent acceptance helps to show that the regret is sincere. The message must combine cordiality with tact.

DECLINING INVITATION PENDING FURTHER THOUGHT. When it is necessary to think about something, keep the letter brief, indicate when you'll give your answer, and close with a positive remark.

Dear Bill:

Just a short note to tell you that I have received your letter of April 24. May I have a few days to think about this?

You will hear from me further within the week, and I hope it will be possible for me to be helpful to you.

Sincerely yours,

DECLINING INVITATION TO BANQUET, LUNCHEON, OR ENTERTAINMENT. Adopt a tone of sincere regret in turning down a special invitation.

Dear John:

For several weeks I have expected that you would be holding the annual Foundation banquet in June, and I've been keeping my fingers crossed in the hope that I could be present. Unfortunately, June 15 is out of the question for me. I'll be in Boston at that time attending a company sales conference.

My sincere thanks, nevertheless, for your gracious invitation. I hope this year's banquet will be the best yet; under your capable guidance, I am sure it will be.

Cordially,

DECLINING A SPEAKING INVITATION. It is not only acceptable, but it is flattering to the recipient for a declination to state that you would like to be considered on another occasion.

> Dear Ms. Connors:
>
> It was good of you to invite me to be your guest speaker at the monthly meeting of the National Office Management Association on March 18. I know I would very much enjoy being with you. However, on that evening I am scheduled to speak in Boston.
>
> I appreciate your thinking of me. Should the occasion arise again, please call on me. I would be very happy to address the members of your group another time.
>
> Sincerely,

DECLINING INVITATION TO SERVE ON CIVIC OR PROFESSIONAL COMMITTEE OR BOARD. Be certain to convey the impression that the declination is not meant to suggest that the activity is unimportant.

> Dear Mr. Cavanaugh:
>
> Thank you for your kind letter of March 6 in which you invited me to become a member of your Committee on Professional Standards in Advertising.
>
> I would like very much to accept the invitation; unfortunately, my present business duties will not permit me to give such an undertaking the time and consideration it deserves. I want you to know, however, that your invitation is deeply appreciated and that you and your associates have my very best wishes.
>
> Yours sincerely,

DECLINING REQUEST TO SUPPORT CHARITABLE OR OTHER ORGANIZATION. These letters must be firm in saying no but simultaneously let the writer appear warm and considerate.

> Dear Mr. Duval:
>
> I just received your letter of December 15 inviting me to participate in the fund-raising program of the Human Welfare Association, and I appreciate your thought in writing to me.
>
> There is no undertaking more deserving of financial aid or any to which I would more gladly contribute than that which you represent. At the same

time, I must tell you that all the funds I have available for such purposes have already been earmarked and that it just is not possible for me to do what you ask at this time. Later, perhaps—but at the moment I do not feel free to make either a current or future commitment.

Although I am not in a position to lend active support just now, I send you my best wishes for success in the fine work you are doing.

Sincerely yours,

Invitations

Many invitations are sent by letter in the business world. However, whether formal or informal, invitations must include all necessary facts.

To ATTEND A SOCIAL EVENT. Include the usual facts of time, date, and place.

Dear Mr. Walker:

The Scott-Miller Company will observe its fiftieth anniversary at an informal banquet to be held in the Langley Hotel junior ballroom at 7 o'clock on May 7, 19—.

We hope that you will attend as a guest of the company. Since you have played a substantial part in its progress, your presence on this happy occasion seems particularly appropriate.

The program following the dinner will be varied and entertaining, and we are sure that you will have a most enjoyable evening.

Cordially yours,

To GIVE AN ADDRESS OR INFORMAL TALK. Include a reason why the person would be an appropriate speaker for the occasion.

Dear Mrs. Serenbetz:

The Board of Directors of the National Office Management Association has asked me to extend an invitation to you to be our guest speaker at the monthly association meeting, Monday, December 7, at the Waldorf-Astoria Hotel at 8:30 p.m.

We have had many inquiries from regional members for updated information in connection with the use and misuse of aptitude, vocational, and personality tests used in modern employment practice. We know of your research work in this field and hope that you will be able to honor us with an acceptance to speak to association members at this time.

I look forward to hearing from you.

Sincerely yours,

Seasonal Good Wishes

Written in mid-December, letters of seasonal good wishes emphasize (1) appreciation of the reader's friendship, confidence, and cooperation and (2) an expression of good wishes for the holiday season and the coming year. Ordinarily, the message of seasonal good wishes should not be more than 150 words. The tone and content are influenced by the relationship involved, but they should all have the essential qualities of informality, friendliness, and sincerity.

Dear Mr. Ramsey:

The association with you during the past year has been so enjoyable that I want to send you this word of good wishes for a happy and successful 19—.

I hope that circumstances in the coming year will afford more opportunities for pleasant contacts between your firm and mine and that I will have the pleasure of further visits with you from time to time.

Sincerely,

Dear George:

As we approach the end of 19—, I realize that the enjoyable association with you has contributed much toward making it a very pleasant year for me.

In sending you these words of thanks for your kindness on several occasions, I wish for you the happiest of holiday seasons. May the New Year bring you continued health, happiness, and success.

Sincerely yours,

Thank Yous

The opportunities to build good relations by saying thank you are limitless. In most cases, a brief note is sufficient.

Dear Mr. Bentley:

It was a rewarding experience for me to tour your plant facilities last week. The efficiency gained by your new assembly robots is truly amazing.

I sincerely appreciated the time you spent with me, Mr. Bentley, and I want to thank you for making my trip so informative and enjoyable.

Best regards,

Dear Erin:

I sincerely appreciated your help in getting out our company newspaper during my stay in the hospital. The issue was one of the best ever, and I'm truly grateful for the time and careful attention you devoted to the project. It really took a big load off my mind.

Many thanks, Erin. I hope I can be of help to you some day too.

Cordially,

PART THREE

HOW TO WRITE CORRECTLY

Chapter 13

Correct Word Usage

PARTS OF SPEECH AND RULES
OF GRAMMAR

Parts of Speech

Noun. A word that names a person, place, thing, idea, action, or quality. It may be preceded by the articles *a* and *the* and may be plural, may show possession, or may be used as the subject of a sentence, as the object of a preposition or verb, or as a predicate noun after certain verbs. See also **Grammatical Terms, Collective noun.**

> The *letters* (plural) were perfect.
>
> The *secretary's* (possession) *supervisor* (subject) was pleased with the *letters* (object of preposition *with*).
>
> The secretary drafted the *letter* (object of verb *drafted*).
>
> She was an outstanding *secretary* (predicate noun).

Pronoun. A word that takes the place of a noun. *I, we, you, he, she, it,* or *they* are personal pronouns used as subjects or predicate pronouns. *Me, us, you, him, her, it,* and *them* are personal pronouns used as objects. *Who* and *whom* are relative pronouns used to refer to persons or animals, *which* to animals or things, *that* to persons, animals, and things. *This, these, that,* and *those* are demonstrative pronouns. *Each, none,* and *some* are examples of in-

437

definite pronouns. *Myself, herself,* and *yourself* are examples of reflexive and intensive pronouns.

> *It* (personal pronoun as subject) is *she* (as predicate pronoun) *who* (relative pronoun) will be in charge.

> To *whom* (object of *to*) do *you* (subject) wish to speak?

> *This* (demonstrative pronoun as subject) is my typewriter.

> *Each* (indefinite pronoun as subject) secretary must prepare *himself* or *herself* (reflexive pronoun referring back to subject) for greater responsibility.

> The manager *himself* (intensive pronoun emphasizing the subject *manager*) will conduct the campaign.

Adjective. A word that modifies (describes or limits) a noun or pronoun. Adjectives usually add *-er* (comparative degree) or *-est* (superlative degree) to mean more or most; they also may be preceded by the words *more* or *most* to express a greater or lesser degree of something. An adjective that is placed after a verb is called a "predicate adjective."

> The *alert* (descriptive adjective) secretary caught the error in time.

> The *bimonthly* (limiting adjective) report is directed toward executive secretaries.

> The new machines are *easier* (comparative degree) to operate than the old ones.

> The new models are the *most reliable* (superlative degree) of all machines in the company.

> Her salary was *substantial* (predicate adjective).

Adverb. A word that modifies a verb, an adjective, another adverb, or a clause or sentence. Some adverbs have an *-ly* ending. Others add *-er* (comparative degree) or *-est* (superlative degree); they also may be preceded by the words *more, most, less,* or *least* to express a greater or lesser degree of something. Adverbs often can be identified in a sentence as the words that answer the question how, when, where, how much, or to what extent.

> He searched the files more (comparative) *thoroughly* (modifies verb *searched*) the second time.
>
> It was an *unusually* (modifies adjective *busy*) busy day.
>
> The report was *exceptionally* (modifies adverb *well*) well written.
>
> *Unfortunately* (modifies sentence), the disk was lost.

Verb. A word that expresses action or state of being. A *transitive verb* has an object; an *intransitive verb* does not. *Auxiliary,* or *linking, verbs* are words used with a principal verb to form a verb phrase. A *regular verb* adds -*d* or -*ed* to the present tense to form a past tense and a past participle. An *irregular verb* uses a completely different spelling of the present tense in its past and past-participle form. A verb must agree with its subject in number and person.

> The secretary *has* (transitive verb) a heavy work load (object).
>
> She *types* (intransitive verb) quickly (no object).
>
> He *passed* (regular verb: *pass, passed, passed*) the exam.
>
> You *write* (irregular verb: *write, wrote, written*) the introduction.
>
> Each student and teacher *was* (*was* agrees in number with the singular subject *Each*) given a chance to speak.

Preposition. A word that connects a noun or pronoun (object of the preposition) with another word(s) and shows the relationship between the two. Some prepositions are followed by a verb, adjective, or adverb. A prepositional phrase is a sentence fragment of two or more words beginning with a preposition and including an object and any modifiers of the object. It may be used as a subject noun, an adjective, or an adverb. Examples of prepositions are *to, of, for, in, on, with, about, between, among, concerning, since,* and *toward.*

> The secretary left *for* (preposition) New York (object).
>
> The orders came *from* (preposition) above (adverb).

> *To understand the issue* (prepositional phrase as a subject) is to understand the alternative solutions.
>
> The office *of the vice president* (prepositional phrase modifying the noun *office*) is closed today.
>
> She worked diligently *to finish on time* (prepositional phrase modifying the adverb *diligently*).

It is better to end a sentence with a preposition than to use an awkward construction, but it is incorrect to place an unnecessary preposition at the end of the sentence.

> Where is the book *at* (unnecessary preposition)?
>
> Now we know what the candidate stands *for* (*not* Now we know *for* what the candidate stands).

Conjunction. A word that connects other words, phrases, clauses, or sentences. *Coordinating conjunctions* such as *and, or, nor, but*, and *for* connect equal elements (words, phrases, clauses, or sentences). The conjunction *and* is frequently misused to connect two verbs when the second verb should be an infinitive, for example: "Try *to finish* (not *and finish*) the chapter." *Subordinating conjunctions* such as *if, as, since, because, while, after, before, when, unless, until, though*, and *although* join a dependent clause to an independent clause. *Correlative conjunctions* such as *either-or, neither-nor, so-as, as-as, whereas-therefore*, and *whether-or* are used in directly related clauses within a sentence. *Conjunctive adverbs* such as *therefore, however, moreover, furthermore, nevertheless, consequently*, and *accordingly* join two elements and also function as adverbial modifiers.

> Mr. Jacobs *and* (coordinating conjunction) Ms. Holt will conduct the seminar.
>
> We will call *when* (subordinating conjunction) the equipment is ready.
>
> *Either* Ellen *or* (correlative conjunction) Linda should go.
>
> Postal rates are scheduled to increase next week; *therefore* (conjunctive adverb) we should complete the mailing by Friday.

Interjection. A word, usually independent of the rest of a sentence, that expresses sudden or strong feeling. Other parts of speech such as exclamatory nouns can also be used as interjections. Some words used as interjections are really slang expressions.

> *Oh* (regular interjection)! Look at that!
>
> *George* (proper noun used as interjection)! Are you
> serious?
>
> *Wow* (slang expression used as interjection)! It's hot
> today!

Grammatical Terms

Adjective. See **Parts of Speech, Adjective.**

Adverb. See **Parts of Speech, Adverb.**

Agreement of verb with subject. A verb should always agree with its subject in number and person. The rule is simple, but the number of the subject is not always clear. Mistakes sometimes occur when two or more subjects are joined by *and* (see **Compound subject**); when two or more subjects are joined by *or, nor,* and the like (see **Alternate subject**); when a noun or a phrase intervenes between the subject and the verb (see **Intervening noun**); and when a verb is followed by a predicate nominative (see **Predicate nominative**).

Alternate subject. Two or more singular subjects in the third person joined by *or, nor, and, not, but, either-or,* or *neither-nor* take singular verbs in the third person.

> *Neither* power *nor* wealth *is* (not *are*) a substitute for
> health.

If two or more subjects differing in number or person are joined by *or, nor, and, not, but, either-or, neither-nor,* the verb agrees with the subject nearer it. (You may also rephrase a sentence to avoid awkwardness).

> *Either* the women *or* the supervisor *has* (not *have*) to
> work late.

Antecedent. Also called "substantive." A noun or pronoun to which another pronoun refers.

> *Janice* (antecedent) organized the office library, but
> *she* (pronoun referring to noun *Janice*) plans to
> expand it for departmental use.

Appositive. A word that explains or identifies another word(s).

> Henry Southby, *sales manager* (appositive), has been
> promoted to vice president, sales.

Article. The adjectives *a* and *an* are known as "indefinite articles"; the article *the* is known as a "definite article."

> *A* (indefinite article) book on *the* (definite article)
> subject of telecommunications is being published
> now.

Auxiliary verb. Also known as "linking verb." A verb that is used with a principal verb to form a verb phrase. Auxiliary verbs are *be, can, do, may, have, shall, will, must, ought*, and sometimes *let*.

> She *must* (auxiliary verb) attend (principal verb) the
> conference.

Case. The relationship of a noun or pronoun to other words. The *nominative case* (subject) denotes the person or thing (noun or pronoun) doing the acting in a sentence. The *objective case* (object of a verb or preposition) denotes the person or thing being acted upon. The *possessive case*, formed by adding an apostrophe (') or apostrophe and *s* (Ms. Burns' house; Carol's house), is used to show ownership.

> *She* (nominative case—subject) sent the report to *him*
> (objective case—object of the preposition *to*).

> The *president's* (possessive case) opening remarks
> were brief.

Collective noun. Singular in form, the name of a group or collection of people or things. Examples are *team, family, audience, community*, and *committee*. A collective noun takes a singular or plural verb according to the intended meaning.

> The American *family* has not disappeared in the
> twentieth century as predicted (singular verb *has* to
> emphasize the family as a unit).

> The *family* were registering to vote (plural verb *were*
> to emphasize the individual members).

Comparative degree. A means of expressing a greater or lesser degree of two persons or things. Adverbs and adjectives both use the comparative degree. See **Parts of Speech, Adjective; Adverb.**

Complement. A word or phrase used after a verb to complete the meaning of a sentence. See **Direct object; Predicate adjective; Predicate nominative.**

Compound personal pronoun. A word formed by adding *-self* or *-selves* to the possessive of a simple personal pronoun.

> She wrote it *herself* (reflexive compound personal
> pronoun referring back to subject).

> The citizens *themselves* (intensive compound
> personal pronoun emphasizing the subject
> *citizens*) wanted higher educational standards.

Do not use a compound personal pronoun in place of the objective case of the pronoun.

> Best regards from George and *me* (not *myself*).

Compound predicate. Two or more connected verbs or verb phrases.

> She *drafted and edited the report.*

Compound subject. Two or more connected subjects (which require a plural verb unless preceded by a singular indefinite pronoun such as *each* and unless the compound subject refers to a single person or thing).

> *Personal progress and success* depend (plural verb)
> on many things.

> *The vice president and treasurer* (single office) is
> (singular verb) out of town.

> *Each officer and member* was (singular verb to agree
> with singular pronoun *Each*) present.

Compound term. Applies to two or more short words written together, joined by a hyphen, or written separately but expressing a single idea. Thus *editor-in-chief, businessperson,* and *attorney general* are all compounds. The authorities differ about whether many compounds should be written as one word.

> *Plurals:* Form the plural of a compound word by adding *-s* to the most important noun in the compound: *editors-in-chief, sons-in-law, attorneys general.*
>
> *Consistency:* When there is a choice, decide whether you want to hyphenate two or more words, write them as one word, or write them as separate words, and follow the form you choose consistently. If your company has a style manual, follow it.
>
> *Meaning:* Use the form that conveys the proper meaning. Although your dictionary might show two or more words joined together or hyphenated, the meaning might differ from the meaning of the same words used separately.
>
> > The *take-off* was smooth. We will *take off* from
> > Kennedy airport.
> >
> > He is very *matter-of-fact.* As a *matter of fact,* I didn't
> > go.
>
> *Usage:* Do not hyphenate or join words together simply because they are frequently used together. Wait until the authorities accept them in compounded form.
>
> *Adjectives:* Hyphenate two or more words used as an adjective when they precede a noun: *two-story* house, *short-term* loan, *no-par* stock, *above-mentioned* law, *well-known* politician. Do not hyphenate compound adjectives that follow a noun.
>
> > The author is *well informed.*
> >
> > The teacher is *civic minded.*

Do not hyphenate color variations used as an adjective, such as *navy blue* dress, *light gray* paint.

Fractions: Hyphenate fractions when the numerator and the denominator are both one-word forms, such as *one-third, three-fourths, one-hundredth*.

Nationalities: Hyphenate two or more words to indicate that the person or thing shares in the qualities of both, as in *Anglo-American, Sino-Japanese, Latin-American, Scotch-Irish*.

Coined phrases: Hyphenate coined phrases, such as *middle-of-the-road, pay-as-you-go, drive-it-yourself, ready-to-wear*.

Adverbs: Do not use a hyphen to connect an adverb and an adjective. Do not use a hyphen to connect an adverb ending in *-ly* and a past participle in phrases such as a *happily married* couple, *brilliantly colored* picture.

Titles: Do not hyphenate titles such as *rear admiral* and *chief of staff*, but do hyphenate *secretary-treasurer* and other coined compounds. Also hyphenate *ex-president, president-elect*, and *vice president-elect*.

Conjunction. See **Parts of Speech, Conjunction.**

Coordinate conjunction. See **Parts of Speech, Conjunction.**

Dangling modifier. A word, phrase, or clause that is misplaced in a sentence so the connection between it and the word it is supposed to modify is not clear.

> *After finishing the report* (dangling), editing began
> (illogically seems to modify *editing*).

> *After finishing the report*, he began editing (correctly
> refers to *he*).

Dependent clause. Also called "subordinate clause." A group of words that has a subject and a predicate but cannot stand alone as a sentence.

> The receptionist *who works at the front desk* will
> direct you to the Sales Department.

Direct object. A noun or noun equivalent that receives a verb's action. It often answers the question "what" or "whom" after the verb.

> She prepared (what?) the *letter*.

Double negative. The use of two negatives to express a negative thought is wrong. Some double negatives, such as *don't want no, doesn't need none, wouldn't never,* are obviously wrong, but the insidious double negatives occur with words that convey a negative idea, such as *hardly, barely, scarcely, but, but that,* rather than with words that are definitely negative in form, such as *no, more, never.* See **Troublesome Words and Phrases, but; but that; hardly; not; scarcely.**

Expletive. A word such as *there* or *it* that fills the position of the subject while the real subject is in the position of the predicate noun. The verb should agree with the actual subject. To avoid a monotonous succession of expletives, rephrase sentences, placing the real subject in its usual position.

> *There* (expletive) are (plural verb to agree with real subject *cartons*) four cartons arriving today.
> *Better*: Four cartons are arriving today.

Future-perfect tense. See **Tense.**

Future tense. See **Tense.**

Gerund. A verbal noun, which is a word derived from a verb and used as a noun. A gerund always ends in *-ing.* If a noun or pronoun precedes a gerund, it must be in the possessive case. A gerund may function as the subject, as the object of a verb or preposition, or as a predicate noun. When you have a choice between a noun form or a gerund, use the noun form. See also **Participle.**

> Your (possessive case, not *you*) *buying* (gerund as subject) the house was a good investment.
>
> Mr. Blakely enjoys *selling* (as object of verb *enjoys*).
>
> Her style of *supervising* (as object of preposition *of*) is effective.
>
> Learning is *experiencing* (as predicate noun).
>
> *Accepting* (gerund form) the position was an ill-advised move. *Better*: *Acceptance* (noun form) of the position was an ill-advised move.

Idiomatic usage. Syntactical, grammatical, or structural form peculiar to the language and accepted because of common use but not because it is consistent with the rules of grammar.

> His art is *worthy of* praise.

Imperative mood. See **Mood.**

Indicative mood. See **Mood.**

Indirect object. A noun or noun equivalent that usually tells to or for whom (or what) something is done. It is placed before the direct object and helps it complete the meaning of the verb.

> The manager gave the *president* (indirect object) his *report* (direct object).

Infinitive. A verb form used as a noun, an adjective, or an adverb, usually preceded by *to.*

Tense. Use the present infinitive, not the perfect, after past conditions such as *would have liked, would have been possible.*

> It would have been possible *to reduce* (not *to have reduced*) the cost at that time.

Split infinitive. It is best not to split the infinitive by placing a word or words between *to* and the verb.

> The company agrees *to increase* (not *to substantially increase*) the salaries substantially.

Split infinitives are preferable to awkwardness or ambiguity.

> *Awkward:* Efforts *to unite firmly* bolters from the party were a failure.
>
> *Improved:* Efforts *to firmly unite* bolters from the party were a failure.

Series of infinitives. If qualifying words separate infinitive phrases, repeat *to* in each phrase; if no qualifying words intervene, do not repeat *to.*

> *To punish* and *expose* the guilty is one thing; *to help*
> the unfortunate is another.

> It is improper for the debtor *to take* an unearned
> discount and then *to refuse* to pay the difference.

Interjection. See **Parts of Speech, Interjection.**

Intervening noun or phrase. The intervention of a noun between the subject and the verb will sometimes cause trouble if the intervening noun is different in number from the subject. Remember that the verb agrees with the subject, not the intervening noun.

> *Celluloid* used as handles on umbrellas and canes *is*
> (not *are*) of high quality.

A phrase coming between a subject and a verb can sometimes cause trouble. The verb agrees with the subject of the main sentence, not with the subject of the phrase.

> The *community*, as well as the owners of the land, *is*
> *interested* in development.

Intransitive verb. See **Parts of Speech, Verb.**

Irregular verb. See **Parts of Speech, Verb.**

Linking verb. See **Parts of Speech, Verb.**

Misplaced modifier. A word(s) positioned in a sentence so it is (they are) awkward or appear(s) to modify the wrong word. See also **Dangling modifier.**

> She *only* (misplaced) ordered the paper back edition.
> *Better*: She ordered *only* the paperback edition.

Modifier. A word or words that restrict or qualify the meaning of another word or words. See **Parts of Speech, Adjective; Adverb.** See also **Dangling modifier; Misplaced modifier.**

Mood. A term referring to the form of a verb that indicates the attitude of the speaker or writer. The three moods are indicative (concerns a fact), subjunctive (concerns the imagined or conditional), and imperative (concerns a command or wish).

> *Indicative*: *Is* this your typewriter? This *is* my typewriter.
>
> *Subjunctive*: If we all *go*, no one will be available to answer the phone. I wish Doug *were* here.
>
> *Imperative*: *Take* the day off. *Have* a good time.

Nominative case. See **Case.**

Nonrestrictive clause. A subordinate clause that is not essential to the meaning of the sentence and is usually set off with commas.

> The lesson plan, *which was more detailed than I expected*, is published with a separate resource manual and reading list.

Noun. See **Parts of Speech, Noun.**

Objective case. See **Case.**

Omission of words. Words may be omitted from a sentence only if they can be supplied clearly and exactly from a parallel portion of the sentence. In two clauses, if one subject is singular and the other plural, do not omit the verb.

> *Wrong*: The sky was clear and the stars bright.
>
> *Right*: The sky *was* clear and the stars *were* bright.

Do not omit part of a verb phrase if it is different in form from the corresponding part of the parallel verb phrase.

> *Wrong*: The company always *has* and always *will give* recognition where it is due.
>
> *Right*: The company always *has given* and always *will give* recognition where it is due.

Do not omit an article, a personal or relative pronoun, or a preposition that is necessary to the grammatical completeness or to the clear understanding of a sentence.

> *Wrong*: He wrote to the chairman and president (two persons).
>
> *Right*: He wrote to the chairman and *the* president (two persons).
>
> *Wrong*: I have great sympathy but no confidence in that class of people.
>
> *Right*: I have great sympathy *for* but no confidence *in* that class of people.
>
> *Better*: I have great sympathy for that class of people but no confidence in them.

See also **Infinitive,** *Series of infinitives,* for omission of *to* in a series of infinitive phrases.

Participle. A verbal adjective, which is a word derived from a verb that modifies a noun or pronoun. The present participle ends in *-ing* (*taking*). See also **Gerund.** The past participle ends in *-en* or *-ed* (*taken*). The past-perfect participle is preceded by the word *having* (*having taken*). A participle that incorrectly does not modify a noun or pronoun is called a "dangling participle."

> The *winning* (participle modifying noun) photograph (noun) was announced today.
>
> *Sending* (participle with object) her (object) the information, I realized how much I had to learn.
>
> *Speaking* (participle modified by adverb) slowly (adverb), he repeated the instructions.

Do not use the present participle for the past-perfect participle, which expresses an action completed at the time indicated by the main verb.

> He *completed* the report on schedule, *having worked* (not the present participle *working*) unusually long hours.

Passive voice. See **Voice.**

Past-perfect tense. See **Tense.**

Past tense. See **Tense.**

Person. Identifies the speaker. The *first person* is the one speaking. The *second person* is the one being spoken to. The *third person* is the person or thing being spoken about.

> *I* (first person) am responsible for incoming-mail distributions.
>
> *You* (second person) are responsible for outgoing-mail duties.
>
> *They* (third person) are responsible for all other mail functions.

Phrasal preposition. Two or more words that are used as a single preposition. See **Parts of Speech, Preposition.**

Prepositional phrase. A preposition, its object, and any modifiers of the object. See **Parts of Speech, Preposition.**

Possessive case. See **Case.**

Predicate. The part of a sentence having the verb and other words that make a statement about the subject.

> Jill and her staff *have a heavy work load during conference registration.*

Predicate adjective. See **Parts of Speech, Adjective.**

Predicate nominative. A noun or pronoun following an intransitive verb (one that does not take an object), thereby completing, or helping to complete, the predicate. As its name implies, a predicate nominative is always in the nominative case. A predicate nominative is also called a "complement." All complements, however, are not predicate nominatives. Forms of the verb *to be* (*am, is, are, was, were*) do not take an object but are followed by a predicate nominative. A common error is the use of the objective case of a pronoun (*me, us, her, him, them*) as a predicate nominative.

> It was *I* (not *me*) to whom you spoke.
>
> It was *he* (not *him*) who delivered the papers.

A verb must agree with its subject and not with the predicate nominative. Difficulty is caused by the use of a singular subject and plural predicate nominative or vice versa.

> A valuable *by-product* (singular subject) of training
> conferences *is* (singular verb) the numerous
> *opportunities* (predicate nominative) afforded for
> management to observe the trainees' reactions.

Preposition. See **Parts of Speech, Preposition.**

Present tense. See **Tense.**

Present-perfect tense. See **Tense.**

Pronoun. See **Parts of Speech, Pronoun.**

Relative pronoun. See **Parts of Speech, Pronoun.**

Restrictive clause. A subordinate clause that is essential to the meaning of the sentence and should not be set off with commas.

> A copier *that can enlarge diagrams* would be useful in
> our office.

Split infinitive. See **Infinitive,** *Split infinitives.*

Subject. A word or group of words in a sentence about which a statement is made.

> *The company* has 500 employees.
>
> *The sales staff and the research staff* worked
> together on the product-development project.

Subjunctive mood. See **Mood.**

Subordinate conjunction. See **Parts of Speech, Conjunction.**

Superlative degree. See **Parts of Speech, Adjective.**

Tense. The time of action expressed by a verb. The six tenses are present, past, future, present perfect, past perfect, and future perfect.

> *Present tense* (denotes action occurring now): I *write*
> slowly in longhand.
>
> *Past tense* (denotes past time): I *wrote* the message
> in shorthand.
>
> *Future tense* (denotes future time): I *shall write* to you
> as soon as the product is available.

> *Present-perfect tense* (denotes action completed at the time of speaking or writing and action that also may be continuing into the present): I *have written* a lot about that subject.

> *Past-perfect tense* (denotes action completed at some definite time in the past): I *had written* a novel by the time I was eighteen.

> *Future-perfect tense* (denotes action to be completed at a definite future time): I *will have written* the press release by the time you need it.

Do not use the future tense for action completed before a future time.

> She *will have finished* (not the future tense *will finish*) the book before next month.

Do not use the past tense for the present-perfect or past-perfect tenses.

> I *was filing* when he returned, but I *had been typing* (not the past tense *was typing*) the report before that time.

In dependent clauses, a permanently true fact is usually put in the present tense even when the main verb is in the past tense. (This rule does not apply to independent clauses or sentences with one verb).

> We *were taught* (past tense) in school that *Hamlet is* (present tense) Shakespeare's greatest tragedy.

The present tense may be used idiomatically to express future action in some cases.

> My vacation *starts* (for the future tense *will start*) next Friday.

Use the progressive form, not the simple present, to express action in progress.

> When I *write* in the morning, as I *am writing* (not the present tense *write*) now, I compose with more facility than in the evening.

After the future tense in a main clause, use the present tense in a dependent clause.

> The chair *will open* the meeting as soon as the
> speaker *arrives.*

When using the past tense, you must use the past-perfect tense to refer to a preceding event.

> He *pledged* the books he *had bought* (not *bought*)
> last week.

Transitive verb. See **Parts of Speech, Verb.**

Verb. See **Parts of Speech, Verb.**

Verbal. A verb form used as another part of speech. See **Gerund; Infinitive; Participle.**

Voice. The quality of a transitive verb that shows when the subject is acting (active voice) or being acted upon (passive voice). Voice is ordinarily not troublesome, but do not mix the voices by shifting from active to passive illogically.

> The jurors *deliberated* for 48 hours before the judge
> discharged them (*not* before they *were discharged*
> by the judge).

The passive voice is less emphatic than the active.

> The publisher *rejected* the manuscript (*not* the
> manuscript *was rejected* by the publisher).

TROUBLESOME WORDS AND PHRASES

a while, awhile (n., adv.). *A while* is a noun phrase meaning a period or interval. *Awhile* is an adverb meaning for a short time.

> I had to wait for *a while* at the airport.

> They talked *awhile* before reaching an agreement.

about (adj., adv., prep.). If you are being precise, use *at*; if you are approximating, use *about*. But if a sentence already indicates an approximation or estimation, *about* is redundant. Never use the combination *at about*. See also **Parts of Speech, Preposition.**

> He will be here *about* (approximately) 9 o'clock and will leave *at* (precisely) noon.
>
> The program will begin *about* (not *at about*) 8:30 P.M.
>
> I estimate that we will sell 2,000 (not *about* 2,000) copies.

above (adj., adv., n., prep.). Preferably used as an adverb or preposition rather than as an adjective or noun.

> *Permissible*: The *above* outline.
>
> *Preferable*: The outline given *above*. The preceding outline.

accede (vb.). When it is followed by a preposition, use *to*.

> He will probably *accede to* the demands.

accompany (vb.). Use *by* when a person accompanies another. Use *with* when the reference is to some intangible thing.

> He was *accompanied by* his wife.
>
> The angry tones were *accompanied with* a pounding on the desk.

according (adj.). Follow by preposition *to*.

> *According to* the instructions, we register here.

adapt, adopt (vb.). *Adapt* means to make fit or suitable, to adjust; *adopt* means to take as one's own, to accept formally.

> Many companies *adapted* their plants to the needs of an expanding economy.
>
> The company *adopted* the suggestions.

addicted to, subject to. *Addicted to* means devoted to persistently, as to a bad habit or indulgence; *subject to* means liable to or conditional upon.

> Jones is *addicted to* alcohol.
>
> This arrangement is *subject to* approval by Mr. Jones.

adept (adj.). When it is followed by a preposition, use *in*.

> He is *adept in* science.

adequate (adj.). When it is followed by a preposition, use *for* when "enough" is meant, *to* when "commensurate" is meant.

> That amount is *adequate for* (enough) her living
> expenses.
>
> That amount is not *adequate to* (commensurate) the
> demands made on her.

adverse, averse (adj.). *Adverse* means in opposition, unfavorable; *averse* means having a dislike for. *Adverse* refers chiefly to opinion or intention; *averse* to feeling or inclination.

> His report was *adverse* to the interest of labor.
>
> He is *averse* to criticism from others.

advise, inform (vb.). Use *advise* in the sense of counsel, warn; use *inform* in the sense of acquaint, tell, communicate knowledge to.

> I will *advise* him not to accept the contract as it now
> stands.
>
> I will *inform* (not *advise*) them that the contract is full
> of loopholes.

affect, effect (n., vb.). The word *affect* is not used as a noun, except as a psychological term; *effect*, used as a noun, means result.

> The *effect* of a sarcastic business letter is to harm
> business.

Affect, as a verb, means to influence, to concern, to change; *effect*, as a verb, means to cause, produce, result in, bring about.

> Passage of this bill will *affect* (influence, concern) the
> entire country.

> Passage of this bill will *effect* (bring about) the
> cooperation of all parties.

Affect is also used in the sense of assuming or pretending.

> He *affects* a blustery manner to hide his shyness.

ago (adj.). When a qualifying clause is used after *ago*, begin the clause with *that*, not *since*.

> It was ten years *ago that* (not *since*) the stores were
> consolidated.

agree (vb.). You agree *with* a person, *to* a proposal, *on* a plan.

> I *agree with* you.
>
> He *agreed to* the suggestion.
>
> The union will not *agree on* a compensation plan.

Also, a thing may agree with another thing.

> The photograph *agrees* with the painting.

agreeable (adj.). Usually, it is followed by *to* but may be followed by *with* when used in the sense of in conformity or in accordance.

> The plan is *agreeable with* (in accordance) my
> understanding of what is expected of us.

alike (adj.). Do not precede it with *both*.

> They are *alike* (not *both alike*).

all (n., pron., adj., adv.). When it is used as a noun, *all* is either singular or plural, depending upon the meaning.

> *All* (everything) *is* forgiven.
>
> *All* (several people) *are* forgiven.

When it is used with a pronoun, *all* is a noun and is followed by *of*.

> Number *all of* them.

When it is used with a noun, *all* is an adjective; *of* is not needed.

> Number *all* (of the) sheets.

all right (adj.). This expression should always be written as two words.

> Are you *all right* (not *alright*)?

allusion, illusion, delusion (n.). An *allusion* is a reference to something; an *illusion* is a false image; a *delusion* is a false concept or belief.

> In his speech he made an *allusion* (reference) to the president's last news conference.
>
> The mirrors gave the *illusion* (false image) of a larger room.
>
> The company's accounting system creates a *delusion* (false concept) about its profits.

amend, emend (vb.). *Amend* means to improve or to make right. *Emend* means to correct or alter.

> The senator wants to *amend* the constitution.
>
> The manager wants to *emend* the foreword to the report.

among. See **between; Parts of Speech, Preposition.**

amounts. Words stating amount (time, money, measurement, weight, volume, fractions) take a singular verb.

> *Five days is* the usual workweek.
>
> *Three feet is* the correct measurement.
>
> *Five yards is* what I ordered.
>
> *Three-quarters* of a pound *is* enough.
>
> *Ten dollars is* more than I expected.

anger (n.). Anger *at* that which hurts or annoys, *toward* a person.

> She expressed her *anger at* having to work overtime.
>
> She expressed her *anger toward* the supervisors.

angry (adj.). Angry *at* a thing, *about* a situation, *with* a person.

> I am *angry at* the computer.
>
> I am *angry about* the tight schedule.
>
> I am *angry with* Louise for backing out.

annoyed (vb.). Annoyed *with* a person, *by* that which annoys.

> I am *annoyed with* her.
>
> I am *annoyed by* her carelessness.

anxious, eager (adj.). *Anxious* is frequently misused for *eager*. To be *anxious* is to be worried; to be *eager* is to anticipate enthusiastically.

> I am *eager* to hear the new director's address.
>
> He is *anxious* (worried) about the outcome of the
>   election.

anyone (pron.), **any one**. Singular, followed by a singular verb and singular pronoun.

> *Anyone* who *is* interested in *his* work *makes* a point of
>   getting to work on time.

Of the two forms, *anyone* and *any one*, the first is correct when *anybody* can be substituted in the sentence with no change in meaning. In other uses, *any one* is the correct form.

> If we send *anyone* (anybody), it should be Mr. Jones.
>
> If we send *any one* of the salespersons, it should be
>   Mr. Jones.

appraise, apprise (vb.). *Appraise* means to estimate something. *Apprise* means to inform someone about something.

> He will *appraise* the property.
>
> She will *apprise* the manager of her progress.

apt, liable, likely (adj.). *Apt* suggests a habitual tendency; *liable* usually means exposed to a risk or unpleasantness. When the sense is simple probability, use *likely*.

> Businesspeople are *apt* (have a tendency) to dictate letters carelessly.
>
> A businessperson who dictates letters carelessly is *liable* to lose (exposed to the danger of losing) his or her customers. (*Note*: Some authorities condemn "liable to do something," allowing only the prepositional instead of the infinitive phrase: "A businessperson is *liable to* the loss. . . .")
>
> He is *likely* to (probably will) vote against the bill.

as (n., pron., conj., prep., adv.). Use *as . . . as* in affirmative statements; use *so . . . as* in negative statements and in questions implying a negative answer.

> This window display is *as* attractive *as* the last one.
>
> This window display is not *so* attractive *as* the last one.
>
> Could any ambitious young man be *so* foolish *as* to turn down the offer (implying a negative answer)?

Use *as* to express comparison when a clause containing a verb follows. See also **like.**

> Copy the report exactly *as* it is written.

As is overworked when used as a substitute for *since, for, because.*

> *Since* (not *as*) the opposition showed no sign of yielding, the minority abandoned its position.

Avoid using *as to* in place of a simple preposition such as *of, about, among, upon.*

> She has no conception *of* (not *as to*) the proper performance of her duties.
>
> The witness testified *about* (not *as to*) the defendant's early life.

as if, as though, like. *As if* is less formal than *as though. As though* is used in the same sense, and like *as if,* it is followed by a verb in the subjunctive mood. *Like* is widely used and misused in informal conversation (*like* I said), but authorities still recommend that it be used as a preposition and with a noun or pronoun that is *not* followed by a verb.

> She hesitated to begin the project *as if* she were afraid it would fail.
>
> He angrily rejected the proposal *as though* it were a personal affront.
>
> The president acts *like* a dictator.

assure, ensure, insure (vb.). See **ensure, insure, assure.**

averse. Not to be confused with *adverse.* See **adverse.**

aversion (n.). Aversion *to* a person, *for* acts or actions.

> He has an *aversion to* the director.
>
> He has an *aversion for* public speaking.

bad (n., adj.), **badly** (adv.). Use the adjective *bad* when it refers to the subject and is simply joined to the subject by the verb. When the verb denotes action, use the adverb *badly* to modify the action.

> He looks *bad* (describes "he").
>
> He was injured *badly* in the accident (describes how he was injured).
>
> He writes *badly* (describes how he writes).

balance (n.). Frequently misused for *rest* or *remainder. Balance* is a financial term and should be used only in reference to the difference between two amounts.

> She gave the *balance* of the money to the Red Cross.
>
> We expect to ship the *remainder* of the order next week.
>
> The *rest* of the audience enjoyed the program.

because. Frequently incorrectly used instead of *that* after "The reason . . . is . . ." See **Parts of Speech, Conjunction.**

> The reason the goods were delayed was *that* (not
> *because*) they were shipped to the wrong zone
> number.

beside (prep., adv.), **besides** (prep., adj., adv.). *Beside* means by the side of, close to; *besides* means additionally, in addition to.

> The letter is on his desk, *beside* (close to) the file.
>
> *Besides* (in addition to) these two bills, several others
> arrived late.
>
> We have these two bills and several others *besides*
> (in addition).

between. Use the objective case after *between*. See **Parts of Speech, Preposition.**

> *Between* you and *me* (never *I*).

Use *between* when reference is made to only two persons or things; use *among* when reference is made to more than two.

> The friendliness *between* the British foreign minister
> and the American secretary of state promoted
> harmony.
>
> The friendliness *among* British, American, and Israeli
> delegates promoted harmony.

Do not use *each* or *every* after *between* or *among* when *each* or *every* has a plural sense.

> Almost all the audience went into the lobby *between*
> scenes (or *between each scene*).
>
> It is essential that harmony prevail *among* the
> departments (not *between every department*).

biannual, biennial (adj.). *Biannual* means twice a year, although not necessarily at six-month intervals; *semiannual* implies an interval of six months; *biennial* means once in two years. (*Biannually, biennially,* are the adverbial forms.)

> The association holds *biannual* (two a year)
> conferences.

> Members of Congress are elected *biennially* (every
> two years)

biweekly, bimonthly (adj., adv.). *Biweekly* means once every two weeks or twice a week; *bimonthly* usually means once every two months. But it is clearer to use *once every two weeks, once every two months.* See **semimonthly, semiweekly.**

blame (vb.) Blame a person *for* something do not blame something *on* a person.

> *Blame* the administration *for* the present difficulty (not
> *Blame it on the administration*).

both (adj., pron., conj.). Plural, followed by a plural verb and plural pronoun. *Both* is unnecessary with the words *between, alike, at once,* and *equally* and should be omitted unless the omission of the other words is preferable.

> *Both* the Democrats and Republicans *are* eager (not
> *equally eager*) to prevent the spread of
> communism. (*Or:* The Democrats and Republicans
> are *equally* eager to prevent the spread of
> communism.)

bring, take (vb.). These words are opposites. *Bring* implies "coming" with some person or thing to another place; *take* implies "going" with some person or thing to another place.

> I will *bring* the book *with* me when I come to your
> office this afternoon.

> I will *take* the book *to* him when I go to his office this
> afternoon.

but (adv., n., prep., pron.). When it is used in the sense of *except,* some writers incorrectly consider *but* as a preposition and follow it with the objective case. The case after *but* varies according to its usage. When *but* and the word that follows it occur at the end of the sentence, the word after *but* is in the objective case. See **Parts of Speech, Conjunction.**

> Everyone *but she* (not *her*) enjoyed the
> entertainment. (*She* did not enjoy it.)
>
> I told no one *but him* (not *he*) about the change. (I told
> *him* about it.)

A common error is the use of *but* after a negative.

> I *can* (not *cannot*) but object to the title.

When *but* is used in the sense of *except*, it may follow a negative.

> *No one but* he went.
>
> He accepted *none* of the shipment *but* the short coats.

But what is correctly used only when *except* could be substituted for *but*. The use of *but what* for *but that* is a colloquialism.

> He said nothing *but what* (or *except what*) any
> honorable person would have said.

but that. A common error is the use of *but that* instead of *that* to introduce a clause after *doubt* (either the verb or the noun *doubt*).

> There is no doubt *that* (not *but that*) the shipment will
> reach you tomorrow.

But that is not interchangeable with *that*. Notice the difference in meaning in the following sentences.

> It is impossible *that* the signatories to the United
> Nations Charter will sanction the move. (They will
> not sanction it.)
>
> It is impossible *but that* the signatories to the United
> Nations Charter will sanction the move. (They are
> sure to sanction it.)
>
> It is not impossible *that* the signatories to the United
> Nations Charter will sanction the move. (They may
> sanction it.)

When *but that* has a negative implication, the subsequent use of *not* is incorrect.

> How do you know *but that* the apparent friendliness of
> our competitor may be (not *may not be*) an attempt
> to probe our methods?

cabinet (n.). When it is used to mean a body of advisors, *cabinet* is a collective noun. See **Grammatical Terms, Collective noun.**

can, could (vb.). *Could* is the past tense of *can*. See **Grammatical Terms, Tenses.** Use *can* with verbs in the present, perfect, and future tenses; use *could* with verbs in the past and past perfect tenses.

> I give/I have given/I will give what I *can*.

> I gave/I was giving/I had given what I *could*.

Use *could*, not *can*, when *would* is used in the main clause.

> He *would* stop in Cincinnati on his way west if he
> *could* arrange to meet you there.

A common error is the misuse of *could* for *might* in conditional sentences. *Could* expresses ability, *might* expresses permission or possibility. See **can, may.**

> If you have not bought the stock, you *might* (not *could*
>) as well forget about it.

can, may (vb.). *Can* denotes ability or power; *may* denotes permission.

> *Can* you (will you be able to) make shipment next
> week?

> *May* we (will you give us permission to) make
> shipment next week?

> I *can* (it is possible for me to) go to Alaska by plane.
> *May* I? (Do I have your permission?)

canvass (vb.), **canvas** (n.). *Canvass* means to scrutinize, discuss, solicit, not to be confused with *canvas*, a heavy cloth.

> You should *canvass* the neighborhood for support.

capital, capitol (n.). *Capital* is a city that is the seat of the government; *Capitol* is the building in which Congress meets or a building in which a state legislature meets. State capitols may be spelled either uppercase or lowercase, but the U.S. Capitol is spelled with an uppercase "C."

> Washington, D.C., is the *capital* of the United States.
>
> I hope the repairs to the *Capitol* are completed when we visit Washington.
>
> The *capitol* at Albany is being repaired.

Capital has several other meanings, for example, accounting assets, but they do not cause confusion.

careless (adj.). Careless *about* appearance and dress, *in* the performance of an action.

> She is *careless about* her dress.
>
> He was *careless in* checking the machine.

class (n.) pl., *classes*. See **Grammatical Terms, Collective noun.** For correct usage in the sense of "kind" or "sort," see **kind.**

client, customer, patron (n.). A *client* is someone who consults a professional person. A *customer* is someone who purchases a product or service. A *patron* is someone who supports a thing or person.

> The lawyer met with his *client.*
>
> The discount store had a red-letter sale for its charge *customers.*
>
> She is a *patron* of the arts.

coincident (adj.). When it is followed by a preposition, use *with.*

> His theory is *coincident with* the facts.

committee (n.). See **Grammatical Terms, Collective noun.**

common, -er, -est (adj.). Preferable to *more common, most common.*

common, mutual (adj.). *Common* refers to something that is shared alike by two or more individuals or species, as *common fear* of war, *common trait* of character. *Mutual* refers to something that is reciprocally given and received, as *mutual agreement, mutual respect.*

> They have a *mutual* (not *common*) desire to
> cooperate.

> A *common* (not *mutual*) effort ensured the success of
> the project.

Mutual can also be used in the sense of "having the same relationship to each other."

> We have *mutual* (or *common*) friends.

compare to, compare with. If you want to suggest a similarity or to state that a similarity exists, use *to*. If you want to indicate specific similarities or differences, use *with*.

> The speaker *compared* the new law *to* a plague.
> (The speaker merely suggested a similarity.)

> The speaker *compared* the British law *with* the
> American statute. (The speaker made a detailed
> comparison.)

complacent (adj.), **-ency** (n.); **complaisant** (adj.), **-ance** (n.). *Complacent* people are pleased with themselves or with things that affect them personally. A *complaisant* person is eager to please by compliance or indulgence.

> Don't let your *complacency* about your work keep you
> from knowing your shortcomings.

> If Congress were in a more *complaisant* mood, the
> president might be able to push the law through.

complement, compliment (n., vb.). *Complement* is that which is required to complete or make whole; *compliment* is an expression of admiration. The noun *complement* is followed by the preposition *of*; the verb *compliment* is followed by *on*.

> This department has its full *complement* (noun) *of*
> workers.

> A gold clip on your dress will *complement* (verb) your
> costume.

> His *compliments (noun) on* my article were gratifying.

> The president *complimented* (verb) him *on* the
> showing made by his department.

complementary, complimentary (adj.). The distinction in meaning is the same as that between *complement* and *compliment*. See the preceding entry. The preposition *to* is used with *complementary; about* or *concerning* is used with *complimentary*.

> Practical experience is *complementary to* theoretical
> training.
>
> Two *complementary* colors mixed together make a
> third color.
>
> His review of the book was not *complimentary*.
>
> *Complimentary* remarks *about* a person's work are
> always appreciated.

compliance (n.). When it is followed by a preposition, use *with*.

> They are in *compliance with* the law.

comply (vb.). When it is followed by a preposition, use *with*.

> You should *comply with* the law.

compose, comprise (vb.). *Compose* means to make up something by combining (the parts *compose* the whole). *Comprise* means to include (the whole *comprises* the parts).

> Twenty chapters *compose* the book. (The book is
> *composed* of twenty chapters.)
>
> The association *comprises* 6,000 members.

concur (vb.). Concur *in* a decision, opinion, belief; concur *with* a person.

> I *concur in* that decision.
>
> I *concur with* you.

conducive (adj.). When it is followed by a preposition, use *to*.

> The machine's rhythm is *conducive to* relaxation.

confidant (n.), **confident** (adj.). *Confidant* is a person to whom secrets are entrusted. *Confident* means assured and self-reliant.

> He was her *confidant*.
>
> She was *confident* the project would be approved.

conform (vb.). When it is followed by a preposition, use *to* or *with*.

> The report *conforms to* Regulation 6-AR.

connect (vb.). Objects, places, or people are connected *with* one another *by* certain means.

> Gimbel's used to be *connected with* Saks *by* a bridge.

connection (n.). The phrase *in this connection* is never good usage; the phrase *in connection with* is considered trite and is overworked. There is no grammatical objection to it when it is the proper phrase to use, but a substitution is preferable. Try *about* as a substitute.

> He talked to her *about* (not *in connection with*) the
>   report.

conscious (adj., n.), **aware** (adj.). *Conscious* emphasizes inner realization; *aware* emphasizes perception through the senses.

> He became *conscious* of the reason for his failure.
>
> He was *aware* of stale air in the room.

consensus (n.). An erroneous expression frequently used is *consensus of opinion*. *Consensus* means agreement in matter of opinion; therefore, the expression is redundant.

> A *consensus* (not *consensus of opinion*) was reached.

consist (vb.). Followed by *of* to indicate the material, by *in* to define or show identity.

> Margarine *consists of* (the materials) vegetable oils
>   and coloring.
>
> The sinking-fund methods *consists in* (may be
>   defined as) the payment of a sum.

> His greatest asset *consists in* (is) his ability to
> understand.

contemptible, contemptuous (adj.). *Contemptible* means despicable, deserving of being despised. *Contemptuous* means scornful.

> The effort to bring pressure to bear on him was
> *contemptible* (despicable).

> His comments on the report were *contemptuous*
> (scornful).

continual, continuous (adj.). *Continual* means occurring in close succession, frequently repeated; *continuous* means without stopping, without interruption. The same distinction applies to the adverbs *continually* and *continuously*.

> *Continual* (frequent) breakdowns in the factory
> delayed production.

> The machinery has been in *continuous* (without
> stopping) operation for 60 hours.

> He is *continually* (frequently) asking for favors.

> He drove *continuously* (without stopping) for 6 hours.

correct (adj.). Not comparable. If anything is correct, it cannot be *more* correct. *More nearly correct* is allowable.

correlative (adj.). When it is followed by a preposition, use *with*.

> The two methods are *correlative with* each other.

could. See **can, could.**

council (n.), **counsel** (n., vb.), **consul** (n.). *Council* applies to a board or assembly and to the meeting of such a body; *counsel* means advice or to advise. *Consul* is a government representative looking after his country's interests in a foreign country.

> The *council* met last Wednesday.

> His job was to *counsel* prisoners.

> He held the position of U.S. *consul* in Argentina.

credible, credulous, creditable (adj.). *Credible* means believable; *credulous* means easily imposed upon, believing too easily; *creditable* means praiseworthy.

> He is not a *credible* witness.
>
> The readers are indeed *credulous* if they believe the editorial completely.
>
> His summation of the case was highly *creditable*.

damage, injury (n.). *Injury* is the broad general term; *damage* is especially an injury that impairs value or involves loss. *Injury* is impairment of utility or beauty and applies generally to persons, feelings, reputation, character, and sometimes to property. *Damage* applies to property only.

> He collected insurance for *injury* to his back and for *damage* to his car.

data (n.). Plural and takes a plural verb and plural adjective pronoun. The singular form *datum* is now seldom used.

> We have proved that *these* (not *this*) data *are* (not *is*) reliable.

dates from. The correct expression is *dates from*, not *dates back to*.

> The artifacts *date from* the sixteenth century.

deduction, induction (n.). *Deduction* refers to reasoning by moving from the general to the particular. *Induction* refers to reasoning by moving from the particular to the general.

> *Deduction*: All computers accept some form of symbolic data; therefore, the XL100 should accept symbolic input.
>
> *Induction*: Having read thousands of business letters, most of which have one or more grammatical errors, I believe that most businesspeople need further education in basic English composition.

defect (n.). Defect *in* a concrete object; defect *of* an intangible quality, such as judgment or character.

The failure to pick up speed is a *defect in* the
machine.

The *defect of* his character is impatience.

depositary, depository (n.). *Despositary* is applied to the person or authority entrusted with something for safekeeping. It may also be used to apply
to the place where something is deposited or stored. *Depository* is applied
only to the place where something is deposited or stored.

The president is the *depositary*; the bank is the
depository.

depreciate (vb.). Do not follow *depreciate* by the words *in value*. If anything
has depreciated, its value is less.

The ring has *depreciated* (not *depreciated in value*).

did (vb.). Sometimes misused in place of *has* or *have*. *Did* represents past
action; *has* or *have* represents action continuing to the present moment.
The misuse usually occurs with *yet* or *already*.

Did you listen to "Town Meeting" yesterday (past
action)?

Have you heard the results of the election yet (not *did
you hear*)?

I *have* not heard (not *did not hear*) the results of the
election yet.

differ (vb.). Used in the sense of unlikeness, *differ* is followed by *from*;
used in the sense of disagreeing in opinion, it is followed by *with*.

My sales campaign *differs from* yours.

I *differ with* you about the value of your sales
campaign.

different (adj.). Do not use it to show separate identity that has already
been established.

Three secretaries (not *three different secretaries*)
asked for a Christmas vacation.

different from. This is the correct form; *different than* is sometimes used when followed by a clause.

> My sales plan is *different from* yours.

> The computer looked *different than* I thought it would.

differentiate, distinguish (vb.). *Differentiate* means to show specific differences in two or more things. *Distinguish* means to point out general differences.

> You can *differentiate* among the fabrics by texture and design.

> You can easily *distinguish* evergreens from deciduous trees.

direct (vb., adj., adv.). The adverb form is *direct* or *directly*. *Direct* is not comparable. If anything is direct, it cannot be *more* direct. *More nearly direct* is allowable.

disappointed (adj.). Disappointed *with* a thing or object; otherwise, disappointed *in*.

> I am disappointed *with* the car.

> I am disappointed *in* the outcome of the election.

disburse, disperse (vb.). *Disburse* means to pay out. *Disperse* means to cause to break up or spread out.

> He *disbursed* the payroll.

> The crowd *dispersed*.

disinterested, uninterested (adj.). *Disinterested* means impartial, without selfish motive or thought of personal gain. *Uninterested* means not interested or enthusiastic.

> The teacher stated the case in a *disinterested* (impartial) manner.

> He seemed *uninterested* (lacking in interest) in his work.

disorganized, unorganized (adj.). *Disorganized* refers to the lack of an orderly system. *Unorganized* means not having an orderly whole.

> He is such a *disorganized* person.
>
> The politician's supporters were *unorganized.*

dissent (vb., n.). When it is followed by a preposition, use *from.*

> He *dissented from* the majority.

do (vb.). Principal parts: *do, did,* and (*has, had,* or *have*) *done.* See **Parts of Speech, Verb.** For the misuse of *did* for *has* or *have,* see **did.**

doubt if, doubt that, doubt whether. *Doubt if* should be avoided in business writing. *Doubt that* is the preferred expression in negative or interrogative sentences when little doubt exists. *Doubt whether* is usually limited to situations involving strong uncertainty.

> I *doubt that* we can meet the deadline.
>
> I *doubt whether* anything will come of it.

due to. Often misused for *owing to. Due* is an adjective and must be attached to a noun or pronoun, whereas *owing to* is now considered a compound preposition. *Due to* means caused by. Test your sentence by substituting *caused by* for *due to.*

> The labor movement is losing prestige *owing to* the methods of some of its leaders. (*Methods* is the object of the compound preposition *owing to.*)
>
> The success of the firm was *due to* (caused by) the ability of its president.
>
> The firm succeeded *owing to* (not *due to*) the ability of its president.

each (pron., adj., adv.). When it is used as a subject, *each* invariably takes a singular verb and pronoun even when followed by *of them* or the like.

> *Each* of the reports made by the committees *was* a tribute to the late president.
>
> *Each carries his* or *her* share of the load.

When *each* immediately follows a plural noun or pronoun, the verb is plural.

> The *officers each take* an oath.

When *each* refers to a preceding plural noun or pronoun, the number of a subsequent noun or pronoun depends upon whether *each* comes before or after the verb. Use the plural when *each* precedes the verb, the singular when *each* follows the verb.

> The *employees each have their* own assignments (precedes the verb).
>
> The *employees are* responsible *each* for *his* or *her* own assignment (follows the verb).

For the use of *each* after *between* or *among*, see **between.**

each other, one another. *Each other* should be used when only two things are referred to and *one another* when more than two are referred to.

> Smith and I see *each other* often.
>
> It will be interesting for the four of us to see *one another* again.

The possessive of *each other* is *each other's*; of *one another, one another's.*

> They did not spare *each other's* (two persons) feelings.
>
> They did not spare *one another's* (more than two persons) feelings.

economics (n.). Usually plural in form but singular in meaning; hence, it takes singular verbs and singular pronouns. See **-ics.**

> Economics *is* of prime importance to every student of commerce. Several courses in *it* are required.

effect. See **affect.**

either (conj.). Singular, followed by a singular verb.

> *Either* of these sales plans *is* excellent.

Use *either* to designate one of two persons or things; use *any one* to designate one of three or more.

> You may choose *either* of the (two) new typewriters
> or *any one* of the (three) old typewriters.

either . . . or (conj.). The construction after correlatives should be the same; for example, if *either* is followed by a verb, *or* must be followed by a verb. The misplacement of *either*, a common error, frequently results in an unbalanced construction after the correlatives.

> You are required *either to register* by the 15th *or to drop* the course (not *either are required to register . . . or to drop*).
>
> *Either you must go* today, *or you must wait* until next week (not *You must either go . . . , or you must wait*).

elicit (vb.), **illicit** (adj.). *Elicit* means to bring out. *Illicit* refers to something illegal.

> The ad *elicited* a negative response.
>
> The harbor was known for numerous *illicit* activities.

else (adj., adv.). A common error is to combine *else* with *but*.

> It was nothing *but* selfishness on his part (not *nothing else but*).

The possessive of *somebody else* is *somebody else's*; of *everyone else*, *everyone else's*; the same form is followed for other examples such as *anyone else* and *no one else*.

emigrate, immigrate (vb.). *Emigrate* means to go *from* one's own country to another for the purpose of living there. *Immigrate* means to go *into* a country or place for the purpose of living there. *Emigrate* is followed by the preposition *from, immigrate* by *to*.

> Thousands of Jews *emigrated from* (left) Germany
> and *immigrated to* (moved to) Israel.

eminent, imminent (adj.). *Eminent* means prominent, distinguished, and is applied to persons. *Imminent* means impending, threatening, close at hand, and is applied to events. See also **immanent, imminent.**

> He is an *eminent* lecturer.
>
> A struggle for power between the two nations is *imminent.*

ensure, insure, assure (vb.). *Ensure* means to make certain. *Insure* means to give or take insurance, and it also means to make certain. American writers tend to prefer *insure,* and British writers tend to prefer *ensure* in the sense of "making certain." *Assure* means to guarantee and is used only in reference to persons.

> They campaigned an extra week to *insure* (or *ensure*) that the measure would pass.
>
> She *assured* them that the deadline would be met.

equally as. Often incorrectly used for *equally . . . with,* for *equally* by itself, or for *as* by itself.

> The Republicans are *as* (not *equally as*) guilty as the Democrats.

-ever. Compounds of *-ever—however, whichever, whoever, whatever*—are not interrogatives. A common error, particularly in speech, is to use these compounds as interrogatives with the thought that they add emphasis to the question.

> How (not *however*) did you find out?
>
> Who (not *whoever*) told you that?

every (adj.). Always singular. Followed by singular verb and singular pronouns.

> *Every* large company in the industry *files its* reports with the trade association.
>
> *Everyone was* trying to better *his* or *her* position.

> *Every one* of the students who participated in the
> demonstration put *himself* or *herself* in the position
> of insubordination.
>
> *Every one* but he *was* at the meeting.

everybody (pron.). Write as one word. Always singular. *Everyone* is preferred.

every (adj.) **one, everyone** (pron.). Write as one word only when *everybody*
is meant. If *of* is used, the expression must be written as two words.

> *Everyone* (everybody) should attend the meeting.
>
> *Every one of* the department heads attended the
> meeting.
>
> All the drawings are excellent; *every one* (*of* the
> drawings) deserves a prize.

See **every** for the correct number of verb and pronoun to use after *every
one* or *everyone*.

everywhere (adv.). Always written as one word. *Every place* is commonly
misused for *everywhere*. See **place**.

expect (vb.). Expect *of* a person; otherwise, expect *from*.

> The company expects loyalty *of* its employees.
>
> They *expect* tornadoes to come *from* the hurricane.

faced (vb.). When it is followed by a preposition, use *by* or *with*.

> She is *faced with* a difficult decision.

farther (adj., adv.), **further** (adj., adv., vb.). Use *farther* to refer to distance;
use *further* to refer to time, quantity, or degree.

> Philadelphia is *farther* from Washington than from
> New York.
>
> We went *further* into the matter.

This distinction, however, is disappearing, and *further* is widely used in all
instances.

fatal (adj.). Not comparable. If anything is fatal, it cannot be *more* fatal. *More nearly fatal* is allowable.

feel (vb.). Followed by a predicate adjective and not by an adverb (see **Parts of Speech, Adverb),** unless it is used in the sense of touching physically.

> I do not *feel well* (predicate adjective modifying *I*).
>
> He telephoned and said that he still *feels* very *bad* (not *badly*) (predicate adjective modifying *he*).
>
> The doctor *felt* the bruise *tenderly* (adverb describing how the doctor touched the bruise).
>
> I *felt sick* when I heard the news (predicate adjective modifying *I*).

few (indef. pron.). Either singular or plural, depending on the meaning. See **less** for the distinction between *less* and *fewer*.

> A *few is* enough.
>
> Many are called, but *few are* chosen.

final (adj.). Not comparable. If anything is *final*, it cannot be *more* final. *More nearly final* is allowable.

firstly (adv.). In formal enumerations, the use of *first, second, third,* or *firstly, secondly, thirdly,* and so on is a matter of personal preference. However, *first, second, third,* is preferable. Do not mix the forms (not *first, secondly, third*).

formally, formerly (adv.). *Formally* means in a formal manner; *formerly* means previously.

> He was *formally* initiated into the club.
>
> He was *formerly* president of this company.

former (adj.). Correct when used to designate the first of two persons or things; incorrect when used to designate the first of three or more.

> Smith and Jones were at the convention; the *former* gave an interesting talk.

> Smith, Jones, and Brown *were* at the convention;
> *Smith* gave an interesting talk.

fractions. See **amounts.** For the use of the hyphen in writing fractions, see **Grammatical Terms, Compound term,** *Fractions.*

-ful. The correct plural of words ending in *-ful,* such as *spoonful, handful,* is *-fuls: spoonfuls, handfuls* (not *spoonsful, handsful*). See also **Grammatical Terms, Compound term,** *Plurals.*

full (adj.). Not comparable. If anything is *full,* it cannot be *more* full. *More nearly full* is allowable. The adverb form is *full* or *fully.* See **Parts of Speech, Adverb.**

further. See **farther.**

generally, usually (adv.). Use *generally* in a general sense or as a whole; use *usually* when you mean in the majority of cases.

> It was *generally* believed that the market would rise.
>
> The market is *usually* erratic in a presidential election year.

good. See **well.**

goods (n., pl.). Always takes a plural verb and plural pronouns.

> The *goods were* damaged in transit before *they were* delivered.

government (n.). In the United States, *government* is constructed as singular; in Great Britain, as plural.

> The U.S. *government is* sending *its* delegates to the meeting.
>
> Her Majesty's *government are* sending *their* delegates to the meeting.

group (n.). See **Grammatical Terms, Collective noun.**

guarantee (n., vb.), **guaranty** (n.). For the verb, always use *guarantee.* Business convention has established a specialized use of *guaranty* as a noun, which is illustrated in expressions such as *contract of guaranty, act of guar-*

anty. However, *guarantee* is never wrong, even in these expressions. A safe rule to follow is: when in doubt, use *guarantee*.

> The manufacturer's *guarantee* expires next year.

habitual (adj.). When it is followed by a preposition, use *with*.

> It is *habitual with* him.

had (vb.). *Had . . . have* is sometimes carelessly used in inverted sentences when only *had* is required.

> *Had* I *been* (not *have been*) on the jury, I would have
> voted to acquit him.

An incorrect use of *had . . . have* occurs when the sentence has not been inverted.

> If I *had been* (not *had have been*) on the jury I would
> have voted to acquit him.

hardly (adv.). This word conveys a negative idea and should not be used with a negative. The error usually occurs when the speaker or writer decides to modify a negative statement.

> The company *can hardly* (not *cannot hardly*) take that
> attitude.

Hardly is used only in the sense of *scarcely*. The adverb of *hard*, meaning firm or solid, is the same as the adjective—*hard*. The following examples illustrate how the use of *hardly* changes the meaning of a sentence.

> His salary as president of the company is *hard*
> earned.

> His salary as president of the company is *hardly*
> earned.

he. Nominative case of third-person singular pronoun. For misuse of *he* instead of *him*, see **Parts of Speech, Pronoun**. For use after forms of the verb *to be* (*am, is, are, was, were*), see **Grammatical Terms, Predicate nominative.**

heavy (n., adj., adv.). The adverb forms are *heavy, heavier, heaviest* or *heavily, more heavily, most heavily*. See **Parts of Speech, Adverb**.

help (n., vb.). Should not be followed by *but* when used in the sense of avoid.

> I cannot *help feeling* (not *help but feel*) that you are
> unwise.

her (pron.). Objective case of *she*. For use as an object, see **Parts of Speech, Pronoun**. For misuse of *her* instead of *she* after forms of the verb *to be (am, is, are, was, were)*, see **Grammatical Terms, Predicate nominative**.

him (pron.). Objective case of *he*. For use as an object, see **Parts of Speech, Pronoun**. For misuse of *him* instead of *he* after forms of the verb *to be (am, is, are, was, were)*, see **Grammatical Terms, Predicate nominative**.

himself. See **Grammatical Terms, Compound personal pronoun**.

hope (n., vb.). Sometimes incorrectly used in the plural after *no*.

> We have no *hope* (not *hopes*) of receiving payment.

When *hope* is used in the passive voice, the indefinite pronoun *it* is always the subject. The error usually occurs when *it* is omitted from the parenthetical expression *it is hoped*, especially in a clause introduced by *what*.

> The region is now experiencing what, *it is hoped* (not
> *what is hoped*), will be a short cold spell. (*What* is
> the subject of *will be*.)

I. Nominative case of first-person singular pronoun. For use of *I* instead of *me*, see **Parts of Speech, Pronoun**. For use after the forms of the verb *to be (am, is, are, was, were)*, see **Grammatical Terms, Predicate nominative**. Avoid use of the editorial *we* instead of *I* in a letter written on behalf of a company. Use *I* when referring to the writer individually and *we* when referring to the company. *I* and *we* may be used in the same letter.

> *I* (the writer) will look after this order, and you may be
> sure that *we* (the company) will ship it tomorrow.

-ics. A few English words end in *-ic—music, rhetoric, logic, magic*—but the normal form is *-ics.* Words ending in *-ics* are sometimes treated as singular and sometimes as plural.

> *Singular when used strictly as the name of a science or study:* Mathematics (the science of) *is* most interesting.

> *Singular when used with a singular noun complement:* Economics *was* a crucial *factor* in his decision.

> *Plural when used loosely and when denoting qualities, usually preceded by his, the, such:* Such politics never *win* an election.

> *Plural when denoting practice or activity:* Superb tactics *were* responsible for our victory.

identical (adj.). When it is followed by a preposition, use *with* or *to.*

> Your suit is *identical to* mine.

if (conj.). Often misused in place of *whether.*

> I am not sure *whether* (not *if*) I can ship the goods on that date.

Avoid the use of *if and when.* Only in rare cases is *if and when* really better in a sentence than *if* or *when.*

> He told the association that *when,* or *if,* the Republicans gain control, conditions will change.

ignorant (adj.). When it is used in the sense of uninformed, follow by *in;* in the sense of unaware, by *of.*

> He treats her as though she were *ignorant in* the subject.

> I was *ignorant of* his interest in the matter.

ill (adj.). When it is followed by a preposition, use *with.*

> He is *ill with* the flu.

immanent, imminent (adj.). *Immanent* means indwelling, inherent. *Imminent* means impending, threatening, close at hand.

> Honesty and fairness are *immanent* in the president's character.

> The passage of the bill is *imminent*.

immigrate (vb.). See **emigrate**.

impatient (adj.). Impatient *at* actions or characteristics; *with* persons.

> I am *impatient at* delays.

> I am *impatient with* Mark.

imply, infer (vb.). *Imply* means to suggest, insinuate, express vaguely. *Infer* means to draw from, deduce from, gather from, or conclude from.

> Your letter *implies* that I have tried to evade payment of the bill.

> I *infer* from your letter that you cannot grant an extension of time.

impossible (adj.). Not comparable. If anything is *impossible*, it cannot be *more* impossible. *More nearly impossible* is allowable.

in, into (n., prep., adj., adv.). *In* denotes position or location; *into* denotes action, motion from without to within.

> He was *in* the sales department but is now *in* the advertising department.

> Put this folder *in* (not *into*) the file drawer before locking it. (The folder itself is passive and takes no action.).

> We went *into* the room.

Do not use *into* for the words *in to* (adverb and preposition).

> He went *in to* the meeting. (You cannot go *into* the meeting.)

> He took her *in to* (not *into*) dinner.

inasmuch (conj.). Always written as one word.

infer. See **imply.**

inferior (adj.). Should be followed by *to*, not *than*.

> Their products are always *inferior to* ours.

inform. See **advise.**

ingenious, ingenuous (adj.). *Ingenious* means clever, skillful; *ingenuous* means frank, innocent, trusting.

> He concocted an *ingenious* (clever) plan to avoid the law.
>
> He is very *ingenuous* (trusting, easily fooled) for a man of his age and background.

insofar as (conj.). *Insofar* is written as one word.

interstate (n., adj.), **intrastate** (adj.). *Interstate* means a highway or between two or more states. *Intrastate* means within one state.

> He traveled *Interstate* 80 between Iowa and Illinois.
>
> They engaged in *interstate* commerce between New York and New Jersey.
>
> They engaged in strictly *intrastate* commerce in Delaware.

investigation (n.). When it is followed by a preposition, use *of*.

> The *investigation of* merger trends is almost over.

its (adj.), **it's.** *Its* is the possessive form of the impersonal pronoun *it*. *It's* is a contraction of *it* and *is* or *it* and *has* and is sometimes incorrectly used as a possessive.

> The company has expanded greatly in recent years; *its* success is attributable to its founders.
>
> *It's* too bad that the books will not be ready for delivery by September.

It's (it has) been three months since we received that
order.

jury (n.). See **Grammatical Terms, Collective noun.**

kind (n.), pl., *kinds*. The explanation here applies also to *class, sort, type, size, breed, brand, quality, variety, species,* and similar words. The singular form is modified by *this* and *that*, not *these* and *those*.

This (not *these*) kind does not grow readily; *that* (not
those) does grow readily.

The expression *kind of* is followed by a singular noun unless the plural idea is particularly strong. The common error is inconsistency.

The *kind of position* (not *positions*) that appeals to me
doesn't interest her.

The *kind of positions* I prefer *are those* that offer a lot
of company benefits.

It is incorrect to follow *kind of* by *a*.

What *kind of* (not *kind of a*) position do you want?

After the plural form *kinds of*, a singular or a plural noun may be used.

The *kinds of* writing that *are* the most lucrative *are*
novels and inspirational books.

The *kinds of* books that they publish *are* novels and
textbooks.

know, realize (vb.). *Know* means to perceive, to understand. *Realize* means to accomplish, to grasp fully, and implies a more thorough understanding than *know*.

I *know* a better route.

I *realize* the implications of our action.

latter, last (adj.). The word *latter* may be used to designate the second of two persons or things previously mentioned but should not be used where more than two have been mentioned.

We are now conducting a special sale of suits and overcoats; the *latter* (not *last*) are particularly good value.

We are now conducting a special sale of hats, suits, and overcoats; the *overcoats* are particularly good value.

Do not use the expression *the latter part of.* The correct expressions are *toward the end of, the last part of.*

The book will be published *toward the end of* next month.

The book will be published *the last part of* next month.

lay, lie (vb.). *Lay* means to put or set down, place, deposit. *Lie* means to rest, to be in a certain position or location. *Lay* takes an object; *lie* confines the action to the subject. Principal parts, *lay: lay, laid, laid, laying.* Principal parts, *lie: lie, lay, lain, lying.* The common error is the use of *lay* or one of its principal parts for *lie* or one of its principal parts. Thus *lay* is used incorrectly in place of *lie.* Remember that you must *lay* something down.

lay, laid, laid, laying:

You *lay* the book on the table, and it *lies* there.

You *laid* the book on the table yesterday, and it *lay* there until Mary picked it up.

I *lay* the *letters* in the same place on his desk each morning.

I *laid* the *letters* on his desk before I left the room.

The brickmason *has laid* the *stones* in an irregular pattern.

The brickmason *is laying* the *stones* in an irregular pattern.

lie, lay, lain, lying:

I *lie* (not *lay*) in the sun for an hour every day.

I *lay* (not *laid*) in the sun for an hour yesterday (past tense).

The book *has lain* (not *laid*) there for a month.

The book *is lying* (not *laying*) here where you laid it.

lead (vb.). Principal parts, *lead, led, led*. See **Parts of Speech, Verb.**

less (prep., adj., adv.). Use *less* only in the sense of a smaller amount. Apply *less* only to things that are measured by amount and not by size, quality, or number.

He has *less* (a smaller amount of) assets than
liabilities.

The staff in the New York office is *smaller* (not *less*)
than that in the Chicago office.

Fewer (not *less*) industrial accidents occurred this
year than last.

liable (adj.), **libel** (n.). See also **apt.** *Liable* means responsible or obligated according to law. *Libel*, as a noun, means a written or oral defamatory statement.

The company is *liable* for the damages.

He sued the writer for *libel*.

like (n., vb., conj., interj., prep., adj., adv.). Commonly misused in place of *such as* when the meaning is *for example*.

In his factory are a number of useful machines, *such
as* (not *like*) cutters and stamps.

Use *like* as a preposition, *as* as a conjunction. *Like* takes an object; *as*, or *as if*, introduces a clause.

You are *like me* in your desire for perfection. (No verb
follows *like*.)

He treats her *as if* (not *like*) she were ignorant.

I wish I could think *as* (not *like*) he (does). (The verb
is understood.)

likely. See **apt.**

live (vb.). Live *in* a town, *on* a street, *at* a certain address, *by* means of a livelihood.

> He lives *in* New York on Tenth Street.
>
> He lives *at* 231 West Tenth Street.
>
> He lives *by* selling family heirlooms.

loan (n., vb.), **lend** (vb.). Many authorities object to any use of *loan* as a verb. It is best to use the word only in connection with formal banking transactions—for example, placing a *loan* through a banker. For general purposes, use *lend*. Never use *borrow* to mean *lend*.

> Will you *lend* (not *loan*) me ten dollars?
>
> He *lent* (not *loaned*) me ten dollars.
>
> The bank *loaned* the money at 12 percent interest.
>
> *Lend* (not *borrow*) me a quarter, please.

loose (adj.). Means unfastened. Frequently confused with *lose* (verb), meaning to misplace.

> The handle is *loose*.
>
> Did you *lose* the pen?

majority (n.). Relates to the greater of two parts regarded as parts of a whole.

> A *majority* (greater number) of my hours are spent on
>   the computer.

In a contest, *majority* means more than half of the votes cast, whereas *plurality* means more votes than any other candidate received but less than half of the votes cast.

> Smith received a *plurality* but not a *majority* of the
>   votes. There were 21,000 votes cast, and Smith
>   received only 10,000. Jones received 7,000, so
>   Smith's *plurality* was 3,000. A *majority* is
>   necessary for election.

Majority is singular or plural depending upon the sense in which it is used. Thus when *majority* is plural, it is followed by a plural verb. When it refers to majority as a whole, it takes a singular verb.

> The *majority* (the majority as a whole) *is* against the new bill.
>
> A *majority* (the larger number as individuals) *are* against the new bill.

many a. Always takes a singular verb, even if it is followed by a compound subject.

> *Many a* newspaper and magazine *has* published his work.

mass (n.). Do not capitalize it in reference to individual celebrations, but do capitalize it in reference to the eucharistic sacrament. A *mass* is offered or celebrated, not held.

> They celebrated *mass* at 6 o'clock in the morning.

mathematics. See -ics.

may. See **can.**

may, might (vb.). When expressing possibility in a simple sentence, these words are usually interchangeable.

> I suggest that we settle the question now; otherwise it *may* (or *might*) cause trouble several years hence.
>
> We *may* (or *might*) decide to order a different make.

Might is the past tense of *may*. In using *may* or *might*, generally observe the proper sequence of tenses. With the present, perfect, and future tenses, use *may*; with the past or past perfect, use *might*.

> I give/I have given/I will give you the information so that you *may* understand the situation.
>
> I gave/I was giving/I had given you the information so that you *might* understand the situation.
>
> As we *have seen*, it *may be* wise to allow the debtor additional credit.

> I *have not heard* what happened this morning, but he
> *may have* persuaded her to adopt his view.
>
> The president *said* that we *might have* a holiday.
>
> The instructions *were* that, come what *might*, the task
> should be completed by the end of September.

Might is conditional. It is used in the main clause of a conditional sentence whether the condition is expressed or implied.

> Anyone *might* learn the facts from the report (if one
> read it).
>
> If the product is successful, it *might be* necessary to
> increase the size of the plant. (The increase is
> conditional upon success.)
>
> If the certificate fails to make provision for the
> issuance of stock in series, it subsequently *might
> be* amended to include that provision.

Might is used in the sense of *would perhaps* in a conditional statement.

> With a little persuasion, Mr. Brown *might* (*would
> perhaps*) agree to that arrangement.

Might is used in the subjunctive to express a supposition.

> He spoke *as though* he *might* sever his connections
> with the company.

May is used in prayer and benediction. The subjective *might* denotes wish without expectation of fulfillment.

> *May* God bless you.

See **can, could,** for the misuse of *could* for *might* in conditional sentences.

me (pron.). Objective case of *I*. For use as an object, see **Parts of Speech, Pronoun.** For misuse of *me* instead of *I* after forms of the verb *to be* (*am, is, are, was, were*), see **Grammatical Terms, Predicate nominative.**

might. See **may.**

minimal (adj.), **minimum** (n.). *Minimal* is that constituting the least possible. *Minimum* means the least quantity or value possible.

> His contribution was *minimal.*

> The *minimum* temperature was below freezing last
> year.

monopoly (n.). When it is followed by a preposition, use *of.*

> They have a *monopoly of* the market.

more than one. Always takes a singular noun and verb, although the meaning is plural.

> More than one *defendant is* involved.

most (n., pron., adj., adv.), **almost** (adv.). *Most* is used with an adjective to express the superlative degree. Do not use *most* for the adverb *almost.*

> He is the *most eager* of the boys.

> *Almost* all senators voted against the bill.

Most in many constructions also changes the meaning of the sentence when it is used incorrectly.

> I am *most ready* to go (more ready than others).

> I am *almost ready* to go (nearly ready to go).

mutual. See **common.**

myself. See **Grammatical Terms, Compound personal pronoun.**

neither (pron., conj., adj., adv.). Singular, followed by singular verb. The use of a plural verb after *neither* is a common error.

> *Neither* of these plans *is* satisfactory.

Use *neither* to designate between one of two persons or things; use *none* or *no* instead of *neither* to designate one of three or more.

> He decided that *neither* of the (two) plans suggested
> was satisfactory.

He decided that *none* of the (five) plans was
satisfactory.

No report submitted to date covers the subject
adequately.

neither . . . nor (conj.). It is always incorrect to use *or* with *neither*. The construction after correlatives should be parallel. The misplacement of *neither* frequently results in unbalanced construction after the correlatives.

The plan meets the approval *neither of* the president
nor of the treasurer.

The plan meets the approval of *neither* the president
nor the treasurer.

news (n.). Plural in form but singular in meaning.

The *news is* good.

nobody (pron.). Always written as one word. *No one* is preferred. Use a singular verb with both *nobody* and *no one*.

No one is working today.

none (indef. pron.). Either singular or plural, depending on the meaning.

We asked for volunteers, but *none* of them *was*
willing to go.

I want *none* of them to go unless *they* want to.

no . . . or. When *no* precedes the first word or phrase in a series and is applicable to each, connect the words or phrase with *or*, not *nor*.

No man, woman, *or* child can be happy without
friends.

Several of the families had *no* fuel to burn *or* money
with which to buy it (no fuel, no money).

not (adv.). *Not* is often superfluous in a subordinate clause after a negative in the main clause. In each of the following sentences, *not* should be omitted.

No one knows how much time may (not *may not*) be
wasted in argument.

Do you think there might (not *might not*) be some
other cause at work here?

Not is correct when its use is necessary to convey the intended meaning, but usually a better construction is the substitution of *no* for *not*.

Is it impossible for you to realize that *no* merger will
be consummated?

He does not believe that there are *no* extenuating
circumstances.

nowhere (n., adv.). Always written as one word. Do not add an *s* to *nowhere; no place* is commonly misused for *nowhere*.

I have gone *nowhere* today.

number (n.). Followed by a singular verb when used collectively, by a plural verb when used distributively.

A *number* of company rules and regulations (as a
group, not specific) *discourages* employee initiative.

A *number* of the company's rules and regulations
(certain ones in the group) *discourage* employee
initiative.

odds (n., pl.). Always takes a plural verb.

The *odds are* against him.

off (prep., vb., adj., adv.). Never follow *off* by *of*.

He gave me 10 percent *off* (not *off of*) the list price.

oneself (pron.). Formerly *one's self* but now preferably written as one word.

Conducting *oneself* professionally is essential in
business.

only (adv., adj.). The meaning that the sentence is intended to convey determines the position of the word *only*.

> *Only his assistant* has authority to sign the payroll
> record.
>
> His assistant has *authority only to sign* the payroll
> record, not to prepare it.
>
> His assistant has authority to sign *only the payroll
> record* (or *the payroll record only*).

Each of these sentences conveys a different meaning. The first states that the assistant is the only one with authority to sign; the second, that the assistant has no authority beyond signing; and the third, that the assistant has authority to sign the payroll record but nothing else.

Only is sometimes erroneously used as a conjunction.

> The *one* (or *only*) difference between your pen and
> mine is the different nib (*not* Your pen is the same
> as mine *only* that the nib is different).

oral (adj.). *Verbal* is often misused for *oral.* See **verbal.**

over (prep., vb., adj., adv.). The expression *over with* is erroneous; the *with* is superfluous.

> Our annual sale is now *over* (not *over with*).

owing to. See **due to.**

people (n.). Singular in form but plural in meaning. The plural *peoples* is used when more than once race or nation is referred to.

> The *peoples* of France and Italy share many
> economic goals.

When referring to a number of individuals, use *persons.* When referring to a group, use *people.*

> Six *persons* were in the room.
>
> Do you know the *people* who live next door?
>
> The American *people* are democratic.

place (n.). Must be used as the subject or as the object of a verb or preposition. *Place* is commonly misused with *any, every, no, some,* after an intransitive verb. The adverbs *anywhere, everywhere, nowhere, somewhere,* are usually better.

> Are you going *anywhere* (not *any place*) this afternoon?
>
> I have looked *everywhere* (not *every place*) for the letter.
>
> I have *no place* to go (object of the transitive verb *have*).
>
> I have *nowhere* to go.
>
> He is located in *some place* in the West (object of preposition *in*).
>
> He is located *somewhere* in the West.

plurality. See **majority.**

practical, practicable (adj.). *Practicable* means feasible, capable of being put into practice; *practical* means useful or successful in actual practice. *Practical* may be used with reference to either persons or things, but *practicable* can be used only with reference to things.

> Jones is a *practical* man. (He is a doer.)
>
> The scheme is *practical.* (It will be successful when it is carried out.)
>
> The scheme is *practicable.* (It can be carried out.)

precede, proceed (n.). *Precede* means to go in front or to surpass. *Proceed* means to continue, to come forth.

> The president *precedes* the vice president in the receiving line.
>
> *Proceed* with the test.

precedence (n.). When it is followed by a preposition, use *of.*

> The vice president has *precedence of* the secretary of state.

precedent (n., adj.). When the noun is followed by a preposition, use *of* or *for*. When the adjective is followed by a preposition, use *to*.

> He set a *precedent for* the others.
>
> It is a *precedent* cause *to* use as a guide.

preclude (vb.). An erroneous expression is *preclude the possibility of* since *preclude* means to render impossible.

> She agreed to the review in an effort to *preclude* (not *preclude the possibility of*) a misunderstanding.

prescribe, proscribe (vb.). The word *prescribe* means to order as a rule or course to be followed or, in medicine, to order as a remedy. The word *proscribe* means to denounce or condemn a thing as dangerous, to outlaw.

> What do you *prescribe?*
>
> Destroying files is *proscribed*.

presently (adj.). Meaning soon, before long. A common error is the use of *presently* when *at present* is meant.

> We expect to complete the book *presently* (soon).
>
> *At present* (now) we are working on your book.

principal (n., adj.), **principle** (n.). The word *principle* is a noun only and cannot be used as an adjective. *Principle* means a fundamental or general truth, a rule. *Principal* is used in all other cases. As a noun, *principal* has a variety of meanings; as an adjective, it means chief, main, most important.

> We have always acted on the *principle* (fundamental truth) that honesty is the best policy.
>
> An agent may bind his *principal* to contracts entered into within the scope of his authority.
>
> The loan, including *principal* and interest, amounted to $350.
>
> The New England states have been our *principal* source of business during the past five years.
>
> The *principal* of the school is here.

proceeds (n., pl.). Refers to a sum of money. Used in the plural and takes a plural verb.

> The *proceeds* were substantial.

prove (vb.). Principal parts: *prove, proved, proved*. The use of *proven* for *proved* is increasing in the United States but is not considered good usage by some authorities.

> He *has proved* his case.

provided, providing (conj.). The use of *providing* as a conjunction is not always sanctioned, although it is commonly used. It is preferable not to use *that* after *provided* except where it is accepted usage in formal documents.

> I will give you the order *provided* (or *providing*) you
> agree to my price.

quality (n.), pl., *qualities*. See **kind.**

quarter (n., vb., adj.). When you are referring to the time of day, the correct expression is *a quarter to*, not *a quarter of*.

reaction (n.), **reply** (n., vb.), **response** (n.). *Reaction* means a response to stimuli. It should not be used to mean attitude, viewpoint, feeling, or response. *Reply* means a response in words. *Response* is a reply, an answer.

> The injection caused a violent *reaction*.
> She sent her *reply* by messenger.
> The client's *response* was positive.

reason (n., vb.). When a sentence begins with "The reason is," the clause giving the reason should begin with *that* and not with *because*.

> Her *reason is that* (not *because*) she does not have
> the money.

reconcile (vb.). When it is followed by a preposition, use *with* or *to*.

> She *was reconciled to* a stressful week ahead.

regard (n., vb.). Do not use *regards* in place of *regard* in the expressions *in regard to, with regard to*.

regardless (adj., adv.), **regardless of** (prep.). *Irregardless* is not a word. Misuse is sometimes caused by confusion with the word *irrespective,* which means "without respect to" and is correct. *Regardless* takes the preposition *of.*

> We should acknowledge all orders *regardless* (not *irregardless*) *of* the amount involved.

relation(ship) (n.). When it is followed by a preposition, use *of, to,* or *with.*

> The *relation of* these parts is not clear.
>
> The *relationship of* the beneficiary *to* the insured is not close.
>
> Strained *relations with* a friend are always a source of concern.

resentment (n.). Resentment *at* or *for* an action, *against* a person.

> My *resentment against* him was *at* (or *for*) his rudeness to me.

retroactive (adj.). When it is followed by a preposition, use *to.*

> The law is *retroactive to* May 14.

riches (n., pl.). Always plural and takes a plural verb.

> The *riches* of life *are* not always monetary.

right (n., vb., adj., adv.). The adverb form is *right* or *rightly.* See **Parts of Speech, Adverb.** *Right* is not comparable. If anything is *right,* it cannot be *more* right. *More nearly right* is allowable.

round (n., vb., prep., adj., adv.). *Round* is not comparable. If anything is *round,* it cannot be *more* round. *More nearly round* is allowable.

same (adj.). Do not use as a pronoun. Businesspersons especially are guilty of the misuse of *same.*

> We will repair the spring and ship *it* (not *same*) to you.

scarcely (adv.). This word carries a negative idea and should not be used with a negative.

> There is *scarcely any* (not *scarcely no*) time left in
> which to fill the order.

seem (vb.). Followed by a predicate adjective and not by an adverb.

> The new machines seem *strange* (not *strangely*).

semimonthly, semiweekly (adj., adv.). Since *semi* means half, *semiweekly* means twice a week, and *semimonthly* means twice a month.

set. See **sit.**

shall (should); will (would) (vb.). *Should* is the past tense of the auxiliary verb *shall; would,* of the auxiliary verb *will.* Traditionally, *shall* and *should* are used in the first person (*I shall*) and *will* and *would* in the second and third persons (*he will, they will*) to express simple futurity. To express determination, the order is traditionally reversed (*I will, he shall, they shall*). However, *will* and *would* are often preferred in *all* persons in contemporary American usage (*I will* instead of *I shall*) as sounding less stuffy.

she. Nominative case of third-person singular pronoun. For misuse of *she* instead of *her,* see **Parts of Speech, Pronoun.** For use after forms of the verb *to be (am, is, are, was, were),* see **Grammatical Terms, Predicate nominative.**

since (conj., prep., adv.). Do not use *since* to begin a clause after *ago.* Begin the clause with *that.* This error is more apt to occur when a parenthetical expression follows *ago.*

> It is more than ten years *ago,* as well as I remember,
> *that* (not *since*) the stores were consolidated.

Be certain that a phrase introduced by *since* is correctly attached to the sentence and is not a dangling participial phrase. See **Grammatical Terms, Participle.**

> *Since I prepared* the report, *new figures are* available.
>
> *Since preparing* the report, *I have found new figures*
> (not *Since preparing* the report, *new figures are*
> available).

> *Since the preparation of* the report, *new figures are* available.

sit, set (vb.). *Sit* means to rest when the subject rests. *Set* means to place an object. *Sit* never takes an object, *set* always does. Principal parts, *sit: sit, sat, sat, sitting.* Principal parts, *set: set, set, set, setting.*

> He *sits* at his desk.
>
> He *sat* at his desk from ten to eleven.
>
> He *has sat* there for two hours.
>
> He *is sitting* at his desk.
>
> I *set* the thermos on his desk every morning.
>
> I *have set* the thermos on his desk every day for a month.
>
> I *set* the thermos on his desk yesterday, as usual.
>
> I *am setting* the thermos on the table.
>
> The thermos *sat* on the table for a week (past of *sit*).
>
> The thermos *has sat* there for a week (present perfect of *sit*).

size (n.), pl., *sizes.* See **kind.** *Size* is a noun; *sized,* an adjective. Either noun or adjective may form a compound adjective.

> *medium-size* or *medium-sized* house.

Since *size* is a noun and not an adjective, it is incorrect to omit the *of* in these and similar expressions.

> that size *of* machine

so. For the correct use of *so . . . as,* see **as.**

some (pron., adj., adv.). For misuse of *some place,* see **place.**

somebody, someone (pron.). Always write *somebody* as one word. *Someone* is preferred. Write *someone* as one word when it is equivalent to *somebody;* otherwise, it is two words.

He will appoint *someone* of outstanding ability.

If *some one* person is designated to head the project,
we can plan accordingly.

When *someone* is singular, it is followed by a singular verb and pronoun:

I know *someone* (or *somebody*) *was* here while I was
away, because *he* left *his* briefcase.

some time, sometime, sometimes (adv.). Either *some time* or *sometimes* may be used instead of *at some time*, meaning a point of time not specified. There is no distinction. The trend is to omit *at* and use *sometime*.

I expect to be there *sometime* (or *some time*) in
August.

Use *some time* when referring to an indefinite lapse of time. It is incorrect to use *sometime* in this sense.

It will take *some time* to prepare the report.

Sometime may be used as an adjective to describe a former state. It is equivalent to *at one time having been*.

Dr. Evatt, *sometime* minister of Australia, is speaking
tonight.

Sometimes, written as one word, means at several indefinite times; on some occasions.

Sometimes she works late.

somewhere (n., adv.). Always written as one word. *Some place* is commonly misused for *somewhere*. See **place.** *Somewheres* is not a word.

sort (n.), pl., *sorts*. See **kind.**

species (n.). Singular or plural depending on the intended meaning.

The *species is* well known.

These *species are* being studied now.

stationary (adj.), **stationery** (n.). *Stationary* means standing still; *stationery* means writing materials.

> Some loading platforms are *stationary*, but others are mobile.

> Don't forget to order the office *stationery*.

straight (n., vb., adj., adv.). The adverb form is *straight*. *Straightly* is rare. *Straight* is not comparable. If anything is *straight*, it cannot be *more* straight. *More nearly straight* is allowable.

subject to. See **addicted to.**

substantive. See **Antecedent.**

such (pron., adj., adv.). Do not use *which, who, that,* or *where* with *such.* The correct combination is *such . . . as.* Frequently, the better usage is to omit *such* or change *such* to *the, that, those,* and the like.

> Some people give only *such* things *as* (not *that*) they do not need.

> Some people give only *those* things *for which* they have no need.

Do not use *such as* in place of *as* to introduce a prepositional phrase.

> Radios that you have previously purchased from us, *as in* (not *such as in*) your last shipment, are out of stock.

suitable (adj.). Suitable *for* a use or purpose, *to* an occasion or requirements.

> The machine is *suitable for* that work.

> The machine is *suitable to* the requirements of your office.

superior (adj.). Should always be followed by *to*, not *than.*

> It is *superior* from every point of view *to* the other material.

surround (vb.). When it is followed by a preposition, use *by*.

> We are *surrounded by* buildings.

tactic (n.), pl., *tactics*. Commonly used in the plural.

> Her *tactics are* questionable.

than (prep., conj.). Never use after *more and more*. See also **different from.**

> The Supreme Court has granted *more* (not *more and
> more*) powers to the federal government *than* was
> originally intended.

thanks (n., pl.). Always takes a plural verb.

> Our *thanks are* directed to all of you.

that (conj.). Use only one *that* to introduce a single clause. A common error is the use of a second *that* when a phrase or clause intervenes between *that* and the clause it introduces.

> I hope *that* when you have reconsidered the matter
> you will cooperate (not *that* you will cooperate).

that, which (rel. pron.). Use *that* to introduce a defining or restrictive clause; use *which* to introduce a nondefining, nonrestrictive clause, a comment, or an additional thought.

> Statutory requirements *that* fix a definite number of
> days for notice must be followed.

> The proposed amendments, *which* increase the value
> of the measure, were adopted unanimously.

them (pron.). Objective case of *they*. For use as an object, see **Parts of Speech, Pronoun.** For misuse of *them* instead of *they* after forms of the verb *to be (am, is, are, was, were)*, see **Grammatical Terms, Predicate nominative.**

there (n., pron., adj., adv.). Often used to introduce a clause in which the verb precedes the subject. The number of the verb is not affected by *there* but depends on the number of the subject.

> *There are* not sufficient *data* (plural subject) available.
>
> *There is* a *mass* (singular subject) of data available.

they. Nominative case of third-person plural pronoun. For misuse of *they* instead of *them*, see **Parts of Speech, Pronoun**. For use after the forms of the verb *to be* (*am, is, are, was, were*), see **Grammatical Terms, Predicate nominative**.

time card (n.). Two words. See **Grammatical Terms, Compound term**.

toward(s) (prep., adj.). Either is correct, but the use of *toward* is more prevalent. *Towards* is the accepted British form.

try (vb.). Often erroneously followed by *and* with a verb in place of an infinitive.

> *Try to come* (not *and come*) to New York.

type (n., vb.), pl., *types*. See **kind**. The noun *type* should not be used as an adjective. It is incorrect to omit the *of* in these and similar expressions: type *of* machine, type *of* building, type *of* person.

uninterested. See **disinterested**.

unique (adj.). *Unique* is not comparable; it means the only one of its kind. You should not say *"most* unique," *"more* unique," *or "very* unique."

unqualified (adj.), **disqualified** (vb.). *Unqualified* means not having the right qualifications. *Disqualified* means deprived of the right qualities.

> He was *unqualified* for the job (not right for it).
>
> She was *disqualified* from the competition (made ineligible).

unquestioned, unquestionable (adj.). *Unquestioned* refers to that which has not been questioned; *unquestionable,* that which cannot be sensibly questioned.

> The statement was *unquestioned.*
>
> His loyalty is *unquestionable.*

unsatisfied, dissatisfied (adj.). *Unsatisfied* means not content and wanting more. *Dissatisfied* means unhappy.

>She is *unsatisfied* with the amount of the research.
>
>She is *dissatisfied* with her job.

us (pron.). The objective case of *we;* sometimes misused for *we.*

>Tell *us* what to do.
>
>They are not as efficient as *we* (are efficient) from the standpoint of accuracy.

valuables (n., pl.). Always used in the plural and takes a plural verb.

>Your *valuables are* safe.

variety (n.), pl., *varieties.* See **kind.**

verbal (adj.). Relates to either written or spoken words. *Verbal* is used often carelessly in place of *oral* with reference to spoken words. To avoid confusion, use *oral* to mean spoken words and *written* to mean written words.

>A contract, whether written or *oral* (not *verbal*), is binding.
>
>He gave *oral* (not *verbal*) instructions.
>
>A few *verbal* (or *written*) changes (changes in words) are necessary.

verb. See **Parts of Speech, Verb.** For agreement of a verb with its subject, see **Grammatical Terms, Compound subject; Alternate subject; Intervening noun or phrase; Predicate nominative.**

very, very much. These words are overworked. Although they are acceptable modifiers, excessive use of them destroys the force of the words modified. *I am pleased* is as emphatic as *I am very much pleased.* Rather than using *very* or *very much,* selecting a stronger word is often the better alternative. Those who insist on using *very* and *very much* should observe correct usage. These terms are not interchangeable. The problem is whether to use *very* or *very much* before a passive participle. Use *very* when the passive participle has the force of an adjective.

>A *very delighted* crowd heard the news.

Use *very much* (or *much*) when the passive participle is used in the predicate with verbal force.

> I was *very much* (or *much*) delighted at the result of
> the game.

> I will be *very much* (or *much*) inconvenienced by the
> delay.

Exception: A passive participle that, although used as a verb, has lost its verbal force by common usage is preceded by *very*.

> I am *very* (not *very much*) tired of hearing about the
> matter.

viable, workable (adj.). *Viable* means capable of existence. *Workable* means practicable, feasible, capable of working or succeeding.

> The new company is a *viable* entity.

> The plan seems *workable* to me.

wait on. Do not use in place of *wait for*.

> We have been *waiting for* (not *on*) her.

walk (vb.). Principal parts: *wake, waked,* or *woke* and *has, had,* or *have waked*.
See **Parts of Speech, Verb.**

way (n., adj., adv.). Do not use *ways* in place of the singular *way*.

> This year's sales are quite a *way* (not *ways*) ahead of
> last year's. *Better:* This year's sales are
> *considerably* ahead of last year's.

we. Nominative case of first-person plural pronoun. For misuse of *we*, see **Parts of Speech, Pronoun.** For use after forms of the verb *to be (am, is, are, was, were)*, see **Grammatical Terms, Predicate nominative.** For the correct use of *we* or *I* in letters, see **I.** *We* is frequently misused for *us* in apposition to a noun in the objective case.

> It is advisable for *us* (not *we*) citrus growers to
> organize an association.

well (adj., adv.), **good** (adj.). *Well* may be either an adjective or an adverb but is usually an adverb except when it refers to a state of health. *Good* is always an adjective.

> He *did* the job *well* (adverb, describing how he did the job).
>
> He looks *well* (predicate adjective, referring to state of health).
>
> The *situation* looks *good* to me (predicate adjective, describing the *situation*).
>
> The upswing in the stock market is a *good indication* that prosperity is still with us (adjective, modifying *indication*).

what (pron., adj., adv.). May be either singular or plural. In the singular, *what* stands for *that which* or *a thing that*. In the plural, *what* stands for *those* (persons) *who* or *those* (things) *that*.

> Singular: *What is* saved in price *is* likely to be lost in service and goodwill.
>
> Plural: My *reasons* for refusing the order *were what* I considered sufficient (*reasons* is the plural antecedent of *what*).

If *what* is singular in the beginning of the sentence, it remains singular. A common error is to make the second verb agree with a plural predicate nominative. In each of the following examples, *what* is definitely established as singular because it is followed by a singular verb. The second verb must also be singular, although it is followed by a plural predicate nominative, which is the complement to *what*.

> *What is* needed *is* houses at prices that the people can afford.
>
> *What seems* to be needed *is* stringent regulations.
>
> *What caused* the delay *was* the three transfers.

In each of the following examples, *what* is used in the plural sense. Test the sentence by substituting *those* (things) *that* for *what*.

He is attempting to show by the chart *what appear*
(not *appears*) to be the reasons for the decrease in
sales (meaning "those reasons that").

The company sold at discount only *what were* (not
was considered refrigerators of second quality
(meaning "only those refrigerators that were
considered").

when (n., pron., conj., adv.). Do not use *when* to define a word.

A sentence is a complete thought (not *when you have
a complete thought*).

Where is frequently misused for *when*. *Where* should introduce an adverbial clause of place; *when*, of time.

When (not *where*) a proxy is given limited power, he
must act within the limitations.

A surplus exists *when* (not *where*) there is an excess
in the aggregate value of assets over liabilities and
capital.

Where the company is building its new offices, a
redwood forest once stood.

where (n., conj., adv.). Sometimes misused in place of *that*.

I see in the paper *that* (not *where*) the corporation has
declared a dividend.

Do not use *where* to define a word.

Perjury is the voluntary violation of an oath (not *where
a person voluntarily violates an oath*).

Where should be used to introduce an adverbial clause of place, not of time; see **when** for an example.

which (pron., adj.). For use of *that* as a relative pronoun instead of *which*, see **that, which**.

while (n., vb., conj.). When it is used most precisely, *while* means "during the time that" or "as long as." It is sometimes incorrectly used as a substitute for *although, whereas*, or *but*.

> *Although* (not *while*) the report is due now, more
>   research is needed.

who, whom (pron.). *Who* is the nominative case and is used as the subject; *whom* is the objective case and is used as the object of a verb or preposition.

> He is the client for *whom* (object of *for*) I prepared the
>   contract.
>
> Mr. Adams is the person *who* (subject) has charge of
>   sales.
>
> Whom (object of *to see*) do you want to see?
>
> Mr. Edwards is the candidate *who* I believe will win.
>   (*Who* is the subject of *will win; I believe* is
>   parenthetical.)
>
> Mr. Edwards is the candidate *whom* I favor. (*Whom* is
>   the object of *favor*.)

will. See **shall.**

would. See **shall.**

write (vb.). When an indirect object follows *write*, without a direct object, precede the indirect object by *to*. If a direct and indirect object follow, *to* is not necessary.

> I will write *to you* as soon as I can.
>
> I will write *you* (indirect object) a *letter* (direct object)
>   as soon as I can.

wrong (n., vb., adj., adv.). The adverb forms are *wrong, wrongly*. See **Parts of Speech, Adverb.** *Wrong* is not comparable. If anything is *wrong*, it cannot be *more* wrong.

yourself (pron.), pl., *yourselves*. See **Grammatical Terms, Compound personal pronoun.**

Chapter 14

Spelling and Word Division

RULES OF SPELLING

Plurals

SINGULAR NOUNS. Usually, the plural is formed by adding *s*.

>   files   telephones   desks

In some cases, it is formed by adding *es*.

>   classes   churches   boxes

WORDS ENDING IN O. Words ending in *o* preceded by a vowel form the plural by adding *s*.

>   folios   trios   studios

Generally, words ending in *o* preceded by a consonant form the plural by adding *es*.

>   potatoes   heroes

A few form the plural by adding *s*.

>   solos   dynamos   memos

Some have both forms.

>   cargoes/cargos   mottoes/mottos   zeros/zeroes

WORDS ENDING IN Y. Most words ending in *y* preceded by a vowel form the plural by adding *s*.

attorneys   days
But: soliloquy/soliloquies

Words ending in *y* preceded by a consonant change the *y* to *i* and add *es*.

ladies   berries   countries   counties

WORDS ENDING IN F, FE, FF. Some nouns ending in *f*, *fe*, or *ff* form the plural by adding *s*. Others change the *f* to *v* and add *s* or *es*; some do not; some have both forms. There is no way to distinguish the groups. When in doubt, consult a dictionary.

roof/roofs	chief/chiefs	loaf/loaves	leaf/leaves
cliff/cliffs	tariff/tariffs	knife/knives	life/lives

WORDS ENDING IN CH, S, SH, SS, X, Z. Add *es* to form the plural of words ending in *ch*, *s*, *sh*, *ss*, *x*, or *z*.

church/churches	bias/biases	dish/dishes
glass/glasses	box/boxes	quartz/quartzes

IRREGULAR NOUNS. Some words are spelled differently in the plural form; others use the same spelling in both the singular and plural forms.

child/children   corps/corps   deer/deer

ABBREVIATIONS. The plural of an abbreviation is usually formed by adding *s*.

mfrs.   mos.   nos.

The plurals of some abbreviations are formed by repeating the abbreviation.

p., pp./page, pages   v., vv./verse, verses

Some, such as metric abbreviations, are considered singular or plural without adding *s*.

mm   kg   cl

FIGURES AND LETTERS. Add *'s* if *s* alone would be confusing.

p's and q's   6's and 7's   Ph.D.'s and Ed.D.'s

In other cases, letters and numbers form the plural by adding *s* alone.

YWCAs   1980s

COMPOUND TERMS. In general, the plural of a compound term is formed by making the most important word plural. The most important word is the word telling what the principal is. Following this general rule, military titles for the most part form the plural by adding *s* to the second word, which is usually the most important. However, *sergeant major* forms the plural on the first word since the rank is really a form of *sergeant*, not major. Civilian titles usually add the *s* to the first word, since the first word usually tells what the person is.

> *notaries* public (they are *notaries*, not *publics*)
>
> major *generals* (they are *generals*, not *majors*)
>
> *adjutants* general (they are *adjutants* [assistants], not *generals*)

The following are examples of forming the plural of a compound term by making the most important word plural:

aides-de-camp	*governors* general
ambassadors at large	judge *advocates*
assistant *attorneys* general	lieutenant *colonels*
attorneys general	*presidents*-elect
bills of lading	*rights*-of-way
brigadier *generals*	*sergeants* at arms
brothers-in-law	*sergeants* major
comptrollers general	*surgeons* general
deputy *chiefs* of staff	trade *unions*
general *counsels*	

When both words are of equal importance, both words take the plural form.

coats of arms   men employees   women drivers

When no word is of importance in itself, the last word takes the plural form.

> forget-me-*nots*   jack-in-the-*pulpits*   pick-me-*ups*

When a noun is compounded with a preposition, the noun takes the plural form.

> *hangers*-on   *listeners*-in   *passers*-by   by-*products*

When neither word in the compound term is a noun, the last word takes the plural form.

> also-*rans*   go-*betweens*   write-*ups*   tie-*ins*

Compound nouns written as one word form their plurals regularly. Words ending in *-ful* are the only ones that cause trouble.

> cup*fuls*   tablespoon*fuls*   bucket*fuls*

When it is necessary to convey the meaning that more than one container was used, write the compound as two words and add *s* to the noun.

> 5 *cups* full   2 *tablespoons* full   4 *buckets* full

Combinations of *i* and *e*

Learn the following rhyme to avoid mistakes in combining *i* and *e*. Use *i* before *e* except after *c* or when sounded like *a* as in *neighbor* and *weigh*.

> believe   receive   weight

Exceptions: either, neither, seize, weird, sheik, leisure, plebeian, financier, specie, conscience.

Suffixes

DOUBLING THE FINAL CONSONANT. Double the consonant before a word ending that begins with a vowel if the word ends in a single consonant preceded by a single vowel and if the accent falls on the last syllable of the word. (For the purpose of this rule, words of one syllable are considered "accented" on the last syllable.) Confusion arises because *all* these conditions must be met before the consonant can be doubled.

> occur/occurred (all conditions are met)
> bag/baggage (all conditions are met)
> ship/shipped (all conditions are met)
> commit/commitment (suffix does not begin with a vowel)
> desert/deserting (word does not end in a single consonant)
> appeal/appealed (final consonant not preceded by a single vowel)
> offer/offered (accent does not fall on the last syllable)

Exceptions: Most of the exceptions are derivatives in which the syllabication changes and the accent of the main word is thrown back on the first syllable.

> de fer'/def'er-ence   re fer'/ref'er-ence   pre fer'/pref'er-ence

But the *r* is doubled when adding *ed* or *ing* to *defer, prefer*, and *refer*.

> deferred/deferring   preferred/preferring   referred/referring

Do not double the final consonant before adding a word ending beginning with a consonant when a one-syllable word ends with a vowel followed by one consonant.

> ship/shipment   joy/joyfully   glad/gladly

WORDS ENDING IN SILENT E. Words ending in a silent *e* usually drop the *e* before a suffix or verb ending that starts with a vowel.

> bride/bridal   argue/arguable
> guide/guidance   owe/owing
> ice/icing   judge/judging
> use/usable (*variant* useable)   sale/salable (*variant* saleable)

Exceptions: dye/dyeing, eye/eyeing, hoe/hoeing.

Words ending in silent *e* usually retain the *e* before suffixes beginning with a consonant, unless another vowel precedes the final *e*.

> hate/hateful   argue/argument   excite/excitement   due/duly

Exceptions: abridgment, acknowledgment, judgment, nursling, wholly.

WORDS ENDING IN CE OR GE. Words ending in *ce* or *ge* usually keep the *e* before adding a word ending that starts with *a* or *o* but drop the *e* before adding word endings that begin with *i*.

> enforce/enforceable courage/courageous
> finance/financial deduce/deducible

WORDS ENDING IN IE. Words ending in *ie* drop the *e* and change the *i* to *y* before adding the *-ing*.

> die/dying lie/lying tie/tying

WORDS ENDING IN Y. Words ending in *y* preceded by a consonant usually change the *y* to *i* before any suffix or verb ending except one beginning with *i*.

> modify/modifying/modifier/modification worry/worrisome/worried
> lonely/lonelier/loneliness

Exceptions: The following exceptions apply:

1. Adjectives of one syllable have two forms in the comparative and superlative.

   > dry: drier/driest or dryer/dryest
   > shy: shier/shiest or shyer/shyest
   > spry: sprier/spriest or spryer/spryest

2. Adjectives of one syllable usually retain the *y* before *ly* and *ness*.

   > shyly/shyness dryly/dryness spryly/spryness

3. The *y* is retained in words with *ship* and *like* and in derivatives of *lady* and *baby*.

   > secretaryship ladylike ladyfinger babyhood

Words ending in *y* preceded by a vowel usually keep the *y* before any verb ending.

> buy/buying employ/employment delay/delayed

Exceptions: day/daily, pay/paid, say/said.

WORDS ENDING IN IC. When a word ends in *ic,* insert a *k* before adding a suffix beginning with *e, i,* or *y.*

> picnic/picnicking/picnicked   traffic/trafficker/trafficking

WORDS ENDING IN AL. When changing an adjective ending in *al* to an adverb ending in *ly,* retain all letters in the original word.

> real/really   practical/practically

WORDS ENDING IN AR, ARY, ERY. Very few words end in ar.

> beggar   calendar   dollar   singular

MANY WORDS, HOWEVER, END IN *ARY* OR *ERY.*

> contrary   stationery   contemporary   cemetery

WORDS ENDING IN SEDE, CEED, CEDE. Only one word in our language ends in *sede—supersede.* Only three end in *ceed—proceed, exceed, succeed.* All the others end in *cede.* Note that *proceed* changes its form in *procedure.*

SUFFIXES ABLE, OUS. Words ending in *e* preceded by *c* or *g* do not drop the final *e* before the suffixes *able* or *ous* but do drop the final *e* before the suffix *ible.*

> service/serviceable   manage/manageable
> courage/courageous   advantage/advantageous
> deduce/deducible   convince/convincible

SUFFIXES ABLE, IBLE. If a word has an *ation* form, it always takes the suffix *able* instead of *ible.*

> application/applicable   reparation/reparable

Many words that do not have an *ation* form also take the suffix *able,* which is far more common than the suffix *ible.* There is no rule distinguishing the groups. But often the letters *ss* precede *ible* (*access/accessible*), and nouns ending in *ion* are frequently changed by adding *ible* (*destruction/destructi-*

ble). When a word ends with a soft *c* or *g*, *ible* is used (*reduce/reducible*). The following are examples of common *ible* adjectives.

accessible	descendible	gullible	indefeasible
invincible	irresistible	negligible	persuasible
plausible	preventible	responsible	visible

SUFFIXES ANCE, ENCE. When the suffix is preceded by *c* having the sound of *k*, or *g* having a hard sound, use *ance, ancy,* or *ant*; when *c* has the sound of *s*, or *g* the sound of *j*, use *ence, ency,* or *ent*.

extravagance	revelancy	significant
convalescence	dependency	persistent

If the suffix is preceded by a letter other than *c* or *g* and you are in doubt about the spelling, consult the dictionary.

SUFFIXES ISE, IZE, YZE. There is no rule governing the use of *ise* or *ize*. The words in the following list, and their derivatives and compounds, are spelled with *ise*.

advertise	advise	apprise	arise
chastise	circumcise	comprise	compromise
demise	despise	devise	disguise
enterprise	excise	exercise	exorcise
franchise	improvise	incise	merchandise
premise	reprise	revise	supervise
surmise	surprise	televise	

The preferred American spelling for other such words is *ize*.

apologize	criticize	realize	summarize

Words ending in *yze* are not common.

analyze	paralyze

Prefixes

The current trend is to write words with prefixes (such as *non, anti, semi, pseudo, pro, post, pre,* and *neo*) closed (*anticlimax*) (1) unless the prefix precedes a proper name (*anti-American*), (2) unless a double vowel might make the word difficult to read if the hyphen is omitted (*antiintelli-*

gence/anti-intelligence), or (3) unless a different meaning is intended (*re-form*, meaning to form again).

PREFIXES DIS, MIS. Words formed by adding the prefix *dis* are frequently misspelled because of doubt about whether the combined form has one *s* or two. If the word to which the prefix is added begins with *s*, the combined form has two *s's*; otherwise, the combined form has only one *s*. The same rule applies to the prefix *mis*.

agree/disagree	appoint/disappoint	appear/disappear
regard/disregard	satisfy/dissatisfy	simulate/dissimulate
spell/misspell	apply/misapply	print/misprint

Numbers and Symbols

NONSCIENTIFIC WRITING. In nonscientific text, follow one of these two styles: (1) spell out *one* through *ninety-nine*, except in paragraphs that have larger uneven numbers, or (2) spell out *one* through *ninety-nine* and large round numbers, except in paragraphs that have large uneven numbers. Follow this principle in using monetary symbols and most other symbols.

> During the past *twenty* years, the price of a lakeside cottage has increased from *$5,000* to *$50,000* (*or* from *five thousand* to *fifty thousand* dollars).

> During the past *twenty* years, the price of a lakeside cottage has increased from *$5,250* to *$50,000*.

> Attending the meeting were *four* teachers and *twenty-five* students.

> Attending the meeting were *4* teachers and *102* students.

SCIENTIFIC WRITING. In scientific and other technical writing, use figures for all numbers above *nine* or *ten*.

> He found *seven* bolts and *nine* taps missing.

> He found *7* bolts and *10* taps missing.

> During the past *20* years the price of coils increased from *$2.50* to *$12.50*.

Exceptions: In general, spell out centuries or decades and governmental designations. Use figures for uneven clock time in informal writing.

> twentieth century   Third Reich   2:30 P.M. (informal)
> half past two o'clock (formal invitation) 2 o'clock *or* two o'clock

Use numbers with *percent* in both scientific and nonscientific writing, unless the number begins a sentence.

> *Ten percent* were absent.
> No more than *10 percent* were absent.

In most tabular matter, numbers are preferred in both scientific and nonscientific usage. In the column heads of tables, however, symbols may be spelled out if desired and if space permits.

> Percentage   Attendance (%)
> of
> Attendance

Possessive Case

Add an apostrophe and *s* to form the possessive of a singular noun if it does not end in an *s* sound.

> worker's insurance   David's car

When the word ends in an *s* sound, add an apostrophe and *s* if pronouncing the possessive causes a new syllable to be formed.

> boss's instructions   witness's comments

If adding an *s* makes the word difficult to pronounce, add only an apostrophe and omit the *s*.

> Jesus' sermon   for appearance' sake

When a plural noun already ends in *s*, add only an apostrophe. If it does not end in *s*, add an apostrophe and *s* the same as you would do for a singular noun.

> Burnses' car   children's toys
> witnesses' testimony   women's rights

HOW TO IMPROVE YOUR SPELLING

Helpful Mnemonics for Accurate Spelling

One of the easiest ways to learn to spell a certain word is to make up a phrase that will call the correct spelling to mind. This device to aid the memory is called a *mnemonic*. A silly phrase or a little rhyme will often make a word stick in your mind even better than a sensible rule. Keep a list of these words and the phrase or rhyme you make up on your desk. Each time you must look up the spelling of a word, add the word to your list with your own phrase or jingle; the next time that word comes up, look at the list instead of in the dictionary. You will be amazed at how quickly you will learn to spell the words on the list.

> A superintend*ent* collects r*ent*.
> *All right* is the opposite of *all wrong* (there is no word *alright* just as there is no word *alwrong*).
> Only a *rat* would sepa*rat*e friends.
> Perhaps he is only a compa*rat*ive *rat*.
> A fri*end* sticks to the *end*.
> My button is lo*ose*; if I am not careful I will l*ose* it and then it will be l*ost*. Or: You g*oose*, your button is lo*ose*.
> Cut me a pi*ece* of *pie*.
> An apartment l*ease* brings p*eace* from rent incr*ease*.
> A letter is written on station*ery*. You stand still when you are station*ary*.
> The princip*al* part is the m*ain* p*art*.
> The para*ll*el lines are in the center of the word (think of the two l's as parallel lines).
> Super*sede* is the only word in the English language that ends in *sede*.
> She is irresistible when wearing l*i*pstick.
> An *able* man is depend*able* and indispens*able*.

List of Commonly Misspelled Words

Certain words are more troublesome than others, and special attention is required to avoid misspellings. This list contains problem words listed in alphabetical order.

absence	already	beginning	compliment
absurd	altogether	believe	compromise
accede	amendment	beneficial	concede
accept	among	beneficiary	conceivable
acceptance	analogous	benefited	concern
accessible	analysis	bookkeeper	concession
accessory	analyze	brilliant	concurred
accidentally	announce	brochure	conference
accommodate	announcement	boutonniere	confident
accompanying	annoyance	budget	confidential
accordance	annual	bulletin	congratulate
accrued	anticipate	buoyant	conscience
accumulate	anxious	bureau	conscientious
accuracy	apologize	business	conscious
accustom	apparel	businessperson	consensus
achievement	apparent	busy	consequence
acknowledgment	appearance	calendar	consignment
acquaintance	appliance	campaign	consistent
acquiesce	applicable	canceled (cancelled)	contemptible
acquire	applicant	cancellation	continuous
across	appointment	cannot	controlling
adapt	appraisal	capital	controversy
address	appreciable	capitol (*building*)	convenience
adequate	appropriate	career	convenient
adjustment	approximate	casualty	cordially
admirable	architect	catalog(ue)	corporation
advantageous	argument	chauffeur	correspondence
advertisement	arrangement	choice	correspondents
advertising	article	choose	council
advice	ascertain	circumstances	counsel
advisable	assessment	client	courteous
advise	assignment	clientele	courtesy
advisor	assistance	collateral	coverage
advisory	associate	column	creditor
affect	assured	coming	criticism
affidavit	attendance	commission	criticize
aggravate	attention	commitment	current
agreeable	attorneys	committee	customer
allotment	authorize	comparable	debtor
allotted	available	comparison	deceive
allowable	baccalaureate	compelled	decide
allowance	bankruptcy	competent	decision
all right	bargain	competitor	deductible
almost	basis	complement	defendant

defense
deferred
deficit
definite
definitely
delegate
dependent
depositor
describe
description
desirable
deteriorate
develop
development
device
devise
difference
director
disappear
disappoint
discrepancy
dissatisfied
eagerly
ecclesiastical
economical
edition
effect
efficiency
efficient
eligible
eliminate
embarrass
emergency
emphasis
emphasize
employee
enclose
endeavor
endorsement
enterprise
enthusiasm
envelope
environment
equipment

equipped
especially
essential
etiquette
exaggerate
exceed
excellence
excellent
except
excessive
exercise
existence
expedite
expenditure
expense
experience
explanation
extensions
extraordinary
extremely
facilities
familiarize
fascinate
favorable
favorite
February
finally
financial
forcible
foreign
forfeit
formerly
forty
forward
fourth
freight
friend
fulfillment
furthermore
gauge
genuine
government
governor
grateful

grievance
grievous
guarantee
handled
harass
hardware
hazardous
height
hesitant
hoping
identical
illegible
immediately
imperative
impossible
inasmuch as
incidentally
inconvenience
incurred
indebtedness
independent
indispensable
individual
inducement
influential
initial
inquiry
installment
intelligence
intention
intercede
interfere
interrupted
inventory
investor
irrelevant
itemized
itinerary
it's (*it is*)
jeopardize
judgment
justifiable
knowledge
laboratory

legible
legitimate
leisure
length
letterhead
liaison
library
license
likable
livelihood
loose
lose
magazine
maintenance
management
manufacturer
manuscript
maximum
medical
memorandum
menus
merchandise
mileage
minimum
miscellaneous
mischievous
modernize
mortgage
necessary
negligible
negotiate
neighborhood
nevertheless
ninety
ninth
noticeable
oblige
occasion
occupant
occurred
occurrence
occurring
offense
offering

official	premium	response	tariff
omission	previous	responsible	temporary
omitted	price list	responsibility	their
opportunity	principal (*adj.*)	restaurant	there
ordinary	principle (*n.*)	ridiculous	thorough
organization	privilege	route	throughout
organize	probably	salable (saleable)	too
original	proceed	salary	tragedy
overdue	professor	satisfactorily	transferred
paid	prominent	schedule	typing
pamphlet	prosecute	secretary	ultimately
parallel	psychology	securities	unanimous
partial	purchase	seized	undoubtedly
participant	pursue	separate	unfortunately
particularly	quantity	serviceable	unnecessary
patronage	questionnaire	shipment	until
percent	quiet	shipping	urgent
permanent	quite	siege	usable
permissible	realize	significant	usually
permitted	really	similar	vacuum
perseverance	reasonable	simultaneous	valuable
personal	receipt	sincerity	various
personnel	receive	someone	vehicle
persuade	recipe	somewhat	vendor
phase	recognize	specialize	vicinity
physician	recognized	stationary	visible
planning	recommend	stationery	volume
pleasant	recurrence	statistics	voluntary
pleasure	reference	strictly	volunteer
possession	referred	submitted	warehouse
practical	referring	subscriber	weather
practically	regrettable	substantial	whether
practice	reimburse	succeed	wholesale
precede	remember	successful	withhold
precision	remittance	sufficient	worthwhile
preferable	renewal	superintendent	writing
preference	repetition	supersede	yield
preferred	representative	supervisor	zodiac
prejudice	requirement	surprise	
preliminary	respectfully	survey	

RULES OF WORD DIVISION

Division of Words at the End of a Line

Divide a word at the end of a line *only* when necessary. Try not to have two successive lines with a divided word at the end, and never have more than two. Never divide the last word on a page except in legal documents, where the word is sometimes intentionally divided to show continuity. Try to avoid dividing the last word in a paragraph.

Syllabication and Pronunciation

The correct division of a word depends on the breakdown of the word into syllables. American dictionaries syllabicate according to pronunciation and not according to derivation. If you do not know the proper division into syllables for a word, look up the word in a definition dictionary or a spelling dictionary. Spelling dictionaries that show pronunciation as well as word division are especially helpful since pronunciation is a basic guide to word division. For example, *pre-sent* means to give or introduce; *pres-ent* refers to a gift.

Basic Rules of Word Division

ONE-SYLLABLE WORDS. Never divide words pronounced as one syllable.

through (*not* th-rough)   drowned (*not* drown-ed)   gained (*not* gain-ed)

FOUR-LETTER WORDS. Never divide a four-letter word.

only (*not* on-ly)   into (*not* in-to)

ONE-LETTER SYLLABLES. Never separate one-letter syllables from the rest of the word.

around (*not* a-round)   alone (*not* a-lone)   caf-e-te-ria (*not* cafeteri-a)

Divide a word with a one-letter syllable within the word after the one-letter syllable, except in the case of the suffixes *able* or *ible*.

busi-ness   sepa-rate   medi-cal   con-sider-able   reduc-ible

Note: There are many words ending in *able* or *ible* in which the *a* or *i* does not form a syllable by itself. These words are divided after the *a* or *i*.

pos-si-ble   char-i-ta-ble   ca-pa-ble

TWO-LETTER SYLLABLES. Do not carry over a two-letter syllable at the end of a word.

caller (*not* call-er)   deeded (*not* deed-ed)   purchaser (*not* purchas-er)

Avoid separating two-letter syllables at the beginning of a word from the rest of the word.

eli-gi-ble (*not* el-igible)   begin-ning (*not* be-ginning)
atten-tion (*not* at-tention)   redeemed (*not* re-deemed)

Always keep three or more characters (including punctuation) on the top line or see that three or more are carried to the next line.

break-up, (Carry over the three characters *up*, to the bottom line.)

CONSONANTS WITHIN A WORD. When the final consonant in a word is doubled before a suffix, the second consonant belongs with the letters following it.

run-ning   occur-ring

Do not carry over to the next line single or double consonants in the root word.

call-ing (*not* cal-ling)   forc-ing (*not* for-cing)
divid-ing (*not* divi-ding)   fore-stall-ing (*not* forestal-ling)

When two consonants occur within a word, divide the word between the consonants.

gram-mar   expres-sive   moun-tain   foun-da-tion

PREFIXES AND SUFFIXES. Divide a word before or after (not within) prefixes and suffixes.

anti-climax (*not* an-ticlimax)
mini-computer (*not* min-icomputer)
over-confident (*not* ov-erconfident)
trust-worthy (*not* trustwor-thy)

HYPHENATED COMPOUNDS. Avoid dividing a compound hyphenated word except where the hyphen naturally falls.

father-in-law (*not* fa-ther-in-law)   self-applause (*not* self-ap-plause)

DASHES. Divide after a dash and keep the dash on the top line.

typing— / and proofreading (*not* typing / —and proofreading)

ABBREVIATIONS AND CONTRACTIONS. Do not divide abbreviations and acronyms.

Ph.D. (*not* Ph.-D.)   YWCA (*not* YW-CA)
isn't (*not* is-n't)   COD (*not* C-OD)

NUMBERS. Avoid dividing numbers. If it is necessary to divide them, divide on the comma and retain the comma.

$1,548,-345,000 (*not* $1,548,3-45,000)

Divide dates in the body of a letter between the day and the year, not between the month and the day. Avoid separating other number-word groups and separate numbers in lists only before the number.

September 19, / 1988 (*not* September / 19, 1988)

page 15 (*not* page / 15)

1100 West / Avenue (*not* 1100 / West Avenue)

(1) typing, / (2) editing, and (3) spelling (*not* [1] typing,
    [2] / editing, and [3] spelling)

NAMES. Do not separate the initials of a name, and avoid separating initials, titles, or degrees from the name; also avoid dividing proper names.

John / Devonshire (*not* John Devon-shire)

A. C. / Davis (*not* A. / C. Davis)

Chapter 15

Punctuation

PRINCIPAL MARKS AND RULES
OF PUNCTUATION

Apostrophe

POSSESSIVES. Use the apostrophe to indicate the possessive case of nouns. Do *not* use the apostrophe to indicate the possessive case of personal pronouns.

John's   Davis'   its   theirs

CONTRACTIONS. Use the apostrophe to denote a contraction or omission of letters. Place the apostrophe where the letter or letters are omitted.

it's for *it is*   *ass'n* for *association*   *'84* for *1984*

But omit the apostrophe in contractions formed by dropping the first letters of a word if the contraction has come into common usage.

phone   plane   though

LETTERS AND SYMBOLS. Use the apostrophe to form the plurals of letters and symbols.

p's and q's   5's and 6's   #'s

WORDS. Use an apostrophe to indicate the plural of a word referred to *as a word*, without regard to its meaning, but use the regularly formed plural if a meaning is attached to the word.

> There are three *but's* in the sentence.
>
> The *ayes* have it.
>
> There are eight *threes* in twenty-four.
>
> There are eight *three's* in the sentence.

ABBREVIATIONS. Use an apostrophe to denote the plural or some other form of an abbreviation.

> three O.K.'s   O.K.'d   V.I.P.'s

Colon

INTRODUCTION TO LISTS, TABULATIONS. The most frequent use of the colon is after a word, phrase, or sentence that introduces lists, a series, tabulations, extracts, texts, and explanations that are in apposition to the introductory words.

> The following is an extract from the report:
>
> These conditions must exist:

But do not use a colon to introduce a series of items that are the direct objects of a preposition or verb or that follow a form of the verb *to be*. In the following example the colon in brackets should be omitted.

> The requirements of a good secretary *are* [:] ability to take rapid dictation and to transcribe it rapidly and accurately, ability to spell correctly and to use the dictionary to the best advantage, and familiarity with basic office procedures.

Note: A colon may precede a *formal tabulation* even when the tabulated words or phrases are the objects of a preposition or verb or follow a form of the verb *to be*.

The requirements of a good secretary are:

1. Ability to take rapid dictation
2. Ability to spell correctly
3. Familiarity with basic office procedures

PAUSES. Use a colon to show a pause between two closely related sentences.

The secretary had one primary goal: she wanted to
advance within the company.

TIME AND RATIOS. Use a colon to indicate clock time and to show ratios.

4:10 A.M.   8:1 ratio

LETTER SALUTATIONS. Business-letter salutations are always followed by a colon.

Dear Mrs. Adams:

FOOTNOTES. Use a colon to separate the name of the city and state of publication from the name of the publisher.

1. Gavin A. Pitt, *The Twenty-Minute Lifetime* (Englewood
Cliffs, N.J.: Prentice-Hall, Inc., 1988), 20.

BIBLE REFERENCES. Use a colon to separate the verse and chapter in biblical references.

Matthew 10:4

DASH AND COLON. Do not use a dash with a colon.

Look at this bulletin—it's amazing. *Not:* Look at this
bulletin:—it's amazing.

Comma

Although many people still overwork the comma, the modern style is to curtail its use and omit it in many cases where its use was formerly mandatory.

APPOSITIVES. Use a comma to set off an *appositive,* an expression that explains or gives additional information about a preceding expression.

> The president of our company, *Mr. Edwards*, is in
> Europe.
>
> My husband, *John*, is an electrical engineer.

But do not separate two nouns, one of which identifies the other.

> The *conductor Bernstein* returned to America today.
>
> The *witness Jones* testified that he saw the defendant.
>
> His *son Carl* graduates today (he may have more
> than one son, so do not set off with commas).

CITIES AND STATES. Use a comma to separate the name of a city from the name of a state and enclose the state in commas.

> Brown Company of Auburn, *New York*, has reduced
> turnover by 50 percent.

COMPOUND PREDICATES. Compound predicates are not separated by commas.

> The total number of children in high school is
> increasing *and* will continue to increase for several
> more years.

COMPOUND SENTENCES. Use a comma to separate the two main clauses joined by the conjunctions *but, and, or, for, neither, nor,* or *either.* The comma precedes the conjunction.

> We appreciate your order of July 16, *but* we are
> unable to accept it because of our established
> merchandising policy.

The comma may be omitted before a conjunction if the clauses are short and closely connected in thought.

> The radios were shipped yesterday *and* the television
> sets will be shipped tomorrow.

DASH AND COMMA. Do not use a dash and comma together.

> He's very bright—or perhaps he's very lucky.
> *Or*: He's very bright, or perhaps he's very lucky.
> *Not*: He's very bright,—or perhaps he's very lucky.

DATES. Separate the day of the month from the year by a comma. Omit the comma after the month if no day is given.

> The dividend is payable March 12, 1988, to the
> stockholders.
> On March 1988 the dividend is payable to the
> stockholders.

ESSENTIAL AND NONESSENTIAL PHRASES AND CLAUSES. An essential, or restrictive, phrase or clause (often introduced by *that* or *who*) is one that is essential to the meaning of the sentence and is not merely descriptive or parenthetic; it cannot be omitted and therefore should *not* be set off by commas. A nonessential, or nonrestrictive, phrase or clause (often introduced by *which* or *who*) is one that adds an additional thought to the sentence but is not essential to the meaning of the sentence; it can be omitted and therefore *should* be set off by commas.

> The car *that was damaged* is being towed away.
> (*essential*)
>
> The lawyer *who argued the case* is a close friend of
> the defendant. (*essential*)
>
> Mr. Ransome, *who argued the case*, is a close friend
> of the defendant. (*nonessential*)
>
> The rule against lateness, *which has been in effect
> many years*, is strictly enforced. (*nonessential*)

INTERDEPENDENT WORDS. A frequent error is the separation of words that belong together and are interdependent, for example, separating a verb from its subject or object or predicate nominative or a limiting clause from its antecedent. In the following examples, the commas in brackets should be omitted.

> The rapid advancement of the company to its present enviable position in the publishing world [,] is attributable largely to the acumen and energy of its founders. (The comma incorrectly separates the subject *advancement* from its verb *is*.)

> The revision combines with the first edition's thoroughness [,] a constructive viewpoint, a wide range of practices, and up-to-date methods. (The comma incorrectly separates the verb *combines* from its objects *viewpoint*, *range*, and *methods*.)

> The leeway allowed to the defendants in this trial, as in all others [,] where justice prevails, is in sharp contrast to the treatment accorded defendants in totalitarian countries. (The *where* starts a limiting relative clause modifying *others*.)

INTRODUCTORY WORDS. Use a comma to separate an introductory word from the rest of the sentence. Words ending in *ly* are usually set off by a comma, as are words such as *however* and *for example*. But it is not necessary to set off brief introductory words such as *thus* and *yet*.

> *However*, the office will be closed.

> *Yes*, the meeting will be held as scheduled.

> *Thus* we took an earlier flight.

> *Usually*, the office is open on Saturday.

OMISSION OF WORDS. Use a comma to indicate that one or more words have been omitted.

> The employer contributed 60 percent; the employees, 40 percent.

NAMES. Do not use a comma between a name and *of* indicating place or position.

> Henderson Manufacturing Company *of* Phoenix,
>   Arizona
>
> Mrs. Edwards *of* Robinson & Co.
>
> Ms. Steinberg *of* counsel

Place a comma between a name and *Inc., Sr.,* and *Jr.* when the person or company uses that style; omit the comma when the subject also omits it. (Do not place a comma before *II* or *III* in a name.)

> Lever Brothers, *Inc.*   R. G. Jones, *Sr.*   R. G. Jones III

NUMBERS. Use a comma when writing figures in thousands *but not* in numbers designating street, room, post office box, postal zip code, telephone, or book page.

> $15,800.65   1381 Vinton Avenue   P.O. Box 4671
> zip code 07632   page 1159   3,800 cars

OH. Use a comma after *oh* if other words follow it.

> *Oh*, he returned the manuscript yesterday.

PARENTHESES AND COMMA. Use a comma after a closing parenthesis if the construction of the sentence requires a comma. Never use a comma *before* a parenthesis or an expression enclosed in parentheses.

> Our incorporators' meeting (the first meeting of our
>   stockholders), which is required by law, will be held
>   November 15.
>
> Our incorporators' meeting (the first meeting of our
>   stockholders) will be held November 15.

PARENTHETICAL WORDS AND PHRASES. Use commas to set off parenthetical words or phrases, such as *I believe, for example,* and *however,* unless the connection is close and smooth enough not to call for a pause in reading.

> *Furthermore*, credit obligations may be paid out of capital items.
>
> The economic condition of the country, *I believe*, is gradually improving.
>
> He was *perhaps* busy at the time.
>
> That make of car is not expensive and *therefore* appeals to potential customers in the low-income brackets.

PARTICIPIAL PHRASES. Do not separate a participle from the noun it modifies when the noun is not the subject and the expression is not closely connected with the rest of the sentence. The commas in brackets in the following sentences should be omitted.

> The operators [,] *having agreed to arbitrate*, the union called off the strike.
>
> The evidence [,] *being merely circumstantial*, the jury acquitted him.

PHRASES WITH A COMMON ELEMENT. Place a comma before a word or words that are common to two or more phrases but are expressed only after the last phrase. In the following examples the commas in brackets are frequently *omitted in error*.

> The report was documented with references to many, if not all [,] of the recent court decisions on the question of interlocking directorates. (The words *of the* . . . are common to *many* and to *all*.)
>
> The sales manager's reports are clearer, more concise, more instructive [,] than those of the advertising manager. (The words *than those* . . . are common to *clearer, more concise*, and *more instructive*.)

Note: If the phrases are connected by a conjunction, the comma is omitted.

> The sales manager's reports are clearer, more concise, *and* more accurate than those of the advertising manager.

QUOTATIONS. Set off direct quotations by commas.

> His reply was, "I am interested in the matter."
>
> "I am not interested in the matter," he replied.

But if a question mark is needed at the end of the quotation, do not use a comma.

> "What is the lowest price you can quote?" he inquired.
>
> *Not*: "What is the lowest price you can quote?," he
> inquired.

QUOTATION MARKS AND COMMA. Place the comma on the *inside* of quotation marks.

> When he spoke of "overtime," I thought he meant
> "over 35 hours."

SERIES. Separate words and phrases in a series by a comma.

> Thus we speak of buying goods on credit, of a
> merchant's credit, and of making a payment by
> credit.
>
> Its membership comprises manufacturers and
> wholesalers of silverware, watches, diamonds, and
> semiprecious stones.

But do not use a comma between two (not a series) parallel constructions joined by a conjunction.

> This amount is equal to the covered loss less (1) the
> coinsurance deduction and (2) the normal loss.
>
> He can ask for changes in the estimate or for a
> completely revised estimate.

Dash

PRINCIPAL USE. The dash is a more forceful mark than most other punctuation. It is used principally to set off explanatory or parenthetical clauses, to indicate abrupt changes in the continuity of expression, and to set off a thought that is repeated for emphasis. But some writers use a dash unnecessarily and excessively when a comma or other punctuation would be more appropriate; such overuse causes a dash to lose its effectiveness and distracts the reader.

> The old typewriter—last year's model—is a better machine than the new one.

> He said that Monday would be fine—or did he say Tuesday?

> She returned my copy—the copy I thought was lost.

SERIES. A dash may be used before or after a clause that summarizes a series of words or phrases, but a colon is more common *after* such a clause.

> "Wage and Hour," "Arbitration," "Union Contracts"—these chapters indicate only a few of the topics discussed in our *Complete Labor-Equipment Services* handbook.

> Our *Complete Labor-Equipment Services* handbook has six chapters: "Wage and Hour," "Employee Relations," "Union Contracts," "Labor Relations," "State Labor Law," and "Pension and Profit Sharing."

DASH AND OTHER PUNCTUATION MARKS. A dash may be used after an abbreviating period. If the material set off by dashes requires an interrogation or exclamation point, retain the punctuation before the second dash. Do not use a dash with a comma or semicolon. Do not use a dash and colon together before a list of items.

> The check is now O.K.—he made a large deposit.

> The head of the personnel department—is his name Donovan or O'Donovan?—said he thought there would be an opening next week.

Ellipsis Points and Leaders

ELLIPSIS POINTS. The marks used to show an omission from a sentence of a word or words that would complete the construction. The marks are usually dots (periods), but they may be asterisks if an entire line (three to five asterisks on a separate line) is used to show the omission of a substantial amount of copy. When you are quoting and want to omit words, use three consecutive dots (. . .) to indicate an omission of words. If a period would ordinarily follow the words omitted, you will then have four dots, one representing the period. Put a space before and after each dot except when the first dot represents a period.

> . . . according to Mr. Burns, . . . the check is past due
> [words omitted at the beginning and in the middle
> of the sentence: three dots, equal space before and
> after each one].

> The report will nevertheless be delayed. . . . Let us
> hope it doesn't happen again [end of the sentence
> or other sentences or paragraphs missing: no
> space before first dot since it represents a period].

> I was wondering . . . [incomplete sentence: three dots,
> equal space after each one].

> The purpose of punctuation is clear. . . . it should be
> respected [end of first sentence and beginning of
> next sentence missing: no space before first dot
> since it represents a period].

The same principles apply to extracts, which are blocks of copy set off from the rest of the text and indented.

> In an extract the first complete [no introductory words
> missing] sentence is *not* indented and is *not* preceded
> by three dots—*if* it falls somewhere within the first
> paragraph you are quoting. But four dots *are* placed at
> the end of the sentence or paragraph to show that
> other words, a sentence(s), or another paragraph(s) is
> missing. . . .
> . . . the second paragraph *is* indented and *is*
> preceded by three dots when the beginning words are
> omitted from a sentence that does *not* open that
> paragraph. Also, three dots are used as always when
> words are missing in the middle of any sentence . . . in
> any paragraph.

LEADERS. A row of dots (periods) or short lines (hyphens) to lead the eye across a space in the line of writing to a related figure or words. Their principal use is in statements of account or other tabulations.

> Accounts Receivable $1,425.72

Exclamation Point

EXCLAMATORY SENTENCES. Place an exclamation point after a startling statement or a sentence expressing strong emotion.

> How incredible that he should take that attitude!
>
> I'm absolutely furious!

EXCLAMATORY WORDS. Place an exclamation point after exclamatory words.

> Oh!   Great!   Stop!   No!

FOR EMPHASIS. If not used to excess, an exclamation point is a good device to lend emphasis or to drive home a point. It is used more frequently in sales letters than in any other business correspondence. But, as with the dash, unless the exclamation point is used sparingly, it loses its effectiveness and distracts the reader.

> Buy now!   And more than 1000 forms!

IRONY AND SATIRE. An explanation point can be used to indicate that a remark is satirical or has an ironic connotation.

> Don't you just love the way she combs her hair!

Hyphen

DIVISION OF WORDS. Use a hyphen at the end of a line to show that part of a word has been carried over to another line.

> govern-   princi-
> ment   pal

COMPOUND TERMS. Use a hyphen as a connecting link in compound terms.

> president-elect   secretary-treasurer

SERIES OF HYPHENATED WORDS. In a series of hyphenated words having a common base, place a hyphen after the first element of each word and write the base after the last word only.

> fourth-, fifth-, and sixth-grade pupils

Use either a closed or a suspended hyphen in numerical descriptions.

> 3- by 5-inch cards (suspended)
>
> 3-by-5-inch cards (closed)
>
> one- to two-year program (suspended)
>
> one-to-two-year program (closed)

TIME. Use a hyphen to indicate a span of time but do not use a hyphen with the words *from* or *between* in relation to a time period.

> The report covers the fiscal year 1985–86.
>
> The report covers the period *from* January 1985 *to* December 1986.
>
> The report covers the period *between* January 1985 *and* December 1986.

Parentheses and Brackets

EXPLANATORY EXPRESSIONS. Use parentheses to enclose parenthetical or explanatory expressions that are *outside* the general structure of the sentence. Parentheses indicate a stronger separation than do commas or dashes.

> The place at which an incorporators' meeting (sometimes called the first meeting of the stockholders) is to be held is determined by statute in most states.

FIGURES. Enclose a figure in parentheses (1) in a legal document when it follows an amount that has been written out in words and (2) when the American equivalent of foreign currency is given.

> Under the will he received £100,000 ($280,000).
>
> The check is for seven thousand five hundred (7,500) dollars.
>
> The check is for seven thousand five hundred dollars ($7,500).

Note: If the figure is written *before* the word *dollars*, or other currency designation, do not use the dollar sign; if the figure is written *after* the word *dollars*, use the dollar sign. (This rule also applies to the percent sign.)

QUESTIONS AND ANSWERS. In testimony (question-and-answer material), use parentheses to enclose matter describing an action and, also, to indicate a person who has not previously taken part in the questions and answers.

> Q. (By Mr. Smith)   Will you identify this
>   handkerchief? (Hands the witness a handkerchief)

ENUMERATIONS. Enclose in parentheses letters or numbers in enumerations run into the text. In general writing, however, it is often preferable to omit the numbers entirely, except in long or complex enumerations.

> Stock may be divided broadly into two kinds: (1)
>   common stock and (2) preferred stock.

SINGLE (CLOSING) PARENTHESES. Parentheses are usually used in pairs, but a single closing parenthesis may be used instead of a period to follow a letter or roman numeral in outlines. Usually, double parentheses (or a period) are preferred even in this case.

> 1) Parentheses
>   a) Brackets
>   b) Explanatory expressions

PUNCTUATION IN PARENTHESES. Commas, periods, and similar punctuation marks belong *within* the parentheses if they belong to the parenthetical clause or phrase. They are placed *outside* the parentheses if they belong to the words of the rest of the sentence.

> The boy ran as if a ghost (and, indeed, he may have
>   been right) were following him.

> She reported the action at once. (She has a strong
>   sense of civic responsibility.)

> He turned in a perfect examination paper. (What an
>   example for the rest of the class!)

BRACKETS. Use brackets to rectify mistakes in quoted material and to enclose parenthetical material *within* remarks already enclosed in parentheses.

> "The fire occurred [*sic*] in 1985."

> Read Chapter 5 ("Real Estate Practice [legal
>   implications] in New York") before you begin
>   writing.

Period

SENTENCES. Place a period at the end of a declarative or imperative sentence.

> The contract was signed last week. (*declarative*)
>
> Hold the shipment until next month. (*imperative*)

INITIALS AND ABBREVIATIONS. Place a period after certain initials and abbreviations. The periods are omitted between initials standing for agencies and other organizations and between the letters of many abbreviations (see the list of abbreviations in Chapter 17) and after letters used as a name.

Ph.D.	ibid.	Chas.
R. E. Smith	NASA	Mr. T

OUTLINES. Place a period after each letter or number in an outline or itemized list unless the letter or number is enclosed in parentheses.

> A. Comma
> > 1. Appositives
> > 2. Cities and states
>
> (A) Comma
> > (1) Appositives
> > (2) Cities and states

OMISSIONS. Omit the period after contractions; roman numerals, except in an outline; sums of money in dollar denominations, unless cents are added; shortened forms of names and words in common use; and letters identifying radio and television stations.

ass'n	sec'y	volume II	George V	$50	$50.25
Ed	Will	ad	memo	percent	photo	NBC

PERIODS AND PARENTHESES. When an expression in parentheses comes at the end of a sentence and is part of the sentence, put the period *outside* the closing parenthesis; if the parenthetical expression is independent of the sentence and a period is necessary, place the period *within* the closing parenthesis.

> The creditor can get a judgment against him and garnishee his wages (see Section 15).

> The creditor can get a judgment against him and garnishee his wages. (The law of garnishment is discussed in Section 15.)

But do not use a period when a complete declarative or imperative sentence is enclosed in parentheses *within another sentence.*

> The honorary chairman of the board (he retired from active duty several years ago) addressed the Quarter-Century Club.

PERIODS AND QUOTATION MARKS. Always place the period *inside* quotation marks.

> Please explain what you meant by the expression "without reservation."

Question Mark

INTERROGATIVE SENTENCES. Place a question mark after a direct question but not after an indirect question.

> Have you heard the decision that was made at the conference? (*direct*)

> Mr. Rogers asked me, "When will the book be ready for publication?" (*direct*)

> Mr. Rogers asked me when the book would be ready for publication. (*indirect*)

REQUESTS. Do not place a question mark after a question that is a request to which no answer is expected.

> Will you please return the signed copy as soon as possible.

QUERIES. A question mark enclosed in parentheses may be used to query the accuracy of a fact or figure. Other punctuation is not affected by this use of the question mark.

> The treaty was signed September 5(?), 1979

SERIES OF QUESTIONS. A question mark is usually placed after each question in a series included within one sentence, and each question usually begins with a capital.

> What will be the significance of our landing on the
> moon if we still cannot get along with others? If our
> cultural endeavors have been sacrificed? If world
> peace is still unstable?

But the question mark is omitted after the various items in a simple series.

> Who is responsible for (1) copyediting the book, (2)
> producing the artwork, and (3) preparing the
> production schedule?

Quotation Marks

DIRECT QUOTATIONS. Enclose the exact words of a speaker or writer in quotation marks, but do not enclose words that are not quoted exactly. The quoted material may be a word or several paragraphs in length.

> On July 15 he wrote, "Please consider the contract
> canceled if the goods are not shipped by the tenth
> of next month."
>
> On July 15 he wrote that we should consider the
> contract canceled if the goods are not shipped by
> the tenth of next month.
>
> He wrote that he was "no longer interested" in the
> proposition.

Do not use quotation marks when the name of the speaker or writer immediately precedes the quoted material or in question-and-answer material.

> MR. EDWARDS: In my opinion the machine is
> worthless.
>
> MS. ROBERTS: Upon what do you base that opinion?

PARAGRAPHS. When quoted material consists of more than one paragraph, place quotation marks at the beginning of each paragraph but only at the close of the last paragraph.

DEFINITIONS. Quotation marks may be used to enclose a word or phrase that is accompanied by its definition, although it is more common to write a word being defined in italics (or underscored in manuscript copy).

> The party against whom garnishment proceedings are brought is called the "garnishee."

> "Bankruptcy insolvency" means that a debtor's total assets are less than his total liabilities.

UNIQUE WORDS OR TRADE TERMS. Quotation marks may be used to enclose a word or phrase the *first* time the term is used in an unusual sense or with a special trade meaning. It is not desirable to use the quotation marks when the term is repeated or when the sense or meaning will be understood by most readers. Many writers use quotation marks excessively and unnecessarily.

> This "pyramiding" was carried to an extreme in the public utility field.

> In "spot" markets, commodities are bought and sold in specific lots and grades with a definite delivery date specified.

TITLES AND NAMES. Use quotation marks to enclose the titles of articles, chapters or part titles in books, unpublished works such as a thesis or conference paper, short poems, songs, and television and radio shows.

> "Heredity in Asian Cultures" (article or chapter title)

> "CAM and CAD Technology in the 1990s" (conference address)

> "Winter's Song" (short poem)

> "Star-Spangled Banner" (song)

> "Murphy Brown" (television show)

Note: Titles of books, periodicals, brochures and pamphlets, operas, paintings, plays and motion pictures, and long poems are italicized in printed material (underscored in manuscript copy).

Do not use quotation marks with or underscore the Bible, names of its books (Psalms), or other parts of it (New Testament); movements of a symphony, concerto, or other long composition or names of numbered compositions (Symphony No. 5 in C Minor); parts of poems or plays (Scene 2); book series titles (Studies in American Literature) and book editions (Second Edition); common titles in a book (Appendix I); notices (No Smoking); and mottoes (One for All and All for One).

SINGLE QUOTATION MARKS. Use single quotation marks to enclose a quotation within a quotation.

> Last week he wrote, "It is understood that delivery
> 'must be made on or before the 30th.'"

PLACEMENT OF QUOTATION MARKS. Always place a period or comma *inside* quotation marks.

> The account was marked "paid," but he never
> received a receipt.
>
> The check was marked "canceled."

Always place colons and semicolons *outside* quotation marks.

> Turn to the chapter "Consideration for Stock"; the
> reference is in the first paragraph.

Interrogation and exclamation points come before or after the quotation marks, depending on the meaning of the text.

> Who is the author of "Up the Down Staircase"? (The
> entire question is not quoted.)
>
> He shouted, "I will never consent to those terms!"
> (The exclamation is part of the quotation.)

Semicolon

COMPOUND SENTENCES. A semicolon may be used to separate the parts of a compound sentence when the comma and conjunction are omitted.

> The adjustment has been made; the file has been
> closed.

LONG, INVOLVED CLAUSES. Use a semicolon to separate long, involved clauses. (The following example could also be written as two sentences separated by a period.)

> A low rate of interest usually reflects easy conditions
> and an inactive industrial situation; a high rate
> indicates money stringency and industrial activity.

PUNCTUATED CLAUSES. Use a semicolon to separate clauses that are punctuated by commas.

> On the other hand, if the turnover is low in
> comparison to the normal figure it shows just the
> opposite; that is, it indicates weaker sales policy
> and poorer purchasing ability and stock control
> than the average.

SERIES. In enumerations or series of items, use semicolons to separate items that contain commas.

> The most important of these services is published by
> Moody's Investors Service, Inc.; Standard & Poor's
> Corporation; and Fitch Publishing Company, Inc.

BEFORE A CONJUNCTIVE ADVERB. Use a semicolon before an adverb that serves the purpose of a conjunction. Examples of conjunctive adverbs are *accordingly, also, besides, consequently, furthermore, hence, however, indeed, likewise, moreover, nevertheless, otherwise, similarly, so, still, therefore,* and *thus.* Omit the comma after a conjunctive adverb preceded by a semicolon, unless it ends in *ly,* and omit the comma after short conjunctive adverbs such as *so* and *thus.* In the following examples the comma in brackets should be omitted in the first example and may be omitted in the second and third examples.

He told his secretary that he did not want to be disturbed; so [,] she did not announce the chairman of the board, whom she did not recognize.

She telephoned that he did not plan to leave until next week; therefore [,] I did not consider it necessary to send the report to him by airmail.

He will attend the meeting; indeed [,] he will be the main speaker at the meeting.

QUOTATION MARKS AND SEMICOLON. Place the semicolon *outside* quotation marks.

As stated in his report, "the department is expanding"; therefore our advertising should reflect this development.

PARENTHESES AND SEMICOLON. Use a semicolon after a closing parenthesis if the construction of the sentence requires a semicolon. Never use a comma or semicolon before a parenthesis or an expression enclosed in parentheses.

The current sales figures are ambiguous (in my opinion); however, new data will be out this month.

Virgule (Solidus)

PRINCIPAL USE. The virgule (also called "solidus" and "slash") is used most often in fractions, in identification numbers, in abbreviations, in place of the word *per*, in dates instead of a hyphen, between nouns of equal weight, to show a time span, and between lines of poetry that are run into the text. Usually, there is no space before or after the virgule unless it is used to separate lines of poetry. (Some authorities recommend that the hyphen instead of the virgule be used to show a time span and between nouns of equal weight.)

7/8 (fraction)	B/R-423	B/L (bill of lading)
miles/hr.	1985/90	owner/operator

Thompson said: "But the rose's scene is bitterness / to him that loved the rose."

Chapter 16

Capitalization

RULES AND PRINCIPLES OF CAPITALIZATION

Abbreviations

Degrees and Titles. Capitalize abbreviations of scholastic degrees and titles. Do not space between the letters of degrees.

B.A.   Ph.D.   M.P.   Dr.   Jr.   Esq.   Lt. Col.

Initials of Names. Capitalize the initials representing names. When a name has two initials, place a space between the letters. When a name has three initials, the space between the letters may be omitted. Do not space between the letters used alone to refer to a person (*FDR*).

R. D. Ellis   R.D.M. Ellis   Mr. T   JFK

One Letter. Capitalize abbreviations of one letter, except most units of measurement and minor literary subdivisions.

F (Fahrenheit)   p. 3 (page 3)   t (ton)

Time and Years. In typewriter or computer preparation, abbreviations designating the time before or after noon are usually lowercase, whereas abbreviations for chronology such as *Ano Domini* are written in all capitals. Small capitals are used for all such time designations in printed material. Do not space between any of the letters. In designations referring to time zones, only the letter representing a proper noun is capitalized. The abbreviation for *meridies* (noon) should be capitalized, because it is one initial— M. Do not use the abbreviations *a.m.* or *p.m.* when the hour is written out; write *four o'clock in the afternoon* or *four o'clock*, not *four p.m.*

> p.m.   B.C.   Pst (Pacific standard time)

COMMON ABBREVIATIONS. Many common abbreviations may be lowercase or uppercase, but the trend is toward lowercase. Abbreviations of organization names and well-known acronyms are usually capitalized (but not general shortcuts such as *PO* or *po* for *post office*). Two-letter postal abbreviations such as *NY* are always capitalized. Do not space between the letters.

C.O.D or c.o.d	FOB or fob	NB or nb	SALT
YMCA	IBM	NJ	

Acts, Bills, Codes, Laws

OFFICIAL TITLE. Capitalize the official titles of specific acts, bills, codes, and laws; also capitalize the accepted title by which a law is generally known.

> Securities Exchange Act, the securities act, the act
>
> Civil Rights Bill, the bill
>
> National Labor Relations Act, the act

Lowercase *bill* or *law* when used with the sponsor's name unless the formal title of the bill is given.

> the Thomas bill, the Thomas wage-hour bill

GENERAL DESCRIPTIVE TERMS. Lowercase *bill* and *act* when they are standing alone, and lowercase abbreviated titles and general descriptive terms designating them.

> the act
>
> the bill
>
> the tariff act
>
> the rent-control bill

FEDERAL, STATE, AND MUNICIPAL CODES. Lowercase federal, state, and municipal codes, but capitalize the formal titles of codes of law.

> building code
>
> Code of Criminal Procedure
>
> Code Napoleon

CONSTITUTION. Capitalize *constitution* when it refers to the specific constitution of a country, but lowercase general references. Capitalize *constitution* immediately following a state name, but lowercase it when it precedes the state name and in general references.

> the U.S. Constitution, the Constitution of the United
> States, the Constitution (of the United States), a
> national constitution
>
> the New Jersey Constitution, the constitution of New
> Jersey, the state constitution, the constitution

AMENDMENTS TO THE U.S. CONSTITUTION. Capitalize amendments to the Constitution when they are referred to by number or by full title, but lowercase them when they are used as general terms or as parts of general descriptive titles.

> Eighteenth Amendment, the amendment
>
> prohibition amendment
>
> Child Labor Amendment, the amendment
>
> constitutional amendment

Computer Terms

GENERAL RULE. Capitalize the official names of computer hardware (brand names) and software (programs) as well as names and designations of languages, commands, operations, and the like. Lowercase terms used in general reference.

> Zenith Data Systems computers, the 80286 Personal
> Computer, the Z-286, the computer
>
> WordPerfect Version 5.1, word processing software

> BASIC, COBOL, FORTRAN (*or* Fortran), Assembler, Pascal, the language
>
> GOTO, DSKSETUP, CONFIGUR, MKDIR, the command
>
> WESTLAW (*or* Westlaw), the legal database
>
> access, debug, format, hard copy, on line

Courts, Judges, Cases

FULL TITLE. Capitalize the full title of a court, but lowercase *court* when it is standing alone or when it is used in a general descriptive sense. Always capitalize references to the Supreme Court of the United States, even when the word *Court* is standing alone.

> the federal courts
>
> Judge Mason's court
>
> U.S. Supreme Court, the Supreme Court, the Court
>
> Court of Appeals of New York, the Court of Appeals (capitalized to distinguish from the U.S. court), the court
>
> Arizona Supreme Court, the supreme court, the court
>
> General Sessions
>
> magistrate's court
>
> traffic court
>
> night court

JUDGES, JUSTICES. Capitalize titles when they precede a proper name, but lowercase *chief justice, associate justice, justice, judge, magistrate, surrogate,* and so on when they stand alone.

> Magistrate Williams, the magistrate
>
> Associate Justice Donaldson, the associate justice
>
> Surrogate Brown, the surrogate

REFERENCE TO THE JUDGE. Capitalize *court* when it refers directly to the judge or presiding officer. Capitalize *Your Honor, His* (or *Her*) *Honor,* when they refer to the Court.

> The *Court* overruled the objection.
>
> In the opinion of the *Court* . . .
>
> If it please *Your Honor* . . .

BAR, BENCH. Capitalize *bar* and *bench* when they are part of a judicial body, but lowercase them in all other instances.

> American Bar Association, the bar
>
> Court of King's Bench, the bench

CASES. Capitalize the main words in the name of a case but not the abbreviation *v.* or *vs.* (versus).

> *White and Stone, Inc.* v. *City of Cleveland*, the *White*
>   case

Education

NAMES OF SCHOOLS. Capitalize the names of schools or colleges and their departments, but lowercase the words *school, college,* and *department* when they are not part of a name.

> Washington Irving High School, the high school
>
> Harvard, the university
>
> Public School No. 1, a public school
>
> Department of History, the history department
>
> College of Liberal Arts, the college
>
> School of Business Administration, the business
>   school

CLASSES. Capitalize the names of classes of a high school, college, or university, but lowercase the word when it refers to a member of a class.

> Freshman Class, a freshman

DEGREES, CHAIRMANSHIPS. Capitalize academic degrees, scholastic honors, chairmanships, fellowships, and the like, whether abbreviated or written in full, if the person's full name is given. Lowercase these words in general usage when they are not part of a name or title.

> John Smith, Ph.D.; John Smith, Doctor of Philosophy; the doctor of philosophy degree
>
> LL.D., the degree of doctor of laws, the doctor of laws degree
>
> M.A., the master of arts degree
>
> Robert Brown Fellowship, the fellowship
>
> Sc.D., the doctor of science degree, the doctorate

COURSES, SUBJECTS. Capitalize the official names of courses, but capitalize the names of subjects only when they are derived from proper names.

> Education II, the education course
>
> Modern History 309, the course in modern history
>
> I am studying history, Latin, and English.

Enumerations

PRECEDED BY A COLON. Capitalize the first word in each section of an enumeration that has been formally introduced if the enumerations are in a complete sentence. Lowercase brief items that do not make sentences, unless they are itemized in outline style.

> A secretary uses the guide under these circumstances: (1) Someone outside the immediate office wants the material. (2) The manager expects to take the material out of the office. (3) The secretary expects to use the material for more than one day.
>
> She listed the following as her qualifications for the position: (1) initiative, (2) intelligence, and (3) tact.
>
> Her qualifications for the position are:
> 1. Initiative
> 2. Intelligence
> 3. Tact

NOT PRECEDED BY A COLON. Lowercase enumerations that are not preceded by a colon.

> The disadvantage is offset to some extent by (1) the limited liability of shareholders and (2) the marketability of ownership in the company.

Foreign Names

GENERAL RULE. Usually articles, prepositions, and conjunctions (such as *du, de, la, le, von, van*) that constitute a part of foreign names are not capitalized unless the name is written without the given name or a title. Some people with foreign names prefer capitals, however, and you should observe the person's preference.

> E. I. du Pont de Nemours
>
> Van Wort, the author
>
> Martin Van Buren (preferred spelling)
>
> Ludwig van Beethoven
>
> Dr. de la Bonne

Geographical Terms

POINTS OF COMPASS. Capitalize names of points of the compass when they refer to a section of the United States, but lowercase them when they denote simple direction or compass points.

> the South, south of here, southern
>
> the Northwest, to the northwest, northwestern
>
> the East, moving east, eastern
>
> the West, a west window, western
>
> the Midwest, midwestern origin

POPULAR NAMES. Capitalize popular names of specific localities. But lowercase *ghetto, fatherland,* and the like.

> Corn Belt, Cotton Belt
>
> East Side, West Side
>
> the Delta
>
> the Loop (Chicago)
>
> Mississippi Valley, valley of the Mississippi
>
> the Continent (Europe), continental Europe, a
>   continent
>
> New York ghetto

REGIONAL TERMS. Capitalize regional terms that are part of a precise descriptive title, but lowercase terms that are merely localizing adjectives.

> the Eastern Shore
>
> the South Shore
>
> South Jersey (definite regional term)
>
> northern China (localizing adjective)
>
> western New York (localizing adjective)

COAST. Capitalize *coast* when it designates a specific locality or stands alone, but lowercase it when it is used with geographic designations.

> West Coast (U.S.), the coast
>
> New England coast, the coast
>
> Pacific Coast (U.S.), the coast
>
> Jersey coast, the coast
>
> Florida coast, the coast
>
> Gulf Coast (U.S.), the coast

DIVISIONS OF WORLD OR COUNTRY. Capitalize most political divisions and major parts of the world or a country but not adjectives derived from them.

> the Old World, the New World
>
> Far East, Near East
>
> New England states
>
> Roman Empire, the empire

the Union (U.S.)

West Africa, western Africa

Arctic, arctic winter

North Atlantic, northern Atlantic

Orient, oriental

Mississippi River, the river

Mississippi and Arkansas rivers

Tropic of Cancer, the tropics

Central America

central Europe (general), Central Europe (World War
I political division)

the East (U.S. region), eastern U.S.

Government and Political Terms

GOVERNMENT, ADMINISTRATION. Lowercase both *government* and *administration* in most cases, but capitalize *government* when it is part of an official title.

Her Majesty's Government, the government in Britain

the U.S. government, the federal government, the
government

the Reagan administration, the administration

the Tennessee government, the government of
Tennessee, the government

FEDERAL. Capitalize *federal* when it is part of a title. When *federal* is used as an adjective referring to institutions or activities of the federal government, use lowercase. Always use lowercase when *federal* is used as a general term.

Federal Register (title of publication)

the federal government

the federal courts

the federal principle of government

NATIONAL. Capitalize *national* when it is part of a title or name of a political party (the word *party* is not capitalized); lowercase it when it is used as a general descriptive term. Also lowercase *nationals,* meaning citizens of a country.

> National Labor Relations Board, the board
>
> the National Socialist party, the party
>
> national customs
>
> The nationals were opposed to the legislation.

STATE. Capitalize *state* or *commonwealth* when it is part of a name; otherwise, lowercase it.

> New York State, state of New York, the state
>
> Commonwealth of Massachusetts, the commonwealth

CITY. Capitalize *city* when it is part of a name, but lowercase it when it is used in transposed form or when it stands alone.

> New York City, the city of New York, the city

COUNTY. Capitalize *county* when it is part of a name, but lowercase it when it is used in transposed form or when it stands alone.

> Westchester County, the county of Westchester, the
>   county

DISTRICT. Capitalize *district* when it is part of a name, but lowercase it when it is used as a general term or when it stands alone.

> District of Columbia, the district
>
> Second Congressional District, the congressional
>   district
>
> Third Assembly District, the district

WARD, PRECINCT. Capitalize *ward* and *precinct* when they are part of a name, but lowercase them when they stand alone.

> Ward 3, Third Ward, the ward
>
> Fifth Precinct, the precinct

DEPARTMENTS, BOARDS, COMMITTEES. Capitalize the full title of governmental departments, boards, committees, commissions, bureaus, and so on, but lowercase *department, board, committee, commission, bureau,* and the rest when they are used alone in place of the full name.

> Police Department, the department
>
> Department of Justice, the Justice Department, the department
>
> Bureau of Standards, the bureau
>
> Council Finance Committee, the Finance Committee (of the council), the committee (the Council Finance Committee), a committee (general reference)

NAMES OF LEGISLATIVE BODIES. Capitalize the names of legislative, administrative, and deliberative bodies, both domestic and foreign.

> U.S. Congress, the Congress
>
> U.S. House of Representatives, the House
>
> U.S. Senate, the Senate
>
> Board of Estimate, the board
>
> House of Lords, the House
>
> Parliament (Br.), parliamentary

Lowercase general or incomplete designations of legislative bodies.

> the city council, Huntsville City Council
>
> the lower house, the House of Commons
>
> the senate (general, no specific state), Iowa State Senate, the Senate (Iowa)
>
> the assembly (general, no specific state), Delaware General Assembly, the General Assembly (Delaware), the Assembly (Delaware)

LEGISLATURE. Capitalize *legislature* when it is part of the name of a specific body. Unless the exact designation is used, there is no need to capitalize *legislature* when it is used with the name of a state.

> Mississippi Legislature (official designation), the legislature
>
> Arkansas legislature (the exact designation is Arkansas General Assembly), the legislature

Headings and Titles

GENERAL RULE. Capitalize all important words (nouns, pronouns, verbs, adjectives, adverbs) in headings and titles of books, articles, lectures, reports, and the like, and lowercase articles, conjunctions, and prepositions.

> Valuable Aids in Letter Writing
>
> Selecting and Operating a Business of Your Own
>
> This Is the Way It Was
>
> Trends in Productive Sales Techniques
>
> Substance Before Style

INFINITIVES. Lowercase *to* in an infinitive.

> How to Build a Better Vocabulary
>
> How to Establish and Operate a Retail Store

PREPOSITIONS. Prepositions of five or more letters may be capitalized, but the trend is to lowercase them. Prepositions with fewer than five letters are always lowercased.

> Let's Talk about Children
>
> Life without Stress
>
> Computers for the Home
>
> Rules concerning Parliamentary Procedure

BREAK IN TITLE. Articles, prepositions, and conjunctions that immediately follow a marked break in a title, indicated by a colon or dash, are capitalized.

> Pick Your Job—And Like It
>
> Television: The Eyes of Tomorrow

Historical Terms

ERAS. Capitalize designations of eras of history and periods in the history of a language or literature. But lowercase informal adjectives in phrases such as *early Victorian* and numerical periods such as *twentieth century*. Lowercase very recent designations such as *space age*.

Dark Ages	Stone Age
Middle Ages	the Exile
Christian Era	Roaring Twenties
the Diaspora	Medieval Latin
Elizabethan Age	antiquity
nineteenth century	baroque period
colonial period (U.S.)	ancient Greece
the Renaissance	a renaissance of poetry

IMPORTANT EVENTS. Capitalize the names of important events. But lowercase *war* unless it is part of the name of a war.

Missouri Compromise, the compromise

World War II, the Second World War, the war

Peace of Utrecht

Battle of the Bulge, the battle

Vietnam War, the war in Vietnam, the war

DOCUMENTS. Capitalize the names of important historical documents.

Magna Carta

Declaration of Independence, the declaration

Atlantic Charter, the charter

Monroe Doctrine, the doctrine

Holidays, Seasons, Feast Days

RELIGIOUS. Capitalize religious holidays and feast days.

Yom Kipper	Passover	Christmas Eve
Good Friday	Hanukkah	Lent

SECULAR. Capitalize secular and especially designated days and weeks. But lowercase descriptive days such as *primary day.*

Thanksgiving Day	Memorial Day
Clean-Up Week	inauguration day

SEASONS. Lowercase names of seasons, unless they are personified.

autumn	spring	summer
midwinter	Spring, with her arms full of flowers . . .	

Hyphenated Compounds

GENERAL RULE. The capitalization of hyphenated compounds varies among authorities. The style indicated here is common in secretarial practice. But whichever style you adopt, be consistent.

HYPHENATED WORDS. Capitalize the parts of a hyphenated word that would be capitalized if the word were not hyphenated.

no-par stock

English-speaking nations

Anglo-Saxon descent

ex-President Johnson

TITLES AND HEADINGS. Capitalize all parts of hyphenated words in titles and headings, except (1) when the second word modifies the first word and (2) when the two parts are considered one word.

Spanish-speaking Students

Self-taught Writers

Sage of Twenty-second Street

Conference of Ex-Senators

Anti-intellectual Bias

Owner-Operator Guidelines

Nineteenth-Century Politics

Non-American Alliances

COMPOUND NUMERALS. Lowercase the second part of a compound numeral, even in titles and headings.

> Eighty-first Congress Convenes
>
> One-fifth of Students on Strike
>
> Twenty-second Victory for Ross

Leagues, Treaties, Pacts, Plans

GENERAL RULE. Capitalize the names of bodies, except adjectives derived from them or incomplete designations. Capitalize *treaty*, *pact*, and *plan* only when part of a specific title.

> United Nations
>
> General Assembly, the assembly
>
> Security Council, the council
>
> Secretariat
>
> Treaty of Versailles, Versailles treaty, treaty at
>   Versailles, the treaty
>
> Marshall Plan, the plan
>
> Pact of Paris, the pact

Lists and Outlines

GENERAL RULE. Capitalize the first word of each item in a list or outline.

> I. Office procedure
>   A. Typing
>   1. Typewriter and computer

Military Terms

NAMES. Capitalize names of military services, but lowercase words such as *army* and *navy* when they stand alone, are used collectively in the plural, or are not part of an official title.

United States Army, the army, the armed forces

United States Navy, the navy

United States Signal Corps, Signal Corps, the corps

United States Marines, the marines

National Guard, the guard

Red Army, Russian army, the army

BRANCHES, DIVISIONS. Capitalize titles of various branches or divisions, but lowercase general references such as *division*.

First Division, the division

Third Army, the army

Company A, the company

Navy Militia, the militia

Second Battalion, the battalion

TITLES. Capitalize a few titles of distinction that refer to a specific person, whether the title is standing alone or is followed by a proper name. Capitalize *Fleet Admiral* and *General of the Army* to avoid ambiguity. But generally lowercase military and naval titles when they are standing alone and are not followed by a proper name.

the Chief of Staff

the General of the Army, the general

the Admiral of the Fleet, the admiral

Admiral Rogers, the admiral

Captain Smith, the captain

the Adjutant General

the Judge Advocate General

the Paymaster General

Commander Roberts, the commander

Money

CHECKS. In writing checks the amount of money is always written out with each word capitalized. In general writing, the amounts are usually not capitalized.

> Two Hundred and No/100
>
> We made two hundred dollars.

LEGAL DOCUMENTS. To ensure accuracy in legal documents, spell out amounts of money and capitalize each word in the amount.

> Eight Hundred Twenty-Five Dollars ($825)

Music, Drama, Paintings, Poetry, Film, Radio

GENERAL RULE. Capitalize the principal words in titles of plays, hymns, songs, paintings, and the like. Lowercase movements of a symphony, concerto, or other musical composition. Lowercase *trio, quartet, quintet,* and so on when they refer to compositions, but capitalize them when they are used in the name of performers. Usually, capitalize the first word in every line of poetry, although some modern poetry is not capitalized in the traditional style. In cases of irregularity, follow the poet's style.

> "Rock of Ages" (hymn)
>
> *A Chorus Line* (play)
>
> "Designing Women" (TV show)
>
> "Posies for a Parlour" (short poem)
>
> Rodin's *The Thinker* (sculpture)
>
> Beethoven's Fifth Symphony, Symphony No. 5 in C Minor
>
> *William Tell* Overture
>
> California Quartet (performers)
>
> "I bridle in my struggling Muse in vain, / That seeks to launch into a nobler strain" (Pope).

Nouns and Adjectives

NAMES. Capitalize the names of particular persons, places, and things (proper nouns).

John Smith   Washington, D.C.   Statue of Liberty

COMMON NOUNS USED IN NAMES. Capitalize common nouns and adjectives used in proper names.

the Liberty Bell   the White House

WORDS DERIVED FROM PROPER NOUNS. Lowercase words derived from the proper nouns that have developed a specialized meaning through use.

anglicize	japan varnish
italicize	bohemian
manila envelopes	roman type, roman numerals

EPITHETS. Capitalize common nouns and epithets used with, or as substitutes for, proper names.

the Canal (Panama Canal)	Peter the Great
the First Lady	Richard Coeur de Lion

NOUNS WITH NUMBERS OR LETTERS. Nouns or abbreviations used with numbers or letters in a title are capitalized. In general writing, the trend is to lowercase common references such as *grade* and *article* (grade 6; article 7, section 5; room 102), although *room, suite,* and so on are capitalized in addresses, and *article, section,* and so on are capitalized in formal documents. Particular designations such as *Psalm 22* are always capitalized.

Sputnik I	World War II
Division IV	Ward 3
Class B	Precinct 4
grade 6, 6th grade	section 6, 6th section

Organizations and Institutions

OFFICIAL NAMES OR TITLES. Capitalize the official names of organizations and institutions. But lowercase the common noun in a name when it is used in the plural with two or more names.

Young Men's Christian Association, YMCA, the
association

Prentice Hall

Ohio University, the university

Ohio and Chicago universities, the universities

Metropolitan Opera, the opera

Independent Order of Odd Fellows, an Odd Fellow,
the order

Southern Railroad, the railroad

Southern and Pennsylvania railroads, the railroads

TERMS NOT PART OF NAME OR TITLE. Lowercase terms referring to organizations or institutions if those terms are not part of a specific name or title, even when the terms stand for specific organizations or institutions. But in formal writing, such as contracts, capitalize the term that stands for a specific organization or institution.

the parent-teacher association, Portland
Parent-Teacher Association

the chamber of commerce, Prescott Chamber of
Commerce

the board of directors (general), the Board of
Directors (formal document)

the company, Newcomb Engineering Company

Pursuant to a resolution of its Board of Directors, XYZ
Corporation, a corporation duly organized,
hereinafter called the Corporation, has adopted . . .

Peoples, Races, Tribes

GENERAL RULE. Capitalize the names of peoples, races, and tribes. But lowercase terms that refer to color or localized designations.

Romans	Aryans	Caucasians
Jews	Negroes	whites
Malays	bush people	blacks

Personal and Professional Titles

GENERAL RULE. Capitalize professional, academic, military, and similar titles or designations preceding names, but lowercase them when following names or used instead of names. Do not capitalize general descriptive titles such as *programmer* even before a name.

> District Attorney Bell, the district attorney
>
> Governor Jones, the governor
>
> Captain Davis, Capt. Mark Davis, the captain
>
> salesman Joe Brown, the salesman

PRESIDENT. Capitalize *president* when it precedes a name; otherwise, lowercase it.

> Mr. Nelson, president of NAM; President Nelson; the
>   president

NATIONAL GOVERNMENT OFFICIALS. Capitalize titles of cabinet members, heads of departments, and government dignitaries when the titles are used with names. *The Speaker* (of the House of Representatives) is usually capitalized, even when alone, to avoid ambiguity.

> Secretary of State Warren Christopher, the secretary
>   of state, the secretary
>
> Ambassador Jones, the ambassador
>
> Tom Foley, Speaker of the House; the Speaker of the
>   House; the Speaker

STATE OR MUNICIPAL OFFICIALS. Capitalize the titles of *governor, chief executive* (of a state), *lieutenant governor, mayor, borough president, senator, assemblyman, alderman,* president of any municipal body, and the like when they are used with proper names. Lowercase these titles when they follow a name or are used as general terms without reference to a specific official or office.

> Governor Smith, the governor
>
> Alderman Rogers; Mr. Rogers, president of the
>   Harrisville Board of Aldermen; President Rogers
>
> Mayor Adams, the mayor
>
> Senator Waltham, the senator

Capitalize heads of state and city departments such as *police commissioner, city counsel, commissioner of education, attorney general,* and *sheriff* and subordinate titles such as *deputy sheriff* and *assistant attorney general* when they precede names. Lowercase them when they follow a name or stand alone.

> Commissioner Edwards, the commissioner
>
> Assistant Attorney General Brown, the assistant attorney general
>
> Sheriff Lewis, the sheriff

BUSINESS AND PROFESSIONAL TITLES. Capitalize business and professional titles when they precede a name. Lowercase them when they follow a name or when they are used instead of a name of a specific office or official. In formal writing, such as contracts and minutes of meetings, titles referring to a specific officer of a specific company or organization may be lowercase or uppercase, but in such writing, you must capitalize *company, corporation,* and the like.

> Professor Stone, the professor
>
> Dr. Carvelli, the doctor
>
> Mr. Edgar Robbins, president of XYZ Company; President Robbins, the president

HONOR OR NOBILITY. Capitalize all titles of honor or nobility when preceding a name. (Some British titles are also capitalized when used without a personal name.) Lowercase them in all other instances.

> Queen Elizabeth, the queen of England
>
> Pope John Paul, the pope
>
> the Princess Royal, the princess
>
> the Duke of Kent, the duke
>
> His Excellency
>
> Your Grace

ACTING, UNDER, ASSISTANT. Capitalize the words *acting, under,* and *assistant* when they are part of a capitalized title that precedes a name. Otherwise, lowercase them along with the rest of the title.

> Acting Secretary of State Mackintosh, the acting
>   secretary
>
> Under Secretary of Labor Collins, the under secretary
>
> Assistant Secretary of Education Monroe, the
>   assistant secretary

WORDS IN APPOSITION. When a common noun precedes a name but is separated from it by a comma, the noun does not have the force of a title and is not capitalized.

> The secretary, John Doe, is on the executive
>   committee.
>
> Secretary Doe is on the executive committee.

COMPOUND TITLES. Capitalize all parts of a compound title if any part is capitalized.

> Vice President Gore
>
> Congressman-Elect Adamson

LISTS OF NAMES. In formal lists such as a mailing list, titles and descriptive designations immediately following the names should be capitalized.

> Ms. Adelaide Horton, President
> Prescott Information Bureau
> 1111 Main Street
> Prescott, AZ 86301

Personification

GENERAL RULE. Personification gives some attribute of a human being to inanimate objects, abstract ideas, or general terms. Capitalize the things personified when emphasis is desired.

> The meeting was called to order by the Chair.
>
> "Low Spirits are my true and faithful companions"
>   (Thomas Gray).
>
> The trees whispered in the wind.
>
> The waves roared as the hurricane approached.

Planets

GENERAL RULE. Capitalize the names of the planets and imaginative designations of celestial objects. But lowercase *stars*, *earth*, *moon*, *sun*, unless they are used in connection with other planets that are always capitalized.

Saturn	Leo	Mars
Milky Way	Big Dipper	

This is a scientific treatise on the relation of Mars to Earth.
The earth is fertile indeed.

Political Parties, Factions, Alliances

NAMES. Capitalize names of political parties, factions, and alliances. Do not capitalize *party*.

Democratic party, the party, Democrats, democratic
  principles

rightists, leftists, the Left, the Right, Left Wing and
  Right Wing (of political parties), left wing of the CIO

Socialist party, Socialists (of the party), socialist
  (general) economy

WORDS DERIVED FROM NAMES. Lowercase words derived from the names of political parties, factions, and alliances.

Communist party, communism, communistic

Socialist party, socialism, socialistic

Democratic party, democratic, democracy

Quotations

DIRECT QUOTATION. Capitalize the first word of an exactly quoted passage if it is a complete sentence, but lowercase quoted parts that do not form a complete sentence.

In his report the president said, "A member will not be
  permitted to remain in service after the normal
  retirement date without the special consent of the
  company."

What did he mean by calling my action
  "reprehensible"?

INDIRECT QUOTATION. Do not capitalize indirect quotations.

> In his report the president said that employees will not
> be permitted to remain in service.

BROKEN QUOTATION. Do not capitalize the second part of a broken quotation, unless it is a complete sentence.

> "If the order is not received by the first," he wrote, "we
> will be compelled to cancel it."

> "If the order is not received by the first, we will be
> compelled to cancel it," he wrote. "We cannot sell
> the goods after that date."

Religious Terms

CHURCH. Capitalize *church* when it is part of the name of an edifice.

> Central Presbyterian Church, the church
> St. Peter's Catholic Church, the church
> The First Lutheran Church, the church
> the Greek Orthodox church
> the Roman Catholic church
> the Baptist church

CHURCH DIGNITARIES. Capitalize the title of a church dignitary when it is used before a name. Lowercase it in other instances.

> the Reverend John Smith, the reverend
> Pope John Paul, the pope
> Mother Angelica, the mother superior
> Cardinal Spellman, the cardinal
> Rabbi Feldman, the rabbi
> Father Williams, the father, the priest
> Deacon Jones, the deacon

DEITY. Capitalize all names and appellations of the one supreme God (Lord) and of other deities (e.g., Zeus). Capitalize the personal pronouns *he, his, him, thee, thou,* and so on when they refer to the deity only in cases when capitalization avoids ambiguity. Do not capitalize the relative pronouns *who, whom.*

> God   Buddha   Allah
> In the Protestant religion, God is all-powerful, and it is
>   he who reigns supreme.

BIBLE. Capitalize all names for the Bible and other sacred books. Also capitalize books and versions of the Bible. Do not underscore or use quotation marks. But lowercase adjectives such as *biblical.*

> New Testament   the Gospels   Talmud, talmudic
> *But:* Koran, Koranic; Vedas, Vedic

DENOMINATIONS. Capitalize the names of all religious denominations.

> Baptists   Mormons
> Gentiles, gentile practices   Franciscan order, the order

Resolutions

GENERAL RULE. In resolutions write every letter in *WHEREAS* and *RESOLVED* in capitals; begin *That* with a capital letter.

> RESOLVED That . . . WHEREAS . . .

Series of Questions

GENERAL RULE. When a series of questions is included in one sentence, each question usually begins with a capital letter.

> What must a secretary do to advance herself? Get a
>   college education? Take an evening course?

Sports and Games

COLLEGE COLORS. Capitalize *gold, maroon, crimson,* and the like when they designate teams and refer to college colors.

> The Crimson Tide triumphed over the Black and Gold.
>
> Their uniforms are blue and orange.

GAMES AND SPORTS. Lowercase the names of sports and games, except when the names derive from proper names or are trade names.

football	Rugby	bridge
Monopoly	going to Jerusalem	

PLAYING FIELDS. Capitalize the names of playing fields and stadiums.

> Yankee Stadium, the stadium
>
> the Bowl
>
> Madison Square Garden, the Garden (capitalized to avoid ambiguity)

CUPS, STAKES. Capitalize *cup, stakes, trophy,* and the like when they are part of a specific title; otherwise, lowercase them.

> Belmont Stakes, the stakes
>
> Davis Cup, the cup
>
> Atlantic Trophy, the trophy

Trade Names

GENERAL RULE. Always capitalize trade names and spell and punctuate them as the manufacturer does.

Teletype	Kleenex
Coca-Cola	Q-Tips Cotton Swabs

PART FOUR

THE SECRETARY'S HANDY INFORMATION GUIDE

Chapter 17

Quick-Reference Guide to Facts and Figures

STUDY OUTLINE FOR CPS EXAM

Professional Secretaries International (PSI) offers a Certified Professional Secretaries (CPS) certificate to qualified secretaries who pass an exam on diverse subjects. Information and study materials are available from PSI,

10502 N.W. Ambassador Drive, P.O. Box 20404, Kansas City, MO 64195-0404.

The following outline summarizes examination content in six key areas:

1. **Behavioral Science in Business.** This part tests the principles of human relations and organizational dynamics in the workplace. It focuses on needs, motivation, nature of conflict, problem-solving techniques, essentials of supervision and communication, leadership styles, and understanding of the informal organization.

2. **Business Law.** This part measures (a) the secretary's knowledge of the principles of business law and (b) knowledge of the effect of governmental controls on business. Understanding of the historical setting in which these controls developed should be emphasized in preference to names and dates.

3. **Economics and Management.** This part consists of 35 percent economics and 65 percent management. Emphasis is placed on understanding of the basic concepts underlying business operations. Key economic and management principles as well as the latest governmental regulations in business are included.

4. **Accounting.** This part measures (a) knowledge of the elements of the accounting cycle, (b) ability to analyze financial statement accounts, (c) ability to perform arithmetical operations associated with accounting and computing interests and discounts, and (d) ability to summarize and interpret financial data.

5. **Office Administration and Communication.** This part measures proficiency in subject matters unique to the secretary's position: (50 percent office administration) executive travel, office management, records management, and reprographics; and (50 percent written business communication) editing, abstracting, and preparing communications in final format.

6. **Office Technology.** This part covers the secretary's responsibilities created by data processing, communications media, advances in office management, technological applications, records-management technology, and office systems.

Insert MARKS OF PUNCTUATION AND MECHANICS
and ROMAN NUMERALS figures on this page

MARKS OF PUNCTUATION AND MECHANICS

´ (é)	Accent, acute	ˇ (č)	Haček
` (è)	Accent, grave	-	Hyphen
' or '	Apostrophe	—	Em dash
*	Asterisk	–	En dash
{ }	Braces	. . . . . .	Leaders
[ ]	Brackets	‾ (ō)	Macron
˘	breve	¶	Paragraph
ˆ	Caret	‖	Parallels
, (ç)	Cedilla	( )	Parentheses
ˆ or ⌢ or ˜ (ô)	Circumflex	.	Period
:	Colon	?	Question mark
,	Comma	" "	Quotation marks
†	Dagger	§	Section
¨ (ö)	Dieresis	;	Semicolon
‡	Double dagger	˜	Tilde
. . .	Ellipsis points	___	Underscore
!	Exclamation point	/	Virgule (*also,* Solidus, Diagonal)

ROMAN NUMERALS

I	1	XI	11	XXX	30	CCC	300
II	2	XII	12	XL	40	CD	400
III	3	XIII	13	L	50	D	500
IV	4	XIV	14	LX	60	DC	600
V	5	XV	15	LXX	70	DCC	700
VI	6	XVI	16	LXXX	80	DCCC	800
VII	7	XVII	17	XC	90	CM	900
VIII	8	XVIII	18	C	100	M	1,000
IX	9	XIX	19	CC	200	MM	2,000
X	10	XX	20				

General Rules for Roman Numerals

1. Repeating a letter repeats its value: XX = 20; CCC = 300.

2. A letter placed after one of greater value adds thereto: VIII = 8; DC = 600.

3. A letter placed before one of greater value subtracts therefrom: IX = 9; CM = 900.

4. A dash line over a numeral multiplies the value by 1,000. Thus $\overline{X}$ = 10,000; $\overline{L}$ = 50,000; $\overline{C}$ = 100,000; $\overline{D}$ = 500,000; $\overline{M}$ = 1,000,000; $\overline{CLIX}$ = 159,000; $\overline{DLIX}$ = 559,000.

ABBREVIATIONS

Abbreviation style varies considerably among businesses, but the trend is toward lowercase letters and few or no periods, unless the period is needed to distinguish an abbreviation (such as *in.* for *inch*) from an actual word (such as the preposition *in*).

Although the use of abbreviations is increasing in technical and specialized writing, it is decreasing in formal or general writing. Follow the preferred style in your office.

General Abbreviations

a to oc	attached to other correspondence
aa	always afloat; author's alteration(s)
a&a	additions and amendments
aap	advise if able to proceed; affirmative action program
aar, AAR	against all risks
a/c	account; air conditioning
A/C	account current
a/c pay.	accounts payable
a/c rec.	accounts receivable
acv	actual cash value
a&d	accounting and disbursing; ascending and descending
a/d	after date
ad fin.	to the end (Latin: *ad finem*)
ad inf.	to infinity (Latin: *ad infinitum*)
ad int.	in the meantime (Latin: *ad interim*)
ad loc.	to or at this place (Latin: *ad locum*)
adsc	average daily service charge
Adt	Atlantic daylight time
ad val., a/v	according to value (Latin: *ad valorem*)
aec	additional extended coverage; at earliest convenience
afc	average fixed cost
ag.	agricultural; agriculture
agb	any good brand
agi	adjusted gross income; annual general inspection

a&i	abstracting and indexing; accident and indemnity
aia	advise if available
AIDS	acquired immune deficiency syndrome
aka	also known as
ald	a later date; acceptable limit for dispersion
a.m.	before noon (Latin: *ante meridiem*)
a&m	agricultural and mechanical; ancient and modern; architectural and mechanical
amr	automatic message routing
an.	above named; annual; arrival notice (shipping)
a/o	account of
aod	as of date
ap	additional premium
a/p	authority to pay
a/r	all risks; against all risks (marine insurance)
as.	at sight
a/s	after sight; alongside
Asl	American sign language
ast	absolute space time
Ast	Atlantic standard time
At	Atlantic time
A/t	American terms (grain trade)
ata	actual time of arrival; air to air
ATM	automated teller machine
atv	all-terrain vehicle
av	acid value; assessed valuation; audiovisual
a/w	actual weight; all-water; all-weather
awol, AWOL	absent without leave; absent without official leave
b.	born; brother
b&b	bed and board; bed and breakfast
b/c	bales of cotton; bills for collection; birth control; broadcast
B.C.	before Christ
bd	bank draft

b/d	barrels per day; brought down (accounting)
b/e, B/E	bill of exchange; bill of entry (bookkeeping)
bf	backfeed; bold face
b/f	black female; brought forward (bookkeeping)
b/l, B/L	bill of lading
bo	back order; blackout; body odor; branch office; buyer's option
b/o	back order; brought over (accounting); budget outlay
bop	balance of payments; best operating procedure
b/p, B/P	bills payable; bill of parcels
b/r, B/R	bills receivable
bs	backspace
b/s, B/S	bill of sale; bill of sight
b/st	bill of sight
bv	book value
b.w.	please turn over (German: *bitte wenden*)
b/w	black and white; bread and water
c	about; calorie; candle; carat; cent; century; chapter; child
C	centigrade
cad.	cash against documents; computer-aided design; contract-award date
CAD	computer-aided design
cad/cam, CAD/CAM	computer-aided design/computer-aided manufacturing
caf	cost, assurance, and freight
cap.	client assessment package; computer-aided production
CB	citizen's band (radio)
cbd	cash before delivery
cbx, CBX	computerized branch exchange; computerized business exchange
cc	carbon copy; chief complaint; color code; command and control

c&d	collection and delivery
c/d	carried down; cash against documents
CD	certificate of deposit
cdst	central daylight saving time
cdt	central daylight time
ceo	chief executive officer
cf.	compare (Latin: *confer*)
c&f	cost and freight
c/f	carried forward (bookkeeping)
cfi	cost, freight, and insurance
cfo	cost for orders
c&i	cost and insurance
c/l	cash letter
c&lc	capital and lowercase (small) leters
cn	credit note; consignment note; circular note
c/o	care of; carried over (bookkeeping); cash order; complains/complaints of
c.o.d., C.O.D.	cash on delivery
cola, COLA	cost-of-living adjustment; cost-of-living allowance
cos	cash on shipment
CPA	certified public accountant
cpi, CPI	consumer price index
CPLS	certified professional legal secretary
CPS	certified professional secretary
crt, CRT	cathode ray tube
c&sc	caps and small caps (capital and small capital letters)
cst	central standard time
ct	central time
c/t	certificate of title
cv	chief value
cwo	cash without order
d	daughter; day; degree; died
d/a	deposit account
db.	debit
dba	doing business as/at
d&c	dilation and curettage

dd	days after date; deferred delivery; delayed delivery; double draft; drydock; due date
df	dead freight
dl	demand loan
dlo	dispatch loading only
dn	debit note
d/n, D/N	debit note
do.	ditto (the same); delivery order
dos	date of sale
dp	data processing; deal pending; departure point; dewpoint; direct part; displaced person; distribution point
dr.	debit; debtor; doctor; dram; drawer; drill; drive
d/s	days after sight
dst	daylight saving time
dtp, DTP	desktop publishing
d/v	declared value
D.V.	God willing (Latin: *Deo volente*)
dwi	driving while intoxicated
eaon	except as otherwise noted
edp, EDP	electronic data processing
edt	eastern daylight time
ee	errors excepted; eye and ear
EE	Early English
eeo	equal employment opportunity
efa	essential fatty acids
e.g.	for example (Latin: *exempli gratia*)
emp	end-of-month payment
eo	by authority of his or her office (Latin: *ex officio*)
eod	every other day
eoe	equal opportunity employer
e&oe	errors and omissions excepted
eoph	except as otherwise provided herein
Esl	English as a second language
est	eastern standard time; electroshock therapy

et	eastern time; educational therapy; elapsed time; electric/electronic typewriter; extraterrestrial
eta	estimated time of arrival
et al.	and elsewhere (Latin: *et alibi*); and others (Latin: *et alia*)
etc.	and so on; and so forth (Latin: *et cetera*)
et seq.	and following (Latin: *et sequens*)
f	family; farthing; father; female
f.	folio; following page
F	Fahrenheit
f/b	feedback; female black; front to back
f&d	freight and demurrage (shipping)
ff.	following (after a numeral)
fifo	first in, first out
filo	first in, last out
fio	free in and out
fka	formerly known as
fl.	flourished (Latin: *floruit*)
foa	free of all average (shipping)
fob	free on board
foc	free of charge
fod	free of damage
fp	floating (or open) policy; fully paid (premium)
ft	free of tax; free trade; full terms
fv.	back of the page (Latin: *folio verso*)
fx	foreign exchange
FY	fiscal year
fyi, FYI	for your information
gnp, GNP	gross national product
hab. corp.	may you have the body (Latin: *habeas corpus*)
hc	hard copy
i&a	indexing and abstracting
ibid.	in the same place (Latin: *ibidem*)
id.	the same (Latin: *idem*)
i.e.	that is (Latin: *id est*)
i/o	in and/or over; input/output; instead of
i&o	input and output

IOU	I owe you
IQ	import quota; intelligence quotient
i.q.e.d.	that which was to be proved (Latin: *id quod erat demonstrandum*)
ISBN	International Standard Book Number
j.	journal
kia, KIA	killed in action
k-o, KO	knockout
l.	line
lc	lowercase (small letters)
lf	lightface; ledger folio
lifo	last in, first out
lmac	let me see correspondence
lp, LP	long play
ls, LS	place of the seal (Latin: *locus sigilli*)
m, M	male; married; masculine; noon (French: *meridies*)
mad., MAD	mind-altering drug; mutual(ly) assured destruction
mbo, MBO	management by objectives
Mesd.	Ladies (French: *Mesdames*)
Messrs.	Gentlemen (French: *Messieurs*)
Mgr.	Monseigneur (French: *Monsignor*); Monsignore (Italian: *Monsignor*)
mia, MIA	missing in action
Mlle.	Miss (French: *Mademoiselle*)
Mlles.	Misses (French: *Mademoiselles*)
m.m.	with the necessary changes (Latin: *mutatis mutandis*)
Mme.	Missus (French: *Madame*)
Mmes.	Ladies (French: *Mesdames*)
MP	member of Parliament; military police; mounted police
ms.	manuscript
mss.	manuscripts
mst	mean solar time; mountain standard time
mt	mountain time
n	note; number
n.	net; note; number
n/a	no account (banking)

NA, N/A	not available
n.b., N.B.	note well (Latin: *nota bene*)
n/c	no charge; numerical control
ncv	no commercial value
nd	no date
ne	not exceeding
nes	not elsewhere specified
nf, n/f, N/F	no funds
n/o	in the name of (finance); no orders (banking)
nol. pros.	do not want to prosecute (Latin: *nolle prosequi*)
non obs.	notwithstanding (Latin: *non obstante*)
non seq.	it does not follow (Latin: *non sequitor*)
nop	not otherwise provided for
nos	not otherwise specified
np	net proceeds; no place; no publisher; notary public; note payable
n.p.	no place; no publisher
ns	new series; not specified
n.s.	new series
NS, N.S.	new style
nsf	not sufficient funds
N/t	new terms
ntp	no title page
ob.	died (Latin: *obiit*)
od	on demand; overdraft (banking)
oe	omissions excepted
OE	Old English
oo	on order
o/o	order of
op. cit.	in the work cited (Latin: *opere citato*)
os	old series; operating system; out of stock
o.s.	old series
o/s	out of stock
OS	old style; on sample; one side
O.S.	old style
ot	overtime
ow	one way
p.	page

pa	private account; particular average; power of attorney
pabx, PABX	private automatic branch exchange
pbx, PBX	private branch exchange
pc	percent; postcard; petty cash
pd	per diem
p&i	principal and interest
p.m.	afternoon (Latin: *post meridiem*)
pn	promissory note
p/n	please note
po, PO	post office
por	payable on receipt
pp	parcel post
pp.	pages
pro tem.	for the time being (Latin: *pro tempore*)
P.S.	written after (Latin: *post scriptum*)
Pst	Pacific standard time
Pt	Pacific time
pto	please turn over
PX	please exchange; post exchange; private exchange
q.e.d.	that which was to be proved or demonstrated (Latin: *quod erat demonstrandum*)
q.v.	which see (Latin: *quod vide*)
r	recto; reigned
rop	run of paper; run of press
rp	return premium; reply paid
Rsvp	please reply (French: *répondez s'il vous plaît*)
R.s.v.p.	please reply (French: *répondez s'il vous plaît*)
r&t	rail and truck
s	son; substantive; second
/s/	signed
sa	subject to approval; safe arrival; without year (Latin: *sine anno*); the year (Latin: *sub anno*)
sae	self-addressed envelope
SALT	Strategic Arms Limitation Talks

sase	self-addressed stamped envelope
s/b	statement of billing
sc	separate; small caps (small capital letters); statistical control
sd	without a day being named (Latin: *sine die*); sight draft
sf	sinking fund
s&l	savings and loan
smsa, SMSA	standard metropolitan statistical area
so	seller's option; shipping order; ship's option
sop, SOP	standard operating procedure
ss	namely (Latin: *scilicet*)
st.	let it (crossed-out copy) stand (Latin: *stet*)
t, T	temperature
td	time deposit
tf	till forbidden (advertising)
tl	time loan
tlc, TLC	tender loving care
u.	university
uc	uppercase (capital letters)
ufo, UFO	unidentified flying object
u&lc	upper and lowercase (capital and small letters)
u.s.	as above (Latin: *ut supra*)
u/w	underwriter
v.	value; verb; verse; verso; versus
v.i.	see below (Latin: *vide infra*)
viz.	namely (Latin: *videlicet*)
vv	vice versa
wa	with average (insurance); will advise
WATS	wide-area telephone/ telecommunications service
wf	wrong font
w/o	without
woc	without compensation
wp	will proceed; without prejudice; word processing; working paper; working party

xp	express paid
z	zero; zone

Technical Abbreviations

a	ampere; arc; atto (prefix: one-quintillionth)
Å	angstrom
abm, ABM	automated batch mixing
abort	abandon activity
ac	alternating current; automatic analog computer; axiocervical
ACC	accumulator
a/d	analog to digital
ADC	analog-to-digital converter
ADDR	address
ADR	adder
ADV	advance
agz	actual ground zero
ah, a-h	ampere hour
Ah	ampere-hour; hyperopic astigmatism
ALGOL	Algebraically Oriented Language; Algorithmic Language
alphanumeric	alphabetical and numerical
alt.	alternator; altimeter
amp.	ampere; amplification; amplifier; amplitude
amr, AMR	automatic message routing
AOC	automatic output control
aoi	angle of incidence
APT	Automatic Programmed Tools (language)
arcos	arc cosine
are., ARE	air reactor experiment
ASCII	American Standard Code for Information Interchange
ASR	answer, send, receive
ast	absolute space time
at., AT	ampere-ton; ampere-turn
at. no.	atomic number
at. vol.	atomic volume

at. wt.	atomic weight
av.	average; avoirdupois
avdp.	avoirdupois
ax.	axial; axes; axiom; axis
az.	azimuth
BAM	basic access method
bar.	barometer; barometric; base address register; buffer address register
BAR	buffer address register
BASIC	Beginner's All-Purpose Symbolic Instruction
BC	binary code
bev, BeV	billion electron volts
bfr	buffer
bhp	boiler horsepower; brake horsepower
bi., BI	binary
bit	binary digit
bn, BN	binary number (system)
bof, BOF	beginning of file
BOS	basic operating system
bot, BOT	beginning of tape
bps	bits per second; bytes per second
bs	backspace; binary subtraction
BS	backspace
btu	basic transmission unit; British thermal unit
Btu, BTU	British thermal unit
bu.	bushel
c	calorie (large); carbohydrates; centi (prefix: one-hundredth); coefficient; computer; cycle; speed of light
C	calculated weight; candle; Celsius; Centigrade
cad.	cartridge-activated device; computer-aided design
CAD	computer-aided design
cad/cam, CAD/CAM	computer-aided design/computer-aided manufacturing
cal	computer-aided learning; conversational algebraic language

cal.	calorie (small)
cam.	central address memory; computer-addressed memory; computer-aided manufacturing
CAM	computer-aided manufacturing
CAN	cancel
Cd	coefficient of drag
cg	center of gravity; centigram
c-h	candle-hour
char., CHAR	character
cl	centiliter
clu_2	central logic unit
cm^2	square centimeter
CMND	command
COBOL	Common Business-Oriented Language
coef.	coefficient
cos.	cosine
cot.	cotangent
cp/m	control program/microcomputers
cpr	cardiopulmonary resuscitation
CPU	central processing unit
crt, CRT	cathode-ray tube
CTRL	control
cbu.	control unit busy
cv	coefficient of variation
cwt	centum weight; counterweight; hundredweight
cx	central exchange; control transmitter
CX	central exchange
cyb.	cybernetics
d	day; deci (prefix: one-tenth)
da	deka (prefix: ten); density altitude; drift angle
dag	dekagram
dal	dekaliter
dam.	dekameter; direct-access method
DAM	direct-access method
dav	data above voice
db	decibel; diode block
dB	decibel

dbu, dBu	decibel unit
dde	direct data entry
del., DEL	delete
dg	decigram
diam.	diameter
dl	data link; deciliter
d/l	data link
DMA	direct memory access
do.	diamine oxidase; dissolved oxygen
dos, DOS	disk operating system
dov, DOV	data over voice
dp	data processing; dewpoint; diametral pitch; diffusion pressure
dr.	dram
dwt	deadweight ton; pennyweight
dyn.	dyne
ecr	energy consumption rate
edp, EDP	electronic data processing
eer	energy-efficiency ratio
efi	electronic fuel injection
ekg, EKG	electrocardiogram
emf	electromotive force
Emos	Earth's mean orbital speed
eo, EO	end of operation
eob, EOB	end of block (character)
eof, EOF	end of file
eoj, EOJ	end of job
eolb, EOLB	end-of-line block
eom, EOM	end of message
eor, EOR	end of record; end of run
eot, EOT	end of tape; end of transmission
esc, ESC	escape (character)
est	electroshock therapy
etb, ETB	end-of-transmission block (character)
etx, ETX	end of text (character)
f	farad; fathom; feedback; feet
F	Fahrenheit; farad; fathom; feedback
f/b	feedback; front to back (ratio)
fc	foot-candle
ff, FF	form feed

fL	foot-lambert
fl. dr.	fluid dram
fl. oz.	fluid ounce
fl. pt.	fluid pint
FORTRAN, Fortran	Formula Translation (language)
ft.	foot; feet
ft.^{2}	square foot; square feet
ft.-lb.	foot-pound
G	gauss; giga (prefix: one billion)
gal.	gallon
Gb	gilbert
gc	geographical coordinates; gigacycle; gyrocompass
GDT	graphic display terminal
gev, GeV	gigaelectronvolt
g gr.	great gross
GHz	gigahertz
gill	gill
gr.	grain; gross
GV, Gv	gigavolt
gw	gigawatt; ground wave
Gw	gigawatt
h	hectare; hecto (prefix: one hundred); height; hour
H	henry
ha	hectare; hour angle; hour aspect; humic acid
hepa	high-efficiency particulate air (filter)
HSP	high-speed printer
hz, Hz	hertz
ic	input circuit; integrated circuit
i gal., imp. gal.	imperial gallon
in.	inch
i/o, I/O	input/output
i/p, I/P	input
i&r	information and retrieval
isr, ISR	information storage and retrieval
J	joule

k	about one thousand (computer-storage capacity); carat (karat); Kelvin; kilo (prefix: one thousand); knot
K	about one thousand (computer storage)
kb	keyboard; kilobit; kilobyte
kc	kilocycle
kg	kilogram
kG	kilogauss
khz, kHz	kilohertz
kΩ	kilohm
kt	karat (caret); kiloton
kv, kV	kilovolt
kva, kVa	kilovoltampere
kw, kW	kilowatt
l	line; liter; locus
L	lambert
LAN	local area network
lb.	pound
lbs.	pounds
lcd	liquid crystal display; lowest common denominator
LCD	liquid crystal display
lm	lumen
lms	least mean square; lumen second; lunar mass spectrometer
log.	logarithm
lsc	least significant character
lsd	least significant digit
m	mega (prefix: one million); meter; milli (prefix: one-thousandth)
m^2	square meter
ma, mA	milliampere
mc	magnetic center; master control; megacycle; metric carat; millicycle
mcg	microgram
mf	medium frequency; millifarad
mF	millifarad
mg	megagram; milligram
mG	milligauss
mh	magnetic heading; millihenry

mH	millihenry
mhz, mHz	megahertz; millihertz
mi.	mile
mK	millikelvin
mL	millilambert
mm	megameter; millimeter; millimicron
modem	modulator-demodulator
mΩ	megaohm
mr, mR	milliroentgen
ms	mean square; metric system; millisecond
msc	most significant character
msd	most significant digit
mv	mean variation; megavolt; millivolt
mV	megavolt; millivolt
mw	megawatt; milliwatt; molecular weight
mW	megawatt; milliwatt
μ	micro (prefix: one-millionth)
μg	microgram
μm	micrometer
n	nano (prefix: one-billionth)
N	newton
NAM	network access machine
NC	numerical control
NL	new line
ns	nanosecond
ocr, OCR	optical character reader; optical character recognition
os	oil solvent; operating system
OS	operating system
oz.	ounce
p	pico (prefix: one-trillionth); probability
Pa	pascal
pot.	point of tangency; potentiometer
pW	picowatt
ql	quintal
qt.	quart
ram., RAM	random-access memory
rem, REM	recognition memory
rms	root mean square
rom, ROM	read-only memory

s/c	short circuit
sop, SOP	standard operating procedure
sq. rt.	square root
t	tonne (metric); troy
T	tera (prefix: one trillion)
tan.	tangent
uhf, UHF	ultrahigh frequency
USASCII	USA Standard Code for Information Interchange
uv, u-v	ultraviolet
v, V	volt
VDT	video display terminal
w, W	watt
xmt, XMT	transmit
yd.	yard
z	zero
zn	zenith

Organizations

AA	Addicts Anonymous; Alcoholics Anonymous
AAA	American Automobile Association
ABA	American Bankers Association; American Bar Association
ABC	American Broadcasting Company; Audit Bureau of Circulation
AEC	Atomic Energy Commission
AFL-CIO	American Federation of Labor and Congress of Industrial Organizations
AHA	American Heart Association; American Historical Association
AIA	Aerospace Industries Association
AIB	American Institute of Banking
AID	Agency for International Development
AMA	American Management Association; American Maritime Association; American Medical Association; Automobile Manufacturers Association
AP	Associated Press

ARC	American (National) Red Cross
ASA	American Standards Association; American Statistical Association
ASE	American Stock Exchange
ASTA	American Society of Travel Agents
BBB	Better Business Bureau
BIAA	Bureau of Inter-American Affairs
BLS	Bureau of Labor Statistics
BTA	Board of Tax Appeals
CAA	Civil Aeronautics Administration
CAP	Civil Air Patrol
CAB	Civil Aeronautics Board
CBO	Congressional Budget Office
CCC	Commodity Credit Corporation
CEA	Commodity Exchange Administration
CEC	Commodity Exchange Commission
CED	Committee for Economic Development
CHR	Commission on Human Rights
CIA	Central Intelligence Agency
CMEA	Council for Mutual Economic Assistance
CORE	Congress of Racial Equality
CPSC	Consumer Product Safety Commission
CSC	Civil Service Commission
DOD	Department of Defense
EEC	European Economic Community
EEOC	Equal Employment Opportunity Commission
EPA	Environmental Protection Agency
FAA	Federal Aviation Agency
FBI	Federal Bureau of Investigation
FCA	Farm Credit Administration
FDA	Food and Drug Administration
FDIC	Federal Deposit Insurance Corporation
FHA	Federal Housing Administration
FMC	Federal Maritime Commission
FPC	Federal Power Commission
FRB	Federal Reserve Board; Federal Reserve Bank
FRS	Federal Reserve System
FTC	Federal Trade Commission

GAO	General Accounting Office; Government Accounting Office
GPO	Government Printing Office
GSA	General Services Administration
HUD	Housing and Urban Development (Department of)
ICC	Interstate Commerce Commission
IFC	International Finance Corporation
IMF	International Monetary Fund
INP	International News Photos
INS	International News Service
IRO	International Refugee Organization
IRS	Internal Revenue Service
ISO	International Standards Organization
IWW	Industrial Workers of the World
KC	Knights of Columbus
KKK	Ku Klux Klan
LWV	League of Women Voters
NAACP	National Association for the Advancement of Colored People
NALS	National Association of Legal Secretaries
NAM	National Association of Manufacturers
NAS	National Academy of Sciences
NASA	National Aeronautics and Space Administration
NATO	North Atlantic Treaty Organization
NBS	National Broadcasting Service
NEA	National Education Association
NGS	National Geodetic Survey; National Geographic Society
NIH	National Institutes of Health
NLRB	National Labor Relations Board
NMB	National Mediation Board
NOW	National Organization for Women
NPS	National Park Service
NRC	Nuclear Regulatory Commission
NSC	National Security Council
NSF	National Science Foundation
OAS	Organization of American States

OECD	Organization for Economic Cooperation and Development
OEO	Office of Economic Opportunity
PC	Peace Corps
PHA	Public Housing Administration
PHS	Public Health Service
PSI	Professional Secretaries International
REA	Rural Electrification Administration
ROTC	Reserve Officers' Training Corps
RRAB	Railroad Retirement Board
SAG	Screen Actors Guild
SBA	Small Business Administration
SEATO	Southeast Asia Treaty Organization
SEC	Securities and Exchange Commission
SGO	Surgeon General's Office
SPCA	Society for the Prevention of Cruelty to Animals
SSA	Social Security Administration
SSS	Selective Service System
TC	Tax Court (of the United States)
TVA	Tennessee Valley Authority
UN	United Nations
UNESCO	United Nations Educational, Social, and Cultural Organization
UNICEF	United Nations Children's Fund
UNRRA	United Nations Relief and Rehabilitation Administration
UPI	United Press International
UPS	United Parcel Service
USDA	United States Department of Agriculture
USIA	United States Information Agency
VA	Veterans Administration
VFW	Veterans of Foreign Wars
VISTA	Volunteers in Service to America
WHO	World Health Organization

Academic Degrees

A.A.	associate in accounting; associate in arts
A.B.	bachelor of arts
A.M.	master of arts

A.Sc.	associate in science
B.A.	bachelor of arts
B.Ag.	bachelor of agriculture
B.Ar.	bachelor of architecture
B.B.A.	bachelor of business administration
B.C.	bachelor of chemistry
B.C.E.	bachelor of chemical/civil engineering
B.C.L.	bachelor of civil law
B.E.	bachelor of education
B.E.E.	bachelor of electrical engineering
B.F.	bachelor of finance/forestry
B.F.A.	bachelor of fine arts
B.L.S.	bachelor of library science
B.Lit(t).	bachelor of literature/letters
B.M.	bachelor of medicine/music
B.Mus.	bachelor of music
B.P.E.	bachelor of physical education
B.S., B.Sc.	bachelor of science
B.T.	bachelor of theology
Ch.D.	doctor of chemistry
D.Ag.	doctor of agriculture
D.C.L.	doctor of canon law/civil law
D.D.	doctor of divinity
D.D.S.	doctor of dental science
D.F.A.	doctor of fine arts
D.Lit(t).	doctor of literature/letters
D.L.S.	doctor of library science
D.M.D.	doctor of dental medicine
D.Med.	doctor of medicine
D.M.V.	doctor of veterinary medicine
D.Mus.	doctor of music
D.O.	doctor of osteopathy
D.P.	doctor of pharmacy/podiatry
D.Pharm.	doctor of pharmacy
Dr.Jr.	doctor of law
D.S., D.Sc.	doctor of science
D.T., D.Th.	doctor of theology
D.V.M.	doctor of veterinary medicine
Ed.B.	bachelor of education
Ed.D.	doctor of education

Ed.M.	master of education
Eng.D.	doctor of engineering
J.C.D.	doctor of canon law/civil law
J.D.	juris doctor; doctor of jurisprudence; doctor of law(s)
Jur.D.	doctor of law
L.B.	bachelor of letters
L.H.D.	doctor of humanities
Lit(t).B.	bachelor of literature/letters
Lit(t).D.	doctor of literature/letters
LL.D.	doctor of laws
LL.M.	master of laws
M.A.	master of arts
M.Ag.	master of agriculture
M.B.A.	master of business administration
M.C.L.	master of civil law
M.D.	doctor of medicine
M.E.E.	master of electrical engineering
M.Ed.	master of education
M.I.E.	master of industrial engineering
M.L.S.	master of library science
M.P.E.	master of physical education
M.Ph.	master of philosophy
M.S., M.Sc.	master of science
M.Th.	master of theology
Mus.B., Mus.Bac.	bachelor of music
Mus.D.	doctor of music
Phar.B.	bachelor of pharmacy
Phar.D., Pharm.D.	doctor of pharmacy
Phar.M.	master of pharmacy
Ph.B.	bachelor of philosophy
Ph.D.	doctor of philosophy
Pod.D.	doctor of podiatry
S.B., Sc.B.	bachelor of science
Sc.D., Sci.D.	doctor of science
Sc.M.	master of science
S.J.D.	doctor of juridical science
S.M., Sc.M.	master of science
Th.D.	doctor of theology
V.M.D.	doctor of veterinary medicine

U.S. Postal Service Abbreviations

Traditional and Two-Letter
State and Territory Abbreviations

	Traditional Abbreviation	Postal Abbreviation
Alabama, State of	Ala.	AL
Alaska, State of	Alas.	AK
American Samoa	Amer. Samoa	AS
Arizona, State of	Ariz.	AZ
Arkansas, State of	Ark.	AR
California, State of	Calif.	CA
Canal Zone	C.Z.	CZ
Colorado, State of	Colo.	CO
Connecticut, State of	Conn.	CT
Delaware, State of	Del.	DE
District of Columbia	D.C.	DC
Florida, State of	Fla.	FL
Georgia, State of	Ga.	GA
Guam	Guam	GU
Hawaii, State of	Hawaii	HI
Idaho, State of	Ida.	ID
Illinois, State of	Ill.	IL
Indiana, State of	Ind.	IN
Iowa, State of	Iowa	IA
Kansas, State of	Kans.	KS
Kentucky, Commonwealth of	Ky.	KY
Louisiana, State of	La.	LA
Maine, State of	Maine	ME
Maryland, State of	Md.	MD
Massachusetts, Commonwealth of	Mass.	MA
Michigan, State of	Mich.	MI
Minnesota, State of	Minn.	MN
Mississippi, State of	Miss.	MS
Missouri, State of	Mo.	MO
Montana, State of	Mont.	MT
Nebraska, State of	Nebr.	NE
Nevada, State of	Nev.	NV
New Hampshire, State of	N.H.	NH
New Jersey, State of	N.J.	NJ
New Mexico, State of	N.M.	NM
New York, State of	N.Y.	NY
North Carolina, State of	N.C.	NC
North Dakota, State of	N.D.	ND
Northern Mariana Islands	No. Mariana Is.	CM
Ohio, State of	Ohio	OH
Oklahoma, State of	Okla.	OK
Oregon, State of	Oreg.	OR
Pennsylvania, Commonwealth of	Pa.	PA

	Traditional Abbreviation	Postal Abbreviation
Puerto Rico	P.R.	PR
Rhode Island and Providence Plantations, State of	R.I.	RI
South Carolina, State of	S.C.	SC
South Dakota, State of	S.D.	SD
Tennessee, State of	Tenn.	TN
Texas, State of	Tex.	TX
Trust Territory	Trust Terr.	TT
Utah, State of	Utah	UT
Vermont, State of	Vt.	VT
Virgin Islands	V.I.	VI
Virginia, Commonwealth of	Va.	VA
Washington, State of	Wash.	WA
West Virginia, State of	W.Va.	WV
Wisconsin, State of	Wis.	WI
Wyoming, State of	Wyo.	WY

Street and Place-Name Abbreviations

Word	Abbreviation	Word	Abbreviation
Academy	ACAD	Clear	CLR
Air Force Base	AFB	Cliffs	CLFS
Agency	AGNCY	Club	CLB
Airport	ARPRT	College	CLG
Alley	ALY	Common	CMM
Annex	ANX	Corner	COR
Arcade	ARC	Corners	CORS
Arsenal	ARSL	Course	CRSE
Avenue	AVE	Court	CT
Bayou	BYU	Courts	CTS
Beach	BCH	Cove	CV
Bend	BND	Creek	CRK
Big	BG	Crescent	CRES
Black	BLK	Crossing	XING
Boulevard	BLVD	Dale	DL
Bluff	BLF	Dam	DM
Bottom	BTM	Depot	DPO
Branch	BR	Divide	DV
Bridge	BRG	Drive	DR
Brook	BRK	East	E
Burg	BG	Estates	EST
Bypass	BYP	Expressway	EXPY
Camp	CP	Extended	EXT
Canyon	CYN	Extension	EXT
Cape	CPE	Fall	FL
Causeway	CSWY	Falls	FLS

Word	Abbreviation	Word	Abbreviation
Center	CTR	Farms	FRMS
Central	CTL	Ferry	FRY
Church	CHR	Field	FLD
Churches	CHRS	Fields	FLDS
Circle	CIR	Flats	FLT
City	CY	Ford	FRD
Forest	FRST	Meeting	MTG
Forge	FRG	Memorial	MEM
Fork	FRK	Middle	MDL
Forks	FRKS	Mile	MLE
Fort	FT	Mill	ML
Fountain	FTN	Mills	MLS
Freeway	FWY	Mines	MNS
Furnace	FURN	Mission	MSN
Gardens	GDNS	Mound	MND
Gateway	GTWY	Mount	MT
Glen	GLN	Mountain	MTN
Grand	GRND	National	NAT
Great	GR	Naval Air Station	NAS
Green	GRN	Neck	NCK
Ground	GRD	New	NW
Grove	GRV	North	N
Harbor	HBR	Orchard	ORCH
Haven	HVN	Oval	OVAL
Heights	HTS	Palms	PLMS
High	HI	Park	PARK
Highlands	HGLDS	Parkway	PKY
Highway	HWY	Pass	PASS
Hill	HL	Path	PATH
Hills	HLS	Pike	PIKE
Hollow	HOLW	Pillar	PLR
Hospital	HOSP	Pines	PNES
Hot	H	Place	PL
House	HSE	Plain	PLN
Inlet	INLT	Plains	PLNS
Institute	INST	Plaza	PLZ
Island	IS	Port	PRT
Islands	IS	Point	PT
Isle	IS	Prairie	PR
Junction	JCT	Radial	RADL
Key	KY	Ranch	RNCH
Knolls	KNLS	Ranches	RNCHS
		Rapids	RPDS
Landing	LNDG	Resort	RESRT
Lake	LK	Rest	RST
Lakes	LKS	Ridge	RDG
Lane	LN	River	RIV
Light	LGT	Road	RD
Little	LTL	Rock	RK
Loaf	LF	Row	ROW
Locks	LCKS	Run	RUN
Lodge	LDG	Rural	R

Word	Abbreviation	Word	Abbreviation
Loop	LOOP	Saint	ST
Lower	LWR	Sainte	ST
Mall	MALL	San	SN
Manor	MNR	Santa	SN
Meadows	MDWS	Santo	SN
School	SCH	Tower	TWR
Seminary	SMNRY	Town	TWN
Shoal	SHL	Trace	TRCE
Shoals	SHLS	Track	TRAK
Shode	SDHD	Trail	TRL
Shore	SHR	Trailer	TRLR
Shores	SHRS	Tunnel	TUNL
Siding	SDG	Turnpike	TPKE
South	S	Upper	UPR
Space Flight Center	SFC	Union	UN
Speedway	SPDWY	University	UNIV
Spring	SPG		
Springs	SPGS	Valley	VLY
Spur	SPUR	Viaduct	VIA
Square	SQ	View	VW
State	ST	Village	VLG
Station	STA	Ville	VL
Street	ST	Vista	VIS
Stream	STRM	Walk	WALK
Sulphur	SLPHR	Water	WTR
Summit	SMT	Way	WAY
Switch	SWCH	Wells	WLS
Tannery	TNRY	West	W
Tavern	TVRN	White	WHT
Terminal	TERM	Works	WKS
Terrace	TER	Yards	YDS
Ton	TN		

CORRECT FORMS OF ADDRESS

U.S. Government Officials

Personage	Envelope and Inside Address (Add Org., City, State, Zip)	Formal Salutation	Informal Salutation	Formal Close	Informal Close	1. Spoken Address 2. Informal Introduction or Reference
The President	The President The White House	Mr. President:	Dear Mr. President:	Respectfully yours,	Very respectfully yours, *or* Sincerely yours,	1. Mr President *or* Sir 2. Not introduced (The President)
Former President of the United States[1]	The Honorable William R. Blank (local address)	Sir:	Dear Mr. Blank:	Respectfully yours,	Sincerly yours,	1. Mr. Blank *or* Sir 2. The Honorable John Blank
The Vice President of the United States	The Vice President United States Senate	Mr. Vice President:	Dear Mr. Vice President:	Very truly yours,	Sincerely yours,	1. Mr. Vice President *or* Sir 2. The Vice President
The Chief Justice of the United States Supreme Court	The Chief Justice The Supreme Court	Sir:	Dear Chief Justice: *or* Dear Chief Justice Blank:	Very truly yours,	Sincerely yours,	1. Chief Justice *or* Sir 2. The Chief Justice
Associate Justice of the United States Supreme Court	Justice Blank The Supreme Court	Sir:	Dear Justice Blank:	Very truly yours,	Sincerely yours,	1. Justice Blank *or* Sir 2. Justice Blank

Note: In this chart the form of address for a man is used throughout except where not applicable. To use the form of address for a woman in any of these positions, use the substitution *Madam* for *Sir* and *Mrs., Miss,* or *Ms.* for *Mr.* Thus Dear *Madam; Mrs.* Blank, Representative from New York; The Lieutenant Governor of Iowa, *Miss* Blank; The American Minister, *Ms.* Blank. The *Mr.* preceding a title becomes *Madam.* Thus *Madam* Secretary; *Madam* Ambassador. Use *Esquire* or *Esq.* in addressing a man or woman where appropriate. (For additional information, see chapter 10.) This chart lists accepted options for correct forms such as spoken address and introductions. For a detailed listing with additional options, consult a current guide to social usage, such as *Protocol* (Devon Publishing, latest edition).

1. If a former president has a title, such as *General of the Army,* address him by it.

U.S. Government Officials continued

Personage	Envelope and Inside Address (Add Org., City, State, Zip)	Formal Salutation	Informal Salutation	Formal Close	Informal Close	1. Spoken Address 2. Informal Introduction or Reference
Retired Justice of the United States Supreme Court	The Honorable William R. Blank Chief Justice of the United States Supreme Court	Sir:	Dear Chief Justice Blank:	Very truly yours,	Sincerely yours,	1. Chief Justice *or* Sir 2. Chief Justice Blank
The Speaker of the House of Representatives	The Honorable William R. Blank Speaker of the House of Representatives	Dear Mr. Speaker:	Dear Mr. Blank:	Very truly yours,	Sincerely yours,	1. Mr. Speaker *or* Mr. Blank 2. The Speaker of the House of Representatives, Mr. Blank
Former Speaker of the House of Representatives	The Honorable William R. Blank (local address)	Sir:	Dear Mr. Blank:	Very truly yours,	Sincerely yours,	1. Mr. Blank 2. Mr. Blank
Cabinet Officers addressed as "Secretary"[2]	The Honorable William R. Blank Secretary of State *If written from abroad:* The Honorable William R. Blank Secretary of State of the United States of America	Dear Mr. Secretary:	Dear Mr. Blank:	Very truly yours,	Sincerely yours,	1. Mr. Secretary *or* Mr. Blank 2. The Secretary of State, Mr. Blank
Former Cabinet Officer	The Honorable William R. Blank (local address)	Dear Mr. Blank:	Dear Mr. Blank:	Very truly yours,	Sincerely yours,	1. Mr. Blank 2. Mr. Blank

2. Titles for cabinet secretaries are Secretary of State; Secretary of the Treasury; Secretary of Defense; Secretary of Education; Secretary of Energy; Secretary of the Interior; Secretary of Agriculture; Secretary of Commerce; Secretary of Labor; Secretary of Health and Human Services; Secretary of Housing and Urban Development; Secretary of Transportation.

U.S. Government Officials *continued*

Personage	Envelope and Inside Address (Add Org., City, State, Zip)	Formal Salutation	Informal Salutation	Formal Close	Informal Close	1. Spoken Address 2. Informal Introduction or Reference
Postmaster General	The Honorable William R. Blank Postmaster General	Dear Mr. Postmaster General:	Dear Mr. Blank:	Very truly yours,	Sincerely yours,	1. Mr. Postmaster General *or* Mr. Blank 2. The Postmaster General, Mr. Blank
The Attorney General	The Honorable William R. Blank Attorney General of the United States	Dear Mr. Attorney General:	Dear Mr. Blank:	Very truly yours,	Sincerely yours,	1. Mr. Blank 2. The Attorney General, Mr. Blank *or* Mr. Blank
Under Secretary of a Department	The Honorable William R. Blank Under Secretary of Labor	Dear Mr. Under Secretary:	Dear Mr. Blank:	Very truly yours,	Sincerely yours,	1. Mr. Blank 2. Mr. Blank
United States Senator	The Honorable William R. Blank United States Senate	Sir:	Dear Senator Blank:	Very truly yours,	Sincerely yours,	1. Senator Blank *or* Senator 2. Senator Blank
Former Senator	The Honorable William R. Blank (local address)	Dear Sir:	Dear Mr. Blank:	Very truly yours,	Sincerely yours,	1. Senator Blank 2. The Honorable John Blank, former United States Senator from (state)

U.S. Government Officials *continued*

Personage	Envelope and Inside Address (Add Org., City, State, Zip)	Formal Salutation	Informal Salutation	Formal Close	Informal Close	1. Spoken Address 2. Informal Introduction or Reference
Senator-elect	The Honorable William R. Blank Senator-elect United States Senate	Dear Sir:	Dear Mr. Blank:	Very truly yours,	Sincerely yours,	1. Mr. Blank 2. Mr. Blank
Committee Chairman—United States Senate	The Honorable William R. Blank, Chairman Committee on Foreign Affairs United States Senate	Dear Mr. Chairman:	Dear Senator Blank:	Very truly yours,	Sincerely yours,	1. Senator Blank *or* Senator 2. Senator Blank
Subcommittee Chairman—United States Senate	The Honorable William R. Blank, Chairman Subcommittee on Foreign Affairs United States Senate	Dear Mr. Chairman:	Dear Senator Blank:	Very truly yours,	Sincerely yours,	1. Senator Blank *or* Senator 2. Senator Blank
United States Representative or Congressman[3]	The Honorable William R. Blank House of Representatives *When away from Washington, D.C.:* The Honorable William R. Blank (local address)	Sir:	Dear Mr. Blank:	Very truly yours,	Sincerely yours,	1. Mr. Blank 2. The Honorable Mr. Blank, Representative from New York *or* Mr. Blank

3. The official title of a "congressman" or "congresswoman" is *Representative.* Senators are also congressmen or congresswomen.

U.S. Government Officials continued

Personage	Envelope and Inside Address (Add Org., City, State, Zip)	Formal Salutation	Informal Salutation	Formal Close	Informal Close	1. Spoken Address 2. Informal Introduction or Reference
Former Representative	The Honorable William R. Blank (local address)	Dear Sir: *or* Dear Mr. Blank:	Dear Mr. Blank:	Very truly yours,	Sincerely yours,	1. Mr. Blank 2. Mr. Blank *or* The Honorable John Blank, former Representative from (state)
Territorial Delegate	The Honorable William R. Blank Delegate of (territory) House of Representatives	Dear Sir: *or* Dear Mr. Blank:	Dear Mr. Blank:	Very truly yours,	Sincerely yours,	1. Mr. Blank 2. Mr. Blank
Resident Commissioner	The Honorable William R. Blank Resident Commissioner from (territory) House of Representatives	Dear Sir: *or* Dear Mr. Blank:	Dear Mr. Blank:	Very truly yours,	Sincerely yours,	1. Mr. Blank 2. Mr. Blank
Directors or Heads of Independent Federal Offices, Agencies, Commissions, Organizations, etc.	The Honorable William R. Blank Director	Dear Mr. Director (Commissioner, etc.):	Dear Mr. Blank:	Very truly yours,	Sincerely yours,	1. Mr. Blank 2. Mr. Blank
Other High Officials of the United States	The Honorable William R. Blank Public Printer (Comptroller General of the United States)	Dear Sir: *or* Dear Mr. Blank:	Dear Mr. Blank:	Very truly yours,	Sincerely yours,	1. Mr. Blank 2. Mr. Blank

U.S. Government Officials continued

Personage	Envelope and Inside Address (Add Org., City, State, Zip)	Formal Salutation	Informal Salutation	Formal Close	Informal Close	1. Spoken Address 2. Informal Introduction or Reference
Secretary to the President	The Honorable William R. Blank Secretary to the President The White House	Dear Sir: or Dear Mr. Blank:	Dear Mr. Blank:	Very truly yours,	Sincerely yours,	1. Mr. Blank 2. Mr. Blank
Assistant Secretary to the President	The Honorable William R. Blank Assistant Secretary to the President The White House	Dear Sir: or Dear Mr. Blank:	Dear Mr. Blank:	Very truly yours,	Sincerely yours,	1. Mr. Blank 2. Mr. Blank
Press Secretary to the President	Mr. William R. Blank Press Secretary to the President The White House	Dear Sir: or Dear Mr. Blank:	Dear Mr. Blank:	Very truly yours,	Sincerely yours,	1. Mr. Blank 2. Mr. Blank

State and Local Government Officials

Governor of a State or Territory[1]	The Honorable William R. Blank Governor of (state)	Sir:	Dear Governor Blank:	Very truly yours,	Sincerely yours,	1. Governor Blank or Governor 2. Governor Blank or The Governor

1. The form of addressing governors varies in different states. The form given here is the one used in most states. In Massachusetts by law and in some other states by courtesy, the form is *His (Her) Excellency, the Governor of Massachusetts.*

State and Local Government Officials *continued*

Personage	Envelope and Inside Address (Add Org., City, State, Zip)	Formal Salutation	Informal Salutation	Formal Close	Informal Close	1. Spoken Address / 2. Informal Introduction or Reference
Acting Governor of a State or Territory	The Honorable William R. Blank Acting Governor of (state)	Sir:	Dear Mr. Blank:	Very truly yours,	Sincerely yours,	1. Mr. Blank 2. Mr. Blank
Lieutenant Governor	The Honorable William R. Blank Lieutenant Governor of (state)	Sir:	Dear Mr. Blank:	Very truly yours,	Sincerely yours,	1. Mr. Blank 2. Mr. Blank *or* The Honorable John Blank, Lieutenant Governor
Secretary of State	The Honorable William R. Blank Secretary of State of (state)	Dear Mr. Secretary:	Dear Mr. Blank:	Very truly yours,	Sincerely yours,	1. Mr. Blank *or* Sir 2. Mr. Blank
Attorney General	The Honorable William R. Blank Attorney General State of (state)	Dear Mr. Attorney General:	Dear Mr. Blank:	Very truly yours,	Sincerely yours,	1. Mr. Attorney General *or* Mr. Blank 2. Mr. Blank
President of the Senate of a State	The Honorable William R. Blank President of the Senate of the State of (state)	Sir:	Dear Mr. Blank:	Very truly yours,	Sincerely yours,	1. Mr. Blank 2. Mr. Blank
Speaker of the Assembly or The House of Representatives[2]	The Honorable William R. Blank Speaker of the Assembly of the State of (state)	Sir:	Dear Mr. Blank:	Very truly yours,	Sincerely yours,	1. Mr. Blank 2. The Speaker of the Assembly of the State of (state), Mr. Blank

2. In most states the lower branch of the legislature is the House of Representatives. The exceptions to this are New York, California, Wisconsin, and Nevada, where it is known as the Assembly; Maryland, Virginia, and West Virginia—the House of Delegates; New Jersey—the House of General Assembly.

State and Local Government Officials *continued*

Personage	Envelope and Inside Address (Add Org., City, State, Zip)	Formal Salutation	Informal Salutation	Formal Close	Informal Close	1. Spoken Address 2. Informal Introduction or Reference
Treasurer, Auditor, or Comptroller of a State	The Honorable William R. Blank Treasurer of (state)	Dear Sir:	Dear Mr. Blank:	Very truly yours,	Sincerely yours,	1. Mr. Blank 2. Mr. Blank
State Senator	The Honorable William R. Blank The Senate of (state)	Dear Sir:	Dear Senator Blank:	Very truly yours,	Sincerely yours,	1. Mr. Blank 2. Mr. Blank *or* The Honorable John Blank, (state) State Senator
State Representative, Assemblyman, or Delegate	The Honorable William R. Blank House of Delegates	Dear Sir:	Dear Mr. Blank:	Very truly yours,	Sincerely yours,	1. Mr. Blank 2. Mr. Blank *or* Delegate Blank
District Attorney	The Honorable William R. Blank District Attorney, Albany County County Courthouse	Dear Sir:	Dear Mr. Blank:	Very truly yours,	Sincerely yours,	1. Mr. Blank 2. Mr. Blank
Mayor of a city	The Honorable William R. Blank Mayor of (city)	Dear Sir:	Dear Mr. Mayor: *or* Dear Mayor Blank:	Very truly yours,	Sincerely yours,	1. Mayor Blank *or* Mr. Mayor *or* Sir 2. Mayor Blank
President of a Board of Commissioners	The Honorable William R. Blank, President Board of commissioners of the City of (city)	Dear Sir:	Dear Mr. Blank:	Very truly yours,	Sincerely yours,	1. Mr. Blank 2. Mr. Blank

State and Local Government Officials *continued*

Personage	Envelope and Inside Address (Add Org., City, State, Zip)	Formal Salutation	Informal Salutation	Formal Close	Informal Close	1. Spoken Address 2. Informal Introduction or Reference
City Attorney, City Counsel, Corporation Counsel	The Honorable William R. Blank, City Attorney (City Counsel, Corporation Counsel)	Dear Sir:	Dear Mr. Blank:	Very truly yours,	Sincerely yours,	1. Mr. Blank 2. Mr. Blank
Alderman	Alderman William R. Blank City Hall	Dear Sir:	Dear Mr. Blank:	Very truly yours,	Sincerely yours,	1. Mr. Blank 2. Mr. Blank

Court Officials

Personage	Envelope and Inside Address (Add Org., City, State, Zip)	Formal Salutation	Informal Salutation	Formal Close	Informal Close	1. Spoken Address 2. Informal Introduction or Reference
Chief Justice[1] *of a State Supreme Court*	The Honorable William R. Blank Chief Justice Supreme Court of the State of (state)[2]	Sir:	Dear Mr. Chief Justice:	Very truly yours,	Sincerely yours,	1. Mr. Chief Justice *or* Sir 2. Chief Justice Blank *or* The Honorable John Blank, Chief Justice of the Supreme Court of the State of (state)
Associate Justice of a State Supreme Court	The Honorable William R. Blank Associate Justice Supreme Court of the State of (state)	Sir:	Dear Justice Blank:	Very truly yours,	Sincerely yours,	1. Justice Blank *or* Sir 2. Justice Blank
Presiding Justice	The Honorable William R. Blank Presiding Justice Appellate Division Supreme Court of (state)	Sir:	Dear Justice Blank:	Very truly yours,	Sincerely yours,	1. Justice Blank *or* Sir 2. Justice Blank

1. If his or her official title is *Chief Judge* substitute *Chief Judge* for *Chief Justice*, but never use *Mr., Mrs., Miss,* or *Ms.* with *Chief Judge* or *Judge.*
2. Substitute here the appropriate name of the court. For example, the highest court in New York State is called the Court of Appeals.

Court Officials continued

Personage	Envelope and Inside Address (Add Org., City, State, Zip)	Formal Salutation	Informal Salutation	Formal Close	Informal Close	1. Spoken Address 2. Informal Introduction or Reference
Judge of a Court[3]	The Honorable William R. Blank / Judge of the United States District Court for the Southern District of (state)	Sir:	Dear Judge Blank:	Very truly yours,	Sincerely yours,	1. Judge Blank / 2. Judge Blank
Clerk of a Court	William R. Blank, Esq. / Clerk of the Superior Court of (state)	Dear Sir:	Dear Mr. Blank:	Very truly yours,	Sincerely yours,	1. Mr. Blank / 2. Mr. Blank

3. Not applicable to judges of the U.S. Supreme Court.

U.S. Diplomatic Representatives

Personage	Envelope and Inside Address (Add Org., City, State, Zip)	Formal Salutation	Informal Salutation	Formal Close	Informal Close	1. Spoken Address 2. Informal Introduction or Reference
American Ambassador[1]	The Honorable William R. Blank / The American Ambassador to (country)	Sir:	Dear Mr. Ambassador: or Dear Ambassador Blank:	Very truly yours,	Sincerely yours,	1. Mr. Ambassador or Mr. Blank / 2. The American Ambassador to (country) (The Ambassador or Mr. Blank)
American Minister (to Central or South America)[2]	The Honorable William R. Blank / The Minister of the United States of America	Sir:	Dear Mr. Minister: or Dear Minister Blank:	Very truly yours,	Sincerely yours,	1. Mr. Minister or Mr. Blank / 2. The Minister of the United States of America, Mr. Blank (The Minister or Mr. Blank)

1. When an ambassador or minister is not at his or her post, the name of the country to which he or she is accredited must be added to the address, for example, *The American Ambassador to Great Britain*. If he or she holds military rank, the diplomatic complimentary title *The Honorable* should be omitted, thus *General William R. Blank, American Ambassador (or Minister)*.
2. With reference to ambassadors and ministers to Central or South American countries, substitute *The Ambassador (or Minister) of the United States for American Ambassador or American Minister*.

U.S. Diplomatic Representatives *continued*

Personage	Envelope and Inside Address (Add Org., City, State, Zip)	Formal Salutation	Informal Salutation	Formal Close	Informal Close	1. Spoken Address 2. Informal Introduction or Reference
American Chargé d'Affaires, Consul General, Consul, or Vice Consul	William R. Blank, Esq. Chargé d'Affaires ad interim of the United States of America	Sir:	Dear Mr. Blank:	Very truly yours,	Sincerely yours,	1. Mr. Blank 2. Mr. Blank
High Commissioner	The Honorable William R. Blank United States High Commissioner for (country)	Sir:	Dear Mr. Blank:	Very truly yours,	Sincerely yours,	1. Commissioner Blank *or* Mr. Blank 2. Commissioner Blank *or* Mr. Blank

Foreign Officials and Representatives

Personage	Envelope and Inside Address (Add Org., City, State, Zip)	Formal Salutation	Informal Salutation	Formal Close	Informal Close	1. Spoken Address 2. Informal Introduction or Reference
Foreign Ambassador[1] in the United States	His Excellency[2] Erik Rolf Blankson Ambassador of (country)	Excellency:	Dear Mr. Ambassador:	Very truly yours,	Sincerely yours,	1. Mr. Ambassador *or* Mr. Blankson 2. The Ambassador of (country) (The Ambassador *or* Mr. Blankson)

1. The correct title of all ambassadors and ministers of foreign countries is *Ambassador (Minister) of (name of country)*, with the exception of Great Britain. The adjective form is used with reference to representatives from Great Britain—*British Ambassador, British Minister.*
2. When the representative is British or a member of the British Commonwealth, it is customary to use *The Right Honorable* and *The Honorable* in addition to *His (Her) Excellency,* whenever appropriate.

Foreign Officials and Representatives *continued*

Personage	Envelope and Inside Address (Add Org., City, State, Zip)	Formal Salutation	Informal Salutation	Formal Close	Informal Close	1. Spoken Address 2. Informal Introduction or Reference
Foreign Minister[3] in the United States	The Honorable George Macovescu The Minister of (country)	Sir:	Dear Mr. Minister:	Very truly yours,	Sincerely yours,	1. Mr. Minister *or* Mr. Macovescu 2. The Minister of (country) (The Minister or Mr. Macovescu)
Foreign Diplomatic Representative with a Personal Title[4]	His Excellency[5] Count Allesandro de Bianco The Ambassador of (country)	Excellency:	Dear Mr. Ambassador:	Very truly yours,	Sincerely yours,	1. Mr. Ambassador *or* Count Bianco 2. The Ambassador of (country) (The Ambassador or Count Bianco)
Prime Minister	His Excellency Christian Jawaharal Blank Prime Minister of (country)	Excellency:	Dear Mr. Prime Minister:	Respectfully yours,	Sincerely yours,	1. Mr. Blank 2. Mr. Blank *or* The Prime Minister
British Prime Minister	The Right Honorable Godfrey Blanc, K.G., M.P. Prime Minister	Sir:	Dear Mr. Prime Minister: *or* Dear Mr. Blanc:	Respectfully yours,	Sincerely yours,	1. Mr. Blanc 2. Mr. Blanc *or* The Prime Minister
Canadian Prime Minister	The Right Honorable Claude Louis St. Blanc, C.M.G. Prime Minister of Canada	Sir:	Dear Mr. Prime Minister: *or* Dear Mr. St. Blanc:	Respectfully yours,	Sincerely yours,	1. Mr. St. Blanc 2. Mr. St. Blanc *or* The Prime Minister

3. The correct title of all ambassadors and ministers of foreign countries is *Ambassador (Minister) of (name of country)*, with the exception of Great Britain. The adjective form is used with reference to representatives from Great Britain—*British Ambassador, British Minister*.

4. If the personal title is a royal title, such as *His (Her) Highness* or *Prince*, the diplomatic title *His (Her) Excellency* or *The Honorable* is omitted.

5. *Dr., Señor, Don,* and other titles of special courtesy in Spanish-speaking countries may be used with the diplomatic title *His (Her) Excellency* or *The Honorable*.

Foreign Officials and Representatives *continued*

Personage	Envelope and Inside Address (Add Org., City, State, Zip)	Formal Salutation	Informal Salutation	Formal Close	Informal Close	1. Spoken Address 2. Informal Introduction or Reference
President of a Republic	His Excellency Juan Cuidad Blanco President of the Republic of (country)	Excellency:	Dear Mr. President:	Respectfully yours,	Sincerely yours,	1. Your Excellency *or* Mr. President 2. The President of the Republic of (country)
Premier	His Excellency Charles Yves de Blanc Premier of the Republic of (country)	Excellency:	Dear Mr. Premier:	Respectfully yours,	Sincerely yours,	1. Your Excellency *or* Mr. Premier 2. The Premier of the Republic of (country), Mr. de Blanc
Foreign Chargé d'Affaires (de missj)[6] in the United States	Mr. Jan Gustaf Blanc Chargé d'Affaires of (country)	Sir:	Dear Mr. Blanc:	Very truly yours,	Sincerely yours,	1. Sir *or* Mr. Blanc 2. The Chargé d'Affaires of (country), Mr. Blanc
Foreign Chargé d'Affaires ad interim in the United States	Mr. Edmund Blank Chargé d'Affaires ad interim[7] of (country)	Sir:	Dear Mr. Blank:	Very truly yours,	Sincerely yours,	1. Sir *or* Mr. Blank 2. The Chargé d'Affaires ad interim of (country), Mr. Blank

6. The full title is usually shortened to *Chargé d'Affaires.*
7. The words *ad interim* should not be omitted in the address.

The Armed Forces/Army

Personage	Envelope and Inside Address (Add Org., City, State, Zip)	Formal Salutation	Informal Salutation	Formal Close	Informal Close	1. Spoken Address 2. Informal Introduction or Reference
General of the Army	General of the Army William R. Blank, USA Department of the Army	Sir:	Dear General Blank:	Very truly yours,	Sincerely yours,	1. General Blank 2. General Blank
General, Lieutenant General, Major General, Brigadier General	General (Lieutenant General, Major General, or Brigadier General) William R. Blank, USA[1]	Sir:	Dear General (Lieutenant General, Major General, Brigadier General) Blank:	Very truly yours,	Sincerely yours,	1. General Blank 2. General Blank
Colonel, Lieutenant Colonel	Colonel (Lieutenant Colonel) William R. Blank, USA	Dear Colonel (Lieutenant Colonel) Blank:	Dear Colonel (Lieutenant Colonel) Blank:	Very truly yours,	Sincerely yours,	1. Colonel Blank 2. Colonel Blank
Major	Major William R. Blank, USA	Dear Major Blank:	Dear Major Blank:	Very truly yours,	Sincerely yours,	1. Major Blank 2. Major Blank
Captain	Captain William R. Blank, USA	Dear Captain Blank:	Dear Captain Blank:	Very truly yours,	Sincerely yours,	1. Captain Blank 2. Captain Blank
First Lieutenant, Second Lieutenant[2]	First (or Second) Lieutenant William R. Blank, USA	Dear Lieutenant Blank:	Dear Lieutenant Blank:	Very truly yours,	Sincerely yours,	1. Lieutenant Blank 2. Lieutenant Blank
Chief Warrant Officer, Warrant Officer	Chief Warrant Officer (Warrant Officer) William R. Blank, USA	Dear Mr. Blank:	Dear Mr. Blank:	Very truly yours,	Sincerely yours,	1. Mr. Blank 2. Mr. Blank
Chaplain in the U.S. Army[3]	Chaplain William R. Blank, Captain, USA	Dear Chaplain Blank:	Dear Chaplain Blank:	Very truly yours,	Sincerely yours,	1. Chaplain Blank 2. Chaplain Blank

Note: Although civilian writers traditionally spell out the rank for all branches of the service, military writers use abbreviations such as *CPT* for *Captain* and *1LT* for *First Lieutenant*.
1. *USA* indicates regular service; *USAR* signifies the reserve.
2. In all *official* correspondence, the full rank should be included in both the envelope and the inside address, but not in the salutation.
3. Roman Catholic chaplains and certain Anglican priests are introduced as *Chaplain Blank* but are spoken to and referred to as *Father Blank*.

The Armed Forces/Navy

Personage	Envelope and Inside Address (Add Org., City, State, Zip)	Formal Salutation	Informal Salutation	Formal Close	Informal Close	1. Spoken Address 2. Informal Introduction or Reference
Fleet Admiral	Admiral William R. Blank, USN Chief of Naval Operations Department of the Navy	Sir:	Dear Admiral Blank:	Very truly yours,	Sincerely yours,	1. Admiral Blank 2. Admiral Blank
Admiral, Vice Admiral, Rear Admiral	Admiral (Vice Admiral or Rear Admiral) William R. Blank, USN[1]	Sir:	Dear Admiral (Vice Admiral, Rear Admiral) Blank:	Very truly yours,	Sincerely yours,	1. Admiral Blank 2. Admiral Blank
Commodore, Captain, Commander, Lieutenant Commander	Commodore (Captain, Commander, Lieutenant Commander) William R. Blank, USN	Dear Commodore (Captain, Commander) Blank:	Dear Commodore (Captain, Commander, Lieutenant Commander) Blank:	Very truly yours,	Sincerely yours,	1. Commodore (etc.) Blank 2. Commodore (etc.) Blank
Junior Officers: Lieutenant, Lieutenant Junior Grade, Ensign	Lieutenant (Lieutenant Junior Grade, Ensign) William R. Blank, USN	Dear Mr. Blank:	Dear Mr. Blank:	Very truly yours,	Sincerely yours,	1. Mr. Blank[2] 2. Lieutenant (etc). Blank (Mr. Blank)

1. *USN* signifies regular service; *USNR* indicates the reserve.
2. Junior officers in the medical or dental corps are spoken to and referred to as *Dr.* but are introduced by their rank.

The Armed Forces/Navy continued

Personage	Envelope and Inside Address (Add Org., City, State, Zip)	Formal Salutation	Informal Salutation	Formal Close	Informal Close	1. Spoken Address 2. Informal Introduction or Reference
Chief Warrant Officer, Warrant Officer	Chief Warrant Officer, (Warrant Officer) William R. Blank, USN	Dear Mr. Blank:	Dear Mr. Blank:	Very truly yours,	Sincerely yours,	1. Mr. Blank 2. Mr. Blank
Chaplain	Chaplain William R. Blank, Captain, USN	Dear Chaplain Blank:	Dear Chaplain Blank:	Very truly yours,	Sincerely yours,	1. Chaplain Blank 2. Captain Blank (Chaplain Blank)

The Armed Forces—Air Force

Air Force titles are the same as those in the army, except that *USAF* is used instead of *USA*, and *USAFR* is used to indicate the reserve.

The Armed Forces—Marine Corps

Marine Corps titles are the same as those in the army, except that the top rank is *Commandant of the Marine Corps*. *USMC* indicates regular service; *USMCR* indicates the reserve.

The Armed Forces—Coast Guard

Coast Guard titles are the same as those in the navy, except that the top rank is *Admiral*. *USCG* indicates regular service; *USCGR* indicates the reserve.

Church Dignitaries/Catholic Faith

Personage	Envelope and Inside Address (Add Org., City, State, Zip)	Formal Salutation	Informal Salutation	Formal Close	Informal Close	1. Spoken Address 2. Informal Introduction or Reference
The Pope	His Holiness, The Pope or His Holiness, Pope (name) Vatican City, Italy	Your Holiness: or Most Holy Father:	*Always Formal*	Respectfully yours,	*Always Formal*	1. Your Holiness 2. Not introduced (His Holiness or The Pope)
Apostolic Pro-Nuncio	His Excellency, The Most Reverend William R. Blank[1] Titular Archbishop of (place) The Apostolic Pro-Nuncio	Your Excellency:	Dear Archbishop Blank:	Respectfully yours,	Sincerely yours,	1. Your Excellency 2. Not introduced (the Apostolic Delegate)
Cardinal in the United States	His Eminence, William Cardinal Blank Archbishop of (place)	Your Eminence:	Dear Cardinal Blank:	Respectfully yours,	Sincerely yours,	1. Your Eminence or Cardinal Blank 2. Not introduced (His Eminence or Cardinal Blank)
Bishop and Archbishop in the United States	The Most Reverend William R. Blank, D.D. Bishop (Archbishop) of (place)	Dear Bishop (Archbishop):	Dear Bishop (Archbishop) Blank:	Respectfully yours,	Sincerely yours,	1. Bishop (Archbishop) Blank 2. Bishop (Archbishop) Blank
Bishop in England	The Right Reverend William R. Blank Bishop of (place) (local address)	Right Reverend Sir:	Dear Bishop:	Respectfully yours,	Sincerely yours,	1. Bishop Blank 2. Bishop Blank
Abbot	The Right Reverend William R. Blank Abbot of (place)	Dear Father Abbot:	Dear Father Blank:	Respectfully yours,	Sincerely yours,	1. Father Abbot 2. Father Blank

1. Sources differ on the use of *The* preceding a religious title. Some churches are no longer using *The*, whereas others retain it in the traditional style. Follow the style of the particular church.

Church Dignitaries/Catholic Faith *continued*

Personage	Envelope and Inside Address (Add Org., City, State, Zip)	Formal Salutation	Informal Salutation	Formal Close	Informal Close	1. Spoken Address 2. Informal Introduction or Reference
Monsignor	The Very Reverend Monsignor William R. Blank	Very Reverend Monsignor:	Dear Monsignor Blank:	Respectfully yours,	Sincerely yours,	1. Monsignor Blank 2. Monsignor Blank
Superior of a Brotherhood and Priest[2]	The Very Reverend William R. Blank, M.M. Director	Dear Father Superior:	Dear Father Superior:	Respectfully yours,	Sincerely yours,	1. Father Blank 2. Father Blank
Priest	*With scholastic degree:* The Reverend William R. Blank, Ph.D.	Dear Dr. Blank:	Dear Dr. Blank:	Very truly yours,	Sincerely yours,	1. Doctor (Father) Blank 2. Doctor (Father) Blank
	Without scholastic degree (but member of religious order): The Reverend William R. Blank, S.J.[3]	Dear Father Blank:	Dear Father Blank:	Very truly yours,	Sincerely yours,	1. Father Blank 2. Father Blank
Brother	Brother John Blank	Dear Brother:	Dear Brother John:	Very truly yours,	Sincerely yours,	1. Brother John 2. Brother John

2. The address for the superior of a Brotherhood depends on whether or not he is a priest or has a title other than superior. Consult the *Official Catholic Directory.*
3. When the order is known, the initials immediately follow the person's name, preceded by a comma.

Church Dignitaries/Catholic Faith *continued*

Personage	Envelope and Inside Address (Add Org., City, State, Zip)	Formal Salutation	Informal Salutation	Formal Close	Informal Close	1. Spoken Address 2. Informal Introduction or Reference
Mother Superior of a Sisterhood (Catholic or protestant)[4]	The Reverend Mother Superior, O.C.A.	Dear Reverend Mother: *or* Dear Mother Superior:	Dear Reverend Mother: *or* Dear Mother Superior:	Respectfully yours,	Sincerely yours,	1. Reverend Mother 2. Reverend Mother
Sister Superior	The Reverend Sister Superior *(order, if used)*[5]	Dear Sister Superior:	Dear Sister Superior:	Respectfully yours,	Sincerely yours,	1. Sister Blank *or* Sister Margaret 2. The Sister Superior *or* Sister Blank (Sister Margaret)
Sister[6]	Sister Mary Blank	Dear Sister: *or* Dear Sister Blank:	Dear Sister Mary:	Very truly yours,	Sincerely yours,	1. Sister Mary 2. Sister Mary

4. Many religious congregations no longer use the title *Superior*. The head of a congregation is known instead by another title such as *President*.
5. The address of the superior of a Sisterhood depends on the order to which she belongs. The abbreviation of the order is not always used. Consult the *Official Catholic Directory*.
6. Use the form of address preferred by the person if you know it. Some women religious prefer to be addressed as "Sister Blank" rather than "Sister Mary" in business situations, but others object to the use of the last name.

Church Dignitaries/Jewish Faith

Personage	Envelope and Inside Address (Add Org., City, State, Zip)	Formal Salutation	Informal Salutation	Formal Close	Informal Close	1. Spoken Address 2. Informal Introduction or Reference
Rabbi	*With scholastic degree:* Rabbi William R. Blank, Ph.D.	Sir:	Dear Dr. Blank: *or* Dear Rabbi Blank:	Very truly yours,	Sincerely yours,	1. Rabbi Blank *or* Dr. Blank 2. Rabbi Blank *or* Dr. Blank
	Without scholastic degree: Rabbi William R. Blank	Sir:	Dear Rabbi Blank:	Very truly yours,	Sincerely yours,	1. Rabbi Blank 2. Rabbi Blank

Church Dignitaries/Protestant Faith

Personage	Envelope and Inside Address (Add Org., City, State, Zip)	Formal Salutation	Informal Salutation	Formal Close	Informal Close	1. Spoken Address 2. Informal Introduction or Reference
Archbishop (Anglican)	The Most Reverend Archbishop of (place) *or* The Most Reverend John Blank Archbishop of (place)	Your Grace:	Dear Archbishop Blank:	Respectfully yours,	Sincerely yours,	1. Your Grace 2. Not introduced (His Grace or The Archbishop)
Presiding Bishop of the Protestant Episcopal Church in America	The Right Reverend William R. Blank, D.D., L.L.D. Presiding Bishop of the Protestant Episcopal Church in America	Right Reverend Sir:	Dear Bishop Blank:	Respectfully yours,	Sincerely yours,	1. Bishop Blank 2. Bishop Blank

Church Dignitaries/Protestant Faith continued

Personage	Envelope and Inside Address (Add Org., City, State, Zip)	Formal Salutation	Informal Salutation	Formal Close	Informal Close	1. Spoken Address 2. Informal Introduction or Reference
Anglican Bishop	The Right Reverend The Lord Bishop of (place)	Right Reverend Sir:	Dear Bishop Blank:	Respectfully yours,	Sincerely yours,	1. Bishop Blank 2. Bishop Blank
Methodist Bishop	The Reverend William R. Blank Methodist Bishop	Reverend Sir:	Dear Bishop Blank:	Respectfully yours,	Sincerely yours,	1. Bishop Blank 2. Bishop Blank
Protestant Episcopal Bishop	The Right Reverend William R. Blank, D.D., L.L.D. Bishop of (place)	Right Reverend Sir:	Dear Bishop Blank:	Respectfully yours,	Sincerely yours,	1. Bishop Blank 2. Bishop Blank
Archdeacon	The Venerable William R. Blank Archdeacon of (place)	Venerable Sir:	Dear Archdeacon Blank:	Respectfully yours,	Sincerely yours,	1. Archdeacon Blank 2. Archdeacon Blank
Dean[1]	The Very Reverend William R. Blank, D.D. Dean of (place)	Very Reverend Sir:	Dear Dean Blank:	Respectfully yours,	Sincerely yours,	1. Dean Blank *or* Dr. Blank 2. Dean Blank *or* Dr. Blank
Canon	The Reverend William R. Blank, D.D. Canon of (place)	Reverend Sir:	Dear Canon Blank:	Respectfully yours,	Sincerely yours,	1. Canon Blank 2. Canon Blank
Protestant Minister	*With scholastic degree:* The Reverend William R. Blank, D.D., Litt.D. *or* The Reverend Dr. William R. Blank	Dear Dr. Blank:	Dear Dr. Blank:	Very truly yours,	Sincerely yours,	1. Dr. Blank 2. Dr. Blank
	Without scholastic degree: The Reverend William R. Blank	Dear Mr. Blank:	Dear Mr. Blank:	Very truly yours,	Sincerely yours,	1. Mr. Blank 2. Mr. Blank

1. Applies only to the head of a cathedral or of a theological seminary.

Church Dignitaries/Protestant Faith continued

Personage	Envelope and Inside Address (Add Org., City, State, Zip)	Formal Salutation	Informal Salutation	Formal Close	Informal Close	1. Spoken Address 2. Informal Introduction or Reference
Episcopal Priest (High Church)	*With scholastic degree:* The Reverend William R. Blank, D.D., Litt.D. *or* The Reverend Dr. William R. Blank	Dear Dr. Blank:	Dear Dr. Blank:	Very truly yours,	Sincerely yours,	1. Dr. Blank 2. Dr. Blank
	Without scholastic degree: The Reverend William R. Blank	Dear Father Blank: *or* Dear Mr. Blank:	Dear Father Blank: *or* Dear Mr. Blank:	Very truly yours,	Sincerely yours,	1. Father Blank *or* Mr. Blank 2. Father Blank *or* Mr. Blank

College and University Officials

Personage	Envelope and Inside Address (Add Org., City, State, Zip)	Formal Salutation	Informal Salutation	Formal Close	Informal Close	1. Spoken Address 2. Informal Introduction or Reference
President of a College or University	*With scholastic degree:* Dr. William R. Blank *or* William R. Blank, L.L.D., Ph.D. President	Sir:	Dear Dr. Blank:	Very truly yours,	Sincerely yours,	1. Dr. Blank 2. Dr. Blank

College and University Officials *continued*

Personage	Envelope and Inside Address (Add Org., City, State, Zip)	Formal Salutation	Informal Salutation	Formal Close	Informal Close	1. Spoken Address 2. Informal Introduction or Reference
President of a College or University	*Without a scholastic degree:* Mr. William R. Blank President	Sir:	Dear President Blank:	Very truly yours,	Sincerely yours,	1. Mr. Blank 2. Mr. Blank *or* Mr. Blank, President of the College
	Catholic Priest: The Reverend William R. Blank, S.J., D.D., Ph.D. President	Sir:	Dear Dr. Blank:	Very truly yours,	Sincerely yours,	1. Doctor (Father) Blank 2. Doctor (Father) Blank
University Chancellor	Dr. William R. Blank Chancellor	Sir:	Dear Dr. Blank:	Very truly yours,	Sincerely yours,	1. Dr. Blank 2. Dr. Blank
Dean or Assistant Dean of a College or Graduate School	Dean (Assistant Dean) William R. Blank School of Law	Dear Sir: *or* Dear Dean Blank:	Dear Dean Blank:	Very truly yours,	Sincerely yours,	1. Dean (Assistant Dean) Blank *or* 2. Dean (Assistant Dean)
	With a scholastic degree: Dr. William R. Blank Dean (Assistant Dean), School of Law	Dear Sir: *or* Dear Dean Blank:	Dear Dean Blank:			Dr. Blank, the Dean (Assistant Dean) of the School of Law
Professor	Professor William R. Blank	Dear Professor Blank:	Dear Professor Blank:	Very truly yours,	Sincerely yours,	1. Professor (Dr.) Blank 2. Professor (Dr.) Blank
	With a scholastic degree: Dr. William R. Blank	Dear Dr. (or Professor) Blank:	Dear Dr. (or Professor) Blank:			

College and University Officials *continued*

Personage	Envelope and Inside Address (Add Org., City, State, Zip)	Formal Salutation	Informal Salutation	Formal Close	Informal Close	1. Spoken Address 2. Informal Introduction or Reference
Associate or Assistant Professor	Mr. William R. Blank *With a scholastic degree:* Dr. William R. Blank Associate (Assistant) Professor	Dear Professor Blank: Dear Dr. (or Professor) Blank:	Dear Professor Blank: Dear Dr. (or Professor Blank):	Very truly yours,	Sincerely yours,	1. Professor (Dr.) Blank 2. Professor (Dr.) Blank
Instructor	Mr. William R. Blank *With a scholastic degree:* Dr. William R. Blank	Dear Mr. Blank: Dear Dr. Blank:	Dear Mr. Blank: Dear Dr. Blank:	Very truly yours,	Sincerely yours,	1. Mr. (Dr.) Blank 2. Mr. (Dr.) Blank
Chaplain of a College or University	Chaplain William R. Blank *With a scholastic degree:* The Reverend William R. Blank, D.D. Chaplain	Dear Chaplain Blank: Dear Dr. Blank:	Dear Chaplain (Dr.) Blank:	Very truly yours,	Sincerely yours,	1. Chaplain Blank 2. Chaplain Blank *or* Dr. Blank

United Nations Officials[1]

Secretary General	His Excellency, William R. Blank Secretary General of the United Nations	Excellency:[2]	Dear Mr. Secretary General:	Very truly yours,	Sincerely yours,	1. Excellency *or* Mr. Secretary General 2. The Secretary General of the United Nations, Mr. Blank
Under Secretary	The Honorable William R. Blank Under Secretary of the United Nations The Secretariat United Nations	Sir:	Dear Mr. Under Secretary: *or* Dear Mr. Blank:	Very truly yours,	Sincerely yours,	1. Mr. Blank 2. Mr. Blank
Foreign Representative (with ambassadorial rank)	His Excellency, William R. Blank Representative of (country) to the United Nations	Excellency:	Dear Mr. Ambassador:	Very truly yours,	Sincerely yours,	1. Mr. Ambassador 2. Ambassador Blank *or* The Representative of (country) to the United Nations, Ambassador Blank
United States Representative (with ambassadorial rank)	The Honorable William R. Blank United States Representative to the United Nations	Sir: *or* Dear Mr. Ambassador:	Dear Mr. Ambassador:	Very truly yours,	Sincerely yours,	1. Mr. Ambassador 2. Ambassador Blank *or* The United States Representative to the United Nations, Ambassador Blank

1. The six principal branches through which the United Nations functions are The General Assembly, The Security Council, The Economic and Social Council, The Trusteeship Council, The International Court of Justice, and The Secretariat.
2. An American citizen should never be addressed as "Excellency."

STANDARD PROOFREADING MARKS

∧	Make correction indicated in margin.	////	Hair space letters.
Stet	Retain crossed-out word or letter; let it stand.	*wf.*	Wrong font; change to proper font.
Stet	Retain words under which dots appear; write "Stet" in margin.	*Qu?*	Is this right?
		lc.	Set in lower case (small letters).
X	Appears battered; examine.	*s.c.*	Set in small capitals.
=	Straighten lines.	*Caps*	Set in capitals.
✓/✓	Unevenly spaced; correct spacing.	*c&sc*	Set in caps and small caps.
‖	Line up; i.e., make lines even with other matter.	*rom.*	Change to roman.
run in	Make no break in the reading; no paragraph.	*ital.*	Change to italic.
		≡	Under letter or word means caps.
No ¶	No paragraph; sometimes written "run in."	=	Under letter or word means small caps.
Out-see copy	Here is an omission; see copy.	—	Under letter or word means italic.
¶	Make a paragraph here.	∼∼∼	Under letter or word means boldface.
tr	Transpose words or letters as indicated.	∧	Insert comma.
✄	Take out matter indicated; delete.	⫯	Insert semicolon.
⫯	Take out character indicated and close up.	:/	Insert colon.
		⊙	Insert period.
lc	Line drawn through a cap means lower case.	/?/	Insert interrogation mark.
⊘	Upside down; reverse.	/!/	Insert exclamation mark.
⊃	Close up; no space.	-/	Insert hyphen.
#	Insert a space here.	∨	Insert apostrophe.
⌄	Push down this space.	∀ ∀	Insert quotation marks.
⊡	Indent line one em.	⌅	Insert superior letter or figure.
[	Move this to the left.	∧	Insert inferior letter or figure.
]	Move this to the right.	[/]	Insert brackets.
⌐	Raise to proper position.	(/)	Insert parentheses.
⌐	Lower to proper position.	-⫲-	One-em dash.
		⫢	Two-em parallel dash.
		⊕	Spell out.

CORRECTED GALLEY PROOFS

HOW TO CORRECT PROOF

It <u>does</u> not appear that the earliest printers had any method of correcting errors before the form was on the press. The learned learned correctors of the first two centuries of printing were not proofreaders in our sense; they were rather what we should term office editors. Their labors were chiefly to see that the proof corresponded to the copy, but that the printed page was correct in its latinity, that the words were there, and that the sense was right. They cared but little about orthography, bad letters or purely printers' errors, and when the text seemed to them wrong, they consulted fresh authorities or altered it on their own responsibility. Good proofs, in the modern sense, were impossible until professional readers were employed, men who had first a printer's education and then spent many years in the correction of proof. The orthography of English, which for the past century has undergone little change, was very fluctuating until after the publication of Johnson's Dictionary, and capitals, which have been used with considerable regularity for the past 80 years, were previously used on the miss or hit plan. The approach to regularity, so far as we have, may be attributed to the growth of a class of professional proofreaders, and it is to them that we owe the correctness of modern printing. More errors have been found in the Bible than in any other one work. For many generations it was frequently the case that Bibles were brought out stealthily, from fear of governmental interference. They were frequently printed from imperfect texts and were often modified to meet the views of those who published them. The story is related that a certain woman in Germany, who was the wife of a Printer, and had become disgusted with the continual assertions of the superiority of man over woman which she had heard, hurried into the composing room while her husband was at supper and altered a sentence in the Bible, which he was printing, so that it read Narr instead of Herr, thus making the verse read "And he shall be thy fool" instead of "And he shall be thy lord." The word not was omitted by Barker, the King's printer in England in 1632, in printing the seventh commandment. He was fined £3,000 on this account.

TABLES OF WEIGHTS, MEASURES, AND VALUES

Long Measure

12 inches = 1 foot
3 feet = 1 yard
$5\frac{1}{2}$ yards or $16\frac{1}{2}$ feet = 1 rod
320 rods or 5,280 feet = 1 mile
1,760 yards = 1 mile
40 rods = 1 furlong
8 furlongs = 1 statute mile
3 miles = 1 league

Common Metric Equivalents

1 inch = 2.540 centimeters
1 foot = 30.480 centimeters
1 yard = 0.914 meters
1 rod = 5.029 meters
1 mile = 1.609 kilometers

Square Measure

144 square inches = 1 square foot
9 square feet = 1 square yard
$30\frac{1}{4}$ square yards = 1 square rod
$272\frac{1}{4}$ square feet = 1 square rod
40 square rods = 1 British rood
4 roods = 1 acre
160 square rods = 1 acre
640 acres = 1 square mile
43,560 square feet = 1 acre
4,840 square yards = 1 acre

Common Metric Equivalents

1 square inch = 6.451 square centimeters
1 square foot = 0.093 square meters
1 square yard = 0.836 square meters
1 square rod = 25.293 square meters
1 square mile = 2.590 square kilometers

Solid or Cubic Measure (Volume)

1,728 cubic inches = 1 cubic foot
27 cubic feet = 1 cubic yard
128 cubic feet = 1 cord of wood
24.75 cubic feet = 1 perch of stone
2,150.42 cubic inches = 1 standard bushel
231 cubic inches = 1 standard gallon
40 cubic feet = 1 ton (shipping)

Common Metric Equivalents

1 cubic inch = 16.387 cubic centimeters
1 cubic foot = 0.028 cubic meters
1 cubic yard = 0.765 cubic meters

Surveyors' Long Measure

7.92 inches = 1 link
25 links = 1 rod
4 rods or 100 links = 1 chain
80 chains = 1 mile

Surveyors' Square Measure

625 square links = 1 square rod
16 square rods = 1 square chain
10 square chains = 1 acre
640 acres = 1 square mile
36 square miles = 1 township

Circular or Angular Measure

60 seconds (60″) = 1 minute (′)
60 minutes (60′) = 1 degree (1°)
30 degrees = 1 sign
90 degrees = 1 right angle or quadrant
360 degrees = 1 circumference

Note: 1 degree at the equator = about 60 nautical miles.

Dry Measure

2 pints = 1 quart
8 quarts = 1 peck
4 pecks = 1 bushel
2,150.42 cubic inches = 1 bushel
1.2445 cubic feet = 1 bushel

Common Metric Equivalents

1 pint = 0.550 liters
1 quart = 1.101 liters
1 peck = 8.809 liters
1 bushel = 35.238 liters

Liquid Measure (Capacity)

4 gills = 1 pint
2 pints = 1 quart
4 quarts = 1 gallon
31.5 gallons = 1 barrel
2 barrels = 1 hogshead
1 gallon = 231 cubic inches
7.4805 gallons = 1 cubic foot
16 fluid ounces = 1 pint
1 fluid ounce = 1.805 cubic inches

Common Metric Equivalents

1 fluid ounce = 29.573 milliliters
1 gill = 118.291 milliliters
1 pint = 0.473 liters
1 quart = 0.946 liters
1 gallon = 3.785 liters

Mariners' Measure

6 feet = 1 fathom
100 fathoms = 1 cable's length as applied to distances or
intervals between ships

120 fathoms = 1 cable's length as applied to
                marine wire cable
7.50 cable lengths = 1 mile
5,280 feet = 1 statute mile
6,080 feet = 1 nautical mile
1.15266 statute miles = 1 nautical or geographical mile
3 geographical miles = 1 league
60 geographical miles   = 1 degree of longitude on the
  or 69.16 statute miles   equator or 1 degree of meridian
360 degrees = 1 circumference

Note: A *knot* is not a measure of distance but a measure of speed, about 1 nautical mile per hour.

U.S.-British Weights and Measures

1 British bushel = 1.0320 U.S. (Winchester) bushels
1 U.S. bushel = 0.96894 British Imperial bushel
1 British quart = 1.03206 U.S. dry quarts
1 U.S. dry quart = 0.96894 British quart
1 British quart (or gallon) = 1.20095 U.S. liquid quarts (or gallons)
1 U.S. liquid quart (or gallon) = 0.83267 British quart (or gallon)

Avoirdupois Measure (Weight)

27.343 grains = 1 dram
16 drams = 1 ounce
16 ounces = 1 pound
25 pounds = 1 quarter
4 quarts = 1 hundredweight
100 pounds = 1 hundredweight
20 hundredweight = 1 ton
2,000 pounds = 1 short ton
2,240 pounds = 1 long ton

Common Metric Equivalents

1 grain = 0.0648 grams
1 dram = 1.772 grams
1 ounce = 28.350 grams
1 pound = 0.454 kilograms
1 hundredweight (short) = 45.359 kilograms
1 hundredweight (long) = 50.802 kilograms

Note: The avoirdupois measure is used for weighing all ordinary substances except precious metals, jewels, and drugs.

1 ton (short) = 0.907 metric ton
1 ton (long) = 1.016 metric tons

Troy Measure (Weight)

24 grains = 1 pennyweight
20 pennyweights = 1 ounce
12 ounces = 1 pound

Common Metric Equivalents

1 grain = 0.0648 grams
1 pennyweight = 1.555 grams
1 ounce = 31.103 grams
1 pound = 0.373 kilograms

Avoirdupois-Troy Measure

1 pound troy = 5,760 grains
1 pound avoirdupois = 7,000 grains
1 ounce troy = 480 grains
1 ounce avoirdupois = 437.5 grains
1 carat or karat = 3.2 troy grains
24 carat gold = pure gold

Apothecaries' Fluid Measure (Capacity)

60 minims = 1 fluid dram
8 fluid drams = 1 fluid ounce
16 fluid ounces = 1 pint
8 pints = 1 gallon

Apothecaries' Measure (Weight)

20 grains = 1 scruple
3 scruples = 1 dram
8 drams = 1 ounce
12 ounces = 1 pound

Common Metric Equivalents

1 grain = 0.0648 gram
1 scruple = 1.295 grams
1 dram = 3.887 grams

1 ounce = 31.103 grams
1 pound = 0.373 kilogram

Paper Measure

24 sheets = 1 quire
20 quires = 1 ream
2 reams = 1 bundle
5 bundles = 1 bale

Counting

12 units or things = 1 dozen
12 dozen or 144 units = 1 gross
12 gross = 1 great gross
20 units = 1 score

United States Money

10 mills = 1 cent
10 cents = 1 dime
10 dimes = 1 dollar
10 dollars = 1 eagle

Comparison of Centigrade and Fahrenheit Temperatures

   0° C = Freezing Point = 32° F
 10° C =   50° F
 20° C =   68° F
 30° C =   86° F
 40° C =   104° F
 50° C =   122° F
 60° C =   140° F
 70° C =   158° F
 80° C =   176° F
 90° C =   194° F
100° C = Boiling Point 212° F

Note: To convert from °F to °C, subtract 32 from °F and multiply by 0.555. To convert from °C to °F, multiply °C by 1.8 and add 32.

Land Measurements

1 rod = $16\frac{1}{2}$ feet
1 chain = 66 feet or 4 rods
1 mile = 320 rods, 80 chains, or 5,280 feet
1 square mile = $272\frac{1}{4}$ square feet
1 acre = 160 square rods
1 acre = $208\frac{3}{4}$ square feet
1 acre = 8 rods × 20 rods or any two numbers (of rods)
        whose product is 160
25 × 125 feet = 0.0717 acre
1 section = 640 acres

TABLES OF METRIC WEIGHTS, MEASURES, AND VALUES

Metric Prefixes and Multiplication Factors

Weight

1 *kilo*gram = 1,000 grams
1 *hecto*gram = 100 grams
1 *deka*gram = 10 grams
1 gram = 1 gram

1 *deci*gram = 0.1 gram
1 *centi*gram = 0.01 gram
1 *milli*gram = 0.001 gram

Length

1 *kilo*meter = 1,000 meters
1 *hecto*meter = 100 meters
1 *deka*meter = 10 meters
1 meter = 1 meter

1 *deci*meter = 0.1 meter
1 *centi*meter = 0.01 meter
1 *milli*meter = 0.001 meter

Volume

1 *hecto*liter = 100 liters
1 *deka*liter = 10 liters
1 liter = 1 liter

1 *centi*liter = 0.01 liter
1 *milli*liter = 0.001 liter

Metric Measurement Conversions

When You Know	Multiply By	To Find
Length		
inches (in.)	2.54	centimeters (cm)
feet (ft.)	30.00	centimeters (cm)
yards (yd.)	0.90	meters (m)

When You Know	Multiply By	To Find
miles (mi.)	1.60	kilometers (km)
millimeters(mm)	0.04	inches (in.)
centimeters (cm)	0.40	inches
meters (m)	3.30	feet (ft.)
meters (m)	1.10	yards (yd.)
kilometers (km)	0.60	miles (mi.)

Area

square inches (in.²)	6.50	square centimeters (cm²)
square feet (ft.²)	0.09	square meters (m²)
square yards (yd.²)	0.80	square meters (m²)
square miles (mi.²)	2.60	square kilometers (km²)
acres	0.40	hectares (ha)
square centimeter (cm²)	0.16	square inches (in.²)
square meters (m²)	1.20	square yards (yd.²)
square kilometers (km.²)	0.40	square miles (mi.²)
hectares (ha (10,000 m²)	2.50	acres

Weight

ounces (oz.)	28.00	grams (g)
pounds (lb.)	0.45	kilograms (kg)
short tons (2,000 lbs.)	0.90	tonnes (t)
long tons (2,240 lbs.)	1.01	tonnes (t)
grams (g)	0.035	ounces (oz.)
kilograms (kg)	2.20	pounds (lb.)
tonnes (1,000 kg)	1.10	short tons
tonnes (1,000 kg)	0.98	long tons

Volume

teaspoons (tsp.)	5.00	milliliters (ml)
tablespoons (tbsp.)	15.00	milliliters (ml)
fluid ounces (fl. oz.)	30.00	milliliters (ml)
cups (c)	0.24	liters (l)
pints (pt.)	0.47	liters (l)
quarts (qt.)	0.95	liters (l)
gallons, U.S. (gal.)	3.80	liters (l)
gallons, Imp. (gal.)	4.50	liters (l)
cubic feet (ft.³)	0.028	cubic meters (m³)
cubic yards (yd.³)	0.76	cubic meters (m³)
milliliters (ml)	0.03	fluid ounces (fl. oz.)
liters (l)	2.10	pints (pt.)
liters (l)	1.06	quarts (qt.)
liters (l)	0.26	gallons, U.S. (gal.)
liters (l)	0.22	gallons, Imp. (gal.)
cubic meters (m³)	35.00	cubic feet (ft.³)
cubic meters (m³)	1.30	cubic yards (yd.³)

Metric Equivalents

Linear Measure

1 centimeter = 0.3937 inch
1 inch = 2.54 centimeters
1 decimeter = 3.937 inches = 0.328 foot
1 foot = 3.048 decimeters
1 meter = 39.37 inches = 1.0936 yards

1 yard = 0.9144 meter
1 dekameter = 1.9884 rods
1 rod = 0.5029 dekameter
1 kilometer = 0.62137 mile
1 mile = 1.6093 kilometers

Square Measure

1 square centimeter = 0.1550 square inch
1 square inch = 6.452 square centimeters
1 square decimeter = 0.1076 square foot
1 square foot = 9.2903 square decimeter
1 square meter = 1.196 square yards
1 square yard = 0.8361 square meter
1 acre = 160 square rods

1 square rod = 0.00625 acres
1 hectare = 2.47 acres
1 acre = 0.4047 hectare
1 square kilometer = 0.386 square mile
1 square mile = 2.59 square kilometers

Volume

1 cubic centimeter = 0.061 cubic inch
1 cubic inch = 16.39 cubic centimeters
1 cubic decimeter = 0.0353 cubic foot
1 cubic foot = 28.317 cubic yards
1 cubic yard = 0.7646 cubic meter
1 stere = 0.2759 cord
1 cord = 3.624 steres
1 liter = 0.908 quart dry = 1.0567 quarts liquid

1 quart dry = 1.101 liters
1 quart liquid = 0.9463 liter
1 dekaliter = 2.6417 gallons
= 1.135 pecks
1 gallon = 0.3785 dekaliter
1 peck = 0.881 dekaliter
1 hectoliter = 2.8375 bushels
1 bushel = 0.3524 hectoliter

Weights

1 gram = 0.03527 ounce
1 ounce = 28.35 grams
1 kilogram = 2.2046 pounds

1 pound = 0.4536 kilogram
1 metric ton = 0.98421 English ton
1 English ton = 1.016 metric ton

Approximate Metric Equivalents

1 decimeter = 4 inches
1 liter = 1.06 quarts liquid
= 0.9 quarts dry
1 meter = 1.1 yards
1 kilometer = 0.625 mile

1 hectoliter = 2.625 bushels
1 hectare = 2.5 acres
1 kilogram = 2.20 pounds
1 stere or cubic meter = 0.25 cord
1 metric ton = 2,200 pounds

MATHEMATICAL TABLES

Mathematical Signs and Symbols

— vinculum (above letters)

÷ geometrical proportion

−: difference, excess

‖ parallel

‖s parallels

≢ not parallels

| | absolute value

· multiplied by

: is to; ratio

+ divided by

∴ therefore; hence

∵ because

:: proportion; as

≪ is dominated by

> greater than

⊏ greater than

≥ greater than or equal to

≧ greater than or equal to

≷ greater than or less than

≯ is not greater than

< less than

⊐ less than

≶ less than or greater than

≮ is not less than

◄ smaller than

≤ less than or equal to

≦ less than or equal to

≥ or ≥ greater than or equal to

≲ equal to or less than

≦ equal to or less than

≤ is not greater than equal to or less than

≥ equal to or greater than

≥ is not less than equal to or greater than

⊥ equilateral

⊥ perpendicular to

⊢ assertion sign

≐ approaches

≑ approaches a limit

⩹ equal angles

≠ not equal to

≡ identical with

≢ not identical with

/НЦ score

≈ or ≑ nearly equal to

= equal to

~ difference

≃ perspective to

≅ congruent to approximately equal

≏ difference between

⧓ equivalent to

(included in

) excluded from

⊂ is contained in

∪ logical sum or union

∩ logical product or intersection

√ radical

√ root

√ square root

∛ cube root

∜ fourth root

/ virgule; solidus; separatrix; shilling

± plus or minus

∓ minus or plus

⁵√ fifth root

⁶√ sixth root

π pi

ε base (2.718) of natural system of logarithms; epsilon

ε is a member of; dielectric constant; mean error; epsilon

+ plus

➕ bold plus

− minus

➖ bold minus

× multiplied by

= bold equal

number

⅌ per

% percent

∫ integral

| single bond

\ single bond

/ single bond

‖ double bond

⦀ double bond

⫽ double bond

⬡ benzene ring

∂ or δ differential; variation

∂ Italian differential

→ approaches limit of

~ cycle sine

⌐ horizontal integral

∮ contour integral

∝ variation; varies as

Π product

Σ summation of; sum; sigma

! or ⌐ factorial product

Source: United States Government Printing Office Style Manual (Washington, D.C.: U.S. Government Printing Office, 1984).

Shortcuts in Multiplication

To multiply by	add		and	divide by	8
1-1/4	add		and	divide by	8
1-2/3	"	0	"	"	6
2-1/2	"	0	"	"	4
3-1/3	"	0	"	"	3
5	"	0	"	"	2
6-1/4	"	00	"	"	16
6-2/3	"	00	"	"	15
8-1/3	"	00	"	"	12
12-1/2	"	00	"	"	8
14-2/7	"	00	"	"	7
16-2/3	"	00	"	"	6
25	"	00	"	"	4
31-1/4	"	000	"	"	32
33-1/3	"	00	"	"	3
50	"	00	"	"	2
66-2/3	"	000	"	"	15
83-1/3	"	000	"	"	12
125	"	000	"	"	8
166-2/3	"	000	"	"	6
250	"	000	"	"	4
333-1/3	"	000	"	"	3

For example, to multiply 5 times 2: add 0 to 2 (20) and divide by 2 (20 ÷ 2 = 10). Thus, 5 × 2 = 10.

Shortcuts in Division

To divide by	multiply by	8	and	divide by	10
1-1/4	multiply by	8	and	divide by	10
1-2/3	"	6	"	"	10
2-1/2	"	4	"	"	10
3-1/3	"	3	"	"	10
3-3/4	"	8	"	"	30
6-1/4	"	16	"	"	100
7-1/2	"	4	"	"	30
8-1/3	"	12	"	"	100
9-1/11	"	11	"	"	100
11-1/9	"	9	"	"	100
12-1/2		8			100
14-2/7	"	7	"	"	100
16-2/3	"	6	"	"	100
25	"	4	"	"	100
31-1/4	"	16	"	"	500
33-1/3	"	3	"	"	100
75	"	4	"	"	300
125	"	8	"	"	1,000
175	"	4	"	"	700
275	"	4	"	"	1,100

To divide by					
375	multiply by	8	and	divide by	3,000
625	"	8	"	"	5,000
875	"	8	"	"	7,000

For example, to divide 5 by 6-1/4, multiply 5 times 16 (80) and divide by 100 (80 ÷ 100 = 0.80). Thus, 5 ÷ 6-1/4 = 0.80.

GREEK LETTER SYMBOLS

Name of Letter	Greek Alphabet	Name of Letter	Greek Alphabet	Name of Letter	Greek Alphabet
Alpha	A a α^1	Kappa	K κ	Tau	T τ
Beta	B β	Lambda	Λ λ	Upsilon	Υ υ
Gamma	Γ γ	Mu	M μ	Phi	Φ ϕ φ^1
Delta	Δ δ ∂^1	Nu	N ν	Chi	X χ
Episilon	E ϵ	Xi	Ξ ξ	Psi	Ψ ψ
Zeta	Z ζ	Omicron	O o	Omega	Ω ω
Eta	H η	Pi	Π π		
Theta	Θ θ ϑ^1	Rho	P ρ	1. Old style character.	
Iota	I ι	Sigma	Σ σ s^2	2. Final letter.	

INTEREST TABLES

Rate of Savings under Various Discount Terms

½%	10	days	net	30	days	=	9%	per annum	
1%	"	"	"	"	"	=	18%	"	"
1½%	"	"	"	"	"	=	27%	"	"
2%	"	"	"	"	"	=	36%	"	"
2%	"	"	"	60	"	=	14%	"	"
2%	30	"	"	"	"	=	24%	"	"
2%	"	"	"	4	mos.	=	8%	"	"
2%	40	"	"	60	days	=	36%	"	"
2%	70	"	"	90	"	=	36%	"	"
3%	10	"	"	30	"	=	54%	"	"
3%	"	"	"	4	mos.	=	10%	"	"
3%	30	"	"	60	days	=	36%	"	"
4%	10	"	"	"	"	=	29%	"	"
4%	"	"	"	4	mos.	=	13%	"	"
5%	"	"	"	30	days	=	90%	"	"
5%	"	"	"	60	"	=	36%	"	"
5%	"	"	"	4	mos.	=	16%	"	"
6%	"	"	"	60	days	=	43%	"	"
6%	"	"	"	4	mos.	=	20%	"	"
7%	"	"	"	"	"	=	23%	"	"
8%	"	"	"	"	"	=	26%	"	"
9%	"	"	"	60	days	=	65%	"	"
10%	"	"	"	90	days	=	45%	"	"

Time in Which Money Doubles Itself at Interest

Rate percent	Simple Interest			Compound Interest			
2	50	years		35	years	1	day
2½	40	"		28	"	26	days
3	33	"	4 months	23	"	164	"
3½	28	"	208 days	20	"	54	"
4	25	"		17	"	246	"
4½	22	"	81 days	15	"	273	"
5	20	"		14	"	75	"
6	16	"	8 months	11	"	327	"
7	14	"	104 days	10	"	89	"
8	12	"	6 months	9	"	2	"
9	11	"	40 days	8	"	16	"
10	10	"		7	"	100	"

Exact Number of Days between Dates

From Any Day Of	To the Same Day of the Next											
	Jan.	Feb.	Mar.	Apr.	May	June	July	Aug.	Sept.	Oct.	Nov.	Dec.
January	365	31	59	90	120	151	181	212	243	273	304	334
February	334	365	28	59	89	120	150	181	212	242	273	303
March	306	337	365	31	61	92	122	153	184	214	245	275
April	275	306	334	365	30	61	91	122	153	183	214	244
May	245	276	304	335	365	31	61	92	123	153	184	214
June	214	245	273	304	334	365	30	61	92	122	153	183
July	184	215	243	274	304	335	365	31	62	92	123	153
August	153	184	212	243	273	304	334	365	31	61	92	122
September	122	153	181	212	242	273	303	334	365	30	61	91
October	92	123	151	182	212	243	273	304	335	365	31	61
November	61	92	120	151	181	212	242	273	304	334	365	30
December	31	62	90	121	151	182	212	243	274	304	335	365

Simple Interest Tables

Interest on $100 at Various Rates for Various Periods

Days	5%	6%	7%	8%	9%	10%	11%	12%
1	0.0139	0.0167	0.0194	0.0222	0.0250	0.0278	0.0306	0.0333
2	.0278	.0333	.0389	.0444	.0500	.0556	.0611	.0667
3	.0417	.0500	.0583	.0667	.0750	.0833	.0917	.1000
4	.0556	.0667	.0778	.0889	.1000	.1111	.1222	.1333
5	.0694	.0833	.0972	.1111	.1250	.1389	.1528	.1667
6	.0833	.1000	.1167	.1333	.1500	.1667	.1833	.2000
7	.0972	.1167	.1361	.1556	.1750	.1945	.2139	.2333
8	.1111	.1333	.1556	.1778	.2000	.2222	.2445	.2667
9	.1250	.1500	.1750	.2000	.2250	.2500	.2750	.3000
10	.1389	.1667	.1944	.2222	.2500	.2778	.3056	.3333
20	.2778	.3333	.3889	.4444	.5000	.5556	.6111	.6667
30	.4167	.5000	.5833	.6667	.7500	.8333	.9167	1.0000
40	.5556	.6667	.7778	.8889	1.0000	1.1111	1.2222	1.3333
50	.6945	.8334	.9722	1.1111	1.2500	1.3889	1.5278	1.6667
60	.8333	1.0000	1.1667	1.3333	1.5000	1.6667	1.8334	2.0000
70	.9722	1.1667	1.3611	1.5555	1.7500	1.9445	2.1389	2.3333
80	1.111	1.3334	1.5555	1.7778	2.0000	2.2222	2.4445	2.6666
90	1.2500	1.5000	1.7500	2.0000	2.2500	2.5000	2.7500	3.0000
100	1.3889	1.6667	1.9444	2.2222	2.5000	2.7778	3.0556	3.3333

Interest on $100 at Various Rates for Various Periods

Days	13%	14%	15%	16%	17%	18%	19%	20%
1	0.0361	0.0388	0.0417	0.0444	0.0472	0.0501	0.0528	0.0556
2	.0722	.0778	.0834	.0888	.0944	.0999	.1056	.1112
3	.1083	.1166	.1251	.1332	.1417	.1500	.1583	.1668
4	.1445	.1556	.1668	.1776	.1889	.2001	.2111	.2224
5	.1805	.1944	.2082	.2224	.2361	.2499	.2639	.2776
6	.2167	.2334	.2499	.2668	.2833	.3000	.3167	.3332
7	.2528	.2722	.2916	.3112	.3306	.3501	.3695	.3888
8	.2889	.3112	.3333	.3556	.3778	.3999	.4222	.4444
9	.3250	.3500	.3750	.4000	.4250	.4500	.4750	.5000
10	.3611	.3888	.4167	.4444	.4722	.5001	.5278	.5556
20	.7222	.7778	.8334	.8888	.9444	.9999	1.0556	1.1112
30	1.0833	1.1666	1.2501	1.3334	1.4167	1.5000	1.5833	1.6668
40	1.4445	1.5556	1.6668	1.7778	1.8889	2.0001	2.1111	2.2224
50	1.8056	1.9444	2.0835	2.2222	2.3611	2.5002	2.6389	2.7780
60	2.1667	2.3334	2.4999	2.6666	2.8333	3.0000	3.1667	3.3332
70	2.5278	2.7222	2.9166	3.1110	3.3055	3.5001	3.6945	3.8888
80	2.8889	3.1110	3.3333	3.5556	3.7778	4.0002	4.2222	4.4444
90	3.2500	3.5000	3.7500	4.0000	4.2500	4.5000	4.7500	5.0000
100	3.6111	3.8888	4.1667	4.4444	4.7222	5.0001	5.2778	5.5556

FLOWCHART SYMBOLS

Program Flowcharting Symbols

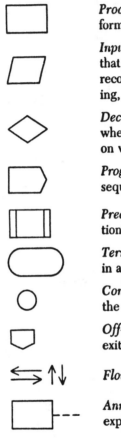

Processing. Group of program instructions that perform a processing function within a program

Input/output. Any function of an input/output device that makes information available for processing, recording, processing information, tape positioning, and so on

Decision. Used to document points in a program where a branch to alternate paths is possible based on variable conditions

Program modification. Instruction(s) that change the sequence of a program

Predefined process. Process, or groups of operations, not specified elsewhere

Terminal. Beginning, end, or point of interruption in a program

Connector. Entry from or exit to another part of the program flowchart

Off-page connector. Used to designate entry to or exit from a page

Flow direction. Direction of processing or data flow

Annotation. Addition of descriptive comments or explanatory notes.

Source: Mary A. DeVries, *Secretary's Almanac and Fact Book* (Englewood Cliffs, N.J.: Prentice-Hall, Inc., 1985).
Note: A *program flowchart* is a diagram that describes a computer program in a series of steps.

System Flowcharting Symbols

Punched card. Punched cards including stubs

Perforated (punched) tape. Paper or plastic, chad or chadless

Document. Paper documents and reports

Magnetic tape.

Transmittal tape. Proof or adding machine tape or other batch-control information

Off-line storage. Of either paper, cards, or magnetic or punched tape

On-line storage. For example, drum or disk storage

Display. Information displayed by plotter or video

Manual input. Information supplied to or by a computer using an on-line device, for example a keyboard

Sorting and collating. Operation using sorting or collating equipment

Clerical or manual operation. Off-line operation not requiring mechanical assistance

Auxiliary operation. Machine operation supplementing main processing function

Keying operation. Operation using a key-driven device

Communication link. Automatic transmission of information from one location to another via communications lines

Source: Mary A. DeVries, *Secretary's Almanac and Fact Book* (Englewood Cliffs, N.J.: Prentice-Hall, Inc., 1985).
Note: A *system flowchart* is a diagram that shows the relationship among events in a data-processing system and describes the flow of data throughout the system.

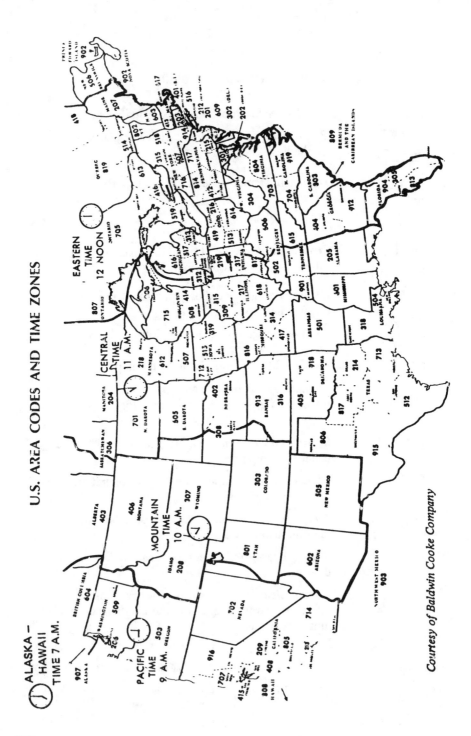

U.S. AREA CODES AND TIME ZONES

Courtesy of Baldwin Cooke Company

652

INTERNATIONAL TIME CHART

Wellington, Auckland	Solomon Islands, New Caledonia	Brisbane, Guam, Melbourne, New Guinea, Sydney	Korea, Japan, Adelaide	Celebes, Hongkong, Manila, Shanghai	Chungking, Chengtu, Kunming	Bombay, Ceylon, New Delhi	Ethiopia, Iraq, Madagascar	Cairo, Capetown, Istanbul, Moscow	Bengazi, Berlin, Oslo, Rome, Tunis, Tripoli, Warsaw, Stockholm	G.M.T.	Algiers, Lisbon, London, Paris, Madrid	Iceland	Rio, Santos, Sao Paulo	Buenos Aires, Santiago, Puerto Rico, Lapaz, Asuncion	Bogota, Havana, Lima, Montreal, New York, Panama, Bermuda	Chicago, Central America (except Panama), Mexico, Winnipeg	San Francisco & Pacific Coast	Tahiti	Alaska, Hawaiian Islands	Aleutian Islands, Tutuila, Samoa
11:30am	11:00am	10:00am	9:00am	8:00am	7:00am	5:30am	3:00am	2:00am	1:00am	0000	MIDNIGHT	11:00pm	9:00pm	9:00pm	7:00pm	6:00pm	4:00pm	2:00pm	2:00pm	1:00pm
12:30pm	MIDI	11:00am	10:00am	9:00am	8:00am	6:30am	4:00am	3:00am	2:00am	0100	1:00am	MINUIT	10:00pm	10:00pm	8:00pm	7:00pm	5:00pm	3:00pm	3:00pm	2:00pm
1:30pm	1:00pm	Mediodia	11:00am	10:00am	9:00am	7:30am	5:00am	4:00am	3:00am	0200	2:00am	1:00am	11:00pm	11:00pm	9:00pm	8:00pm	6:00pm	4:00pm	4:00pm	3:00pm
2:30pm	2:00pm	1:00pm	NOON	11:00am	10:00am	8:30am	6:00am	5:00am	4:00am	0300	3:00am	2:00am	Medianoche	MIDNIGHT	10:00pm	9:00pm	7:00pm	5:00pm	5:00pm	4:00pm
3:30pm	3:00pm	2:00pm	1:00pm	MIDI	11:00am	9:30am	7:00am	6:00am	5:00am	0400	4:00am	3:00am	1:00am	1:00am	11:00pm	10:00pm	8:00pm	6:00pm	6:00pm	5:00pm
4:30pm	4:00pm	3:00pm	2:00pm	1:00pm	Mediodia	10:30am	8:00am	7:00am	6:00am	0500	5:00am	4:00am	2:00am	2:00am	MINUIT	11:00pm	9:00pm	7:00pm	7:00pm	6:00pm
5:30pm	5:00pm	4:00pm	3:00pm	2:00pm	1:00pm	11:30am	9:00am	8:00am	7:00am	0600	6:00am	5:00am	3:00am	3:00am	1:00am	Medianoche	10:00pm	8:00pm	8:00pm	7:00pm
6:30pm	6:00pm	5:00pm	4:00pm	3:00pm	2:00pm	12:30pm	10:00am	9:00am	8:00am	0700	7:00am	6:00am	4:00am	4:00am	2:00am	1:00am	11:00pm	9:00pm	9:00pm	8:00pm
7:30pm	7:00pm	6:00pm	5:00pm	4:00pm	3:00pm	1:30pm	11:00am	10:00am	9:00am	0800	8:00am	7:00am	5:00am	5:00am	3:00am	2:00am	MIDNIGHT	10:00pm	10:00pm	9:00pm
8:30pm	8:00pm	7:00pm	6:00pm	5:00pm	4:00pm	2:30pm	NOON	11:00am	10:00am	0900	9:00am	8:00am	6:00am	6:00am	4:00am	3:00am	1:00am	11:00pm	11:00pm	10:00pm
9:30pm	9:00pm	8:00pm	7:00pm	6:00pm	5:00pm	3:30pm	1:00pm	MIDI	11:00am	1000	10:00am	9:00am	7:00am	7:00am	5:00am	4:00am	2:00am	MINUIT	Medianoche	11:00pm
10:30pm	10:00pm	9:00pm	8:00pm	7:00pm	6:00pm	4:30pm	2:00pm	1:00pm	Mediodia	1100	11:00am	10:00am	8:00am	8:00am	6:00am	5:00am	3:00am	1:00am	1:00am	MIDNIGHT
11:30pm	11:00pm	10:00pm	9:00pm	8:00pm	7:00pm	5:30pm	3:00pm	2:00pm	1:00pm	1200	NOON	11:00am	9:00am	9:00am	7:00am	6:00am	4:00am	2:00am	2:00am	1:00am
12:30am	MINUIT	11:00pm	10:00pm	9:00pm	8:00pm	6:30pm	4:00pm	3:00pm	2:00pm	1300	1:00pm	NOON	10:00am	10:00am	8:00am	7:00am	5:00am	3:00am	3:00am	2:00am
1:30am	1:00am	Medianoche	11:00pm	10:00pm	9:00pm	7:30pm	5:00pm	4:00pm	3:00pm	1400	2:00pm	1:00pm	11:00am	11:00am	9:00am	8:00am	6:00am	4:00am	4:00am	3:00am
2:30am	2:00am	1:00am	MIDNIGHT	11:00pm	10:00pm	8:30pm	6:00pm	5:00pm	4:00pm	1500	3:00pm	2:00pm	Mediodia	NOON	10:00am	9:00am	7:00am	5:00am	5:00am	4:00am
3:30am	3:00am	2:00am	1:00am	MINUIT	11:00pm	9:30pm	7:00pm	6:00pm	5:00pm	1600	4:00pm	3:00pm	1:00pm	1:00pm	11:00am	10:00am	8:00am	6:00am	6:00am	5:00am
4:30am	4:00am	3:00am	2:00am	1:00am	Medianoche	10:30pm	8:00pm	7:00pm	6:00pm	1700	5:00pm	4:00pm	2:00pm	2:00pm	NOON	11:00am	9:00am	7:00am	7:00am	6:00am
5:30am	5:00am	4:00am	3:00am	2:00am	1:00am	11:30pm	9:00pm	8:00pm	7:00pm	1800	6:00pm	5:00pm	3:00pm	3:00pm	1:00pm	Mediodia	10:00am	8:00am	8:00am	7:00am
6:30am	6:00am	5:00am	4:00am	3:00am	2:00am	12:30am	10:00pm	9:00pm	8:00pm	1900	7:00pm	6:00pm	4:00pm	4:00pm	2:00pm	1:00pm	11:00am	9:00am	9:00am	8:00am
7:30am	7:00am	6:00am	5:00am	4:00am	3:00am	1:30am	11:00pm	10:00pm	9:00pm	2000	8:00pm	7:00pm	5:00pm	5:00pm	3:00pm	2:00pm	NOON	10:00am	10:00am	9:00am
8:30am	8:00am	7:00am	6:00am	5:00am	4:00am	2:30am	MIDNIGHT	11:00pm	10:00pm	2100	9:00pm	8:00pm	6:00pm	6:00pm	4:00pm	3:00pm	1:00pm	11:00am	11:00am	10:00am
9:30am	9:00am	8:00am	7:00am	6:00am	5:00am	3:30am	1:00am	MINUIT	11:00pm	2200	10:00pm	9:00pm	7:00pm	7:00pm	5:00pm	4:00pm	2:00pm	MIDI	Mediodia	11:00am
10:30am	10:00am	9:00am	8:00am	7:00am	6:00am	4:30am	2:00am	1:00am	Medianoche	2300	11:00pm	10:00pm	8:00pm	8:00pm	6:00pm	5:00pm	3:00pm	1:00pm	1:00pm	NOON
11:30am	11:00am	10:00am	9:00am	8:00am	7:00am	5:30am	3:00am	2:00am	1:00am	2400	MIDNIGHT	11:00pm	9:00pm	9:00pm	7:00pm	6:00pm	4:00pm	2:00pm	2:00pm	1:00pm

INTERNATIONAL TIME DIFFERENTIALS

**To determine STANDARD TIME overseas
add (+) to or subtract (-) from
EASTERN STANDARD TIME as indicated:**

	E.S.T.		E.S.T.		E.S.T.
Afghanistan	+9½	Finland	+7	Norway	+6
Albania	+6	Formosa	+13	Pakistan	+10 (5)°
Algeria	+6	France	+6	Panama	0
Argentina	+2	Germany	+6	Paraguay	+1
Aruba	÷½	Ghana	+5	Peru	0
Australia	+15 (1)°	Great Britain	+5	Philippines	+13
Austria	+6	Greece	+7	Poland	+6 (6)°
Azores	+3	Guatemala	-1	Portugal	+5
Belgian Congo	+6 (2)°	Haiti	0	Puerto Rico	+1
Belgium	+6	Hawaii	-5	Rhodesia	+7
Bermuda	+1	Hungary	+6	Roumania	+7
Bolivia	+1	Iceland	+4	Salvador (El)	-1
Borneo (Br)	+13	India	+10½	Saudi Arabia	+8 (7)°
Brazil	+2 (3)°	Iran	+8½	Singapore	+12½
Bulgaria	+7	Iraq	+8	Spain	+6
Burma	+11½	Irish Republic	+5	Surinam	+1½
Canal Zone	0	Israel	+7	Sweden	+6
Ceylon	+10½	Italy	+6	Switzerland	+6
Chile	+1	Japan	+14	Syria	+7
China	+13 (4)°	Korea	+13½	Thailand	+12
Colombia	0	Lebanon	+7	Tunisia	+6
Costa Rica	-1	Luxembourg	+6	Turkey	+7
Cuba	0	Madagascar	+8	Union of South Africa	+7
Curacao	+½	Malaya	+12½	Russia	+8 (8)°
Czechoslovakia	+6	Morocco	+5	Uruguay	+2
Denmark	+6	Netherlands	+6	Venezuela	+½
Dominican Republic	0	Netherlands Antilles	+½	Vietnam	+12
Ecuador	0	Newfoundland	+1½	Virgin Islands	+1
Egypt	+7	New Zealand	+17	Yugoslavia	+6
Ethiopia	+8	Nicaragua	-1		

Note: (1)° Brisbane, Canberra, Melbourne,
　　　　　New South Wales, Sydney, Queensland.
　　　(2)° Leopoldville.
　　　(3)° Rio de Janeiro, Sao Paulo, Santos.
　　　(4)° Hong Kong, Peiping, Shanghai, Tientsin.
　　　(5)° Karachi   (6)° Warsaw   (7)° Djeddah   (8)° Moscow

FOREIGN MONEY

Country or Area	Basic Monetary Unit Name	Symbol	Principal Fractional Unit Name	Abbreviation or Symbol
Afghanistan	Afghani	Af	Pul.	
Albania	Lek.	L	Quintar	
Algeria.	Dinar	DA	Centime	
Andorra.	French franc.	FRF	French centime. . .	
	Spanish peseta	ESP	Spanish centimo. .	
Angola.	Kwanza	NKZ	Lwei.	
Antigua and Barbuda. . .	Dollar.	EC$	Cent	C
Argentina	Peso	m/n$	Centavo	Ctvo
Armenia.	Tram		Luma.	
Australia	Dollar.	$A	Cent	C
Austria.	Schilling.	ATS	Groschen	
Azerbaijan.	Manat			
Bahamas, The.	Dollar.	B$	Cent	C
Bahrain	Dinar	BD	Fil.	
Bangladesh	Taka.	Tk	Paisa (Poisha) . . .	
Barbados	Dollar.	BD$	Cent	C
Belarus (Belorussia). . . .	Ruble.	R	Kopek	
Belgium.	Franc.	BFr	Centime	
Belize.	Dollar.	$B	Cent	C
Benin.	Franc.	CFAF		
Bermuda.	Dollar.	BD$	Cent	C
Bhutan.	Ngultrum	Nu	Chetrum	
Bolivia	Boliviana.	$b	Centavo	Ctvo
Bosnia-Herzegovina	Dinar	Din	Para	
Botswana	Pula.	P	Thebe	
Brazil.	Cruzeiro	Cr$	Centavo	Ctvo
Brunei	Dollar.	B$	Cent	C
Bulgaria.	Lev.	BGL	Stotinka (Stotinki)	C
Burkina Faso	Franc.	CFAF		
Burma	Kyat	K	Pya	
Burundi	Franc.	FBu	Centime	
Cambodia.	Riel.	R	Sen	
Cameroon.	Franc.	CFAF		
Canada	Dollar.	$, Can$	Cent	C
Cape Verde	Escudo	CVE, CV Esc	Centavo	Ctvo
Cayman Islands	Dollar.	$K	Cent	C
Central African Republic	Franc.	CFAF		
Chad	Franc.	CFAF		
Chile	Peso	Ch$, CLP	Centavo	Ctvo
China.	Yuan	¥	Jiao/Fen	
Colombia.	Peso	Col$, COP	Centavo	Ctvo
Comoros.	Franc.	CF	Centime	
Congo	Franc.	CFAF		
Cook Islands	Dollar.	NZ$	Cent	C

FOREIGN MONEY Continued

Country or Area	Basic Monetary Unit Name	Symbol	Principal Fractional Unit Name	Abbreviation or Symbol
Costa Rica	Colón	₡	Céntimo	Ctmo
Croatia	Krone			
Cuba	Peso	$, CUP	Centavo	Ctvo
Cyprus	Pound	£C	Cent	C
Czech Republic	Koruna	Kčs	Haler	
Denmark	Krone (Kroner)	DKr	Øre	
Djibouti	Franc	DF	Centime	
Dominica	Dollar	EC$	Cent	C
Dominican Republic	Peso	RD$	Centavo	Ctvo
Ecuador	Sucre	S/		
Egypt	Pound	£E	Piastre	
El Salvador	Colón	₡	Centavo	Ctvo
England	Pound	£	Penny (Pence)	
Equatorial Guinea	Franc	CFAF		
Estonia	Kroon			
Ethiopia	Birr	EB	Cent	C
Falkland Islands	Pound	£	Penny (Pence)	
Fiji	Dollar	$F	Cent	C
Finland	Markka	Fmk	Penni	
France	Franc	FF	Centime	
French Guiana	Franc	F	Centime	
French Polynesia	Franc	CFPF		
Gabon	Franc	CFAF		
Gambia, The	Dalasi	D	Butut	
Georgia	Ruble	R	Kopek	
Germany	Deutsche Mark	DM	Pfennig	Pf
Ghana	Cedi	₡	Pesewa	P
Gibraltar	Pound	Gib£	Penny (Pence)	
Greece	Drachma	Dr	Lepta	
Greenland	Krone (Kroner)	DKr	Øre	
Grenada	Dollar	EC$	Cent	C
Guadeloupe	Franc	FF	Centime	
Guatemala	Quetzal	Q	Centavo	Ctvo
Guinea	Franc	GF		
Guinea-Bissau	Peso	GWP	Centavo	Ctvo
Guyana	Dollar	G$	Cent	C
Haiti	Gourde	G	Centime	
Honduras	Lempira	L	Centavo	Ctvo
Hong Kong	Dollar	HK$	Cent	C
Hungary	Forint	Ft	Fillér	
Iceland	Króna	Kr	Aurar (Eyrir)	
India	Rupee	Rs	Paisa (Paise)	
Indonesia	Rupiah	Rp	Sen	
Iran	Rial	Rls		
Iraq	Dinar	ID	Fil	
Ireland	Pound	£, IR£	Penny (Pence)	

FOREIGN MONEY Continued

Country or Area	Basic Monetary Unit		Principal Fractional Unit	
	Name	Symbol	Name	Abbreviation or Symbol
Israel.................	Shekel................	ILS	Agorot..........	
Italy..................	Lira...................	L, Lit	Centesimo.......	Ctmo
Ivory Coast...........	Franc.................	CFAF		
Jamaica..............	Dollar................	J$	Cent...........	C
Japan................	Yen..................	¥	Sen.............	
Jordan...............	Dinar................	JD	Fil.............	
Kazakhstan...........	Ruble................	R	Kopek..........	
Kenya................	Shilling..............	KES, Sh	Cent...........	C
Kiribati...............	Australian dollar.......	A$	Cent...........	C
Kirghizia.............	Ruble................	R	Kopek..........	
Korea, North.........	Won.................	W	Jun.............	
Korea, South.........	Won.................	W	Chon...........	
Kuwait...............	Dinar................	KD	Fil.............	
Kyrgyzstan...........	Ruble................	R	Kopek..........	
Laos.................	Kip..................	Kp	Att.............	
Latvia...............	Lats.................			
Lebanon.............	Pound...............	£Leb	Piastre.........	
Lesotho..............	Loti (Maloti).........	M	Lisente (Sente)...	
Liberia...............	Dollar................	$, LIR	Cent...........	C
Libya................	Dinar................	LD	Dirham.........	
Liechtenstein.........	Franc................	SwF	Centime........	
Lithuania............	Litas................			
Luxembourg..........	Franc................	LUF	Centime........	
Macao...............	Pataca...............	P	Avo.............	
Macedonia...........	Denar................		Deni...........	
Madagascar..........	Franc................	MGF		
Malawi...............	Kwacha..............	K	Tambala........	
Malaysia.............	Ringgit...............	M$	Sen.............	
Maldives.............	Rufiyaa..............	Rf	Laari...........	
Mali.................	Franc................	CFAF		
Malta................	Pound...............	£M	Cent...........	C
Marshall Islands.......	Dollar................	$	Cent...........	C
Martinique...........	Franc................	FF	Centime........	
Mauritania...........	Ougulya..............	UM	Khoum.........	
Mauritius............	Rupee...............	Rs	Cent...........	C
Mexico...............	Peso................	M/n$, Mex$	Centavo.........	Ctvo
Micronesia...........	Dollar................	$	Cent...........	C
Moldavia.............	Leu..................			
Monaco..............	Franc................	FF	Centime........	
Mongolia.............	Tugrik...............	T	Möngö..........	
Montenegro..........	Dinar................	Din	Para...........	
Montserrat...........	Dollar................	EC$	Cent...........	C
Morocco.............	Dirham...............	DH	Centime........	
Mozambique..........	Metical (Meticais)......	M	Centavo.........	Ctvo
Myanmar.............	Kyat.................	K	Pya.............	

FOREIGN MONEY Continued

Country or Area	Basic Monetary Unit		Principal Fractional Unit	
	Name	Symbol	Name	Abbreviation or Symbol
Namibia...............	Dollar.................	N$		
Nauru................	Dollar.................	$A	Cent	C
Nepal.................	Rupee	Re	Pais(a)	
Netherlands	Gulden (Guilder)	f	Cent	C
Netherlands Antilles	Gulden (Guilder)	NAf	Cent	C
New Caledonia	Franc.................	CFPF		
New Zealand	Dollar.................	$NZ	Cent	C
Nicaragua.............	Córdoba	NIO	Centavo	Ctvo
Niger	Franc.................	CFAF		
Nigeria................	Naira	₦	Kobo............	k
Northern Ireland	Pound	£	Penny (Pence) ...	
Norway	Krone (Kroner).........	Kr	Øre	
Oman.................	Rial..................	OMR	Baiza............	
Pakistan	Rupee	PR	Paisa............	
Panama...............	Dollar.................	$	Cent	C
Papua New Guinea	Kina	K	Toea	
Paraguay	Guarani	G		
Peru..................	Nuevo Sol.............	S/	Centavo	Ctvo
Philippines	Piso	₱	Sentimo	
Pitcairn Island	Dollar.................	P$	Cent	C
Poland................	Złoty (Złotych).........	Zł	Grosz(y)	
Portugal...............	Escudo	Esc	Centavo	Ctvo
Qatar.................	Riyal.................	QR	Dirham	
Réunion...............	Franc.................	FF	Centime	
Romania	Leu (Lei).............	L	Ban(i)	
Russia................	Ruble................	R	Kopek	
Rwanda...............	Franc.................	RWF	Centime	
St. Helena	Pound	£	Penny (Pence) ...	
St. Lucia..............	Dollar.................	EC$	Cent	C
St. Pierre and Miquelon	Franc.................	FF	Centime	C
St. Vincent and the Grenadines	Dollar.................	EC$	Cent	C
San Marino............	Lira..................	L, Lit	Centesimo	Ctmo
São Tomé e Príncipe...	Dobra.................	Db	Centimo	
Saudi Arabia	Rial (Riyal)	R	Halala...........	
Scotland	Pound	£	Penny (Pence) ...	
Senegal...............	Franc.................	CFAF		
Serbia	Dinar	Din	Para	
Seychelles	Rupee	SR	Cent	C
Sierra Leone	Leone	Le	Cent	C
Singapore.............	Dollar.................	S$	Cent	C
Slovak Republic	Koruna...............	Kčs	Haler............	
Slovenia	Tola(r)			
Solomon Islands	Dollar.................	SI$	Cent	C
Somalia...............	Shilling (Shilin).........	So Sh	Cent	C

FOREIGN MONEY Continued

Country or Area	Basic Monetary Unit		Principal Fractional Unit	
	Name	Symbol	Name	Abbreviation or Symbol
South Africa	Rand	R	Cent	C
Spain	Peseta	Ptas		
Sri Lanka	Rupee	RE	Cent	C
Sudan	Pound	£S	Girsh	
Suriname	Gulden (Guilder)	Sf	Cent	C
Swaziland	Lilangeni (emalangeni)	E	Cent	C
Sweden	Krona (Kronor)	SKr	Öre	
Switzerland	Franc	Sfr	Centime	
Syria	Pound	£Syr	Piastre	
Tadzhikistan	Ruble	R	Kopek	
Taiwan	New Taiwan dollar	NT$	Cent	C
Tajikistan	Ruble	R	Kopek	
Tanzania	Shilling (Shilingi)	Sh	Cent (Senti)	C
Thailand	Baht	B	Satang	
Togo	Franc	CFAF		
Tonga	Pa'anga	T$	Seniti	
Trinidad and Tobago	Dollar	TT$	Cent	C
Tunisia	Dinar	D	Millime	
Turkey	Lira	TL	Kurus	
Turkmenistan	Ruble	R	Kopek	
Tuvalu	Dollar	A$	Cent	C
Uganda	Shilling	USh	Cent	C
Ukraine	Ruble	R	Kopek	
United Arab Emirates	Dirham	Dh	Fil	
United States	Dollar	$	Cent	C
Uruguay	Nuevo Peso	N$	Centesimo	
Uzbekistan	Ruble	R	Kopek	
Vanatu	Vatu	Vt		
Vatican City	Lira	L, Lit	Centesimo	Ctmo
Venezuela	Bolívar	Bs	Centimo	
Vietnam	Dông	D		
Wales	Pound	£	Penny (Pence)	
Western Samoa	Tala	WS$	Sene	
Yemen	Rial	YR	Fil	
Yugoslavia	Dinar	Din	Para	
Zaïre	Zaïre	Z		
Zambia	Kwacha	K	Ngwee	
Zimbabwe	Dollar	Z$	Cent	C

Note: Some countries, such as the new republics of the Commonwealth of Independent States, were in the process of forming their own currencies as of 1992. For up-to-date currencies on emerging countries, consult a current edition of the *MRI Bankers' Guide to Foreign Currency*, *Statesman's Year-Book*, or other source that reports international currency information.

PART FIVE

GLOSSARY OF IMPORTANT BUSINESS TERMS

18. Glossary

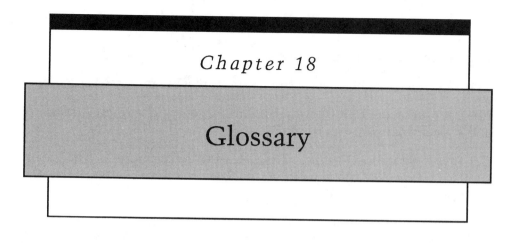

Chapter 18

Glossary

OFFICE TECHNOLOGY

Address. A number that identifies a location in the computer's memory, which enables the computer to find specific data or instructions.

Analog. The representation of data by continuously variable quantities such as voltages (compare with **digital**).

ASCII. American Standard Code for Information Interchange, a code for representing symbols as **binary** digits.

Bar code. A code recorded on labels of products and other material that can be read by a wand or **scanner.**

BASIC. Beginner's All-Purpose Symbolic Instruction Code, a standard, high-level, easy-to-learn programming language commonly used for developing programs to run on microcomputers.

Batching. Processing a group of documents at one time together as a unit.

Binary. Consisting of two things or two parts, such as binary numbers, which are written in a number system that uses only two digits: 0 and 1.

Bit. Short for **binary** digit (0 or 1).

Buffer. A device where data are stored temporarily, such as a computer buffer where data are held until a printer is ready to receive it.

Bug. An error in a computer program.

Byte. A group of eight adjacent **binary** digits that are processed as a unit.

Central processing unit (CPU). That part of a computer where arithmetic and logic operations are performed.

CD-ROM. Short for **Compact Disk–Read-Only Memory;** a small disk similar to a musical CD where data, images, or sound can be stored, for example, an encyclopedia.

Database. Also known as "databank." Any collection of data, such as an address file, stored on a **disk** or other computer medium. Sometimes used also in reference to **hard-copy** storage of data collections.

Desktop publishing. The production of documents (text and graphics) in-house through the use of a microcomputer and printer that can fit on a desk, often by way of a **software** program especially designed to provide the appearance of traditional typesetting and printing.

Digital. The representation or calculation of data by discrete units or in the form of numerical digits (compare with **analog**).

Disk(ette). A computer memory device for storing information. Hard disks are permanently installed or attached to a computer, whereas disk-ettes are small, removable media resembling a musical CD disk or small phonograph record.

Downtime. A temporary halt in machine production or worker performance resulting from equipment breakdown or some other condition affecting normal operations.

Electronic mail. Mail prepared by computer at one terminal and sent to another **terminal** either over the telephone lines or directly from machine to machine wired together on a **local-area network.**

Ergonomics. Human engineering, or the science of effective human-machine interaction.

Facsimile. A copy of text or graphics transmitted electronically; also, the machine that transmits the material. See **Transceiver.**

Fax. Short for **facsimile.**

Feedback. The output from a machine, process, or system used as input for another machine, process, or system.

Filename. A series of characters or a designation that identifies a particular file in a computer's memory.

Hard copy. A computer printout of text or graphics on paper; also used broadly to refer to any paper copy.

Hardware. The mechanical and electronic equipment, wires, circuits, and other physical parts of a computer system, as opposed to the **software.**

Interface. The connection or interaction between two devices or systems, such as the link between a computer and a **modem.**

Local-area network (LAN). A system in which interoffice electronic equipment is connected, usually by direct wiring, to form a network within a common area, such as a building.

Macro. A single computer instruction that consists of a sequence of operations, usually carried out in repetitive work by one keystroke that takes the place of several keystrokes that would otherwise be required.

Mainframe. A large computer that serves as a central processor for many **terminals** or users that are connected to it.

Megabyte. One million **bytes.**

Micrographics. The technique or process of reducing information to a microform medium (e.g., film) for storage and retrieval.

Microprocessor. A microcomputer; a computer's **central processing unit** contained on a single integrated-circuit silicon chip.

Modem. Short for "modulator-demodulator," a device connecting computer systems long distance by converting data in the sending system into signals that will travel over the telephone lines and then converting those impulses back into computer data in the receiving system.

Mouse. A handheld device connected to a computer that is rolled along a hard surface to move or edit text and graphics on a computer display screen (monitor).

Off line. Not interacting directly with the **central processing unit** of a computer, as opposed to direct **on-line** interaction.

On line. The direct connection with or interaction with the **central processing unit** of a computer, as opposed to **off-line** operation.

Optical character recognition. The reading of information recorded on paper by a **scanner** that converts the data into **digital** form that can be used by a computer.

Qwerty keyboard. A keyboard on which the keys are arranged in the same pattern as that used on traditional typewriters.

Random-access memory (RAM). The main memory of a computer where data can be stored, retrieved, edited, and returned to storage; a computer memory device that permits stored data to be located in any order desired, as opposed to sequential retrieval. See also **Read-only memory.**

Read-only memory (ROM). The memory of a computer containing instructions that can be read but not edited. See also **Random-access memory.**

Real time. A reference to the time involved when a response to a request occurs immediately or at essentially the same speed as that of the input of data.

Scanner. A device that can sense characters or graphics recorded on paper and transfer it to a computer.

Software. The programs that instruct or tell a computer what to do, as opposed to the **hardware.** *Systems software* directs the overall operations of the computer; *applications software* enables the computer to perform specific applications, such as word processing.

Telecommunications. Communication between two or more people or machines by transmission of signals over the telephone lines, by television, or by other means of transmission.

Telecommuting. The process of working at home and transmitting information to the office by computer and **telecommunications** channel (e.g., telephone line).

Teleconferencing. Exchanging information by using **telecommunication** links.

Telematics. Derived from the French term *télématique,* meaning information technology.

Terminal. A device whereby data can be sent and received over a communications channel, often consisting of a keyboard and a video display (monitor) connected to a **central processing unit** and printer; a terminal that cannot function fully on its own is a *dumb terminal.*

Tie line. A private transmission channel for voice or data, usually leased from a common carrier, that connects two or more locations. Also called *leased line* or *tie trunk.*

Time sharing. Use of a device, such as a computer, for two or more purposes or by two or more customers.

Transceiver. A **facsimile** machine that can both transmit and receive data.

Voice mail. An electronic message system whereby voice messages can be sent and stored for later access by the addressee.

BUSINESS ORGANIZATION
AND MANAGEMENT

Affiliated companies. Companies that are related by a community of interest or by way of a **parent corporation's** ownership of their **stock.**

Agency. A relationship in which one person authorizes another to act in his or her behalf.

Alien corporation. A business organization incorporated outside the United States and its territories.

Annual report. A report prepared by a **corporation** at the close of its fiscal year containing audited financial statements and other information.

Arbitration. The submission of a dispute to a third party whose decision is binding.

Articles of incorporation. The document, also known as *certificate of incorporation* or *charter*, that creates a private **corporation** and states what the organization is authorized to do.

Bankruptcy. The procedure by which the property of a debtor is taken over by a receiver or trustee for the benefit of the creditors, thereby relieving the debtor of all debts.

Bill of lading. A document giving evidence of a contract between a shipper and carrier for the transport and delivery of goods.

Business corporation. A **corporation** organized to conduct business for profit.

Bylaws. The rules adopted by an organization to establish and regulate its conduct and that of its stockholders, directors, and officers.

Cartel. A close association of companies engaged in similar business.

Certificate of incorporation. See **Articles of incorporation.**

Charitable corporation. A **corporation,** also known as an *eleemosynary corporation,* that is organized and operated for charitable or nonprofit purposes.

Charter. See **Articles of incorporation.**

Close corporation. A **corporation** whose capital **stock** is held by a limited group and not sold to the general public.

Conditional sale. An installment sale in which a buyer gives the seller a promissory note, and title to the goods remains with the seller until all payments have been made.

Consignment. Transferring goods to another party for shipment or sale but retaining ownership and title to the consigned goods.

Consolidation. Combining individual **corporations** into a new corporation.

Corporation. A legally established organization created to carry out some specified purpose.

Corporation service company. A company that provides services for **corporations** that they are unable to provide or do not wish to provide for themselves.

Cumulative voting. A system of voting for directors in which each share of **stock,** or each person, has as many votes as there are directors to be selected.

Domestic corporation. A **corporation** doing business in the state in which it was incorporated.

Dummy incorporators. Persons who initially serve as incorporators to set up a **corporation** in a particular state and then drop out.

Eleemosynary corporation. See **Charitable corporation.**

Featherbedding. The illegal practice of paying for services not performed or not to be performed.

First in, first out (FIFO). A method of valuing goods that assumes those first acquired are those to be sold first.

Foreign corporation. A **corporation** doing business in a state other than the one in which it was incorporated.

Holding company. A company organized to control other companies by owning and holding their **stock.**

Incorporated partnership. See **Close corporation.**

Individual proprietorship. See **Proprietorship, sole.**

Interested director. A director who has a personal interest, which may cause a biased vote, in some matter potentially profitable for the **corporation.**

Interlocking directorates. Boards of directors of two or more organizations that have one or more directors in common.

Investment company. A company that invests in other companies' securities and sells its own shares to the public.

Joint adventure (venture). An association of two or more persons in a joint business endeavor without the usual requirements of a formal **partnership.**

Joint stock company. A company created by an agreement of the parties and similar to a **corporation** except that all owners are liable for company debts.

Last in, first out (LIFO). A method of valuing goods that assumes those last acquired are those to be sold first.

Limited partnership. A **partnership** in which a partner's liability for the firm's debts is limited to the amount of his or her investment.

Liquidation. Distributing assets of a dissolved **corporation** to the stockholders after payment of all corporate debts.

Markdown. The reduction of the price of goods below the original retail price.

Markup. The amount of the selling price of goods above cost or in addition to the original retail price.

Massachusetts trust. A business association set up in the form of a trust, with permanent trustees similar to directors and beneficiaries similar to stockholders.

Merchandising, retail. Buying merchandise, controlling it, and selling it to consumers.

Merger. Uniting one or more **corporations** with another one that retains its identity while the others become part of the existing corporation.

Merit rating. The change in state unemployment insurance tax according to a company's stabilization of employment, with higher rates imposed on employers with heavy labor turnovers.

Moneyed corporation. A **corporation** that deals in money or lending of money.

Nonprofit corporation. A **corporation** organized for some purpose other than making money for its members.

Nonstock corporation. Any **corporation** other than a corporation that has capital stock, such as an educational institution.

Palletization. Shipping goods on lightweight wooden platforms to enable the shipment of several units as one large unit.

Parent corporation. A **corporation** that owns the majority of the **stock** of another corporation and fully controls it.

Partnership. An agreement between two or more persons to conduct business together for profit as co-owners, with each owner fully liable for all partnership debts.

Preemptive right. The right of existing stockholders to purchase their relative share of new **stock** to retain their interest in the **corporation.**

Promoters. Persons who form a new **corporation** and occupy a position of trust until the stockholders elect an independent board of directors.

Proprietorship, sole. A form of business organization in which ownership is held by one person.

Public corporation. A **corporation** organized by the federal or a state government to serve as a governmental agency.

Public service corporation. A **corporation,** also known as a *public utility company,* that supplies public services such as power and is regulated by a public service commission.

Public utility corporation. See **Public service corporation.**

Pyramiding. The process by which a few persons who control a top holding company gain control over vast properties by investing relatively small amounts in a number of interrelated companies.

Quasi-public corporation. See **Public service corporation.**

Registered office. An office set up by a **corporation** in a state in which it does business or where it is only nominally incorporated to meet that state's statutory requirements.

Resident agent. An employee or agent who resides in a state where a **corporation** is incorporated but only nominally in residence in order to perform the services required by the state's statutes.

Retailing. See **Merchandising, retail.**

Rights. An existing stockholder's right to purchase additional shares of **stock** at a stipulated price before a certain date.

Silent partner. A partner who has no voice in the **partnership** management but is fully responsible for the debts of the business.

Stock. Identical units called *shares* that represent ownership in a **corporation.**

Stock certificate. The written evidence of shares of ownership in a **corporation.**

Stock corporation. A **corporation** that has its ownership divided into shares of **stock** and is authorized to distribute to the holders of this stock proportional amounts of profits in the form of dividends.

Stock insurance company. An insurance company organized like a business **corporation,** with net earnings distributed to stockholders.

Stock ledger. A permanent record of each stockholder's interest in the **corporation** and all transfers of the stockholder's interest.

Subsidiary. A company controlled by a **holding company** or **parent corporation** that owns all or a majority of its **stock.**

Trademark. A mark, symbol, or design that legally identifies a company or its products.

Transfer agent. A person, bank, or trust company that maintains a **corporation's stock ledger,** records all **stock** transfers, and ensures that the transfer is properly executed.

Vetoing stock. A class of **stock** that has no right to elect directors but carries the power to vote on certain other matters.

Voting trust. A method of concentrating a company's control in the hands of a few people through an agreement whereby stockholders transfer their **stock** and voting rights for a specified period.

Voting trust certificate. A certificate of interest given to stockholders in a **voting trust** who have agreed to transfer their **stock** and voting rights to the trustees for a specified period.

ACCOUNTING AND FINANCE

Accounts payable. The amount an individual or a business owes to creditors for merchandise and services purchased on open account.

Accounts receivable. The amount due to an individual or a business from customers that purchased merchandise or services on open account.

Accrual accounting. A method of accounting that allocates income and expenses to the period to which they apply regardless of whether the income was actually received or the expenses actually paid.

Adjustment entries. Journal entries made at the end of an accounting period to correct errors and assign income and expenses to the correct period.

Amortization. The gradual reduction of a debt until it is extinguished by a series of periodic payments to a creditor.

Annuity. A series of periodic payments made to a named person(s) for a certain number of years or for life.

Assets. Anything of value that is owned by a business or an individual.

Audit. An examination of accounting records to verify the **assets, liabilities,** and **capital** of a business as of a certain date and to verify its financial transactions during the fiscal period just ended.

Balance sheet. A detailed statement of the **assets, liabilities,** and **capital** (**net worth**) of a business organization on a given date.

Bank draft. A check drawn by one bank against funds deposited to its account in another bank.

Bill of exchange. A written document issued and signed by one party that requires another party (the addressee) to pay a specified amount to a third party.

Book value. The price of **assets** as reported on a **financial statement.**

Books of original entry. An accounting book or computer file, such as a **journal,** in which each transaction is first recorded.

Capital. The excess of **assets** over **liabilities;** in a corporation, **net worth.**

Capital stock. An account that shows the amount received from stock sales regarded as legal capital; in a corporation, evidence of ownership in the form of certificates.

Capitalization. The total accounting value of **capital stock, paid-in capital in excess of par value,** and borrowed capital; in a corporation, the total amount of its securities outstanding in the form of capital stock and long-term bonds.

Cash accounting. A method of accounting that records income at the time it is actually received and expenses at the time they are actually paid.

Cash disbursements journal. An accounting book or computer file in which each payment is initially recorded.

Cash journal. An accounting book or computer file in which all transactions are initially recorded.

Cash receipts journal. An accounting book or computer file in which each receipt of cash (e.g., bank deposits) is recorded.

Certificates of deposit. Written evidence that a specified sum of money is deposited on interest for a certain period.

Circulating capital. See **Working capital.**

Closing entries. Entries in a **journal** at the end of an accounting period to transfer income and expense account balances to the **balance sheet** accounts.

Collateral. Something of value pledged to a lender to secure the repayment of a loan.

Common stock. Evidence of unlimited interest in a corporation's profits and assets.

Control account. A **general ledger** account that summarizes the information of a **subsidiary ledger.**

Credit. The entry in **double-entry bookkeeping** that records increases in the **capital,** income, and **liability** accounts and decreases in the **asset** accounts.

Cross-footing. Totaling the columns in books (or computer files) of accounts.

Current assets. Assets that will be realized or converted within an accounting period.

Current capital. See **Working capital.**

Current liabilities. Debts and obligations that are met within the accounting period by using **current assets** or incurring additional liabilities.

Debit. The entry in **double-entry bookkeeping** that increases **asset** and **expense accounts** and decreases capital and liability accounts.

Demand deposits. Deposits payable to the depositor at any time desired.

Depreciation. Periodic loss of value of limited-life assets due to wear and tear, obsolescence, and so on.

Double-entry bookkeeping. A system of recording each transaction twice, as a **debit** and as a **credit.**

Draft. See **Bill of exchange.**

Expense account. A record of someone's expenses during a specified period for a specified purpose.

Financial statement. A summary of financial data, such as a **balance sheet,** prepared from the accounting records.

Fiscal year. The one-year accounting period (any twelve successive months) of business operations.

Fixed assets. Permanent **assets,** such as land and buildings.

Footing. See **Cross-footing.**

General ledger. The accounting book or computer file in which all financial transactions are finally summarized in separate accounts (except those kept in a **subsidiary** or private **ledger**).

Gross income. The total income an individual or business enterprise receives before any deductions are taken.

Gross profit. The excess of income over the cost of merchandise sold and the expense of doing business.

Imprest fund. See **Petty cash.**

Income statement. A summary of the income and expenses of a business that shows the **net profit** or loss in a specified accounting period.

Individual retirement program (IRA). A long-term savings program allowing tax-deductible contributions to a personal interest-bearing account, until money is withdrawn and taxed after retirement.

Installment sale. A contract establishing equal payments, or installments, at regular intervals until a debt is fully paid.

Intangible assets. Items of value other than tangible property or the direct right to tangible property, such as patents and franchises.

Journal. Any accounting book or computer file in which each financial transaction is initially recorded.

Ledger. A book (or computer file) of final entry in which financial transactions are summarized in separate accounts.

Liabilities. The debts and obligations of a business.

Negotiable instrument. A written instrument signed by the person who draws it that contains an unconditional promise or order to pay a certain sum of money.

Net assets. The excess of the book value of **assets** (the price as reported on a **financial statement**) over **liabilities.**

Net income. Gross, or total, **income** derived from performing services minus all expenses involved in performing those services.

Net profit. Gross, or total, **income** derived from the sale of merchandise minus all expenses involved in doing business and minus income taxes.

Net worth. Book value of the **assets** of a business minus **liabilities.**

No-par stock. Stock that has no face value on the stock certificate.

Notes payable. A **general ledger** account showing the amount of promissory notes, or the **liability** of notes, given by the business.

Notes receivable. A **general ledger** account showing the amount of negotiable promissory notes a business received from its customers and other debtors.

Overhead. General and administrative expenses of a business such as rent and insurance.

Over the counter. A method of trading securities without using any recognized exchange service.

Paid-in capital in excess of par value. Contributions of **capital** by stockholders that are not credited to **capital stock.**

Par value stock. Stock that has been given a face value on the stock certificate.

Payroll. The record of all employees wages, salaries, deductions, and net pay for a specified period.

Payroll journal. A book or computer file where all payroll information is systematically recorded.

Petty cash. A limited amount of cash kept on hand for disbursements too small to justify the use of checks.

Portfolio. An individual's or organization's holdings of stocks and bonds.

Posting. The process of transferring entries from **journals** to **ledger** accounts.

Preferred stock. Stock that is entitled to earnings before **common stock** payments.

Profit and loss statement. See **Income statement.**

Puts and calls. Options to buy or sell a certain number of securities at a specified price within a specified time.

Sight draft. A commercial draft that is payable on presentation.

Single-entry bookkeeping. A method of accounting that records transactions with debtors and creditors as a single entry rather than two equal **debit** and **credit** entries.

Spreadsheet. A manual or computer table of numbers arranged by row and column and used to perform accounting and financial calculations.

Straight loan. A loan for a specific number of years, at a specific interest rate, payable in full at maturity without advance payments of principal.

Subsidiary journal. A specialized accounting book or computer file, such as a **petty cash** journal used to record similar transactions that occur regularly and frequently.

Subsidiary ledger. A specialized accounting **ledger,** such as a plant and equipment ledger, used to summarize similar **journal** entries.

Time deposits. Deposited funds that a customer may withdraw at a specified date, for example, thirty days from the date of deposit.

Trial balance. Listing debit and credit balances taken from **ledger** accounts and totaling them to prove that total **debits** equal total **credits.**

Usury. Lending or receiving money at more than the legal rate of interest allowed by law.

Variable annuity. An **annuity** contract that provides for payments in units of income that vary from time to time.

Working capital. The excess of **current assets** over **current liabilities**; in a business sense, the **capital** an organization or individual keeps to pay for daily working needs.

Yield. The annual rate of return on an investment in securities, computed as a percentage of the amount invested.

BUSINESS LAW

Abrogation. Annulling or repealing a law by an authoritative act.

Acceleration clause. A section of or statement in a contract that makes an entire debt become due and payable immediately when some condition of the contract is breached.

Acknowledgment. Signing a legal instrument and declaring before an authorized official, such as a notary public, that you executed the instrument.

Affidavit. A written statement sworn to, by the person making it, before someone officially authorized to administer an oath.

Allegation. A statement made by someone who claims it can be proved as a fact.

Allonge. A piece of paper attached to a negotiable instrument that provides space to write **endorsement** when there is no room on the instrument itself.

Answer. A defendant's formal written response, signed by his or her attorney, to charges and demands made in a plaintiff's formal written complaint.

Antitrust laws. Laws to protect trade from monopolies and to prohibit conspiracies and trusts that restrain **interstate commerce**.

Assignment. The transfer of property or rights to property from one party to another.

Attachment. Taking or seizing a debtor's property to place it under control of a court.

Attestation. Witnessing the signing of a written instrument and signing it yourself to signify that you so witnessed that act.

Bailment. Delivery of property by the owner to another person for temporary care.

Bill of sale. A formal document given by a seller to a buyer as evidence of the transfer of property the bill describes.

Binder. A temporary agreement or insurance contract providing coverage until the actual policy is written.

Blue-sky laws. Laws regulating and supervising stock sales and similar transactions to protect the public from fraudulent deals.

Breach of contract. Failure to perform some act a contract calls for.

Breach of warranty. Failure of a vendor to provide what a **warranty** promises.

Caveat emptor (*Latin*). "Let the buyer beware"; a **common law** doctrine that imposes on buyers the duty of examining goods before buying them.

Certiorari (*Latin*). "To make sure or to be made certain about something"; a writ issued by a superior court directing an inferior court to send the record of a particular case.

Chattel. Any property other than land and its improvements.

Chose in action. (*French*). A right to recover a debt or receive damages that can be enforced in court.

Civil law. Law handed down from Roman laws under Justinian.

Common law. Law derived from the decision of judges based on accepted custom and tradition.

Complaint. The formal written statement of a plaintiff in a **civil lawsuit.**

Constructive. That which legally amounts to an act or is implied, even if the act itself has not actually been performed.

Deed. A formal written instrument by which one person transfers title to real property to another person.

Del credere (*Italian*). An agent who sells goods for someone and guarantees that the buyer will pay for the goods.

Disaffirmance. The repudiation of prior consent.

Earnest money. A buyer's deposit to show good faith and to bind a sale.

Eminent domain. The right of government to take private property for public use or the public welfare.

Endorsement. Writing your name, with or without additional words, on a negotiable instrument or **allonge**.

Equity. That which constitutes fairness or fair dealing in a particular situation.

Escrow. Money, property, or documents held by someone, possibly a third party, until an act is performed by another person.

Estoppel. A barrier that stops someone from taking a certain position that is inconsistent with previous acts or statements.

Ex parte (*Latin*). Done by or for one party.

Fee simple. Absolute ownership of **real property**.

Garnishment. A legal proceeding taken by a creditor, following judgment against a debtor, to compel a third party to pay money to the creditor instead of the debtor.

Guaranty. A contract that guarantees that one party will be responsible to another for payment of a debt or performance of a duty by a third party.

Holder in due course. The legal holder of a negotiable instrument who acquired it in good faith, believing it to be valid.

Indemnity. An express or implied contract to compensate another party for possible or actual loss or damage.

Indenture. A formal written instrument, such as a lease, that defines reciprocal rights and duties.

Interstate/intrastate commerce. *Interstate commerce* is any business transaction conducted directly or indirectly across state boundaries; *intrastate commerce* is any business transaction conducted entirely within a state.

Joint and several. Both together and individually; for example, two parties might be held liable for something either individually or together, depending on the option of a third party.

Libel and slander. *Libel* is written or published defamation or injury to the reputation of another person. *Slander* is oral defamation of another person in the presence of a third party.

Lien. A charge or claim against property that makes the property serve as security until some obligation is discharged.

Liquidated damages. An amount that parties to a contract agree on to satisfy the loss resulting from a breach of contract.

Mechanic's lien. A worker's legal claim to property until monies due to him or her are paid by the owner.

Option. An agreement whereby one person pays a certain amount of money for the right to buy or sell something within a specified time.

Patent. A right granted by the federal government to make, use, and sell an invention during a specified period.

Personal property. A legal right or interest in something movable, not land or anything permanently attached to land.

Pledge. Placing personal property with a lender as security for a debt until the debt is paid.

Power of attorney. A written instrument giving someone authorization to act for the person signing the document.

Privity. Close, mutual, or successive relationship to the same right of property or the power to enforce a promise or **warranty.**

Protest. A formal certificate attesting someone's refusal to pay a negotiable instrument you presented for payment.

Quasi (*Latin*). "Sort of" or "analogous to," as a quasi corporation.

Quiet title, action to. Proceedings to establish clear title to land.

Quo warranto (*Latin*). "With what authority"; a proceeding that questions a person's right to do something.

Real property. Land and anything that is attached to it.

Rescission. An action whereby a court annuls or cancels a contract.

Restrictive covenant. A clause in an agreement that limits the action of one of the parties to the agreement.

Slander. See **Libel and slander.**

Statute of frauds. State laws that require certain contracts to be signed and in writing to be valid.

Statute of limitations. State laws that set a time limit within which legal action may be brought.

Statutory law. Rules brought into law by legislative action.

Substantive law. Law that concerns rights and duties, such as contract law, as opposed to procedural law, such as law of pleading.

Summary proceeding. A short form of legal proceeding in which established procedure is disregarded.

Summons. A written notice that informs a defendant that a lawsuit is being brought against him or her.

Supplementary proceeding. The legal procedure by which a judgment creditor conducts an in-court examination of the debtor and others to determine if any assets are available to pay the debt.

Tenancy in common. An estate held by two or more persons by separate and distinct titles but with unity of possession.

Tenancy by the entirety. An estate held by husband and wife by title acquired jointly after marriage.

Tort. A civil wrong done to another person that does not involve a contract, for example, **libel.**

Trust. Holding property and applying it and its income for the benefit of someone named by the person who created the trust.

Ultra vires. (*Latin*). "Without power"; outside the scope of or in excess of something.

Uniform laws. Similar laws adopted by various states.

Waiver. Voluntarily giving up a right.

Warranty. A promise or affirmation made by a seller to induce a buyer to purchase something.

Without recourse. A phrase used by an endorser of a negotiable instrument meaning that he or she will not be liable if the other party refuses to accept payment.

Worker's compensation. Laws giving protection against injury and death occurring on the job.

Writ. A court order or judge's order authorizing or compelling someone to do something.

"Yellow-dog" contract. An illegal employment contract in which the employee agrees not to join a union.

Index

A

Abbreviations, 582-604
  academic degrees, 602-4
  alphabetizing, 13-14
  and apostrophe, 530
  capitalization, 551-52
    common abbreviations, 552
    degrees/titles, 551
    initials, 551
    one-letter, 551
    time/years, 551-52
  general abbreviations, 582-92
  organizations, 599-602
  and period, 543
  plural spellings, 512
  technical abbreviations, 592-99
  U.S. Postal Service, 605-8
  and word division, 527
Abstract, reports, 98
Academic degrees, abbreviations, 602-4
Acceptance letters, 423-24
  membership in professional/civic organization, 424
  speaking invitation, 423-24
  special event, 423
Accommodations:
  employer's preferences:
    air-travel arrangements, 221
    train-travel arrangements, 223
  meeting/conference visitors, 187-88

hotel rooms, 187
  travel, 187-88
Accounting:
  accrual basis vs. cash basis, 256
  bookkeeping compared to, 256
  confidentiality in, 268-70
  cost assignment, See Photocopy log; Electronic calendars
Account numbers, placement on envelopes, 347
Accrual basis accounting, cash basis accounting vs., 256
Acknowledgment:
  of expression of sympathy, 314-16
  footnotes, 106
  of legal document, 252
Acknowledgment letters, 396-98
  that also answer, 397-98
  without answer, 396-97
Acting official, correct form of address, 351
Acts/bills/codes/laws:
  capitalization rules, 552-53
  Constitution, 553
    amendments to, 553
  federal/state/municipal codes, 553
  general descriptive terms, 552
  official title, 552
Address, envelopes, 345
Address, forms of, 347-52

Air Force personnel, 624
Army personnel, 622
church dignitaries:
  Catholic faith, 625-27
  Jewish faith, 628
  Protestant faith, 629-30
Coast Guard personnel, 624
college/university officials, 630-32
companies, rules for, 348
court officials, 617-18
foreign officials/representatives, 619-21
general rules, 347-48
  degrees, 347-48, 351
  esquire, 348
  titles, 347
Marine Corps personnel, 624
men, titles, 348-49
Navy personnel, 623-24
officials:
  acting, 351
  former, 351
  spouses of, 351-52
prominent persons, 351-52
scholastic degrees, persons with, 347-48, 351, 556, 602-4
state/local government officials, 614-17
United Nations officials, 633
U.S. diplomatic representatives, 618-19
U.S. government officials, 609-14
women: